THE GREAT WAR FOR PEACE

THE
GREAT WAR
FOR PEACE

WILLIAM MULLIGAN

YALE UNIVERSITY PRESS
NEW HAVEN AND LONDON

For information about this and other Yale University Press publications, please contact:
U.S. Office: sales.press@yale.edu   www.yalebooks.com
Europe Office: sales@yaleup.co.uk   www.yalebooks.co.uk

Set in Adobe Caslon Pro by IDSUK (DataConnection) Ltd
Printed in Great Britain by TJ International Ltd, Padstow, Cornwall

Library of Congress Cataloging-in-Publication Data

Mulligan, William, 1975
    The Great War for peace/William Mulligan.
      pages cm
    ISBN 978-0-300-17377-2 (cl : alk. paper)
    1. World War, 1914–1918—Peace—Social aspects.   2. World War, 1914–1918—
Protest movements.   3. Peace movements—Europe—History—20th century.
    4. World War, 1914–1918—Diplomatic history.   I. Title.
    D613.M825.2014
    940.3'12—dc23
                                                                              2013041983

A catalogue record for this book is available from the British Library.

10 9 8 7 6 5 4 3 2 1

CONTENTS

ILLUSTRATIONS

MAPS

CHAPTER 1

INTRODUCTION

In late December 1915 the American Society of International Law held its annual conference in Washington. The committee had postponed the gathering from its customary date in April in order that the Society could participate in the Pan-American Scientific Congress, a recent addition to the numerous international associations that had flourished since the late nineteenth century. However, the presidential address of Elihu Root, the former Republican Secretary of State, New York senator, and Nobel Peace Prize winner in 1912, concentrated on the war in Europe, 'where the moral standards of the Thirty Years' War have returned again . . . with the same dreadful and intolerable consequences'.[1] The bonds of international peace, from 'skillful balances of power' to 'human sympathy', had been swept away in July and August 1914. Each side justified its own violation of international law by the outrages of their opponents, tearing down the fragile and often imperfect peace of the late nineteenth and early twentieth centuries. Aggression overwhelmed conciliation, hatred goodwill, and belligerence the love of peace. Yet Root did not despair. 'It was during the appalling crimes of the Thirty Years War,' he told his audience, 'that Grotius wrote his *De Jure Belli ac Pacis* and the science of international law first took form and authority. . . . We may hope that there will be again a great new departure to escape destruction by subjecting the nations to the rule of law.'[2]

In light of the subsequent history of Europe during the first half of the twentieth century, Root's reference to the Thirty Years War appears unfortunately prescient. In the telling phrase of American diplomat and historian George Kennan, the First World War was the 'seminal catastrophe' of the twentieth century. The war, in his reading, 'lay at the heart of the failure and decline of this Western civilization'. Kennan, who served in the Moscow embassy in the 1930s and was interned in Germany during the Second World War, witnessed the catastrophic legacies of the First World War. The barbarization of men in the trenches overflowed into post-war politics, setting the scene for the decline of democracy and the collapse of the rule of law. Revolution and Bolshevik dictatorship in Russia, the rise of Fascism in Italy, and the racist Nazi regime were only the most notably repressive and violent political consequences of the war. One act of violence begat another in a vicious spiral, from the assassination of the Archduke Franz Ferdinand in Sarajevo on 28 June 1914 to the dropping of nuclear weapons on Hiroshima and Nagasaki in August 1945. The Holocaust was undoubt-edly a singular event, but it was part of a larger pattern of politics, in which populations were segregated, deported, exchanged, resettled, and murdered along ethnic and national lines. The ethnic cleansing of Muslims from the Balkans in 1912 and 1913, the Armenian genocide of 1915, and the exchange of population between the new Turkish Republic and Greece in the early 1920s constitute part of this history, rooted in the First World War.[3]

Kennan was a deeply pessimistic person. He forever fretted over the travails and dangers of the modern world. What he called civilization was a fragile construct, at risk from its own stepchildren – nuclear weapons, pornography, and urbanization, to name but some of the perceived threats. He coined the phrase 'seminal catastrophe' at the height of the Cold War in the early 1980s, when fear of nuclear war stalked the world.[4] By his own admission Kennan would have felt more comfortable living in an eighteenth-century agrarian society than an industrialized twentieth-century one. At Princeton, where he became a fellow of the Institute of Advanced Study at the recommendation of Robert Oppenheimer (one of the architects of the atom bomb), and even more so on a large farm he bought, Kennan could put some distance between himself and the temptations and perils of modern America. He was not alone in viewing the First World War as the event that gave birth to the self-destructive tendencies of modern civiliza-tion. Contemporaries and later historians sought explanations for the catastrophes that had befallen the world of the early twentieth century. Technology and science, bureaucracy and government, businesses and civil society could no longer be seen simply as progressive forces, working towards the continual improvement of the human condition. In short, the history of the twentieth century, particularly its first half, mocked the aspi-rations of figures like Root.

Explaining the violent twentieth century has been one of the most pressing issues in the study of modern history. In the aftermath of the

Second World War there was a tendency to identify German political culture as the source of Europe's ills. In 1947 the Allies abolished the state of Prussia, which had come to symbolize aggressive militarism in foreign and domestic politics. The sources of two world wars could be traced back to the absence of a democratic revolution, the role of military force in unifying Germany, and the authoritarian dispensation of the Kaiserreich. Germany's *Sonderweg*, or 'special path', had led to catastrophe.[5] Yet part of the shock of war in 1914 was that people considered Germany to be a 'civilized' society. Its economic dynamism, progressive urban politics, social reforms, and innovative cultural scene were admired throughout Europe before 1914. Far from following a peculiar historical path, Germany appeared as progressive (and repressive in other ways) as the other major powers.[6]

By the end of the twentieth century, wars in Yugoslavia, growing popular awareness of the violent legacies of empire, and confrontation with the moral and political evasions in the transition from the Second World War to Cold War Europe focused attention on broader trajectories of violence in European history, which embraced but extended beyond German national history. The First World War marked the beginning of the path for the 'dark continent'.[7] Mark Mazower argues that the decade of conflict beginning in the Balkans in 1912 was 'the catalyst for genocide, ethnic cleansing, and massive forced population movements for the first time in history'. Ian Kershaw argues that during the period between 1914 and 1950 'violence had an epochal quality; it determined the age.' Although the roots of this violence lay in the development in the nineteenth century of nationalism, colonial imperialism, and socialism, he concluded that 'without the searing impact on mentalities of these dreadful years [of the First World War] it would be impossible to explain the politics of violence and the extent of the appalling inhumanity this would bring in the following decades'.[8] The mechanics and motivations behind what Alan Kramer has called the 'dynamics of destruction' of the war have been reconstructed with immense scholarly care.[9] Despite or perhaps because of the large body of scholarship, the relative significance of the Balkan wars, the shock of violence against civilians in 1914, the Armenian genocide, the rigours of industrial mobilization, the repression of domestic opposition to the war, the two Russian revolutions of 1917, and the peace treaties of 1919 and 1920 remain a source of contention in historical debates about the escalation of violence in the twentieth century.[10]

Given this catastrophic narrative of the First World War and its place in twentieth- century history, it may seem somewhat naive or even perverse to place peace at the centre of the story. In one of the great books about the war, *Civilization, 1914–1917*, Georges Duhamel, who served as a stretcher-bearer in the French Army, recounted the story of Cousin, a cheerful and courageous amputee. 'Whenever I sat down on his bed,' Duhamel wrote, 'Cousin would tell me about his little [business] affairs. He always carried the events up to the point where the war had interrupted them, and he had a natural tendency to unite the beautiful past of peace with a not less delicious future. Over the troubled and bloody abyss he loved to portray the life of other days into the life that was coming. Never verbs in the imperfect tense, but an eternal and miraculous present.'[11] Rather than ignoring the 'troubled and bloody abyss', by dividing war and peace into radically separate conditions, it is important to explore how the prospect of peace – the 'delicious future' – became interwoven with the violent experience of war.

Peace was at the centre of the First World War, providing meaning to the conflict. In turn, peace was imagined and constructed in new ways that had an enduring legacy in twentieth-century international relations. War aims ranging from the establishment of international law to the consolidation of welfare reform at home were central to the mobilization of socialists and trade unions in the conflict. Of course the defence of the state was the central war aim in all belligerent societies and governments, but people also believed that they were fighting to build a better, more peaceful future. In the midst of war, humanitarian sensibilities survived, or were even sharpened. The International Red Cross and the Vatican worked to attenuate the hatreds caused by the war, suffering, and atrocities, while new associations, such as the Women's International League for Peace and Freedom, emerged during the conflict. The experience of war and criticisms of the pre-war international order led politicians, diplomats, and others to rethink the meaning of security with a greater stress on international law, society, and institutions in place of more conventional understandings based on relative military power. Nor were these changes restricted to Europe. The war upset assumptions about European civilization and stoked demands for reform of colonial rule. In the 1920s governments and societies sought to make peace work. Although their ideas, institutions, and practices ultimately failed, they continued to inform peace-making throughout the rest of the century.[12]

Peace does not simply mean the absence of fighting. Peace became a conceptual repository, a short-hand for peoples' aspirations for a better, more just, and more prosperous world. Its meaning expanded in the First World War. For example, in his speech in late December 1915 Elihu Root spoke of 'skillful balances of power' and 'human sympathy', reconciling power politics and deterrence with human sociability and international associations, two very different approaches to peace.[13] In an appeal to boost post-war housing supply, the Trade Union Congress in 1917 called on the British government to build 1 million 'Dwellings of the Great Peace', modern houses with kitchens, plumbing, and small gardens, a tangible representation of peace.[14] In November 1948, speaking in Brussels, Alcide De Gasperi – born in the Trentino (northern Italy) in the Habsburg empire – a leading Catholic politician in post-First World War Italy, an internal exile under Fascist rule, and prime minister (1945–53) of the Italian Republic, spoke of a trinity of 'liberty-justice-peace'. His view was influenced by the experiences of two world wars. 'To save liberty it is necessary to save peace,' he claimed, updating arguments made during and after the First World War, 'but the regime of liberty cannot be saved without effecting economic reconstruction, which is the basis of social justice. The circle is therefore closed and this proves that all democratic action, by the very reason of its existence, must tend towards peace.'[15]

How did understandings of peace expand in the First World War? Peace, organized around the great powers in the late nineteenth century, came to embrace a much wider and deeper set of social and international relations, including labour regulations, the principle of nationality, constitutional reform, trusteeship, welfare, transnational associations, and international institutions. Understandings of peace connected diverse elements of private, domestic, and international relations, so that, for example, the family became an essential element in making peace. There were fears that soldiers, brutalized by their experiences, could not return to 'normal' family life. 'You won't be able to appreciate the peace of home anymore', one despairing woman in Hamburg warned her soldier husband in October 1914. Peace had a double meaning, of domestic calm and social stability.[16] Upholding family affections enabled the demobilized soldier to reintegrate into post-war society, to take up once again the bonds of community, including work, and to provide a basis for social stability. Equally, the family could serve as a source of empathy between former enemy societies, as images of the enemy were deconstructed and replaced by images of common bonds of affection between man and wife and parents and children. That said, family policy was also geared to higher birth rates, to produce the next generations of soldiers who would defend the state.

This expansive understanding of peace resulted from the experience of the war and the ways in which contemporaries made sense of the broader historical meaning of the conflict. The term 'total war' was not used until the 1930s, when it was popularized by the leading figure in the German Army during the First World War, Eric Ludendorff. Since the 1930s both the First and Second World Wars have often been described as total wars. Although the concept of 'total war' privileges certain experiences and evidence and marginalizes others – for example, the reluctance of some belligerents to mobilize women in the labour force – it remains the case that the First World War had an unprecedented impact on European societies, indeed, as we will see, on societies and politics around the globe. The mobilization of soldiers and workers, the rupturing of communities, the economic and commercial dislocation, the expansion of the state, food shortages, the mass experience of death and grief, and the violent face of occupation and internment had not occurred in living memory in Europe. Outside Europe there had been recent wars, such as the Spanish-American War (1898), the South African War (1899–1902), and the Russo-Japanese War (1904–5). For the European (and American) societies involved, however, mobilization for these wars was limited. Personal experience of warfare was much more evident in colonized societies, but it is significant that Europeans and Americans defined these regions as 'uncivilized' while claiming their wars served the civilizing mission. The experience of war after 1914, therefore, created expectations that peace would transform these aspects of daily life. The conditions of war also created specific social categories, including the veteran, the war-wounded, the orphan and war widow, and the refugee. Their fate established a claim on the state and society in the reconstruction of the post-war world.

Mobilization on this scale, in an era of popular politics and a vibrant transnational public sphere, led many to view the war as having a purpose, often connecting sacrifice with future redemption and peace. From the outset the war became a conflict of ideas.[17] The politics of war went beyond great power rivalries. In December 1915 Walter Lippmann, then a rising figure in the American intellectual firmament, rejected notions that his journal, The New Republic, was pro-German because of the absence of hatred of Germany in its articles. The war, he argued, was not about fighting against a particular state, but for political principles. 'The moral issue,' he concluded, 'is whether we can make the war count for or against a civilized union of nations.'[18] Many of these ideas, such as 'civilization' and international law, were framed in terms of the future peace. While the preservation of the state was of primary concern, war aims often anticipated far-reaching political transformations, including constitutional reform to the development of new international institutions. Institutional reforms and innovations served a wider agenda of remaking the moral framework of politics, of preserving 'civilization', and creating a political ethic conducive to peace. Governments claimed to defend not just the nation and the state, but broader values, such as 'civilization' or 'Europe', while socialists, liberals, and conservatives viewed the purpose of the war in distinctive ways. One of Germany's leading intellectuals, Max Weber, condemning Anglophobia amongst the German nationalist right in 1916, argued that the most fearful threat came from Russia, which 'threatens not just our state, but our whole culture, indeed world culture, as long as it is as degenerate as it is now'.[19] The visions of future peace proliferated as interest groups, such as trade unions, business, academics, and churches, made various claims about the reconstruction of international politics. While the precise contours of the future international order were contested, it is striking, as President Woodrow Wilson pointed out in 1916, that both sides in the war often claimed to defend the same set of values.

Of course one could dismiss the speeches, pamphlets, and books as rhetoric, useful to mobilize societies to fight, but relatively unimportant when set beside the more material and immediate concerns about the security of the state. The importance of material factors in the international order – geographical location, number of soldiers, military technology, financial resources, and so on – can hardly be denied. Yet these forms of power were deployed in a political context, in which the stakes of the war were defined in terms that went beyond state security to encompass the defence of civilization, international law, European values, and the principle of nationality, to name but some. Immanuel Kant had argued in *Perpetual Peace*, written during the French revolutionary wars in 1795 and an important source for peace debates in the First World War, that the principle of publicity created its own political dynamics. 'This hommage that every state pays the concept of right (at least verbally),' he wrote, thinking of the public declarations of states and politicians in the French revolutionary wars, 'nevertheless proves that there is to be found in the human being a still greater, though at present dormant, moral predisposition to eventually become master of the evil principle [of offensive war] within him.'[20]

First, it was significant that the First World War had to be justified in terms that went beyond arguments rooted in the defence of a state's material interests, its territorial integrity, and its military security. These concerns were central to debates about war aims, but they were articulated within a wider framework of principles that shaped the international order. Second, behind closed doors, abstract principles, such as international law and international labour regulation, framed policy-making. Politicians were aware that measures had to be justified against the political and moral principles at stake in the war. These principles were bent, often to the point of destruction, but they provided political vocabularies in which more specific measures were communicated. Third, this pervasive talk of peace and its associated principles led to the emergence of norms that structured the international order. The tendency of Kant's publicity principle was to bring political behaviour closer to the dictates of moral codes.

The prospect of perpetual peace, paradoxically, worked to intensify violence during the First World War. George Bernard Shaw, in an introduction in 1916 to Fabian proposals for international government, denounced the idea of a war to end war as an 'oxymoron'. Such slogans, he argued, 'can be taken only literally by ignorant and simple persons to whom a European war is simply a football match conducted with cannons'.[21] Two years earlier Shaw's friend, the science fiction writer H. G. Wells, had written *The War that Will End War*, a collection of his articles in the first months of the conflict. 'This is now a war for peace,' he declared. It was a war to change the German mind, by which he meant the attitudes of the German military and political elite. 'We fight not to destroy a nation, but a nest of evil ideas. . . . The real task of mankind is to get better sense into the heads of these Germans, and therewith and thereby into the heads of humanity generally, and to end not simply a war, but the idea of war.'[22] The idea of a war to end wars became a bitter mockery of Wells's better aspirations, but during the conflict these ideas were taken seriously. The vision of a balanced and harmonious world order justified each side believing itself to be the sole guardian of virtue against an inherently evil enemy, in making ever greater efforts to win a decisive victory rather than compromising and having to fight once again in the foreseeable future. The sacrifices of the war could only be redeemed through total victory, leading to total peace. As each side defined its struggle in moral, as well as security, terms, it reduced the scope for a negotiated settlement. Moral values could not be spliced and diced like territory and reparations. Even territorial and financial issues, on the face of it material issues, were framed as part of a moral contest. While both sides claimed to represent a set of values that went beyond the strictly national, this was more emphasized amongst British, French, and later American meanings of the war. As the self-proclaimed champions of civilization, these states had to destroy not only the armies but also the political systems of

Germany, Austria-Hungary, and the Ottoman empire, which corrupted international politics with their barbaric attitudes to military force. According to this logic peace and war were not polar opposites, but mutually dependent. Violence, contemporaries argued, could serve progressive ends.

Many of these ideas were circulating in the late nineteenth century, but this story begins in the summer of 1911 with the Second Moroccan Crisis and the Italian government's decision to invade the two north African Ottoman provinces of Tripolitania and Cyrenaica. The book concludes with the domestic and international settlements between the Treaty of Washington in 1922 concerning the Pacific and East Asia and the Treaty of Locarno in 1925 dealing with Europe. This period between 1911 and 1925 constitutes the Long First World War. During these years there took place a transformation of international politics from the European great power and imperial order to a global order based on international institutions, nation states, multilateral security systems, arms limitation agreements, restored economic interdependence, and transnational associations. By no means were all problems resolved by 1925 – an impossible definition of peace, in any case; rather, a framework existed that enabled further peace work.

The Italian invasion of north Africa in 1911 began a series of wars in the eastern Mediterranean and Balkans that demonstrated the failure of the great power peace of the late nineteenth and early twentieth centuries. These wars and the failures of the great powers to manage political change created the immediate conditions for the outbreak of a general European war in 1914. Coincidentally, though of importance for understanding the global transformations of this period, the Mexican Revolution had begun in 1910, and the Qing dynasty fell in China in 1911, inaugurating a period of instability in East Asia. Both of these events revealed the limits of European imperial power on the eve of the First World War. While the armistices ended the war in November 1918, the transition to peace was jagged and often violent. From conventional wars, such as the Soviet–Polish War in 1919–20, to the violent suppression of anti-imperial movements, to the paramilitary violence across much of central and eastern Europe, the violent legacies of the First World War shaped these conflicts and the post-war system as much as the treaties concluded at Paris in 1919 and 1920.[23] Between 1922 and 1925 post-war regimes consolidated their power, from the Irish Free State to the Turkish Republic, from Soviet Russia to Fascist Italy. At the same time international peace was slowly constructed, culminating in the Treaties of Washington in 1922 and Locarno in 1925.

This longer chronological view is accompanied by a broad geographical perspective. While the war's epicentre was in Europe and the decisive theatre turned out to be the Western Front, the most revolutionary consequences of the war were arguably felt elsewhere. This was particularly evident in 1917. 'The world is not only at war,' wrote Lippmann, 'but in revolution as well. That revolution goes deeper than any man had dared to guess. The overturn in Russia, the intervention of America, the stirring of China, stupendous as they are, may be merely the prelude to events more drastic still.'[24] The map of central and eastern Europe changed more radically than that of western Europe, while the territorial changes in the Middle East following the collapse of the Ottoman empire were more radical still. Mapping political values and identities was part of the process of establishing a new global order. Notions about 'civilization', race, and barbarism were territorially bounded, but those boundaries shifted over the course of the war. Even an ostensibly geographical term such as 'Europe' contained within it political and cultural assumptions associated with 'civilization', Christianity, and nationality. The entangled connections and relationships between different parts of the world are important in understanding the global transformations of the long First World War. Ideas discussed in one part of the world were reworked in another part, to suit the local context. Decisions and events in one region could have unintended consequences elsewhere. Nor were these entanglements restricted to inter-state relations. The richly textured internationalist culture of the pre-war years, from scientific congresses to commercial, labour, and religious associations, survived throughout the war. This internationalism was diverted into new paths as societies mobilized for war and considered new ways of making and sustaining peace. The persistent international connections meant that governments paid close attention to civil society in other states, while interest groups in one society interacted with their counterparts elsewhere, including in enemy states. Tracing these connections and interactions involves jumping around different parts of the globe, but in doing so, it demonstrates how the First World War was part of a remaking of the global, as well as the European, order. But first let us start with the collapse of the great power peace between 1911 and 1914.

CHAPTER 2

THE FAILURE OF GREAT POWER PEACE, 1911–1914

AT THE HEIGHT of the Second Moroccan Crisis, the Chancellor of the Exchequer, David Lloyd George, used the traditional forum of the Mansion House Speech on 21 July 1911 to warn German leaders that the British government would defend its interests, in this case its entente with France. The speech was carefully choreographed. Lloyd George was on the radical wing of the Liberal Party, associated with constitutional and social reform rather than with an assertive foreign policy. His warning would compel German leaders to adopt a more conciliatory stance in negotiations over Morocco. As Lloyd George rose to give his speech, 'a young man in evening dress who sat at a table near the door, asked to be informed of the intention of the Government in regard to Women's Suffrage. He was at once removed and taken in charge by the police. He admitted that he had come to the banquet uninvited but pleaded, as if in mitigation of his conduct, that he had not tasted any of the things provided.'[1] *The Times* lingered no longer on the disruption, but the intrusion of the young man was a reminder of one of the many issues that crowded domestic and international politics in 1911. The coronation of a new king, George V (on 22 June), was an opportunity to rethink the structure and purpose of the British empire. The imminent Home Rule crisis raised the issue of the place of national minorities in multi-national states, a matter that was relevant across Europe. The meeting of the First Universal Races Congress in London in July signalled the increasing importance of notions of race in international politics. Further afield, the Qing dynasty in China would be engulfed in revolution by the end of the year. Meanwhile in Mexico, the revolution that started in late 1910 had become increasingly radical.

Confrontation between the European great powers took place within a wider remaking of international politics. The international order over the forty years since the end of the Franco-Prussian War (1871) had depended, in large part, on the ability of the great powers to manage changes in domestic, international, and imperial politics. Between 1911 and 1914 the capability of the great powers to restrain their own rivalries and manage change had failed. This failure became evident in the Italo-Ottoman War of 1911–12 and the two Balkan Wars of 1912 and 1913. The origins of the First World War were part of a larger transformation of global politics, in which the institutions, norms, and practices that had developed since the late nineteenth century were challenged and eroded, and new ideas about the international order became increasingly prominent.

* * *

There was a vibrant debate in the early twentieth century about the future direction of the European and global order. Many advocates of change in international politics were idealists, who looked forward to a more peaceful and just world. They were often marginal to the formal decision-making processes in international relations, but as new ideas percolated into mainstream debate about international politics, they challenged the conventions of great power politics. This contest of ideas was important not because of their intrinsic merits but because, in the global crisis ignited by the First World War, people reached for alternative ideas that expressed their experiences and their aspirations for a better future. To take just three examples centred on London in the summer of 1911: in June leaders from around the British empire gathered in London to celebrate the coronation of George V and discuss ways of strengthening imperial bonds. The following month around a thousand delegates met at the First Universal Races Congress to discuss the promotion of friendly relations between different races. It was 'the greatest event of the twentieth century', according to the African American activist William E. DuBois.[2] In August, Britain along with France signed arbitration treaties with the United States. President William Taft and his Secretary of State, Philander Knox, both lawyers, promoted these treaties assiduously, though they later foundered in the Senate.[3]

The processions of proposals for a new international order, based variously on notions of humanity, civilization, power, and law, derived from a dense network of international associations, intellectual exchange, and cheap and reliable communications. Internationalism, in its various guises, operated on a different plane to great power politics. There were international associations for lawyers, humanitarians, trade unionists, social reformers, missionaries, academics, and business people. International networks were important props to the promotion of their own interests, be they better working conditions or the conversion of heathens. Figures such as Paul Otlet, the Belgian founder of the Union of International Associations, were unusual in viewing internationalism as an end in itself. At government level, there were international agreements on the regulation of posts and telegraphs, cooperation in eradicating or at least managing epidemics, and the establishment of common standards regarding time and weights and measures.

Whether internationalism could tame the rivalries between states remained an open question. In June 1913 the Russian composer Sergey Prokofiev travelled to London. His journey was emblematic of the global connections centred on Europe, and especially London, on the eve of the war. He was particularly struck by the advertisements in shipping line offices for voyages to India and the Americas. 'Such appetizing displays, beckoning from afar, are not to be found in St Petersburg or even Paris, and they make London seem somehow more closely connected to the world, so that a trip to India or South America, which seems to a Russian a virtually impossible fantasy, here appears a relatively normal, even simple under-taking.' Later that day Prokofiev was in Hyde Park when the French President, Raymond Poincaré, and George V trundled past in 'magnificent antique carriages. The crowd welcomed them with cheers, while the band thundered out the Marseillaise, breaking into the English national anthem after three bars.'[4] In London the gestures of great power politics – the state visit – jostled with the ephemera of a globalized world – the alluring adver-tisements for foreign travel.

This process of globalization in the late nineteenth century was largely the product of European ideas, power, and institutions, which in turn faced challenges from around the globe. In 1910 and 1911 two revolutions, in Mexico and China respectively, also marked significant changes in global politics. By undermining conventional patterns of European (and American) political influence and reworking ideas about constitutional reform, race, and political economy, the Mexican and Chinese revolutions can be viewed as part of a changing world order on the eve of the First World War. If we think about the First World War not just as a conflict between the European great powers, but as a remaking of ideas, institu-tions, and geopolitics, then affairs in both the western hemisphere and East Asia become important to understanding the transformations of this era.

Both revolutions were driven in part by a rejection of the state's position in world politics and the economy. In Mexico the oligarchical dictatorship of Porfirio Díaz faced rising middle-class criticism which was led by a rich and idealistic landowner from northern Mexico, Francisco Madero, who campaigned for a restoration of constitutional liberties. The rural masses also rose to support him, due in part to their appalling working conditions, which had been shaped by the integration of Mexico into the global economy. Mexico, a recipient of massive foreign investment mainly from the United States and Britain, exported minerals and agricultural products grown on vast *haciendas* or estates. In addition, from the early twentieth century oil companies bought exploration rights and expelled indigenous inhabitants from areas in northern Mexico. Poor harvests in 1908 and 1909, and the slowdown in the American economy following the financial crisis of 1907, exposed the imbalances in the Mexican economy. Unable to contain the revolt, Díaz resigned in May 1911 and Madero became president-elect in November of that year.[5]

Likewise international politics shaped the Chinese Revolution. After the country was defeated by Japan in the war of 1894–5, the Qing dynasty joined the list of what Lord Salisbury called the 'dying empires'. Nor would Qing China be left to die in peace. The Boxer Rebellion of 1900 led to occupation by European, American, and Japanese forces. A combination of the weakness of the state and continued foreign intervention doomed planned reforms. In October 1911 army officers in the Wuhan province rebelled and imperial officials fled. On 12 February 1912 Yuan Shikai, the leading Chinese general, who identified George Washington as his model, declared China a republic. Chinese revolutionaries wanted to modernize the country so that it could participate effectively in international politics, rather than remain a passive object of great power politics. Power, rather than political economy, was at the core of the Chinese Revolution's relationship with the international system. Yang Du, an intellectual and supporter of Yuan, coined the phrase 'gold-ironism' to describe his theory that the modern world was based on economic strength and military power. The revolutionaries believed that making China an effective power would require social and cultural change. Hence the adoption of the solar calendar and Western dress codes symbolized China's ambition to become an equal state within the international system – but also one that could defend its interests.[6]

Domestic unrest had provided a long list of opportunities for foreign intervention in the past, but in the case of the Mexican and Chinese

Revolutions, the great powers, including the United States and Japan, were hesitant and divided. The failure of the great powers to manage transformations in these states marked a departure from the previous practices of international politics. There was some sympathy for Madero's reforming project, though most foreign observers predicted he would fail. Paul von Hintze, the German minister in Mexico City, called Madero 'a good and noble person'. 'His cardinal error lies in his belief,' Hintze argued, 'that the Mexican people can be ruled like one of the advanced Germanic nations [William II marked this 'correct']. This raw people, of semi-savages without religion and a thin upper elite of superficially civilised half-castes, cannot bear anything other than the rule of enlightened despotism.'[7] The slow pace of reform, in part due to Madero's concern not to provoke foreign intervention by radical measures, undermined his political base. In February 1913 General Huerta led a military coup against Madero, who was then murdered.

Yuan, sworn in as president on 10 March 1912, was determined to centralize power in China. His authoritarian instincts cut across the new participatory politics. Political rivals were intimidated and even murdered, and constitutional restraints on presidential power were cast aside. Yuan was also willing to conclude the so-called six-power loan with banks from six states – Japan, the United States, Russia, Britain, France, and Germany. Loans reduced his dependence on parliamentary government.

The Mexican and Chinese Revolutions provided the stage for Woodrow Wilson's introduction to international politics. In November 1912 he won the presidency in a race against Teddy Roosevelt and Taft. A former president of Princeton University and governor of New Jersey, Wilson had run on 'new freedom', a slogan devised by Louis Brandeis, whom Wilson would later appoint as the first Jew to the Supreme Court. 'New freedom' entailed a criticism of the concentration of economic power in corporations and special interests. This concentration of economic power endangered the individual's political liberty. Moreover, powerful economic interest groups exploited the political system to enhance private profit. Excessively high tariffs, which protected certain producers and pushed up prices for consumers, were one of Wilson's particular targets. He famously remarked that it would be 'an irony of fate' if foreign policy dominated his presidency.[8] Nonetheless he had certain general ideas about American foreign policy, based in part on his prescriptions for the domestic political economy. American interests could be advanced by commercial freedoms and the attractiveness of its democratic ideals. 'You will establish the supremacy of America as we wish it to be established,' he had declared to the National

League of Commission Merchants in January 1912, 'not by force of arms, not by the conquest of aggrandizement, . . . but by the free injection of our enthusiasm, our love of mankind, our confidence in human liberty.'[9]

On entering office, Wilson faced important decisions concerning China and Mexico. Would the United States recognize the Chinese Republic? Would Wilson support the loan agreement with China? Would the United States recognize General Huerta's regime in Mexico? Wilson's first move was to reverse Taft's decision to participate in the six-power loan to China. Far from strengthening China, Wilson argued that the loan would further infringe Chinese sovereignty. Control of the budget would pass from the elected representatives to foreign bankers. American bankers were free to lend money to China, but they would receive no support from their own government. Less than two weeks after the decision on the six-power loan, Wilson decided in March 1913 to recognize the Chinese Republic. 'The awakening of the people of China,' he said, 'to a consciousness of their possibilities under free government is the most significant, if not the most momentous, event of our generation.'[10] Wilson's support for Yuan's government married principle and interest. The rejection of the loan, which Yuan badly needed to rebuild China, risked a loss of American influence in East Asia. However, the diplomatic recognition of China was a means of building links on the basis of shared political principles of freely elected representative government. In reality there was a vast gulf between American and Chinese political visions and circumstances. Nonetheless, language mattered. Wilson declared himself 'stirred and cheered' when Yuan asked Christian churches to set aside a day of prayer to 'guide China'.[11]

It was also significant that Wilson had recognized the Chinese Republic without prior consultation with the other powers. The Russian ambassador to Washington was at pains to point out that the European powers had followed the American lead on whether to recognize the Mexican government or not. However, Wilson disputed the comparison, on the grounds that Yuan was a legitimately elected president and parliamentary elections had taken place in China, whereas murder and a military coup were the basis of Huerta's regime in Mexico. Wilson and the Russian ambassador were talking at odds – for Wilson, political legitimacy was the key point, not geographical spheres of influence.[12] Wilson refused to recognize Huerta's regime until elections had taken place. The absence of recognition prevented Huerta from raising a loan. As pointed out by the British minister in Mexico City, Francis Strange, who liked to walk around with a parrot on his shoulder, this exacerbated the collapse of the Mexican state and the rise of lawlessness. Even a man with a 'consuming passion for parrots', as his American colleague Henry Lane Wilson put it, could be right.[13] British frustration at Wilson's policy increased throughout 1913, but the Foreign Secretary Edward Grey recognized that American friendship was more valuable than the futile championing of Huerta's claims. Huerta's decision to dissolve the Chamber of Deputies and hold elections was criticized by Wilson's administration. On 27 October 1913 Wilson gave his first major foreign policy address in Mobile, Alabama, in which he braided together the themes of constitutional liberty and economic freedom. He condemned American business groups for supporting dictatorships in Latin America. Constitutional government, he argued, had to be won; it could not be conferred from above.[14]

In April 1914, following the arrest of American sailors by Huerta's forces at the eastern Mexican port of Tampico, Wilson ordered American marines to the port of Veracruz further south in order to prevent the importation of arms destined for Huerta's troops. The bombardment of the town killed 126 Mexicans. John Reed, a radical journalist (best known for his coverage of the Bolshevik Revolution and *Ten Days that Shook the World*), criticized Wilson's decision to send marines to Veracruz. He denounced the attitudes of cultural superiority and financial greed, which, he claimed, shaped American intervention in Mexico and elsewhere. Imperialism abroad was the product of corrupt government at home. 'In Mexico, as well as at home, the idle money of foreign speculators is of more importance than the wishes, independence, and ideals of the people who gave it to them.'[15]

By the outbreak of the First World War neither the Mexican nor the Chinese Revolution had resulted in stable government. The war would shape these revolutions, especially in China. Yet it is also worth bearing in mind that these revolutions signalled changes within the international system. The influence of European powers in Mexico and China was considerably restricted when compared to the second half of the nineteenth century. The world that Europe had made was less and less amenable to its control, even as societies adopted European conventions – from dress to the Chinese reworking of Otto von Bismarck's adage about 'blood and iron'. The election of Woodrow Wilson had coincided with these revolutions and in this context he first set out some of his foreign policy ideas, notably the stress on constitutional government, his suspicion of military force, and the promotion of trade.

* * *

Lloyd George's intervention in the Second Moroccan Crisis momentarily heightened tensions between Britain and Germany, while the dilatory pace of Franco-German negotiations over the summer of 1911 sapped confidence in a peaceful resolution. Most of the German press considered war as a likely outcome, though their editorials did not view the prospect of war in positive terms.[16] The uncertainty was captured by the British ambassador to Berlin, Edward Goschen, who told a French diplomat that 'I regarded the present situation like I regarded ghosts. I don't believe in them but I am frightened of them. So I don't believe there will be war – but I am deadly anxious about it.'[17] It was unlikely that the Moroccan crisis would lead to a general European war. Military action remained confined to Morocco, where French troops had marched on the northern city of Fez in March 1911 to suppress a revolt against the Sultan of Morocco, whilst also exploiting the collapse of the Sultan's authority to establish a French protectorate. The German Foreign Secretary, Alfred von Kiderlen-Wächter, whose normal mastery of diplomatic calculation was absent in this crisis, never countenanced war as a serious option in 1911. The stakes were too low and it was difficult to justify waging a war over Germany's interests in Morocco to domestic and international opinion. In Paris, once the Chief of the General Staff, Joseph Joffre, told the premier, Joseph Caillaux, that France stood a 70 per cent chance of winning a war against Germany, the French government decided on a negotiated settlement. French and German diplomats eked out an agreement by early November. France transferred part of Cameroon to Germany's colonial empire, while Germany recognized the French protectorate over Morocco.

The successful resolution of the Moroccan crisis masked a more serious deterioration in the international system. In May 1916 Stephen Pichon, sometime French Foreign Minister and close associate of Georges Clemenceau, remarked that 'the war became inevitable after the march on Fez. This decision released Italy, which wanted Tripolitania. This then led to war between Italy and Turkey. Then the Balkan states raised their standards under the protection of Russia. Everything unfolded fatally.'[18] Coming from a senior French politician in the midst of the war, this was a remarkable assessment. The Moroccan crisis led the Italian government to invade Tripolitania, present-day Libya, which was then part of the Ottoman empire. The subsequent war between Italy and the Ottoman empire weakened the latter and gave the Balkan League – Serbia, Bulgaria, Greece, and Montenegro – an opportunity to destroy the remnants of Ottoman power in the Balkans in 1912. However, in 1913 the Balkan League collapsed, as

Bulgaria fought and was defeated by its erstwhile allies. These wars destroyed a system of European states that had maintained general peace for over four decades. The responsibility for the collapse of peace between the great powers lay not simply in what the great powers did, but in what they failed to do: they failed to manage the process of change. The maintenance of peace was not a default position. Peace required the management of political change, an often painstaking and tedious process of diplomatic engagement.

Remarkably there were politicians, diplomats, and journalists who foresaw the disastrous repercussions of an Italian invasion of Ottoman territory in north Africa. Although the provinces of Tripolitania and Cyrenaica (present-day eastern Libya) were remote from the core of the empire, an Italian invasion was bound to weaken the prestige and authority of the Ottoman government, which had been attempting to revive the state's fortunes since the Young Turk Revolution of 1908. When the Italian ambassador to Vienna, the Duke of Avarna, claimed that an Italian occupation of Tripolitania would not constitute a threat to peace, the Austro-Hungarian Foreign Minister, Count Aehrenthal, noted the 'incalculable moral danger, which lay in the repercussions of such an Italian step in Tripoli on the powers and the Balkan states'. By violating the status quo in one region, Italy made it much more difficult to defend the status quo in other regions of the Ottoman empire.[19] Given the intervention of the great powers in the Ottoman empire – the British occupation of Egypt since 1882 and the Austro-Hungarian annexation of Bosnia-Herzegovina in 1908 being the two most notable examples – Aehrenthal's pious defence of principle seemed hollow. Days before the Italian invasion, Kiderlen-Wächter made a half-hearted attempt to persuade the French government to intervene with Germany in Rome in urging peace. 'The outcome is uncertain,' he told Jules Cambon, the French ambassador to Berlin, 'and it will be impossible the moment it breaks out to hold back Bulgaria, Serbia, and Greece. The Albanians and the Arabs in Yemen will revolt, and Austria perhaps will be compelled to intervene in the conflict, which will set fire to the whole of the Orient: it will be general war.'[20]

Not only did the Italian invasion undermine diplomatic principle and geopolitical arrangements, it threatened to provoke a war characterized by ethnic and religious violence. This war was not a traditional 'cabinet war' (a decisive and short conflict fought for limited political aims) between two standing armies, the type fought between Austria and Prussia in 1866 and the German Confederation and France in the summer of 1870. Violence against civilians, justified on the grounds of religious and ethnic identity, would not be subject to the same control by professional officers. An editorial in the leading Viennese newspaper, *Neue Freie Presse*, on 25 September 1911, predicted that the war in north Africa would reach Europe. 'Racial hatred' would thrive as the Ottoman empire expelled Italian citizens from its territory, the war would cost numerous lives, and trade would be destroyed. Yet it was futile to oppose Italy at this point: 'the Italian people wish it and we live in an era of people's rule'.[21] Violence against civilians, justified by racial, religious, and ethnic difference, had been a feature of imperial politics throughout the late nineteenth century. Within Europe ethnic and religious wars had been contained and localized, as Balkan states and the Ottoman empire were subject to the majesty of the great powers. Now the *Neue Freie Presse* and other papers were no longer confident about the great powers' ability to contain this type of violence. In north Africa the restraints of European great power politics intersected with the violence of imperialism.

Given the risks, why did Italian leaders decide to invade Tripolitania in September 1911? In March of that year Giovanni Giolitti had formed a new government. Born in Mondovì, near Turin, in 1842, Giolitti was the dominant figure in Italian politics in the early twentieth century. A master of *traformismo* – the practice of clientelism and parliamentary management – he had already served as prime minister on three occasions. In his fourth term he intended to widen the basis of the Italian political system by introducing universal male suffrage and social reforms. As reform required stability, imperial expansion was not a priority.[22] Moreover, Giolitti was acutely aware of the dangerous repercussions that an Italian attack on Ottoman territory carried. 'The integrity of what is left of the Ottoman empire is one of the principles upon which is founded the equilibrium and peace of Europe,' he told his friend the journalist Guglielmo Ferrari. 'And what if, after we attack Turkey, the Balkans move? And what if a Balkan war provokes a clash between the two groups of powers and a European war? Is it wise that we saddle ourselves with the responsibility for setting fire to the powder?'[23] Others echoed these concerns. Avarna, despite his assurances to Aehrenthal about a decisive Italian success, noted on 28 July 1911 that the 'truly capital and delicate point of the question' was the reaction of the Balkan states. North Africa and the Balkans were connected spheres, part of a larger map of European geopolitics. If the Balkan states acted and the status quo became untenable, he predicted that Austria-Hungary would seek compensation in the Balkans. Italy risked losing ground in the Balkans, while it grabbed territory in north Africa. In a highly secret memorandum written on the same day, read only by Giolitti and the king, Victor Emmanuel, the Foreign Minister, Antonio di San Giuliano, also underlined the risks of repercussions in the Balkans.[24]

Yet Avarna and San Giuliano also offered cogent reasons for an Italian invasion of Tripolitania in the same documents as they warned of the possible consequences of a general European war. In part, Italy had to expand in order to maintain its position amongst the great powers and the balance of power in the Mediterranean. 'At many points around the world,' Avarna wrote on 28 July, 'European powers are undertaking activities, which must lead to an increase in their territory. The intrigues of Russia in Persia serve this end. The current Moroccan crisis will probably lead to a territorial extension of France, Germany, and Spain in the Mediterranean basin, the equilibrium of which is one of the cornerstones of our foreign policy.'[25] The logic of international politics gave Italian leaders a desperate choice. The extension of French influence in Morocco required a similar prize for Italy. Great powers did not merely protect their territory and patrol their spheres of influence, they had to pursue expansionist policies. Standing still equated to decline. This dynamic competition could be accommodated within the European states system as long as expansion took place in far-flung parts of the globe. However, this dynamism ran counter to the restraint exercised by the great powers within Europe. Of course, states had expanded their territory in Europe, notably the Balkan states and Austria-Hungary at the expense of the Ottoman empire. Expansion occurred at moments when the Ottoman empire was undergoing crisis and it was also sanctioned by the European great powers – Austria-Hungary's annexation of Bosnia-Herzegovina was an important exception to this pattern, but Austro-Hungarian soldiers and officials had occupied and administered these two provinces since the Treaty of Berlin in 1878. Giolitti and San Giuliano feared provoking a major crisis in the Ottoman empire, but they considered that they had little choice, owing to the need to secure Italy's interests as a great power.

Indeed, successive Italian governments had secured agreements from other great powers to its sphere of influence in Tripolitania. The most important of these agreements was concluded in 1902 between the Italian Foreign Minister, Giulio Prinetti, and the French ambassador to Rome, Camille Barrère. According to this agreement, France and Italy could develop their 'spheres of influence' in Morocco and Tripolitania respectively. This show of Franco-Italian cooperation in north Africa failed to perturb Italy's partner in the Triple Alliance, Germany, as the then Chancellor, Bernhard von Bülow, remarked that a man would not object to his wife dancing with another man, as long as she went home with her husband at the end of the evening. In October 1909 the Italian and Russian Foreign Ministers had agreed to support the status quo in the Balkans, but if the status quo was upset, the principle of nationality would dictate the territorial settlement in the Balkans.[26] The establishment of a French protectorate in Morocco, the most likely outcome of the Moroccan crisis by the late summer of 1911, meant Giolitti's government now had to cash in the 1902 agreement. Giolitti reckoned that there would be no meaningful opposition from any of the great powers. San Giuliano hoped that this absence of opposition, coupled with the difficulty the Ottoman empire faced in defending its territory, would enable Italian forces to invade and control Tripolitania rapidly. A decisive military success could limit the risk of complications in the Balkans.

Aside from the pressures of the international system, Giolitti also faced an increasingly vociferous nationalist movement. In 1910 the Italian Nationalist Association had been founded in Florence. The year 1911 was the fiftieth anniversary of the foundation of the Italian state, commemorated in Rome by the construction in monumental style of 'Il Vittoriano' between the Piazza Venezia and the Capitoline Hill. This was hardly an atmosphere conducive to restraint. *La Stampa*, a nationalist paper in Turin, ran a campaign urging Giolitti to invade Tripolitania. One of its journalists, Giuseppe Bevione, cruised along the coast of Tripolitania, looking through a telescope at what he described as a lush territory.[27] Mixing stories of outrages against Italian settlers and families there with demands for action to assert Italy's interests, the nationalist press added to the pressure on the government to order an invasion.[28] The role of the state was to protect honour – the intimate, private honour of the family as well as the public honour of the nation.

La Stampa criticized the idea of 'pacific penetration' – this term referred to the use of economic means by a great power to assert its influence in a given territory. France in Morocco and Britain in Egypt had established their influence through financial institutions, trade, and technical experts, before using military force to secure their interests. Tripolitania offered less scope for exerting commercial influence, but Italian firms complained that they were shut out by Ottoman officials, who favoured German and French businesses. In reality most Italian firms were not strong enough to support an effective policy of 'pacific penetration'. Giolitti's government was even more reliant, therefore, on the Italian Army to assert its claims to Tripolitania. In other words, the decision to resort to military force was partly born out of Italian weakness in what is nowadays called 'soft power'.

The Ottoman government sought to conciliate the Italian government, while bolstering its defences in the region. Earlier in the year the Grand Vizir, Ibrahim Hakki Pasha, had replaced the *vali*, or governor, of Tripolitania, who was accused of obstructing Italian commercial interests in the province.[29] Ottoman leaders were determined to defend their territory. Following the Young Turk Revolution of 1908, successive governments had sought to mobilize the different religious, ethnic, and national groupings under the banner of Ottomanism, a broad tent that could accommodate the diversity of the empire in a single, more centralized state.[30] However, this imperial vision was under attack from within as well as without the empire. In 1911 Ottoman troops were fighting against rebels in Albania and Yemen, which weakened the empire in two ways as it prepared for conflict with Italy. First, military resources were severely overstretched on the eve of the war in 1911. Second, Ottoman forces committed atrocities during the suppression of the Albanian revolt, including the rape of women and the burning of villages. 'A scandal to the 20th century', these atrocities reinforced older notions that the Ottoman state was inherently cruel and did not belong within the moral sphere of European powers.[31] Assessing the implications of the war, Winston Churchill, then Home Secretary under Prime Minister Herbert Asquith, noted that 'we [Britain] must prefer Italy to Turkey on all grounds – moral and material'.[32]

The decision for war was essentially taken by two men, Giolitti and San Giuliano. Over the summer they had minimized contact with foreign diplomats. 'We have had a quiet summer in Italy,' the British ambassador Rennell Rodd reported on 14 September, 'particularly as the heat washed out all one's energy, but now things are beginning to grow more lively with Tripoli – and the outcome of the Moroccan question.'[33] On the same day Giolitti and San Giuliano met and agreed to invade Tripolitania in November. Their timetable soon accelerated. On 28 September the Italian ambassador presented an ultimatum to the Ottoman government. It combined the language of national interest with the imperial civilizing mission. It was in Italy's 'vital interest' that it occupy Tripolitania, an area which should 'enjoy the same progress as that attained by other parts of North Africa'. The ultimatum was designed to be rejected and the Ottoman government duly did so. The following day, 29 September 1911, Italy declared war.[34]

The immediate reaction around Europe was telling. William II, on his hunting estate in Rominten, near Königsberg in northeastern Germany, said the news 'landed like a bomb'. He predicted the collapse of the Ottoman government, the massacre of foreigners in the Ottoman empire, and war in the Balkans, 'the unleashing of a *Weltbrand* (world fire) with all its terrors.'[35] The popular Austro-Hungarian ambassador to London, Count Mensdorff, was at the royal retreat of Balmoral when the news arrived. George V's entourage condemned Italy's action as 'immoral', while John Morley, by now one of the grand old men of the Liberal Party and Gladstone's biographer, told Mensdorff that compared to Italy, Germany – in poor standing following the Moroccan crisis – was like a 'sweet lamb'.[36] The *Manchester Guardian* echoed Morley's sentiments. 'There can surely be few parallels in history to the indifference towards the opinion and conscience of civilised States which the aggressor has shown in entering this quarrel', declared the editorial. It concluded that 'disregard of public laws is contagious and the infection grows worse as it spreads'.[37] The Austrian liberal and Anglophile Josef Redlich described Italy's attack on the Ottoman empire as a 'street mugging'. International law was exposed as pious and irrelevant.[38] The next day, 30 September, he met the British journalist William Stead, who called for the boycott of Italian commerce until the Italian government submitted its dispute with the Ottoman empire to arbitration. 'The idea is magnificent, but it is not practical politics or even common-sense', commented the editorial in *The Times* on 5 October. 'The truth is that these and other provisions in Peace Conventions are only effective in a world given over to Realpolitik, if and when, the parties invoking them are able and willing to assert them by armed force. They cannot in the present, imperfect state of civilization be a substitute for that force. This, perhaps, is the most valuable, as it is the most direct, lesson taught to us and to others by events in the Mediterranean. We trust that it will not be thrown away upon the nation or even upon all of our eminent peacemakers.'[39]

The Times was right to underline the centrality of power in the international system, power that could be measured in ships and battalions. 'Moral force' seemed impotent in the face of military power, but the language, which framed the diplomatic exchanges and public debates, was of crucial importance to the development of the international system. Power required legitimacy – indeed, legitimacy was an element of power in the international system. The language of civilization and atrocity, international law and military force, and empire and nation carried heavy political freight. Vague as these ideas were, they provided a framework for action in the international sphere. Political acts required public justification – and not just to a domestic audience, but also to an international one. Hypocritical as it may appear, the ability of France to portray its actions in Morocco as part of a civilizing mission gave it an advantage over Italy, whose claims did not enjoy similar credibility in Europe. For example, by early 1914 German, French, and British politicians were speaking of their common civilizing mission in Africa, one element in the rapprochement that took place between the three states after the Moroccan crisis.[40] Moreover, language provided a means for thinking about international politics, how they operated and how they could be remade. Stead's plea for arbitration was ignored in 1911, but the idea was on the agenda of international politics. As the ideas, practices, and institutions that had shaped the international order since the late nineteenth century began to fail, specific forms of expression, often conceived in couplets such as 'civilization and barbarism' or 'white and yellow', provided a framework for imagining a different world.

And so on 29 September 1911 four decades of general peace in Europe came abruptly to an end. The Italian government's justifications for its action were flimsier than usual, without even an immediate threat to public order in Tripolitania, long a staple excuse for European powers to intervene in the Ottoman empire. While the European powers harboured long-term ambitions to carve out spheres of influence in the Ottoman empire, they had no wish to hasten that process and risk war in the Balkans. Yet it must also be remembered that Giolitti and San Giuliano faced a stark choice in September 1911, one that would torment European statesmen over the next three years. Could they reconcile Italy's claims to be a great power, claims that demanded military action in Tripolitania, with the interests of maintaining stability within the European states system, interests that demanded restraint? In the end they privileged Italy's great power status over the requirements for stability. They hoped that decisive military victory would square the circle. In this sense they anticipated the far riskier decisions made in Vienna, St Petersburg, and Berlin between 1912 and 1914. Giolitti and San Giuliano did not set out to provoke a general European conflagration, but they were willing to run the risk and in the process eroded the practices, norms, and institutions that had preserved general peace in Europe since the 1870s.

* * *

Had Italian forces won a decisive victory, paving the way for a quick political settlement, then the repercussions of the Italo-Ottoman war might have been limited. Colonial wars, however, rarely went to plan. Italy's defeat at Adowa in Ethiopia in 1896 was only the most notable of many setbacks, which European and American forces suffered from southern Africa to the Philippines. The Italian military effort in north Africa turned into a counter-insurgency war as Italian forces fought against Berber guerrilla forces in a struggle that lasted into the 1920s.[41] The conduct of the Italo-Ottoman war and the subsequent Balkan Wars in 1912 and 1913 further destroyed the great power peace in Europe. The use of irregular forces, the escalation of political aims and military means, the use of extreme violence against civilians, and, especially in the Balkan Wars, the practice of ethnic cleansing anticipated some features of warfare after 1914. Moreover, it confirmed the argument set out in the *Neue Freie Presse* and elsewhere that violence in the twentieth century was less amenable to the forms of professional control that had existed in the wars of mid-nineteenth-century Europe. Violence on this scale destroyed the social and international order. Of course there were claims that the violence of these wars was specific to their context – the wide open spaces of the Libyan desert and the alleged inherent belligerence of Balkan societies. Finally, Europeans invested these wars with the moral categories and language of civilization and barbarism, law and brute force, Christianity and Islam, nation and empire, and European and Asian.

On 5 October Italian sailors landed at Tripoli, paving the way for the arrival of the expeditionary force on 11 October. As the Ottoman garrison had fled, the campaign had started auspiciously. But hopes for a quick victory were soon confounded. The scope of the territory, the caution of General Caneva, the leader of the Italian forces, the unexpected popular resistance by local Arabs (whom Italian planners had fondly believed would welcome the invading forces), the expansion of Italy's war aims, and the improved organization of the Ottoman military ensured the war would be longer, more vicious, and less decisive than San Giuliano and Giolitti had hoped. By mid-October Italian forces faced stiff resistance in Benghazi and Homs. Outside Tripoli, Italian units dug trenches and piled up the barbed wire. As Italian forces marched east of Tripoli, they were attacked by local tribesmen and Turkish officers on 23 October. Over the next few days Italian forces suffered hundreds of casualties, some of whom, it was discovered, were mutilated, crucified, and even buried alive. Fearful, Italian forces began summary executions of Arabs found to be carrying weapons.[42] The Ottoman resistance was organized by Enver Pasha, a leading figure in the Committee of Unity and Progress (CUP) and future Minister of War, as well as Mustafa Kemal, later the founder of the Turkish Republic and better known as Atatürk. Although the CUP was largely a secular movement, it adopted religious poses as a means of mobilizing the population.[43] The cooperation between the Ottoman officers and groups such as the Senussi, a Muslim political order, contributed to European notions of a broader conflict between Christianity and Islam

On 5 November 1911 Giolitti dramatically widened the scope of the war when he declared that the Italian state would annex Tripolitania and Cyrenaica.[44] Whereas Britain and Austria-Hungary had first occupied Ottoman territory (Egypt and Bosnia-Herzegovina respectively) before annexing it over three decades later, Giolitti proposed to complete the process in one fell swoop. This was important because it limited the scope for peace negotiations between Constantinople and Rome. Giolitti's decision was an example of how events on the battlefield and political aims could combine in a process of cumulative radicalization. The reports of the massacre of Italian soldiers at Sciara Sciat and popular Arab resistance led Giolitti to conclude that announcing the planned annexation would deprive the local population of any hope of an Italian retreat, and therefore dampen their resistance and shorten the war. However, by removing the possibility of a compromise settlement, Giolitti deprived the Ottoman government of any reason to negotiate and therefore lengthened the war.

The war also served the nationalist purpose of completing Italian unity. Nationalists considered the unification of the Risorgimento to be incomplete. Imperial expansion and military glory would combine to forge Italians. The annexation of the two provinces in north Africa served as a tangible achievement for this remaking of the nation. 'We Italians have celebrated in the most splendid fashion,' La Stampa declared on 6 November, 'the fiftieth anniversary of our political resurrection. We have celebrated it with a new moral, political, and military resurrection, with a new and great immortal episode in our history, which is a history of civilization and progress, certainly not inferior to those of other peoples.'[45]

In order to achieve these more radical aims, Italy extended military operations, including the use of air power against military and civilian targets.[46] The navy undertook operations in the eastern Mediterranean and the Red Sea, and Italian land forces occupied the Dodecanese islands in the Aegean Sea. The navy even attempted to force a passage through the Dardanelles in April 1912. This extension of the war had three profound consequences. First, Ottoman politics, unstable since the Young Turk Revolution, was further radicalized. The CUP lost credibility as the

Ottoman empire continued to fracture in Albania, Yemen, and now Tripolitania. As opposition gathered under the Party of Freedom and Understanding, the CUP responded by removing the political liberties introduced after the 1908 revolt. After the intervention of a group of officers, the Saviour Officers, the CUP leaders resigned from government in July 1912.[47] Second, the basis of Liberal Italy was also undermined. Changes, such as Giolitti's introduction of universal male suffrage in 1912, were already in the pipeline. At the same time the war deepened divisions in Italian politics, particularly between those who believed that the war was a distraction from domestic reforms and a threat to political liberties, and those who saw the war as a means of making an Italian nation. Attitudes to foreign policy and war would remain fluid. For example, the socialist Gaetano Salvemini opposed the war in Libya but supported Italian entry into the First World War in 1915.[48] The most immediate blow to Liberal Italy was the collapse of fiscal stability. This led to chaotic tax policies and inflation, which ultimately discredited parliamentary government. It marked the unmooring of financial restraints across Europe in this era.[49]

The third consequence of the war was that it gave the Balkan states the time and opportunity to strike at the weakened Ottoman empire in the Balkans. The prospect of war in the Balkans, evident from the early summer of 1912, compelled Italian and Ottoman diplomats to negotiate, finally concluding the war with the Treaty of Lausanne on 18 October 1912. This treaty acknowledged Italian sovereignty over Tripolitania and Cyrenaica, while in return Italy agreed to recognize the Caliphate's religious authority in the provinces, pay a small indemnity, and withdraw from the islands in the Aegean.

The Balkan states – Bulgaria, Serbia, Greece, Montenegro, and Romania – derived their legitimacy from the principle of nationality. In 1912 Bulgaria, Serbia, and Greece viewed Ottoman weakness as an opportunity to assert their claims to territory in Macedonia, western Thrace, and Albania, which they claimed as part of their national domains.[50] Macedonia had been at the core of tensions in the Balkans, both between the Balkan states themselves and with the Ottoman empire. In the 1890s Macedonian revolutionaries had established the Internal Macedonian Revolutionary Organization (IMRO), which developed links with Balkan states, principally Bulgaria. It waged a guerrilla campaign against Ottoman rule. Atrocities by IMRO as well as severe Ottoman reprisals fuelled a cycle of ethnic violence as well as nationalist demands in the Balkans for the liberation of these territories from Ottoman rule.[51] In December 1911, following the killing of between fifteen and twenty Christians, the leader of the opposition National Liberal Party in Bulgaria, Vasil Radoslavov, mocked the passivity of the government: 'We have not spent 950 million leva on the army just to look at it on parade.'[52] The prime minister, Ivan Geshov, needed little encouragement. He was already conducting negotiations for an alliance with Serbia, which was concluded in February 1912. By May Greece had joined to complete the Balkan League. On the same day that the Treaty of Lausanne between Italy and the Ottoman empire was concluded, 18 October 1912, the Balkan League declared war on the Ottoman empire.

The Balkan states rapidly defeated the demoralized Ottoman forces. Greek forces arrived in Salonica, northern Greece, just ahead of their Bulgarian allies, who had surrounded Edirne (Adrianople), the last significant city on the path to Constantinople, by late October. Meanwhile Serbian forces occupied large swathes of Macedonia. Military and paramilitary units undertook the ethnic cleansing of Muslims from the Balkans. The consequences of these atrocities rippled long after the wars were over. 'The spectacle of Moslem refugees, men and women and children, fleeing from the fire and sword of the enemy, the slaying of prisoners of war, their mutilation and starvation, atrocities and massacres perpetrated on the civilian population – the first of their kind in twentieth- century warfare – inflicted wounds far deeper than the defeat itself,' recalled the Turkish novelist Halide Edib.[53] Civilians and soldiers suffered from artillery fire, disease, and hunger. In Edirne the imam at one of the mosques, Hafız Rakım Ertür, recorded in his diary that 'Being besieged within a fortress is an experience that resembles none other on this earth – neither prison nor exile. ... A thousand lies are concocted daily.'[54] The Ottoman Refugee Commission counted a total of 413,922 Muslim refugees, who arrived in Constantinople from the Balkans. In towns and villages across the Balkans, Bulgarian, Serbian, and Greek forces, sometimes regular, but often irregular units, massacred thousands of Muslims. They also forced Muslims to convert to Christianity, raped Muslim women, and destroyed mosques and property.[55]

This was the result of policies purposefully adopted by Bulgarian, Serbian, and Greek commanders. The atrocities were part of the nation-making project, which in turn formed the basis of these states' domestic and international legitimacy. The consequences for Ottoman politics were predictable. There was a further radicalization, as the CUP seized power in a coup in January 1913. By the spring of 1913 the CUP's vision of Ottoman identity had become more limited. It focused on the Anatolian heartland of

VIENNA

A U S T R O -

RUSSIA

BUDAPEST   DEBRECEN

H U N G A R I A N

JASSY

ODESSA

Lake Balaton

E M P I R E

ZAGREB

BELGRADE

R O M A N I A

BOSNIA-
HERZEGOVINA
*(annexed by
Austria-Hungary,
1908)*
SARAJEVO

BUCHAREST

VARNA

S E R B I A

Black Sea

MONTENEGRO

*Adriatic
Sea*

SOFIA

B U L G A R I A

BURGAS

SKOPJE

ADRIANOPLE

CONSTANTINOPLE

TIRANA

ALBANIA

SALONIKA

Corfu

G   R   E   E   C   E

O T T O M A N

*Aegean
Sea*

SMYRNA

I T A L Y

E M P I R E

Mediterranean Sea

PATRAS   ATHENS

*Dodecanese
(Italian,
1912)*   *Rhodes*

Crete

OUTCOME OF THE BALKAN WARS

Ottoman Empire, 1912

Ottoman Empire, 1914

——— Frontiers, 1914

the Ottoman empire while Islam now became integral to the CUP's vision of Ottoman identity. Religious conviction could provide the basis for the renewal of the empire; in particular religious conviction would mobilize ordinary soldiers in defence of the empire. Enver Pasha emerged as the key figure in the new dispensation. 'Revenge, revenge, revenge,' he wrote to his wife in May 1913. Against whom would this vengeance be directed? Christians in general were seen as a foreign and dangerous element in the new Ottoman political community. Many CUP figures, including the future Turkish leader Mustafa Kemal, or Atatürk, came from the Balkans. Now their Christian neighbours had hunted them out of their homelands. Hundreds of thousands of refugees had gathered in Constantinople having witnessed the atrocities, perpetrated in the name of nation and religion. One such figure was Mehmed Nâzım, a doctor in Salonica. Arrested by Greek authorities in October 1912, he had been imprisoned and humiliated and told that his family had been exterminated. On his release in 1913 he called for retaliation against Christians within the Ottoman empire – and there remained a substantial Christian population, especially in Armenia.[56]

The First Balkan War removed the Ottoman empire from all but a tiny sliver of the European continent, admittedly an important one, around Constantinople and the Bosphorus Straits. It marked a forced disengagement from any residual sense of belonging to a broader European community. Ottoman identity was now more geographically bound to Anatolia and the emphasis on Islam was also incompatible with European identities, which drew on Christianity. Yet this disengagement also marked the failure of Europe. Ottoman intellectuals, on the periphery in geographical and cultural terms, perhaps saw the demise of the nineteenth-century European order more clearly than others. The editorial in the Izmir daily, *Ahenk*, declared, 'We must now fully realise that our honour and our people's integrity cannot be preserved by those old books of international law but only by force.'[57] In the late nineteenth century, European great powers had intervened to stop atrocities committed by Ottoman forces against Christians in the Balkans and Armenia. They had also acted to preserve the Ottoman empire or at least manage its decline. The Young Turk Revolution had aimed to modernize the empire by adapting models of reform from the French Revolution and the Prussian Reform Era. CUP leaders were steeped in European thought. Kemal's education and outlook were informed by Social Darwinism, science, and materialism.[58] But now in the twentieth century, European powers did not intervene to halt the invasion of Ottoman territory or the murder of Muslims. In losing their political capacity to act, the great powers also lost the legitimacy that underpinned their dominance of the international system.

The First Balkan War was not just a war between Balkan Christians and Ottoman Muslims. It was also a war between emerging nation states with their own rival claims to territory. In particular, Bulgarian leaders were dissatisfied with the territorial settlement established by the Treaty of London on 30 May 1913. The Greek control of Salonica deprived Bulgaria of an important port, while Serbian forces controlled Macedonian territory, initially destined for Bulgaria under the terms of their 1912 treaty. In Serbia the prime minister, Nikolai Pašić, struggled to assert civilian control over the military. Colonel Dimitrijević, nicknamed the Bull, who had played a central role in the 1903 coup – which replaced the Obrenović with the Karadjordjević dynasty and turned Serbian foreign policy away from cooperation with to hostility towards Austria-Hungary – had founded the Black Hand movement in March 1911 with a view to engaging in a more vigorous assertion of Serbian interests in Macedonia. He and other officers now wanted to expel the Bulgarian forces from their positions in the province. In the end the Bulgarian forces moved first. Greece and Serbia, joined by the Ottoman empire and Romania, rounded on their erstwhile ally. Within weeks Bulgaria was defeated and the Second Balkan War concluded with the Treaty of Bucharest on 10 August 1913. The Ottoman empire regained Edirne, Serbia extended its territory to include central Macedonia, while Greece gained southern Macedonia. Bulgaria lost the region of Dobrudja between the Lower Danube and the Black Sea to Romania.[59]

* * *

The wars between 1911 and 1913 attracted considerable attention in Europe. The atrocities troubled Europeans, particularly liberals and socialists. Atrocities raised questions about a progressive view of human nature and modern society. Was this violence culturally specific to these societies or was it inherent in human nature? Did the codes of behaviour and the internalized restraints on aggression, developed over the course of the nineteenth century, really constitute what the German sociologist Norbert Elias later called 'the civilising process'? Or did more malevolent and destructive instincts lurk near the surface of ordinary men and women? Peace in the nineteenth century had rested on assumptions about human nature. Controlling aggression in war was important because it prevented the commission of atrocities that would fuel hatred and further conflict. In addition it also prevented the brutalization of the citizen soldier, who, after all, if he survived, was expected to return to civilian society, to his family, and to work. 'Compared to the battle fury of the Abyssinian warriors – admittedly powerless against the technical apparatus of the civilized army – or to the frenzy of the different tribes at the time of the Great Migrations,' argued Elias, 'the aggressiveness of even the most warlike nations of the civilized world appears subdued.'[60]

For some the conduct of war in the Balkans and north Africa had no bearing on the changes in warfare in the twentieth century. The Balkans were just as distant from the imagined values of Europe as the African and Asian societies colonized in the nineteenth century. Western Europeans had long viewed the Balkans as a distinctively violent society. 'A Montenegrin would be just as likely to go for a stroll down the village without his entire arsenal,' explained the *Penny Illustrated Press*, 'as an Englishman would be likely to walk down Piccadilly without his collar.'[61] Dress provided a key to the cultural mores of a society, so the reader instantly knew that violence was as inherent in the Montenegrin village as politeness was on the London streets. Another explanation that comforted readers in London, Berlin, and Paris rested on the institutional differences between military formations in the Balkans and western Europe. In addition to conscript armies under professional officers, all sides in the Balkan Wars deployed irregular units. Not subject to the conventions of European military discipline, armed bands were more likely to commit atrocities. The different cultural and institutional environment of the Balkans and north Africa meant that atrocities were geographically bounded – they were not part of a moral conception of Europe. Commenting on the murder of women and children, the liberal German newspaper *Die Vossische Zeitung* claimed that the 'era of the Enlightenment has not yet arisen for the Balkans. The wildest barbarism reigns there and the war provides an opportunity to educate Europe about this.'[62] Violence against women and children and the destruction of the family stood outside the realm of civilization, as defined by the European powers. Reports, such as the one about Bulgarian soldiers digging up the body of a Muslim girl before raping the corpse, suggested that the wars were shaped by cultures and environments that were not perceived as European. During the Second Balkan War, the *Daily Telegraph* argued that the 'young Slav peoples have astounded the admiration of the world, they now forfeit the whole of that esteem for when civilization honours the soldier it is for other and more noble qualities than those of pugnancy and recklessness.'[63]

For others the Balkan Wars served as a warning to the rest of Europe of the destructiveness of modern warfare. Leon Trotsky, reporting for the liberal *Kievskaya Mysl*, wrote that these wars were the 'first real, authentic instance . . . of ruthless extermination. In the circumstances of the organised brutality of war, men quickly become brutalised without realising it.'[64] Modern warfare was the product of civilization, of technological advance, bureaucratic organization, and nationalism. On this reading civilization contained the seeds of its own destruction. Jean Jaurès, the French socialist leader and one of the foremost thinkers on military affairs in Europe before the First World War, addressed these issues in a series of articles in 1912. In April 1912 he condemned the civilizing pretensions of European imperialism, particularly the French and Italian military campaigns in Morocco and Tripolitania. Instead of a 'glorious protectorate', France was establishing an 'atrocious regime' in Morocco. Barbarism and atrocity were inherent in the act of civilizing another society through the use of military force. 'The policy of plunder and conquest produces its own consequences,' he argued:

> From the invasion to revolt, from the riot to repression, from deceit to treachery, the sphere of civilization grows. Decidedly we have nothing to envy Italy and she knows what our decency is worth. But if the violence of Morocco and Tripolitania succeed in stirring the wounded feelings of Muslims, in Turkey and throughout the world, if Islam one day responds with a ferocious fanaticism and a vast revolt of global aggression, who will be surprised? Who will have the right to be indignant? If the repercussions of these unjust enterprises disturb the peace of Europe, with what heart will the people support a war, which has its origins in the most revolting crime?[65]

Jaurès did not reject an interventionist foreign policy, but he called for one based on 'French idealism' rather than military force, one that would promote democratic institutions and human dignity.

In November 1912, as tensions mounted throughout Europe in the wake of the First Balkan War, Jaurès returned to the relationship between civilization and modern warfare. Far from attenuating the worst excesses of violence, civilization exacerbated the consequences of violence. 'The events in the Balkans,' he argued, 'provide an idea of what a general war would be like. In a war that has barely lasted a month, one third of the strength of armies has been destroyed. 150,000 men out of 500,000 have been rendered hors de combat. It is a proportion without precedent in modern wars. It is the reproduction in a civilized age of the great destructiveness of barbaric times when entire armies of people disappeared.' Jaurès concentrated on the suffering of ordinary people, the destruction of the intimate sphere of everyday life – family, homes, work, and local communities. This was a view of war rooted in concrete reality, rather than more abstract frameworks of capitalism, imperialism, and nationalism. The pain of the individual became a way of mobilizing against war. The overflow of the wounded from hospitals, refugees dying on roads, people becoming delirious through thirst, and the spread of cholera through army camps were some of the vignettes that composed Jaurès' vision of modern war.

Perhaps, Jaurès wondered, a new order would emerge in the Balkans based on a democratic Ottoman state and a confederation of Balkan nation states. 'But this order is born in a mass grave,' he warned:

> And the odour of this mass grave begins to spread over Europe, and Europe begins to say to itself: 'If such are the disasters of war in the Balkans with a limited conflict, with a figure of 500,000 combatants, with its essentially agrarian peoples whose economic life is less easily disrupted, what would it be like when millions and millions of men, from the west and the east of Europe pile and collide into each other, and when the prodigious and delicate capitalist and financial industrial societies are halted by such a formidable commotion?' And the social revolution emerging from this chaos, instead of being the supreme expression of progress, like a higher act of reason, of justice, and of wisdom, will be part of a universal crisis of the mind, an attack of contagious fury derived from the suffering and violence of war.[66]

In his final comment Jaurès criticized the views of socialists who saw a general European war as an opportunity for revolution. Friedrich Engels in the late nineteenth century and Vladimir Ilyich Lenin in the First World War were two of the most notable advocates of this strategy, but for the vast majority of socialists in Europe on the eve of the war, reform within established political structures was the goal. Violence, in their view, would only serve to corrupt socialist achievements.

The atrocities of the Balkan Wars were investigated by a Commission of Inquiry funded by the Carnegie Endowment for International Peace.[67] By documenting the atrocities and assessing the crimes against the 1899 and 1907 Hague Conventions on the conduct of war, the Commission intended that the report would shame the belligerents and reinforce the rules of war.

Public opinion was also an instrument to enforce the norms, practices, and laws of the international system. The Commission represented an alternative means of conducting international politics, distinct from the great powers, which were bound by national interests. Although drawn from the European great powers and the United States, the commissioners represented a particular vision of Europe. Paul Miliukov was the Liberal leader of the Cadets in the Russian Duma, or Parliament, who had been exiled from Tsarist Russia in the 1890s. The Liberal politician and historian Joseph Redlich was the Austro-Hungarian representative, though he did not travel to the Balkans. Paul-Henri D'Estournelles de Constant, winner of the 1909 Nobel Peace Prize, acted as president of the Commission, while Nicholas Murray Butler, the president of Columbia University and acting director of the Carnegie Endowment for International Peace, wrote the preface to the report. Embedded in networks of international lawyers, pacifists, parliamentarians, and academics, these men conceived of themselves – and were widely regarded – as representative of civilized world opinion. Miliukov declared that the Commission's report was the 'voice of Europe'.[68] Membership of this moral community had political benefits, making it easier to legitimize certain measures and mobilize support. This was why the Balkan states reacted to the Commission. Miliukov was thrown out of his hotel in Athens, before wandering through the streets of Piraeus, the port quarter of Athens, where he 'found somewhat poorer lodgings in a hole for sailors where newspapers were not read'.[69] The belligerents also published and translated their own investigations into atrocities committed by their opponents and allies.

The report was published in February 1914. Its detailed examination of atrocities was designed to compel the 'contemplation of the individual and national losses due to war and to the shocking horrors which modern warfare entails'. By concentrating on the destruction and suffering of warfare, rather than martial glory, Murray Butler argued that states would move closer to the 'substitution of justice for force in the settlement of international differences'.[70] Yet the detailed descriptions of the atrocities could just as easily confirm the view of some readers that the wars were of little relevance to the rest of Europe. The different readings of the Balkan Wars were summed up in an exchange between Miliukov and Justin Godart, the French lawyer and politician, who was president of the inquiry, on their train journey to Paris in 1913. 'We exchanged impressions,' recalled Miliukov. 'No matter how horrible these impressions were, I said, we ought at least to take one comfort from them. If a military clash should occur between the more civilized countries of Europe, we would not witness extremes like the ones we had studied. Godard remained silent; then he answered curtly, "I'm not so sure." [71]

In contrast to this apocalyptic vision of the Balkan Wars as the harbinger of destruction in Europe, others interpreted the outcome of the war as part of the reordering of Europe on national principles. The legacy of Mazzini's vision of a Europe of nation states enjoyed support amongst European liberals. Liberal representative institutions at home and borders determined by national sentiment would ensure peace in Europe. It was the principle, rather than the violent means of achieving it, that nationalists sought to imitate. In Ireland nationalists were attracted by the success of small nations carving out their independence within the European states system. The vast majority of Irish nationalists supported Home Rule, achieved through the Westminster Parliament, rather than full independence achieved through an unlikely military conflict with British forces. Despite these differences the Balkan states signalled the shift of the international system to the principle of nationality.[72]

In marking the triumph of the principle of nationality in the European states system, the greatest impact of the Balkan Wars was felt in Austria-Hungary. Here leaders of national minorities, such as Thomas Masaryk and Karel Kramář, argued that the Habsburg empire had to take into account the large Slav populations – Czech, Slovak, Serb, Croat, Slovene, and Romanian – in constitutional reform. As in the United Kingdom, most national minority leaders in Austria-Hungary sought autonomy, rather than independence. Alcide De Gasperi, elected to the Reichsrat in 1911 as one of ten members of the Italian Popular Catholic Party, sought to preserve Italian cultural autonomy in the Trentino, northern Italy, within the empire, rather than direct a separatist gaze at Rome. Stjepan Radić, the leader of the Croat Peasant Party, argued autonomy could strengthen the Austro-Hungarian empire. Like leaders of other peasant parties in Europe, such as Alexander Stamboliski in Bulgaria, Radic feared that radical change would lead to war, in which peasants would suffer most. On 15 April 1914 he predicted that Serbia's expansion would provoke a 'flood of blood and the real hell of a world war'.[73]

Austria-Hungary, with its dual monarchy and national minorities, offered a different model of political organization. Diotima, the beautiful muse in Robert Musil's novel of ideas, *The Man without Qualities* (1930–42), was quarrelling with her husband about the presence in her salon of a German industrialist, Arnheim, a figure loosely modelled on the

German-Jewish businessman Walther Rathenau, when she offered this quintessential defence of the Habsburg monarchy: 'the world would find no peace until it was as permeated by a universally Austrian spirit as the ancient Austrian culture that embraced all the people, with their different languages, within the borders of the monarchy'.[74] Imperial, sometimes oppressive, often chaotic, the leaders of the Habsburg monarchy saw in the outcome of the Balkan Wars a challenge to its geopolitical security and legitimizing ideals. In Musil's novel the characters plan to honour Emperor Franz Joseph's seventieth year on the throne in 1918 by celebrating it as a year of peace (in reality, he died in 1916), the singular ethos of the Habsburg empire. In the real world, however, Austro-Hungarian leaders doubted whether the conflict between Serbia and the monarchy could be settled peacefully. The Austrian Foreign Minister and grand seigneur, Leopold von Berchtold, instructed the minister to Bucharest, Otto Czernin:

> They recommend to us moderation, goodwill, economic and political compromise. Such palliative means are, however, unsuitable to restore our relationship with Serbia. Between us and today's Serbian state stands the great South Slav problem, which demands increasingly urgently a definite solution. This solution – according to human judgment, given the determination, intrepidness, and care with which Serbia pursues the greater Serbian ideal, it can only be a violent solution – will leave only small traces of the current Serbian state or it will shake Austria-Hungary to its foundations.[75]

* * *

The *Irish Times* called the great powers 'Les grandes impuissances', as the editorial warned that the 'smaller nations of Europe will develop a perfectly legitimate contempt' for the Concert of Europe if the great powers failed to enforce their own demands – as in the case of the evacuation of Serbian forces from Scutari (in present-day Albania) during the First Balkan War, following an ultimatum from Austria-Hungary.[76] The paper's pithy diagnosis of European politics pointed to one of the central features between 1911 and the outbreak of the First World War – the failure of the great powers to manage political change in Europe. This failure was particularly significant given the predictions of 'world fire' by Emperor Wilhelm II and others in late summer 1911. Politicians, diplomats, and journalists had some sense of the direction that European politics would take if the great powers proved ineffective in managing change. Moreover, the great powers had acted in previous crises to manage political change and humanitarian emergencies. Indeed, this was essential to the legitimacy as well as the power of the Concert of Europe. More often than not, the great powers were slow to act, had different interests, and failed to resolve fully the problems of European politics. Equally, their combined weight ensured that crises were localized and that violence was eventually restrained. The purpose of the Concert was not to resolve a problem fully, but to fudge its way to peace, no matter how uneasy or temporary. Between 1911 and 1914, however, the great powers failed to intervene; or when they intervened, they were ineffective in implementing their decisions; or when they implemented their decisions, they were divided, and therefore individual great powers began to defect from the Concert of Europe. From this perspective the origins of the First World War lay not in the conscious decisions of political and military leaders in any single capital to destroy the European states system; rather they issued from the erosion and collapse of that system through passivity and ineffectiveness, which led decision-makers to look for new means to achieve their security.

As Giolitti and San Giuliano had prioritized Italian prestige and power in the Mediterranean over broader concerns about the deterioration of the international system, decision-makers in Berlin, Vienna, London, and Paris privileged alliance concerns, military security, and bilateral deals. These choices were not made with historical hindsight. In choosing a limited conception of security, based on alliances and military power, over the vaguer assurances of the viability of the international order, statesmen began to undermine the very restraints that the order and ultimately their security rested upon. The Foreign Ministers of Germany and Austria-Hungary, Kiderlen-Wächter and Aehrenthal respectively, and other diplomats in Berlin and Vienna, faced a particularly difficult choice in 1911. Germany and Austria-Hungary were allies of Italy (the Triple Alliance dating from 1882), but they – especially Germany – had significant political and commercial interests in the Ottoman empire. They risked either the break-up of the Triple Alliance, which was due for renewal, or a loss of influence in the Ottoman empire. Kiderlen-Wächter and Aehrenthal agreed that an Italian invasion of Tripolitania was 'disturbing', but the German Foreign Minister in particular failed to exercise any meaningful restraint on Italy. Kiderlen-Wächter was severely hampered by the Moroccan crisis, which made it impossible to bring Britain and France into a joint great power mediation between Italy and the Ottoman empire. Without French and British cooperation in any mediation, there was an unacceptable risk that Italy would depart from the Triple Alliance and cosy up to the Triple Entente (France, Great Britain, and Russia). The German ambassador to Rome, Gottlieb von Jagow, pleaded for the German press to tone down its sharp criticisms of the Italian invasion. Mustering every stereotype he could, he wrote:

> The Italian is a primadonna, used to and needy for applause; that the Tripolitanian Bravo aria, of which she expected the greatest success, has instead been whistled at, most sharply by her friends, has caused an hysterical collapse of nerves, during which she throws fragile objects at her friends. The director must reckon upon such conditions of the spoilt actress. The lady will change her mind for the better and return to the arms of her old admirer. Because the benefit, which the others offer, is too vague.[77]

Shaken by the Moroccan crisis, German leaders sought to bolster security in the autumn of 1911 by introducing a massive increase in the size of the army and reaffirming the Triple Alliance.

Edward Grey, the Liberal Foreign Secretary, was equally reluctant to intervene. His good friend and fellow Liberal, Richard Haldane, believed that Grey 'had a first rate judgment, with an old man's caution'.[78] Intervention, Grey contended, was the responsibility of Italy's allies, Germany and Austria-Hungary. Above all, he was concerned that 'neither we nor France should side against Italy now'. Meanwhile the British ambassador in Rome, Rennell Rodd, saw the war between Italy and the Ottoman empire as an opportunity to detach Italy from the Triple Alliance. 'The bidding for Italian friendship at the international auction may have to be rapid,' he told Grey on 4 September 1911.[79] At the very least British diplomacy aimed to exploit the Italo-Ottoman war to unsettle the Triple Alliance.

The French Foreign Office was bound by its previous agreements with Italy, specifically that of 1902. No matter that they realized complications would ensue or that the chargé d'affaires in Constantinople, August Boppe, reported on the indignation of the Young Turk press that the Ottoman empire, having adopted a constitutional regime, was now denied the security of international law as set out in the Hague Conventions. The French Foreign Office held strictly to the line that it would honour the 1902 agreement with Italy.[80]

The only great power to make a significant attempt to intervene was Russia. In September 1911 Russian politics was in turmoil as the prime minister, Piotr Stolypin, was assassinated in a theatre in Kiev.[81] His murder was a significant blow to reformers, who struggled with the autocratic pretensions of Tsar Nicholas II and the continued imposition of martial law over large swathes of the country. As the Ottoman government threatened to close the Bosphorus Strait in November 1911, Russian diplomats began to adopt a more activist stance. They proposed amending the conventions governing the Straits to enable Russian warships to pass through to the eastern Mediterranean. On Christmas Day 1911 Sergei Sazonov, the Foreign Minister, who had just returned from convalescence in Switzerland, proposed a joint great power intervention. Sazonov's proposal, however, satisfied neither the Ottoman nor the Italian government and henceforth Russian diplomacy concentrated on keeping the Straits open for commercial shipping, which was important for its agricultural exports.[82]

In the end it was the prospect of war in the Balkans that brought Italian and Ottoman diplomats to negotiate the Treaty of Lausanne. Affairs in the Balkans further exposed the inadequacy of the great powers. As already discussed, Bulgaria and Serbia had concluded an alliance in February 1912. Russia, the great power with pretensions to dominate the region, failed to shape the politics of the Balkan League. The common assumption in the early twentieth century was that the great power dominant in a particular region took responsibility to ensure that the smaller states did not disrupt or overturn the norms and practices of the international system. President Teddy Roosevelt had given his name to this assumption in the western hemisphere when he added the Roosevelt corollary to the Monroe Doctrine. He pointed out that the United States could only expect European states to desist from intervening in the western hemisphere if it ensured that the smaller states followed the rules – in this particular case, Venezuela had to pay British and German creditors. There was an expectation that Russian diplomacy would influence the Balkan states. 'The Balkan dogs will not bite, as long as the great, white Papa in St Petersburg doesn't want them to; they will only yap,' remarked Kiderlen-Wächter in 1910.[83] When Anatolii Nekludoff, the Russian minister in Sofia, first heard Bulgarian politicians speak of an alliance with Serbia in September 1911, he had arranged to meet Sazonov, then recuperating in Davos. For Sazonov the prospective alliance was 'perfect', as it would mean 'five hundred thousand bayonets to guard the Balkans' against Austrian or German invasion.[84] As we have seen, the Balkan states had very different designs. The Slavic identity of the Balkan states was only one aspect of their self-representation and did not hinder their pursuit of national interests.

As the First Balkan War started in October 1912 with rapid military successes for the Balkan states, the great powers scrambled to find a solution. The central issues for the great powers were the growth of Serbian power, its claim to a port on the Adriatic Sea, and Austria-Hungary's vehement objections. One possibility was a renewal of détente in the Balkans between Austria-Hungary and Russia. Public opinion in Russia pushed Sazonov towards support of Serbian claims, but he admitted that Russia had 'no vital interest' in the question of Serbian access to the sea. Moreover, Russian diplomats were anxious about Bulgarian progress towards Constantinople – seeing a 'little brother' snatch this prize would have been a humiliation for Tsarist Russia.[85] An Austro-Russian rapprochement might have been the best outcome from the point of view of the great powers, but throughout November Russian policy hardened in support of Serbian claims.

Another alternative was rapprochement between Austria-Hungary and Serbia. On 30 October, Berchtold, the Austrian Foreign Minister, acknowledged that the status quo in the Balkans could no longer be preserved. He proposed a customs union between Austria-Hungary and Serbia, which would protect Austrian influence in the Balkans. Economic power would secure political goals. In return, Austria-Hungary would countenance Serbian territorial expansion. It was an imaginative solution, redefining security and influence through commerce.[86] Alas, it was also unfeasible. Austria-Hungary's commercial relations with Serbia had deteriorated since the Pig War of 1906. Blocked from exporting to the Habsburg empire, Serbian farmers had exported to Germany and France instead. Banks and firms from those two states also dominated Serbia's economy. A commercial union with Austria-Hungary made little sense. The Serbian prime minister, Nikolai Pašić, also rejected the proposal on the grounds of Austria-Hungary's deep unpopularity in Serbia. Austria-Hungary's lack of soft power – in economic and cultural terms – hindered its influence in the Balkans.

As relations between Austria-Hungary and Serbia and Russia deteriorated, Paul Cambon, the French ambassador, urged Edward Grey to call a conference of the great powers to resolve the crisis in the Balkans. Grey agreed, inviting the ambassadors of the great powers in London to a conference in December 1912. British policy was facilitated by German interests in maintaining peace between Russia and Austria-Hungary. In addition it was an opportunity to improve Anglo-German relations, a process that had begun earlier in the year. The Concert of Europe had emerged by December 1912 as a means of resolving the immediate crisis, but also as an institution that could sustain great power peace in Europe. Its prospects rested on three factors. First, shaken by the Moroccan crisis and the possibility of an 'inadvertent' conflict, British and German politicians sought to improve relations between the two states. Although some historians have dismissed the détente as 'hollow' because of the failure to negotiate a naval agreement or resolve Britain's stance in the case of a continental war, the immediate aim of the German Chancellor, Theobald von Bethmann Hollweg, Grey, and others was to preserve great power peace. While neither Bethmann Hollweg nor Grey would abjure war as an instrument of policy, both feared the revolutionary consequences of a general European confrontation. Only in defence of a narrowly defined vital interest would either man be prepared to countenance war.[87] Britain and Germany were also the most powerful states in their respective blocs. Britain had not concluded a defensive alliance with either France or Russia, which enabled Grey to warn those governments that Britain's position in a general European war would be determined by the specific occasion for the war. In other words, Britain would not underwrite a military aggression by either of her entente partners. Just as Britain restrained Russia, Bethmann Hollweg restrained Austria-Hungary. While Wilhelm II declared his support of Austrian policy in the Balkans, Kiderlen-Wächter and Bethmann Hollweg poured a 'cold shower of water' on Berchtold, warning him that Berlin and Vienna had to consult with each other on Balkans policy.[88] For the moment, German policy was made by the Chancellor and the Foreign Secretary, rather than the Kaiser. In short, German diplomacy would support Austria-Hungary's territorial integrity, but it would not sponsor a war against Serbia. German and British interests coincided and their formidable strength made them powerful pillars of a renewed Concert of Europe.

The success of the Concert of Europe depended on two other factors. 'Diplomatically we have passed the biggest rocks,' Grey noted as the conference of ambassadors met in London on 21 December.[89] The process of sitting down around a table committed the great powers to finding a peaceful solution. It was possible for one of the ambassadors to walk out, but in an age of public diplomacy walking out of a conference meant risking being blamed for its failure – and for a general European conflict. By no means was the conference 'open diplomacy' *avant la lettre*, but the gesture of great power conference diplomacy was reinforced by an international public sphere. The final element of the Concert was the implementation of its decisions by the great powers and the dutiful obedience of the small states. In November 1912 Grey had warned Serbia that the rights of the great powers 'should not be rudely challenged.'[90] The great powers hoped to impose their will through diplomatic pressure, but the prospect of military mobilization in support of the Concert's decisions was an important instrument.

The ambassadors' conference soon agreed to the establishment of an autonomous Albanian government and some form of Serbian access to the sea. In retrospect these issues appear insignificant, but they were of enormous importance in European politics between 1912 and 1914. First, the creation of Albania blocked the territorial expansion of Serbia and Greece and gave Austria-Hungary a bastion of influence on the east coast of the Adriatic. Austro-Hungarian diplomats even argued that Albanians wanted their own government and therefore could not be placed under either Serbian or Greek rule, as this would violate the ethnic and national principles on which the political map of the Balkans was being redrawn.[91] Second, access to the sea was considered an essential element of national independence, as this would guarantee commercial independence. How access to the sea was to be secured remained open to debate, though diplomats proposed imaginative solutions, such as establishing certain ports as international territories and guaranteeing rail access to them. Third, and most significantly, the detailed implementation of these decisions tested the effectiveness of the Concert of Europe and it was in the details that divisions emerged between the great powers. The 'dreary steeples of Fermanagh and Tyrone' – to use Winston Churchill's phrase about the debate over the exclusion of Ulster from an Irish Home Rule settlement in the summer of 1914 – had their equivalents in the town of Scutari in northern Albania and the villages of Epirus in the south.

The Concert soon fractured and collapsed as the great powers struggled to impose their decisions on the Balkan states. During the First Balkan War, Montenegrin forces had surrounded and then occupied the town of Scutari on the southern tip of Lake Scutari, which drained into the Adriatic. Given the close relationship between Serbia and Montenegro, possession by the latter was considered to give Serbia effective control over the port. The powers agreed by February 1913, however, that Scutari would be part of Albania, ensuring that state's viability and depriving Serbia of direct access to the Adriatic. With Montenegrin troops in Scutari, the powers now had to implement their decision. In Vienna military leaders wanted to exploit the crisis to declare war on Serbia. In Russia public support for the Montenegrin occupation of Scutari meant Sazonov could only offer diplomatic weight to the great powers, rather than military power. Russia was the only great power not to join the naval demonstration in support of the Concert's demands that Montenegrin troops evacuate the city. As this naval demonstration proved ineffective, Berchtold issued an ultimatum, threatening the use of military force. On 4 May 1913 King Nikita of Albania ordered Montenegrin troops to withdraw from Scutari, but the episode exposed the fragility of the Concert. Sazonov's adherence to the Concert was limited by popular sympathy for the Balkan nations, while Berchtold drew the lesson that unilateral action was more effective than the slow pace of Concert diplomacy.[92]

Austria-Hungary's defection from Concert diplomacy was confirmed in October 1913. Following an uprising in Albania, Serbian troops had moved into the north of the country. Although Pašić justified Serbian actions on the grounds of providing humanitarian assistance and restoring order, Berchtold feared Serbia would exploit the occupation to expand its territory. The Hungarian prime minister, István Tisza, claimed that events on the Serbian–Albanian border posed the question as to 'whether we will remain a vital and capable power or give ourselves up to ridiculous decadence.' Between 13 and 18 October, Austro-Hungarian ministers drafted an ultimatum, which gave Serbia one week to withdraw from northern Albania.[93] Not only was this ultimatum successful in forcing Serbian forces to evacuate, but it was also issued without German approval, let alone the support of the other great powers. Berchtold and his colleagues had lost faith in the Concert and even in the support of their ally. Convinced that a war against Serbia was inevitable, Berchtold had now cast aside the restraints on Austro-Hungarian policy. It was also significant that the geographical horizons of policy-makers in Vienna were increasingly restricted to the Balkans, rather than Europe.

The failure of the Concert was compounded by the Second Balkan War. Just four weeks after the Treaty of London, Bulgaria attacked its erstwhile allies on 29 June 1913. Although the territorial grit in this war – Macedonia – had not been the subject of the Treaty of London, the Balkan states' dissatisfaction with the settlement imposed by the great powers had exacerbated tensions in the region. That the war was settled in Bucharest rather than London and that the great powers accepted this outcome further symbolized the inability of the great powers to manage the European states system. Finally, the expansion of Serbian territory confirmed in the Treaty of Bucharest further alarmed already nervous leaders in Vienna. Serbian success, in their view, attracted the attention of South Slavs within the Habsburg empire, who were subjects of allegedly dubious loyalty.

The miserable outlook in Vienna, one might have expected, would be a source of joy for Russian diplomats. In 1913 the Tsarist regime celebrated the 300th anniversary of the Romanov dynasty. While Bruce Lockhart, the British consul in Moscow, reported the 'overwhelming' reception Nicholas II received in that city, other events underlined the gap between nation and monarch. 'We clearly live in those times,' said A. A. Mosolov, head of the court chancellery, to his father, 'when faith and love for the Tsar and father-land have died out.'[94] Military parades emphasized the importance of the projection of power abroad to the dynasty's legitimacy at home.

Russian diplomats, politicians, and journalists, however, looked back on a litany of failures. In the Balkans the failure to support Serbian claims to a port on the Adriatic rankled. More importantly, Sazonov had suffered a series of setbacks in the Ottoman empire. The failure to get a seat on the Ottoman debt council, the appointment of a German general to reform the Ottoman Army after its defeats between 1911 and 1913, and the Armenian reform agreement between Russia and the Ottoman empire on 8 February 1914 were all seen as setbacks, even defeats, for Sazonov's foreign policy.[95] According to his own analysis, these setbacks were the result of the loose diplomatic arrangements of the Triple Entente, Russia's reputation for pursuing a policy of peace at any price, and the failure to flex its military power, given that it lacked alternative instruments of soft power to achieve its end. In the first six months of 1914, Sazonov sought to remedy these defi-ciencies. A meeting of political, naval, and military leaders on 21 February 1914 confirmed plans to seize Constantinople in the event of the collapse of the Ottoman empire, which could be precipitated by a general European war. Further, Sazonov also sought to remake the Triple Entente and ensure Britain supported Russian ambitions, rather than restrained her, as had been the case in 1912 and 1913. Sazonov, like Berchtold and Giolitti, was not actively seeking a general European war. Rather, the significance of his deci-sions was their departure from the restraints that had sustained great power peace between 1911 and 1913.[96]

By spring 1914 the bonds of peace in Europe had frayed to breaking point. Leaders in Austria-Hungary and Russia believed that the operation of the international system was eroding their great power status and secu-rity, and therefore they had little incentive to prop up the system. Britain, France, and Germany, the three powers close to conflict in the summer of 1911, had repaired their relations. The Anglo-German détente was the final pillar of peace that remained in the spring of 1914. Its effectiveness depended on continued trust between London and Berlin and their diminishing ability to restrain their diplomatic partners. The Balkan states challenged the international system, asserting their own claims to agency and legitimacy on the basis of nationality. The conduct of the wars between 1911 and 1913 undermined notions of civilization and international law. Europe, as a set of political ideas, practices, and institutions, was in flux. The concept of Europe remained important as a means of asserting political claims and mobilizing support, but what Europe meant was contingent on shifting political circumstances and contested on the eve of the First World War.

CHAPTER 3

THE END OF CIVILIZATION, 1914

'WILD DREAMS ON the night of New Year's Eve,' noted Leopold von Berchtold, the Austrian Foreign Minister, in his first diary entry for 1914. A postcard from the German publicist Maximilian Harden reassured him that Europe had passed through its worst crisis during the Balkan Wars of 1912 and 1913 and could look forward to a better future.[1] Despite the talk since 1911 of a general European conflagration, the outbreak of war still came as a surprise to many Europeans and others around the world. The shock of violence, as societies mobilized and Europeans committed atrocities against each other, led contemporaries to recast their conceptions of civilization and barbarism, the meaning of peace, and the construction of a new international order. Even before the declarations of war, during the crisis in July 1914 that followed the assassination of the Archduke Franz Ferdinand, the future belligerents were casting the forthcoming conflict in moral as well as geopolitical terms.

* * *

Harden's confidence in January 1914 was not unfounded; indeed, it was shared by perceptive observers. Arthur Nicolson, the Permanent Under-Secretary at the Foreign Office, wrote to Maurice de Bunsen, the British ambassador in Vienna, on 19 January: 'I myself really have no fears that there will be any serious friction between European powers, divergent as their views may be on many questions.'[2] Nicolson believed that confrontation could be accommodated within the existing international order. In addition the attention of governments, he claimed, was directed towards internal problems – having married into a Unionist family from County Down in Ulster, the Home Rule crisis in Britain was very much on his mind. The Zabern affair in Germany, resulting from a clash between soldiers and civilians in the Alsatian town now known as Saverne, stoked a constitutional crisis about civil–military relations, while the perennial instability of French governments and the persistent tensions within the Habsburg empire meant that domestic political concerns had the first claim on their attention. The issues on the horizon, such as the friction between Greece and the Ottoman empire over the disposition of islands in the Aegean and the drawing of the Albania border, could be resolved through the standards channels of great power diplomacy.

The maintenance of great power peace through the tumultuous Balkan Wars contributed to Nicolson's confidence. In particular, the improvement in Anglo-German relations since 1911 enabled the great powers to manage crises in south-east Europe. Just over a year following the Second Balkan War, Germany, Britain, Austria, Russia, and France were at war. The assassination of Archduke Franz Ferdinand on 28 June in Sarajevo, the capital of Bosnia, had triggered an unforeseen crisis and conflict. It is plausible that if the assassination attempt had not succeeded, great power peace would have been sustained throughout the whole of 1914. By the time the next major crisis erupted – and crises will always happen – the contours of international politics could have changed. The continued improvement of Anglo-German relations, détente between France and Germany, an end to the cycle of the arms race, and the gradual stabilization of the Balkans were identified as probable developments over the coming years.

The assassination of the Archduke was significant because of when it happened. In June 1914 the international order had deteriorated to such an extent that it was no longer capable of accommodating the different interests of the great powers. Leaders in Vienna and St Petersburg had already lost confidence in the international order by early 1914. The breakdown of the Anglo-German détente in May and June 1914 meant that the great powers lacked the diplomatic capacity to resolve the July crisis peaceably. The breakdown of détente was the crucial shift in the international system that separated Nicolson's optimism in continued peace from a general European war. Once détente broke down, German leaders, most notably Chancellor Bethmann Hollweg, considered that only robust support of Austria-Hungary could protect German security. By June 1914 three powers – Austria-Hungary, Russia, and Germany – were pursuing an aggressive defence of their vital national interests. That decision-makers believed that defensive aims could only be achieved through aggressive measures demonstrated the collapse of any meaningful system of peace between the great powers *before* the assassination of the Archduke. Moreover, it is important to appreciate the emphasis on the defensive intentions of policy-makers in the summer of 1914, because the notion of a defensive war became central to the moral debate about the origins and purpose of the conflict.

The end of Anglo-German détente was marked neither by a great dramatic incident nor a major public row. Rather it was the quiet consequence of a move to shore up Anglo-Russian relations, which had been fraught following the Balkan Wars, tensions over the Ottoman empire, and barely contained conflict in Persia. In spring 1914 the British cabinet agreed that the Admiralty should open a dialogue with their Russian counterparts. The Anglo-Russian naval conversations never took place before the outbreak of war. The conversations had very little naval significance and were conceived as part of what Churchill, First Lord of the Admiralty, called the 'nods and winks' of international politics. In a further irony the major advocates of this gesture, Nicolson and the British ambassador in St Petersburg, George Buchanan, viewed the consolidation of the Anglo-Russian entente as bolstering peace. Not only would better relations enhance British interests in central Asia, where expanding Russian influence in Persia concerned the Indian government, it would also strengthen the Triple Entente in Europe, preserve the balance of power, and deter any possible German aggression. Recent studies of British and French foreign policy criticize the failure of diplomats and politicians in London and Paris to think about the repercussions of their diplomatic manoeuvres on the system.[3] The British Foreign Secretary Edward Grey was undoubtedly nervous that any sign of stronger naval or military ties between Britain and Russia would alarm German leaders. Yet the alternative was to allow the Anglo-Russian entente to erode further, which, some feared, could lead to the formation of a German–Russian bloc. Such an outcome would have been even more pernicious for the stability of European politics. The equilibrium between the great powers was so unstable that either a consolidation of the Triple Entente or the emergence of a new bloc, likely based on a rapprochement between Germany and Russia, could undermine the security of one of the great powers to such an extent that it might precipitate a preventive war.

Grey tried to couple the consolidation of the entente with Russia with an affirmation of the Anglo-German détente. After the German Foreign Office was informed of the Anglo-Russian naval conversations through Benno von Siebert, who was both an attaché and a spy in the Russian embassy in

London, the German ambassador Prince Lichnowsky was instructed to find out more about this new development. At a meeting on 24 June, just four days before the assassination of the Archduke, Grey dissembled when asked about the naval conversations, before discussing Anglo-German détente and how it might function to stabilize great power peace in Europe. 'As new developments arose,' he assured Lichnowsky, 'we should talk as frankly as before, and discuss them in the same spirit as we had discussed things during the Balkan crisis. Let us go on as we had left off when that crisis was over. I was most anxious not to lose any of the ground that had been gained then for good relations between us.' Grey outlined how he saw the Anglo-German détente in relation to the two blocs in Europe: 'The British government belonged to one group of Powers, but did not do so in order to make difficulties greater between the two European groups; on the contrary we wished to prevent any questions that arose from throwing the groups, as such, into opposition.'[4] Grey was prepared to stick with détente.

Meanwhile in Berlin, Bethmann Hollweg viewed the naval conversations as something of a closed fist rather than 'a nod and a wink'. Siebert transmitted information about the conversations to Berlin from the Russian embassy in early May. Siebert, whose mother was German, favoured a rapprochement between Germany and Russia. Like many Russian conservatives, he feared that the entente would lead Russia into the mire of an Anglo-German war.[5] In short, he too saw himself as working (or spying) towards peace. When his report reached Berlin on 11 May, there was consternation. Bethmann Hollweg viewed the Anglo-German détente as bankrupt. His pessimism was reinforced by Grey's evasive answers to questions about the naval conversations. The Chancellor's British policy had counted on Grey restraining Russia from aggressive measures in the Ottoman empire, central Europe, and the Balkans. The naval conversations indicated that Britain could no longer restrain Russia and Bethmann Hollweg's policy was bankrupt. He was also undergoing a personal crisis at the time as his wife died in May, an event that compounded his sense of foreboding and pessimism. He now reoriented his foreign policy. German security became more dependent on the alliance with Austria-Hungary, which required Berlin to offer more support to Vienna in operations in the Balkans. On 15 July Gottlieb von Jagow, the German Foreign Secretary, told Lichnowsky that it was a 'vital interest' to uphold the 'world position' of Austria-Hungary due to the improvement in Anglo-Russian relations.[6]

* * *

So when Gavrilo Princip, a Bosnian Serb, shot and killed Franz Ferdinand and his pregnant wife Sophie on 28 June, there were no diplomatic resources with which to prevent the outbreak of war. What type of war – local, European, or world war – would result from the crisis remained an open question in late June. When Raymond Poincaré, the French president, was told of the assassination, he simply turned back to watch the horse-racing at Longchamps. Albert Hopman, a senior official in the German Admiralty, was having dinner with British sailors when he heard of the murder, 'whose political consequences are unforeseeable'.[7] The murder was a 'world-historical event', noted Josef Redlich, the Austrian liberal and Anglophile, in his diary. Yet the only lesson he derived on 28 June was the impossibility of coexistence between Austria-Hungary and Balkan nationalisms.[8] The choices made in Vienna and Berlin, then in St Petersburg and Paris, then again in Berlin, and finally in London reveal a complex interaction of diplomatic moves and geopolitical expectations. Diplomatic moves were also heavily freighted with moral judgements.[9]

Berchtold was on his estate in Buchlau when he received news of the assassination. He rushed back to Vienna. Over the next few days, three positions emerged. 'War, war, war' urged Franz Conrad von Hötzendorff, Chief of the General Staff of the Habsburg Army, when he met Berchtold on the evening of 29 June. Conrad's conception of war was rooted in a fatalistic view of the monarchy. The monarchy and army were doomed, in his opinion, yet it was necessary to wage a 'hopeless struggle' against Serbia and Russia because 'such an ancient monarchy and a glorious army could not disappear ingloriously'. The purpose of the war, from this perspective, was to choreograph the preordained collapse of Austria-Hungary.[10] Berchtold also tended towards war against Serbia, but he wanted to secure German diplomatic support before undertaking any military measures. Failure to act, Berchtold argued, would be a fatal admission of Austro-Hungarian decrepitude, encouraging further attacks and ultimately 'world war'. Berchtold hoped for a limited, localized war that would ensure the monarchy's survival. The final position was represented by the Hungarian prime minister, István Tisza. He wanted to exploit the crisis to score a decisive diplomatic success by improving relations with Bulgaria and Romania and isolating Serbia as an outlaw state. Launching a war against Serbia would make Austria-Hungary the guilty party in European eyes.[11]

The moral dimension of the crisis was important to policy-makers in Vienna. Partly from conviction and partly from tactical considerations, they conceived of their response as a defence of the peace of Europe against criminals. Punishment of Serbia went beyond a narrow defence of the state's interest. The immediate origins of the moral arguments, so central to war cultures in Europe, were cast in Vienna in early July.[12] At stake in this crisis were the definition and protection of European values. Berchtold spoke of exploiting the 'immediate impression of the loathsome murder on Europe's public opinion'. Oskar von Montlong, the head of the Press Bureau at the Ministry of Foreign Affairs, told the editor of the Reichspost, Friedrich Funder, that the response was 'about the existence or not of the monarchy. ... We have no plans for conquest, we only want to punish the criminals, and to protect the peace of Europe in the future against such crimes.'[13] Legal and judicial terms – atrocity, murder, criminal, and investigation – seeped into Austria-Hungary's diplomatic language. Berchtold and others arrogated to themselves the role of judge and ultimately executioner. They had already pronounced a guilty verdict on Serbia, which had placed itself outside Europe and deserved none of the normal courtesies extended to a sovereign state.

Berchtold won the debate in Vienna in early July and chose Alexander von Hoyos, one of the rising hawks in the Ministry of Foreign Affairs, to undertake the mission to Berlin. In meetings with Bethmann Hollweg, Emperor Wilhelm II, and officials from the Foreign Office, Hoyos secured the 'blank cheque'. German leaders had agreed to underwrite Austro-Hungarian military action against Serbia. The most important figure in this decision was Bethmann Hollweg. Since late 1912 the emperor had urged Austro-Hungarian leaders to take action against Serbia, but his advice had always been countered by the restraining counsels of the Chancellor. At this point, in July 1914, Bethmann Hollweg was willing to countenance a general European war, but he did not expect one. He told Hoyos 'that it was not Germany's affair to give us advice regarding our policy towards Serbia. It [Germany] would cover our backs with all its power and fulfil its alliance duties in every way, if we found it necessary to act against Serbia. If I wanted to know his personal view regarding the opportunity of the moment, he would tell me that if war was inevitable, then the current moment was better than a future one.'[14] Yet on 5 and 6 July German leaders believed that there would not be a general war. They expected Austria-Hungary to launch a quick and decisive military action against Serbia, presenting Europe with a fait accompli. They put forward various arguments as to why the Russian government would not support Serbia. Wilhelm II claimed that Russia was not 'militarily ready'. Nor would the Tsar support 'the murderer of kings'. Colonel Hans Georg von Plessen, who was close to the emperor and present at the meeting on 5 July, noted: 'Amongst us the view is that the sooner the Austrians get going against the Serbians the better and that the Russians – although friends of Serbia – will not join in.'[15] Yet the emperor and Bethmann Hollweg also doubted whether the 'Austrian government is really in earnest, even though its language is undeniably more resolute than in the past'.[16] The lack of clarity in German policy in early July 1914 is striking. Wilhelm II had not discussed the timing of any action or the content of any ultimatum. Berlin had abdicated its leading role in the alliance in order to preserve that alliance.

However, when the Common Ministerial Council of the Habsburg empire met on 7 July, there were still divisions.[17] Tisza remained opposed to war. He predicted that Russia would support Serbia on the grounds of prestige, leading to the 'frightful calamity of a European war'. The Hungarian prime minister also feared the impact of a war on his country's border with Romania in the Siebenburgen region. Here a large ethnic Romanian population lived, whetting the claims of irredentist politicians in Bucharest. The empire's Minister of Finance Leon Bilinski warned that the assassination in Sarajevo and subsequent pogroms against Serbians in the monarchy, had embittered the South Slav population. Serbia presented an alternative locus of loyalty for South Slavs and until the 'greater Serbian ideal' was crushed, Austria-Hungary could never enjoy domestic stability. In short, the monarchy was caught in a bind. The logic of nationality politics suggested incompatible options, either offensive measures or caution, depending on the perspective from Vienna and Budapest.

On 9 July Berchtold presented Emperor Franz Joseph with three options following the ministerial meeting. Austria-Hungary could launch an immediate military attack; it could present an ultimatum to Serbia; or it could undertake a more moderate diplomatic offensive in the Balkans. The emperor chose the second option. The ultimatum would either lead to a major diplomatic success or more likely war. Interestingly, the option of an immediate offensive (imitating Japan's attack on Russia in 1904), which General Alexander von Krobatin had urged on 7 July, was rejected because it would place Austria-Hungary in the dock of European opinion. Berchtold noted that an ultimatum, by ostensibly leaving open the possibility for peace, would improve the diplomatic position and political justification for military action.[18]

Between the ministerial meetings on 7 July and 19 July, diplomats worked on a draft ultimatum to Serbia. The text was sent on 20 July to Baron Giesl von Gieslingen, the Habsburg minister in Belgrade, to be presented three days later to the Serbian government. It was a list of criminal charges against the Serbian state. The government was held responsible for tolerating and supporting 'acts of terrorism', 'the criminal doings of diverse societies and associations directed against the Monarchy', and 'subversive plans'. The assassination showed 'all the world the horrible consequences of such toleration'. The ultimatum then listed various demands, from the suppression of Narodna odbrana (National Defence, a secret society dedicated to the union of all Serbians in one state) and anti-Habsburg ideas in the press and schools, to the participation of Austro-Hungarian officials in the investigations into the complicity of the Serbian state with terrorists. The language of criminal prosecution rather than international law permeated the text. Austro-Hungarian leaders did not regard Serbia as an equal sovereign state, but as a criminal menace.[19] As Jovan Jovanović, the Serbian minister in Vienna, put it, he feared Austria-Hungary would 'put the Serbs from Serbia and the Yugoslav nation on trial'.[20] Tisza and Berchtold realized that war against Serbia was almost certain. 'Owing to the shamelessness of the Serbians,' wrote Tisza to his daughter-in-law on 21 July, 'we must act seriously because it is impossible to put an end to this. The thing can pass without war. God grant that it is so. However I cannot give you full assurances that it will not come to war.'[21] Moreover, most diplomats in Vienna recognized that a general war, not just a limited war, was the likely outcome, although they certainly wished to avoid it. Only a few, however, opposed the ultimatum. On 13 July Heinrich von Lützow, the former ambassador to Rome, denounced the ultimatum as certain to lead to 'world war', which would 'gamble the entire existence of the monarchy'. He was so incensed that he discussed the ultimatum with the British ambassador, Bunsen, one of the channels through which the Triple Entente knew about Vienna's plans.[22]

On 23 July Giesl issued the ultimatum to the Serbian Finance Minister, Lazar Paču. His initial reaction was that the ultimatum was unacceptable. 'There is nothing left,' he said, 'but to die.' The Serbian response framed the crisis in an alternative reading of law and European values. Even before the ultimatum, Serbian politicians had prepared their defence. They too framed the issue as a criminal affair. However, Serbians could not be held collectively guilty for the 'mindless act of a young fanatic'. They promised to extradite any Serbians, 'of whose complicity in the crime of Sarajevo proofs are forthcoming', for trial in Austria-Hungary. They stressed the investigations undertaken by Serbian authorities into the crime and promised further action to stamp out anti-Habsburg propaganda. In other words,

Serbia was acting as a responsible sovereign state. As such it could not allow Austro-Hungarian officials to participate in the investigation on Serbian sovereign territory. Instead the government offered to submit the dispute to arbitration at The Hague or to the great powers. In addition the response depicted Serbia's 'pacific and moderate policy during the Balkan crisis' as evidence of 'the sacrifice that she has made in the exclusive interest of European peace'.

Behind the language lay clear political calculations. For a start, Serbian opinion was unanimous that full acceptance of the ultimatum would constitute a massive infringement of their sovereignty, which had been recently asserted and defended in two bloody wars. Nikola Pašić, the prime minister, was possibly aware of the assassination plot, but efforts to stop covert military support for the plotters had been blocked by powerful groups in the Serbian military. Since 1903 the military had been an important, if fragmented, group, which constrained Pašić's freedom for manoeuvre. Finally, and most importantly, Pašić was confident, though not certain, of Russian support. In February 1914 he had visited St Petersburg, where Nicholas II had assured him 'We will do everything for Serbia.' Were Russia to enter the lists, then Serbia would have a chance to preserve her independence.[23] From the Serbian perspective the choice was between war, destruction, and independence on the one hand, and peace, humiliation, and loss of sovereignty on the other. Only through military resistance could Serbia affirm its sovereignty. National self-determination was based on the (imagined) collective will of the nation *and* its resistance to foreign rule. Paču was only partly right – Serbia had to die in order to live once again.

Giesl delivered the ultimatum in the afternoon on 23 July. The German backing for Austria-Hungary and Serbia's rejection of the ultimatum meant that, at the very least, there would be a localized war in the Balkans, the first time a great power had fought in Europe since Russia's war against the Ottoman empire in 1877–8. The war could only remain localized if Russia refused to support Serbia. Early in July German and Habsburg diplomats had counted on the Tsar's distaste for regicide and military unpreparedness. On receiving the text of the ultimatum Sergei Sazonov, the Russian Foreign Minister, declared war to be inevitable. At a meeting of the Council of Ministers on 24 July, ministers agreed that Russian prestige and interests in the Balkans dictated support for Serbia. Prestige was a vague but pervasive term in great power politics before 1914. In this case it was both the currency with which Russia purchased influence in the Balkans and its more general reputation as a great power. Since 1912 Russian ministers and diplomats had been increasingly worried by what they considered a string of one-sided concessions and a 'peace at any price' reputation. 'The only hope of influencing Germany,' declared Alexander Krivoshein, the influential Minister of Agriculture, to his colleagues on 24 July, 'was to show them, by making a firm stance, that we had come to an end of the concessions we were prepared to make. In any case, we should take all the steps, which would enable us to meet an attack.'[24] Sazonov was even more explicit: 'The moment had come when Russia, faced with the annihilation of Serbia, would lose all her authority if she did not declare herself the defender of a Slavonic nation threatened by powerful neighbours. ... Our policy had always been directed towards the defence of the Slavs. If Russia failed in her historic mission, she would be considered a decadent state and would henceforth have to take second place among the powers.'[25]

By the time Sazonov met other ministers on 24 July, he had spoken to Maurice Paléologue, the French ambassador, and Buchanan, the British ambassador. Paléologue reaffirmed the guarantees of support, which Poincaré had extended to Nicholas II and Sazonov during the state visit between 21 and 23 July. French policy privileged the alliance over the maintenance of peace, though Poincaré and others believed that through a policy of firmness it was possible to reconcile these twin considerations. Just before departing, Poincaré had offered a toast to his hosts: 'On all the questions, which are currently posed every day to governments and which need the concerted activity of their diplomacy, accord has always existed, and will not cease to exist, as the two countries have the same ideal of peace in power, honour, and dignity.' The president had already agreed that France would warn Austria-Hungary not to infringe Serbian sovereignty.[26] In supporting Russian policy in the Balkans, Poincaré was aware that the crisis could escalate into a general European war. Since coming to office in 1912, he had consolidated the alliance with Russia and supported her Balkan policy. Yet while Poincaré understood the risk of war – and was willing to run it – he thought that a policy of firmness towards Germany and Austria-Hungary would likely force these powers to back down. Firm support of Russia served multiple aims in French policy. It provided the basis for deterrence of German and Austro-Hungarian aggression and it reaffirmed the value of the alliance with Russia. If war did break out, then the Franco-Russian alliance would enter the war united, providing a political platform for victory. Buchanan, for his part, refused to assure Sazonov of British support, opening a breach within the Triple Entente, which was not fully repaired until British entry into the war. Grey could no longer restrain Russian policy, though this was because he was unable rather than unwilling.

Following the ministerial meeting, on 25 July Nicholas II ordered partial mobilization in Odessa, Kiev, Kazan, and Moscow. Directed against Austria-Hungary, this partial mobilization represented a step in the diplomatic dance as well as a military threat, a means of signalling the seriousness with which a great power viewed a crisis. Partial mobilization could be managed and calibrated, sometimes with great difficulty. Leaders in Berlin and Vienna viewed Russia's partial mobilization in political terms. They still hoped that Russia could be deterred from entering the conflict, so German civilian and military leaders did not yet mobilize their own forces, and Conrad even moved an additional army corps to participate in the offensive against Serbia, leaving the Habsburg border with Russia more exposed.[27] However, I. N. Danilov, who had drawn up Russia's war plan in 1912, objected to partial mobilization. Military concerns began to intrude into the diplomatic calculations, as Danilov argued that partial mobilization against Austria-Hungary would leave Russia exposed to an attack by Germany. Assuming that war against both Germany and Austria-Hungary was the likely outcome, Danilov pushed for full mobilization. On 28 and 29 July the chances of resolving the crisis receded. Austria-Hungary began its attack on Serbia on 28 July, British offers of mediation were rejected by Germany, and Count Friedrich von Pourtalès, the German ambassador in St Petersburg, warned Sazonov on 29 July that Germany would mobilize if Russia did not cease its military activities. Believing war against Germany to be inevitable, Sazonov pressed Nicholas II to order full mobilization. On 30 July the Tsar issued the order, which was implemented the following day.[28]

Russian mobilization involved the concentration of troops, not the invasion of enemy territory. Deterrence, the last refuge for great power peace, was about to be tested to destruction. At each stage in the crisis, the costs of backing down had escalated. German leaders were increasingly concerned at reports of partial mobilization, though Bethmann Hollweg had managed to resist demands from Erich von Falkenhayn, the Prussian Minister of War, for German mobilization. Only when intelligence about Russia's general mobilization reached Berlin did the scales tilt towards German mobilization, which involved the invasion of other states, rather than mere concentration of troops.[29] The Russian mobilization was enormously significant in framing Germany's mobilization and declarations of war – against Russia on 1 August and France two days later. First, German military planning depended on relative speed – more rapid mobilization would give German forces an advantage in the initial battles. If Russian mobilization stole a march, then East Prussia would be increasingly vulnerable. Second, German war plans required an offensive in the west. German diplomacy, in a quandary, manufactured an excuse to declare war against France. Third, the Russian mobilization enabled Bethmann Hollweg to persuade the SPD (Social Democratic Party) and the population in general that the Reich was waging a defensive war. The notion of a justified response to Russian mobilization provided an important starting point for this narrative.[30]

Britain's entry into the war transformed the conflict into a global war. Doubts remained over British entry until 2 August. This caused particular anxiety among French leaders and diplomats, notably Paul Cambon, the French ambassador to London and brother of Jules, the ambassador in Berlin. Fearing Britain would remain neutral, Paul Cambon had flounced out of Grey's office, asking whether honour had any meaning in the English language. Speaking two years later, Lloyd George claimed that Cambon 'is a great man. He had much to do with our coming into the war. He came and wept; and the German ambassador came and wept – but he wept like a German. He wept tears like German sausages. Cambon wept like an artist.'[31] The tears revealed the stress experienced by diplomats, soldiers, and politicians, but the decision for British entry was shaped by security concerns, party politics, and the German invasion of Belgium on 4 August. From late July, as Grey pondered the increasing likelihood of war in Europe, he believed that Britain would have to intervene on the side of France and Russia. He and Foreign Office officials, such as Eyre Crowe, reasoned that if Britain stayed out and Germany won the war, they could expect little gratitude from Wilhelm II. If Russia and France were victorious, they could exert pressure on British imperial interests in Africa and Asia as payback for what they saw as betrayal. British security interests around the globe, therefore, were bound up with European politics. Only by entering the war, calculated Grey, could Britain thwart German ambitions and manage Russian and French aims. Grey, supported by Liberal prime minister, Asquith, was the key decision-maker in London.

However, British entry was shaped by two other considerations. First, the Conservative leader Andrew Bonar Law had written to Asquith on 2 August assuring him of Conservative support for a British declaration of war. Most of the Liberal cabinet had doubts about British entry into the war, but they also realized that Asquith and Grey would resign if Britain stayed out, bringing about the collapse of the Liberal government and the installation of a Conservative cabinet; and this Conservative cabinet with the support of Liberal imperialists would bring Britain into the war. In other words, the Liberal cabinet could only protect liberalism – as a set of political values and as a party – by entering the war. Second, the invasion of Belgium by Germany was important not simply because it gave Lloyd George, then Chancellor of the Exchequer, and his wing of the party a reason to justify Britain's entry into war, but also because it added a twist to the definition of British interests in the war. This was a war in defence of small nations and international public law against an aggressive militarist state. Of all the belligerents in 1914, Britain faced the least immediate threat to its territory, yet the government was able to frame the war as defensive.

By 4 August seven states in Europe were at war. Each claimed it was waging a war of defence. In some cases – Serbia, Belgium, France, and Germany (in East Prussia) – the claim was made easier by the invasion of enemy forces. These claims to a war of defence were important in shaping the war cultures of the different belligerents. Nor can the claims be simply dismissed as cynical propaganda. That each state claimed to wage a war of defence and the vast majority of its citizens, and even leaders, largely or wholly believed this, suggests that the international system could no longer accommodate the rival interests of the various powers. The great power peace of the late nineteenth and early twentieth centuries had failed.

The costs of that failure were clear to statesmen and soldiers around Europe. Famously, Grey, looking out of a window of the Foreign Office one evening in early August, told John Alfred Spender, editor of the *Westminster Gazette*, that the 'lamps are going out all over Europe, we shall not see them lit again in our lifetime'. Wilhelm von Schoen, the German ambassador to Paris, lamented to a French friend that the war 'will be horrible, it is Europe's suicide'.[32] Europe, as represented by the pre-1914 diplomatic and military castes, was on the verge of extinction.

* * *

The rupture between peace and war was experienced most intensely during the mobilization of armies in the belligerent states in August 1914. The departure of conscripts, reservists, and volunteers to join their units marked the intrusion of war into the workplace and family dwellings. The normal rhythms of everyday life broke down. 'Commerce and transport have come to a complete halt,' the German-Jewish businessman Walther Rathenau wrote to his father. 'The cities begin to empty'.[33] Of course this was an exaggeration. The trains were running overtime to bring soldiers to their units and people bustled around cities. Behind Rathenau's claim stood the city as the essential site of modern civilization. The eeriness and ambiguity of the empty urban space had been depicted in early 1914 by Giorgio de Chirico, the Greek-born Italian surrealist painter, in *Gare Montparnasse: The Melancholy of Departure*. When war broke out in 1914 de Chirico was one of many foreign artists who left Paris. Others, such as the German sculptor Wilhelm Lehmbruck, were transformed from artist into an enemy alien. An admirer of Auguste Rodin, Lehmbruck returned to Berlin in 1914, where he took up service in a military hospital. Rathenau was not thinking in such specific terms as the fracturing of international artistic groups, but his comment hinted at the catastrophe that had befallen shared notions of European civilization. In exploring the immediate reaction of Europeans to the outbreak of war, it is possible to identify what the war experience meant in terms of everyday life – and how that experience redefined daily life, from family relationships to the workplace, as part of new ideas about peace. In addition these experiences provided the basis for mobilization by the state and the self-mobilization of society for the war effort.

Mass popular enthusiasm remains one of the images associated with 1914. Europeans did gather in towns and cities, waving flags and singing boisterously. In Munich crowds, amongst them Adolf Hitler, who had come to the city the previous year, gathered in front of the Feldherrenhalle at the Odeonsplatz, the monument to Bavaria's military past. From there they surged to the recruiting office. After an address from Munich's deputy mayor and a few bars of the patriotic song, 'Watch on the Rhine', the volunteers including Hitler were enrolled into the Bavarian Army.[34] Similar scenes were acted out across Germany, an enthusiastic performance by a nation united in defence of the Fatherland.[35]

A young student touring through the Rhineland in July 1914 wrote to his mother describing the scenes in Duisburg, even before war had been declared:

In the evening we went to the most fashionable café in the town. You cannot imagine the excitement, the tumult which reigned there. Each time a new dispatch was made public, the orchestra began to play with delight patriotic songs, which were sung by the whole crowd in chorus, including the people gathered in the square below. At one moment, it was announced that France had, apparently, mobilised. . . . Thereupon frenetic shouts had rung out, various cries such as 'Frankreich kaput' and 'À Paris'.

The orchestra struck up 'Watch on the Rhine', which was sung by everyone
with great gusto.

This was written by Pierre Viénot, a seventeen-year-old French student,
who continued:

> I had to listen to these songs standing up; half an hour before our arrival,
> they had thrown out someone, who had remained seated, half-lynched
> him and flung him down the stairs. I was obliged to raise my glass to
> several 'Hoch' to the health of the emperor. . . . This is lamentable because
> it is creating such an agitation that if things get worse, it will be public
> opinion that will force the government into war.[36]

Viénot returned across the Rhine and volunteered for the French Army.

In London on 3 August a crowd estimated at between 6,000 and 10,000,
favouring intervention in the European war, gathered outside Buckingham
Palace. Patriotic enthusiasm had seeped into gestures of everyday life. A
restaurateur, Eustace Miles, noted that everything was 'awful' and 'thrilling'.
'There are small and subtle changes too,' he noted. 'I notice people in the
streets are now singing the "Marseillaise" and "God Save the King" and
"Rule Britannia": the very children are marching instead of walking and
carrying bits of stick as bayonets and using old pieces of pencils as drums.'[37]
In Britain, where conscription was introduced only in 1916, volunteering
was sometimes an act of patriotic war enthusiasm. By 22 August over
100,000 men had volunteered. Raymond Asquith, a talented barrister, and
his brother Herbert, with an inclination towards romantic poetry, both
sons of the prime minister, were among the volunteers in 1914. War, to
adapt Herbert Asquith's phrase, was an opportunity to break a lance in 'life's
tournament'. Public support for the soldiers was also evident in the parades
that saw them off. One newspaper compared the sending-off to the cele-
brations that had greeted the liberation of Mafeking during the Second
Boer War.

Yet war enthusiasm was limited. Indeed, some of the boisterous scenes
resulted from drinking and the camaraderie of a sing-song. Some, like the
clerk in Asquith's verse, wanted adventure and release from the drudgery of
daily life. For the future British prime minister, Harold Macmillan, his main
preoccupation appeared to be the social status of his regiment. Patriotic
duty merged with social strategy. His mother's influence ensured he served
with the Grenadier Guards.[38]

Resignation, tears, and anxiety were the dominant emotional registers. The war tore apart carefully constructed and fragile lives. Max Lotz, a man who had fallen on difficult times, had written to Rathenau earlier that year looking for work in one of the industrialist's German factories. Lotz described the world as harsh and unfeeling and himself as an 'Opfertier' (sacrificial animal). In June he got a job at AEG's factory in Oberschöneweide, a manufacturing area of Berlin. He had barely settled into the job when he was called up and sent to the Eastern Front. 'Unfortunately we are sitting here in lazy inactivity,' he wrote to Rathenau on 24 August. 'Hopefully the decisive blow will fall in France very soon. Then there will be no delay with the Russians. It cannot last for too long, otherwise the social ruin of every country will lead to catastrophe.'[39] The bonds of civilization were being unpicked by the war. The disruption of daily life was considered the prelude to social chaos and revolution.

Misery and fear took very specific forms. At train stations, families gathered to wish their husbands, sons, and fathers well. Separation, the prospect of death and injury, and the struggle of the family left behind shaped the response to mobilization across belligerent societies. A study of Russian children's essays about the mobilization noted that they were generally 'sombre'. 'My God, how many tears flowed at our departure,' recalled one Russian soldier. 'Daddy, why are you leaving us, who will earn money, and buy bread for us?' One woman was crushed to death as she said goodbye to her husband.[40] In Bremen a seventeen-year-old recorded 'the grim songs of departure' of young married couples. Death and slaughter were the preoccupations of ordinary people, rather than patriotic heroism.[41] Dominik Richert, an Alsatian soldier in the German Army who was conscripted in 1913, did not have an opportunity to say goodbye to his family. Unlike the other soldiers in his barracks, he had no interest in drinking and singing when the mobilization decree was issued, 'because I thought that in war one can be nothing as good as shot dead. That was an extremely unpleasant outlook. Also I was scared when I thought of my relatives and my Heimat, which lay on the border and ran the danger of being destroyed.'[42] One woman in Kenya in 1969 recalled the recruitment of porters to sustain the war in east Africa: 'Their mothers were crying as they went. The son of a man who was hated was taken. The son of a man who was respected was hidden by Kinyanjui wa Gatherimu. Ropes were put through their ears and tied together. We were left weeping, mourning.'[43] Maurice Barrès, one of the leading French nationalist writers of the era, could not avoid anxiety as his son Philippe, eighteen years old, went off to war in late August, though he derived some comfort from the interweaving of his personal life and 'the life of France'.[44]

Economic disruption also threatened millions of individuals. Unemployment, food shortages, and other forms of economic privation were expected. Certain groups were hit particularly hard. Agricultural communities had lost large numbers of young men to military service. But work had to go on. Elderly peasants had to resume the kind of labour that they hoped to have given up.[45] In Georges Duhamel's book *Civilization*, a recuperating invalid reaches the summit of the hill before looking into the fields below to see a 'population of old people struggling with the earth'.[46] The socialist press in Germany and Britain contrasted the war enthusiasm of the middle class with the struggles of the working class. Workers, it was claimed, were more connected with the daily struggles of life than, say, middle-class mothers raising their children. The war threatened to inflict pain, poverty, and misery on workers. 'The people think in reality,' wrote a pastor from the working-class quarter of Moabit in Berlin, 'and the distress lies heavily on the people.' The *Daily Herald* contrasted the 'maffiking crowds' outside Buckingham Palace with mothers in the East End of London 'huddling their babes to their breasts'.[47]

Although the European middle classes demonstrated their patriotism more vigorously and bore the economic privations more easily than the working classes, many of them recognized the dangers to body and property. On the eve of the war, Prokofiev had returned to St Petersburg after spending a month in London. Having arranged for the transfer of his share certificates from St Petersburg to a bank in Moscow on 31 July, he went to a concert in Pavlovsk, just outside St Petersburg. During the second half of the concert a man interrupted the performance to read out the news of war. 'The audience became agitated, there were loud cries of "Hurrah", flags were unfurled, and the concert was transformed into a demonstration,' Prokofiev recorded in his diary:

> One poor music lover complained that his enjoyment was being spoiled, but the crowd turned on him and he barely managed to make his escape from the belligerence of the mob. Someone else was weeping, on the street there were shouts of 'Down with Austria' and a violinist I knew clutched me anxiously by the sleeve. I boarded the train back to St Petersburg, where a bath was waiting for me, and I could not avoid noticing the number of serious, worried faces all around; war with Germany is now certain. There are two ways of looking at it: the conventional point of

view is that it is such an appalling catastrophe that one's hair stands on end with the horror of it; but from the historical perspective it is terribly interesting.[48]

Mobilizing on the basis of these diverse experiences and emotional reactions was a challenge for each belligerent power. The mobilization train timetables, plotted by the General Staff in the years before 1914, ran to plan. Mobilization was a broader and continuous process than simply getting troops to the front. It also required popular commitment to the war, social cohesion, and the transfer of economic resources from the demands of peacetime to the necessities of wartime. The diversity of the initial reactions to the war anticipated the jagged and incomplete process of mobilization. The state could coerce its citizens and subjects, but mobilization also drew on the consent of Europeans to wage war. Governments recognized that social cohesion required the satisfaction of material needs, the integration of diverse and often conflicting political and social interests into a single war effort, and investing war with a moral purpose. Mobilization reshaped the complex relationships between individuals, civil society, the state, and the international order, which created a new context for imagining future peace.

For the most part, conscripts did not seek to evade military service in 1914. In Russia where nearly 10 per cent of the draft pool had failed to turn up in 1913 and some men had been known to starve themselves to evade conscription, 3,915,000 men, over 95 per cent of the pool, mobilized on schedule in 1914.[49] A combination of patriotism and a sense of duty helped to sustain mobilization. In the province of Viatka, in central Russia, the mood was solemn. Peasants accepted the war as one of national defence against the 'monster William'.[50] A stoic sense of duty mingled with tears. Driving from the Elysée Palace in Paris to his home in Pargnan in Picardy, Gabriel Hanotaux, historian and former Foreign Minister, recorded his impressions of mobilization:

We followed, step by step, the order of general mobilization which had been issued at 4 pm. Leaving Méaux, we were warned by the reddened eyes of the women. As we went along the men quit their work, the peasants their carts, and the women gathered and cried. The gendarmes arrived in the villages and posted the order of mobilization; and then, the nation began, so to speak, to put itself on a war footing and to take on the soul of the warrior. It was a display of extraordinary simplicity and grandeur. As men do not change, I suppose this was the effect on Gaul by the fires which Vercingetorix lit.[51]

Though most French people did not share Hanotaux's historical allusions (or even illusions), the patriotic connection between citizens, soil, and history sustained the sense of duty that underpinned mobilization in 1914.

Families also negotiated their mobilization. Returning briefly to Viatka, one Russian peasant petitioned for the release of his eldest son, Iakov, from military service on the grounds that his two other sons were in the army and that Iakov had a young child. Family survival required tailoring mobilization to specific needs.[52] It is worth bearing in mind that Robert Menzies, the future Australian prime minister and then a nineteen-year-old student with a commission in the University of Melbourne's militia unit, resigned his commission. It was later argued that since his two brothers had volunteered, the family had made their collective sacrifice to the imperial war effort. The family unit was the basis of social organization, so that states, when mobilizing, had to go with the grain of family life. Moreover, conscripts made sense of the abstract claims of national defence by associating the war effort with the defence of their families and homes.[53] The preservation of family became a key component of national mobilizations.

Successful mobilization required belligerent states to provide financial support to families, particularly in states with conscription where men had little or no control over their enlistment. Welfare states had expanded in pre-war Europe. The war deepened the state's role in the provision of welfare, but it also reworked the social contract. Military service became a means of asserting rights to welfare provision, while governments, political parties, and social reformers held out the prospect of improved working conditions and welfare services after the war. In Russia a law passed in 1912 gave the dependants of every soldier the right to a monthly food allowance. Wives and children simply needed to present their claim, though some beneficiaries continued to think of welfare as a form of charity rather than a right.[54] Austria had also passed a law in 1912 which gave a wife the right to a twice-monthly payment if her husband was the main earner and was drafted. By the end of the war there were 467,321 applicants for state support in Vienna alone.[55] By the end of 1914, 2,750,000 German husbands had left home to serve in the army. As family incomes in Germany plummeted, local authorities distributed Family Aid. By late 1915 over 4 million families, or 11 million individuals, received Family Aid subsidy in Germany. Though the financial support was often inadequate, the scale of support

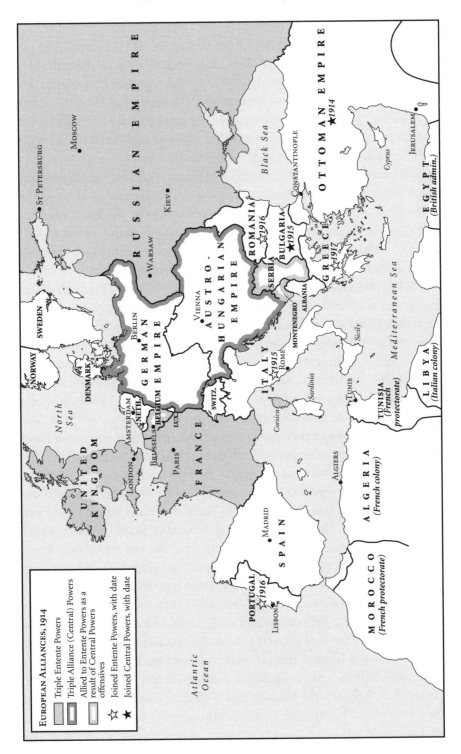

EUROPEAN ALLIANCES, 1914

Triple Entente Powers

Triple Alliance (Central) Powers

Allied to Entente Powers as a
result of Central Powers
offensives

☆ Joined Entente Powers, with date

★ Joined Central Powers, with date

had created a new social relationship, in which state, soldier, and family were bound by mutual obligations.[56] On 10 August 1914 the British government introduced a separation allowance, paid directly to the wife of a soldier. By the end of the war 1,500,000 British wives were receiving this allowance. In France financial support was extended to all the dependants of a soldier (including elderly parents, for example). In addition to the standard rate of 1.25 francs a day, a soldier received an extra 50 centimes for each dependent child.[57] Although the payments operated in different ways in each state, protection of the family had become a test of the state's legitimacy and authority. The family became a site connecting soldiers to the home front, society to the state, and present misery to the future expectation of peace. As the disruption of family life was one of the central experiences of mobilization, the preservation of the family during the war and its renewal after the conflict became a central element in imagining peace.

Mobilization was also mediated by a range of religious, political, social, and economic associations standing between the individual and the state. Churches, political parties, trade unions, commercial associations, charities, and intellectuals provided the social basis for national mobilization. Of course, these groups represented very different interests, but the demands of war required a vision of national unity. There was no time to negotiate national unity between the different associations and states in August 1914 – in fact, the idea of political negotiations between the state and different interest groups would have negated the purpose of national unity, which was to pretend that domestic political differences had been suspended or even overcome. Instead, national unity was asserted and labelled – as in the Burgfrieden, or civil peace, in Germany, the Union Sacrée in France. Those negotiations would take place in coming years, after the mythical moment of national cohesion. However, the forging of national unity in 1914 entailed the assertion of claims by these groups of what the war was about. These claims ranged from the defence of certain material interests to the definition of the moral purpose of the war and the future conditions for peace.

Even for the two small powers embroiled at the very beginning of the conflict, Serbia and Belgium, which could claim to have taken up arms in defence of their national integrity, the assertions about the moral purpose of the war went beyond the national. Pašić sought to cast the war as a defence of Balkan nations against a common threat from the Germanic powers.[58] In Belgium, the Flemish and Walloons joined in defence of what they both called 'la patrie'. A sense of national unity was forged in defence against 'the brutal behaviour of Germany', as one Flemish man put it. The

Belgian Workers' Party, which had waged a frustrated campaign for universal male suffrage before 1914, voted for war credits. On 3 August its manifesto urged 'the cause of democracy and political liberties in Europe ... against militaristic barbarism.' Emile Vandervelde, who joined the government as a minister of state in August, and other socialists claimed that they were fighting for democracy.[59] Liberty abroad could only thrive if democracy was secured at home. Given that the socialists had criticized the restrictions on suffrage before the war, their claim to defend democracy was essentially one about the future implementation of voting reform.

With the exception of Austria-Hungary the belligerents presented themselves as nation states. Wilhelm II had famously told the Reichstag that he no longer recognized parties, only Germans. The notion of national unity had a powerful claim on the European imagination in 1914, as national cohesion was considered a precondition for military success. The interests of national minorities did not disappear; rather they were now invested into the war as part of a set of reciprocal expectations concerning the future domestic and international political order.

In Ireland, for example, the threat of civil war over the Home Rule bill first introduced in 1912 receded quickly, but it did not mark an end to political divisions. Unionists and nationalists asserted their own rival claims through their commitment to the British war effort. The Ulster Volunteer Force, set up to defend Ulster against the threat of Home Rule, now joined the British Army en masse to fight Germany. As a verse of doggerel put it: 'And wherever the fight is hottest, and the sorest task is set, ULSTER WILL STRIKE FOR ENGLAND, AND ENGLAND WILL NOT FORGET.' From the perspective of the *Cork Free Press*, British soldiers (including the Ulstermen) were fighting for the 'integrity of small nations'. Supporters of Home Rule placed the Irish question in a European context. Participation in the war was a means of achieving Home Rule by demonstrating Irish nationhood through military service. In making this connection nationalists reworked the idea of the nation in arms for an Irish context. By associating their claims for autonomy with the defence of Belgium and Serbia, they associated their cause with conceptions of 'Europe' and 'civilization' that underpinned British and French war cultures. Tom Kettle, an Irish Home Rule nationalist, was in Belgium trying to buy guns for the Irish Volunteer Force, which had been established in response to the Ulster Volunteer Force. He witnessed the German invasion, the atrocities, and the destruction of Louvain, events which left him in no doubt that he must join the British Army in 'defence of our civilization'.[60] In order to maintain national unity, Asquith ensured that the Home Rule bill was given Royal Assent in September, but that it would not be implemented until the war had ended. Although Edward Carson, leader of the Ulster Unionists, claimed he could not decide whether Wilhelm II or Asquith was the 'worst blackguard', the prime minister's finesse worked, the party truce between the Liberals and Conservatives held, and recruitment rates remained reasonably high in Ireland, especially in Ulster.[61]

For the moment Irishmen were not fighting each other. For Polish nationalists the position was greatly complicated by the presence of Poles on opposing sides. The partition of Poland in the late eighteenth century had been sustained by cooperation between Russia, Austria, and Prussia (later Germany). The complex geopolitics of the Polish question divided national leaders. For some, such as Roman Dmowski, the founder of the National Democratic Party, the future of Polish nationalism required co-operation with Russia. Dmowski viewed Germany as a greater threat to Polish nationalism on the grounds that it could Germanize Poland, whereas Russia could not Russify Poland. In a war against Germany, Russia would require Polish support. On 14 August the Russian Grand Duke Nicholas's manifesto to the Polish nation appeared to confirm Dmowski's political calculations. This manifesto was adorned with high-flown language, with a vague promise that Poland would be 'free in its faith, language and self-government'.[62] Moreover, the alliance between Russia, Britain, and France enabled Dmowski to set the Polish national question in the context of a liberal alliance, fighting for the rights of nations.

In the other camp stood Josef Pilsudski, soldier and leader of the Polish Socialist Party. Before the war he had based himself in Cracow, in Austria-Hungary, where he enjoyed the protection of local officials. Pilsudski favoured cooperation with the Central Powers on the grounds of their likely victory over Russia and the more benign political regime for Poles in the Habsburg empire. On the outbreak of war he took command of several units, which advanced from Cracow into Congress Poland in the Russian empire. In part this manoeuvre was a nationalist gesture, an attempt to create a martial national moment, which would legitimize Polish nation-alist claims. When one of Pilsudski's units arrived at the home of the great Polish writer Henryk Sinkiewicz, he accused them of associating with the Germans, to which one of the soldiers replied that he would 'even go with the devil, the main issue is a free Poland'.[63] Wilhelm II assured Bogdan von Hutten-Czapski, a Polish aristocrat, of his support for the Polish nation. The war had reopened the Polish question, creating space for the claims of

Polish nationalists. The working-out of those claims remained as vague as the promises issued in the Grand Duke's manifesto and Wilhelm's conversation with Hutten-Czapski, but the Polish question had become one of the major geopolitical and ideological issues in the war, a test of the place of nationalism in a Europe for now dominated by great powers and empires. For the moment, most Poles supported their empire, some more heartily than others.

In eastern and western Europe the vast majority of national minorities saw the war as an opportunity to further their goals of autonomy and cultural rights. Empires provided security for small nations. The overrunning of Belgium and Serbia in 1914 reinforced the concern for security amongst national minority politicians in Europe. In Austria-Hungary the majority of Czechs, Slovaks, Slovenes, Serbs, and Romanians rallied to the Habsburg monarchy in July 1914. The Catholic Party in Moravia declared their loyalty to the state and emperor, which provided the 'most secure guarantee' for the development of different nations. In Prague, Social Democrats were alarmed at the prospect of being drawn into Tsarist Russia's orbit, given its record of suppressing workers' rights. 'The Czech nation,' the party declared in August, 'has to rely on Austria in the future, and it must work for a reform of the state according to its needs. It is in the situation of a man who temporarily occupies small rooms in the house best suited to his requirements. His endeavour should not be directed towards either demolishing the house or moving somewhere else, but to negotiate better living conditions for himself.'[64] However, there were pockets of resistance. In Prague conscripts of the 28th Regiment, drawn from areas dominated by the Czech National Party, were heard singing: 'We are marching against the Russians, but no one knows why.' Eight months later the soldiers from the regiment deserted.[65]

Across Europe, Jewish leaders pledged loyalty to their state. Military service provided an opportunity to demonstrate that Jews were equally loyal to their state as any other subject and therefore deserved equal rights. Zionists remained marginal to Jewish political and social life; indeed, British figures like Lucien Wolf, a journalist and member of the Conjoint Foreign Committee, an Anglo-Jewish group campaigning against the persecution of Jews in Russia and Romania, and Edwin Montagu, a Liberal politician, feared that Zionism, with its goal of a Jewish homeland, would provide anti-Semites with an excuse to challenge the loyalty of Jews in Britain (or any other society). When Walter Rathenau volunteered his services to Chancellor Bethmann Hollweg, he did so as a businessman who had

an extensive knowledge of international politics, rather than as an affirmation of a German Jew's loyalty to the Kaiserreich, a question that would
have barely crossed his mind in 1914.[66]

The rallying of socialist and trade union leaders to the war added
another layer of claims as to the purpose of the conflict. The majority of
socialists and trade unionists had long been prepared to support a defensive war. In this case, defence denoted the protection of social and political
reforms as well as national territory. Tactical calculations and political
belief led socialists to support their national war effort. For example, the
SPD leadership in Germany had major doubts about the conduct of foreign
policy during the July crisis, but these were secondary to the defence of the
Fatherland against oppressive Tsarist Russia. Workers defended German
democracy, welfare, and economic prosperity against Tsarist autocracy and
Russian barbarism. Socialists were undoubtedly caught up in the sense of
national unity once war had been declared. This unity provided the SPD
and trade unions with an opportunity to emerge from their political isolation in imperial Germany. In turn, by integrating into the political system,
the SPD could defend workers' interests more effectively, while also pushing
for reforms that reflected their understanding of the war as the defence of
political liberty. On 24 August, Eduard David, on the right of the party, told
the Reich Interior Minister Clemens von Delbrück that only reform of the
restrictive Prussian electoral laws would constitute reasonable compensation for the people's sacrifice.[67]

In France the funeral of the socialist leader Jean Jaurès, attended by
figures as diverse as the nationalist Barrès, the Archbishop of Paris, Cardinal
Ammette, and the leader of the Confédération Générale du Travail, Léon
Jouhaux, enabled a public display of national unity. French socialists cast
the war in a revolutionary context. 'Do not forget,' Joseph Paul-Boncour
told his audience, 'that you are going to defend the Paris of the Commune.'
More generally, however, socialists shared the view that this was a war in
defence of civilization and against militarism. The move from a war in
defence of national territory to a war in defence of a set of ideals was part of
an expansion of the purpose of the conflict. The French cause was fused
with that of humanity. French socialists, claiming the legacy of the
Revolution, looked forward to the potentially emancipatory consequences
of war. Jouhaux spoke of the 'social remaking' that, he believed, would be
the inevitable consequence of the 'murderous shock' of war. Social progress
was dependent on political liberty at home and abroad. The defence of civilization required the destruction of German militarism. What this entailed

was not yet explained in August 1914, but it implied the overthrow of the German domestic political system. It was not sufficient to defeat German armies, which would recover in due course. French socialists believed that the crushing of German militarism in this war would provide the foundation for a more enduring peace and enable more attention and resources to be directed towards social and political reform. Like the Belgian Workers' Party, French socialists were able to combine the political aims of defending the rights of small nations with social reform. And just as Vandervelde became a minister in the Belgian cabinet, so too Jules Guesde and Marcel Sembat entered the French cabinet.[68]

In Britain, Ramsay MacDonald, the Scottish leader of the Labour Party, bucked the trend of other reforming socialists in Europe and opposed entry to the war. Whereas German and French socialist leaders accepted, for the most part, that their nation was waging a legitimate war of national defence, MacDonald argued that British entry was dictated by the 'balance of power'. Without this moral dimension, MacDonald – no pacifist – could not support the war.[69] Nevertheless, on 5 August 1914 the Labour Party decided to support the British war effort and MacDonald resigned as leader. He was replaced by Arthur Henderson, who initially had opposed British entry but supported the government once war was declared. The General Federation of Trade Unions and the Trades Union Congress made clear their support on 5 August, the same day that they and the Labour Party established the War Emergency Workers' National Committee, which was designed to defend workers' conditions during the war. In contrast to MacDonald, Ben Tillett of the General Federation of Trade Unions identified the German aristocratic military elites, supported by socialists and liberals, as the culprits for the war, who had to be 'eliminated from civilization'.[70]

The various versions of the Union Sacrée were completed by the commitment of churches, businesses, nationalist associations, and liberals to the war. Their immediate reaction at the outbreak of the conflict focused on national defence. 'No matter what our attitude toward the government's domestic policy,' Paul Miliukov wrote in the Cadet Party's manifesto of support for the Tsarist government, 'our first duty is to preserve the unity and integrity of our country, and to defend its position as a world power. . . . Let us postpone our domestic disputes; let us not give our adversary even the slightest excuse for relying on differences which divide us.'[71] The promise of national unity, drawing on the myth of war enthusiasm, had implications for forging a new political community. This could require the exclusion as well as inclusion of certain social, ethnic, and religious groups, though few people articulated this exclusionary dimension in August 1914. 'It is a joy to be alive', declared a special issue of the *Alldeutsche Blätter* on 3 August. However, Heinrich Claß, the Pan-German leader, complained the following day that internal reform of the Reich was made more difficult by the Jews and Social Democrats, because 'they are so unusually loyal'.[72] Claß's conception of national cohesion was shared by other nationalists across Europe, who prized a homogeneous society – a single people or Volk, undifferentiated by creed, class, or language – as the basis for the projection of national power. Both Miliukov and Claß would soon call for domestic political reforms in order to wage war more effectively, but their proposals veered in different directions. Miliukov sought reforms that would bind minorities to the state by giving them rights; Claß sought to diminish the rights of minorities, workers, and others.

Not all Europeans rallied to their state in 1914. Some national minority and socialist leaders actively opposed their state and pursued more radical goals. For example, the Czech nationalist leader and professor of philosophy Thomas Masaryk went into exile in late 1914 and campaigned for the independence of Czechoslovakia from Austria-Hungary.[73] Croat supporters of a South Slav state, such as Ante Trumbic, also went into exile. The Irish Republican Brotherhood, controlled by Tom Clarke and Sean McDermott, welcomed the war as an opportunity to launch a rebellion against the British government. 'The name of Ireland,' the *Irish Volunteer* asserted, 'must now or never be written on the scroll of nations.'[74] In 1914 Vladimir Ilyich Lenin, the Bolshevik leader, also went into exile, leaving Cracow for Switzerland. Socialist supporters of the war, according to Lenin, had forgotten that the 'working class have no country'. They betrayed the international socialist movement by supporting a war that was rooted in a capitalist economic system. According to Lenin, war could only be brought to an end by a revolutionary war against capitalist bourgeois governments.[75]

Revolutionary war was Lenin's version of the war to end all wars. Given his policies after 1917, it is easy to dismiss the references to peace, a United States of Europe, and other benign-sounding terms as mere political slogans. Yet these words and other such as 'humanity', 'civilization', and 'barbarism' reveal important features of European war cultures as states and societies mobilized in August 1914. The emotional register of mobilization was dominated by the contradictions of sadness, anxiety, relief, and euphoria. This experience was immediately translated into expectations. Some of these expectations concerned the war – the possibility of death, injury, or captivity, and the concern for family and employment. The private emotional register of mobilization did not provide a basis for a sustained war effort. The state intervened to provide financial support. More significantly, however, the moment of mobilization also created expectations about the purpose of the war. And, paradoxically, many of these expectations concerned peace, domestic political reform, and the reordering of the international system. These expectations were bound up with terms such as 'civilization', 'humanity', 'barbarism', 'militarism', 'nation', 'democracy', 'family', and 'social reform'. These terms had no defined content. They were used by different people, often on different sides, and often in contradictory ways. This does not render them irrelevant. The war was partly a struggle to give shape and content to these terms. Indeed, the expectation that a better world could be created justified the intensification of the war effort. 'I am convinced', Carl Legien, the German trade union leader, told an audience in Kiel in January 1915, 'that this will be the last war.'[76] The moment of mobilization in July and August 1914 had created expectations of 'total peace', which would follow this final war. Peace would embrace all facets of existence, from family life to territorial settlements. It was an inflated and unattainable notion of peace, but it mobilized societies and legitimized violence. Experiences and expectations of peace and war were interwoven from the outset of the conflict.

* * *

Beyond Europe the outbreak of war immediately raised questions about power and identity in a changing global order. Stefan Zweig wrote a powerful account of the confusion that war caused to notions of racial order, civilization, and personal fate in *Journey into the Past*, a novella then written in 1924 (though then unpublished) about Ludwig, a talented young man who fell in love with his boss's wife and was sent from Germany to Mexico to manage the firm's business affairs. He had booked his return home when there 'came the disastrous day that pitilessly tore up not only his calendar but, with total indifference, the lives and thoughts of millions, leaving them in shreds'. Personal upheaval was mirrored by the unsettling of normal relations between European and American managers and Mexican workers. 'The few white settlers had left their work and were standing around the station in the midst of a shouting, questioning, stupidly gaping throng of mestizos and native Indians.'[77] The war was viewed as an opportunity to recast the world order, although it also entailed enormous difficulties for poorly developed economies tied into the European commercial system. 'Fifty years work gone in an hour,' remarked one German merchant in Peru, watching fifty steamers lie idle.[78]

Amongst the crowded tenements on the Lower East Side of Manhattan, where many European immigrants first found shelter on arriving in the United States, Lillian Wald, a progressive social reformer and head of the Henry Street Settlement, articulated what many Europeans felt on the outbreak of war. War, she said, was a 'demon of destruction and a hideous wrong – murder devastating home and happiness.'[79] However, while some progressives viewed the war as a catastrophe, many other Americans viewed it as an opportunity, even a providential moment, to establish American commercial and political dominance over the western hemisphere – to replace the unfortunate German merchant in Peru. It was also a chance to make money from the warring European states.[80] President Woodrow Wilson was in no position to take any immediate policy decisions in early August 1914 beyond proclaiming American neutrality, as he was at the bedside of his dying wife. In any case, American aims did not require any immediate decisions. Business would come to the United States.

Across Europe's overseas empires, nationalist politicians faced similar choices and made similar decisions to nationalist leaders in Ireland, Poland, and Bohemia. In Canada, Australia, and New Zealand, prime ministers pledged immediate support for Britain. The empire offered a guarantee of their security and imperial unity was also sustained by notions of shared Britishness. Archibald T. Strong, a professor at the University of Melbourne and a leading intellectual in Australia, contended that the liberal values underpinning representative democracy in Australia were endangered by the prospect of German hegemony and the values of Prussian militarism. He urged Australians to fight to a 'clean finish', by which he meant the destruction of the Hohenzollern dynasty. Only the British empire provided the security for the flourishing of liberal values. The German threat was a fusion of ideological and geopolitical anxieties.[81]

In South Africa the relationship between empire, race, and nation took on a particular twist in a war waged in the name of 'civilization'. British and Afrikaner politicians were constructing a new state, and the dominant South African Party, led by Louis Botha and Jan Smuts, who had fought against British forces during the Boer War, decided to support the British empire. While they sought to build a white South Africa within the empire, the South African Native National Congress, formed in 1912 in opposition to the racist treatment of blacks by the new Anglo-Boer dispensation, offered to raise a contingent of troops. By fighting for civilization in Europe, they hoped to achieve the rights associated with civilization in South Africa.[82] Indian nationalist leaders also rallied to support Britain. At the Indian National Congress in December 1914 the president, Bhupendra Nath Bose, argued that India was fulfilling her destiny, 'written in the blood of her sons'. Martial prowess served 'the great principles of equality and justice', which, in practical terms, meant greater representation of Indians in their own government and administration and more autonomy from London.[83] Yet whiteness remained a signifier of the competence for self-government, both individually and collectively. Responding to a vote of loyalty presented by Kaseva Pillai, a journalist and nationalist politician on the Madras Legislative Council, Harold Stuart, a British civil servant in Madras, thanked the Indian population for their support in the 'great fight for freedom . . . so far as their limited capabilities permitted'.[84]

Japan had declared war on Germany in August. In East Asia the geopolitical implications of 'Europe', 'whiteness', 'Asia', and Christianity had particular consequences. As European empires turned on each other, the conflict opened up possibilities for the reordering of East Asian politics. The concept of 'Asia for the Asians' had emerged in late nineteenth-century Japan; it was not always a disingenuous slogan to disguise Japanese expansion into China, though Japanese intellectuals and leaders considered themselves the natural leaders and defenders of Asian interests. In China, Sun Yat-sen, a rival to Yuan Shikai and dependent on Japanese aid, saw the war as an opportunity, because 'Europe would have no time to pay attention to the East'.[85] Sun's reference to 'Europe' revealed the insight of those looking in from the outside – the distinctions between French republicanism and German militarism, between Russian autocracy and British liberalism looked less important than what had bound Europeans together and enabled them to shape the late nineteenth-century world. 'From our perspective as Asians,' said General Terauchi Masatake, a leading Japanese general, 'it is a war between Christians and, if we borrow their words, heathen peoples.' He went on to spell out the geopolitical implications in East Asia: 'Although we will not insist upon excluding Europeans and Americans, it is proper to inform Westerners that, up to a point, Asia should be under control of the Asians.'[86] What this meant remained to be worked out. There were competing visions of East Asian politics both between and within China and Japan, but the outbreak of war had accelerated the process already evident during the first years of the Chinese Revolution, the ebbing of European power in the region.

* * *

Robert Dubarle, captain of the 68th Battalion of *Chausseurs alpins*, was perhaps a particularly reflective soldier. Born in 1881 near Grenoble, he wrote frequently to his wife, sisters-in-law, and parents. 'It is necessary to love one's country,' he wrote to his sister-in-law, Charlotte, on 9 November 1914,

> but that is not a reason to hate others and to only dream of massacres. The other day when I took down my German, I was very satisfied, at first because the poor devil had tried to kill me, and afterwards because it happened during combat. But with combat finished, I see the German corpses, I feel emotion and pity. Indeed recently I saw the corpse of a German NCO killed the previous day, the palour of wax, resting on his side with a young and charming face. I could not stop myself from expressing my compassion to the great astonishment of a sergeant who had accompanied me and who looked at the body (he had killed him the previous day in an ambush) with the greatest possible joy. Today the weather will be delicious, fresh, soft, and hazy. How exquisite autumn always is in these mountains, and how this nice temperature and delicate sun on the green and red forests seems the opposite to the savageries of war. Was Rousseau really wrong when he exalted nature and contrasted it to the nastiness of man?[87]

The shock of violence raised larger issues concerning the war, some of which Dubarle mentioned in his letter. Could nationalism only be expressed in hatred of the enemy? Did empathy have a place on the battlefield? Had the war revealed the inherent brutishness of man or had war brutalized man? The war cultures, which had taken shape during mobilization, were further sharpened in the last months of 1914 as soldiers committed atrocities against civilians, refugees fled war zones, and prisoners of war went into captivity.

The shock of violence might have mattered less had one or other side scored a decisive military victory. In the west, the German Army's advance into France came to a halt at the battle of the Marne, fought between 6 and 10 September. Already slowed down by the delay in capturing Liège and the timely arrival of the British Expeditionary Force, a gap opened between the 1st and 2nd German Armies. Joseph Joffre, the French commander, ordered a counter-attack against the German 1st Army, which retreated back across the River Marne. In France relief combined with euphoria in celebration of the miracle of the Marne.

Barrès saw the Marne as a moment in which France was restored, forty-four years almost to the day after the battle of Sedan: 'We return to the true France. We are exiles who have found our country again.'[88] 'It is as quiet as a mortuary in the school-buildings in Luxembourg [the head-quarters of the General Staff],' noted Karl von Wenninger, the Bavarian military plenipotentiary, on 10 September, 'one tip-toes around, the General Staff officers rush past me with their eyes cast down – best not to address them, not to ask.'[89] Helmuth von Moltke, suffering from a nervous breakdown, was replaced as Chief of the General Staff by the Prussian Minister of War Erich von Falkenhayn. By November, after the first battle of Ypres, the front had stabilized and a rudimentary trench system was constructed. Germany had gained considerable territory in Belgium and northern France, a potential bargaining chip and a source of raw materials. On the other hand, by holding out, France and Britain could now bring their greater combined economic and demographic resources to bear on the war.

On the Eastern Front, Russian forces advanced into East Prussia. After losing confidence in the commander of the German 8th Army in mid-August, Moltke appointed Eric Ludendorff and Paul von Hindenburg to take charge of the defence of East Prussia. The Russian 1st and 2nd Armies lost contact with each other and were poorly coordinated. 'How disastrously the conditions of warfare had changed,' lamented Alexander Samsonov, the commander of the Russian 1st Army in Alexander Solzhenitsyn's fictional account, *August 1914*, 'making a commander as impotent as a rag doll.'[90] Yet the disparity between the performance of the Russian and German commanders showed that leadership was not a lost art in 1914. Better-trained soldiers, more effective communication, and reliable supplies enabled the German 8th Army to defeat Samsonov's forces. After sustaining 140,000 casualties Samsonov walked into woods nearby and committed suicide.[91] Although the battle of Tannenberg – as Hindenburg christened the victory, as a kind of historical revenge for the defeat of the Teutonic Knights by Polish forces five hundred years previously – provided the basis for the duumvirate of Hindenburg and Ludendorff to become key figures in German politics until 1918, it was not a decisive victory. Russia remained very much in the war, with vast reserves of men and territory.

Meanwhile the Austro-Hungarian government had generously allowed the Serbian Chief of the General Staff, Radomir Putnik, to return home from his spa holiday in Gleichenberg, Bohemia. Over the following months the front moved back and forth. On 2 December Habsburg forces captured Belgrade but by the end of the year the Serbian army had forced them to withdraw.[92] In a war of attrition, however, Austria-Hungary had a decisive advantage over Serbia. Only in East Asia was there a decisive victory in this period when Japanese forces captured Tsingtao, a German colony, on 7 November. However, Japanese possession was directed as much against Chinese claims as against German ones.[93]

The experience of violence was a shock. The visceral experience of battle, captivity, occupation, and flight was new for the vast majority of Europeans in 1914, including soldiers. The conflicts before the First World War had provided some sense of what modern warfare might entail, but the actual physical experience of violence proved shocking, disturbing human-itarian sensibilities. These sensibilities were not expressed simply through references to codes of international law, but rather reflected the peaceful-ness of early twentieth-century Europe. This is not to say that violent death was absent from Europe before 1914 – but it was either the product of natural catastrophes, such as the earthquake in Messina in 1908, industrial accidents, such as the collapse of mines, or murder. War, however, was viewed as an organized form of violence that transformed the institutions of civilization into iron cages of destruction. Duhamel's lacerating descrip-tion of wounded men forming a queue at the medical station demonstrated the bitter incongruity of violence and order. 'The great European massacre,' he wrote, 'insists on order. Every act of the drama is regulated with minute exactness. As fast as the men filed past, they were counted and enveloped in red tape; secretaries verified their identity with the cold exactness of custom-house clerks. As for them they answered with the patience of the eternal public at the administrative wicket.'[94] Anyone who wants war, one Bavarian soldier wrote in October 1914, 'is no longer human'.[95] The point is not that morale collapsed – soldiers' morale held up remarkably well until about 1917 – but that violence shocked most Europeans, at least early in the war.

Soldiers transmitted the experience of violence around the continent. Letters and returning home on leave were two obvious means, but wounded soldiers and prisoners of war represented for civilians a direct encounter with war. In Merseyside one woman was upset when she saw a hospital ship coming into port. 'It seemed to bring home the pitilessness of it all,' wrote her daughter. 'It is a queer old world [and] we are queer people in it trying to kill each other – what good is it all?'[96] Owing to the war of movement, large numbers of prisoners were taken in late 1914, particularly by German forces. The International Red Cross reported in spring 1915 that there were over 750,000 prisoners of war in Germany. There is evidence of the killing of prisoners in the immediate aftermath of capture, though such incidents remained rare. Prisoners were shocked at their journey into captivity. At Clermont-Ferrand in France the 'crowd shouted angrily at the prisoners and sang the Marseillaise', while French and British prisoners were also exposed to the hostility of civilians in Germany. 'Old German women can spit,' wrote one British prisoner.[97]

The war of movement in late 1914 also witnessed violence against civilians. In the final chapter of Joseph Roth's novel about the end of the Habsburg empire, *The Radetzky March* (1932), in the first days of the war the main protagonist, Trotta, comes across three civilians, including an Orthodox priest, hanged outside a graveyard. Trotta 'looked at their swollen faces. He thought he could recognize in them various of his own men. They were the faces of people with whom he dealt on a daily basis.'[98] Trotta cut down the corpses and buried them in a shallow grave, a hurried act of respect that marked the passing of his pre-war world. The work of John Horne and Alan Kramer on German atrocities in Belgium and north-east France has underlined the centrality of this violence to the emerging war cultures. Violence against civilians occurred on each front. Between 5 and 8 August, German forces killed 850 Belgian civilians and razed 1,300 buildings to the ground. After Belgian troops withdrew from Louvain, a university town and centre of Catholic culture, on 19 August, the German 1st Army occupied the town. On the evening of 25 August, after some shooting – most likely friendly fire between German soldiers – troops broke into the library and set it ablaze. Over the following days, German soldiers killed 248 civilians. The destruction of the library stood as a symbol of the German assault on civilization. In total 5,146 civilians were killed in north-east France and Belgium in August and September 1914 alone.[99] Less detailed figures and research exist for other fronts. In Kalisz on the Prosna river in Congress Poland, German troops bombarded the city, executed several inhabitants after occupying it, and deported hundreds of others.[100] In East Prussia one German report estimated that Russian troops killed 101 civilians. Anti-Semitic pogroms and the killing of Romanians accompanied the Russian occupation of Bukovina and Galicia in the Habsburg empire in autumn 1914.[101] Austro-Hungarian forces killed 3,500 Serbian civilians in the first weeks of the war, proportionately more than the Germans in Belgium and north-east France. The atrocities included mass executions and the burning of dwellings.[102]

Far more civilians fled the advancing armies than were killed, creating the new social and political category of the refugee. By December 1914 an estimated 100,000 refugees had crowded into Warzaw. 'Well-to-do people,' reported one observer, 'have become poverty stricken refugees; those with large families have lost children en route and have been forced to leave behind their sick relatives.'[103] Six hundred thousand Belgians fled to France, Britain, and the Netherlands, as the news of atrocities spread in advance of the German forces. 'One only had one thought,' recalled two sisters, 'to be far away, to flee them, to move ahead of them, these accursed. To put oneself out of their clutches. To flee the atrocities.'[104]

This shock of violence shaped the debate about the moral purpose of the war. Intellectuals and others responded to violence by framing the war as a struggle about the future of humanity. Visions of peace, refracted through the violence of war, were at the core of international exchanges in late 1914. H. G. Wells, the colourful author of scientific romances, set out his reasons for supporting Britain's participation in the conflict in *The War that Will End War*. War was stripped of its glories, redefined as 'unprecedented slaughter' and 'hideous butchery'. This sensibility to suffering led Wells both to hate war and also to demand the intensification of the war effort. The violence could only be justified if the moral purpose of this war was to end war. War aims escalated to embrace 'the war of the mind'. 'We fight not to destroy a nation,' he argued, 'but a nest of evil ideas.' He reiterated that the war was directed against the German leaders, who embodied the ideals of militarism. 'Our grievance is the grievance of every decent life-loving German, of every German mother and sweetheart who watched her man go off under his incompetent leaders to hardship and mutilations and death.' Indeed, German society was the 'most civilized' because people cherished domesticity. Peace was defined by what war destroyed – families, homes, and bodies. 'It is not a war of nations,' Wells wrote in the introduction, 'but of mankind. It is a war to exorcise a world-madness and end an age . . . this is now a war for peace.'[105]

The Allies tended to adopt universalist language, framing their war as a defence of peace, civilization, and humanity against militarism and barbarism. This seeped into diplomatic discourse and radicalized the discussion of war aims. Théophile Delcassé, the French Foreign Minister, promised that French armies would bring the fight onto German soil so that the Allies could impose reparations 'and set up in Europe a new condition, which would guarantee the peace of the world for many years'.[106] Discussing war aims, Nicholas II told Maurice Paléologue, the French ambassador, that the primary goal was the 'destruction of German militarism'. The radical aims – territorial dismemberment and regime change in Germany – could only be legitimized by the larger moral purpose of peace. 'Our work will only be justified by history,' the Tsar continued, 'if it is dominated by a moral idea, by the preoccupation of assuring for a very long time the peace of the world. Therefore it means the end of the German empire.'[107] Wells conflated moral purpose and territorial aims when he wrote that 'We are fighting for a new map of Europe if we are fighting for anything at all.'[108] Redrawing the map of Europe was both a conventional geopolitical task and a moral one, which would secure the values the Allies claimed to represent.

The invitation card to the Lord Mayor's Banquet in London in November 1914 was altered to represent the flags of the five Allies intertwined. Arthur Balfour, the former Conservative prime minister, told the audience that the Allies were united by the shared values of 'civilization'. Allied victory would secure the 'sacredness of international law and the rights of international freedom'. An international system defined by these norms would enable small states to thrive and develop their own 'ideals' without fearing foreign intervention. The German government could no longer call itself civilized, following the invasion of Belgium, the atrocities, and the brutal occupation.[109] The atrocities in Belgium figured prominently in denunciations of German barbarism and the Allies' self-depiction as the guardians of civilization, in Russia as well as in Britain and France.[110] The Allied presentation of the atrocities dramatized more abstract concepts of international law and civilization by tying them to the defence of family and home. Indeed, contemporary understandings of international law were shaped by humanitarian concerns rather than a strict reading of the Hague Conventions.[111]

The violence drew on imperial languages and images in ways that excluded Germany from the moral map of Europe and carried the language of the civilizing mission into the war. Before 1914, uncontrolled violence against civilians had been associated with the 'barbaric' conduct of war in Africa or the conflicts of the Middle Ages. In Belgium, however, the German army had violated the precepts of European civilization. Speaking at the Académie des Sciences Morales et Politiques, Henri Bergson argued that pillage, arson, the destruction of monuments, and the murder of women and children marked a 'return to barbarism', crimes that were an affront to the values represented by the Académie. The German way of warfare involved the destruction of populations, the result of the triumph of might over right in the Kaiserreich.[112]

German and Austro-Hungarian intellectuals, academics, and artists responded to these denunciations. They also claimed to defend international law and blamed the civilian populations in occupied territory for attacking and mutilating soldiers. Civilian participation in violence transgressed the norms of European warfare. Soldiers in both Austria-Hungary and Germany claimed that they operated within the constraints of international law. The 'cultural level' of the Balkans had, according to one Austro-Hungarian commander, led to the 'brutal, deceitful actions of the Serb military and population against our troops, which violated every norm of war and all laws of humanity'.[113] The German military and Foreign Ministry investigated the reports of atrocities, aware of the disastrous impact these reports had on Germany's international reputation. While figures such as Bethmann Hollweg were aware that atrocities had been committed, the general defence was that the civilian population had engaged in a people's war (*Volkskrieg*). Evidently, the Central Powers could not denounce the war, but they sought to represent themselves as defenders of a carefully codified conduct of warfare. This was based on a different reading of nineteenth-century humanitarianism, in which the purpose of the laws of war was to contain violence, rather than abolish war.[114]

German writers defended militarism against Allied charges, most notably in the Appeal to the Civilized World. Published on 4 October and signed by ninety-three prominent figures from the arts, universities, and politics, the Appeal became one of the most controversial polemics of the war. The text was drafted by Ludwig Fulda, a brilliant theatre producer who broke off work on his translation of Ibsen's *Peer Gynt*. Fulda and other signatories, such as Lujo Brentano, the economist, had been critics of Wilhelmine cultural policies before the First World War. The Appeal claimed that militarism was essential to the defence of the German people and culture. Germany, according to the Appeal, had been encircled by the Triple Entente before the war. It justified the invasion of Belgium by claiming that French and British war plans involved the violation of Belgian neutrality. Belgian civilians had then cruelly shot German troops, often in the back. 'It is not true', the text argued,

> that our conduct of war violates the rules of international law. It [conduct of war] does not recognise any unrestrained cruelty. However in the East, the earth drinks the blood of women and children slaughtered by Russian hands and in the West dum-dum bullets tear the breasts of our warriors. Those who are allied to the Russians and the Serbians and who offer the

world the shameful show of inciting the Mongolians and Negroes against the white race have the least justification to portray themselves as defenders of European civilization.[115]

The reference to colonial troops fighting in the French and British armies showed how German writers could frame their war effort as a defence of Europe, not just of Germany and Austria-Hungary. Indian troops fought at Festubert in north-eastern France in December 1914, while just under 500,000 French colonial troops fought in Europe during the First World War. The employment of these troops, according to publicists in the Central Powers, violated the laws of war, white racial solidarity, and the claims of the civilizing mission. Socialists, such as the Austrian Karl Renner, argued that the use of such troops was the final proof of imperial exploitation. A pamphlet produced by the German Foreign Ministry in 1915 claimed that the 'brutality and cruelty [of these troops were] a shame to the conduct of war in the twentieth century'. On this reading colonial troops were so culturally backward that they could not internalize the restraints that underpinned the laws of war. Stories of mutilation and bestial imagery accompanied German propaganda against them. Moreover, colonial troops would recognize the divisions amongst the white European powers and get used to the idea of killing white men, thus weakening the legitimacy of European imperial rule.[116]

Karl Lamprecht, a liberal German economic historian, turned the universal claims of British and French writers against them in a brilliant analysis in late August. His own career had combined methodological innovation, intense research into German history, and the cultivation of international academic networks and friendships. He contrasted two trends of the early twentieth century. The first was the development of a 'cosmopolitan sense', based on economic interdependence. The key figure in this process was the businessman, 'the hero of peace'. At the same time the rise of the nation state, which Lamprecht associated with the emergence of the bourgeoisie, fuelled national sentiment. The atrocities committed during the Balkan Wars and against Belgian and French civilians represented these political values. Yet the war was not simply the product of a conflict between national types and the failure of internationalism. Indeed, Lamprecht concluded that the conflation of national with universal claims had led British and French governments to extend their rule. Hence the British and French champions of humanity bore responsibility for the war and the radicalization of war aims.[117] Lamprecht's defence of German policy cost him friendships. Henri Pirenne, the leading Belgian medieval historian, refused to see Lamprecht when the latter visited the occupied region. Lamprecht's argument anticipated later German writings, which claimed that universal values threatened the national distinctions that constituted Europe.

The idea that Germany and Austria-Hungary were the defenders of Europe entered diplomatic and high political language. For Bethmann Hollweg the challenge of the war was to accommodate German power within a European order. Driving through the battlefields on 4 September his adviser, Kurt Riezler, contrasted the calm of nature with the burnt villages and injured prisoners. 'It will be the collapse of Europe,' he reflected, 'if Europe does not find in this opportunity any form of permanence and common ground.'[118] Bethmann Hollweg's first draft of German war aims, completed on 9 September, remains one of the most controversial documents of the war, over fifty years after the historian Fritz Fischer first wrote about it. While Fischer saw the September programme as a coherent statement of hegemonic wars that shaped German policy until 1918, more recent research has stressed its contingent character, the centrality of economic aims, and its attempt to forestall a more radical territorial programme. While annexations of French and Belgian territory were important to the proposal, the central feature was the guarantee of German security in Europe through the economic subjugation of other states. The Chancellor would observe the niceties of nation states and equal sovereignty in the formation of a European customs union, but this would serve German political and commercial pre-eminence. It may be an exaggeration to call it 'the Kaiser's European Union', but Bethmann Hollweg appreciated the limits of German power. This was the beginning of a conversation in which he repeatedly struggled to reconcile German security with broader conceptions of Europe.[119] In Vienna, meanwhile, the notion of Austria-Hungary as a European necessity persisted. Its supporters considered it a model for maintaining peace between the different national and ethnic groupings in Europe.[120]

Europe, even as it split apart in 1914, remained an important category for thinking about the international system. Romain Rolland, the French author and opponent of the war, wrote in despair in September 1914 of 'the European war, this sacrilegious melée, which offers the spectacle of a demented Europe, climbing on to the funeral pyre and ripping off its own hands, like Hercules'.[121] The personification of Europe allowed Rolland to describe what he saw as Europe's suicide. Civilization was destroying itself in two ways. First, the technologies and bureaucracies that underpinned civilization enabled a radical intensification of violence. Second, the stakes in the war had been raised beyond the territorial claims of previous wars between the great powers. War aims were imagined and negotiated through visions of the future of Europe, civilization, culture, international law, and humanity. These terms encoded different and competing visions of a lasting peace. Walter Rathenau, who refused to cooperate with Rolland's plans for an intellectual international based in Geneva, considered the war, at least in the first few months, as a crisis in which Europe and Europeans would be remade.[122] The shock of violence had destroyed a European order, but it had not destroyed the idea of one. People were fighting for the power to define the new European order.

CHAPTER 4

EMPIRES AND NATIONS, 1915

'THINK OF IT,' Thomas Masaryk said, 'the very question of this war is graphically not represented, though day by day for over a year past endless discussions, alike in the press and on the public platform, turn upon the question of nationality.' The Czech nationalist leader was speaking at his inaugural lecture at the newly founded School of Slavonic Studies, King's College London. He reconciled his vision of a Europe of nation states with the claims of 'humanity' and 'democratic internationalism'. He derived this vision of the nation as the guarantor of democracy at home and peace abroad from his reading of the French revolutionary model. It was also a means of presenting Czechoslovak claims to independence to an audience that remained ambivalent towards the establishment of new nation states. Masaryk acknowledged that 'national and racial fragments' characterized societies in central Europe, the Balkans, and western Russia. In addition, as a product of the late nineteenth-century Habsburg empire, he noted that 'sovereignty is relative, for the economic and cultural interdependency of all nations is growing'. As he spoke he was aware that the future of Serbia was threatened by the autumn offensive of the Central Powers. Masaryk wondered whether his lecture had any value, when what Serbia really required was military aid – a none too subtle dig at the failure of the Allied great powers to support Serbia – but he comforted himself with the thought that a 'good word is a good deed'.[1]

Did words matter in shaping political decisions and the international order? More conventional calculations concerning relative military power, bargaining between cabinets, and territorial security shaped some of the key decisions in the war in 1915. Between November 1914 and September 1915 the Ottoman empire, Italy, and Bulgaria entered the conflict, while

Greece underwent a constitutional crisis owing to the pressures of foreign policy. The position of the neutral United States began to weigh more heavily on the belligerents as a result of the Allied blockade of Germany and the German submarine campaign, while in the Far East the tensions between Japan and China were cast as part of the wider global conflict. Nonetheless, the decisions of the political elites were framed by questions about the principle of nationality and multi-ethnic empires, the role of international law in an interdependent world, and civilization as a code for ascribing hierarchies within world politics. Security, dependent on social cohesion, embraced issues of identity as well as military power. Urgent military and political demands intersected with claims about the moral purpose of the war and the reordering of international politics.

* * *

The pivot of the war in the first half of 1915 was the Ottoman empire, which had entered the conflict on the side of the Central Powers the previous November. Often viewed as a futile exercise on the periphery of hostilities, the battle of Gallipoli epitomized the global dimensions of the conflict, involving troops from Arab lands, New Zealand, Australia, and French West Africa.[2] 'The question today,' wrote the Austro-Hungarian ambassador to Constantinople János von Pallavicini, 'is whether Constantinople and therefore predominance in the Near East will fall to one or the other group of powers. For this reason it is my view that the decision of the war will happen here in Constantinople.'[3] Of course, a diplomat is prone to stress the centrality of his posting to wider global affairs. The collapse of the Ottoman empire would not have led to the defeat of Germany and Austria-Hungary. The stakes of the war, however, were not planted solely on the Western Front. The future of the Ottoman empire was a question of vital importance to the European belligerents and neutrals on the cusp of entering the war, such as Italy, Greece, and Bulgaria. The geopolitical stakes in the Ottoman empire were refracted through the claims of empire and nation as the basis of domestic communities and international order.

Since the Young Turk revolution in 1908, the Committee of Union and Progress (CUP) leadership had sought to modernize the empire. The wars between 1911 and 1913 altered their vision of the domestic basis of the empire and its geographical extent. Enver Pasha, who had taken control of the government in a military coup in January 1913, and Talaat Bey, the Interior Minister, accepted the loss of the Balkan territories. The Balkan Wars made CUP leaders more suspicious of the loyalty of Christians to the empire. CUP writers argued that the empire could only be revitalized by instilling citizens with national values. Although this model of national revival was based on the French Revolution and the Prussian Reform Era of the early nineteenth century, Ottoman intellectuals associated nationalization with the promotion of Islam. For Mustafa Kemal, Islam had an instrumental function – it was a means to instil patriotic commitment. By redefining the Ottoman empire as a Muslim nation, the CUP leadership excluded Christians from the political community.

CUP fears about the loyalty of Christians were also a product of foreign policy considerations. For decades the great powers had intervened in the Ottoman empire on the grounds that they needed to defend Christians against persecution. The agreement on the Armenian reforms, concluded in February 1914, was the latest step in this process. From the perspective of the CUP, foreign states and Christian minorities allied to undermine Ottoman sovereignty. From the perspective of minorities, only foreign surveillance could prevent periodic massacres. On the eve of the war Ottoman leaders had considered population transfers as a solution to ethnic tensions.[4]

Having entered the war in November 1914, CUP leaders anticipated Christian betrayal and began to repress Christian groups, notably the Armenian population living on the border with Russia. Even before the defeat of the Ottoman 3rd Army by Russian forces at Sarikamish on 29 December, Talaat Bey had ordered the dismissal of Armenian police officers and government officials from their posts in the provinces of Erzurum, Bitlis, and Van. Fear of Christian revolt mingled with the desire for revenge. The Young Turk journalist Hüseyin Cahit Yalçin argued that the war was an opportunity to avenge the defeats in the Balkans and the treachery of Christians. The presence of over 400,000 refugees from the Balkans, who had personal experience of ethnic cleansing, ensured that there was a large reservoir of highly motivated men prepared to pursue revenge. These men were organized into paramilitary formations called the Special Organization.[5] War provided a reason and an opportunity to make the demographic basis of the Ottoman empire more homogeneous.

The decision to enter the war owed much to the reading of recent international history by CUP leaders. Internal reform required external security, which Enver Pasha believed could only be achieved by combining with one or other power bloc. This assumption – based on the fear that the empire would be partitioned after a general European war even if it remained neutral – limited the room for Ottoman diplomacy. He would only require

Ottoman benevolent neutrality. Enver also wanted to abolish the capitulations – humiliating restrictions on the sovereignty of the Ottoman empire,
which allowed Europeans special privileges and rights, incompatible with
conceptions of the modern nation state. In discussions in late July and early
August, Enver and Hans von Wangenheim, the German ambassador, negotiated a series of agreements, which kept the Ottoman empire out of the war
but clearly favoured Germany and threatened Russia. While Enver remained
cautious and sought to avoid entry, German military leaders pressed for an
Ottoman offensive either against British positions in Egypt or the Russian
empire. 'We are caught vacillating in the middle,' Talaat told a cabinet
meeting on 16 September. 'Each passing day we lose the confidence of our
allies while compounding the enmity of others. That's called eating up your
capital; therefore we must make up our minds.'[6] The option of an alliance
with Russia was briefly explored, but differences over Armenia and the
Bosphorus Strait were too great to bridge. Throughout September and
October the Ottoman and German governments finalized agreements on
military aid. On 29 October Admiral Wilhelm Souchon, commander
of the battlecruiser *Goeben*, which had escaped British patrols in the
Mediterranean to reach the Black Sea in August, launched an attack on
Russian ships. This prompted the Russian declaration of war on 2 November.
As in July 1914 in other capitals, decision-makers viewed the war both as a
risk and an opportunity. 'I believe that it is the Turks' ultimate duty,' wrote
Cemal Pasha, the Naval Minister, on 2 November, 'either to live like an
honourable nation or to exit the stage of history gloriously.'[7]

As Ottoman entry into the war on the side of the Central Powers looked
increasingly likely, Allied diplomacy prepared the partition of the Ottoman
empire. On 20 September the Russian Foreign Minister, Sergei Sazonov,
agreed to arm Armenian groups inside the Ottoman empire, while several
days later Krivoshein, the Minister for Agriculture, told Buchanan, the
British ambassador, that Russia could only 'obtain any material satisfaction'
from this war by annexing Ottoman territory.[8] Amongst the Liberal cabinet
in Britain, feelings ran high against the Ottoman empire. 'In feeling [Lloyd]
George is not strongly anti-German,' noted the editor of the *Manchester
Guardian*, C. P. Scott, on 27 November 1914. 'He said he should have much
greater pleasure in smashing Turkey than in smashing Germany.'[9] In his
Guildhall speech on 9 November Asquith declared that the 'death-knell of
Ottoman authority, not in Europe only, has been rung out by Ottoman
hands.'[10] Geopolitical interest and moral imperative were beginning to fuse
into radical prescriptions for the remaking of the Middle East.

The prime minister's speech had placed the Ottoman leaders on notice that the empire faced extinction. 'I have no commiseration of any kind for these wretched Turks,' Charles Hardinge, Viceroy of India, wrote to Arthur Nicolson at the Foreign Office on 6 January 1915, 'and would like to see them wiped out from Europe. But it is very imprudent of people in the position of Asquith to say such things.'[11] Hardinge, who was mourning the death of two sons – Alexander, who had died following an operation in July 1914, and Edd, his elder son, who died from his wounds in December – had personal experience of violent resistance to imperial rule, having been badly injured in an assassination attempt by a Bengali terrorist in 1912. He and others feared that the entry of the Ottoman empire into the war presaged a worldwide uprising of Muslims in India, central Asia, and north Africa against the Allied empires. However, notions of Muslim political unity were much exaggerated in the febrile imaginations of European politicians. German hopes and Allied fears that a global Muslim uprising would take place never materialized.[12]

The proclamation of jihad read out at the Mosque of Mehmet the Conqueror in Constantinople on 14 November aimed to mobilize Ottoman subjects while preserving the unity between the Arab and Turkish parts of the empire. In that sense it was a defensive move as much as an offensive one. CUP leaders and others recognized that jihad could undermine the mobilization of the empire's resources by denying Christian and Jewish subjects a stake in the struggle. Yet they were also reacting to the attempts of the European great powers to detach Muslim Arabs from the Ottoman empire. In 1911 Italian officers in Tripolitania and the Red Sea region and British agents distinguished between Arab and Turk as a means of winning over local Arab communities. The Ottoman response was to stress the common religious bonds between Arabs and Turks. The nineteenth-century confrontation between Christianity and Islam, central to imperial politics and resistance, seeped into the war cultures of the First World War.[13]

From the Allied perspective Ottoman entry into the war offered new operational opportunities. The Western Front remained the primary focus of British and French military efforts, but already political leaders were shocked at the levels of casualties and the indecisive character of trench warfare. Dismayed by the destruction and frustrated by the stalemate, Winston Churchill, First Lord of the Admiralty, looked towards the Dardanelles as an alternative route to military success. Lloyd George, of similar temperament, supported Churchill's plan for a naval attack on the Dardanelles on 8 January 1915.[14] In Paris the idea of peripheral operations against the Ottoman and Habsburg empires attracted some attention, particularly from Aristide Briand, the Minister for Justice. He was sceptical about the value of further offensives on the Western Front and argued that an Anglo-French military presence in the eastern Mediterranean could win over neutral Balkan states.[15]

In fact, the focus of French-led intervention in the Balkans, Greece, turned into a political and military quagmire for the Allies. Different nationalist agendas proved divisive in Greece. Several fissures ran through Greek politics, most significantly on the foreign policy alignment of the state and the balance between the monarchy and parliament. Eleftherios Venizelos, the prime minister and dominant civilian politician in the country, favoured cooperation with France and Britain, while King Constantine, backed by the officer corps, tended towards pro-German neutrality. The split between the popularly elected Venizelos government and the monarchy supported by the military had obvious resonance in the wider ideological confrontations in Europe. Venizelos was anxious to enter the war to secure further territorial gains and he negotiated secretly with the Allies. Yet opportunities to enter the war in the spring and autumn of 1915 passed by, as the king remained wedded to neutrality. However, Venizelos's secret diplomacy paved the way for the Allies to land forces at Salonica in September. The Allies backed Venizelos, who was able to form a counter-government in Salonica in 1916. The Greek officer corps also split in two, as Ioannis Metaxas, then a captain, founded the royalist National Reservists League, while General Panagiotis Danglis founded the pro-Venizelos National League of Greek Reservists.[16]

Aside from failing to get Greek support, Allied planning for the Gallipoli campaign was undermined by poor intelligence about Ottoman defensive preparations and a lack of clarity about the military and political goals. The results of the naval attacks in February and March were derisory. On 25 April, following the failure to force the Straits by naval bombardment, landings of British, French, and ANZAC troops took place at five beaches on the Dardanelles peninsula. 'Captain French of the Dublins told me afterwards,' noted Captain Geddes of the Munster Regiment in his diary, 'that he counted the first 48 men to follow me [off HMS *River Clyde*], and they all fell. I think no finer episode can be found of the men's bravery and discipline than this – of leaving the safety of the *River Clyde* to go to what was practically a certain death.'[17] Once on the beaches the Allied forces had to scramble up steep inclines to reach Ottoman positions. The troops were inadequately trained and supported, but enthusiasm (and a lack of any alternative) carried them forward. One officer in the Australian Imperial Force, Major Darnell, noted how it was 'mad, wild, thrilling', charging over Ottoman trenches, as 'men dropped all round me'.[18] These soldiers were facing a much improved opponent. The Ottoman Army had been transformed after its defeats between 1911 and 1913, so that the 5th Army offered effective resistance to the Allied landings. One of the officers leading that resistance was Mustafa Kemal, who joined his regiment on the peninsula in February 1915. His tenacity in holding off Allied attack earned him a promotion, but the plaudits went to more senior figures in the Ottoman forces. Only later did his role in the battle assume a critical importance in his presentation as a charismatic military and national leader.[19]

That the Ottoman defences would hold out was not obvious in March and April 1915. 'The Turk will have to leave Constantinople and Europe', Nicolson wrote on 11 March.[20] Expelling the Ottomans from the city raised difficult questions about how to replace them. Imperial rivalries between Russia, France, and Britain were central to discussions about the future of Constantinople that took place between 3 and 10 March. These negotiations laid the basis for the destruction of the Ottoman empire in Asia as well as Europe, as each ally asserted claims to territory in a classic example of imperial diplomacy. A few diplomats and politicians made decisions, there was no reference to the wishes of the inhabitants of the territories being distributed, and conventional concerns about imperial security and maintaining a wartime alliance dominated the diplomatic calculations. It is also worth bearing in mind that these agreements were contingent – they were more significant for what they revealed about diplomatic practice in 1915 than they were in determining the shape of the territorial settlement after the war. On 22 February, at a meeting of political and military leaders, Sazonov announced that Russian possession of Constantinople was a war aim. In addition to the long-standing arguments concerning the strategic advantage of possessing the city, the Foreign Minister also hoped to sustain Russian public support for the war, following the defeat of the Russian 10th Army by German forces in early February. Losses had amounted to 100,000 dead and 110,000 prisoners of war, and it proved more demoralizing than the defeat at Tannenberg as the Russians blamed pro-German circles in the Tsar's court.[21]

In British and French diplomatic circles, a combination of imperial opportunism and fear of the growth of Russian power produced an uncertain response. Dogged advocates of closer relations with Russia favoured supporting Sazonov's ambitious war aims in return for concessions on

British and French imperial ambitions in Persia, Mesopotamia, and Syria. 'We shall never have so good an opportunity,' Buchanan wrote on 24 February, 'of settling all Asiatic questions with Russia as we shall have something to bargain with.'[22] The recipient of this letter, Nicolson, agreed wholeheartedly. The Foreign Secretary, Edward Grey, also considered the moment opportune for establishing agreement over more general war aims in the Ottoman empire. In his note, on 10 March, acceding to Sazonov's demands about Constantinople, Grey stated that he expected Russian support for British and French aims elsewhere in the Ottoman empire.[23]

In March 1915 the French Foreign Minister, Théophile Delcassé, was more reluctant to accept Sazonov's demands on the grounds that Russia's military performance did not warrant such a prize. In addition he was anxious about the enormous expansion of Russian power.[24] However, Delcassé and Grey also needed to keep Russia in the war by supporting its claim to Constantinople. At the same time as Grey and Delcassé were negotiating with Sazonov about the future of Constantinople, they were also demanding that the Russian Foreign Minister accept Italian claims to areas of Dalmatia, which cut across Russian support for Serbia. The need to win the war was creating an increasingly complex set of agreements and promises, held together by the bargaining style of cabinet diplomacy.

Working out the partition of the Ottoman empire in the Middle East involved contradictory imperial bargains and local agreements. Imperial politics tended to ignore the aspirations of local communities, or at least to subordinate them to the dictates of alliance politics. However, the business of waging war in the region led British officials into a much more complex set of relationships. In January 1916 Mark Sykes, an 'excitable' Catholic Conservative MP who had travelled extensively in the Ottoman empire, and François Georges-Picot, a diplomat and member of the Comité d'Asie Française, completed the plans for the partition of the Ottoman empire. Under the terms of their agreement, Britain would receive Mesopotamia and Jordan, France would receive Syria and Lebanon, and they would share control of Palestine.[25] Yet before this agreement Sharif Husayn of Mecca and Henry MacMahon, the British High Commissioner in Egypt, negotiated an agreement, between June 1915 and March 1916, whereby Sharif Husayn would lead an Arab revolt against the Ottoman empire in return for a British guarantee of an Arab kingdom in Mesopotamia and Syria. This cut across the promises made to France. A belief that ethnicity drove politics also informed Britain's final wartime commitment in the region, the Balfour Declaration of November 1917, which favoured the establishment of a 'national home for the Jewish people' in Palestine. The skilful diplomacy of Chaim Weizmann, president of the British Zionist Federation, and Foreign Office belief in Jewish political importance in the United States and Russia – then on the eve of the Bolshevik Revolution – shaped the British decision.[26] The confusion in British policy stemmed from the multiple agents at work, the often contradictory practicalities of winning the war and keeping the alliance together, and different conceptions of British imperial politics.

These plans for partition intersected with the fortunes of battle and ethnic and religious tensions with catastrophic effects in the Ottoman empire in 1915. The prospect of partition raised the already enormous stakes for the CUP leadership. Defeat at Sarikamish and the arrival of Allied ships and soldiers in the Dardanelles heightened the sense of emergency. To survive the empire had to create a homogeneous community, a cohesive nation. This led to the deportation and murder of citizens considered unreliable on the basis, for the most part, of their religious identity. An estimated 100,000 Greek Orthodox subjects were deported from north-west Anatolia into the interior. Deportations covered a multitude of crimes, including the rape and execution of deportees.[27] The Christian Armenian population, which lived in Armenia bordering the Russian empire, Cilicia, a target of French imperialists, and Constantinople, the heart of the Ottoman empire, were targets of repression, then sporadic massacres, and ultimately genocide, in a process that Donald Bloxham has called 'cumulative radicalization'.[28] CUP and military leaders identified Armenians as a threat to Ottoman security.[29] There were some limited connections between Russian military plans and Ottoman Armenians. Five Armenian volunteer battalions fought in the Russian Army in 1915, while arms were smuggled across the border. Some Armenian leaders, such as Boghos Nubar, who had championed the cause of Armenian reform on the international stage in 1913, claimed that only through rebellion could Armenians prove that they deserved nationhood. Without resistance they would lose their right to self-determination, even if that resistance brought about catastrophe.[30] However, the overwhelming majority of Armenians were not involved in any form of resistance to the Ottoman empire.

This mattered little to Ottoman officials, whose policy was shaped by perceptions, experience, and deeply held convictions about the twin threat of great power partition and internal revolt. In mid-March 1915 the CUP expanded the Special Organization, a paramilitary force charged with the suppression of internal enemies and staffed by refugees from the Balkans.

On 25 March Mehmed Reshid, a doctor, was appointed governor of Diyarbekir, a province between the Euphrates and Tigris rivers. His parents had fled from the Russian invasion of the Caucasus to Constantinople in 1874, the year after his birth. In his previous post in Balikesir in the Marmara region, he had expelled Greek Orthodox civilians. Now in Diyarbekir, the Armenians represented a collective enemy: 'Either they us, or we them. In this situation I thought to myself: "Hey Dr Resid! There are two alternatives: Either the Armenians will liquidate the Turks or the Turks will liquidate them!" Faced with the necessity of having to choose, I did not hesitate for long. My Turkishness triumphed over my identity as a doctor.'[31] After arriving in Diyabekir, he ordered mass arrests, closed off Armenian districts, and shut down their businesses. Some 27,000 Armenians were killed between November 1914 and April 1915.

From late April Ottoman policy became more systematic. On 24 April Armenians living in Constantinople were arrested. On 27 May the government promulgated a law authorizing the deportations of civilians in the interests of military security. Between then and the middle of 1916 it is estimated that 1 million Armenians died. Some were murdered, others died from exhaustion, starvation, and thirst. On 30 May Major Rüşdü handcuffed over 800 Armenian notables and escorted them to a barge on the River Tigris. After sailing downstream for one hour, he and other members of the Special Organization massacred their prisoners. The corpses were thrown into the river. Aghavni Kassabian's father, a merchant, was tortured and murdered before she and her mother were deported. Her mother died on the journey. She was abducted by a Kurdish nomad, to whom she bore two children, before she escaped and made her way to the United States.[32]

The existential threat to Ottoman security in 1915, the experience of the Balkan Wars in 1912 and 1913, and the complex interaction between ethnicity and the international system since the late nineteenth century shaped the Armenian genocide. It was also part of a project to nationalize the Ottoman empire. Intellectuals close to the CUP argued that Turkish nationalism provided the state's legitimacy. Amongst these was Mehmed Ziyâ Gökalp, from the Diyarbekir region, appointed the first professor of sociology at Istanbul University in 1915. He called on all citizens to use the Turkish language and customs. He argued that some social groups, such as the Kurds, could be assimilated into the new Turkish nation, but others including the large Arab population in the empire were not capable of becoming 'Turkish'. This cut across the proclamation of jihad, which had stressed the Muslim unity of Turk and Arab. Becoming a nation involved redefining the territorial boundaries of the empire and its demographic composition.[33] It was a violent process of territorial truncation and genocide.

CUP leaders saw this process as the only way of saving the empire in a world of nation states. Their definition and practice of Ottoman identity – in geographical and ethno-religious terms – had shrunk so dramatically by 1915 that the Ottoman empire in its early twentieth-century guise had effectively ceased to exist, while new national identities were emerging. Genocide was the apotheosis of this process of nation-making. In trying to become part of an international community of nation states, Ottoman leaders were charged with atrocities, which excluded the empire from the international order, at least in the view of Allied politicians and commentators. The Armenian genocide fitted readily into an Allied narrative of the war as a struggle between civilization and barbarism, established by German atrocities in Belgium and north-east France in 1914. The scale, circumstances, and policies were not comparable, though this did not stop some Allied commentators making the connection. Following the capture of Erzinjan in the Caucasus in July 1916 by Russian forces under General Nikolai Yudenich, *Le Temps*, a French paper close to the Ministry of Foreign Affairs, lamented that it was too late for the Armenians, 'a small nation', who were 'methodically exterminated by the Turks, under the direction and manifest complicity of Germany'. The application of modern bureaucratic order to the massacres of Armenians was considered to be particularly 'German' – 'one more piece to place in the file of Kultur'. Another article claimed that the massacres cleared territory for the settlement of German colonists, 'the most monstrous holocaust' ever perpetrated to advance a state's interests.[34]

The idea that the Allies were fighting for humanity shaped the diplomatic response to the Armenian genocide. Sazonov prevailed on the British and French governments to send a note to the Ottoman government, which threatened to prosecute individuals guilty of 'those new crimes of Turkey against humanity and civilization'.[35] In the nineteenth century the great powers intervened to protect Christians in the Ottoman empire. Activists in humanitarian campaigns in the late nineteenth century remained involved in the debates during the First World War. However, the terms of the argument had evolved. The religious identities of the victims were more marginal, the categories of 'humanity' and 'civilization' more prominent. The language had more in common with the anti-slavery campaigns of the late nineteenth century and the assumptions of the civilizing mission.

These ideas of a war for humanity and civilization had already gained trac-
tion in 1914, as Britain and France defined their ideological conflict with
Germany in these terms. By transposing these ideas of a conflict between
civilization and barbarism to the war against the Ottoman empire, the
Allies denied the empire membership of the international order. The genocide reinforced the claims of those who wished to break up the empire.

The Allied claims against the Ottoman empire were both territorial and
moral. These derived from the imperial ambitions and cultures of the late
nineteenth and early twentieth centuries. The Ottoman empire lay at the
intersection of imperial and European politics. This imbrication of geopolitics and moral claims can be seen in the work of Andrej Mandelstam, a
Russian diplomat who had served in Constantinople until 1914 and had
shaped the Armenian reform agreements of February 1914. 'Turkey, having
violated the Rights of Man and of the Nation regarding the non-Turkish
peoples under its domination,' Mandelstam wrote in his 1917 book *Le sort
de l'empire ottoman* (*The Fate of the Ottoman Empire*), 'the international
community has to declare that it has no right any more to the tutelage over
these people. . . . Delendum est imperium ottomanorum.'[36] Whereas the
Allied note in 1915 had specified the prosecution of individuals, Mandelstam
considered the Ottoman empire itself to be guilty.

* * *

In Rome diplomats followed the battle on the Dardanelles peninsula closely.
On 6 March Giacomo de Martino, the Secretary General at the Consulta,
told the French ambassador to Rome, Camille Barrère, that the arrival of
the Allied fleet at the Straits meant that the Italian government could not
long delay its decision to intervene.[37] Two days earlier Guglielmo Imperiali,
the ambassador in London, had transmitted Italy's demands for entry into
the war to Grey. In Vienna the ministerial council met on 8 March. At this
meeting ministers discussed whether Austria-Hungary should make territorial concessions in return for guarantees of Italian neutrality. Although
Russian forces besieged the Galician fortress of Przemsyl, the Austrian
Foreign Minister, István Burián, described the Anglo-French naval attack
as 'an event of much greater political significance because the whole Balkans
will be unsettled by the possibility of the capture of Constantinople'. He
feared that a successful Allied attack against the Straits would lead neutral
states to rush into the war, eager to assert their claims.[38]

Timing was vital in shaping the entry of neutrals into the war. On
17 September 1914 Antonio Salandra feared the defeat of the Central

Powers, especially Austria, before Italy could choreograph her entry. 'No doubt about it,' remarked the prime minister, 'we should almost wish her [Austria-Hungary] a little victory.'[39] Allowing a decent interval to pass between the burial of the Triple Alliance and the announcement of the engagement to the Allies required considerable diplomatic skill. The essence of wartime Italian diplomacy has often been captured in the phrase 'sacro egoismo.' Salandra had uttered this phrase at a meeting with officials at the Ministry of Foreign Affairs in Rome on 18 October 1914. He had taken over the ministry on an interim basis from the recently deceased San Giuliano and soon he appointed Sidney Sonnino, a man with an irascible temper and perfect English, to the post. However, a closer reading of Salandra's speech reveals that behind the diplomatic calculation lay a fierce sense of patriotic commitment. He promised to uphold the 'real interests of the country'. Foreign policy had to be stripped 'of all preconceptions, of all prejudices, of all sentiment, which is not the exclusive and unlimited devotion to our country, of the sacro egoismo, for Italy'. In 1922, as Liberal Italy was collapsing, Salandra returned to the subject to explain what he meant. It was not a war for justice, democracy, or humanity, but for nations. Men would not have fought for universal abstract values, he argued, but only for their nation.[40]

Leading German and Austro-Hungarian politicians and soldiers routinely dismissed their Italian counterparts as little better than criminals, transforming the pursuit of the national interest into a transgression. 'Bandits' and 'street thieves', exploded Moriz von Lyncker, Chief of the Military Cabinet.[41] There was nothing particularly Italian about this search for security. Responding to denunciations of Italian diplomatic chicanery, Bernhard von Bülow noted that Italian diplomats had learned devious diplomacy from Frederick II and Bismarck as well as Machiavelli and Giucciardini. 'People are the same everywhere,' he concluded.[42] The politics of Italy's entry into the war, played out between August 1914 and May 1915, emphasized the complex connections between security, cabinet politics, the claims of nation, and notions of a European order.

Under the terms of the Triple Alliance, Italy was under no obligation to enter the war on the side of Austria-Hungary and Germany. There was a consensus amongst the political elite that Italy needed to emerge from the war with territorial gains. Some, such as the former prime minister Giovanni Giolitti, believed that Italy could achieve these gains through negotiations with Austria-Hungary, whereas others, such as Salandra and Sonnino, were prepared to countenance entering the war on the Allied side. Liberal Italy was closely wedded to its self-presentation as a great power. The country, its leader argued, needed foreign policy achievements in order to ward off their domestic enemies – the socialists and the Catholics. Sonnino told German and Habsburg diplomats that in the absence of territorial gains the monarchy would fall. In other words this conservative and limited, if undoubtedly patriotic, view of the nation and the state underpinned diplomatic calculations.[43] Concerns about the future territorial settlement in the Balkans also preoccupied San Giuliano and later Sonnino. Italian statesmen considered Italy a Balkan as well as a Mediterranean power. The prospect of Austro-Hungarian expansion or the emergence of a South Slav state required compensation for Italy. The centrality of the Balkans in Italian thinking was illustrated by the conclusion of an agreement with Romania on 23 September 1914, in which both parties agreed to consult with each other in the event of the collapse of Austria-Hungary. Two days later San Giuliano warned Italian ambassadors of the 'danger of serious conflicts in the future with Slav states', an early indication of Italian concerns about successor states.[44]

On 9 December 1914, just days after Austro-Hungarian forces occupied Belgrade – temporarily as it transpired – Sonnino issued a demand for compensation. His aim was to establish Italian demands, but he did not want an agreement with Austria-Hungary. He feared, rightly, that the Central Powers might pay now and reclaim later.[45] Sonnino kept his demands vague, enabling him to raise them continually and eventually to break off the negotiations. Yet the negotiations between Sonnino and Germany and Austria-Hungary were not simply a charade. There were politicians waiting in the wings such as Giolitti, who would have come to an agreement with Austria-Hungary.

Moreover, Sonnino's demands placed an enormous strain on the Central Powers. Since the outbreak of war Bethmann Hollweg, the German Chancellor, and Gottlieb von Jagow, the Foreign Minister, had urged Austria-Hungary to concede territory in Trieste and Trentino, which Italian irredentists claimed on the grounds of the principle of nationality. German leaders, fearing that the entry of Italy into the war would lead to the collapse of Austria-Hungary, became advocates of the nationalist principle. From the very beginning of the conflict, strategic interest dictated support for the claims of Italian irredentists. Anton von Monts, the former German ambassador to Rome, wrote to Josef Redlich, the Austrian liberal, on 26 August arguing that Austria-Hungary should surrender the Trentino to Italy and then recapture it later. Urging the surrender of South Tyrol two weeks later, he commented that 'I would prefer to hack off my hand than my arm.'[46] Monts undertook a mission to Vienna in early 1915 to urge concessions to stave off an Italian entry into war. German fury towards the Austro-Hungarian monarchy rose throughout early 1915, as the obstinate refusal to make timely concessions to Italy appeared to invite disaster. 'They would rather go down "with honour"', Lyncker noted with bitterness, 'and carry us into the abyss. Nice outlook, that!'[47] The mood at German headquarters could change quickly. 'Very depressed atmosphere,' noted Admiral Georg Alexander von Müller, Chief of the Imperial German Naval Cabinet, on 6 March. The following day he reported 'some very satisfactory news' as it appeared that Austria-Hungary and Italy might reach agreement on the Trentino.[48]

The willingness to consider the transfer of territory to Italy represented a major change in Austro-Hungarian foreign policy and its self-depiction in European politics. The application of the national principle threatened the legitimacy of the monarchy. Austria-Hungary had gone to war to defend itself, but was now being asked to dismember itself. German demands to make territorial concessions to Italy amounted to more than the slicing off of territory. The Austro-Hungarian elite asserted a vision of empire that allowed different nations to live alongside one another, while subordinating national interests to the stability of the monarchy. The domestic legitimacy of this vision was underpinned by the monarchy's role in the European order, where it acted as a restraint on war. In response to German pressure, Franz von Matscheko offered a stout defence of the importance of being Habsburg for the European order. 'The domestic right to existence of the monarchy,' he wrote in a memorandum dated 21 December 1914,

> lies in the fact that the peace of Europe would be subjected to continual shocks in that area where the great European races – Germans, Romans, north and south Slavs – meet in interwoven fusion, if there existed no strong great power, which had arisen and consolidated over the course of centuries and incorporated the isolated Hungarian block. All the neighbouring states must forego the realization of their national ideals in favour of this European necessity, just as the individual peoples in the monarchy necessarily accept limitations, in a national sense.[49]

At his first meeting with Bethmann Hollweg on 20 February, Burián made a similar argument that any transfer of territory on the principle of nationality 'would be the first step to the dissolution of the empire and would provoke disastrous unrest in the ranks of the Austro-Hungarian army in the midst of battle'.[50]

Great power prestige was one of the bonds holding together the multi-national empire. Foreign intervention in the domestic affairs of a small state was considered humiliating, but now Austro-Hungarian leaders faced pressure from their ally, Germany, and neighbours, Italy and Romania, to make concessions. At stake, argued the Hungarian prime minister István Tisza, was Austria-Hungary's status as a great power. Domestic reforms undertaken in response to external pressure would only invite more demands. 'Right now,' he told his colleagues at a meeting of the ministerial council on 8 August 1914, 'when prestige plays such an important role in our foreign policy, we have to appear strong and give neither Romania nor Bulgaria any opportunity to pursue their policy of extortion.'[51] In many ways, Austro-Hungarian leaders were trapped by their own experiences, assumptions, and fears. Any concessions were seen as a sign of weakness, leading to death by a thousand cuts. The retreat of the Habsburg empire during the nineteenth century produced a sense of historical inevitability about its further decline.

Burián, who succeeded Berchtold as Habsburg Foreign Minister in January 1915, also rejected an alternative way out of the crisis, namely the cynical ploy of surrendering territory now with a view to turning on Italy after the war. 'What is lost in battle, can perhaps be rescued,' he argued, 'what one gives up is lost forever.'[52] From his perspective the logic of the nation state was irreversible. Fighting, even in a lost cause, legitimized future claims in the international public sphere. It enabled ministers to argue – as French politicians did in the case of Alsace-Lorraine – that the loss of territory was the result of brute force rather than the legitimate transfer of territory. In addition transferring territory on the grounds of the principle of nationality would forever alienate the inhabitants of the Trentino and South Tyrol from the Habsburg monarchy.

Yet on 8 March ministers agreed to negotiate the transfer of territory to Italy. This change was largely due to the deterioration of the military situation in the first few months of the year. The fortress of Przemsyl was about to fall, while Tisza and Stürgkh, the Austrian prime minister, both identified the Allied attack on the Dardanelles and possible collapse of the Ottoman empire as 'a very serious moment in the overall situation'. Tisza's change of policy was the most striking. In January he had resisted Berchtold's entreaties that Austria-Hungary should transfer territory to Italy. With tears in his eyes, Tisza warned that the monarchy's future was at stake and berated Berchtold for his passivity. Berchtold was replaced as Foreign Minister by Burián, another Hungarian close to Tisza.[53] The succession of defeats in 1915 had eroded ministers' confidence in Austria-Hungary's great power status and made the monarchy more dependent on German military and political support. Austro-Hungarian power was ebbing away. This was the result of a longer-term process, in which its self-presentation as a multi-national empire, which was a European necessity and guarantor of peace, enjoyed less and less legitimacy throughout Europe, and a shorter-term process, in which its comparative military weaknesses had been exposed by defeats against Russian forces. Indeed, the decline of Matscheko's vision of a multi-national empire as a guarantor of European peace was evident in the ministerial council. General Alexander von Krobatin, after confirming that the Austro-Hungarian Army would not be able to fight on a third front against Italy and agreeing to the transfer of territory in the South Tyrol, urged the expulsion of remaining Italians from the Austro-Hungarian monarchy. Population transfer was the only means to become 'master in one's own house' and to avoid later irredentist claims, he argued.[54]

In addition to the worsening military situation, Bethmann Hollweg sweetened the pill by offering Burián compensation in the form of parts of Prussian Silesia (taken from Austria in the 1740s) and Sosnowiec, with rich coal resources, in Congress Poland. The Prussian government had initially resisted the proposed compensation, but Bethmann Hollweg stressed that it was the only means to strike a deal between Austria-Hungary and Italy, keeping the latter out of the war. Burián accepted this compensation and also received a loan into the bargain on 7 March, the day before the vital ministerial council meeting. It was a classic stroke of cabinet politics, designed to ease the transfer of territory on the principle of nationality, all in the service of winning the war – or staving off defeat.

Four days before the ministerial council met in Vienna, Sonnino had opened negotiations with the Allies. Imperiali presented to Grey the Italian demands – these included possession of the Trentino and the South Tyrol, border changes in Isonzo, Istria, and Trieste, and the establishment of a dominant position in the Adriatic by possession of Dalmatia and the Albanian port of Valona. These aims went far beyond irredentist ambitions. Indeed, Sonnino was more preoccupied with military security than with nationalist politics. The establishment of a hegemonic position in the Adriatic Sea was the principal aim.[55]

The Italian demands tested the Allied claims to be champions of the principle of nationality and small nations. Indeed, Italian demands in the

Adriatic were directed against Serbia and the potential emergence of a Yugoslav state. On 7 December 1914 the Serbian National Assembly, meeting in Nis and reeling from the loss of Belgrade, had issued the Declaration of Nis. This document remobilized Serbian society in support of a war of liberation for the South Slavs, including Croats and Slovenes, and laid claim to the Dalmatian coast. Croat supporters of the Yugoslav project endorsed the war of liberation, with Franz Supilo, a Croatian journalist and nationalist leader, warning that Italy would 'swallow us up like macaroni' if the South Slav nations remained politically divided.[56] In an extensive note, rejecting what he considered to be excessive Italian demands, Sazonov repeatedly invoked the idea that the Allies were fighting for the 'principle of nationalities', which the Italian demands now threatened. In an aide-memoire – though it was more of a grand statement – that fused the legitimacy of the Allied war effort with geopolitical ambitions, the Russian Foreign Minister did

> not hesitate to recall that Russia, France, and England had taken up arms in the current war precisely to defend the weak and to ensure the triumph of the principles of balance [équilibre] and equity. This attitude has gained for the three Allied powers the general sympathy and has turned towards them the eyes of all the peoples oppressed by Austria-Hungary, who hail them as their liberators. The desire to lessen the horrors of war obliges the powers now to make some sacrifices to Italy. At the least it is necessary to reduce as much as possible the sacrifices, so that, by moving away to a certain extent from the national principle, they do not lose the sympathies and confidence of the peoples of Austria-Hungary by placing them against their will under Italian domination, which would be nothing more for them than a new yoke, perhaps harsher than the old one.[57]

Of course, political interests informed Sazonov's objections to Italian demands. The Russian government had partly justified its entry into the war as a defence of Slav interests. Although Constantinople was the pre-eminent prize for Russian diplomacy, protecting its influence in the Balkans remained an important goal. Moving the debate onto the terrain of the principle of nationality had distinct advantages for Sazonov, as it had for French politicians, who feared an expansion of Italian power and subsequent rivalry in the Mediterranean.[58]

Allied politicians recognized that Italian entry into the war would add to the difficulties of making peace, 'but first it is necessary to win, and as soon as possible', as Delcassé said on 8 March. 'Above all,' Barrère repeated a few days later, 'it is necessary to win.'[59] Grey tended to agree, though it helped that Italian claims did not pose a challenge to British interests. Fearful that Sazonov's aide-memoire would derail the negotiations with Italy, Grey decided to retire to his Northumberland estate for a few days: 'It is essential that I should have some rest and I am therefore going away for a few days,' he told the Foreign Office on 31 March.[60] After his recuperation Grey reverted to the language of imperial bargaining, pointing out that Britain had made major concessions to Russia on Constantinople and he now expected Sazonov to facilitate Italy's entry into the war by agreeing to Sonnino's demands.[61] The business of winning the war concentrated Russian minds. By early April the flush of capturing Przemsyl had faded, while the threat of a German offensive loomed. Sonnino reduced his demands, leaving the southern half of the Dalmatian coast, including the port cities of Split and Dubrovnik, to a future Yugoslav state. On 26 April 1915 Italy and the Allies signed the Treaty of London.[62]

The treaty was a triumph of cabinet politics. The principle of nationality was honoured as much in the breach as in the observance. Italian claims included territories with large majorities of Germans, Slovenes, and Croats. Sonnino had also excluded towns with Italian majorities – notably Fiume (Rijeka). There was a whiff of embarrassment about the treaty's clear contradiction of the Allies' publicly proclaimed principles.[63] Yet the Treaty of London was not the last word on the territorial settlement in the Adriatic. Like other wartime agreements it was contingent and its implementation was dependent on the outcome of the war. The principle of nationality, having shaped though not determined the negotiations in March and April 1915 between Italy and the Allies, would continue to inform geopolitics in the Adriatic.

The relationship between nationalism and Italy's entry into the war was not confined to its territorial ambitions. Indeed, the popular debate about entry reshaped competing notions of Italian national identity. Most Italians, including members of parliament, supported neutrality. Although differentiated by region and economic activity, the majority of peasants opposed the war. The Catholic Church also supported neutrality, both on the grounds of humanitarian opposition to war in general and of the Papal affection for the Habsburg monarchy, the only Catholic great power in Europe. In April 1915 Salandra asked prefects to report on local attitudes towards war. It is clear from these reports that the majority of Italians had a well-founded belief that 'the great sacrifices in men and money', in the words of the prefect of

Novara in north-west Italy, 'would not be adequately compensated even assuming a favourable outcome'. In Ferrara the prefect blamed the propaganda of the socialists for the widespread opposition to intervention.[64]

Interventionists denounced the pragmatic scepticism of opponents of war as apathy and cowardice. War had creative potential, out of which a new man could be forged, one who left behind the materialist preoccupations of the pre-war period. 'We love war,' Giovanni Popini wrote in *Lacerba*, an avant-garde journal in Florence, in October 1914. Unashamedly elitist in his writings, Popini echoed the ideas of other radical militarists in Europe. 'Brothers are always prepared to kill brothers,' he continued, 'and the civilized to turn back to savagery; men do not renounce the wild beasts who gave birth to them. . . . We love war and imbibe it like gourmets as long as it lasts. War is frightening – and precisely because it is frightening and tremendous and terrible and destructive, we ought to love it with every bit of our masculine hearts.'[65] Other intellectuals and artists such as Popini's close collaborator Giuseppe Prezzolini, the writer Renato Serra, the futurist Filippo Marinetti, and the artist Umberto Boccioni, shared these assumptions about the creative potential of war.

While futurist and avant-garde intellectuals and artists saw in the war the opportunity to produce a new man and morality – in contrast to the vast majority of intellectuals, writers, and public commentators who argued that war brutalized man – nationalists and syndicalists saw the conflict as an opportunity to remake the nation. They constituted the majority of interventionists in early 1915. Nationalist interventionists primarily came from the student and professional middle classes. They challenged Liberal Italy and the cautious conservative style of Salandra and Sonnino. Campaigning for intervention in the war was a means for nationalists to assert their claims to represent the nation. The generational gap lent different cadences to interventionist rhetoric. Giuseppe Mazzoni, a literature teacher born just after the unification of Italy, reacted with a sense of resigned duty. 'I hope that the war will be short,' he wrote to his wife on 11 May, two weeks before war was declared, 'but short or long, it is certain that it will cost our country immense sacrifices of blood and treasure, and for this we must be prepared.' His son Gino, born in 1897, was much more enthusiastic, enrolling in the Arditi, the elite Italian formation.[66] For young nationalists like Gino Mazzoni, neither the elite of Liberal Italy nor parliament represented the nation. In May 1915, as the crisis over intervention reached its height, thousands demonstrated – 5,000 in Palermo, 10,000 in Parma, and 30,000 in Milan. Their nation had moved onto the streets.

There were also counter-demonstrations in Italy, often led by trade unionists and socialists. The left had split in Italy since the outbreak of the war. The majority of socialists opposed participation and criticized the diplomatic flirtations of Sonnino and Salandra with the belligerents. The Socialist manifesto, issued on 20 October 1914, blamed the bourgeoisie for the war, stressed the suffering of millions of mourning families, and condemned the French and German socialists for supporting their respective governments. The Italian socialists clung to an internationalism that existed on the margins of the European left.[67] Within Italy a minority of socialists supported entry to the war. These viewed the conflict as an ideological confrontation, in which liberty and civilization were represented by France and Britain, while Germany and Austria-Hungary represented militarism. A manifesto issued on 5 October by the Fascio rivoluzionario d'azione internazionalista, a group that included syndicalists and future Fascists of the first hour such as Michele Bianchi and Amilcare De Ambris, praised the liberal and revolutionary political traditions of Britain and France and the heroism of Belgium, states 'which represent the cause of liberty and peace in Europe'. In the fight against barbarism, authoritarianism, 'German feudalism', and Austro-Hungarian clericalism, the manifesto appealed to workers to support the Allies for 'the triumph of the working-class cause and social revolution, the fraternity of peoples, and the end of all wars'.[68] Gaetano Salvemini represented a different strain of left-wing interventionism, which saw the war as a struggle for democracy and national liberty. Salvemini blamed German militarism for the outbreak of the war. His aims were clear – the support of democracy, represented by the Allies, the incorporation of the Trentino and South Tyrol into Italy on the principle of nationality, and the support of nationalities elsewhere in Europe as the basis of a peaceful order. 'War today,' he argued in September 1914, 'is the only way to make peace and to curtail military spending in the aftermath.'[69]

Democratic interventionists argued that security could be achieved by balancing the different interests of nationalities in the Balkans and the Adriatic. They opposed Sonnino's vision of security, which brought Italy into conflict with Serbian and Yugoslav claims. Benito Mussolini, who had been sacked as the editor of the Socialist paper in November 1914 after coming out in support of interventionism, initially shared the democratic interventionist view on Italian–Serbian relations. He argued that an entente between Italy and Serbia, with the latter (or Yugoslavia) in possession of the Dalmatian coast, would ensure peace and security in the Adriatic. Good relations and the presence of minority but influential Italian communities in towns on the Dalmatian coast provided opportunities to secure Italian cultural and commercial dominance in the region.[70]

In May 1915 Italian politics was deeply fractured. Interventionists had wildly diverging visions of the Italian nation, its territorial extent, and domestic institutional basis. The majority of Italians favoured neutrality and for a brief few days in May it appeared as though Salandra and Sonnino would fail to bring Italy into the war. Giolitti emerged as the alternative leader of a neutral cabinet. On 13 May Salandra and Sonnino resigned. At the same time German diplomacy made one final effort to increase Austro-Hungarian concessions to Italy, a move designed to bolster Italian parliamentary and popular support for neutrality by confirming Giolitti's argument that Italy could gain more by negotiations than by war. On 10 May the two German representatives in Rome, Bülow and Matthias Erzberger, the Catholic Centre Party leader, chased Karl von Macchio, the Austro-Hungarian ambassador and a man of 'pitiful irresolution', through hotels and clubs in order to secure his signature to a deal offering the Trentino, Valona, a free hand in Albania, and cultural reforms in Trieste to Italy.[71] In the end, however, this last-minute intervention in Italian domestic politics weakened Giolitti rather than strengthened him. In any case he was unable to put together his own parliamentary majority. On 16 May Salandra and Sonnino were reappointed. On 23 May Italy declared war on Austria-Hungary.

Several months earlier, Sonnino had told Bülow that Liberal Italy faced a choice between 'war and revolution'.[72] For syndicalists such as De Ambris and Bianchi war meant revolution. From the other side of the border, 700 ethnic Italians from the Trentino had joined the Italian Army, including Giuseppe Battisti, a separatist leader, who was executed by the Habsburg authorities after being taken prisoner of war in 1916. Some 55,000 Trentiners served in the Habsburg forces and over 100,000 ethnic Italians were made refugees as the borderlands became a battlefield. Alcide de Gasperi of the Italian Popular Catholic Party served on the Habsburg refugee commission, seeking to improve living conditions in camps.[73] Italy's entry into the war had multiple meanings and implications for domestic and international politics that went far beyond 'sacro egoismo'. Individuals ascribed their personal and political expectations to the conflict. The challenge of national mobilization was to fashion these meanings and experiences into a cohesive political community.

* * *

By the time Italy declared war the military situation in eastern Europe had been transformed in favour of the Central Powers. In early May, Walther Rathenau was confident that the Central Powers could withstand Italy's entry into the war.[74] In late March following the surrender of Przemsyl to Russian forces with 120,000 prisoners taken, the attacks on the Dardanelles, and the likely entry of Italy, the Central Powers had faced a military and political crisis. In the Carpathians the conditions for Russian and Habsburg soldiers were appalling. 'Hundreds froze to death daily,' wrote Colonel Georg Veith, 'every wounded soldier who cannot get himself back to the lines is irrevocably sentenced to death. Riding is impossible. Entire lines of riflemen surrender in tears to escape the pain.'[75] Erich von Falkenhayn, the Prussian Minister of War, reversed his decision to launch an offensive on the Western Front and decided to undertake a counter-offensive on the Eastern Front in order to stave off an Austro-Hungarian collapse. He set up a new army, the German 11th Army under General August von Mackensen and Colonel Hans von Seeckt as the Chief of Staff. The operational plan depended on the coordination of artillery and infantry, surprise, and precise timing. The 11th Army recaptured Przemsyl on 3 June. By September, German and Austro-Hungarian forces had occupied Russian Poland.[76] The operational success of Mackensen's army, however, did not translate into a decisive political success and a separate peace with Russia.

German victories on the battlefield nevertheless redefined politics in eastern Europe and Russia in the second half of 1915. The violence of war – on the battlefield and on the home front – recast the relationship between ethnicity, nation, domestic political institutions, and the international system. The German and Austro-Hungarian occupation of Poland, the refugee crisis, the crisis of the Russian state, and the decision of Bulgaria to enter the war in September 1915 changed the possibilities for the re-ordering of politics in eastern Europe. In a region where different nationalities intermingled and jostled alongside each other, indeed where nationality had not necessarily been the most important marker of political allegiance, the claims of the nation became the primary means of creating political communities. This worked to Germany's advantage. Germans were the dominant nation in central and eastern Europe, in terms of numbers and the power of the Reich. Nationality also tended to undermine the cohesion of the multi-national empires, Russia and Austria-Hungary.

The Tsarist regime was many things to many people – defender of Slavdom, the embodiment of the Russian nation, and a multi-national empire.[77] These self-representations of the Tsarist regime were over-whelmed by the experience of war and the nationalizing logic of violence and politics in 1915. 'In Germany they built fortresses, while we traded in vodka,' reflected one peasant.[78] Military failure meant more conscription, and only sons, previously exempt from service in order to work on farms, were liable to the draft from September 1915. The government also imposed a tax on non-Russian subjects exempt from military service on 1 August. Less than a year later, when conscription was extended to Turkestan, in the hope of recruiting 250,000 soldiers, it triggered a rebellion, in which 60,000 Kazakhs, Uzbeks, and Turcomen were killed and a further 350,000 civilians left their homes, some escaping to Persia and China.[79] The state was also blamed for its mismanagement of food supplies and welfare support. Soldiers and their families alleged corruption in the distribution of allow-ances. 'In my opinion,' wrote one soldier to his wife, complaining about the allowance system, 'all the authorities are Germans.'[80] The threads of the moral economy of war, a set of reciprocal obligations and expectations designed to support family, nation, and the Tsarist regime, were being unpicked.[81]

As ever, violence created new realities on the ground, ones that were particularly pernicious to the Tsarist regime. First, the numbers of refugees soared in the summer of 1915. Some 220,000 people fled Riga by November 1915, while in the Smolensk region the population of the town of Roslavl increased from 28,000 to 80,000. The refugees constituted a humanitarian crisis. In some areas, epidemics inflated mortality rates to 50 per cent. 'Our children fell down and died from hunger on the street,' reported one observer in Tbilisi. There were reports of mothers, close to death, who drowned their own children in swamps, despairing of their future care. The refugees were a visible condemnation of the Tsarist regime's failure to defend its population and of its incapacity to care for the refugees. Civil society groups, primarily the Union of Zemtsvos and the Union of Towns, responded by establishing a Joint Section for Refugee Welfare on 22 August. As one member of the Union of Towns, Sergei Bakhrushkin, argued, the state could deal with war, while the 'educated society and people' could devote their attention to the welfare of the refugees. The politics of humani-tarian relief extended to claims about who represented the nation. The state established its own bureaucracy to manage the refugee crisis, a new arena in which state and civil society competed in late Tsarist Russia.[82]

Second, the succession of defeats led to violence against ethnic minori-ties in Russia, mainly Germans and Jews. This violence had an ostensibly nationalizing logic, which undermined the imperial regime. The nation, rather than the Tsar, became the focal point of popular Russian loyalties. One explanation for defeat was betrayal, epitomized by the case of Lieutenant Colonel Sergei Nicholaevich Miasoedev. Born into a well-connected family in 1865, Miasoedev led a colourful life before 1914. The circumstances of his pre-war life – his marriage to the daughter of a German-Jewish immigrant, his participation in Wilhelm II's hunting parties at Rominten just a few miles from his posting on the German–Russian border, and his expensive dalliances with beautiful women – were transformed in the context of military failure in 1915. Now Miasoedev stood accused, wrongly, of being a German spy and he was executed on 3 May 1915.[83] Russia's defeat, according to this narrative, was explained by the presence of pro-German officials at the court and in the senior echelons of the state bureaucracy. The fact that Empress Alexandra, the wife of Nicholas II, was German added to the fury of conspiracy theories circulating from 1915. The logic of these theories gave rise to violent incidents directed against 'Germans'. For example in early June in Moscow, the wives and widows of soldiers gathered to receive sewing work. On being told that there was no work available, rumours spread that the Grand Duchess, Elizaveta Fedorovna, had given the work to a German firm, Mandl. Tensions rose and other workers demanded the sacking of all German employees. A crowd drowned the Swedish manager of one factory because he was a 'German'. The violence against Germans escalated into full-blown riots and by the time order was restored, 579 subjects, often from minorities, had been killed. Rioters were motivated by the chance to loot rather than to kill Germans. Some rioters 'were drinking straight from the barrel,' recalled one man. 'That was some party! Like never before, almost all Moscow was drunk.'[84] That the state failed to prevent the riots compounded the erosion of its authority.

The nationalizing process also involved the deportation of enemy aliens, another social category created in the war. This was a process, always coercive and often violent, of unpredictable consequences. A total of 600,000 enemy subjects were deported from the provinces of western Russia. The violence extended to ethnic Germans, who had been born in Russia. The military viewed ethnic Germans as a major threat to the Russian war effort, as a 'prepared base for German conquest' in the words of Nikolai Ianushkevich, the chief of staff.[85] Russian Jews were also subject to deportation on the grounds of suspected disloyalty. During April and May 1915, pogroms broke out, mainly instigated by troops. The deportation of Russian

Jews had unexpected consequences. Far from cleansing the nation of the fantasy of a Jewish threat, the military's deportation orders led Jews to settle in areas from which they were previously excluded. Their right to settle in these areas was confirmed by a decree of 15 August, though they were still excluded from Petrograd and Moscow.[86] Anti-Semitic violence damaged Russia's international reputation. French and British diplomats were concerned that violence against Russian Jews tarnished the Allies' reputation in the United States as the defenders of civilization. Many assumed, on the basis of their own crude assumptions, that a Jewish lobby in America exercised an important influence on public opinion and politics.[87]

Finally, liberals in the Duma and the Unions of Towns and Zemtsvos asserted their claims to participate in government on the grounds of the 'national cause'. For many their commitment was deeply personal. Paul Miliukov was mourning the death of his son, Sergei, in fighting near Cholm in Galicia in July 1915. He had advised his son to take an assignment on Russia's western front rather than slip off to a safer posting in the Far East. 'I never forgave myself,' he wrote in his memoirs, 'for not advising him to go to the Far East. This was one of those wounds which do not heal. . . . It is bleeding even now.'[88] Miliukov became the leader of the Progressive Bloc, which was formed by the Cadets, the Octobrists, and Progressive parties. The Progressive Bloc published its programme on 21 August. The proposals amounted to a call for a constitutional revolution. The government would be made responsible to the Duma; basic political freedoms, such as the right to free expression, would be safeguarded; restrictions on the civil rights of Russian Jews would be abolished; and reforms would give nationalities, such as the Poles and Finns, more autonomy. Miliukov, steeped in the history of liberal thought, sought to transform the state and the nation. Only by limiting the arbitrary power of the incompetent state could the nation mobilize successfully to defend itself in the European war. Yet for Miliukov reforms extended beyond the question of military power. Political reform would also make Russia a full member of European society. Principles were both a means and an end for Miliukov and his allies. Hence his call in June 1915 – 'the law is our only weapon' – for an investigation into the violation of international laws by the military during the Russian retreat from Galicia.[89] The Zemtsvos also joined the calls for political reform in the summer of 1915. While Miliukov sought to remake Russians through grand schemes of constitutional reform, philanthropic associations promoted moral reform through changing the habits of everyday life, from setting up local libraries to encouraging temperance.[90] Whereas the first Congress of Zemtsvos in March 1915 had pledged its loyalty to the sacred national union and the Tsar, the second meeting in June suggested a cleavage between the government and the nation. Prince Lvov, the leader of the Union of Zemtsvos, declared that the 'great national cause is not being pursued according to those principles which assure its success. . . . The final victory can only be assured by a total exertion of all the national forces, given complete mutual trust between the government and the country.'[91]

Between June and September 1915 Nicholas II dithered. In June he sacked unpopular ministers, including the Interior Minister, Nikolai Maklakov, an avowed opponent of the Duma, and the Minister of War, General Sukhliminov, held responsible for the defeats earlier in the year. The Tsar also announced the meeting of the Duma in August. This raised expectations of further reform, but Nicholas II dashed these hopes in August and September 1915. He refused to appoint ministers responsible to the Duma. The reactionary drift of the Tsar's politics was confirmed by the appointment in January 1916 of Boris Stürmer, described by Maurice Paléologue, the French ambassador, as a man of 'third rate intellect, mean spirit, low character, doubtful honesty, no experience, and no idea of State Service.'[92] The Tsar's view of his relationship with the Russian nation was encapsulated by his decision to take over command of the army, the embodiment (or at least one possible embodiment) of the nation. His mystical vision of the relationship between emperor and nation was completely at odds with the experience and meaning of war for many Russians. On 6 November he decorated himself with the Cross of St George, 4th degree. 'The whole day,' Nicholas noted in his diary, 'I walked around as if intoxicated.' His remaining supporters bolstered his image by attributing the successful Russian defence to the Tsar's skills. 'The Russian Emperor, according to the ancient belief of the Orthodox people, the Anointed of God, the All-Russian autocrat,' one book recorded, 'taking the sword into his own hand, halted the invasion.'[93] Such notions had less and less purchase on the imagination of the Tsar's subjects. His credibility was now hitched to military success. Yet the divisions amongst his critics, the lingering authority of the throne if not the person, and his continued control of court and cabinet politics ensured that he remained emperor, albeit an emperor without a nation.

The Russian retreat from Poland and the establishment of German and Austro-Hungarian occupation regimes cracked open the question of Poland's place in the future European order. The split between Polish nationalists over whether to support the Allies or the Central Powers, already evident in 1914, persisted throughout the war. It was an unpalatable choice. One poem compared the choice between a Poland bound to Russia and one bound to Germany as akin to the choice between plague and cholera. Occupation gave Germany and Austria-Hungary a massive advantage in forging Poland's future, though the conditions of occupation undermined their claims to defend Polish interests. Over 500,000 Poles were deported to Germany to make good labour shortages, while in the Habsburg occupied region local civilians only retained 11 per cent of the coal they mined and 40 per cent of the food produced.[94]

The major decisions about the future of Poland were not taken until 1916, but Polish nationalists, Allied politicians, and German and Austro-Hungarian leaders located the issue within a wider conception of a general European settlement as well as the moral categories of civilization and barbarism. In their appeals to Allied governments, Polish nationalists stressed the principle of nationality, historical friendships with the western European powers, and the shared democratic values. Poland became a site in the contest over political values between the Allies and Central Powers. In late May, Jan Styka issued an appeal to the French people. Styka, who had achieved fame for a cycloramic painting, the Racławice Panorama commemorating a battle between Polish and Russian forces in 1794 during the partition of Poland, drew heavily on notions of a shared Franco-Polish history, based on military alliances and the historical support of France for Polish independence. He compared the German occupations of Poland and Belgium: 'She suffers for the same cause, she defends herself against the same enemy, she bears the same fate as Belgium and the north of your country.' Joseph de Lipkowski, an emigré Polish politician in France, stressed the common democratic and national political values of Poland, France, and Britain, but warned that Polish nationalists would soon choose the concrete if disappointing offers of autonomy under the Central Powers over the vague promises of the Allies.[95]

The Polish question posed particular dilemmas for the western Allies. The British and French governments were sympathetic to proposals for Polish autonomy on the grounds of the principle of nationality and the more pressing need to win the war. Russian concessions to Poland would rally Poles in Europe and the United States to the Allied cause, and provide the basis for a more stable political settlement in eastern Europe. On 3 November 1915, days after becoming the President of the Council, Aristide Briand set out his vision of France's struggle for 'civilization and the independence of peoples'. Progress in civilization, he argued, required the 'liberties of people enjoying their full autonomy'.[96] Briand avoided mentioning Poland in this speech as the Tsarist government had warned their Allies against interference in domestic affairs. Sazonov had been working on plans for Polish autonomy even before 1914. In late November 1914 the Council of Ministers had accepted his proposal for limited autonomy for Poland, under which a Polish government would control cultural, language, and education policy, while foreign, military, and commercial policy would remain under Petrograd's control. The retreat of 1915 put paid to these plans. Now the promises of autonomy, which the deeply conservative prime minister Ivan Goremykin made on 1 August 1915, carried little weight with Polish nationalists.[97]

Sazonov understood the international dimension of the Polish question. The claim to absolute sovereignty over Poland could only be maintained as long as the three partitioning powers – Russia, Austria-Hungary, and Germany – remained at peace. Bethmann Hollweg also understood this international dimension. It provided an opportunity to present German war aims as part of a remaking of Europe on the basis of the principle of nationality and a defence of culture. In a speech on 19 August the German Chancellor mocked the Allies' claims that they fought for small nations and civilization. The scorched-earth policy employed by some Russian generals and the deportation of civilians were the latest acts in Allied hypocrisy that stretched back to the British occupation of Egypt and the Boer War. The occupation of Poland provided, he claimed, the basis for improved relations between Germans and Poles, though he was vague about the future of Poland. A strong Germany was essential to Europe's future peace. Weak and divided, Germany and central Europe would become a battlefield, whereas a strong Germany could secure peace and order. Germany was, he concluded, 'a shield of peace, and of the freedom of great and small nations'.[98] There was a strong element of calculation in Bethmann Hollweg's speech. Partly a rhetorical gesture towards the principle of nationality, it was also deliberately vague about Poland's future, as he had not yet ruled out a separate peace with Russia – at Poland's expense.[99] Yet his speech also married principle and political advantage. The Chancellor reasoned that the German Reich could not absorb the smaller nationalities on its borders. Better to pose as their defender and to exert control over them through commercial ties. Bethmann Hollweg's conception of a new European order took account of the restraints on and limits of German power while ensuring that the future settlement would provide security to the great power in the centre of

Europe. In German discussions about the future of Poland, others offered more radical solutions, including the expulsion of Poles from certain regions and the resettlement there of German colonists. This radical nation-alizing project was constrained by divisions within the German leadership, as well as by the ambitions of Austria-Hungary to expand its territory in Poland, issues that were teased out in negotiations throughout 1916.

The final consequence of the Russian defeats in 1915 was the Bulgarian entry into the war on the side of the Central Powers in September, which added a further layer of complexity to the politics of nationality in the Balkans. In the first half of the year, Arthur Nicolson had argued that the decisions of the Balkan states would be dictated by the progress of the war rather than the territorial concessions either alliance offered.[100] Such mili-tary calculations were central in the decision of King Ferdinand of Bulgaria and his prime minister, Vasil Radoslavov, but they also extracted a high price to enter the war. Throughout 1915 they played the Allies off against the Central Powers, as they pushed for claims based on historic rights and ethnicity. Under the terms of the treaties concluded in September with Germany, Austria-Hungary, and the Ottoman empire, Bulgaria would make good the losses suffered in 1913 by retaking the Dobrudja area ceded to Romania, getting the territory it considered its due under the 1912 treaty with Serbia, and modifying the border with the Ottoman empire.[101]

Siding with the Central Powers posed risks for Ferdinand. In late 1914 Nicholas II had warned the new Bulgarian minister in Petrograd that his country would be 'excluded from the Slav family' if it attacked Serbia.[102] Entry to the war, therefore, amounted to a choice about Bulgarian identity as well as its territorial future. 'Some of the streets had Russian names,' Sergey Prokofiev noted as he stopped in Vienna on his way to Rome to meet Diaghilev in February 1915, 'and there was a statue of Alexander III in the main square, but the newspapers are full of articles against Russia and spilling such filth that it is painful to read.' In Bulgaria attitudes towards the war were as divided as in other neutral states. Henry Bax-Ironside, the British minister in Sofia, claimed that the peasants supported Russia, while major opposition parties, such as the Radicals, Nationalists, and Progressive Liberals, favoured the Allies. King Ferdinand, on the other hand, undoubt-edly supported the Central Powers.[103] However, the majority of Bulgarians were weary of war after the experiences of 1912 and 1913. Alexander Stamboliski, the leader of the Bulgarian Agrarian National Union (BANU), claimed that Ferdinand's policy of 'adventurism will lead Bulgaria to the grave'. As in other belligerent societies mobilization was a wrenching affair, as a largely peasant army accepted reluctantly military duty to a nation that was less important to their identity than family and village. The connection between the experiences of the Balkan Wars, the expectation of further suffering, and the pain of departure was captured in Ivan Lazarov's 1915 sculpture, *To War Again*, which depicted a peasant soldier, marching off, resigned but stoic, and his wife tugging fearfully at his tunic.[104]

The military convention between Bulgaria and the Central Powers was directed against Serbia. Weakened by a year of fighting and an outbreak of typhus that had claimed the lives of an estimated 100,000 civilians, 30,000 soldiers, and 30,000 prisoners in the spring, Serbian forces offered little effective resistance. In addition the Allies considered Bulgaria's entry into the war to be due to the refusal of Serbia's prime minister, Nikola Pašić, to make timely concessions to Sofia, so they offered little support. General Mackensen, commanding German and Austro-Hungarian forces, attacked on 6 October. On 14 October Bulgarian forces launched their offensive. The conflict over territory was only the first stage in this war. It was also a war about values and identities that underpinned future political orders. For the Serbian government the only issue was how to preserve the nation. At a meeting at Kruševac, the government decided against a separate peace with the Central Powers. Instead they choreographed the army's retreat, turning it into a national epic. The essence of the nation was located in the army, rather than the people or the territory. The army made its way through the mountains to the Albanian coast, where they awaited evacuation to Corfu in December 1915. 'The state lives', the declaration on 25 November read, 'it still exists, albeit on foreign land, wherever the ruler, the government and the army are to be found.'[105]

King Peter of Serbia was more dubious, telling a French officer that 'even if Serbia survives, I fear there will be no more Serbs'.[106] Austro-Hungarian occupation policy sought to 'denationalize' the Serbian mind, in the words of one historian. This was to be achieved through instilling a sense of 'justice and law' in the civilian population. Expressions of Serbian national identity were considered a threat to law and order and thousands were interned. In anticipating opposition, a draconian occupation policy provoked popular resistance.[107] Bulgarian occupation policy aimed to nationalize the local civilian population. The violent logic of the principle of nationality became quickly apparent in the Bulgarian occupation. The authorities banned the use of Serbian language, promoted Bulgarian language and culture, and executed thousands of intellectuals and priests, the backbone of Serbian national sentiment. Surnames were changed

– Petrovic became Petrov for example – and children were instructed to say how happy they were to be Bulgarian again.[108]

* * *

The lines of trenches on the Western Front had been drawn since November 1914. As David Stevenson has argued, a triple deadlock – military, political, and social stalemate – created its own dynamics, as belligerents sought out new ways to win the conflict.[109] Operational stalemate prompted military leaders on both sides to rethink their doctrine, a process that would continue until 1918 and change the composition and functioning of the armies dramatically. There were occasional expressions of optimism. 'We have only a shell opposed to the French and ourselves,' wrote Douglas Haig, commander of the First Army, to his wife Dorothy on 13 December 1914.[110] Others had given up on the possibility of breaking through in a decisive battle. William Robertson, the new Chief of the Imperial General Staff, had used his remarkable intellect to rise from humble beginnings in Lincolnshire. Now he applied this to the study of warfare on the Western Front. On 8 February he concluded that German forces 'must be beaten by a system of slow attrition'.[111] Marshal Joseph Joffre also began to use the French term 'usure', or attrition, in 1915. Generals in the Allied armies developed related operational concepts to achieve attrition at the strategic level. Ferdinand Foch and Philip Pétain understood that changes in German defensive doctrine made breakthrough impossible. German defensive lines had been deepened, so that the seizure of the first line of trenches was of little significance in determining the outcome of a battle. As hostile forces broke through defensive positions, they faced strongpoints and further lines of trenches. Foch and Pétain now advocated 'methodical battle', while Henry Rawlinson, commander of the 4th Army, called it 'bite and hold'. Small advances would be secured before another offensive was undertaken, supported by careful artillery preparation.[112] Divisions within the Allied military leadership meant that the application of innovative military doctrines remained patchy. In addition the refinement of German defensive tactics and the inherent advantage of defence in the technological and topographical conditions of the Western Front ensured stalemate.

The military stalemate was compounded by the comparative political cohesion of Britain, France, and Germany. Politics was far from stagnant in these states; indeed, the British and French states and societies adapted well to the challenges of war. Political tensions and changes were accommodated within the structures of national unity established in 1914. Albert

Thomas, a prominent French socialist, became Undersecretary of State for Artillery and Munitions in May 1915, giving the French left a greater stake in the war effort. 'Pacifist becomes producer of guns,' ran *The Times* headline over an interview with Thomas in November 1915. Briand replaced Viviani – 'as limp as a rag' in the words of Poincaré – as President of the Council in October 1915, forming the broadest political cabinet in the history of the Third Republic.[113] In Britain, Asquith formed a coalition in May 1915, bringing leading Conservatives into the cabinet. The collapse of the Liberal government reflected general frustration over the conduct of the war, following a scandal over shell shortages and the resignation of Admiral Jackie Fisher.[114] In Germany divisions about war aims between the SPD and right-wing parties and associations, and the intrigues swirling around the military and political elite, were accommodated, for the moment, by Bethmann Hollweg's skilful political management.

Deadlock in western Europe disguised a dramatic widening of the war in 1915 in the west, bringing the United States to the fore of world politics. Both sides expanded the war by instituting a naval blockade (in Britain and France's case) and launching a submarine war (in Germany's case). The war at sea radicalized the conduct of war in humanitarian, commercial, and legal terms as both the blockade and the submarine campaign were aimed at enemy civilians and economies and contravened established international law.[115] This radicalization of warfare reshaped the debate over the future international order as the blockade and the submarine campaign threatened American commerce, lives, and interests. All four powers (though France was the least important in this debate) cast their political aims and military conduct in terms of a broader order, based on humanitarian concerns and international law. Even before the entry of the United States into the war in 1917, it played an important role in the political, ideological, and economic struggle. Owing to its latent power other states had to take American interests into account, while the American government and groups in civil society tried to craft an alternative vision of the international system.

The British government instituted a blockade of Germany in a series of stages between September 1914 and March 1915. The blockade stretched or breached pre-war agreements and law, notably the London Declaration of 1909. Prior to the war the Royal Navy had considered itself the guardian of world trade, but within a few months from the onset of the conflict its adversaries were regarding it as a threat to the freedom of the seas. The legal and maritime underpinnings of economic interdependence were unravelling. On 2 November the British government had announced its blockade of the North Sea, thereby setting up a distant blockade in contravention of international law. This meant that Royal Navy vessels could blockade Germany from bases in Britain rather than risk being sunk in a close blockade of German ports. On 7 November the German Chief of the Admiralty Staff, Admiral Hugo von Pohl, suggested responding to the British move by launching unrestricted submarine warfare. On 4 February 1915 the German government declared the waters around the British Isles a war area, in which neutral ships could be sunk without warning. The German submarine campaign was also a clear violation of international law, one justified by a tit-for-tat argument, which showed how successive decisions by both sides could lead to a cumulative radicalization of violence.

The escalation of the war on (and underneath) the sea constrained the space for humanitarian and international legal norms. An article by Matthias Erzberger published on 18 February, entitled 'No Sentimentality', encapsulated the shift towards an international system based on the application of military power. Pointing to the Allied blockade and use of colonial troops, Erzberger urged his fellow countrymen to apply naval and military force ruthlessly. 'The greatest ruthlessness in the conduct of war,' he argued, 'provided it is applied rationally, actually constitutes the greatest humanity. It would be more humane, if one had the chance, to destroy all of London with one blow than to allow a single fellow-German to bleed to death on the battlefield; the application of radical measures is the quickest road to peace.'[116] Conventional notions of humanity and international law were subverted as both sides dehumanized their opponents and justified their conduct of the war as a defence of universal abstractions, such as civilization and culture.

Yet the employment of these concepts demonstrated their continued importance in shaping the international order. Each side's claims to represent these universal values were tested against its actions before a domestic and international audience. Moreover, these notions of humanity and international law continued to be important in the American understanding of the war and presentation of its own national and commercial interests. A vibrant public debate took place in the United States about the remaking of the international order. In May 1915 a delegation of American suffragettes, including leading Progressives, such as Jane Addams and Carrie Chapman Catt, attended an international conference at The Hague called by the Dutch suffragette Aletta Jacobs. Empathy and humanitarianism were at the core of their vision of peace. Speeches and petitions concentrated on suffering – the crippled young men, the women raped, the orphans. 'Everywhere we were conscious of a certain revolt,' wrote Addams, 'not of nationalistic feeling nor of patriotism, but of human nature itself.' Catt hoped that 'our women will not emerge from the war with such hate in their hearts that we cannot go on with our international movement'. The institutionalization of what Addams called these 'higher human affections' was to be achieved through the implementation of female suffrage and the formation of international associations.[117] In July 1915 in Philadelphia the former president, William Taft, established the League to Enforce Peace, which drew on some of his pre-war ambitions for a system of international arbitration. Law, rather than empathy, was at the core of the League's vision of a future international order. According to Abbott Lawrence Lowell, the president of Harvard and influential member of the League, it had four aims – the codification of international law, the requirement that all states submit disputes to an international court, the submission of non-justiciable disputes to a committee of conciliation, and the application of economic and military sanctions to states that refused to follow these rules. These sanctions were essential to the project of making international law effective.[118]

The casting of an alternative international order was given dramatic expression by the opening of the Panama Canal in August 1914 and the hosting of a Panama–Pacific International Exposition in San Francisco in 1915. The exposition celebrated American industrial and technological prowess, its expansion westwards, and freedom. Visitors walked down the Avenue of Progress at the specially designed park, while the progressive Republican governor of California, Hiram Johnson, used the event as a showcase for his state and a platform for his Senate campaign the following year. The Liberty Bell was transported across the country from Philadelphia to San Francisco, viewed by huge crowds along the way – such was the scale of the crowds that one unfortunate woman was trampled to death in Memphis.[119] The procession linked the American past and present as well as the geographical expanse of the continent. The opening of the Panama Canal and the hosting of the Exposition at San Francisco underlined the diverse geopolitical preoccupations of the United States, facing across the Pacific and south as well as towards Europe. Herbert Hoover, a mining magnate, an engineering graduate of Stanford University, and the organizer of the American food relief programme for Belgium, argued that the Canal signalled the triumph of Anglo-Saxon civilization over Hispanic societies in the western hemisphere.[120]

President Woodrow Wilson was wary of making such claims, recognizing they would alienate states in Latin America. Nonetheless he pursued a Pan-American policy that served multiple purposes in his general foreign policy. In December 1914 Wilson proposed a mutual guarantee of political independence and territorial integrity for states in the western hemisphere, transforming the Monroe Doctrine into a multilateral pact. Although it was rejected by the Chilean president Enrique Villegas, Wilson continued to pursue multilateral cooperation with Latin American states. It was, as Villegas suspected, partly a means of establishing American commercial and political dominance on the continent. It also blocked the western hemisphere off from European intervention. Finally, the United States held up Pan-American cooperation as an alternative model for international politics. Pan-American cooperation was an 'example to the world in freedom of institutions, freedom of trade, and intelligence of mutual service'.[121] Robert Lansing, the Secretary of State, reaffirmed the exemplary importance of Pan-American cooperation at the Scientific Congress in Washington in December 1915:

Pan-Americanism is an expression of the idea of internationalism. America has become the guardian of that idea, which will in the end rule the world. Pan-Americanism is the most advanced as well as the most practical form of that idea. It has been made possible because of our geographical isolation, of our similar political institutions and of our common conception of human rights. Since the European war began other factors have strengthened this natural bond and given impulse to the movement. Never before have our people so fully realized the significance of the words 'Peace' and 'Fraternity'. Never before have the need and benefit of international cooperation in every form of human activity been so evident as they are today.[122]

At the same Congress, Lansing's nephew, the future Secretary of State, John Foster Dulles, claimed that 'American solidarity' enabled the substitution of law for force in resolving international disputes in the western hemisphere, a model for broader reform of international politics.[123]

American policy violated this ethos of cooperation when the country intervened in Haiti and the Dominican Republic in 1915 and 1916.[124] However, American self-presentation, national interests, and its view of the future world order compelled Britain and Germany to modify their naval policy in successive crises in 1915. In these crises the considerations of the conduct of war, national interests, international law, and abstractions such as 'Europe', 'humanity', and 'civilization' were interwoven. On 7 May 1915 a German submarine sank the *Lusitania* a few hundred miles off the south-west coast of Ireland. A total of 1,198 people died, including 128 Americans. It took just eighteen minutes for the ocean liner to sink to the seabed. The event was inserted into the narrative of German atrocities against civilians.

The violent speed of the sinking of the *Lusitania* belied the complexity of the political situation. 'I wish with all my heart,' Woodrow Wilson told William Jennings Bryan, Lansing's predecessor as Secretary of State, 'I saw a way to carry out the double wish of our people, to maintain a firm front in respect of what we demand of Germany and yet do nothing that might by any possibility involve us in the war.'[125] Yet without the threat of military force, Wilson knew any protest would appear weak and would undermine American interests. The vast majority of Americans did not view the sinking as a *casus belli*, but they expected a stout protest. Bryan wanted to present a parallel protest to the Allies about the blockade, which would preserve American even-handedness. Instead, in a note sent to the German government on 13 May, the American government protested against the submarine campaign, which was bound to lead to greater loss of life, and violated 'those rules of fairness, reason, justice, and humanity, which all modern opinion regards as imperative.'[126] Germany's reply was unsatisfactory, so Wilson, in early June, penned a stronger protest. This prompted the resignation of Bryan, who believed that American policy was veering towards a war against Germany. Wilson appointed Lansing as Secretary of State, marking the beginning of a difficult relationship. Lansing's view of the war had been transformed by the sinking of the *Lusitania*, which he considered 'a crime against civilization, which is without palliation or excuse. A government, which permits acts of this nature, is barbarous.'[127] On 9 June, Lansing sent the second *Lusitania* note to Germany.

Although the two American notes had separated the submarine campaign from the naval blockade, the implicit links between the two issues were well understood in Washington, Berlin, and London. Working out the crisis involved calculations about the relative importance of military and naval power and law in the international order. Although advocates of submarine war in Germany claimed that it was a means to win the war, rather than simply a retaliation to the blockade, the campaign was justified by the blockade. Moreover, the submarine campaign became a diplomatic tool to pressure the United States into action against the blockade. Before the sinking of the *Lusitania*, Kurt Riezler, the adviser to Bethmann Hollweg, had complained that the United States was doing little to prevent the British infractions of international law. 'I told the Chancellor,' he noted in his diary on 20 March, 'that he should send a great note, an historic document to the Americans, in which he would go through the spiralling breaches of international law on the basis of the submarine blockade and he would come finally to the starvation and the evacuation of Belgium if necessary.'[128] Bethmann Hollweg did not take up this option in the spring of 1915, but the connection between power and international law remained one strand of German thinking during the *Lusitania* crisis. Law provided a framework, within which power politics operated. Ranged against this conception of the international order were naval and military leaders, as well as right-wing associations such as the Pan-German League. Throughout the summer of 1915, Bethmann Hollweg and the German Foreign Ministry clashed repeatedly with the Admiralty over the operational limitations on submarine warfare. There were already material restraints on Germany's submarine capacity – in the spring of 1915 an average of six submarines out of a total of thirty-seven were on active patrol each day. While they inflicted losses of over 250,000 tons, they also suffered five losses of their own. In other words the submarine was not a war-winning weapon.[129] Aware of the limitations of German power, Bethmann Hollweg saw an advantage in promoting more general constraints on naval power by means of international legal rules and norms.

Wilson, in conversations with the German ambassador, Johann von Bernstorff, hinted that he would link the cessation of German submarine warfare to increased American pressure on Britain to cease its blockade of certain items, notably food.[130] More remarkable, however, was the British willingness to entertain restrictions on the blockade, one of their principal weapons of war.[131] Earlier in the spring Edward Grey and Edward House, Wilson's closest adviser, had discussed the easing of the blockade in return for the ending of submarine warfare. On 6 June the British ambassador in Washington, Cecil Spring Rice, sent a telegram to the Foreign Office setting out the American opposition to the British food blockade of Germany, a poisonous fusion, in his view, of commercial interests, misplaced humanitarianism, and German-American ethnic politics. Grey had departed on holiday, but Spring Rice's telegram triggered an intense discussion in the Foreign Office about the relative importance of law and force in British security and the international order. Eric Drummond, Grey's private secretary, drafted a paper on 7 June based on discussions between Grey and

House earlier in the spring. In it he argued for a 'League of Peace', an international legal framework governing the use of force on land and sea. Drummond saw advantages in Britain accepting the freedom of the seas, even during war. Britain would be free to import food and vital raw materials and the Royal Navy, deprived of its functions to block enemy and neutral trade, would no longer be seen as an offensive weapon, but one restricted to the naval defence of the British Isles. 'If however by freedom of the sea,' Drummond continued, 'Germany means that her commerce is to go free upon the sea in time of war, while she remains free to make war upon other nations at will, it is not a fair proposition. If on the other hand Germany would enter after this war some League of Nations, where she would give and accept the same security that other nations gave and accepted against war breaking out between them, then expenditure on armaments might be reduced and new rules to secure the freedom of the seas made.'[132]

Drummond's vision of peace underpinned by international law and financial retrenchment and reform at home was a classic expression of a liberal world order. He enlarged upon his ideas in a further memorandum on 11 June. He emphasized popular opposition to the war and expenditure on armaments, which had undermined social reforms before 1914. Popular support for the war in Britain, France, and Italy, he argued, was predicated on the notion that this was a war to destroy German militarism. Although previous attempts to prevent war had failed, Drummond offered a progressive narrative: 'World conditions are entirely different. Nations have become far more civilized and democratic and the horrors of war come home more clearly to each individual. War also affects the community at large to a much greater degree than has been the case in the past. The best answer to those who object on this ground [historical experience of periodic wars] is that some war must be the last war, and that it is possible that this war may be, and worthwhile attempting to ensure that it shall be.' His analysis fused British security, international organization, and legal norms into one grand synthetic view of the future international order. 'There has, however, never been a league of such a kind formed between nations as apart from rulers, and if any one nation attempted to break away from it and embark on an aggressive war, self-interest and self-security would force the others to take definite action even if their pledged word was not sufficient to make them do so.'[133]

Drummond's views did not go unanswered. A memorandum, entitled 'Freedom of the Seas', set out a fundamental objection to his vision, based on an alternative reading of war cultures. The critical issue was whether states, even if they signed up to a League of Peace, would support their pledges with military force in the case of another state embarking on aggressive war. While the aggressor was pillaging a defenceless state, the members of the international community would be bogged down in debates about the finer distinctions of international law. The memorandum expressed suspicion of the United States, whose policy 'would suit its own pocket'. International institutions and legal restraints offered no basis for a stable and peaceful world order because they ignored human nature. 'Men do not fight,' the document claimed in an echo of Salandra's justification of *sacro egoismo*, 'in support of abstract principles. They only fight when they believe that some vital concern of their own is at stake. Even if a nation could be induced in cold blood to make war on another in support of some international code, its soldiers would not fight. It is believed that every writer on military affairs of every nation has dwelt on the overwhelming importance of the moral factor in war, and this is entirely ignored in the proposals under consideration.' The writer concluded in proof of his thesis that the neutral states in the present war had only condemned German violations of international law when their own nationals or commerce had been endangered.[134]

Grey supported easing the blockade in return for the cessation of the submarine campaign. The Foreign Secretary saw in this bargain a means of improving Anglo-American relations, central to his vision of the emerging international order. In addition, securing the freedom of the seas had long-term advantages for British security and power if it denied rivals the opportunity to wage submarine warfare, which had undermined the technological and geographical advantages of blockade.[135] As Nicholas Lambert has shown, the blockade was only partially effective. British goods, shipped to neutral states, still found their way to Germany. The increasingly influential secretary to the cabinet, Maurice Hankey, led the charge against Grey's suggestions. He had already opposed Grey earlier in the year, on the grounds that the blockade represented the best means of choking off Germany's food supply. In addition, he had little faith in the utility of American friendship. Towards the end of July the cabinet decided not to alter its blockade policy – the exigencies of winning the war and the primacy of military and naval power had trumped more exotic notions of a new world order, based on law, democracy, and disarmament – for now.[136]

In Germany the outcome was different. Throughout the summer of 1915 the submarine campaign was gradually restricted amid bitter disputes between Bethmann Hollweg and Admiral Alfred von Tirpitz. The sinking of the British passenger ship, the *Arabic*, on 19 August had led to the deaths of three Americans. On 26 August Bethmann Hollweg and Tirpitz arrived at their headquarters in Pless (in present-day Poland) for a showdown over the submarine campaign and the crisis in relations with the United States. 'When they were summoned by the Kaiser at one o'clock,' recorded Alexander von Müller, 'the conflict of opinions was in full swing and the conference was in the nature of a battle royal.'[137] The Chancellor defeated his bitter rival, Tirpitz. On 1 September the German government informed the United States that its submarines would no longer attack passenger ships. At one level Bethmann Hollweg's victory was rooted in conventional calculations of power politics. The risk of war with the United States and the limited capabilities of the German submarine fleet to destroy British commerce and food supplies outweighed the unlikely benefits of persisting with the campaign. In addition the succession of military victories over Russia, including the capture of Bialystok and Brest Litovsk on the eve of the conference at Pless, favoured caution on the broader Western Front. Behind these calculations lay assumptions about the future international order and German power. Bethmann Hollweg viewed international politics as taking place within an order, which restricted military power. Because German power was limited – particularly on a global scale – he sought to reshape the order in ways that increased German security. The principle of nationality, commercial exchange, and international law were constituent parts of an international order, in which German power could flourish. Moreover, for the moment, he had overcome the advocates of unrestrained power politics, those who assumed the international system was an anarchical arena without rules and constraints.

The failure of the German leadership to agree on a conciliatory response to the United States earlier in the *Lusitania* crisis meant that the opportunity to get Wilson to press Britain for changes in blockade policy passed. The American president was increasingly irritated by the succession of German notes in the summer of 1915 – and worried that the United States might have to enter the war. At a cabinet meeting on 20 July, Wilson avoided issuing an ultimatum, but he also began the campaign of preparedness, increasing American naval power and military training. Preparedness was designed to demonstrate to Germany the mounting seriousness of the crisis. Protecting American commercial and political interests required military and naval power. Franklin D. Roosevelt, the Assistant Secretary to the Navy, feared 'economic death' if the United States was cut off from world trade and supported preparedness measures.[138] The crisis in the summer of 1915 added weight to this argument. Receiving the Liberty Bell at San Francisco, the Republican Speaker of the House, Champ Clark, called for doubling the student intake at West Point and introducing military drills in schools and universities. 'Human nature,' Clark told the crowd, 'has not changed a jot or tittle since Adam and Eve were driven with flaming swords from Paradise.'[139] The war had confirmed the rapaciousness and nastiness of man, in Clark's view, a lesson that necessitated military preparation. Even if the United States was not attacked, its role in shaping the international order required power. On this a Progressive like Walter Lippmann could agree with Roosevelt. 'How is it possible to create the beginnings of international order out of the nations of the world?', he asked in November 1914. 'Not out of a world of pacifists, out of a world of Quakers, but out of this world, which contains only a small minority of pacifists and Quakers. For it is peace on earth that men need, not peace in heaven, and unless you build from the brutalities of earth, you step out into empty space.'[140] Other Progressives had already protested against preparedness, such as Lilian Wald's New York Henry Street Group, which became the core of the American Union against Militarism. Wilson had not surrendered his vision of a reformed international order, but the crisis in the summer of 1915 had confirmed the centrality of military power in the operation of international politics.[141]

* * *

The Japanese victory over German forces and the occupation of Shantung province in November 1914 had created new opportunities for implementing the ambitions of rival statesmen in Tokyo to establish Japanese primacy in the Far East. In January 1915 the Japanese government presented a document known as the Twenty-One Demands to President Yuan's Chinese administration. These demands included privileges for Japanese political and commercial interests in Manchuria and Shantung. The fifth group of demands, the most controversial ones, stipulated that China employ Japanese political, financial, and military advisers. Japan would also have the right to station police in certain provinces. These demands aimed to secure Japanese influence over the Chinese government, whereas the other demands were similar to the periodic demands that the European, American, and Japanese governments had issued to China since the late nineteenth century. On 8 May Yuan's government accepted the demands, with the exception of the fifth group, which the Japanese minister to Beijing,

Hioki Eki, had dropped. This agreement provided the basis for Japanese claims to Shantung, as the first demand had committed China to accepting any arrangement between Japan and Germany after the war for the disposition of German territory and rights in the province of Shantung.

The Twenty-One Demands showed how the reordering of East Asian politics was part of the wider world war. The war had accelerated the diminishing power of European states to control international politics in East Asia. Allied to Japan and without significant military forces in the Far East, the European Allies had little option but to follow Japanese policy.[142] Otherwise Japan could come to terms with Germany, which would place enormous pressure on Russia's eastern flank.

Although the Twenty-One Demands appeared to confirm the dominance of Japan in the newly emerging East Asian order, the domestic political bases for this order in both Japan and China were destabilized by the tensions between the two states. In Japan rival groups competed for the control of foreign policy, which, in turn, provided the basis for dominance in domestic politics. In Tokyo the genrō, the elder statesmen of Japanese politics, who had shaped the Meiji Restoration, and the army sought to challenge the civilian leadership under Prime Minister Okuma and Foreign Minister Katō. The genrō favoured an expansionist foreign policy in China, the improvement of relations with Russia, and a return to more authoritarian government structures. The army supported territorial expansion in China for security reasons and the prospect of increased budgetary allocations. Between January and May 1915 Katō outmanoeuvred his domestic opponents and controlled the foreign policy process. Although he succeeded in toning down the more aggressive stance of rival groups, the ultimatum issued in May 1915 reflected an aggressive turn in Japan's policy towards China and marked the beginning of a more assertive intrusion into Chinese domestic politics. The purpose was to keep the Chinese state weak and divided, unable to resist Japanese influence and encroachments.[143]

While Katō may have congratulated himself on moderating the more aggressive Japanese claims, the popular reaction in China demonstrated the anger at the demands. For some the Twenty-One Demands were both a personal and national tragedy. Ch'in Li-chun, who had studied Japanese and now worked for a Japanese railway company in Shantung province, committed suicide. 'The Japanese language I had studied in Japan for ten years,' he wrote in his suicide note, 'suddenly went out of my mind due to the stimulus on May 7; I was therefore not able to serve the company. I could not provide food and clothes for my family so I had to die.'[144] Songs

written in condemnation of the Japanese demands had a distinctive militaristic message.[145] The mobilization of popular politics, underway since 1911,
was given a fresh fillip. Students organized demonstrations, businesses
arranged the boycott of Japanese goods, and new associations were established. Chinese students in Japan and the United States mobilized as part of
a transnational protest against the Japanese demands, while 232 branches
of the Salvation Fund were founded throughout China to raise money to
'save the nation' – though it was unclear precisely how these groups proposed
to do that.[146]

The acceptance of the Twenty-One Demands suggested that the protests
had been futile. Yet the very fact that the demands had been leaked into the
public sphere by Yuan amounted to a setback for the methods of secret
diplomacy employed by Katō. Governments feared testing the claims of
secret agreements in the public sphere. War cultures, shaped by notions of
nation, culture, civilization, international law, and barbarism (amongst
many other concepts), subjected treaties to the standards of these concepts,
vague and fluid as they were. The popular condemnation in China of the
Japanese demands prepared the ground for future discussions. Claims that
the demands were imposed by the threat of force on a defenceless state and
that they violated national sovereignty had an importance in the long diplomatic game.[147] In addition, Chinese leaders developed two other strategies
to counter Japanese claims. First, Xia Yiting, a Foreign Office official,
argued that China needed a seat at the peace conference to defend her
interests. The surest way to get this seat was to join the war. This was an
attempt to extend the moral claims of the war to East Asia. By entering a
world war, the most extreme test of power politics, China could escape
power politics in East Asia. The second strategy was to appeal on the
grounds of international law and national sovereignty to the United States,
the only power in a position to restrain Japan. In 1915 both of these strategies came to nought. The United States refused to recognize the Japanese
demands, but did not support the Chinese government either. The European
powers deferred to the Japanese interest in blocking China's entry into the
war.[148] However, the day of national humiliation, 7 May, the day when Yuan
agreed to the Japanese demands, was part of a process. So while the war in
Europe opened new spaces for the assertion of Japanese interests, the moral
claims of the war provided Chinese diplomats with instruments to stifle
Japanese demands.

The Japanese demands destabilized politics in China, making the establishment of a new order in East Asia more complicated. The popular

protests soon faded, but they signalled the decline of pan-Asian ideals. Before 1915, increasing numbers of Chinese students had gone to Japan to pursue their studies, but these numbers dropped after the presentation of the demands. Even Sun Yat-sen, the increasingly influential figure in South Chinese politics and a rival to Yuan, was embarrassed by Japanese financial and political backing and sought to keep this secret. National sentiment, the desire to strengthen social cohesion, and a belief in the necessity of power politics, ideals prominent since the revolution of 1911, were intensified. Yuan, weakened by his acceptance of the demands, sought to stabilize the state – and increase his own power – by planning to make himself emperor. Yet his decision to accept the offer of the imperial throne in December 1915 only served to trigger the break-up of China and the onset of civil war and warlordism. Not only did the Japanese government oppose the creation of an imperial state in China, so too did powerful regional leaders and military factions. Before the year was out Cai E, one of the leaders of the 1911 revolution, declared the independence of Yunnan province, the birthplace of the revolution in southern China. In April 1916 Guangdong province in South China and the eastern coastal province of Zheijiang followed suit. The death of Yuan on 6 June 1916 simply exacerbated the break-up of China, a paradoxical outcome of the attempt to make a nation out of the Qing Chinese empire, part of a wider breaking and making of empires and nations accelerated by world war.[149]

CHAPTER 5

MAKING WAR AND OFFERING PEACE, 1916

BETWEEN 6 AND 8 DECEMBER 1915 Allied military leaders met at Chantilly, just under 40 kilometres from Paris. These Allied conferences had begun in the summer of 1915 as a means of coordinating the military campaign more effectively. At this meeting Marshal Joffre presented his proposals for military operations in 1916, including the resumption of the offensive on all fronts, the simultaneous coordination of the offensives, and an increased contribution by France's allies to the military effort. Joffre proposed to elevate the doctrine of attrition from the operational to the strategic. With fewer resources the Central Powers could be worn down, provided that the Allies coordinated their offensives and prevented their opponents from exploiting their interior lines and moving troops from one front to the other to shore up their defensive positions. The Allied military leaders agreed to the general thrust of Joffre's proposals and anticipated a coordinated offensive after March 1916.[1] Three days before they met at Chantilly, Erich von Falkenhayn, Chief of the German General Staff, had travelled to Pless to meet Wilhelm II. Here he broached his military plans for the forthcoming year. Falkenhayn's proposal gave a particular twist to the concept of attrition. He proposed that the German army should undertake a limited offensive, surround the town of Verdun, and then compel the French army to launch a counter-offensive. The French army would be 'bled white' by German defensive military power. The Triple Entente would 'attack us in the west and thereby bleed themselves'.[2]

These were the origins of the great battles of 1916 – Verdun, the Brusilov Offensive, and the Somme. The strategy of attrition required even greater efforts in mobilizing business and manpower, remaking domestic and international political economy. The relationship between trade unions, business, and the state changed, while states also considered forming economic blocks, threatening the pre-war multilateral system of trade. The changing fortunes of battle shaped domestic and international politics, as leaders looked for ways to end the war while also justifying the continuation of the struggle. Verdun and the Somme came to epitomize some of the characteristic features of combat associated with the First World War. Although more soldiers died in mobile warfare in 1914 and 1918, the meat grinder of Verdun and the 50,000 British casualties on the first day of the Somme captured the idea of brutalization and mass death in the this conflict. Paradoxically, these experiences made a compromise peace seem more urgent than ever, yet also threatened a legacy of hatred and violence rendering any diplomatic settlement meaningless in terms of achieving an enduring peace.

* * *

The interaction of different military plans, fronts, and battles upset the calculations of military leaders across Europe. During January 1916, Falkenhayn and the Chief of Staff of the German 5th Army, Constantin von Knobelsdorf, planned the operations for Verdun. Falkenhayn, who had pursued an unusual career path, including a stint in suppressing the Boxer Rising in China in 1900, was not popular amongst the military elite. Moreover, his concept of attrition contrasted with the offensive spirit in the German officer corps. The 5th Army went into battle on 21 February with its Chief of Staff at odds with Falkenhayn over the operational goals. In the days before the attack the French army had bolstered its defences. 'I ask only one thing,' Joffre had told another officer on 8 January, 'that the Germans attack me, and that if they attack, that it be at Verdun.' Leaving aside the revealing personalization of the defence, Joffre was confident that a German offensive would wear itself down and make their army an easier target for the combined Allied offensive.[3]

The German 5th Army made good progress in the initial offensive at Verdun, capturing Fort Douaumont on 25 February. As Falkenhayn had expected, French leaders decided to fight for Verdun. The prime minister, Aristide Briand, rushed to the front on the evening of 24 February to instruct Joffre not to order French forces to fall back to the west bank of the River Meuse, while Philippe Pétain was appointed commander in charge of the defence of the Verdun region the following day. Defence of national identity centred on Verdun, the site of the treaty in 843 between Emperor Charlemagne's three surviving sons, which had divided the Carolingian empire into what many believed were the origins of modern France and

Germany. The battle became an act of heroic grandeur, especially for those who were not there. At La Scala in Milan, which hosted a 'French evening' on 13 March, Gabriel Hanotaux, then on a French diplomatic mission to Italy, reported the 'electric jolt' amongst the audience when Verdun was mentioned. 'Verdun fills thoughts,' he wrote, 'excites hearts, raises emotions, anxieties, and hopes. How France has grown during these past twenty days is somehow inexplicable. She has become the elder sister, the teacher of peoples.'[4] Verdun's monumental scale dwarfed the hundreds of thousands of individuals involved in the battle. Falkenhayn's strategy was to kill or maim them, destroy the nation's morale soldier by soldier and family by family. Joffre understood this strategic assumption, which he summarized as attacking 'the principal enemy [France], not with the hope of putting it out of action, but with the thought of breaking the enemy's morale'.

However, the failure of the German 5th Army to capture the heights overlooking the River Meuse was a serious blow to Falkenhayn's plan. Pétain was able to bring in reinforcements without facing German artillery fire from these dominant heights. This defensive effort was enormous, as only a narrow-gauge rail line connected Verdun to Bar-le-Duc (birthplace of Raymond Poincaré). Between 22 February and 7 March over 190,000 men, 22,500 tons of ammunition, and 2,500 tons of supplies and food were brought to the front. Altogether almost 12 million artillery shells were fired during the battle. The front at Verdun stabilized. Falkenhayn's strategy of attrition transformed men into a form of war materiel, but his plan failed on this count too. Although he refused to issue figures for German losses, it was clear that he had overestimated French casualties and under-estimated German ones. Some 315,000 French soldiers and 281,000 German soldiers were casualties at Verdun.[5]

The battle of Verdun disrupted Allied planning for a coordinated attack. Stunned by the initial German success, Joffre asked France's allies to under-take minor offensives in order to pin down German and Austro-Hungarian troops. Coordination was difficult to achieve. Luigi Cadorna, the Chief of the Italian General Staff, launched an offensive on the Isonzo river between 11 and 16 March, while the offensive of Russian forces at Lake Narotch on the northern front ended in failure. After attending a perfor-mance of Prokofiev's 1912 polytonal composition, 'Sarcasms', on 21 March in St Petersburg, the French ambassador Maurice Paléologue reflected on its 'wealth of intellect, colour, and delicate feeling', but despaired at Russian composers' obsession with theory and ventured that the 'epic of Verdun' was a humiliating illustration of Russian military impotence.[6]

Meanwhile Joffre placed increasing pressure on General Douglas Haig, now commander of the British Expeditionary Force, to accelerate the beginning of the offensive. Even at the end of March 1916, Haig, who had taken two hours of French lessons each day to improve his communications with the French generals, was concerned that the British army was not yet adequately trained for large-scale offensives.[7]

The battle of Verdun altered the conditions in which the Chantilly proposals were implemented. The Russian offensive was brought forward to help ease the pressure on French forces at Verdun and Italian forces, which were retreating in May after Franz Conrad von Hötzendorff, Chief of the General Staff of the Habsburg Army, had ordered the so-called 'punishment expedition'. What became known as the Brusilov Offensive on Russia's south-western front was originally conceived as a diversionary operation in preparation for a larger offensive on the north-west front against the German army. General Aleksei Brusilov prepared the offensive carefully, taking account of the experiences on the Eastern and Western Fronts. He ordered the construction of assault trenches close to the enemy front line, used artillery to destroy enemy trenches and prevent the introduction of reserves into battle, and concentrated the attacks on four sectors, each between 15 and 20 kilometres in breadth. The offensive began on 4 June. Within days the Habsburg 7th Army had lost 133,000 men, Russian forces had crossed the river Styr, advancing 45 kilometres, and the town of Lutsk in the Ukraine was recaptured. Having suffered from a typhus epidemic in 1915, the inhabitants now witnessed the destruction of much of their town. 'The pressure raised the roofs of houses,' one observer wrote, which 'rattled and fell in splinters on the street. Flames shot up from the row of munitions dumps built from several hundred ancient, giant Volhynien trees. The rich scent of the earth bubbled up, glowed, swelled, and dispersed.'[8]

As the Habsburg 4th Army lost 54 per cent of its troops and the 7th Army 58 per cent of its troops within a few days, the Brusilov Offensive became the main thrust of Russian operations in the summer of 1916. Following Falkenhayn's refusal of German support, Conrad transferred two divisions from Italy to the Russian front on 8 June.[9] On 19 June Brusilov ordered his armies to consolidate their gains and prepare for a further offensive in July. The exploitation of the initial victory was hindered by the perennial problems of limited mobility. On the Eastern Front too much space was an impediment to decisive victory. Military politics also thwarted Brusilov's ambitions, as Russian commanders in the north, Aleksei Kuropatkin and Aleksei Evert, refused to accelerate their planned offensives, demonstrating a lack of energy which Brusilov condemned as 'criminal'. Brusilov got re-inforcements of four army corps, including the Imperial Guards, an elite formation whose soldiers were reputedly at least six foot tall and 'the finest human animals in Europe', the ambiguous compliment of the British mili-tary attaché in St Petersburg, Alfred Knox.[10] On 4 July Brusilov resumed his offensive. Despite superior infantry numbers and the low morale of the Austro-Hungarian forces, evident in the increasing rates of desertion among national minorities, Brusilov's forces made only limited gains. Attacking through the Pripet marshes, which divided the Eastern Front between north and south, was a treacherous undertaking. The Russian armies forced the German and Austro-Hungarian troops to retreat behind the Stochod river, but were unable to pursue them further through the muddy plains. 'The wounded sank into the marsh,' Knox recalled, 'and it was impossible to send them help.'[11]

Although Brusilov's offensive stalled, it had the most significant political repercussions of any battle in 1916. The Eastern Front was the major pre-occupation for the Central Powers in the summer of 1916, not the Somme or Verdun. 'Yet again in Pless,' wrote Moriz von Lyncker, Chief of the Military Cabinet, to his wife on 26 July, 'but much more anxious than before. It is not yet clear how the negotiations will go. Everything seems so simple, but the difficulties are immense. The military situation on the eastern front is very serious. Austria, in the view of its own statesmen, is facing imminent collapse. If so, the war would be lost for us. Yesterday they went back and forth. Heavy attacks are coming in the east; we certainly know that. The western front is holding better, or even well.'[12] The military developments on the Eastern Front had three consecutive consequences. First, the Austro-Hungarian army was placed under German command, with Paul von Hindenburg appointed as the commander of the Central Powers on the Eastern Front. Second, the Romanian government decided to enter the war on 4 July. Ion Bratianu, the prime minister, was reluctant to commit, but the military situation appeared to give the Allies a decisive advantage and a fillip to supporters in Bucharest. 'Thank God, I have an excellent doctor in the person of Brusilov,' remarked the terminally ill Conservative leader and supporter of intervention, Nicolae Filipescu. Romania declared war on 27 August. This, in turn, produced the third consequence, the resignation of Falkenhayn and the appointment of Hindenburg as the Chief of the General Staff and of Erich Ludendorff as Quartermaster General on 29 and 30 August. Hindenburg's enormous popularity reshaped the basis of German politics, as Wilhelm II's monarchical authority and Bethmann Hollweg's style of political management faced a challenge from the duumvirate of Hindenburg and Ludendorff.[13]

Between the two phases of the Brusilov Offensive the battle of the Somme began on 1 July. The purpose of the battle within Allied strategy had changed since early 1916. Partly aimed at relieving pressure on the French forces at Verdun, the offensive was now primarily a British affair, rather than one dominated by the French army. In addition the planning process was complicated by differences between Haig and General Henry Rawlinson. Rawlinson proposed a cautious plan along the lines of his doctrine of 'bite and hold'. Disappointed with his subordinate's lack of adventure, Haig pushed a more ambitious plan. At one point he told Rawlinson that he hoped to use his cavalry 'on the lines of 1806', a reference to Napoleon's decisive victory over Prussia at the battle of Jena. Inadequate infantry training and a poor grasp of artillery doctrine compounded the unrealistic plan. Underpinning the preparations for the battle was a vast logistical exercise, which enabled British artillery to fire between 1 and 1.6 million rounds in the week before the offensive and lay 50,000 kilometres of telephone cable.[14] The French 6th Army was also involved in the battle, though its commander, Marie Émile Fayolle, was sceptical about the chances of success. 'The approaching battle will cost 200,000 men,' he wrote on 21 May, 'and I wonder if there is any interest in admitting it. Attrition, is it such that we can hope for a decisive success? I don't think so. . . . Will it be necessary to spend another year in the trenches? Yes.'[15]

Fayolle's fears were justified by the unfolding battle on 1 July. The casualties were enormous, though French casualties, despite the battles of Verdun and the Somme, were lower in 1916 with 350,200 missing or dead than in the five months of 1914, when 454,000 died, or 1915 when 391,000 were lost.[16] The British 3rd and 4th Armies suffered 57,000 casualties in the battle of the Somme, including 19,240 killed and a further 2,000 missing on the first day alone. As a result of German artillery fire, 30 per cent of British casualties occurred behind their own lines. Military historians have now scotched the idea that troops simply sprung out of their trenches and walked, shoulder to shoulder, across no-man's-land. Nonetheless, despite better tactics, the casualties were horrific.[17] The offensives continued in a series of stages. Between 2 and 13 July British forces suffered a further 25,000 casualties and between 15 July and 12 September 126,000 casualties for gains of 6 square miles of territory. Amongst the British dead in the battle of the Somme were Raymond Asquith, son of the prime minister, and Donald Hankey, brother of Maurice and nicknamed the 'student in arms'. Maurice Hankey, secretary to the War

Cabinet, was dictating to his stenographer, F. W. Owens, when he received a phone call. 'Donald's gone,' he said as he hung up the receiver, before, after a brief pause, asking 'Where was I, Owens?' Lloyd George could see beyond political rivalry to acknowledge that Raymond Asquith's death had hit the prime minister 'hard', so hard that Asquith wept daily.[18] Whatever their reactions, the political and military elite were exposed to the suffering of this war. On 1 August Churchill described the losses as 'disastrous' and the territorial gains as 'barren'.[19] The diversion of some German divisions from Verdun could only have been small comfort.

In the light of these casualties it appears astonishing that the confidence of the British troops in ultimate victory was still pronounced after the battle of the Somme. One officer, impressed by the quality of artillery and aircraft support, said of his troops in September: 'They can beat the Boche when and where they like.'[20] The battle of the Somme epitomized the industrialization of warfare. Yet this did not mean that the infantryman had become redundant. Ernst Jünger, who fought at the Somme, later claimed that the battle and industrialized warfare had created a 'new man', in which soldier and technology merged. The previous year the Italian futurist painter Gino Severini, able to observe the departures of soldiers and materiel from his apartment in Paris, had painted *Armored Train in Action*, in which the faceless soldiers merged with the artillery train, so that it was difficult to see where humanity began and machine ended.[21] Although the majority of deaths and wounds were inflicted by artillery, fighting could also be highly personal. Richard Tawney, a Christian socialist and educational reformer, was wounded on the first day of the Somme. He had volunteered in November 1914 to fight a war in defence of civilized values. As he had advanced on 1 July he felt the 'palaeolithic savage' rise within him. He enjoyed 'aiming at anything that moved, though since manhood the pleasure has been sneaking and shamefaced', a hint that killing remained a transgression even while it was an act of pleasure. But then he was wounded and he hoped to die quickly, like the wounded he had come across earlier that day, who had begged him to kill them.[22] The intensity of the fighting also led to a number of atrocities on both sides against prisoners. One British soldier hacked off the head of a German prisoner with a shovel, while another stomped on the head of a wounded prisoner so severely that he died. One German officer later recalled that the British troops were 'not like soldiers, but a horde of savages'.[23]

* * *

This fusion of technology and savagery shaped war cultures and the visions of the future international order. Many Europeans (and others) feared that the violence of the battlefield would seduce civilized man back into savagery, to use Tawney's term. The catastrophe of the war, contemporaries argued, was that the revival of barbaric codes and practices was made more destructive by modern technology and bureaucracy. The experience of the battlefield was brutalizing and exposed man to violent instincts that stripped away the civilizing process of the nineteenth century. The war had the potential, on this reading, to produce an anthropological revolution, in which man's nature changed. Wilhelm Lehmbrück's sculpture, *The Fallen Man* (*Der Gestürzte*), completed in 1916, embodied the perceived degeneration of the human condition, the shame at the violence of war, and the sense of hopelessness. His work was partly inspired by his experiences as a nurse in a military hospital in Berlin. Harold Macmillan, a soldier in the Grenadier Guards regiment, told his mother that one of his friends read Homer's *Iliad* to make ' him fierce', whereas the future British prime minister saw 'the traditions of classic culture' as a way to 'keep myself civilised'.[24] The delicate restraints on human conduct – empathy for others, respect for life, domestic manners, and so on – had been torn aside. The discipline of family, work, and daily routine were undone by the chaotic upheaval of battle. If man's nature changed, the bonds of affection and empathy that had constituted part of the European peace order before the First World War would be transformed into hatreds that would fuel further war. In short, the intimate face of battle was interwoven with wider considerations about war and peace.

One of those fighting at the Somme was the German private Norbert Elias. In September, near Péronne, he was badly wounded. 'Things were never as terrible for me', he recalled in an interview towards the end of his life. 'I probably had a shock. . . . I am incapable of telling you anything else about this subject at the moment. I retain a very precise memory of the journey towards the front – the carcasses of horses, some bodies of soldiers, and the shelter of the trench. And I have the impression of having suffered some kind of important shock, but then my memory fails me. I do not even know how I returned.'[25] Nor could Elias remember enrolling at university two years later, as he began an academic career that resulted in one of the most influential works of scholarship in the twentieth century, *The Civilizing Process*. In this book, written during the mid to late 1930s partly in exile in Britain, he said little about the First World War. In one intriguing passage, examining the development of manners that restricted the use of a knife to eating at the table, a process emblematic of a wider civilizing process, Elias recalled that during the war, soldiers in the conditions of the trenches had eaten with their knives and hands. Yet this merely constituted a 'regressive moment', not the beginning of a new development in personal manners and social etiquette, because, after the war, the returning soldiers slipped back into the conventional table manners. A new code of manners might have been consolidated, but it was not because the internalized codes of behaviour proved stronger once men had been removed from the conditions of the trenches. Instead of downplaying the brutalizing consequences of the war that could result in trauma, Elias considered the conflict to be comparatively unimportant – it was a regressive moment, but it had not given rise to a new man and codes of behaviour that privileged violence and brutality.[26]

Sigmund Freud presented a much more pessimistic interpretation of these issues in two essays written in March and April 1915 – 'The Disillusionment of War' and 'Our Attitude to Death' – which connected the war, its impact on human beings, and international politics.[27] In Freud's account of contemporary European society, he argued that certain instincts about death, sex, and other basic human experiences had been restrained by 'high norms of moral conduct', internalized by individuals. These moral codes were the basis of sociability and modern states. Moreover, these conditions of social stability provided the foundation for international relations, at least between 'the great world-dominating nations of white race'. Sharing similar moral codes enabled the flourishing of a cosmopolitan culture amongst civilized states. The great powers, Freud claimed, had acquired 'so much comprehension of what they had in common, and so much tolerance for their differences, that "foreigner" and "enemy" could no longer be merged, as they still were in classical antiquity, into a single concept'. This was a world in which people moved easily and communicated easily – the world of the early twentieth-century academe, for example. These networks had created a 'new and wider fatherland'.

While Freud's vision of a common 'civilized humanity' reflected a particular and narrow experience of early twentieth-century European society and politics, it offered an important construct for analysing the significance of the war. For Freud the war had proved shocking and disorientating. In particular he identified the conduct of war as a threat to the 'development of ethical relations between the collective individuals of mankind – the peoples and states'. Atrocities stood at the centre of his interpretation of the war, fusing experience and meaning. Armies had disregarded international law and humanitarian considerations in their treatment of wounded prisoners, civilians, and property, so that the conduct of the war was 'as cruel, as embittered, as implacable as any that has preceded it. . . . It tramples in blind fury on all that comes in its way, as though there were to be no future and no peace among men after it is over. It cuts off all the common bonds between the contending peoples, and threatens to leave a legacy of embitterment that will render any renewal of those bonds impossible for a long time to come.' The bonds of affection were replaced by 'hate and loathing', draining European societies of the emotional resources necessary to construct peace. 'Indeed,' Freud continued, 'one of the great civilised nations [Germany] is so universally unpopular that the attempt can actually be made to exclude it from the civilised community as "barbaric", although it has long proved its fitness by the magnificent contributions to that community which it has made.' From the nation to the individual, passions rather than reason determined action.

In his second essay Freud considered the significance of changing attitudes to death resulting from the mass killings of the war. According to him, 'the civilised adult' had ignored death, as though thinking about it seemed 'wicked'. In pushing death aside, modern man had forgotten how to live and die, whereas primeval man had invented spirits and other notions to deal with death. This preoccupation with death had given rise to ethical rules – most notably the commandment 'Thou shalt not kill'. This commandment had expanded to encompass family, then strangers, and finally enemies. By firstly marginalizing death and then embarking on mass killing, civilized man had demonstrated the consequences of losing his 'ethical sensitiveness'. Primeval characteristics had been exposed by the war, but without the corresponding sensitivity to death. This created a dilemma for Freud. At the end of the war, a civilized man who survived would return home and experience the joy of seeing his family again. But he would also be 'unchecked and undisturbed' by his participation in killing. The brutalizing experiences of war would persist, even in the heart of civilized society. War, Freud argued, 'strips us of the later accretions of civilization, and lays bare the primal man in each of us'. In a pessimistic conclusion he suggested that, as war could not be abolished, it was necessary to change attitudes to death: 'Si vis vitam, para mortem.' This could mean that he foresaw war as a permanent condition, but it more likely meant that only by confronting death, and reasserting the ethical sensitivities to death of primeval man, could violence be restrained. In other words, the ethics of the putative savage would become the basis for political and social order.

In his own idiom Freud gave voice to concerns that were shared across geographical boundaries and social divisions about the rupture of empathy and toleration, the brutalization of soldiers and societies, and the emotional legacies of war for the future international order. James Bryce, a Liberal peer who had undertaken investigations into the German atrocities in Belgium and northern France and then into the Armenian genocide, explored the moral and legal issues of the war in two presidential addresses delivered to the British Academy, in June 1915 and July 1916. The shock of the return to the 'Stone Age', as Bryce put it, coursed through the two lectures. In his July 1916 lecture he argued that the bonds of peace – religion, democracy, commerce, and sympathy for humanity – had been inadequate. Christianity had contributed to more peaceful conditions over the previous two centuries, but its ethos was less relevant to government action and morality, while Bryce condemned Islam as a warlike religion. The majority of people suffered in war, for democracy was prone to powerful passions and had not restrained belligerence as liberals had expected. The significance of free trade lay in the cultural exchange between societies rather than in an increase in prosperity, but in the previous three decades tariff barriers had been erected as people wanted the state to protect their particular economic interests. The humanitarian impulse had reached its zenith in the abolition of the African slave trade and slavery, but since the late nineteenth century, Bryce argued, the circle of empathy had been increasingly restricted to one's own nation.

These reflections led him to consider the construction of a future peace. 'That the hatred and horrors conspicuous today grieve us all the more because they seem to be a reversion to a dark and cruel past,' he suggested, 'is of itself a testimony to the progress which mankind had made, and raises in some minds the hope that what we say may be transient and the next change for the better.' Bryce veered between a progressive reading of human nature and an unchanging one, in which greed and arrogance were as wide-spread as they had been in previous centuries. He doubted whether peace could be founded on international law; politics, rather than law, was the source of war and therefore the solution lay in changing international polit-ical culture. Bryce the lawyer ceded way to Bryce the academic. Empathy provided the resources for making peace. He called for the development of a feeling of allegiance to humanity, an interest in the welfare of other states and societies, and the creation of an international public opinion. Academic exchange had a particular role to play in forging these international bonds and restoring reason to its central place in European political culture.

'Nations cannot be enemies forever,' Bryce concluded. 'The time must come when a knowledge of the true sources of these calamities will, even there where hatred is now strongest, enlighten men's minds and touch their hearts.'

Of course there were many who argued that war produced a higher morality, but this was largely defined in terms of a national political order. The subordination of the individual to the nation and the willingness to sacrifice one's life in defence of the nation formed the basis for the perpetuation of the national community and its protection against external enemies. Freud, Bryce, and others feared that violence and consequent brutalization made it more difficult to construct peace. Finding ways to constrain this brutalization of millions of individuals was an enormous challenge, but it anticipated the 'demobilization of the mind' that would take place after 1918, in which empathy between erstwhile foes in some cases replaced the national hatreds. The work of re-imagining a more peaceful world, therefore, began during the war, as civil society associations sought to preserve space for empathy, international law, and humanitarianism.[28]

The International Red Cross, established during the European wars of the mid-nineteenth century, saw its primary goal as the implementation of the Geneva Convention. The purpose of the Convention was humanitarian, to attenuate the suffering of war and ease the restoration of peace. Two weeks after the outbreak of the war, the International Red Cross set up an agency to supervise the treatment of prisoners of war. They undertook regular visits to prisoner-of-war camps, which, while not eliminating mistreatment, acted as a restraint. They helped families identify whether relatives had been killed or taken prisoner. The International Red Cross organized the repatriation of severely wounded prisoners of war. In 1915 two trains, one with French prisoners, the other with German prisoners, passed each other in Switzerland. The prisoners exchanged salutes and sang the 'Marseillaise' and 'Deutschland über Alles'. 'For us Swiss', the *Bulletin of the International Red Cross* stated, 'this sounded like the hope of peace and reconciliation.'[29] By 1918 the International Red Cross had sent 1,370,000 letters to family members of prisoners of war with details of their condition and location. As Europeans came to terms with mass killing, the work of the International Red Cross was of enormous importance to millions of individuals, whose relatives were missing or captured.

A criticism levelled at the International Red Cross was that by trying to make war humanitarian it rendered war more acceptable. Jeanne Halbwachs, a French feminist and pacifist, articulated this argument most trenchantly.

Instead of promoting peace, she claimed, the International Red Cross contributed to the fiction of a humanitarian war. Pacifists meanwhile campaigned against war by revealing its full horrors. Yet the pacifists' criticism misunderstood the logic of the International Red Cross during the war. It sought to limit the brutalization of societies with a view to the future construction of peace. Its bulletins regularly denounced the reciprocal intensification of violence and the threats of reprisals, such as the mistreatment of prisoners and occupied civilian populations and the aerial bombardment of urban areas. 'The war itself is a sufficiently terrible scourge,' the bulletin noted on 12 July 1916, 'without adding to the ills by measures of an inhumane character and futile severities. If the nations hope to achieve a durable peace after this struggle is ended, will the rapprochement not be that much more difficult, if hatred has been stoked in the hearts, not by open and loyal combat, but by the suffering imposed coldly and by calculation on defenceless unfortunates?'[30]

The Vatican also played an important role in promoting humanitarian relief during the First World War. Elected Pope just a month after the outbreak of hostilities, Benedict XV followed a policy shaped by the conventional interests of the Vatican as a state and the broader commitment to Catholics and Christians in general on all sides of the conflict. He saw the war as a catastrophe for Christian Europe and spoke of 'the suicide of civilized Europe'.[31] He condemned violations of the laws of war on the same grounds as the International Red Cross – that building peace would be thwarted by the emotional legacies of hatred and vengeance caused by atrocities. The purpose of the laws of war was not merely to regulate its conduct, to render it more humane as Halbwachs had argued, but to provide a humanitarian and legal space in which future peace could be forged.

These restraints on the conduct of the conflict did have some impact in shaping war cultures and experiences. Elias argued that the civilizing process had shaped the experience and meaning of the war. First, the internalized prohibitions on killing and inflicting pain remained powerful constraints on violence, which governments and armies had to overcome by 'carefully concerted propaganda'. There was little joy in killing, according to Elias.[32] Second, violence was managed and organized, so that even in the chaos of the battlefield soldiers acted within certain constraints.[33]

Yet the atrocities against prisoners, on the Somme and other battlefields, were just a number of many incidents that belied Elias's contention. The killing was gratuitous and spontaneous. The battlefield, prisoner-of-war camps, and occupied territories were sites on which different nationalities confronted each other, and the opportunities for mistreatment and atrocity threatened to burden the process of peace-making. The experience of violence has been well documented in recent scholarship on the First World War, but the results point in different directions. Given that there were at least 7 million prisoners of war in Europe by 1918 and many more civilians who were living under military occupation, it is impossible to generalize. 'Let them hate us, so long as they fear us,' said one German commandant of a prisoner-of-war camp, which housed Russians.[34] Prisoners were at more risk of dying from starvation, disease, and neglect than from the violence of camp guards. Typhus epidemics claimed the lives of 17,000 prisoners in the Russian camp of Somara, while in Mauthausen in Austria-Hungary an outbreak of typhus killed 12,000 prisoners in the winter of 1914–15.

Occupation regimes were repressive, especially in eastern Europe. The Austro-Hungarian regime in Serbia executed civilians for minor infractions. One woman was executed for having told two men that there was money in a neighbour's house, which the men then proceeded to steal.[35] In imposing self-proclaimed German cultural values of 'work' and 'order' in the occupied territories in Poland and the Baltics, occupation authorities humiliated local inhabitants. German military authorities also developed forced labour regimes. Work battalions were involved in building infrastructure and suffered from high mortality rates.[36] In 1916 the German Army began to deport Belgian workers to Germany to make up for labour shortages. One outraged young man wrote to the mayor that working for the Germans meant 'working against my brothers, that makes me weep with rage'. The process of deportation, in which families were separated, was compounded by the sense that one might make the bullet or shell that killed a relative. The daily hardships of life in occupied territories fuelled resentment. When German authorities imposed a tax on dogs, some owners killed their dogs as an act of resistance. In February 1916 Clémence Leroy, who called this the 'holocaust of our unhappy dogs', claimed that 'Sultan has also died for France.'[37]

Such experiences hardly seemed to provide the basis for remaking a peaceful Europe. Yet Leroy's reaction to the sight of wounded German soldiers in October 1916 reveals how empathy for the enemy could persist despite such experiences. 'Although these are the enemy and the cause of all our ills,' Leroy wrote on 29 October, 'a deep pity seizes us at the sight of these unfortunates who are already in the shadow of death. They are there, laid out on pallid stretchers, without movement, no longer appearing to have a breath of life. One of them did not have any legs. And there, my God, on the other side of the terrible barrier, the same scenes are reproduced. And it is ours who are lying there, wounded, dying. Oh, the war, the war! What an accursed horror.'[38] The shared experiences of suffering provided a basis for empathy.

This empathy was reflected in the attitudes of soldiers towards their foes across no-man's-land. Notions of war cultures based on hatred between nations unravelled as soldiers on both sides shared similar experiences. Soldiers' self-presentation was remarkably fluid in that they could inhabit the roles of fighting men, members of a national community, and/or husbands. They could divert hatred for their direct foes into contempt for and anger against civilians on the home front and the governments that directed military policy. An Italian soldier, writing from the front line on 17 January 1917, paused to reflect on what the term 'enemy' meant. 'I say enemy [referring to Austro-Hungarian troops in trenches opposite him], but they are, however, Christians and innocents like us; the barbarians and the assassins are the infamous governments, responsible for the human slaughter.'[39] The death of 100,000 Italian prisoners of war in captivity further illustrates the complex dynamics of empathy and hatred in the First World War. The Italian government considered prisoners to be deserters and hindered their relatives from sending them parcels via the International Red Cross, an important means of sustenance. The responsibility for the mistreatment of Italian prisoners lay with the government in Rome as well as in Vienna.

During the war new identities were created by often violent experiences. Yet the meaning attributed to those experiences could lead to surprising results, including the forging of empathetic bonds between 'enemies'. The humanitarian sensibilities of the nineteenth century proved enduring and provided a basis on which the bonds of affection could be knitted back together or created from scratch after the war. Moreover, war experiences forged peace cultures, in which the common experience of suffering became a potential reference point for those who warned 'Never again'.

* * *

The battle of the Somme epitomized the concept of the *Materialschlacht*, or battle of materiel, that arose during the First World War. The requirements for vast numbers of soldiers, artillery shells, and logistic support accelerated the mobilization of the war economies. As belligerents mobilized, they also kept an eye on the future peace settlement and its economic dimensions. Institutions and practices designed to prosecute the war also served as experiments for peacetime. Pre-war notions of a global economic order based on international commerce, underpinning international peace, were challenged by technocratic visions in which governments, capitalists, and trade unionists would cooperate in planning national and international economic production. Across the barbed wire, trade unionists, economists, and businessmen exchanged ideas in a vibrant transnational debate.

Socialist and trade unionist support for the national war effort, especially in Germany, France, and Britain, derived in part from the welfare reforms and improved labour conditions that had been implemented since the late nineteenth century. Socialists and trade union members participated in the war to protect these gains and to expand their influence in the state and economy. 'The social recasting, which will be the inevitable consequence of these murderous shocks,' claimed Léon Jouhaux, the French trade union leader, 'must be favourable to the emancipation of peoples, of this we are certain.'[40] Defending the SPD's support of the war, the German trade union leader Carl Legien argued that some trade union demands on shift labour and pay, dating from before the war, had been implemented during the first few months of the conflict. 'Although the war is a misfortune,' he said, 'that should not prevent us from getting what is good for the working class.'[41]

First, however, the trade unions sought to protect their members' interests from the dislocation caused by war. The strength of trade unions was based on male-dominated working-class communities, but these communities were undermined by the conflict. Workers were recruited into armies, women, peasants, adolescents, and immigrants took jobs in the war economy, and working practices changed with longer hours and greater flexibility. Trade unions mounted a conservative defence against these changes. While their leaders recognized the importance of flexibility given the demands of the war economy, they negotiated agreements to restore pre-war working arrangements in peacetime. This was essentially a conservative stance that defined women, immigrants, and others as threats to the skilled working-class man. In addition, workers were also subject to strict discipline. In each belligerent society trade unions operated in a context where their centrality to the war economy was recognized, but strikes and other forms of labour disruption carried heavy penalties.[42] The French Army returned 500,000 skilled workers from the fighting front to factories on the home front by the end of 1915, but these men remained subject to military discipline.[43] Striking workers risked losing their exemption from military service, imprisonment, or deportation. David Kirkwood, a shop steward at Beardmore's gun plant in Glasgow, led a strike in March 1916, after which he had the misfortune to be deported from Glasgow to Edinburgh.[44]

Within these confines trade unions and socialists negotiated reforms that opened up new possibilities for industrial relations. The most notable change was the increased presence of the state in industrial relations. Albert Thomas, the French Socialist Undersecretary of State for Armaments, considered the development of the state's role in arbitrating in disputes between employers and workers as part of a longer-term reform of industrial relations. Arbitration eliminated the disruption of strikes, which benefited workers, employers, and, in wartime, the state. In late 1915 Thomas recognized that the limitation of mobilized workers' rights meant that the 'State therefore is morally their guardian, so to speak, and its intervention is not only legitimate, but often helpful. The high cost of living is making itself felt, some demands may be justified, and the decisions of arbitrators, expressed with tact and moderation, may be very useful.' In speeches to workers, Thomas regularly referred to the post-war industrial order. The 'ideal of justice and liberty', for which the nation was fighting in the war, would be carried into the ethos of post-war social reform. In January 1917 Thomas introduced compulsory arbitration in case of disputes about wages. Complaints were heard by a committee with an equal number of worker and employer representatives, with the Ministry of Armaments appointing a representative as the chair.[45]

Trade unions in each belligerent state increased their influence on labour policy and compared to their pre-war situation had a privileged position. Not only employers but also the unions received recognition from the state, being partners in industrial relations. The system of arbitration marked a shift from the confrontational system of industrial relations, in which employers could draw on the power of the state to support a corporatist system with set rules and procedures. In March 1915 the Amalgamated Society of Engineers, one of the most important trade unions in Britain, concluded what became known as the Treasury Agreement with Lloyd George, the Chancellor of the Exchequer. The Treasury Agreement entailed the suspension of strikes, the establishment of an arbitration system, and a promise to restore the privileges of skilled labour after the war. This was reinforced by the passage of the Munitions Act in June 1915, which restricted workers' rights but also introduced compulsory arbitration and statutory wage regulation.

In Germany the demands of the Supreme Command for a twofold increase in armaments production – the so-called Hindenburg Plan of December 1916 – had implications for labour policy. In return for restrictions on labour mobility, the trade unions won the right to sit on committees in each of the

Reich's military districts. This limited employers' control over their employees and gave the trade unions, for the first time, a statutory role in industrial relations. Legien and other trade union leaders supported the Auxiliary Service Law as a means of increasing trade union influence in the war economy as well as offering longer-term benefits in a future peacetime economy.[46] While the operation of the Hindenburg Plan proved chaotic, the establishment of arbitration committees and the statutory role of trade union representatives in factories provided a model of industrial relations for peacetime.

In August 1915 the Italian government militarized parts of the workforce. Yet officials recognized that even under military discipline it was necessary to ensure 'fair treatment' of workers in the interests of efficient production. Even in unequal relationships there was scope for negotiation. FIOM, the Federation of Metal Workers, was able to secure some concessions such as overtime and the regulation of working hours in 1916. 'It will certainly not be in vain,' noted General Alfredo Dallolio, the Undersecretary of State for Munitions in November 1916, 'if, when the war has ended, the labourers will retain a positive, grateful memory of Industrial Mobilization.' However, the FIOM and the Italian Socialist Party kept a greater distance from the state than their counterparts in other belligerent states.[47] In Russia the Special Council that managed the war economy, the OSO, rejected proposals to militarize workers on the grounds that it would require granting them a greater role in the management of factories and workplaces.[48]

The new developments in industrial relations did not bring an end to strikes or workers' sense of unfair treatment. For example, William Sharp of the Boilermakers' Union condemned the 'narrow, miserable, one-sided manner' of implementation of the Munitions Act. Others, however, saw the arbitration machinery as a means of balancing the sacrifices in the national community. Thomas Fyfe, a commercial lawyer and judge on the Glasgow tribunal, who had lost two sons in the war, noted in a judgment in 1917 that 'these awards did not contemplate that operatives any more than any other class of the community were to be entirely relieved of their quota of the war sacrifice, which was common to all classes.'[49] The integration during the war of trade unions into state systems of arbitration raised two problems. First, the process took place as a result of a wartime crisis and the solutions reflected the fluidity of wartime politics. Second, the leaders of trade unions had to mediate between their members, the state, and employers. In this context their responsibility to their members and the maintenance of labour mobilization created tensions. As living conditions worsened, the ability of trade union leaders to control their members and participate in the emerging system of industrial relations was challenged.

Hugo Stinnes, one of the leading industrialists in Germany, expressed concerns about the concessions made to the trade unions and the SPD in the Auxiliary Labour Law. The role of large corporations also changed during the war. 'The capitalist was being robbed by the state of his useful function as a merchant,' wrote G. D. H. Cole, a member of the Fabian Society, in November 1916, 'and was becoming a mere supervisor of manufacture.'[50] In a market dominated by the state the purpose of the merchant was less and less useful. However, governments were generous to large corporations, on which they relied to produce the large quantities of military supplies. They offered firms long-term contracts and high prices so that they would invest in the production facilities required. This enabled firms to make large profits, which in turn threatened the moral economy of wartime society. One response was the introduction of excess profits taxes, as happened in France and Britain during the war. The Italian parliament set up a Consultative Commission for Price Review in 1917. These measures had limited effect. In general, governments had decided that the exigencies of wartime required a bargain with industrialists, who devoted their productive capacities to the needs of the state in return for bumper profits.[51] Despite these financial windfalls industrialists remained wary of the intrusion of the state into the economy, fearing the loss of business autonomy.

During the war reforms in working conditions took place at the national level, but trade unionists and socialists developed ambitious plans for the international regulation of labour relations. The internationalization of labour regulation had its origins in international trade union institutions, networks of social reformers, and agreements between states concerning the rights of migrant labourers, most notably a treaty between France and Italy in 1904.[52] The war framed the debate in three particular ways – as a problem of the capitalist system, as a means of tying the working classes into a peace settlement, and as a means of preserving civilization and culture, the great abstractions for which the war was being fought. Ideas were exchanged at two conferences. The first was the Allied trade unions conference in Leeds in August 1916 and the second was the conference of the trade unions from the Central Powers and some neutral states in Bern in October 1917. First, trade unionists on both sides argued that the war was, in part, the result of a capitalist economic system. National commercial rivalries stoked tensions between states. In addition, workers suffered due to this international economic competition as employers sought to keep costs down by depressing wages, imposing longer working hours, and failing to improve working conditions.

Second, as the character of war changed, so too did the character of diplomacy and peace-making. As this was a people's war, it would also be a people's peace. Trade unionists claimed that any future peace could only enjoy legitimacy if it earned the support of the working classes. By late 1915 when Jouhaux spoke of compensation for the sacrifices made by the working class in the war, he had international as well as national regulations for labour relations in mind. 'Nearly all other wars,' William Appleton wrote to Asquith on 30 August 1916, 'have ended with treaties which conserved the rights of kings, the boundaries of nations, and the privileges of property. The poor people have had no part in the making of war or peace; they have suffered, they have endured contumely, and they have died, but never yet has a monarch or a statesman made their situation a determining factor in a treaty of peace. The time has arrived for better methods; for the consideration of the common rather than the particular interest; for the wide conception of human rights rather than the narrow one.'[53]

Third, the claims to international labour agreements were presented as part of a wider contribution to the strengthening of civilization, which had several implications in this context. Not least amongst the considerations of European trade unionists was that international standards governing working hours, female labour, and social insurance could stave off industrial competition from countries such as China and India. For Jouhaux international labour regulation would reinforce the French claims to fight a war in defence of civilization. It was necessary to insert clauses governing labour standards into the peace treaty, he argued, because 'the proletarians of all countries will benefit from these clauses, because it will raise a little the standard of living of the European working class and our country will have the glory of having sowed in the world the ideas of justice and solidarity.'[54]

In October 1917 trade unionists from the Central Powers and neutral states met at Bern, where they essentially agreed to the resolutions passed at Leeds in August 1916. As one might expect, there were criticisms of the Allied labour movements. Otto Bauer, the German delegate, condemned the 'chauvinistic spirit' of William Appleton, mocked British claims to be a civilized power by pointing to British atrocities in Ireland and colonial wars, and denounced the naval blockade as a 'war against the women and children of Germany'. Yet beyond the evident bitterness and gulf in moral perception between the trade union movements in the Allied states and those in the Central Powers, there was substantial agreement about the importance of labour regulation in a future peace treaty. When Legien presented the resolutions of the Bern conference to the Reichstag on 25 November 1917, he argued that they represented the united will of the international working class, including the Allied powers.[55] Moreover, the arguments put forward at Bern echoed those advanced by Allied Socialist leaders in 1916. Labour regulation would both attenuate the impact of international commercial rivalry on working conditions and aid reconstruction after the war. One delegate urged governments to protect young workers because 'they are the fathers and mothers of the future generations, which will have to fill up the gaps beaten into humanity'. The Bern conference called for the introduction of compulsory insurance schemes for workers to protect against illness, accidents at work, and unemployment, as well as equal pay for men and women, the banning of child labour, a maximum of a ten-hour day (eight hours in some industries), and common health and safety practices.[56]

The inclination of European trade unions to favour more international regulation reflected assumptions that the world economy would return to its interdependent pre-war pattern of trade, capital flows, and migration after the conflict. Yet the war challenged the intellectual assumptions that underpinned the interdependent world economy before 1914. Patterns of trade, migration, and capital flows were altered profoundly by the outbreak of the war, while considerations of national security and power dominated economic policy. However, individual national economies remained too small and narrowly based to provide economic stability and prosperity. Moreover, leading businessmen remained attached to the pre-war world economic system. By 1916 the debate over the future world economic order reached its zenith. Politicians and businessmen started from different assumptions – for some the restoration of commercial prosperity took priority, for others security and political balance between different economic interests were the key criteria. A return to the interdependent world economy, the division of the world into economic blocs based on the wartime alliances, and the tightening of imperial economic ties were the main options.[57]

The difficulties in imagining the future world economy are well illustrated in the inconclusive debates in Germany. Initially, Bethmann Hollweg viewed his country's commercial policy from the vantage point of national security, in which German economic strength would reinforce its geopolitical position in Europe. As Germany was the dominant economy on the

European continent, a customs union that included Austria-Hungary and possibly other states, such as France, Italy, and the Scandinavian countries, was an instrument for political domination. This fusion of military, political, and commercial considerations into a grand scheme of a German-dominated Europe echoed in much more radical ways the war aims documents produced in 1915 by economic interest groups. The most notable of these was the 'Sechser Eingabe' of 20 May 1915, a submission by the League of Agrarians, the German Farmers' League, the Westphalian Farmers' Association, the Central League of German Industry, the League of German Industry, and the German Middle Class (*Mittelstand*) Association. This called for colonization of the agrarian east and the annexation of key industrial centres and sources of raw materials in France and Belgium. German economic dominance in Europe also required the maintenance of the balance between the agrarian and industrial sectors of the domestic German economy.[58]

This vision of a German-dominated, self-sufficient economic area on the continent alarmed several businessmen. The pre-war international economy retained a seductive attraction for political and commercial reasons. Walther Rathenau, who had given serious consideration to an economic *Mitteleuropa* before the First World War, now had doubts about its viability.[59] Businesses that had strong pre-war commercial ties to Germany's current enemies and previously largest trading partners were concerned that their firms would lose export markets, access to raw materials, and be tied into a weaker economic sphere in central Europe. *Mitteleuropa* made little commercial sense for German export industries. In the Rhineland local political figures, such as Konrad Adenauer, elected mayor of Cologne in 1917, recognized that the region's economic vitality rested on its international connections.[60] In addition, figures such as Prime Minister István Tisza in Austria-Hungary feared that a customs union with Germany would further increase the Habsburg empire's dependency on its ally. He bitterly resented Austria-Hungary's humiliating position as a supplicant to Germany. 'A customs union or something similar with Germany,' he told the Ministerial Council meeting in June 1915, 'means not only the economic dependency on Germany, but it would also entail political consequences for our great power status.'[61] In November 1915 the Habsburg Foreign Minister, István Burián, rejected Bethmann Hollweg's proposals for a customs treaty.[62]

As German commerce had profited from the pre-war international economic order, French and British firms favoured restrictions on

NORWAY
OSLO
SWEDEN
STOCKHOLM
TALLINN
PETROGRAD

March 1918,
following
Brest-
Litovsk

North Sea

UNITED
KINGDOM

DENMARK
Baltic Sea

COPENHAGEN

RIGA

VILNIUS

LONDON
AMSTERDAM
HAMBURG
DANZIG
KÖNIGSBERG
BERLIN

RUSSIAN

MINSK

NETH.

GERMANY

WARSAW

EMPIRE

BRUSSELS
BELGIUM

BREST-
LITOVSK

KIEV

PARIS
LUX.
VERDUN

1914

Sep. 1915

PRAGUE

FRANCE

AUSTRIA -

VIENNA
BUDAPEST

Dec. 1916

SWITZ.

HUNGARY

Nov. 1917
CAPORETTO

BELGRADE
ROMANIA
BUCHAREST

Corsica

ROME

SERBIA
SOFIA
BULGARIA

MONTENEGRO
Dec. 1915

Sardinia
TIRANA
ALBANIA
ISTANBUL

SALONIKA

PROGRESS OF THE WAR

Frontiers, 1914

Central Powers

Extent of Central Powers
advance, with date

GREECE
TURKEY

Sicily

ATHENS

competition from Germany. Indeed, the liberal economic order was under as much threat from the Allies as from the Central Powers. The British blockade strategy, incomplete as it was, signalled the power of the Royal Navy to disrupt world trade. By 1916 French and British ministers were engaged in detailed discussions about wartime cooperation and the future of the world economy. In part these talks represented a turn to a techno-cratic vision of economic planning, both at the national and international level. The practical business of coordinating the different Allied war econo-mies provided a lesson in the possibility of international economic coopera-tion. 'It was in effect a new problem,' Jean Monnet recalled, 'a problem of the twentieth century, which a mind without prejudice, without the memories of the past, could better discern than the experts fed on the conceptions of the nineteenth century. These did not know that the forms of power had changed, that the machine of war was called to crush all the resources of a nation and that it was necessary to invent unprecedented forms of organisa-tion.'[63] Monnet, whose family from western France had long been involved in the international cognac trade, had spent time in the United States and Canada before the war. By temperament and experience he was open to new ideas about the management of the international economy. In 1914 he had volunteered to go to London to help coordinate Allied economic efforts. He made friends there with like-minded young British officials, such as Arthur Salter. Monnet also became close to Etienne Clémentel, who was appointed Minister of Commerce in Briand's cabinet in October 1915. Trained as a painter, Clémentel became the most powerful advocate of a planned inter-national economy, in which cooperation would replace rivalry.

Clémentel was inspired by a particular reading of German economic power, which stressed that its success was rooted in cooperation between German firms and the active support of government. Moreover, he took seriously German proposals for an economic *Mitteleuropa*. The German model was to be feared and emulated.[64] Clémentel's views were supported by a cohort of economic academics, such as Georges Blondel, Edmond Théry, and Henri Hauser. They fused their experience of the war economy with a vision of the future economic order. The campaign of economic attrition, in which the Allies cooperated and denied Germany access to materials and markets, provided the basis for post-war security.[65] In Britain similar charges had been laid against sharp German commercial practice since the 1890s, but the dominant political, intellectual, and economic position of free trade had prevailed against those who wished to introduce tariffs and create an imperial trading preference zone. The war, however, had revived ideas about imperial preference and other forms of international economic cooperation.

On 20 December 1915, just two weeks after the Chantilly conference of military representatives, Clémentel approached Briand to suggest an Allied economic conference. Briand supported the idea as part of a wider consolidation of the Allied war effort. In the first half of 1916, Clémentel prepared the ground for such a conference. While much of these preparations and the Allied conference on future economic cooperation held in June 1916 were devoted to wartime economic cooperation, Clémentel and Briand tried to push the agenda on post-war economic cooperation. At a meeting of Allied leaders on 27 March the Belgian prime minister, Charles de Brocqueville, argued that it made no sense to win the military campaign but then to lose the economic peace. Germany, he argued, would be relatively economically stronger after the war, given the destruction of industry in Belgium and northern France.[66]

The conference in June was very much a French initiative. Briand placed the discussions in the context of German plans for economic war and subjugation of the Allies. The purpose of the war, he claimed, was to restore commercial liberties, but in a twist, this meant the exclusion of Germany from international commercial agreements and restrictions on German trade. Briand and Clémentel had longer-term ambitions to restructure the international economy by developing Allied economic cooperation. This would provide France with access to markets and raw materials and ensure economic security against a revival of German power. 'We are at the beginning of a new economic era,' Clémentel told the assembled Allied representatives, 'which permits the application of new methods, based on management, collaboration, and everything that enables cohesion in production. If the Allies know how to turn these ideas into practice, they will have founded a new order of things, which will mark one of the dominant stages in the economic history of the world.'[67] Clémentel's ambitions were belied by the more modest resolutions of the conference, but nevertheless it provided the basis for deepening Allied economic cooperation and significant restrictions on post-war German economic power. Whereas Bethmann Hollweg's ambitious September 1914 memorandum, proposing a European customs union, had aimed to control the French economy by integrating it into a German-dominated sphere of influence, French policy during the war sought the exclusion of and restraint on German commerce. The Allies agreed to harmonize their blockade measures against the Central Powers and to cooperate in the reconstruction of destroyed areas. They also planned to deny Germany the hallmark of the liberal international economic order, the 'most favoured nation status' clause, for a number of years after the war. The Allies agreed to share access to raw materials and to undertake measures to improve their long-term economic cooperation.[68]

These resolutions fell short of Clémentel's aims to secure an Allied economic sphere, based on managerial principles. As with Bethmann Hollweg's plans for economic cooperation in central Europe, there were significant political and economic obstacles to Clémentel's vision. For a start, the Russian and Italian governments did not want to be shut out from the German market and access to technical expertise after the war. Although both economies were financially dependent on Britain by 1916, the pre-war connections to the German manufacturing and banking industries stoked the promise of post-war cooperation. In addition, businesses in France and Britain had an eye on reviving their profitable trade with German firms. The Comité des Forges, the powerful association of French metallurgical and mining employers, considered the revival of trade with Germany central to their business interests. In late 1915 Robert Pinot, a leading figure in the Comité des Forges, noted that 'It is important to maintain between France and Germany the necessary economic relations.' French industry purchased coke from Westphalia and sold minerals to industries there.[69] Finally, British and Dominion politicians would not privilege Allied economic cooperation over imperial preference. In the spring of 1916 the Australian prime minister William Hughes, a powerful advocate of imperial preference and anti-German measures, was in London where he added his weight to discussions of the future economic order.

While the Paris conference was directed against German commerce, it also had repercussions in the United States. Elected to the presidency on the platform of New Freedom in 1912, Woodrow Wilson viewed the integration of the United States into the world economy as the most effective means of advancing American national interests. Lowering tariffs had dual benefits – it reduced the scope of economic special interest groups and it advanced American trade interests abroad. However, under the pressure of war, Wilson had rowed back on his economic reform agenda. In 1916 the Webb-Pomerene Act relaxed earlier anti-trust legislation against firms whose business centred on exports.[70] Even those favourable to the Allied cause were suspicious of Allied economic plans. 'The British idea of cooperation,' the American banker Willard Straight told the diplomat Edwin Morgan in June 1916, 'is that the other fellow does what the Britisher wants him to do, takes as much of the profit as he can get and for this, in the Englishman's mind, he ought to be grateful.'[71] Although the American economy benefited from the war, many Americans feared that the division of the world into economic blocs would restrict their commercial expansion. Of course, the American economy was vibrant and comparatively less dependent on exports than the smaller European economies. Moreover, American firms had captured markets from their European rivals, particularly in Latin America, a proto-economic bloc in the western hemisphere. Nonetheless the discussion of tariff policy and economic blocs in Europe echoed across the Atlantic and, as we shall see, provided one of the themes of the presidential election later in 1916.

Allied economic discussions also added to the tendency in Japanese foreign and commercial policy to see East Asia as its zone of expansion. The Twenty-One Demands had a strong commercial dimension. In 1916 Gotō Shinpei, the Japanese Home Minister, and Nishihara Kamezō, a businessman with interests in Korea, developed plans to promote Japanese commercial primacy in China. Both men were pan-Asianists and close to General Terauchi, who now favoured the use of economic, rather than military, power to carve out a Japanese sphere of influence in East Asia. On 3 July Nishihara presented the 'Outline of Economic Mechanisms in Response to the Situation in China', which argued that Japanese expansion could best be served by lending money to the Chinese government. Crucially, Nishihara and Gotō argued that Japan should issue these loans on a unilateral basis, removing Japan from the constraints of the pre-war financial consortium. This proposal was not a direct response to the Paris economic conference, but it represented a shift in economic thinking and policy, in which the world was divided into economic blocs that combined commercial expansion with geopolitical security.[72]

Whereas most statesmen thought in terms of future economic spheres, Lenin saw the models of economic mobilization in the war as proof that economies and therefore socialism could be organized on a national level. This had implications for the future of revolutionary socialism. Russian Social Democrats had long argued that socialism was impossible in Russia unless there was a simultaneous revolution in western Europe. In addition, the war had demonstrated the interdependence of the world economy. Nikolai Bukharin and Leon Trotsky contended that imperialism had laid the basis for socialism by creating a world economy and then provoking the war, leading to revolution. Lenin initially shared this analysis, arguing in November 1914 for a United States of Europe as 'it is impossible to make the transition from capitalism to socialism without breaking the national frameworks'. However, by August 1915 his analysis had shifted. The revolution could occur in one country – Russia. By December 1916, Lenin viewed the organization of the German war economy as evidence of the viability of distinct national economic units. Lenin's insight into economic mobilization did not mean that he gave up on the project of an international revolution. Rather it offered him an alternative means of organizing revolutionary socialism in Russia, should the revolution not spread to other European states.[73]

* * *

The Allied military planners at Chantilly had intended that their combined offensive would compel the Central Powers to sue for peace. Those plans had been disrupted in the first half of 1916, but by early summer German leaders were losing confidence in the war effort. Following the failure at Verdun, the stalling of the Austro-Hungarian offensive against Italy, and the revival of Russian offensive military power, Bethmann Hollweg appeared caught in a political cul-de-sac. 'The Chancellor spoke of the nightmare of revolution after the war,' his close adviser Kurt von Riezler noted in his diary on 14 June, 'which burdened him. Immense claims of the returning troops, disappointment over the peace. The uselessness of the bourgeois parties, who can only maintain themselves against the left by stoking up passions, but have been internally hollowed out, and have nothing more to say.'[74] On the same day at the St Louis Coliseum, the Democratic National Convention opened. In a hall festooned with American flags and ringing with the sounds of patriotic songs, William Bryan, the former Secretary of State, told the crowd that 'I join the American people in thanking God that we have a President who does not want this nation to be plunged into war'.[75] Just over two months later, the Chief of the Russian General Staff, Mikhail Alekseev, urged Britain and France to maintain their offensive on the Somme in conjunction with the Russian offensive on the Eastern Front. The Central Powers, 'substantially weakened, will begin by breaking and the war will approach its end'.[76] In London Asquith ordered the first formal drafting of British war aims in August in preparation for the possible ending of the war. International politics between July and December were shaped by rapidly shifting fortunes on the battlefield, domestic political vicissitudes, and visions of the future international order.

Bethmann Hollweg's pessimism, entirely characteristic of the man and befiting the gravity of the military situation, led him to grope towards a proposal for a compromise peace. Between June 1916 and January 1917 his plans would interact with Wilson's efforts to mediate between the belligerents and the war aims of the Allies. The flurry of documents, proposals, and decisions amounted to more than the hard-headed assertion of national interests. They reflected broader visions of the international order, whereby principles of nationality, commercial rights, and international law provided frameworks in which security would be enhanced. In 1916 versions of realpolitik accounted for relative military power and territorial dispensations, but they also incorporated more layered conceptions of the international order. The visions of a future order were not based on an anarchical collection of states, but on one in which the use of military power was constrained by legal and political norms. Moreover, the struggle to remake the international order was reflected in domestic political upheavals and contests. The change of military leadership in Germany, the death of Franz Joseph, and the succession of Karl I in Austria-Hungary, the presidential election in the United States, and the rise of Lloyd George in Britain intersected with international politics.

After meeting the Chancellor on 20 August, Henning von Holtzendorff, the Chief of the Admiralty Staff, complained that 'he is obviously not up to it'. Bethmann Hollweg's bearing, slouched and grimacing due to stomach pains, doubtless made a miserable impression, but his political outlook disturbed Holtzendorff even more. 'He is obsessed,' he wrote to Admiral von Müller, Chief of the Naval Cabinet, 'heart and soul with his worries and his desire for peace.' Bethmann Hollweg told Müller that 'we must make peace soon, while we are in the position of victors'. He suggested that Germany should even swap some territory in Alsace and Lorraine in return for the iron ore fields at Briey to sweeten the deal for France.[77] The Chancellor's conversations with Riezler during the summer of 1916 reveal even deeper wells of pessimism than Holtzendorff and Müller suspected. Bethmann Hollweg had questioned the purpose of the war on several occasions since 1914. The war's futility went beyond the possibility of a German defeat. The conflict threatened to destroy the restrained politics of the late nineteenth century, the basis of social and political stability. The Chancellor despaired of the 'terrifying stupidity of the narrow national, blind chauvinistic errors of all sides'. This was a European phenomenon, he claimed, though it was embodied in his pithy dismissal of one of the leading Pan-German figures, Count von Reventlow, 'as nothing other than the piazza'.[78]

The coarsening of political behaviour and rhetoric, on this reading, was the consequence of the intense violence. It was the equivalent of the brutalization of the individual soldier and connected the physical violence of the battlefield to the emotional violence of national politics. Bethmann Hollweg, when he considered peace in the summer of 1916, had a much broader conception of what it entailed than the exchange of territory. The Chancellor groped towards a solution that would ensure German security, establish a legitimate and stable political order in Europe, and enable commercial exchange to thrive. It would be a German peace, but within a European framework. In a fascinating reflection, Riezler, on 6 July, recalled the warning of one of Bismarck's opponents, Constantin Frantz, in 1873 that a central European state based on force and conquest was inherently unstable. Such a state would alienate its neighbours and encounter domestic resistance. While Riezler believed that Bismarck's 'iron-and-blood' solution to the German question had been necessary, these methods had been transformed from the level of political tactics into an ethos that degraded the older values of central European politics. No state, Riezler recognized, could live by force alone. The question remained how to incorporate Germany into Europe. 'In the middle of Europe,' he wrote,

> belongs a state, which on all sides, is federative and attractive, not repellent and aggressive. In the Middle Ages, despite the misery of the old Reich, that was the political talent of the Germans – the Prussian state, which rescued Germany from the old imperial misery, necessarily stood in opposition to such a spirit. If Germany is not to be destroyed in the next war or the one after that, there must be a new synthesis out of this opposition with the old political virtues of the Germans. Out of it the saving of Germany, which is also the saving of Europe, must emerge. We are in the middle of it.[79]

The musings of the Chancellor and his advisor remained vague at this point, but they reflected a conception of a peace embedding Germany in a European order that, especially compared to Pan-German plans, privileged restraint and tolerance over force and chauvinism.

Bethmann Hollweg recognized that any compromise peace reflecting these values would disappoint large swathes of German opinion. To give himself political cover for his peace initiative, he turned to Hindenburg, the most popular figure in Germany. It also signalled an alternative option for German politics, in which the army and nation remobilized to fight to the end if a compromise peace failed. Hindenburg personified the 'will to victory', even if he personally doubted that the German Army could dictate a peace to the Allies.[80] In fact, the political values that Hindenburg held – militarism, authoritarian populism, contempt for Poles and socialists – were so much at odds with Bethmann Hollweg's conception of the future political order that the Chancellor's judgement in supporting Hindenburg must be questioned. That said, however, Bethmann Hollweg's relations with Falkenhayn had worsened throughout the first half of 1916. So when Romania entered the war on 27 August, Bethmann Hollweg (and others in the political and military elite) seized the opportunity to force Wilhelm II to dismiss Falkenhayn and replace him with the duumvirate of Hindenburg and Ludendorff.[81]

The entry of Romania into the war unnerved the Kaiser. It 'means the end of the war,' he told his entourage on the evening of 27 August. Lyncker and Rudolf von Valentini, the head of the Imperial Civil Cabinet, warned that an immediate peace settlement would involve the evacuation of French and Belgian territory, the cession of Alsace and Lorraine to France and Heligoland to Britain, and the loss of colonies. 'We couldn't do that,' they told the Kaiser. 'It would be better to suffer complete defeat.'[82] This reasoning – based on the logic of total victory or total defeat – was diametrically opposed to Bethmann Hollweg's political outlook and temperament. The heightened emotion of late August was captured in a letter on 29 August from General Hans Georg von Plessen, General Adjutant of the Imperial Headquarters, to the Countess von Brockdorff: 'My soul breathes freely again! I foresee the happy continuation and result of the war and the saving of the Fatherland and our dynasty. I have trust again. Big Hindenburg is a magnificent fellow! You cannot imagine how happy I am!' Plessen transposed this personal joy to the whole German nation, whose 'pride' and 'powerful elemental force' would be inflamed to new and incomparable acts of heroism. Invoking a common understanding of the stakes of the war, as a conflict between German culture and western European materialism, he wrote that the 'miserable, rotten world, decaying of Mammon, will get to know the famous militarism of the Prussian. The categorical imperative and the Potsdam watch drill, the basis of our sense of duty, by this the German nation will defeat our enemies.' Plessen concluded the letter by anticipating a rousing speech by Bethmann Hollweg to the Reichstag, which would mobilize the German nation in its fight for its existence.[83] Immanuel Kant's universal prescription – the categorical imperative – was now invoked as the basis of national duty to fight for a German peace. The Reichstag did not meet for another month and even then the Chancellor did not use the occasion as a platform to speak to the nation. Instead

Bethmann Hollweg engaged in the prosaic work of setting out the basis for his peace initiative by providing some substance to his conception of a European order.

As the sense of crisis enveloped the German imperial headquarters, the Allies struck a more confident tone. 'There must be no question,' wrote Haig on 17 July, 'of discussing peace conditions. We must dictate peace terms to the Germans.' William Robertson, Chief of the Imperial General Staff, even wondered whether Britain's greatest challenge in making peace would be reining in her Allies and preserving Germany as a great power in the European equilibrium. In this context, the Foreign Office began to work out some ideas for a future peace settlement. The first comprehensive analysis of British war aims was written by Ralph Paget and William Tyrrell.[84] Paget, minister to Belgrade before the war, had been engaged in humanitarian-diplomatic work in Serbia in 1915, before returning to London where he was appointed Assistant Undersecretary at the Foreign Office. Tyrrell had been on sick leave for part of 1915, following the death of his son, Francis, a lieutenant in the Coldstream Guards, and exhaustion from overwork. Though their views did not represent the unified voice of the Foreign Office, let alone the cabinet, Paget and Tyrrell articulated positions and ideas that would recur in subsequent debates.[85] The document was suffused with ideas about the principle of nationality, international law and institutions, and disarmament and the crushing of militarism, ideas that echoed in British (and Allied) war cultures. Indeed, the public declarations of successive British ministers that 'all the States of Europe, great and small, shall in the future be in a position to achieve their national development in freedom and security' provided the starting point for Paget and Tyrrell. Publicly stated aims, vague as they were on details, mattered. These ideas governed the possibilities of the territorial dispensation and the reordering of the international system. Diplomatic proposals and decisions were measured, by friend and foe alike, against a public record. While Paget and Tyrrell acknowledged the importance of secret treaties, such as the Treaty of London with Italy, in instances where these treaties and the principle of nationality conflicted, the general and the British interest were to guide political decisions.

The principle of nationality – including access to the sea in order to provide nation states with commercial freedom – was easier to apply in some instances than others. Paget and Tyrrell proposed the restoration of Belgium and German reparations, though they doubted Germany could pay those reparations in full. As for Alsace-Lorraine, they proposed accepting French demands for its restoration, but any further French annexations required consultations with the inhabitants. Germany would retain Holstein, but Schleswig might be returned to Denmark on the nationality principle. Indeed, the principle of nationality could be used to restrain the more expansive demands of Britain's allies. The future of Poland was an international question and Paget and Tyrrell favoured an independent Polish state. As a buffer between Russia and western Europe, the creation of Poland would serve a broader purpose in the remaking of Europe. An independent Poland, they argued, would 'add to the number of States in the future composition of Europe whose desires and interests will all tend in the direction of establishing the rule of right over the rule of might. In other words we shall assist in creating nations that will be keen in their sympathy, with our desire for a rule of peace, which shall materially decrease the burden of armaments that so heavily hampered the national and economic aspirations of the people of Europe.' That Paget and Tyrrell were mapping political values, as well as ethnic and national boundaries, became evident in their discussion of the possible future of Austria-Hungary and Germany. In one scenario the Habsburg empire would collapse and Austria could be united with Germany. By creating a powerful southern Catholic bloc in Germany, 'the natural play of political forces' would diminish the Prussian 'capacity for evil'. In the Balkans Paget and Tyrrell proposed a Yugoslav state, while stressing the generous treatment of Bulgarian national goals in Macedonia and Thrace, which would further them in Russia. As for the Adriatic, Paget and Tyrrell saw only minimal changes to Italian claims under the Treaty of London, but hoped that Yugoslavia would incorporate northern Albania and the port at Split.

Consolidating the peace settlement, Paget and Tyrrell argued, would require a normative revolution in international politics. 'If the Allies can succeed in substituting for this doctrine [militarism] the principle that brute force is not entitled to override everything,' they wrote, 'that a country possessing the physical means to impose its will, irrespective of right or wrong, is not entitled to do so, but can promote in its stead the doctrine that no community can exist which is based on physical force alone, one of the main objects for which they went to war will be achieved. In other words, one of the essential elements towards securing a reduction of armaments will be the conversion of the German people to these views.' This transformation in the norms that underpinned international relations would require the destruction of the military party in Germany, effectively regime change, disarmament, and the establishment of a League of Nations, incorporating the United States. Paget and Tyrrell recognized that such a peace would be constructed slowly – after all, their vision of peace involved changing political assumptions and codes of behaviour, rather than slicing and dicing territory. International institutions and the commitment of the great powers to uphold the peace provided the context for this transformation. They compared the subordination within states of individual interests to the general interest to the process that might take place in the international order, a process they called 'the development of what we call the civilized condition of things'. There were nevertheless significant absences in the document, with no discussion for example of the future of the Ottoman empire or the colonial settlement, the regions where British war aims were most expansive. Paget and Tyrrell also only hinted at changes to international maritime law and the freedom of the seas.

By no means did Paget and Tyrrell's memorandum represent a unified British foreign policy. Although the Foreign Secretary, Edward Grey, welcomed the document and circulated it to the War Committee, there were fractures in British foreign policy between diplomats, ministers, and soldiers in the late summer and autumn of 1916. Differences over the conduct of the war and the prospect of mediation led to cabinet divisions between September and November over Lloyd George's 'Knock-Out Blow' interview. One of the paradoxes of these divisions was that a liberal peace required the intensification of the war effort, whereas a compromise and more immediate peace was essentially a conservative settlement.

On 28 September Lloyd George had given an interview to Roy Howard, president of the United Press of America. Just over a week previously Lloyd George had been to France and he was well aware of the high casualties British forces had suffered at the Somme. Nonetheless he was concerned that Asquith, Grey, and Reginald McKenna, the Chancellor of the Exchequer, were considering American mediation and a negotiated settlement with Germany. 'He says,' noted the newspaper proprietor George Riddell in his diary after playing golf with Lloyd George at Walton Heath, 'he believes his recent interview was none too soon and that there has been "peace-talk".'[86] In general Lloyd George was much more preoccupied with the management of the war effort than with specific war aims. With the exception of the dismemberment of the Ottoman empire, he tended to speak of war aims in ideological terms, such as the destruction of militarism and the defence of international law.[87] The implication of this, however, was the overthrow of the German constitution. His interview was directed towards Woodrow Wilson, in case the American president might intervene in advance of the closely contested presidential election in November, and towards his fellow cabinet members. In the interview Lloyd George justified the continuation of war to a decisive victory with the vision of lasting peace. The 'inhumanity and pitilessness' of war were necessary to defend 'civilization' against the revival of German militarism. Only then would the sacrifices of Britain's 'citizen army' be rendered worthwhile. And for good measure he cited a French woman, who having lost four of her five sons said 'The fight will never have gone on long enough until it should have made a repetition of this horror impossible.'[88]

Grey censured Lloyd George's intervention in foreign policy, but rows erupted over a month later. In late October Asquith asked the cabinet members to present their war aims. On 13 November Lord Lansdowne, the Conservative predecessor to Grey, suggested that the government consider mediation. His reasoning reflected the pessimistic turn in Allied fortunes over the previous two months. The summer offensives had petered out and Romania now stood on the verge of defeat. British credit and shipping were under immense strain. In these circumstances Lansdowne wondered whether the Allies could win the war and win it quickly to 'enable us to beat our enemy to the ground and impose upon him the kind of terms which we so freely discuss'. Prolonging the war would merely prolong the suffering to no good effect; better, then, to invite mediation. After all, Lansdowne noted, Asquith's and Grey's recent speeches had laid down general principles, concerning adequate reparation for wrongs done and guarantees against future aggression, but 'the outline was so broadly sketched and might be filled up in many different ways'. Lansdowne's brand of Conservative humanitarianism came under attack from Robertson, who, at the prompting of Lloyd George, condemned the 'cranks, cowards, and philosophers' who believed that 'we stand to gain more by losing the war than by winning it'.[89]

The implication of Lansdowne's proposal was that Britain would compromise with Wilhelm II's regime. Yet the ideological dimension to British war aims – the establishment of the rule of law and the crushing of militarism – was incompatible with a compromise peace. On 27 November Lord Robert Cecil, Grey's Undersecretary of State at the Foreign Office, called for the continuation of war. For Cecil, a decisive victory would justify the moral purpose of the war and provide the basis for a new international system, based on the rule of law and international institutions. In October he had drafted 'Proposals for Diminishing the Occasion of Future Wars'.[90] His views were informed by a humanitarian sensibility for the destructiveness of war.

The atrocities against civilians, the genocide of the Armenians, and the starvation of the Syrian population were part of a broader humanitarian catastrophe involving the 'death by torture' and 'maiming or blinding' of hundreds of thousands of young men. This suffering was compounded by the 'anxiety, the grief, and the bereavement' of the families of dead and wounded soldiers. In short the private tragedies of the war were the starting point of Cecil's vision of the future international system. 'It is not too much to say,' he argued, 'that it [the war] has endangered the fabric of our civilization and if it is repeated, the whole European system may probably disappear in anarchy.' Cecil identified militarism as the major threat to a future peace settlement, but he argued that militarism was the result of territorial disputes and domestic unrest. Militarism, therefore, could appear in any country, including Britain, but he believed it was most likely to undermine peace in central and eastern Europe. The peace treaties, he argued, would establish the territorial settlement and the instruments of arbitration and international conference to which any disputes had to be submitted. The signatories to the peace treaty would be required to defend it by imposing economic sanctions and by force of arms. Cecil believed that such international treaties backed by force would create an embryonic regime of international law, which in turn would transform the normative environment in the international system and enable the reduction of armaments, ideas that echoed the arguments of the League to Enforce Peace in the United States.

Eyre Crowe, one of the dominant officials in the Foreign Office, criticized Cecil's proposals. The present war, he claimed, had exposed the thin reed of international treaty law and world opinion in the face of German aggression. Only a preponderance of military power could sustain political order. Moreover, economic sanctions worked too slowly to deter aggression. Yet Crowe did concede that pledges to defend the territorial status quo and the use of conferences would 'promote the feeling that any Powers embarking on war without previously pleading its cause before a parliament of nations commits an offence against the community of States, for which the penalty may be a general combination against the offender'. As Cecil noted, 'I do not claim substantially more than this.' Force and law did not rest at opposite ends of the spectrum; rather the use of force to defend international law would constitute a new departure in international politics.[91]

In Paris, where discussions about French war aims had been prompted by a conversation in August between Grey and Paul Cambon, the French ambassador, the language of power politics was inserted into a conception of the international order that took account of French assertions that civilization, international law, and the principle of nationality were at stake in the war.[92] At a November meeting in Paris of the Comité National d'Etudes Politiques et Sociales, Léon Bourgeois, the French delegate to The Hague conferences, set out his vision of an international system based on the rule of law in a debate with Henri Bergson. Bourgeois argued that it was unrealistic to believe that German politics would immediately drop its infatuation with military force. Instead the Allies would have to establish an international system, in which law was upheld by military force. This would constitute a civilizing environment, in the same way as the justice system rendered violence between two individuals unacceptable. 'It is necessary,' Bourgeois told his audience, 'that the mental evolution of nations is raised bit by bit to the higher level, on which we believe we are placed. But I think this evolution will be slow. In the case of Germany, it will be very slow and if one does not help this evolution, it will not occur within any useful timeframe.' Moreover, he pointed out that French credibility in the international system would be undermined if, at the moment of victory, policy turned away from the declared purpose of promoting law and justice towards the use of unrestrained military power. Bourgeois, therefore, saw international law as a means of preserving the alliance, drawing in powerful neutrals, notably the United States, and gradually creating a new environment in which arbitration became the dominant mode of international politics.[93]

On the other hand, territorial expansion and the break-up of Germany offered a path to French security. The return of Alsace-Lorraine was taken as a given by French policymakers. French politicians argued that the violent annexation of Alsace and Lorraine over four decades ago disqualified the immigrant German population from any say in the dispensation of the provinces. Claims to the Rhineland were much more contentious, but publicists and some diplomats made valiant efforts to assert French rights on the grounds of historical relations and notions of a shared civilization. Conventional understandings of the principle of nationality confronted arguments that Napoleon had modernized the Rhineland, only for the transfer of the region to Prussia in 1815 to prompt a wave of repressive brutality that cut the Rhineland off from its natural place in western European civilization.[94] The tortuous justification of French claims to the Rhineland demonstrated the pervasive importance of the principle of nationality – and the ways in which that principle might be manipulated.

These different visions of French security – one based on international institutions and law, the other on expansive territorial claims – were trotted out at a lunch at the Elysée Palace on 7 October to discuss French war aims and security. It was attended by the President Poincaré, the prime minister Briand, the erstwhile premier and now cabinet minister Charles Freycinet, Bourgeois, Deschanel, the president of the Chamber of Deputies, and Antonin Dubost, president of the French Senate. The meeting did not reach any clear conclusions. Instead Briand instructed the French ambassadors and brothers Jules and Paul Cambon to prepare a document. Both the annexationist and legalist vision of the international order remained options in French foreign policy.

However, by the time French leaders gathered at the Elysée Palace in October the initiative lay with Berlin. The shock of Romania's entry into the war was soon reversed by German and Bulgarian military successes in September 1916. By 6 December German forces under Falkenhayn entered the capital Bucharest. The remaining Romanian forces were forced into Moldova, from where they offered nominal resistance.[95] For the Allies the reversal of fortune was a shock. 'This Rumania business is horrible,' wrote C. P. Scott, editor of the *Manchester Guardian*, to the former Liberal minister Charles Hobhouse on 25 November, 'the fourth little state to go down in dust on our side and no finger raised to help. . . . The crass stupidity of the military chiefs and incompetence of the Government are enough to make one despair.'[96] The Allies, the self-proclaimed protectors of small nations, did not have the power to demonstrate their credibility. Indeed, Allied actions in Greece since 1915 had undermined these claims, while the suppression of the Easter Rising in Ireland in 1916 further tarnished British claims in the international public sphere.

Bethmann Hollweg had the opportunity to present Germany as the shield of small nations in Europe. Having driven Russian forces from Congress Poland in summer 1915, the Central Powers had the initiative in the Polish crucible of European politics. 'To deny the international meaning of the Polish question,' Sergei Sazonov warned Nicholas II, 'would be to close one's eyes to reality.' The Foreign Minister still harboured hopes in 1916 that Russia could make a bold declaration in favour of Polish unity. This would ease Russia's relations with the western Allies, go some way towards improving relations with Poland, and enable Russia to shape the territorial settlement in eastern Europe. Supported by generals Alekseev and Brusilov, Sazonov had convinced the Tsar by mid-July to issue a manifesto to the Polish nation. Within weeks he had been dismissed, brought down by Boris Stürmer, Prime Minister since January 1916, and Grigori Rasputin, the self-proclaimed holy man, who urged Nicholas II to recover his autocratic nerve and drop the proposed manifesto.[97] The conservative turn in Russian politics and the reluctance of the western Allies to press for a resolution of the Polish question ensured that the Central Powers controlled that agenda. For over a year German and Austro-Hungarian leaders had wrestled with the complexity of the Polish question, a nation divided between three empires. The resolution of the Polish question had implications for the domestic balance in both states, their future relations with Russia, and the remaking of the European states system. Moreover, winning Polish affections would contribute to the remobilization of the Central Powers, if Bethmann Hollweg's peace initiative failed.

The resolution of the Polish question fitted into the Chancellor's peace initiative in three ways. First, the public declaration of support for a Polish state marked the end of any aspiration to a compromise peace with Russia. On 2 October, after having received indications that the new Russian Minister of the Interior, Alexander Protopopov, was interested in a separate peace, Bethmann Hollweg and Wilhelm II agreed to postpone any declaration. By early November these faint hopes had evaporated. On 3 November Müller noted in his diary that the Central Powers would issue the Polish proclamation in a matter of days 'since Russia has no inclination to make a separate peace'.[98]

Second, Bethmann Hollweg presented the solution of the Polish question as part of a wider reordering of Europe. The presentation of German policy and its overarching conception were important in the autumn of 1916. The declaration represented a break with older Prussian conceptions of the political order in eastern Europe, fastened together by dynastic co-operation, towards one shaped by the principle of nationality and autonomy for smaller nations. This served Germany's national interest. Surrounded by weaker states, it would become a 'central point of crystallization, which would lead to a united states of Europe', in Riezler's heady formulation.[99] Read in this light, the Chancellor's policy in eastern Europe rejected the nationalist ambitions of the radical right and presented Germany as the champion of European culture. This conception drew on a strand in German war cultures, which emphasized its European mission rather than a purely national one. 'Any policy, which is Realpolitik,' Max Weber argued in October, 'on the eastern side of our border is inevitably west Slavic policy, not German nationalist policy.' In other words, German security was enhanced by cooperation with the Polish nation, for Weber saw Poland as a buffer against the Russian threat to territorial integrity and culture. He concluded that Germany should present itself as 'the liberator of small nations, even if we do not wish to be'. Taking a global view, Weber mocked the Allied claims to be the defenders of small nations by pointing to British, French, and Russian oppression of nations in Egypt, Morocco, India, South Africa, Indochina, Tunisia, Ireland, Poland, the Ukraine, and the Baltics.[100] Bethmann Hollweg shared this belief that Germany had a European mission. The notion of Europe – as a common political space and set of values – was certainly adopted by statesmen to cover narrower interests, but the pervasive use of the concept of Europe underlined its continuing appeal and political relevance. The Chancellor believed that the Allies were responsible for the 'self-destruction' and 'the bleeding white' of Europe, in a war that would benefit the United States and the 'yellow races'.[101]

The meeting between the German and Austro-Hungarian military and political leadership at Pless between 16 and 18 October further clarified the relationship between the Polish proclamation and the peace initiative. At this meeting the two governments agreed how the Polish state would be organized. Both occupying powers would introduce similar administrative practices and laws, with a view to uniting the two occupied areas in the future. Germany would control the organization of the Polish Army. In addition, Burián, the Habsburg Foreign Minister, proposed peace conditions, which Bethmann Hollweg accepted for the most part, though both men expected these conditions to be modified in the course of any peace negotiations. Strategic considerations were clearly central to the proposed conditions. Whereas in 1915 Bethmann Hollweg had opposed plans for Germany to annex Lithuania and Kurland from Russia, he now supported this proposal. These provinces, with Poland, would provide a large buffer zone between Germany and Russia. Serbia would be reduced to a rump state, as Austria-Hungary proposed annexing Belgrade, while Bulgaria would retain its zone of occupation. Other territorial proposals were more limited, including minor changes on the border between Italy and Austria-Hungary, the exchange between Germany and France of parts of Alsace-Lorraine for Briey, and the securing of German guarantees in Belgium. Additionally, commercial freedoms would be restored, the freedom of the seas secured, and the capitulations – the one-sided commercial treaties between European powers and the Ottoman empire – abolished.[102]

At the centre of these conditions stood the recognition of the kingdom of Poland. On 5 November General von Beseler issued the proclamation, which promised that the Central Powers would create an independent (*selbständig*) Polish state, under a constitutional hereditary monarch, at the end of the war.[103] This left open the future constitutional relationship between the Polish state and the Central Powers, with the possibility that Poland might become part of a restructured Habsburg monarchy. In April 1916 Burián had warned Austria-Hungary that it 'must either lose Galicia or bring Congress Poland into some sort of close connection with the monarchy'.[104] The proclamation led to an intense debate in political salons and journals in Austria, in which a bewildering variety of territorial proposals were spun out. The common assumption, however, was that Galicia would be united or integrated in some form with the new Polish state. This could either destroy Austria-Hungary or, as the Austrian businessman Julius Meinl and others hoped, offer an opportunity for the Habsburg monarchy to reinvent itself in a war for the principle of nationality. Poland's future, as debated in these political circles, transformed the Allied claims to defend the freedoms of small nations into a political credo for the Central Powers and the Habsburg monarchy in particular.[105]

The reaction to the Polish proclamation by Prussian conservatives – ministers such as Friedrich Wilhelm von Loebell, the Minister of the Interior, and party politicians such as Kuno von Westarp – was begrudging, shaped by the belief in an historical conflict between Germans and Poles. Perhaps most significantly many Poles were sceptical about the value of the proclamation, bereft as it was of constitutional details. At the town hall in Warzaw local dignitaries cried out 'Posen lives', a reference to the Prussian province, which would not be part of a future Polish state, despite Poles constituting the majority of the population. For the most part the new Polish Army did not inspire the Polish population. All Polish parties agreed, according to Beseler, that Poles would only spill their blood for a Polish government.[106]

Two days after the Polish proclamation, Americans went to the polls. In the late summer Wilson had been confident of victory over his Republican challenger, the former governor of New York, Charles Hughes. After Hughes's opening campaign speech fell flat, Wilson told Bernard Baruch, one of the few businessmen with whom he enjoyed a good relationship, that he made it a 'rule never to murder a man, who is committing suicide'.[107] However, the election was closely contested and foreign policy issues, including tariffs and Wilson's policy in Mexico, were at the fore in the debate. Having recognized the Carranza government in October 1915, Wilson looked forward to the stabilization of Mexican politics. The upheavals of the revolution were not calmed so easily, as peasant bandit groups remained mobilized. One of these, led by Pancho Villa, attacked the town of Columbus in New Mexico on 9 March 1916. Six days later Wilson ordered General Pershing to pursue Pancho Villa across the Mexican border. As Pershing followed Villa 350 miles inside Mexican territory, Carranza protested against the American intervention and Latin American states saw it as further proof of heavy-handed American dominance in the western hemisphere. Within domestic American politics, Wilson's decision alienated pacifistic progressives, such as the American Union against Militarism. On the other hand Hughes invoked Wilson's vacillations over Mexico to charge him with failing to protect American interests and honour.[108] Republicans also charged Wilson with undermining American economic interests by lowering tariffs. Economic prosperity, they claimed, was the result of war, after which Europeans would put their experience of economic planning to use and regain markets around the world from American firms.

'It is a great disappointment,' wrote the journalist Arthur Bullard to Colonel Edward House, Wilson's closest advisor, on 8 November, having read in his local paper that Wilson had been defeated by Hughes.[109] His anxiety was soon allayed, but Wilson had won by one of the narrowest margins in American history. In California he won by 3,806 votes out of 1 million – Hughes's defeat there was popularly ascribed to an unintentional snub he had given to the governor and now senator-elect, Hiram Johnson. In a close election, European diplomats feared that Wilson might intervene to pose as peacemaker in order to win important political and ethnic constituencies. Wilson kept his counsel, but nonetheless he refined his view of the international order during the year, most notably in his speech in May 1916 to the League to Enforce Peace, led by his Republican predecessor, William Taft. Wilson developed three related ideas. First, Americans 'are participants, whether we would or not, in the life of the world. The interests of all nations are our own also.' Second, military power was essential if the United States wished not only to defend itself but to play a role in constructing a new world order. Finally, he articulated the basis of that new world order, in which 'every state has the right to choose the sovereignty under which they shall live'; states, large and small, had equal rights to sovereignty and territorial integrity, and the United States was 'willing to become a partner in any feasible associations of nations formed in order to realise these objects and make them secure against violation'.[110] Although the details of Wilson's policies remained vague, his commitment to international organization after the war was appealing to League of Nations advocates in Britain and France.

By early December, Wilson had begun work on a note to the belligerents. Before he could dispatch it, however, Bethmann Hollweg had sent his own peace note to the leading neutral states, who were asked to forward it to the Allies. On the same day, 12 December, he spoke to the Reichstag. He was committed to exploring the possibility of a compromise peace. He doubted that German forces could win a decisive military victory, while he was continually reminded of deteriorating conditions in the Habsburg empire. Franz Joseph had died on 22 November and the new emperor, Karl I, sought ways to end the war and his empire's dependency on Germany. In early December, Bethmann Hollweg returned to the perennial theme of the limits of German military power. Although the results of the Polish proclamation had been disappointing, the Chancellor continued to believe that central European political order, based on constitutional reforms, could be secured. Military power, he contended, would only bring about short-term solutions.[111] In addition, Bethmann Hollweg had spent the autumn fending off demands from the admiralty, the Pan-German League, and others to launch unrestricted submarine warfare, which, he feared, would bring the United States into the war, hastening Germany's defeat. Although Germany's military position had improved between August and December, the Chancellor wanted to exploit these military successes in support of his peace initiative.

The chances of success were limited, particularly since the fall of Asquith and the ascent of Lloyd George as prime minister on 7 December, just days before Bethmann Hollweg spoke in the Reichstag. Even if the peace initiative were rejected in the short term, he hoped that it would have longer-term consequences, either by undermining the will to continue the armed struggle, especially in France and Italy, or by starting an exchange of notes. In the absence of a peace settlement, Allied rejection would serve the domestic political purpose of convincing the German people that they were fighting a defensive war, prolonged by the Allied ambition to destroy Germany's existence.[112]

The note and speech captured this kaleidoscope of options. The internal shifts from humanitarianism to hubris were jarring, a reflection of the competing strains in German high politics. 'This catastrophe,' the note began, 'which the bond of a common millennia-old civilization cannot restrain, strikes humanity in its worthiest achievements. It threatens to leave in ruins the spiritual and material progress, which was the pride of Europe at the beginning of the twentieth century.' Then the note asserted that the Central Powers had proven themselves invincible. 'Prepared for war, but ready for peace,' Germany invited the Allies to submit their peace conditions. Bethmann Hollweg had decided against including his conditions, fearing that it would reveal the German and Austro-Hungarian negotiating hand to the Allies and that it would infuriate nationalists. Should the Allies reject this proposal, the Chancellor argued they would be responsible for the continuation of the struggle, a weak attempt to provoke a second war guilt debate to match the moral intensity of the debate about the responsibility for the origins of the conflict.[113]

While the Allied governments were digesting Bethmann Hollweg's peace initiative, they received a note on 18 December from Wilson, asking that each belligerent state their terms. He observed that the publicly declared aims of both sides were 'virtually the same' – the rights of small states, the development and security of the great powers, and the willingness to consider the formation of a League of Nations. House was aghast, noting 'that one sentence will enrage them [the Allies]'.[114] Wilson's observation was not as outrageous as it seemed to House and others at the time. Even in private discussions, the moderate aims of the belligerents offered scope for negotiation. Their public declarations, as Wilson noted, espoused remarkably similar principles. The president wasn't naive. His note was the product of fear that the United States might get dragged into the war, disgust at the humanitarian catastrophe, and an understandable eye on his historical reputation as a peacemaker. The note steered clear of any grand exposition of a post-war order, concentrating instead on the immediate task of bringing an end to the conflict.

Writing to her husband Georges on 23 December, Blanche Duhamel asked him what he thought of Wilson's message. She hoped the Allies would accept the proposal, but 'I pass between the alternatives of hope and despair.'[115] What Wilson neglected, however, was the deep sense of a moral chasm between the two belligerents, one that began at the outbreak of war and had widened through atrocities, submarine campaigns, naval blockades, and brutal occupation measures. The conduct of the conflict had produced its own war cultures, in which each side claimed to fight for universal values and denounced their opponents as the embodiment of evil. These war cultures shaped the Allied response to Bethmann Hollweg's peace initiative and Wilson's note. Even as the Chancellor prepared his peace initiative, the deportation of workers from occupied France and Belgium underlined, from the Allied perspective, the moral stakes of the war. Schoolchildren in the Parisian district of Montmartre drew pictures of Belgian children being forced to work for the German war effort, while *Le Figaro* condemned the 'monstrous razzias of slaves in the Nord' as further affirmation of the organized, scientific barbarism of the German state.[116]

Infused with the civilizing mission, British and French war cultures could not accommodate any compromise with Germany. They were fighting a war for peace against militarism, an idea etched into the fabric of the imperial German state.

This language shaped and seeped into the Allied response, drafted primarily by British and French politicians in late December 1916. They considered the German note a trap. 'Germany was selling at the top of her market,' according to Lloyd George. Paul Cambon thought Bethmann Hollweg's note was designed to exploit victory in Romania and political turmoil in Britain and Russia by sowing division among the Allies. Nonetheless he recognized the importance of framing the response in such a way that undermined German credibility.[117] Allied diplomats had considered simply ignoring the German note, but this was a war conducted in the public sphere and reliant on popular support.[118] The second significant decision taken was that France would lead the diplomacy of the response to the German note. Britain's relations with the United States had been strained throughout 1916 due to the executions of Irish nationalist leaders after the Easter Rising, the consequences of the imposition of the blockade policy for American commerce, and Lloyd George's belligerent interview, the 'Knock-Out Blow'.[119]

Aristide Briand set about drafting a response to the German and American notes. His draft was a statement of the moral stakes of the war. Germany and Austria-Hungary had purposefully prepared for this war for years, had committed atrocities and violated international law, and now prostituted the language of peace in a note, as a 'manoeuvre de guerre'. After condemning Bethmann Hollweg's failure to state specific terms, the French prime minister summarized Allied goals in language familiar from public declarations: 'They [the Allied governments] affirm once again that having been odiously attacked, they will pursue this struggle until reparations for the violations of law and liberty, the retaking of all their invaded territory, the free existence of small nations in a pacific, organized, and guaranteed equilibrium, and of a Europe shielded from the brutal lusts of Prussian militarism is assured.'[120] Briand's draft reply to Wilson's note acknowledged the importance of a League of Nations, but claimed that a premature peace would fail to prevent a recurrence of war. He disputed Wilson's moral equivalence between the two belligerents, citing German violations of international law from the moment of the invasion of Belgium to the policy of occupation.[121] Briand's note was deliberately polemical, but Francis Bertie, the British ambassador to Paris, believed that it could embarrass the Allies, who had their own expansionist ambitions, while the Italian Foreign

Minister Sidney Sonnino complained that it focused too much on French suffering and made no mention of the principle of nationality.[122]

Striking the right tone was proving difficult. Philippe Berthelot, the leading official in the Ministry of Foreign Affairs, the socialist Albert Thomas, and Alexandre Ribot, Minister of Finance, shuffled across the Channel for a conference at 10 Downing Street on 26 December with Lloyd George, George Curzon, and Robert Cecil. Rejecting immediate peace while claiming to fight for an enduring peace was an awkward circle to square. The participants were aware of the connections between their diplomatic reply and popular support for the war. Thomas connected what he called 'the domain of ideology', that is the 'principle of nationalities', with the restitution of invaded territories. 'We must remember,' he advised, 'that as soon as we have finished exchanging these notes, it will be necessary to motivate nations and armies once again for the struggle. With these great ideas, we can do it.'[123] Lloyd George viewed the response as an address to the American people. Each ally – Belgium, France, Serbia (he omitted Russia) – could speak to the American public and government on a different basis. Arthur Balfour, now Foreign Secretary, invoked the vision of an enduring peace as a justification for continuing the war and destroying the hopes of the aggressor. Instead of setting out territorial conditions, the conference members agreed to stress 'principles' in their reply. This amounted to a remobilization of Allied energies for the war effort. 'I wish it would finish,' Blanche Duhamel wrote to her husband at the front on 28 December. 'Your letters are good, but I know little about you. Can we never fill this emptiness? This evening I heard some sinister news [referring to the Allies' rejection of mediation]. I expect it will be confirmed. Bad news is often confirmed.'[124]

The Allied response to the German note, on 30 December, reiterated their moral interpretation of the war. Their analysis tied past, present, and future in a grand synthesis. Germany and Austria-Hungary bore responsibility for the war. They had violated treaties and agreements and blocked disarmament on the grounds that 'necessity knows no law', a doctrine that constituted an enduring threat to peace and civilization in Europe. They now had embarked on a 'new series of crimes' in occupied territories and on the high seas. A repetition of this war could only be prevented once the Allies had won 'effective guarantees for the future security of the world' as well as the principles of nationalities, international law, and the sovereign rights of small states.[125] The Anglo-French response to the American note, on 10 January 1917, went further, enumerating some of the territorial claims of the Allies. These included the restoration and indemnification of Belgium, Serbia, and Montenegro; the evacuation of Romanian, Russian, and French-occupied territory; the return of Alsace-Lorraine to France; the liberation of Slavs, Romanians, Czechs, Slovaks, and Italians from 'foreign domination'; and the expulsion from Europe of the Ottoman empire, considered inimical to 'western civilization'. In addition, the response noted the Tsar's declaration to Poland. Finally, and crucially, the Triple Entente claimed that while they aimed to liberate Europe from the 'brutal covetousness of Prussian militarism', they did not seek the 'extermination of the German peoples and their political disappearance'.[126]

Admiral von Müller was not surprised that the Allies had rejected Bethmann Hollweg's peace initiative, but the text was 'even more impertinent than we expected'. Wilhelm II was 'amazed at the harshness of the tone'. Riezler described the reply as 'coarse, but not out of strength'.[127] Visions of peace were at the core of international politics in late 1916, but mediated through national and allied war cultures the diplomatic exchanges and public representations of policy revealed a moral chasm between the Central Powers and the Allies. Those, such as the Duhamels, who were exhausted by the war, wanted peace to relieve the humanitarian catastrophe of the conflict and to restore the more prosaic but fundamental bonds of society, for example those of family. Perhaps the conservative statesmen, such as Bethmann Hollweg and Lord Lansdowne, had more insight into this dimension of the war experience than their opponents, be they radical militarists or liberal internationalists. Notions of peace veered between the concrete, such as the international regulation of the working day, and the abstract, such as international law. Belligerent societies now remobilized to fight for the great abstractions of peace.

CHAPTER 6

GREAT MOVEMENTS FOR PEACE, 1917

IN THE latrines, trenches, and on the walls of buildings in German positions in Flanders, graffiti expressed soldiers' desire for peace. The General Commander of the Marine Corps had been concerned that the peace initiative would legitimize these hopes, but now that the Allies had so 'brusquely' rejected Bethmann Hollweg's initiative, he no longer tolerated any talk of peace – by which he meant a compromise peace. 'War to the end and unconditional victory as the aim,' he told his men, 'are the solution. Only our complete victory can lead to the German peace. The simple logic should be clear to every man.'[1] The Allied response to the German Chancellor's peace initiative and Woodrow Wilson's note amounted to more than a diplomatic rejection. It was also a presentation of the moral purpose of the war, in which the continuation of the struggle for a particular vision of future peace was the basis for the remobilization of civilian populations and armies. The governments of the Central Powers also set out to remobilize their populations. From the outset the Central Powers had claimed it was a war of defence and this theme was underlined in Wilhelm II's appeal to his soldiers on 5 January 1917: 'In justified fury at the enemy's presumptuous sinfulness, with the will to defend our sacred possessions and secure for the Fatherland a happy future, you will become steel.'[2] Visions of peace remained at the centre of war cultures in 1917, shaping the revolutions in Russia between March and November, the entry of the United States into the war in April, the peace debates and initiatives in the summer of 1917, and the remobilization of war-weary belligerent societies.

* * *

The revolution in Russia in March 1917 was both an act of remobilization for war and, simultaneously, the act of a war-weary society desiring peace. This paradox was partly the result of the different voices and strands within the revolution, but it also reflected the uncertain place of the Russian state and nation in the international order.

Since September 1915 Nicholas II had commanded the Russian armies, but he failed to remobilize the Russian nation in support of his romantic, historical vision of the war's purpose. Of course, the Tsar still inspired loyalty in some important institutions, such as the court and parts of the officer corps.[3] However, his bases of support at court and in the army were detrimental to his position in the nation. Defeats in 1915 had been ascribed to treacherous elements at court and in the upper echelons of the army. Rumours continued to mill around the Tsar's coterie in 1916. These were corrosive, not least because it was difficult, if not impossible, to argue against conspiracy theories that provided neat explanations of military disasters. In April 1916 General Sukhliminov, the former Minister of War, was arrested on suspicion of treason. Six months later he was released, following the intercession of Empress Alexandra and Rasputin, who was sleeping with Sukhliminov's wife. The public reaction was one of fury. Sukhliminov's release appeared to confirm the suspicions that German spies and sympathizers were destroying the Russian war effort from the highest stations in the land.[4] At the very least Nicholas II appeared weak and susceptible to foreign influences.

The mismanagement of the war effort, both the real and the imagined failings of the Tsarist regime, provided the context for attacks in the Duma by the Progressive Bloc in November 1916. Critics demanded the reform of the Russian state in order to channel national energies into the war effort. Paul Miliukov wanted constitutional change within the Tsarist system, rather than its overthrow. The appointment of conservative nonentities, such as Boris Stürmer, demonstrated the failure of the state's capacity to reform itself. In his speech to the Duma on 14 November, Miliukov asked whether the failings of the regime were due to 'treason or stupidity'. Citing the 'shameful delay in the Polish question' and the failure to mobilize national support for the war, Miliukov suggested that stupidity explained the inept conduct of the war. However, his reference to treason resonated in the febrile atmosphere in Petrograd in late 1916. Two days later Vasili Maklakov, a conservative reformer, offered an insightful analysis of the failure of the Tsarist regime. Given the stable military situation and the gathering exhaustion of the Central Powers, the pervasive anxiety reflected the loss of confidence in the Tsarist regime, not the material position of the Russian empire. A year previously Maklakov had compared the regime to a 'crazy driver' and the Russian people to a passenger, who faced the choice of doing nothing and hoping the journey would end safely or trying to grab hold of the steering wheel, but risk careering off the road. 'The old regime and the interests of Russia,' he now told the Duma in November 1916, 'have now separated, and before every member there stands a dilemma: if he is chosen, will he serve Russia or the regime, for serving both is as impossible as serving Mammon and God.' Maklakov, a friend of Leo Tolstoy and the brother of the former conservative Interior Minister, Nikolai Maklakov, was a thoughtful critic of the Tsarist regime, but by late 1916 he was close to those willing to overthrow the Tsar. Fearful that revolution would lead to mob rule, he and others now believed that a palace coup or elite revolution was necessary to prevent popular unrest. 'The Emperor will not change,' a leading officer told Bruce Lockhart, the British consul. 'We shall have to change the Emperor.'[5]

These criticisms of the Tsar were repeated in towns and villages across Russia. 'What kind of sovereign is this,' one peasant asked, 'while there's war, he only goes around to clubs, he is not master in his home, he's absolutely stupid.'[6] The homespun wisdom made this critique, with its veiled references to Rasputin's malign influence and the Tsarina's alleged infidelities, devastating. Peasant, soldier, and worker experienced the failure of the regime in material ways that escaped some members of the Duma and court elite. The popular revolt against the regime owed much to war-weariness. Soldiers and peasants expressed increasing anger at the military draft, which upset conventional notions of the moral economy. Soldiers' wives bridled at the exemption of railway officials from military service, while others turned on the families of soldiers, jealous of their receipt of state support. One man even accused the three sons of a neighbour of lying in a trench, waiting to receive German money![7] The state's control of food supplies undermined the legitimacy of the regime. In August 1916 the Special Food Council decided to imitate the German model of state monopoly control of grain supplies on the grounds that the 'war has advanced the social life of the state as the dominant principle, to which all other manifestations of social life must be subordinated.'[8] Normal supply chains were destroyed by state intervention, local hoarding, and choked transport systems. By the summer of 1916 there were increasing numbers of subsistence riots in urban centres. Women, struggling to find food for their families, were at the fore of these protests. The state had failed to uphold its side of the bargain. In November

1916 the governor of Moscow reported that soldiers' wives complained 'they are slaughtering our husbands and sons at the front, while at home they want to do us in with hunger'.[9]

From the beginning of 1917 there was a wave of strikes, concentrated in Petrograd. On 7 March 30,000 workers were locked out of the Putilov armaments plant in the city. The following day, International Women's Day, women gathered in the Vyborg working-class district to protest against high bread prices. They marched past Finland Station towards Nevsky Prospect, by which time the strikers numbered 100,000. 'Down with the war! Down with the high cost of living! Down with hunger! Bread for the workers!', they cried as they marched through the city. The protesters connected their experience of war with much broader political claims. Although the crux of their complaints was the food supply crisis, this material experience of war had political implications, including the overthrow of the Tsarist regime and an end to the war. It was possible, in theory, that the food supply system could be reformed, but the strikers knew the Tsarist regime could no longer reform itself.

On 8 and 9 March the strikes continued. The army proved ineffective at restoring order, and the soldiers unwilling. Coming out of a bank on 9 March, Sergey Prokofiev was surprised to see crowds on Nevsky Prospect. Cossack soldiers would occasionally charge at the crowd, but in general they treated the people 'as gently as they could'.[10] Many of the soldiers in Petrograd were from the region. In some cases they knew the protesters. Women pleaded with them that they had husbands at the front. There was some empathy between the crowds and the soldiers, based on shared experiences of war, though on 11 March soldiers killed hundreds of protesters. That evening the NCOs of the Volynsky Guard Regiment, who had fired on the crowd earlier that day, decided that they would refuse to carry out further orders and they shot their commanding officer, Captain Lashkevich. By 12 March the soldiers had turned on the regime. Crowds targeted state officials. Prokofiev recorded a group ransacking the apartment of a police chief, throwing furniture out of the window: 'The crowd bayed with unholy glee. "Bloodsucker! That's our blood he's been drinking!" '[11]

Plans for palace coups were now redundant, as popular protests overwhelmed Nicholas II's regime. The revolution in March created two distinct problems. First, it destroyed one source of political authority, but it failed to establish a single new source. Members of the Duma gathered at the Tauride Palace in Petrograd on 11 and 12 March, where they decided to establish a Temporary Committee of State to restore order. This was essentially a

Provisional Government. Miliukov became Foreign Minister. Prince Lvov was nominated as prime minister at the suggestion of Miliukov, who later confessed that he only knew him superficially and came to view him as a 'wet rag'. However, the Provisional Government accepted the establishment of the Petrograd Soviet as an alternative source of authority. The Soviet, not yet a bastion of Bolshevik power, was headed by Nikolai Chkheidze, with Matvey Skobolev and Alexander Kerensky, both members of the Duma, acting as the vice-chairmen. For liberals, such as Miliukov, establishing a single legitimate source of authority was of supreme importance. Without it the revolutionary state was prone to crisis. One final source of authority was the army. The General Staff officers, who considered themselves representatives of the Russian nation, had approved to a man of the abdication of Nicholas II. However, the very first order of the Petrograd Soviet – Order No. 1 – allowed soldiers to elect councils in their units. This undermined the power of the officer corps, hindered the army from acting as a single institution in domestic politics, and limited its use as an instrument of foreign policy.[12]

The revolution was immediately dramatized by contemporaries as an epochal moment, on to which they could project their aspirations for a better world. Peasants in the Orlov district of Viatka, on hearing that Nicholas II had abdicated, sang the Marseillaise. Lvov, speaking in early May, merged the national and universal missions of the revolution:

> The freedom embodied in the Russian revolution is permeated by elements of a global, universal character. Its ideas, sprung from the tiny seeds of freedom and equality sown on our rich dark soil a half century ago, embraces not only the interests of the Russian people, but the interests of all peoples throughout the world. The soul of the Russian people has turned out to be, in its very essence, the soul of world democracy. It is prepared not only to merge with democracy around the world but to stand its vanguard and to guide it along the road leading to the development of humanity on the great principles of liberty, equality, and fraternity.[13]

The British pacifist Bertrand Russell argued that the revolution inspired hopes for a 'better Europe', as the overthrow of Tsarist despotism removed the justification for other autocracies and for militarism.[14] A postal censor in France concluded, in sharp contrast to Russell, that the 'dominant note is one of joy to see our ally freed from German influence and hence able to be fully devoted to the war'.[15] It was between these two poles – pacifism and hopes for Russian remobilization – that revolutionaries had to carve out their place in the world.

While the first order of the Petrograd Soviet weakened the army, one of the first proclamations of the Provisional Government promised to fight the war to a 'victorious conclusion'. Herein lay the second problem of the March revolution: the divisions over revolutionary Russia's place in the world. The first major crisis of the Provisional Government, principally between the Foreign Minister, Miliukov, and the Petrograd Soviet, arose over foreign policy. This reflected the different purposes of the revolution – one that sought to improve living conditions, even at the price of a compromise peace, and one that sought to remobilize Russian society to fight alongside France and Britain. Miliukov, both a liberal and a nationalist, recast Russia's war aims. He sought to reconcile the principle of nationality with Russian security. For example, the Manifesto of Finland restored the constitution of Finland and guaranteed its 'domestic independence', while retaining control over foreign and military policy. Miliukov proposed that the Polish question, the central geopolitical and ideological issue in the war in eastern Europe, be resolved by giving Poles the 'full right to define their own destiny by their own free will'. An independent Polish state would ensure a 'durable peace in the New Europe'. Yet this state would join Russia 'in a free military alliance', acting as 'a firm bulwark against the pressures of the Central Powers upon the Slavic world'.[16] Miliukov, long an advocate of rights for nationalities within the Russian empire, believed that giving Poles greater liberty would secure their support for the Russian war effort. His policies also had to adapt to realities on the ground: on 17 March, Ukrainian nationalists, of different political hues, set up the Rada, or council, a step towards claiming autonomy.[17] The Tsarist regime's failure to resolve the Polish question had frustrated their allies, perturbed liberals, and given Germany and Austria-Hungary an opportunity to represent themselves as defenders of small nations. Miliukov adopted a programme that accommodated Russian security within a new European order, based on the principle of nationality.

Miliukov made clear to Allied representatives that the new Russian regime would adhere to its treaty commitments and war aims, notably the annexation of Constantinople. Although he denied that Russia was fighting a war of expansion, his use of terms such as 'guarantees and sanctions' alarmed socialists in the Soviet. The Petrograd Soviet developed an alternative view of the international system that became increasingly influential during 1917. This was partly due to some rhetorical similarities with Woodrow Wilson's call on 22 January for peace without victory. On 2 April

Irakli Tsereteli, a Georgian Menshevik who had been in exile in Siberia, returned to Petrograd, where the Soviet was engaged in a debate on ending the war. Tsereteli offered a solution, which became known as 'revolutionary defencism'. The Soviet should call for a 'peace without annexations or indemnities', based on the self-determination of peoples. In addition, it could appeal to international socialism to end the war, while defending Russia and its precious revolution from German imperialists.[18] The deceptive simplicity of the phrase 'peace without annexations or indemnities' resonated amongst the war-weary population. Tsereteli's doctrine of revolutionary defencism opened up the war aims debate in Russia and around Europe.

The politics of reconciling Miliukov's and Tsereteli's foreign policy doctrines led to the first major crisis in the revolution. Tsereteli wanted a joint appeal, supported by the Provisional Government as well as the Soviet, to European peoples. He also believed that the army would only continue to fight in an explicitly defensive war. At a joint meeting Miliukov objected to the proposed appeal, but he was overruled by his fellow cabinet members, including Kerensky and Lvov. Miliukov then delayed the declaration for a month and when he issued it, appended a note that stressed Russia's commitment to its treaty obligations and the importance of 'guarantees and sanctions' for any durable peace. Albert Thomas, the French socialist, had proposed this last phrase, but it was read, correctly, as a code for annexations.[19]

Miliukov now became the focus of protests and demonstration. One soldier bitterly claimed that if Miliukov, General Brusilov, and others wanted to fight a war in Britain's interest, they should fight it themselves: 'Regiments 753 and 756 aren't going to take their dear comrades' places in the trenches because the blood is ours and the money is ours, but the words are yours [Miliukov's]. Give us peace. A soldier's word is true. Whoever wants war should go into the trenches and fight for the good of England, but we don't need anyone else's good, we've got enough of our own.'[20] As Tsereteli suspected, the majority of soldiers, workers, and peasants supported a defensive war, defined by the absence of annexations and indemnities. Popular petitions demonstrated a readiness to defend Russia and the revolution against German aggression. The revolution, born out of a spontaneous strike, was now conceived as a means of ending war and re-establishing peace. Popular notions of peace did not extend to nebulous 'guarantees and sanctions'. In many ways peace was defined by the experience of war. Peace meant food, family, and work. 'We are also extending our hand to women and mothers the world over,' declared the Smolensk

Initiative Group of Women and Mothers in May, after Miliukov's ill-judged declaration. 'We are deeply convinced that our extended hand will meet the extended hands of mothers the world over. No annexations or indemnities can compensate a mother for a murdered son.'[21] Empathy, rooted in the wartime experience, provided a register for discussing peace.

Miliukov resigned as Foreign Minister in mid-May, which effectively marked the end of Russia's willingness to fight anything other than a war to defend the revolution. The revolution led other belligerents to modify and adapt their war aims and views of the international order. The new French premier, Alexandre Ribot, quickly accepted that a deal struck only in February giving France a free hand in western Europe and Russia a free hand in eastern Europe was void. Ribot was prepared to accept more limited gains, the return of Alsace-Lorraine rather than the more expansive French border of 1790. Likewise British ministers considered a revision of war aims; at a cabinet meeting on 9 May, Lloyd George even wondered about a separate peace with Austria-Hungary, depriving Italy of promised gains under the Treaty of London.[22]

The impact of the Russian revolution went beyond calculations of power politics. The revolutionaries, from different backgrounds, had raised issues that demanded debate. In terms of his ideological ambitions, Lloyd George was able to accommodate the Russian revolution, initially, into his conception of a liberal world order. During a discussion on 16 March with C. P. Scott, editor of the *Manchester Guardian*, Lloyd George claimed that he had three aims – 'the destruction of the barbarous domination of the Turks', the 'establishment of popular government as a basis of international peace', and the 'destruction of militarism – i.e. of reactionary military government'. The Russian revolution had contributed to the latter two aims and he predicted that militarism in Germany would be destroyed by revolution.[23] On the other side of the barbed wire, the Habsburg Foreign Minister, Otto Czernin, was willing to consider the formula of peace without annexations and indemnities as a basis for negotiation, whereas the results of a conference in Kreuznach, attended by German military and political leaders, insisted on annexations in the Baltics. However, Bethmann Hollweg wanted to explore the elasticity of 'self-determination', which alarmed Czernin, given its implications for Habsburg internal politics.[24]

That the Russian revolution coincided with the crisis in American–German relations had important implications. The revolution was inserted into a narrative that portrayed the war as a conflict between political values. Woodrow Wilson had broken off diplomatic relations with Germany in

February. For over two months he considered American options. The revolution in Russia enabled those who favoured entry into the war to stress the liberal values that now underpinned the Allies. On 17 March Edward House, his closest confidant, urged Wilson to support democracy in Russia, recognize the Provisional Government, and end the potential 'peril' of an autocratic alliance between Germany, Japan, and Russia. 'You will come out of this war as its central figure,' House wrote to Wilson, 'and largely because you stand easily to the fore as the great liberal of modern times.' Robert Lansing, the Secretary of State, who was inclined to view the war in terms of a clash between good and evil, claimed that American entry into the war would strengthen democracy in Russia, sustain liberal Britain and France, and 'put heart into the democratic element in Germany'. American influence in the world depended on 'prompt, vigorous, and definite action in favor of Democracy and against Absolutism'. Wilson was not immune to these arguments, given the importance of representing American participation in the war as a struggle for liberty against militarism. At a cabinet meeting on 20 March he 'spoke of the glorious act of Russians, which in a way had changed conditions, but he could not give that as a reason for war'. The revolution alone did not determine Washington's policy, but this epochal event made it much easier for Wilson to cast his decision as being in defence of democracy, as well as of American interests.[25]

* * *

The American debate over entry into the war was also responding to the renewal of unrestricted submarine warfare by Germany at the end of January 1917. The military and ideological remobilization of the German war effort, following the Allied rejection of their peace initiative, shaped the American decision to enter the war by, most obviously, threatening its interests, but also by framing the American war effort as one in defence of international law, humanitarian values, and liberty against a militaristic regime. Though never monolithic, the German and American policies, as they developed in the first months of 1917, derived from very different assumptions about the international order.

As Bethmann Hollweg prepared his peace initiative from the summer of 1916, German admirals, generals, and nationalist political leaders began to call for the resumption of unrestricted submarine warfare. Its advocates assumed that the war would end either in decisive victory or catastrophic defeat. A negotiated, compromise peace had little purchase on the imagination of admirals such as Alfred von Tirpitz and Henning von Holtzendorff, or pan-German leaders such as Heinrich Class and Count von Reventlow. They viewed international politics as a continual struggle, in which military power provided the only means of security. In public debate, groups such as the Independent Committee for a German Peace, set up by Dietrich Schäfer to promote the war aims of nationalist intellectuals and businessmen, claimed that unrestricted submarine warfare was the only means of winning the war. If the options were conceived as Belgium being 'either a German or an English bulwark', then concerns about international law and other restraints on the use of military force were redundant.[26]

The rejection of the peace initiative bolstered the nationalist contention that the Allies were bent on the destruction of Germany, and therefore the self-denying ordinance on unrestricted submarine warfare had neither moral nor political purpose. On 19 January 1917 the Independent Committee for a German Peace held a mass meeting in Berlin. The choice was between 'triumph and collapse'. The speakers, including Schäfer and Gustav Stresemann, concentrated their criticisms on Britain, as they urged the German government to return to the campaign of unrestricted submarine warfare.[27] The rejection of the peace initiative also weakened Bethmann Hollweg's position. He had disposed of previous demands for unrestricted submarine warfare on the grounds that the peace initiative, if rejected, would create better conditions to justify the resumption of the campaign, as the Allies would carry responsibility for prolonging the war. Now, as Admiral von Müller noted on 8 January, the submarine campaign was the 'last shot in our locker'.[28]

As Ludendorff and Hindenburg concluded that the German armies would remain on the defensive in the west in 1917, unrestricted submarine warfare offered an offensive alternative. By Christmas 1916 they had signalled their approval of the Admiralty plans. On 22 December the Chief of the Admiralty Staff, Holtzendorff, had sent Hindenburg a memorandum setting out the rationale for resuming unrestricted submarine war. Distilling months of Admiralty debate and analysis, his argument rested on three assumptions. First, the war of attrition threatened to exhaust Germany before its enemies collapsed. If Germany did not win by the end of 1917, then the war would 'end in disaster for us'. Second, breaking Britain's 'backbone' was the only way for Germany to achieve a decisive victory. Britain was dependent on shipping, which brought raw materials and most importantly food to fuel its war effort. The plan was to starve the British people into surrender. According to Holtzendorff, the poor harvest of 1916 had created an opportunity, as the British people were even more reliant on supplies from Argentina, Australia, and India. Based on a careful analysis of shipping tonnage and food supplies, Holtzendorff claimed that the submarines could destroy 600,000 tons of shipping each month, deter neutral shipping from making good the difference, and bring Britain to her knees within five months. For good measure, he also assumed that British people would not be able to bear the privations and food shortages as Germans had. Third, he argued that the threat of American entry into the war 'should not lead us to recoil from making use at the decisive moment of a weapon that promises victory for us'.[29]

The certainty of the analysis, contained in careful calculations of tonnage and food supply, appeared overwhelming. It appealed to a cast of mind that counted on power, rather than those less certain men for whom political judgement was hemmed in by the question 'What if?' Bethmann Hollweg was the foremost opponent of unrestricted submarine war, principally because he feared the consequences of American entry into the war. His judgement rested not only on the outcome of the war itself, but also on the post-war world. Even if the submarine campaign defeated the Allies, the United States, having entered the war, would remain hostile to Germany. The Chancellor found support from the erstwhile advocate of unrestricted submarine warfare Matthias Erzberger, the leading figure in the Catholic Centre Party. Always suspicious of so-called experts, Erzberger doubted whether the German Navy could sink the requisite tonnage or whether British stomachs and morale were as feeble as Holtzendorff claimed. Erzberger's shift was part of a broader change in his policy that would see him become a leading advocate of a compromise peace in 1917.[30]

On 9 January the decisive meeting took place in Pless. Bethmann Hollweg, having lost the support of Wilhelm II on this issue, was a defeated man. The only argument he could muster was the risk that Switzerland, infuriated by the cutting off of all supplies, might declare war on Germany. The Chancellor failed to challenge the experts' analysis. 'It was not so much approval as acceptance of the facts,' wrote Müller in an unintentionally revealing summary of the Chancellor's view. The participants also accepted the likelihood of American entry into the war. The Kaiser 'remarked in passing that he expected a declaration of war by America. If it came – and the Chancellor should if necessary make concessions to American passenger liners to avoid it [virtually impossible given the operational doctrine of unrestricted submarine warfare] – so much the better.' Later in the month Kurt Riezler agreed that American entry was inevitable, commenting 'The outcome is unforeseeable. Triumph or defeat.'[31]

The German government did not inform the United States of its resumption of unrestricted submarine warfare until 31 January. When Johann von Bernstorff, the German ambassador, shook hands as he was leaving his meeting with Lansing in Washington late that afternoon, the Secretary of State noticed tears in the German diplomat's eyes.[32] The decision to resume the submarine campaign shocked Wilson, though Lansing had anticipated it. On 24 January he noted rumours that Germany was accelerating its submarine construction programme. A German diplomat had told a friend, whose wife had embarked on a voyage to Europe: 'For God's sake, why did you let her go? You knew she ought not to go now.' Lansing was determined to bring the United States into the war on the side of the Allies and wanted to use the first sinking of an American ship as the trigger for a declaration of war.[33]

The decision, however, lay with Wilson. Even after the rejection of his peace note, the president remained opposed to American participation in the war, though he wanted to ensure his role in shaping a new international system. 'This country does not intend to become involved in this war. We are the only one of the great white nations,' he told House, 'that is free from war today and it would be a crime against civilization for us to go in.'[34] For Wilson, the struggle for civilization would take place after the war, in the work of constructing a new world order – erected, in part, on racial categories and hierarchies. In the first two weeks of January the president worked on a speech, setting out his view of a new international order. His peace note had avoided grand statements about the future, concentrating instead on ending the immediate conflict. In going beyond the peace note, he intended to speak to peoples as well as governments. His speech in May 1916 to the League to Enforce Peace had been directed towards the American people. Having sent his current speech to foreign governments on 15 January 1917, he identified his new audience a week later in the Senate: 'I am speaking for the silent mass of mankind who have as yet no place or opportunity to speak their real hearts out concerning the death and ruin they see to have come upon the persons and homes they hold most dear.' Wilson set out a number of principles underpinning his conception of the new international order – the equality of nations, the consent of the governed (he identified, rather ambiguously, 'a united, independent, and autonomous Poland', as an example of the application of this principle), freedom of the seas, and the limitation of armaments. Rather than set out an institutional framework that would consolidate a peace based on these principles, he spoke of a 'covenant' of peace, a term with distinctive religious connotations that suggested moral reciprocity, rather than the legal bonds that the League to Enforce Peace and figures such as Léon Bourgeois preferred. And with a nod to Martin Luther, in the four-hundredth anniversary of the Reformation, Wilson concluded 'These are American principles, American policies. We could stand for no others.'[35]

The speech became known by one of its many catchy phrases – peace without victory. Herbert Croly, a progressive journalist and founder of the *New Republic*, described the speech as the 'greatest event in his own life'. Robert La Follette, the progressive Republican senator from Wisconsin, called it a 'very important hour in the life of the world'. Wilson's words echoed loud and clear throughout Europe, particularly amongst liberals and socialists, while the idea of 'peace without victory' was given more substance, as we have seen, by the Petrograd Soviet.[36] The American president recognized that peace had to be constructed in people's minds, as well as in the territorial and economic settlements that followed war. Yet the speech was also important because its ideas shaped Wilson's sense of purpose in the war. He did not know that he would lead the United States into war in just over two months, but his vision of the international order, set out on 22 January, became a starting point for his war aims. In addition, he had reinvigorated his progressive supporters, which rallied them to his cause in April 1917 and gave meaning to their war.

Wilson was playing golf on 31 January when he heard of Germany's resumption of unrestricted submarine warfare. He was shocked, even perplexed that Germany's 'peace chat' had ended. On 1 February the president and House arranged to meet Lansing. While they waited, Wilson 'nervously arranged his books and walked up and down the floor. Mrs Wilson spoke of golf and asked whether I [House] thought it would look badly if the President went on the links. I thought the American people would feel that he should not do anything so trivial at such a time.' Wilson himself described his feeling that the 'world had reversed itself' and he could no longer find his balance. He was 'haggard and worried', according to Louis Lochner, a journalist, who met the president on 1 February.[37] On 2 February Wilson met his cabinet, which agreed unanimously that the United States break off diplomatic relations with Germany. The racial framing of the crisis was striking. 'With the terrific slaughter taking place in Europe,' Wilson asked his cabinet, 'if we also entered the war, what effects would the depletion of man-power have upon the relations of the white and yellow races? Would the yellow races take advantage of it and attempt to subjugate the white races?'[38] The epic scale of the crisis, however, prevented any decision beyond severing diplomatic ties with Germany. Wilson's remarks about race and civilization went further than casual talk. He genuinely believed that the United States had a mission as the guardian of white civilization. In 1917 the question centred on how best to protect the achievements of that civilization. Wilson hoped his warning to Germany, delivered to Congress on 3 February, would enable the United States to remain at peace, but if submarines sank American vessels and took American lives then war remained the only means of saving civilization, of following the 'dictates of humanity'.[39]

Wilson's hopes that he could steer through this crisis in American–German relations were given another abrupt jolt in late February when a telegram from Arthur Zimmermann, the secretary at the German Foreign Office, to the Mexican government, proposing an alliance, was intercepted by British intelligence and transmitted to the State Department. The Mexican president, Venustiano Carranza, had floated the idea of an alliance with Germany in late 1916, when negotiations between the United States and Mexico over the withdrawal of General Pershing's expedition were in difficulties. Then the German government had dismissed the proposal. It was revived by the German Foreign Office following the failure of the peace initiative, the launching of the submarine campaign, and the expectation of war against the United States. The terms – Mexican support in case of a war between Germany and the United States, and German support for the reconquest of Texas, Arizona, and New Mexico, lost to the United States in the war of 1846–8 – were less important than the sense that German ambitions threatened the United States in the western hemisphere. The news speeded up the adoption of a bill to arm American merchant ships, a step towards a declaration of war.

The crisis also shed light on the evolving relationship between Mexico and the United States. In January 1917 Wilson had ordered the withdrawal of Pershing's 'punishment expedition' from Mexico. Lansing later argued that Pershing's withdrawal was due to Wilson's nervousness about the deterioration of relations with Germany. The decision, however, had its own roots. Carranza's government had restored stability in Mexico and suppressed banditry, the original reason for Pershing's expedition. On 1 February, four days before Pershing crossed back into the United States, a new constitution was promulgated. It revealed how the war fomented global ideas, which were then reworked in a local context. The constitution included a host of measures regulating labour, strikingly similar to the ideas discussed by Allied trade unionists at Leeds in 1916. These included an eight-hour day and the protection of women and children in the work-place. Significantly, Article 27 claimed that ownership of the lands and waters in Mexican territory was originally vested in the nation, which could expropriate property in the public interest. This had implications for foreign-owned mines and other enterprises in Mexico. American busi-nesses with property in Mexico were outraged, but Wilson was not inclined to intervene on their behalf – nor was he able to do so once the crisis with Germany had escalated.[40]

By mid-March German submarines had sunk three American ships. Wilson remained reluctant to declare war, but step by incremental step he moved from armed neutrality to a declaration of war. The president concluded that he could defend American interests and remake the inter-national order if the United States entered the war. As he put it in late February to Jane Addams, a progressive and pacifist, he could only 'call through a crack in the door' at any peace conference if the United States stayed out. Making peace first required making war. On 2 April Wilson addressed Congress. He started with an examination of the submarine campaign and the American response to it. The German campaign was effectively an act of war against the United States, which having tried and failed to defend life and property with armed neutrality, now had no option but to declare war formally. He then placed the declaration of war in a wider context, taking up and reworking the ideas broached in his speech on 22 January. The United States had joined an alliance of democracies, fighting against German autocracy. The quarrel was with the German government, not the German people, implying that most radical of war aims, the overthrow of an enemy's regime. The democratic allies – and he made much of the Russian revolution in this context – provided the basis for a 'steadfast concert of peace'. Only democracies could be trusted to keep their 'covenants', which hinted at Wilson's particular conception of a League of Nations based on political bonds and public opinion, rather than laws and military sanctions. The principles of democracy, the consent of the governed, and the equal sovereignty of all states were the foundations of his vision of the international order.[41]

What had been his vision for peace in January was now presented as the moral purpose of the war. His supporters in the Progressive movement and other political allies, central to his re-election in November 1916, could rally to this purpose, identifying foreign and domestic political goals in Wilson's universalist rhetoric. In February, Walter Lippmann, then a young journalist, called on the United States to defend what he called the 'Atlantic world', a moral and geopolitical community of states and societies that embraced North and South America, Britain, France, Scandinavia, the Low Countries, Spain, Italy, and Germany. The war was directed against the German elites, in order to bring the German people 'back to the civilization to which she belongs'. This Atlantic community, strengthened by the reintegration of Germany, would defend itself against Japan and Russia, which had not yet rendered itself acceptable by revolution.[42] W. E. B. DuBois, a leading intellectual and activist, supported the war as an opportunity to demonstrate that African Americans were capable of full citizenship in the American Republic. Fighting for democracy abroad would enable African Americans to assert their claims to full civil rights at home.[43] The southern states, dominated by Democrats and home to racist Jim Crow laws, also rallied to the flag. The themes of American honour, democracy, and Christianity were reworked in a regional cadence. Senator John Sharp Williams dismissed any opponent of the war as a coward, who would not even fight 'if a man stepped into his front door and slapped his wife's face'.[44] The American Federation of Labor (AFL), under its British-born leader, Samuel Gompers, supported American participation. Gompers had already been integrated into the agencies undertaking military preparedness measures. The war had demonstrated the centrality of the workers to the war effort and the AFL did not shy away from demanding the extension of labour rights, including equal pay and the regulation of the length of the working day.[45] Lilian Wald, the director of the Henry Street Settlement, resigned from the American Union against Militarism, sensing the progressive purpose in Wilson's war policy.[46]

The majority of Republicans applauded Wilson. After the president's speech to Congress, Henry Cabot Lodge, a bitter Republican opponent, was one of the first to congratulate him. Charles Hughes, the defeated presidential candidate, spoke in support of Wilson's call for universal military service, arguing that unity at home was the prerequisite to the successful prosecution of the war.[47] William Taft saw American participation in the war as strengthening the possibility of a League of Nations. At this point the differences between the League to Enforce Peace and Wilson remained latent. Speaking to a meeting of the Red Cross at the Boston Opera House on 19 June, Taft embraced the certainty of American virtue in this war. 'We have entered this war in no lightness of spirit', he told the audience, 'in no jingo desire to take part in the world quarrel. We are not like the Irishman who walking down the street found two men quarrelling, and inquired whether this was a private fight or whether any man might join in.'[48]

Although he argued that the United States was not in the business of imposing democracy on other states, he also said that if Wilhelm II and Karl I were replaced by republican constitutional governments, there would be peace within two weeks. The path to peace led through revolution and regime change.

* * *

Wilson staged himself and the American entry into the war as a global event, in which American principles and interests merged with universal ones. His success in doing so reflected the tremendous growth of American power in the early twentieth century. This power was based on its economic dynamism, technological modernity, and self-proclaimed political values.[49] The future Cold War warrior, John Foster Dulles, believed that Wilson's speeches had a 'new and revivifying influence' on the Allies and a 'moral effect upon the German and Austrian peoples'.[50] In embracing Wilson's ideas, other states and groups used his language to assert their own claims. American war cultures interacted with those already in existence. Intellectuals, artists, and politicians from Allied countries visited the United States, asserting a community of moral purpose and establishing a form of international moral economy, in which the blood already spilled by the Allies constituted political credit. At the banquet of the Franco-American Society in New York on 12 March, Henri Bergson spoke of the lasting friendship between the two countries, based on 'the same deep and inde-structible love of justice and liberty'. He left no doubt in the audience's mind that France was fighting America's and the world's war. The victory at the Marne in 1914 had 'preserved from moral degradation the whole of the human race'.[51] Stéphane Lauzanne, the editor of Le Matin, gave lectures entitled 'Fighting France' to audiences in New York, Chicago, and San Francisco, recalling the historic alliance between the two countries. He depicted French and Allied aims as embodying the principles of 'freedom, humanity, and international law'.[52]

The global dimensions of American entry into the war can be seen in the unfolding of events in China. Wilson's language was simultaneously inclusive and exclusive. He regularly invoked terms such as 'mankind', 'humanity', and 'civilization', but he betrayed the imaginative limits of those communities when he spoke of 'yellow races' while taking no meaningful action within the United States to ease the restrictions on African American rights. His rhetoric crossed ethnic and racial boundaries, appealing to audi-ences Wilson had barely considered. Chinese politicians used the American rupture with Germany to assert their own claims to equal membership of the international community. The Foreign Minister, Wu Tingfong, argued that China should associate itself with the American note. 'Since Germany has violated international law and hurt our national interest,' he argued on 7 February 1917, 'China, for the sake of its status in the world, should not remain silent. China will take this opportunity to enter a new era of diplomacy, become an equal member of the international community, and through a firm policy win favourable treatment from the Allies.'[53] The Chinese Foreign Ministry presented the protest to Germany two days later, but its politics was directed at the Allies and especially Japan. Wellington Koo, educated at Columbia University and China's minister in Washington, argued that the United States was a geopolitical and ideological ally for the young Republic.

Chinese diplomacy sought to transform the normative environment of the international system. The declaration of war against Germany on 14 August justified China's entry on the grounds of international law, which governed the 'family of nations'. The representation of China's war drew heavily on Allied and American notions. Germany, Koo argued, was emblematic of an international system based on force. The origins of the war were recast, pointing to the occupation of Kiachow in south-east China in 1897 as Germany's first step away from international legal restraints. Atrocities committed by German forces in China were compared to those committed in Belgium. As claimed by Dr Tyau, an expert in international law, the entry into the war served to place China 'on an equal footing with the nations fighting for civilization'. American and Allied notions of equal sovereignty between states and the consolidation of international law were reworked in Chinese diplomacy to defend the Republic against the depredations of Japan.[54]

The reaction to China's entry into the war demonstrated how the transformation of the normative environment worked in practice. Indeed, the principles of international law and equal sovereignty hardly seemed to matter at all, certainly in the short term. The United States and the Allies discouraged China from declaring war, wary of her claims to a seat at the peace conference. The discomfort of the United States and the Allies suggested that they understood the gap between their stated ideals and their diplomatic practice, which undermined the credibility of the new post-war international order. Participation, especially fighting, created a moral claim, which was difficult to dismiss. On the other hand they simply did not consider China as an equal member of the international community, due in part to racial understandings of civilization but also due to China's lack of power. The immediate exigencies of war trumped principles. In August 1918 John Jordan, British minister to China, told W. Langley, Assistant Undersecretary of State, 'With all our world-wide preoccupation at present we cannot afford to antagonize the Japanese, and without antagonizing her, we cannot get the principles for which we are fighting in Europe extended to the Far East.'[55] Jordan neatly encapsulated the conflict of power, geography, and identity in the shaping of a new international order. In November, Lansing concluded an agreement with Ishii Kikujirō, the Japanese special envoy to the United States, recognizing Japan's special rights in China and claims to post-war privileges, while in March the Allies had guaranteed Japan's claim to the Shantung peninsula.

In addition, the entry into war exacerbated the civil conflict in China between Duan Qurui and Sun Yat-sen. Duan had opposed Japan's Twenty-One Demands issued in 1915, even urging military resistance. He became prime minister after Yuan's death in June 1916, promoting modernization and centralization. Entry into the war was a domestic political project in Duan's eyes, in which he intended to strengthen the Chinese state. Sun, Duan's major rival, was opposed to entry into the war, distrusted the Allies, and favoured better relations with Japan. From the spring of 1917 China moved towards civil war, as parliamentary processes broke down and Duan invited warlords – the men who had led the revolution in 1911 – to Beijing to consult on political affairs. By the end of the summer of 1917, following a botched restoration of the Qing dynasty and the collapse of army unity, Duan launched an offensive against regional power centres in South China. This inaugurated the era of 'warlordism' in Chinese politics, in which military power became the basis for political authority and legitimacy. The collapse of constitutional structures at home further diminished Chinese diplomats' efforts to shape a new order in East Asia.[56]

Instead, civil war in China created opportunities for Japanese politicians to exploit. Having secured agreement from the Allies and the United States to Japan's claims to the Shantung peninsula, the Japanese government now supported Duan's military efforts, offered loans, and provided technical assistance. In September 1917 in return for loans, Duan accepted that Japanese troops could continue to stay in Shantung after the war. This compromised Chinese diplomatic assertions that the Japanese claims to Shantung had been imposed by force. In other words, civil war in China had enabled Japan to establish its own treaty-based claim to the Shantung peninsula. These gains for Japanese diplomacy were countered by increasing concerns that the authoritarian structures of Japanese politics were outmoded. 'The tidal wave of world thought,' exclaimed General Terauchi Matasake, the prime minister after the American entry into the war, 'may destroy all order and damage the essence of our National Polity. . . . If at some point German militarism is destroyed by this, we must prevent the misfortune of this engulfing the empire.' These anxieties were heightened by what he and others viewed as the sudden collapse of the Tsarist regime, which had based its legitimacy on 'an enormous army and international renown.'[57]

* * *

The entry of the United States into the war and the Russian revolution reshaped the context for imperial reform in Britain and to a lesser extent France. Mobilization for the war had already created a new context for anti-colonial agitation. In August 1917 Edwin Montagu, recently appointed Secretary of State for India, announced the 'gradual development of self-governing institutions with a view to the progressive realization of responsible government in India as an integral part of the British empire.'[58] As Lord Curzon recognized, 'the free talk about liberty, democracy, nationality, and self-government which have become the common shibboleths of the Allies' meant that changes in imperial rule were necessary, though he hoped change would take place slowly.[59] British policy towards Ireland took into account American attitudes.[60]

That said, imperial reforms had their own logic, beyond the implications of the revolutionary events of 1917. The language of civilization, justice, and law employed by the French and British governments in Europe echoed around their empires. In addition, the mobilization of colonial societies established expectations of future political reform. Politicians in settler colonies, such as William Hughes, the Australian prime minister, and Robert Borden, his Canadian counterpart, expected that the Dominions would have a greater say in imperial policy. For the first two years of the war the Dominion governments had concentrated on providing men and materiel, but the growing burdens of war led to greater participation in imperial government. Between March and May 1917 the Imperial War Conference met. The delegates of the Dominions and the Government of India were represented in the Imperial War Cabinet with equal status to British ministers. Jan Smuts, representing South Africa, made the most significant impression and stayed on in London for the rest of the war. The Imperial War Conference was, in many ways, a heightened version of the pre-war imperial gatherings. However, it was celebrated in 1917 as an event pregnant with the possibility of institutionalizing the power and authority of the empire in a more formal and enduring way. In France colonies elected representatives to the Assembly. Here the issue lay in the restricted rights of Africans. The French government, pressed by the West African deputy, Blaise Diagne, introduced new citizenship laws in 1915 and 1916, extending equal citizenship to colonial soldiers including voting rights.[61]

Wartime reforms did not meet the expectations of many imperial subjects and Irish nationalists. The Montagu Declaration marked a revolutionary new approach in British politics towards India, but for Indian nationalist politicians its promises seemed too vague, condescending, and distant to meet their demands. The term 'responsible government' rather than 'self-government' also failed to recognize the importance of India achieving equal status to the Dominions. Efforts to solve the Irish question after the Easter Rising foundered on British party politics and the shrinking support for Home Rule in Ireland. Finally, the encounter between Africans, Asians, and Europeans in the daily grind of war changed the contexts of racial and social relations and hierarchies. Military and labour service offered a potential path to equal status with white Europeans. This was not prescribed in particular political rights, but rather in a sense of dignity and proud achievement. Kande Kamara, from a prominent Susu family in Guinea, who served with the French Army, said that before the war 'a black man couldn't look straight in the eyes of a white man'. The courage and skill of African soldiers, in his view, made for a more equal register of esteem between Europeans and Africans.[62] However, distinction between forms of service could also undermine notions of dignity. The British and Indian governments distinguished between 'martial' sepoys and 'menial' workers, such as stretcher-bearers and saddlers, recruited from India. Indian and Chinese labourers were disgusted at their treatment. Letters home reflected this bitterness: 'though well-clothed and fed, we are treated like animals. Nobody takes any notice of us . . . we get no credit for the work we do.'[63]

Ho Chi Minh, the future leader of the Vietcong, had arrived in France in 1911. After flitting between France and Britain, he returned to France in late 1917, most likely as a delegate for the Overseas Workers' Association. In the last year of the war he launched his anti-colonial campaign amongst workers recruited from the colonies to work in France. One of the staple themes of Ho Chi Minh's criticism of French imperialism was the daily humiliation inflicted on Vietnamese people, which made a mockery of the 'civilizing mission' and republican ideas about liberty, fraternity, and equality.[64] The war undermined the structures of empire, from the justifications of the civilizing mission to the local arrangements that sustained a thin layer of colonial administration.

* * *

The entry of the United States into the war and the Russian revolution intersected with war-weariness across the belligerent societies in the first half of 1917. Strikes, soldiers' mutinies, and food riots were the most obvious expressions of frustration and anger at the conditions of daily life in the trenches and on the home front. War-fatigue reflected a sense of apathy. The war, as Jean-Jacques Becker has pointed out in the case of French society, had come to seem habitual, a constant state that had to be endured. Yet this limited the political consequences of war-weariness. Strikes and other manifestations were largely apolitical, in the sense that people protested against specific conditions in their everyday lives, but they did not seek to overthrow their government or bring the war to an end with 'peace at any price'. Nonetheless governments and other institutions acknowledged the political consequences of these sentiments, they gathered detailed reports about morale, and they took measures to shore up social cohesion. After all, in its most radical form war-weariness could fuel revolution, as events in Russia had demonstrated. Moreover, inducing war-weariness in enemy society was one of the major purposes of campaigns of attrition. If the goal of the war was to last fifteen minutes longer than the other side, then the politics of everyday life became part of the high politics of strategy.

These experiences of hunger, pain, grief, and tiredness were important because they structured popular expectations of peace. Enduring the privations of the war was conditional on the promise of a better future, whether that be national autonomy, constitutional change, or reforms of labour laws. The bonds of reciprocity between the state, social groups, and the individual had already been woven together in 1914. Promises had been framed in the language of national salvation as well as the larger abstractions for which the war was being fought – humanity, civilization, and democracy, for example. War-weariness tended to moderate aims and to focus on material concerns, such as the justifications for territorial claims and reparations.

In June 1917 and on his first day in Paris, General Pershing laid a wreath at the tomb of Lafayette, declaring to the French hero of the War of Independence, across the centuries as it were, 'Lafayette, we are here.'[65] The arrival of American force gave a morale boost to the French war effort, which had been badly shaken in April when a number of units had muti-nied during the disastrous Nivelle Offensive in the department of the Aisne. Robert Nivelle, a French Protestant with excellent English, had been appointed commander of the Army of the North-East in December 1916, in a reform of the high command that saw Marshal Joffre kicked upstairs. Nivelle's condescending attitude to General Haig also suited Lloyd George, who held the British commander in contempt but could not get rid of him. Nivelle's plan relied on an artillery offensive destroying the German system of defence in depth. Unfortunately for Nivelle, and more unfortunately for the troops taking the field, Hindenburg and Ludendorff had completed Operation Alberich, named after the dwarf in the medieval epic poem *Das Nibelungenlied*. German forces were now ensconced in a specially constructed defensive system. Commenting on the relative lack of French artillery for the proposed operation, Philippe Pétain observed that 'even the waters of Lake Geneva would have but little effect if dispersed over the length and breadth of the Sahara'.[66]

A total of 11 million rounds of artillery had a limited impact on German defences and by the end of April French casualties numbered 30,000 dead, 100,000 wounded, and 4,000 taken prisoner. Senegalese troops alone lost 6,300 men out of a 10,000-strong force on the first day. The futility of the operations led troops to disobey orders, in what became the first major mutiny of the war. This uncovered a complex relationship between military operations, daily life, and the purpose of the war, which structured the rela-tionship between soldier, society, and the state. Soldiers demanded better food and support for their families, while they were suspicious that French colonial troops were bedding their wives as they fought. They expressed a desire for peace, but not at any price. The return of Alsace and Lorraine was considered a just war aim, but they rejected prolonging the war to impose an indemnity on Germany or annex territory. These ideas echoed, in a French context, the proclamations of the Petrograd Soviet and of Woodrow Wilson for a peace without victory. At one level, therefore, the soldiers' service was conditional upon compensations that ranged from the concerns of daily life to war aims. At another level, the state compelled service. Pétain made concessions on leave and food supply, as well as operational changes that stressed defence in depth – this reflected his own operational ideas. Court martials tried 3,427 soldiers and passed 554 death sentences, of which 49 were carried out.[67]

The French mutinies of April 1917 were an extreme manifestation of the war-weariness that all European armies experienced. This was expressed in different ways from army to army and even within armies. One Italian officer, Silvio d'Amico, recounting how wide the mental chasm was between middle-class officers and peasants from the south, recorded in his diary:

> The driver confided in me about which animals he had ridden, and which was the best of all of these, and then after other arguments he finished: 'Signor, is it true that peace is near? In my country a man found a shell, inside which was written: 24 May 1917. Is that not a miracle? Does that not mean that it is the date of peace?' I gave him my lecture on the necessity of meriting peace with a beautiful victorious attack. He went back to talking to me about his animals.[68]

In some ways both options for ending the war – a successful offensive and a miracle – were equally fantastic, though the peasant's thoughts had the merit of being infinitely more humane. Morale in armies worsened in 1917. In the German Army officers reported that new recruits were more despondent about the war than veterans. They were also less healthy than the recruits in 1914 and 1915, having endured food shortages on the home front. Optimism faded. 'If we emerge from this war with one black eye,' wrote an enthusiastic volunteer from 1914, Lieutenant Heinrich Genscher, following American entry in 1917, 'we will have had some damn good luck.' Whereas British soldiers had remained optimistic during the battle of the Somme in the second half of 1916, the failure of the Third Ypres Offensive in autumn 1917 gave rise, according to the postal censor report of the 3rd Army, to a 'feeling of uncertainty as to the progress of our arms to an ultimate victory, and a growing inclination to believe that military enterprise must give rise to political ingenuity'.[69] The postal report of the German 5th Army, on 12 July, concluded that soldiers wanted peace, though not at any price, for otherwise their sacrifices and those of their dead comrades would be rendered futile.[70]

On the home front living conditions provoked war-weariness. Food was central to the politics of war as governments sought to manage scarce supplies. It is worth bearing in mind that civilian populations suffered premature death, largely due to malnutrition, on a massive scale in Europe between 1914 and 1918. Excluding the Spanish flu epidemic of 1918, the estimated civilian 'excess deaths' – meaning the number of people who died in a given year above the average pre-war death rate – amounted to 600,000 in Italy, 200,000 in Belgium, and 300,000 in Germany. In Vienna the annual death rate for women rose each year of the war. A total of 15,390 women died in the city in 1913, gradually escalating to 23,898 in 1918. The death rate in Vienna remained well above average in the years immediately after the war.[71] In Bulgaria the amount of land under cultivation fell by 12 per cent during the war. Prices rose elevenfold between 1910 and 1918, a much more severe increase than in western European states. While Alexander Stamboliski, the prominent opponent of Bulgaria's entry into the war (October 1915), languished in jail, his wife Milena participated in a food riot in February 1917.[72] The politics of food shortages was worked out in the letters between wives and husbands serving at the front, in queues, attacks on food shops, and petitions to local authorities.

Because food shortages were so obviously a consequence of the war, ending the war was seen as a way of restoring an adequate food supply. For example, during a series of demonstrations lasting several days in May 1916 in Vienna, women cried out 'We want peace.'[73] In June 1917 the Berlin police report on morale in the city observed that only a minority were interested in the war aims debate, the dominant topic in the Reichstag that summer, whereas for the 'largest majority only one question seems important: When will the war come to an end?'[74] The distinction between the war aims debate and the ending of the war revealed, perhaps unintentionally, that the war-weary were less preoccupied by the construction of a new international order than by the simple ending of the war. In France trade union leaders and prefects reported grumbling about food price inflation.[75] The consumption of fats and proteins in Britain dropped precipitously between October 1917 and January 1918, by roughly half in the case of cheese and butter, for example. 'The world was poorer for the disappearance of the muffin,' recalled one Dorothy Peel.[76]

Strikes were a particular form of protest at the deteriorating living conditions. In Germany 300,000 workers went on strike in March and April 1917. In France major strikes in Paris in January were followed by a much larger wave of strikes in the spring. About 100,000 workers went on strike in the Paris region in May and June. In Italy in late August a mass strike in Turin ended with the army opening fire on strikers, killing 50 and wounding 200. The demands of the strikers were often specific, related to working practices and living conditions rather than to broader political concerns. For example, in Germany strikers concentrated their demands on bread supply, attacking bakeries. The strikes in the Paris area in May and June resulted from the doubling of the price of coal and an increase in the price of vegetables by 150 per cent from the beginning of the year. Women, those most affected by the chores of organizing household consumption as well as labouring in factories, were at the forefront of these strikes, accounting for 75 per cent of the walkouts in Paris. As trade unions had failed to integrate women into their organizations, many strikes were spontaneous rather than planned. This, in turn, reinforced the tendency to strike in the interests of a specific demand rather than an abstract principle.

Nonetheless one could hear political overtones in the songs that strikers sang, such as 'The International', and their cries of 'Long live peace! Down with war.'[77] In the German city of Magdeburg, a member of the SPD recorded that 'It has gone so far that the workers are saying: "It's all the same to us, however this affair turns out. We want to have peace, we want to eat, no matter how the war turns out." '[78] Filippo Turati, the Italian Socialist leader, came to this conclusion about the attitudes of mostly female protesters: 'They want to end the war immediately, they want their men back.'[79]

Children occupied a prominent place in war cultures, representing the future, peace, and innocence. A story in May 1917 from a French trench journal, L'echo du boqueteau, recalled how a child had wandered into the unit's quarters in the rear zone while its men rested for a few days: 'Joseph! A little scrap of a plump and dimpled boy. . . . This little chap was a whole chapter of delight and idleness for us, eight days of home life in three years of wandering. And his name, to which such happy memories are attached, recalls a series of red-letter days in our quiet lives. Joseph! . . . It means rest, well-being, a table and a bed, and we have forgotten all this . . . Joseph will slip into our minds to remind us that we did have a few hours of peace in our life at war!'[80] If the purpose of the war could be embodied in part by the child, the future of the nation, then the malnutrition that children suffered during the war tended to undermine any sense of purpose whatsoever. Hunger led children to participate in demonstrations and even riots. In a working-class quarter of Vienna around 300 children of school age attacked bakeries on 16 July, shouting 'We are hungry.' In addition the absence of fathers, fighting at the front, stimulated fears that children were running amok and bereft of paternal discipline. In fighting the war, societies risked losing their future. One Austrian journalist commented in 1916: 'So much for the Century of the Child [declared by Franz Joseph in 1900]. . . . We are on the verge of raising a stock of moral weaklings, criminals, and idiots.'[81]

War-weariness reflected the corrosion of the moral economy of war, in which sacrifice was supposed to be distributed fairly across social groups. The moral economy was a vague reckoning, calculated in the different currencies of blood and treasure, but people knew when their sense of fairness and justice had been violated. The Munich historian Karl Alexander von Müller reported that the Bavarian peasantry regarded the war as a swindle perpetrated by social elites. 'Therefore we will think hard about bringing children into this world in the future and raising them with care only so that the top brass can slaughter them for no reason.'[82] In Italy the prefect of Ferrara reported that the working class wanted 'the immediate end of the war, represented as of benefit to the possessing classes and therefore wanted only by them at the expense of the poorer classes.'[83]

On the other hand, the professional and business middle classes resented the increased wages paid to workers. In Britain, by 1917, a skilled munitions worker earned more than an office clerk, which upset established notions about status and pay. As it became harder to afford the middle-class lifestyle, the relative change in salaries between working and middle-class groups went beyond economic argument to reflect the fear of changing social status.[84] Anti-Semitic charges that Jews were evading their obligations became prevalent in belligerent societies. The Prussian Ministry of War undertook the so-called Jewish census in 1916 to find out whether Jews were shirkers. Yet when the results showed that German Jews served and died in the war in proportion to their size of the German population, the government suppressed the results. The moral economy fractured in multiple directions – between urban and rural populations, between classes, between generations, between women and men, along religious lines, and between different ethnic groups. The actual experience of these different groups did not matter. People did not have access to the mass of statistics that historians have used to reconstruct the social history of the war. In the moral economy, the reckoning of accounts was based on rumour, prejudice, and one's own individual experience. As tensions escalated, the erosion of social cohesion threatened to undermine the war effort and spill over into revolution.

'The war finishes, each of the combatants is going to get out of the trenches, filled with horror, with an immense desire for peace,' imagined the writer Maurice Barrès in the spring of 1917 in his journals.[85] In Ferrara three people were arrested in November 1917 for urging Italian soldiers to surrender on the grounds that 'you would be better off under the Germans than the thieves in our government'.[86] War-weariness led people to imagine alternative endings to the war, which did not depend on cabinet negotiations or a decisive military victory. The Russian revolution that began in March, even though it did not bring an end to Russia's participation in the war, demonstrated how popular protests could profoundly alter the course of the war. War-weariness had led people to question the purpose of the conflict and to call for a sharper definition of war aims. The suspicion that the struggle was being fought for the benefit of certain interest groups corroded the sense of national unity and the moral economy that sustained the war effort. The conjunction between the Russian revolution, American entry into the war, and the growing sense of weariness provided the context for a series of debates and initiatives in the summer of 1917.

* * *

In December 1916 Walther Rathenau had written of the 'great peace movement, which goes through the world'. Although he predicted the rejection of Bethmann Hollweg's peace initiative, the longing for peace 'can not remain without consequences'.[87] In the summer of 1917 Rathenau's prediction was born out as the politics of peace assumed new dimensions in the unfolding of three separate, but related, initiatives. The Socialist Peace Conference at Stockholm (May–July), the Reichstag Peace Resolution (July), and the Papal Peace Note (August) revealed new political alignments in the belligerent states. Socialists withdrew from government in Paris and London, while a new parliamentary grouping, including the SPD, the Catholic Centre Party, and the Progressives, emerged in Germany. These political changes were, it must be recognized, partly contingent, born out of war-weariness, domestic political calculations, and the injection of new ideas from the United States and revolutionary Russia into the political debate. The impact of these changes was limited by high political machinations. Yet the new alignments also anticipated ideas, networks, and political constellations that would recur again in the history of the long First World War.

Each initiative had its own origins. The proposals for the Stockholm Conference lay in the remnants of the pre-war Socialist International. While Emile Vandervelde had joined the Belgian coalition government as Minister of Procurement, his fellow Belgian Socialist leader, Camille Huysmans, sought to preserve international socialism by moving the International Socialist Bureau to The Hague. There was a cooperative rivalry between the two men – Vandervelde did the work of winning the war, while Huysmans did the work of sustaining international socialism. 'Despite my identity as a Belgian,' wrote Vandervelde to Albert Thomas in December 1915, 'I know that I am a functionary at everyone's service. . . . The International must have a politics that is detached from the position of the armies.'[88] On 15 April 1917 a meeting of the Dutch delegation of the International decided to move the headquarters of the International Socialist Bureau from The Hague to Stockholm. This move was accompanied by a proposal to hold a conference to which socialists from the belligerent and neutral states would be invited to discuss peace terms on the 'standpoint of Kerensky and Wilson', including autonomy for Poland and Armenia, the resolution of the passage through the Dardanelles, and the establishment of an economic league.[89]

On 30 April the Dutch delegation of the International Socialist Bureau issued its appeal to socialists in all belligerent countries. Referring to the 'hecatombs of victims' and the mounting debts, the appeal also underlined the importance of the Russian Revolution (which began in March) in instigating the Dutch initiative. The proposal for the Stockholm Peace Conference, therefore, became closely associated with the politics of Russia's continued participation in the war. On 15 May the Petrograd Soviet had called for an international socialist conference to discuss peace.[90] Where Dutch socialists saw 'Kerensky's standpoint' as the basis for a negotiated settlement, the Petrograd Soviet had a dual purpose in mind when it adopted Tsereteli's 'revolutionary defencism'. It constituted the basis for a peace settlement, but also a statement of defensive war aims, around which Russian society could reunite and mobilize. Socialists in Britain, France, and Belgium now faced a dilemma. Their governments regarded the proposal for the Stockholm Conference as a plot hatched by the Central Powers to fracture national unity within each Allied state. Leading socialists, such as Thomas, Arthur Henderson, and Vandervelde, remained deeply committed to their nation's war effort, but they also faced minority socialists critical of what they viewed as the Allies' expansionist war aims. Finally, Russia's continued participation in the war was increasingly dependent on a clear statement of defensive war aims.

Allied socialists had already made clear their opposition to the Dutch proposal, but in order to keep Russia in the war a number of leading socialists made their way to Russia in May and June 1917. Henderson reached Petrograd, where his speech, including a reference to the death of his own son, was warmly received on 15 June. Yet he also objected to an 'untimely peace' that left German militarism free to menace Europe in the future. Russia and the Allies had to bear 'a few months of fighting and suffering' for a 'lasting peace'. During his stay Henderson quickly became convinced that Russia's continued participation in the war depended on the Allied socialists supporting the proposed Stockholm Conference.[91]

As it happened three French socialists, including Thomas, attended the meeting of the Petrograd Soviet that decided to issue the invitation to the conference. For Thomas, as for Henderson, the purpose of the conference was to provide a rallying point for the left in the Allied states. Thomas had been in Petrograd since 22 April. He agreed that French socialists would have to discuss war aims, but the Soviet proposal of 'no annexations, no indemnity' was unacceptable.[92] Other groups within the French Socialist Party, however, argued that socialists had a duty to consider any possible route to peace. 'Europe,' declared the branch of the Haute-Loire, 'has been nothing but an immense abattoir for men for the past three years.'[93] On 28 May the National Council of the French Socialist Party decided to accept the invitation to the conference and set up a commission to work out their war aims. This document devoted considerable attention to the issue of responsibility for the war, a reminder of this question's continuing purchase on the moral imagination within the Allied states and its perceived relevance to future peace. While the existence of oppressed nationalities and imperial capitalist rivalries were the structural causes of the war, the proximate cause was German militarism, which viewed international relations as a contest of unfettered military power. The solution to an enduring peace lay in the rights of people to self-determination. This principle inevitably drew on the French revolutionary tradition of the rights of man, but the document also acknowledged Kant's idea that men formed communities which should have a right to self-determination. Disputes between states should be submitted to the League of Nations, whose members would be obliged to use military force to support its operation. This went further than even the League to Enforce Peace, as French socialists pointed out, but this view was compatible with middle-class supporters of the League of Nations in France, such as Léon Bourgeois and the Ligue des Droits de l'Homme. The document also called for the freedom of the seas, the reduction of armaments, and free and fair international commerce, including international agreements about the regulation of labour.[94]

The Belgian delegation – including Vandervelde, Louis de Brouckère, and Hendrik de Man – arrived in Petrograd on 18 May and opposed the Stockholm Conference from the outset. Vandervelde recounted how on the boat journey to Russia, the delegation witnessed a debate between Trotsky, returning from exile in Canada, and some Russian doctors, returning from captivity in German camps. Trotsky contended that it was the revolutionary duty of the working class to end the war, whereas the doctors recounted the beatings and mistreatment they had suffered at the hands of their German captors. This was grist to Vandervelde's mill – that the conflict between the Central Powers and the Allies was one of principle, 'a civil war in the Society of Nations'. The war pitted the democratic Allies against semi-feudal Central Powers. The Belgian delegation, drawing on Woodrow Wilson rather than the Petrograd Soviet, argued that future peace depended on international law and institutions. States could only be members of this international community if they were subject to popular control. 'We can conceive of no durable peace being possible,' claimed the Belgian memorandum to the Dutch-Scandinavian Committee, 'while the Hohenzollerns and the Habsburgs keep their present power.' The Belgian delegation distanced themselves from the slogan of peace without annexations or indemnities, by claiming that the return of Alsace and Lorraine to France was undoing a previous illegal annexation, while the completion of Italian national unity and the formation of a Yugoslav state were justified on the principle of nationality.[95]

Allied socialists were partly justified in their suspicions of the Austrian and German socialists. Czernin, the Habsburg Foreign Minister, and Bethmann Hollweg saw tactical advantages in supporting German and Austro-Hungarian socialists at the conference. Czernin was willing to consider a compromise peace based on no annexations and no indemnities, and both he and the German Chancellor sought a separate peace in the east. They also believed, correctly, that the conference would test unity within and between the Allies.[96] That said, the German and Austrian socialists who attended meetings in Stockholm in late May and June wanted peace, though not at any price. Upset by a debate over German and SPD responsibility for the war, Friedrich Ebert, chairman of the SPD, and his fellow socialists concluded that the value of the conference lay in setting out the basis for future negotiations. Austro-Hungarian diplomats also considered the conference a valuable forum to shape the image of the empire and to challenge Allied interpretations of the emerging norms that were shaping the international system.[97] Both the Austrian and German delegations offered their interpretation of various principles, such as free commerce and national self-determination. Fearing economic exclusion from global markets, the SPD denounced any continuation of economic war after the conclusion of peace. Karl Renner, the Austrian socialist, argued that Austria-Hungary protected small nations, rather than suppressed them. Individuals were autonomous within the empire, Renner claimed, and therefore any reorganization of the Habsburg empire was a domestic rather than an international issue.[98]

The divisions within the socialist movement, between the *majoritaires* and *minoritaires* in France and between the Labour Party and the Independent Labour Party in Britain, had their echoes in Germany. On 6 April the split in German Social Democracy was confirmed when the

Independent Socialist Party of Germany (USPD) was formally founded at a conference in Gotha. This party was led by Hugo Haase, the son of a Jewish shoemaker from East Prussia, who had studied law at Königsberg. A reluctant supporter of the war in 1914, he had voted against war credits since late 1915 and along with his fellow dissidents had been expelled from the SPD. The formation of the USPD represented a challenge to the SPD, which needed to reaffirm the defensive character of the war. The daily miseries of the conflict were rendered more intolerable by the concerns about its political purpose. Hedwig Ducklinski, the niece of the German trade union leader Carl Legien, wrote to him on 11 July 1917: 'How long will this misery last, because the economic situation will soon be unbearable. However one could gladly bear all, if only the murder ceased.'[99] Participation at the Stockholm Conference served to underline the SPD's credentials in the war aim debate within Germany, where the assertions of the nationalist right about territorial expansion in the east and west unnerved moderate voices.

When the SPD delegation went to Stockholm, its members found themselves defending not just their own policies since 1914, but also German state policy. The Stockholm Conference raised questions, for each belligerent, about who represented the state and the nation. This had become a particularly significant issue in German politics in the spring of 1917, culminating in the Reichstag Peace Resolution and resignation of Bethmann Hollweg in July, and divisions about Germany's place in the world. The question of who represented Germany – the military, the Reichstag, the Kaiser, the SPD, the Pan-German League – was at the core of the ideological stakes in the war. Constitutional reform, therefore, connected foreign and domestic politics not merely in terms of specific war aims but also in the representation of German political values.

Since the beginning of the war the SPD had indicated that they sought constitutional reform to strengthen the role of the Reichstag and abolish the three-class electoral law in Prussia, which minimized socialist representation in Germany's most important state. In October 1914 Clemens von Delbrück, the Interior Minister, had argued that popular support for the war demonstrated the necessity of widening the political basis of the state, to integrate fully former 'enemies of the Reich' such as workers, Catholics, and Poles.[100] Bethmann Hollweg had avoided constitutional reform, although he consistently argued that only a government drawing support from the centre and left of the political spectrum could sustain an effective foreign policy. By 1917 the pressure to introduce meaningful reforms had led to a major crisis. One of the most prominent advocates of reform, Max Weber, argued that Germany's constitutional system privileged an inert bureaucratic ethos, whereas the combative parliamentary systems in Britain and the French Third Republic produced more imaginative leaders. Weber rejected the view that Germany and the Western Allies were separated by a deep ideological divide, lamenting the way in which the ambitions of the Pan-German League were taken to represent German opinion as a whole.[101] Matthias Erzberger also viewed constitutional reform as a means to rebut the claims of Woodrow Wilson and other Allied leaders that they were fighting against autocracy. The war aims debate and constitutional reform were the means of contesting the assertions of the Pan-German League that it represented the essential identity of the nation. 'One cannot pay any attention to the Pan-Germans,' Erzberger said in exasperation, 'let them go berserk. It is cheaper to build sanatoria for them than to continue the war for another year.'[102]

Bethmann Hollweg drew on the relationship between constitutional reform and the representation of Germany to the wider world when he justified his plans for Prussian electoral reform at a cabinet meeting on 5 April. Domestic political circumstances necessitated change, but 'the decisive point lies in foreign policy. England has understood how to make the world believe that the war is being fought against Prussian militarism. Recently this struggle has been supported by the Russian revolution and now Wilson, in his declaration of war, is trying to explain to the world that America has nothing against the German people, only against the autocratic German government.'[103] However, the reform of the Prussian electoral system, announced in Wilhelm II's Easter message two days later, was limited. It was further watered down by Prussian Conservatives in late 1917 on the grounds that military service did not make a man fit to vote and endangered the state by empowering 'the propertyless, undifferentiated masses', as Ernst von Heydebrand, the Conservative leader, put it. Significantly, Socialist speakers condemned Conservatives and some National Liberal opponents of the reform as enemies of the German people, implying that members of the SPD or USPD were the true representatives of Germany.[104]

The twin issues of constitutional reform and war aims moved to the Reichstag in July. The immediate trigger was a vote on war credits, which posed particular political difficulties for the SPD. The party could only vote for further war credits if it was able to present German war aims as defensive. To enable the SPD to support the vote, Erzberger decided to present a peace resolution to the Reichstag. This sparked a crisis because the Supreme

Command opposed the peace resolution. Who represented Germany? The majority parties in the Reichstag – the SPD, the Centre Party, and the Progressives – or the Supreme Command and its supporters in the Pan-German League and other nationalist associations and parties? Neither Erzberger nor socialist leaders, such as Philipp Scheidemann, expected that the peace resolution would lead to an immediate conclusion of the war. The resolution was both a political manoeuvre to enable the SPD to continue its support of the war and a longer-term political strategy to recast German domestic politics and its international image. On 6 July Erzberger set out his stall in a dramatic speech to the Budget Committee of the Reichstag, in which for the first time he detailed the failure of the campaign of unrestricted submarine warfare. The consequences of this failure were enormous as Germany faced another winter of war against increasingly strong enemies. Erzberger had travelled a long way from his ambitious war aims of 1914. Now he eschewed annexing Russian territory, favoured a compromise peace, and dismissed the claims of Pan-Germans to represent the people. The Reichstag must demonstrate the popular will, transforming the parliament into the source of political legitimacy. Scheidemann echoed many of these ideas in his speech to the Reichstag the following day. He singled out the Pan-Germans as the source of Germany's ill repute abroad. The British and French governments, he argued, exploited Pan-German propaganda. By demonstrating German reasonableness, the Reichstag majority parties hoped to undermine popular hatred of Germany.[105]

The Reichstag Peace Resolution, passed on 19 July 1917, set out three major principles. First, territorial expansion could not be imposed by force of arms – though this left the way open for territorial changes on the grounds of self-determination, which German political leaders believed could be turned to the advantage of the Reich in the Baltics. Second, economic peace had to be secured by freedom of the seas and the prohibition of economic exclusion against countries. Third, the resolution supported the creation of an international legal organization.[106] Granted, these principles remained vague, but they filled in the concept of defensive war in greater detail than before. They were also underpinned by speeches, designed to appeal to the liberals and socialists in Allied states.

The Reichstag Peace Resolution intersected with the third initiative in the summer of 1917, the Papal Peace Note, issued on 1 August. In late April Erzberger had informed the Vatican that the SPD were posing as the champions of peace. Benedict XV, wary of a peace settlement erected on socialist principles, decided to launch his own peace initiative. The politics of the

Pope's proposal were clear. It contested socialist claims to be the sole propo-
nents of peace in Europe, it offered cover to Erzberger as he dragged the
Centre Party to support the Peace Resolution, and it chimed with the turn
towards a peace policy in Austro-Hungarian politics under Karl I and
Czernin. The Pope also intended that his initiative should coincide with the
Reichstag Peace Resolution to give added impetus to the push for a peaceful
settlement in the summer of 1917. However, Benedict XV was not simply
the 'boche Pope' of Allied legend. His initiative also derived from Christian
humanitarian ideals, which had found expression in the works of the
Vatican on issues such as prisoners of war. Power and principle could not
be disentangled. Benedict XV, like many others, saw the war as a European
civil war, whose consequences would destroy the affective bonds of
Catholics and Christians across the continent. In a Papal letter to bishops
on 5 May 1917 he wrote of the 'suicide of European civilization'. Without
attributing responsibility to either side, he stressed the tragic dimensions of
the war, the atrocities, the loss of human life, and the grief experienced by
millions.[107]

Pietro Gasparri, the Cardinal Secretary of State, and Eugenio Pacelli, the
Papal nuncio in Germany and the future Pope Pius XII, were charged with
the diplomatic preparations for the Papal Peace Note. The diplomatic talks
with Bethmann Hollweg and Karl I concentrated on the terms of the territorial settlement in western Europe. The German Chancellor was willing to
consider full independence for Belgium, though he indicated the domestic
political obstacles to this solution. Karl I favoured a compromise peace with
Italy. In addition, Gasparri considered the freedom of the seas, limitations
on armaments, and a system of international arbitration as central compo-
nents of a new international order; while a peace conference would settle
economic issues, the future status of Alsace and Lorraine, the border
between Italy and Austria-Hungary, and the territorial boundaries and
sovereign status of Poland, Serbia, and Romania. In early July, Pacelli and
Gasparri believed that there was an opportunity to achieve peace. Their
proposed terms looked remarkably similar to those proposed by socialists
and liberals, although the ethos underpinning the Vatican's initiative was
rooted in Christian humanitarianism and neglected crucial issues such as
the future of the Ottoman empire and the imperial settlement.

Two days after the Reichstag passed the peace resolution, Wilson told
House that American conceptions of the future international order were
very different from those of the French and British governments. 'If there is
an interchange of views at all,' he said, 'it ought to be between us and the

liberals in Germany, with no one else brought in.'[108] This was an off the cuff, but revealing, comment. Wilson understood that peace would be constructed by an international coalition. In each belligerent faction there were war parties and peace parties. The general principles of a new world order, debated in Stockholm, Berlin, and the Vatican over the summer of 1917, looked remarkably similar – self-determination, commercial freedom, and international arbitration. They echoed ideas deployed in the Russian revolution and debates over American entry into the war, as well as the claims of different belligerents about the purpose of the conflict since 1914. These were the vague but emerging norms of the international system.

Of course, the devil was in the detail. These principles were open to a wide range of interpretations when it came to their practical application. Moreover, making peace required ending the war in the first instance. There remained a huge chasm between opposing war cultures. Socialists, Catholics, and liberals were unable and unwilling to construct transnational alliances on any significant basis until the moral accounts of the war had been settled. For example, in a House of Commons debate on 26 July only nineteen Members of Parliament supported the contention of Labour's Ramsay MacDonald that the Reichstag Peace Resolution represented the principles for which Britain was fighting.[109]

Moreover, ending the war remained a task for governments rather than transnational associations. In his contribution to the debate on the Reichstag Peace Resolution, Asquith, the erstwhile prime minister, argued that militarism was still thriving in Germany. Pierre Renaudel, the editor of the French socialist paper *L'Humanité*, was equally robust in denouncing the lack of democracy in Germany.[110] Asquith and Renaudel pointed to the resignation of Bethmann Hollweg as Chancellor on 13 July and his replacement by Georg Michaelis as evidence of the dominant position of militarism in Germany. Even had this change not taken place, it is highly unlikely that the Reichstag Peace Resolution or the other initiatives that summer would have ended the war. Nonetheless the high political machinations in July and August that finally ended the peace initiatives in Stockholm, Berlin, and the Vatican placed the domestic basis of international peace politics in sharp relief.

The Reichstag had passed the Peace Resolution by 212 votes to 126, representing a large majority of the parliament and probably popular opinion. However, the representational politics of the resolution had already been undermined by the resignation of Bethmann Hollweg and the appointment of Michaelis, a law professor and head of the Reich Cereal

Office. The Chancellor crisis of July 1917 demonstrated the growing power of the military, based on Hindenburg's charismatic authority and popularity in Germany. The Supreme Command opposed the peace resolution on the grounds that it undermined national confidence in victory and it presaged the parliamentarization of the Reich by arrogating to the Reichstag a role in foreign policy, the prerogative of the Kaiser. Constitutional politics centred on the question of Germany's place in the world, and whether it would be secured by military power or by international agreements. Hindenburg threatened to resign on two occasions in the summer of 1917, effectively forcing Wilhelm II to choose between his Chancellor and his generals. Hindenburg therefore contested the claim of the Reichstag majority parties to represent Germany. His popularity, the embryonic Hindenburg myth, extended into the constituencies that supported the majority parties – the working classes, liberals, and Catholics. However, its foundations rested on his appeal to the national right. Pan-Germans claimed that the Reichstag, through its approval of the peace resolution, had betrayed the German people, cost the lives of thousands of soldiers by offering the Allies hope that Germany was weakening, and potentially prepared the way for Germany's collapse. Only the reassertion of German values, embodied in Hindenburg, could save the country. In September 1917 Pan-German leaders, along with conservative agrarians and businessmen, established the Fatherland Party, a mass movement that claimed up to 1,200,000 members in 1918. In the contest over the representation of Germany, Hindenburg's decisive advantage, however, lay in the constitutional structures that enabled him and his closest advisers, Ludendorff and Max Bauer, to manipulate the Kaiser and evade the control of the majority parties in the Reichstag.[111]

The resignation of Bethmann Hollweg undermined the careful diplomatic preparations of the Vatican. On 24 July Pacelli presented the details of the proposed peace note to Michaelis. Originally, Gasparri had hoped that Germany would accept the proposals and then the Vatican could issue the note to the Allies on the back of a German commitment. Michaelis consulted the General Staff, and Gasparri, unwilling to allow Hindenburg and Ludendorff to kill the proposal before it had even been aired in public, decided to issue the note to the Allies. Dated 1 August, it was sent on 9 August. The French and Italian governments accused the Papacy of trying to undermine the morale of their Catholic soldiers. On 23 August the British Foreign Office declared that a German withdrawal from Belgium was the precondition to any negotiations. Wilson justified the

Un Peuple est devenu par son Orgueil
L'ÉTERNELLE MENACE
DU GENRE HUMAIN

Personne ne peut nier le génie d'organisation de l'Allemagne.
Sa " Kultur " dont elle tire vanité n'est pas une fiction.

mais...

...... et c'est là ce qui distingue nettement l'Allemagne des autres nations, toutes ses facultés créatrices, tant dans l'ordre moral ou social, que dans l'ordre scientifique, commercial ou industriel, *ont toujours été tendues vers un but égoïste.*

Il n'est pas une Nation au Monde qui puisse dire :
Je dois ma liberté ou une amélioration de mon sort à l'Allemagne.

Ses dispositions législatives sont le dernier refuge du despotisme; son commerce d'exportation, grâce à un habile mais perfide système bancaire, *drainait vers l'Allemagne les produits et les richesses des autres peuples* et ses forces guerrières ne sont utilisées que pour asservir, détruire et persécuter.

Or, de l'égoïsme, naît l'orgueil. La plus égoïste des nations devait donc devenir la plus orgueilleuse. L'Allemagne n'a pas failli à sa destinée, et son cri de ralliement :

Deutschland über alles ! L'Allemagne au-dessus de tout !
a montré au monde d'où venait la menace.

LE DESSIN CI-DESSOUS EXPOSE DEUX CONCEPTIONS DE L'ORDRE MONDIAL

Quel est le pays libre qui ne se sente pas visé par la doctrine allemande.
Le jour où ses intérêts seront en opposition avec ceux de l'Allemagne,
au nom du maintien de l'ordre mondial, celle-ci le contraindra à se mesurer avec elle.

COMBATTRE LE PANGERMANISME
C'EST DONC LUTTER POUR LE DROIT DES PEUPLES ET
GARANTIR LA PAIX DU MONDE

Extrait de la brochure " ... et LA LUMIÈRE se fait... ", pages 44 et 45.

Typographie Ad. Mericbel, 11A, Quai de Jemmapes, Paris.

5

1. 'By their pride a people has become an eternal menace for the human race': the war aims debate is given expression in posters. This example contrasts Allied claims to fight for a world order, based on law and justice, with German doctrines of domination through brutal force, dismissing Germany's claims to be a cultured nation.

2. 'Are we the barbarians?': a German propaganda poster rejects Allied claims about barbarism, contrasting Germany, Britain, and France in social spending, illiteracy rates, school spending, book publication, Nobel prizes, and patents. The profile at the top represents Goethe, so that the poster fuses German social and cultural achievements to reject charges of barbarianism.

3. 'The battle for Tsingtao': a Japanese soldier stands beside a destroyed German post in Tsingtao. The quick Japanese victory over small German forces in China was arguably the most decisive military encounter of 1914, enabling the assertion of expansionist Japanese aims in China.

4. 'SMS *Goeben* in harbour on the Bosphorus'. The SMS *Goeben* and SMS *Breslau* escaped the pursuit of the Royal Navy and took refuge in Constantinople. Here they entered the Ottoman navy, though the crew remained composed of German sailors. Their presence in the Black Sea contributed towards the Ottoman leaders' decision to enter the war on Germany's side in November 1914.

5. (above) 'Industry during the
First World War. Belgian workers,
Elisabethville.' The outbreak of war
in 1914 triggered a massive refugee
crisis. Refugees became a powerful
symbol of competing war cultures,
but governments also used them
to replace workers conscripted into
the army. Here Belgian refugees,
living at Elisabethville, worked at
the National Projectile Factory in
Birtley in County Durham.

6. (right) 'A woman carries a
sack of coal up a flight of stairs
at a London gas works.' From
employment patterns to labour
conditions, the war transformed
the world of work. Women
were employed in more heavy
manual labour. The expansion
of female employment was not
always experienced as a form of
emancipation.

7. 'Archduke Joseph August on an inspection of the Romanian front in the Carpathians'. Following a series of defeats on the Eastern Front, the Austro-Hungarian army became increasingly dependent on German military support. In late 1916 joint German-Austro-Hungarian forces, led by Falkenhayn, conquered Romania, ending a year of campaigns that had included the battles of Verdun and the Somme and the Brusilov Offensive. Archduke Joseph August was briefly Hungarian head of state in 1919.

8. 'Der Gestürzte' (The Fallen Man).
Wilhelm Lehmbruck completed this sculpture in 1916, a commentary on the degeneration of the human condition, shame at the violence of war, and a forbidding sense of hopelessness.

9. 'The consequences of the rejected peace offer': produced a year after Bethmann Hollweg's December 1916 peace offer, this poster claims that the course of the war in 1917 has favoured the Central Powers, showing territory captured in the Baltics and Italy and the casualty rates of the Allied forces. While it notes the sinking of nine million tons of Allied shipping, it fails to mention American entry to the war.

10. '1776–1917'. This poster, attributed to the French artist and ceramist René Buthaud, depicts the Franco-American partnership in the First World War. The historic alliance between the thirteen American colonies and France in the American Revolution was an important element in the representation of the common purpose and political values of the Allies and the United States after 1917. However the alliance was concluded in 1778, whereas the revolution had started two years previously in 1776.

11. 'You're the one I'll talk to', 24 January 1918. William H. Walker was a cartoonist for *Life Magazine*. He composed this cartoon after Wilson's fourteen points speech. He suggests that the American president would be willing to negotiate with a government representative of ordinary Germans, but not with the authoritarian, militarist government. It is worth noting that both German figures, 'Fritz' and William II, look ridiculous, even contemptible.

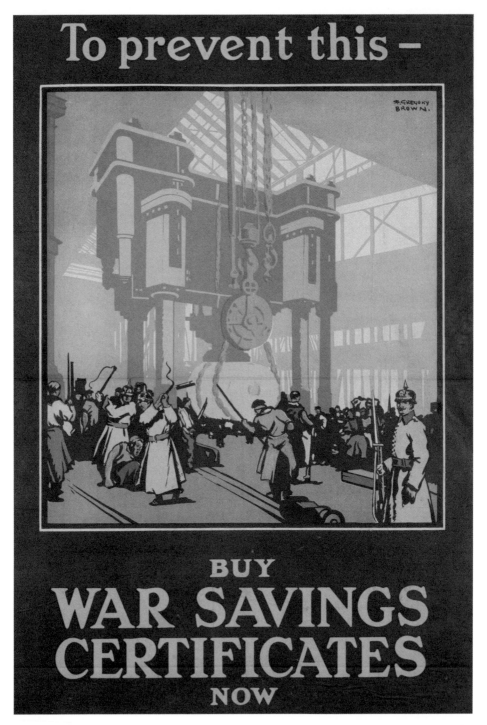

12. 'To prevent this –': a 1918 poster by F. Gregory Brown, urging British people to buy war bonds emphasises the brutal treatment of Belgian workers at the hands of the German occupation forces. In 1916 and 1917 the deportation of Belgian workers to work in German factories fitted into Allied claims of atrocities and German barbarism. Brown also designed posters for the London underground and major companies.

THEIR HOME !

BELGIUM 1918

BUY
National War Bonds
and protect YOUR HOME

13. 'Their home! Belgium 1918'. Although the destruction of Belgian towns and villages was most prominent in Allied war propaganda in 1914 and 1915, the theme of fighting for the sanctity of hearth and family remained important throughout the war, as this 1918 poster, also designed by Brown, illustrates. The background shows the ruins of Ypres and its cloth hall.

14. 'Kindergarten', 6 February 1919. Making peace not only involved a territorial, military, and financial settlement, but it also required social and cultural transformations. Here Walker suggests that making peace involves educating Germans, whose allegedly stunted development in the arts of civilization and democracy are represented by caricatures of officers dressed in bearskins.

15. 'Sitzender Jüngling' (Seated Youth), 1916/17. Lehmbruck made this statue in 1916 and 1917. He refused to design a more heroic figure for the war cemetery in Duisburg. In 1922, three years after Lehmbruck's suicide, the city placed this statue in the cemetery.

American rejection of the note on the grounds that peace could only be made with a representative government, not an autocracy. Safe in the knowledge that the proposal was already doomed, the Central Powers generously promised to support the general principles in the note, such as the freedom of the seas, but, to be on the safe side, rejected the immediate measures, such as the evacuation of occupied Belgian and French territory.[112]

The final unravelling of the peace initiatives in the summer of 1917 came in Paris and London, where the governments refused to issue passports to the socialist delegates bound for the conference at Stockholm. Both Ribot, the French premier, and Lloyd George had been sceptical about the conference from the outset, but their decision to block the participation of French and British socialists was more significant in terms of the realignment of domestic politics than in delivering a fatal blow to the Stockholm Conference. Socialists withdrew from both governments. Henderson resigned from the British cabinet in August and Thomas resigned from the French government in September. Though the overwhelming majority of socialists and trade unionists continued to support their national war efforts, they were increasingly sceptical about Allied war aims. In October 1917 the French Socialist Party conference affirmed its commitment to defeating German imperialism, but it also urged the French government to support the principles of national self-determination and the formation of the League of Nations. On 20 August, just over a week after Henderson's resignation, the National Executive Council of the Labour Party instructed Sidney Webb, the Fabian reformer, to draft a document on war aims. Webb, together with MacDonald and Henderson, wrote the Memorandum on War Aims, which was put to a special Labour Party and trade union conference in December 1917. While the conference committed its support to the British war effort, it envisioned an international order based on parliamentary control of foreign policy and the League of Nations. This statement of Labour war aims was also part of a general strategy to redefine the party within British politics, which culminated in the ratification of a new party constitution in February 1918.[113]

Although the peace initiatives in the summer of 1917 had failed to end the war, in assessing their significance three issues should be borne in mind. First, it is important to differentiate between 'peace talk' and wanting to end the war immediately at any price. This distinction was easily lost, when contemporaries accused those who set out principles for future peace of undermining the war effort. The vast majority of people who supported the peace initiatives in the summer of 1917 continued to support their national war effort, precisely because they hoped that victory would provide the platform to build a better world. Hence the SPD's decision to vote through the war credits in July 1917 was eminently compatible with the Reichstag's Peace Resolution, just as the Labour Party and Trade Union Congress continued to support the British war effort after Henderson left the cabinet.

Second, the initiatives provided an opportunity for a vibrant debate about the principles that would form the basis of the future international system. Taken together the initiatives echoed many of the ideas articulated by Wilson and the Petrograd Soviet. Self-determination, economic freedoms, international law, arbitration, and organization were the foremost principles that shaped these debates. Of course, there were different interpretations of these principles – Michaelis had endorsed the Reichstag Peace Resolution with the rider 'as I interpret it', and it is possible to argue that these principles were simply a rhetorical sham. Yet politicians had to assert and justify claims within the language and logic of these principles, so while there was disagreement about their implementation, they constituted the emerging normative environment of the new international order. These norms set the parameters of legitimate political aims and, in doing so, they both restrained power politics and constituted power. It is also worth bearing in mind that these debates in the summer of 1917 were restricted to the European states system, including the United States. They drew on assumptions about a society of nations, based on notions of civilization, humanity, the 'white races', and Christianity.

Finally, the peace initiatives had revealed the large constituencies that supported these general principles in the various belligerent states. The socialists were the most notable and cohesive supporters, but the range of support extended to members of liberal, conservative, and confessional parties. In eastern Europe peasant parties, led by the Croatian Stejpan Radić and the Bulgarian Alexander Stamboliski, were also attracted to these principles as a means of stopping war, limiting the armaments burden on their societies, and enabling them to modernize their political and economic institutions.

* * *

One of the purposes behind the participation of French and British socialists at the Stockholm Conference was to keep Russia in the war. By the time that Lloyd George and Ribot refused to issue passports to the socialist delegations, Russia's position had deteriorated further. The Western Allies

began to ignore Russia as a factor in the war. There was no Russian representative at the meeting on 7 August of French, British, and Italian military
leaders, who discussed plans for military operations in the autumn. War
aims quickly changed, as the Allies scrambled for solutions to the territorial
redrawing of eastern Europe. As early as 4 June, Ribot and Paul Painlevé
were arguing that France had to support an independent Polish Army,
while on 20 September Ribot recognized the Polish National Committee as
the official representative of the Polish nation.[114] Hopes that the revolution
would reinvigorate the Russian war effort were dimmed by the fall of Paul
Miliukov, the continued existence of competing centres of power in the
Petrograd Soviet and the Provisional Government, and the failure of the
Kerensky peace offensive.

The unfolding revolution continued to be shaped by the pressures of the
international system. Increasingly ineffective in fighting terms, revolutionary Russia could not ignore the war. Yet in attempting to define Russia's
role in the war and the world, each step the Provisional Government and
Petrograd Soviet took radicalized the revolution. It was a perpetual
dilemma, in which the twin demands of the consolidation of the revolution
at home and the assertion of sovereignty abroad had to be reconciled. After
all, the revolution had to defend its political achievements against foreign
threats, as 'revolutionary defencism' stressed. Tsereteli and other socialist
members of the Petrograd Soviet had begun to think in terms of a 'peace
offensive' in May 1917. The logic of the peace offensive involved demonstrating Russia's residual military strength in order to compel the Central
Powers to accept the necessity of negotiating peace, rather than imposing
their terms on a war-weary nation. However, rousing the army to a final
peace offensive had become more difficult following Order No. 1, which
undermined the authority of the officer corps. The ardour of soldiers to
undertake one final offensive, as a prelude to peace negotiations, was damp-
ened by the tone-deaf rhetoric of Kerensky, who told soldiers: 'I summon
you not to a feat but to death.' The peace offensive also lacked support in
Petrograd, where Bolsheviks organized anti-offensive demonstrations with
up to 500,000 people. The offensive in Galicia, which began on 1 July, ended
in disaster as units simply refused to follow orders to attack.[115]

The failure of the offensive led to popular demonstrations in Petrograd,
as crowds returned to the Tauride Palace to demand that the Soviet dismiss
the Provisional Government. This would have ended the system of dual
authority in revolutionary Russia, but the Soviet leaders were able to rely on
loyal troops to restore order and arrest leading Bolsheviks, held responsible

for the demonstrations. Lenin, having returned to Russia with German aid in April, fled to Finland. However, his position was strengthened in the long term. First, the Bolsheviks were the only major left-wing party not associated with the Provisional Government, which contained members of the Menshevik Party and the Socialist Revolutionaries. This enabled Lenin to carve out a distinctive space within the revolution. His conception of the Bolsheviks as an elite that would forge the revolution is well known, but since returning to Petrograd in April he had also paid attention to the mood of the crowds, which he summarized in the slogan 'Peace, Bread, Land'.[116] Petitions from workers, peasants, and soldiers revealed an increasing sense that the war was being fought for the good of others. Hence the resolution of the workers employed in the Peterhof district of Petrograd claimed that 'ruling circles' had 'artificially and criminally prolonged' the war, while letters from soldiers claimed that Russia was now fighting Britain's and France's war.[117] The meaning of peace reflected the experience of war, so that peace was associated with stable food supply and land reform. Lenin sought to exploit this meaning of peace to further his revolutionary goals. The long-term value of the July Days, from the Bolshevik perspective, lay in the association between the party and peace.

The other dimension to the July crisis was the principle of nationality, which worked to pull apart the Russian empire. Defending the Russian national interest had been an important goal of liberals who supported the revolution. It had acted as a bridge between the Tsarist regime and the revolution, a thread of continuous meaning in a period of intense rupture. Liberals now found themselves on the right of a shifting political spectrum and their criticisms of the revolution pointed to the failure to strengthen Russia. When Miliukov had called for autonomous regimes for minorities, such as Poles and Finns in the empire, his proposals aimed to strengthen the Russian state by rallying its diverse population to one flag. In March, Ukrainian politicians had set up the Rada, or parliament. Its leading politicians, such as Simon Petlura, sought autonomy within the Russian empire, but frustrated by the lack of substantial negotiations, the Rada declared autonomy unilaterally. The attention of politicians to the constitutional status of the Ukraine weakened the revolution in that region, as pressing questions of land reform were ignored. Moreover, the Rada's unilateral declaration led to a crisis in the Provisional Government in Petrograd. It compounded the sense that the revolution was unable to protect the interests of the Russian state. On 15 July the Cadet members resigned from the Provisional Government and five days later Prince Lvov followed suit. Kerensky became head of the Provisional

Government, but it remained unstable, while the drift towards the left led industrialists, officers, and conservatives to re-emerge as critics and even opponents of the revolution.[118]

The July Days shaped the main coalitions, which would fight the Russian Civil War between 1918 and 1921. On the left the Bolsheviks pressed for further revolution, while on the right a counter-revolutionary plot emerged around the figure of General Lavr Kornilov. His attempted coup in August further polarized the revolution, as it confirmed the previously unfounded fears on the left that counter-revolution was a significant threat. Kornilov aimed to impose a dictatorship that would restore law and order. The attitudes of Miliukov and Alexander Guchkov encapsulated the rapidly shifting perspective of revolutionary politics and its relationship with Russia's international position. Having supported the revolution in March in order to reinvigorate the war effort, they had resigned in May due to the Petrograd Soviet's victory in the war aims debate. Now in August they supported – Guchkov more so than Miliukov – Kornilov's counter-revolutionary coup as a means of restoring the strong state required to defend order at home and national interests abroad. Kornilov feared further disorder and revolution if he failed to act. However, his coup fizzled out and further undermined the fragile authority of the Provisional Government and even the Petrograd Soviet. When Kornilov's troops marched on Petrograd, workers mobilized themselves to block the coup. They stopped the railways from running and the printing presses from producing declarations favouring Kornilov. Ordinary soldiers had no enthusiasm for the coup and the structures of command had collapsed. Kornilov aborted the coup before soldiers had reached Petrograd. Yet because it had been halted by the self-mobilization of workers at factory level, the coup revealed the weakness of the Provisional Government and the Soviet. By late August state authority in Russia had fractured even further.[119]

On 1 September German forces captured Riga, opening the way for a march on Petrograd. This immediate foreign policy context was inescapable in Lenin's thinking about revolution in autumn 1917. In his hands peace became an instrument of politics. Within Russia he identified the desire for peace as a means to mobilize war-weary civilians and soldiers for revolution. The revolution needed to be defended against its enemies abroad, Germany and Austria-Hungary in the immediate term, the imperialist capitalist world in the longer term. Having fled the country in July, Lenin had returned, in disguise, to Petrograd in October so that he could more effectively manage events. In 'The Tasks of the Revolution', written on

9 and 10 October, he identified, as the third of seven revolutionary tasks, the issuing of a declaration of 'democratic' peace terms to all peoples, including the right of Ukrainians and Finns to secede from Russia. Peace without annexations and based on the consent of the people was similar to the proposal of the Petrograd Soviet in May. However, Lenin planned to make an immediate break with the Allies, who, he claimed, supported Russia 'in exactly the same way as a rope supports a man who has been hanged'. Lenin saw the peace declaration in tactical terms. He predicted that it 'will meet with such tremendous sympathy on the part of all peoples and will cause such a great world-wide outburst of enthusiasm and of general indignation against the continuation of the predatory war that it is extremely probable we shall at once obtain a truce and a consent to open peace negotiations'. In case his audience doubted the credibility of this analysis, Lenin claimed that, in the event of a refusal, revolutionary Russia would wage a just revolutionary war aided by the 'oppressed peoples of the whole world'.[120] Within the party, Grigory Zinoviev and Lev Kamenev opposed Lenin's policy of immediate revolution and doubted the probability of a general European revolution.

While Zinoviev and Kamenev wanted to await the elections to the Constituent Assembly and Lenin wanted to exploit the revolutionary moment, Trotsky had never lost sight of the need for military force in an insurrection. The Bolsheviks controlled the Petrograd Soviet's Military Revolutionary Committee, established after the Kornilov coup to defend the revolution. As German forces advanced towards Petrograd, on 24 October according to the Julian calendar or 7 November according to the Gregorian calendar, Trotsky directed the Military Revolutionary Committee, which no longer trusted Kerensky to defend Petrograd or the revolution against Germany, to seize power in the city. This also coincided with the scheduled Second Congress of the Soviets, which Lenin exploited to legitimize the seizure of power. On the afternoon of 8 November the Military Revolutionary Committee seized the Winter Palace, where the remnants of the Provisional Government were ensconced. The second Russian revolution of 1917 threatened to transform the international, as well as the social, order.

CHAPTER 7

VICTORY AND DEFEAT, 1918

In January 1918 on the Montenegrin coast at Kotor, one of the three main bases of the Austro-Hungarian navy, a drunken officer, champagne glass in hand, had toasted 'To ten more years of war'. By the end of the month sailors, already irate at the gap in living conditions between them and the officers, were shouting 'The war must stop! The people want bread!' The mutiny started on 1 February, on the *Saint George*. Delegates to the mutineers' council had a cascade of demands. Some reflected the daily grind of service in a short-staffed navy – better food, fairer work schedules, and more frequent leave. Other demands drew on two of the key statements about the international system – Lenin's peace decree, issued in November 1917, and Wilson's fourteen-point speech, delivered on 8 January 1918. The mutineers sought immediate peace, without annexations and indemnities, the right to self-determination, and democratic reforms. They threatened revolution because, 'as in Russia, the system must be broken'. The mutiny petered out by 3 February. The mutineers were divided and some non-commissioned officers had remained loyal to the empire. Forty mutineers were put on trial and four – Franz Rosch, Anton Grabor, Jerko Šižgaric, and Mak Brničević – were executed after Karl I refused an appeal for clemency.[1] Just nine months later a mutiny in the navy in Kiel provoked the German revolution, the abdication of the Kaiser, and the ceasefire that ended the First World War. The war ended in weariness, expectations of revolution, and geopolitical chaos.

*   *   *

The war ended first on the Eastern Front. The negotiations at Brest-Litovsk between the Bolshevik delegates, led by Trotsky, the divided Central Powers, the nascent Ukrainian state, and the rump Romanian state were dominated by the right to self-determination, significant for several reasons. First, the meaning and application of national self-determination were contested. The concept provided ample scope for the great powers and nationalities to assert their claims. The negotiations showed how power was both advanced and constrained by principle. Second, the representation of governments, in this case as champions of self-determination, constituted an important part of the negotiating process. Making peace in the east provided a platform for addressing wider questions about the international order. Third, the negotiations shaped Woodrow Wilson's fourteen-point speech on 8 January 1918 to Congress, as well as Lloyd George's speech to the Trade Union Congress in Caxton Hall, Westminster, on 5 January. Wilson's speech, in particular, echoed throughout the rest of the war and beyond.

Having witnessed the failure of the Provisional Government to negotiate peace, Lenin accorded ending the war the highest priority. In the proclamation announcing the Soviet assumption of power on 7–8 November, Lenin's first aim was to propose 'an immediate democratic peace to all the nations and an armistice on all fronts'.[2] On 8 November Lenin issued the decree on peace. 'We must remember', he told the Soviet, 'we are not living in the depths of Africa but in Europe, where news can spread quickly.' Although Lenin had retained the option of a revolutionary war, he saw peace as an instrument to secure the revolution in Russia and foment revolution abroad. He combined the language of revolutionary peace with other conceptions of peace. He appealed to the war-weary, who, after being 'exhausted, tormented, and wrecked by the war', wanted an immediate ceasefire. The decree repeated the appeal for a peace without indemnities and annexations. Drawing on certain liberal and socialist criticisms of pre-war diplomacy, Lenin promised to abolish 'secret diplomacy' and 'to conduct all negotiations quite openly in full view of the whole people'. He extended the principle of self-determination from Europe to 'distant overseas countries', a radical attack on European empires. The decree concluded with the clearest statement of its revolutionary intent, as it appealed to the working classes in Britain, France, and Germany, the 'most advanced nations of mankind', to pressure their governments to end the war 'and at the same time emancipate the labouring and exploited masses of our population from all forms of slavery and all forms of exploitation'.[3]

Lenin expected that revolution in Russia would be followed by revolution across Europe. In the month following the seizure of power, these expectations were disappointed. At a meeting of the Central Executive

Committee on 21 November, Trotsky reported that the peace decree appealed to the sentiments of war-weary Europeans, but that the great powers remained committed to war. As yet there was little evidence of revolution. Only Germany, Trotsky thought, was interested in peace. The prospect of making a separate peace with Germany alarmed Bolshevik leaders, owing to the enormous disparity in military power between revolutionary Russia and the Central Powers. On 27 November the Bolshevik government issued another peace appeal, warning against the 'ruin of the whole European culture' if the war continued.[4]

Leaders in the Central Powers saw the Bolshevik seizure of power as an opportunity to end the war on the Eastern Front on favourable terms. Armies concluded local ceasefires along the front (before a general ceasefire was concluded on 2 December). In these negotiations German and Austro-Hungarian officers emphasized their commitment to peace. Ludendorff instructed officers to draw attention to the decrees issued by the Bolsheviks, particularly those on peace and land reform. He hoped, rightly, that this would diminish the fighting capacity of the remnants of the Russian Army. Peasant soldiers, fearful that land would be redistributed before they were demobilized, drifted home. The propaganda disseminated by the Central Powers also emphasized their own commitment to peace, citing their (half-hearted) response to Benedict XV's peace note and blaming the Triple Entente for prolonging the war. The Bolsheviks responded with their own propaganda campaign, distributing the peace decree amongst German and Austro-Hungarian troops. The reception of the peace decree – one soldier wrote that 'peace is being born there [Russia] and will come to us' – raised fears about the reliability of troops who had been exposed to dangerous Bolshevik doctrines.[5]

Georg von Hertling, appointed Chancellor of Germany in October 1917, responded to the second peace appeal. Although he had reforming inclinations, Hertling was considered to be under the sway of Hindenburg and Ludendorff by the autumn of 1917. On 29 November Hertling announced the acceptance of the Bolshevik appeal for peace negotiations. In a crucial paragraph, cheered by the Centre Party and the SPD, he claimed that Germany supported the 'right to self-determination' of countries previously oppressed by the Tsar – Poland, Lithuania, and Courland, in present day Latvia. 'We expect,' he said, 'that they will give themselves the form of state, which corresponds to their relations and the direction of their culture.'[6] Two weeks earlier the Bolsheviks had issued 'Declarations of the Rights of the Peoples of Russia'. This document promised to remove discrimination against minorities, to support the development of minority rights, and to grant to all peoples in Russia the right of self-determination, even to the point of secession.[7] These exchanges between the German and Bolshevik governments placed the issue of national self-determination at the fore of the political agenda in early 1918.

Each side sought to exploit the principle to maximize their power and influence in the peace settlement. The Bolshevik government was playing a far weaker hand. The Russian empire was dissolving even before the declaration on nationalities was issued. The process accelerated after November 1917. On 20 November the Central Rada proclaimed the Ukrainian People's Republic. The new Republic imagined that it would form part of a Russian federation and the Rada issued decrees on land ownership, state control of production, and the eight-hour day similar to those issued by the Bolsheviks. On 4 December, two days after the ceasefire, the government in Kiev decided to send delegates to the peace negotiations in Brest-Litovsk. The Bolshevik government responded by setting up a Congress of Soviets in the Ukrainian city of Kharkiv and dispatching a military force towards Kiev. In a report on the national question, Joseph Stalin revealed the tactical thinking behind the Bolshevik conception of self-determination, when he claimed that the clash between Bolsheviks and nationalities resulted from class conflict, rather than claims to national independence. 'The principle of self-determination,' argued Stalin, 'should be a means in the struggle for socialism and should be subordinated to the principle of socialism.'[8] In other words self-determination could take place only on terms that advanced the power of the Bolshevik revolution. Ukrainians constituted one of the largest minorities in Europe on the eve of the First World War. Some 22,400,000 Ukrainians lived in Russia in 1900 and another 3,800,000 in Austria-Hungary (they were sometimes called Ruthenians in the Habsburg empire). Aside from the weight of numbers, the Ukraine also produced 20 per cent of the world's wheat crop and 90 per cent of Russia's wheat crop. Food was of enormous importance in the diplomatic negotiations and calculations of military power in early 1918, strengthening the position of Ukrainian nationalists at Brest-Litovsk.

Although the emerging Ukrainian Republic had grain, it did not have effective military forces. Moreover, it lacked popular support amongst a large peasant population due to the Rada's failure to implement land reform, which had been promised since the March revolution. Faced with the Bolshevik military threat, Ukrainian nationalists sought German aid. Since at least October 1917 officers in the German Supreme Command considered Ukrainian independence as a means of weakening Russia and extending German influence. The project of the independent Ukrainian nation also fitted in with one strand of German policy in eastern Europe, according to which the principle of national self-determination weakened Russia, legitimized the establishment of buffer states, and increased German security and influence. Before the end of the year Ludendorff indicated his support for an agreement with an independent Ukraine. Having secured German support, the Rada declared independence on 22 January 1918.[9]

The Austro-Hungarian Foreign Minister, Otto Czernin, was also pushing his interpretation of self-determination at Brest-Litovsk. Lenin's peace decree was both a threat and an opportunity for Austria-Hungary. Since coming to office in late 1916, Czernin had explored various avenues to achieve peace. On 10 November he urged Hertling to accept Lenin's formula of peace without annexations. He saw the negotiations as a prelude to a broader settlement, in which principles tested at Brest-Litovsk could find application elsewhere. Yet while peace without annexation served the Habsburg empire, the extension of the principle of national determination threatened its integrity. On Christmas Day 1917 Czernin issued a declaration setting out Austro-Hungarian principles and challenging not just Lenin and Trotsky, but also the Western Allies and the United States. He claimed that the Central Powers accepted the principle of peace without annexations or indemnities, but that this required application in western Europe as well as on the Eastern Front. He also redefined self-determination as a domestic political issue, not subject to international supervision. Nations that did not constitute an independent state would work out their constitutional arrangements within existing state and constitutional structures. This reading of the principle prevented foreign intervention in Austro-Hungarian nationality politics. Czernin was right to be concerned at the repercussions of negotiations for the Habsburg empire. On 6 January 1918 Czech deputies in the Reichsrat declared the 'Czechoslovak nation' to be free from any duties to the Dual Monarchy. Since the reopening of the Austrian parliament in May 1917, Czech, Polish, and South Slav deputies had raised the potential of national self-determination.[10]

Czernin's reworking of self-determination reflected the views of leading political thinkers within Austria-Hungary, such as Josef Redlich. They adapted the older argument of an Austro-Hungarian model of multinational coexistence for Europe to the principle of national self-determination. In July 1917 Redlich had suggested granting autonomy to nationalities within the empire. The journalist and parliamentarian Ernst Victor Zenker emphasized the necessity of constitutional reform as a means not only of resolving Austria-Hungary's internal crisis, but also of offering a paradigm in European politics of different national communities united within a single state.[11] In the absence of constitutional reform, however, this representation of Austria-Hungary as a crucible of an alternative interpretation of national self-determination lacked credibility.

Czernin, in his Christmas Day reply to the Bolshevik delegation, claimed that the Central Powers did not plan to annex territories occupied during the war, including the Baltic and Polish provinces. This infuriated Ludendorff, but it did not go far enough for the Bolsheviks. Adolf Joffe, their leading negotiator before the new year, had argued that self-determination required the withdrawal of occupying forces from these regions, after which a referendum would decide the status of the territory. The Central Powers aimed to exploit their occupation of these territories in order to influence elections, referenda, and other votes. Richard von Kühlmann, the German Foreign Minister, and General Max Hoffmann, the representative of the Supreme Command, viewed the combination of German occupation and self-determination as the essential means of expanding German interests in eastern Europe. Joffe was shocked, recognizing that this meant the loss of vast swathes of the former Russian empire – though the Central Powers used the Bolshevik decree on the rights of nationalities to press their claims that Russia had already recognized the right of these provinces to secede. On 27 December 1917 Kühlmann demanded that the Bolshevik government recognize the separation of Poland and the Baltic provinces from Russia. The following day negotiations were suspended.

The suspension of negotiations revealed the divisions within the Central Powers. Advocates of unrestrained military power and annexations confronted those who favoured a solution, based on the exploitation of self-determination. Ludendorff warned that relations in the east had to be clarified in advance of the offensive he was planning in the west. Clarity, in his view, required the resumption of military operations, the annexation of the Baltic provinces, and the incorporation of a large slice of Polish territory with 2 million Poles into the Reich. Hoffmann and Kühlmann objected to Ludendorff's demands in meetings with Wilhelm II in the first days of January 1918, arguing in favour of minor border adjustments with Poland and the right of self-determination in the former provinces of the Russian empire. On this occasion the Kaiser sided with Kühlmann against Ludendorff. Meanwhile Czernin was frantic, lest the chance to conclude peace be lost. He even considered a separate peace, denouncing the extremism of the German Supreme Command. One of the Austrian diplomats at Brest-Litovsk, Prince Johann Schönburg-Hartenstein, wrote to Czernin on 3 January: 'A large part of Germany and a smaller section of Austria-Hungary still believe that they can compel peace militarily. The greater the military-technical dimensions present themselves, the less England will want to know about peace, and the greater German claims. . . . in this vicious circle, the war can still last a long time, and the means to break out of this accursed ring unfortunately cannot be seen in Brest Litovsk.'[12] Yet it was the German refusal to resume military operations in early January that was striking. As events would show several weeks later, the Central Powers had the military capacity to impose their will on the Bolsheviks. The exercise of power for now was framed by the politics of self-determination, which would legitimize – in their view – a settlement in eastern Europe and buttress German and Austro-Hungarian influence in the region.

* * *

This was the context for the programmatic statements by Lloyd George and Wilson on 5 and 8 January 1918. They were a response to the claims of the Central Powers and part of the international debate about self-determination. Only later in the century were Wilson's fourteen points considered to be the first exchange in the rivalry between liberal capitalism and communism. Lenin's peace decree and Wilson's fourteen points became foundational texts in the international order, but they were the product of a debate taking place at Brest-Litovsk.

Lloyd George, first into the breach, devoted much of his speech at the Trades Union Congress to engaging with Czernin's Christmas Day declaration, though he also acknowledged the Labour Party's memorandum on war aims, itself a product of the politics of the Stockholm Conference. At a lunch after the speech Lloyd George cast his delivery as a challenge to the German terms presented at Brest-Litovsk. 'I went as near peace as I could,' he told the newspaper proprietor George Riddell. 'It was the right moment. The time had come to speak definitely.'[13] On 29 December Maurice Hankey, secretary to the War Cabinet, had woken up at 6 a.m. with the 'brainwave' that the British government should reply to the German peace offer at Brest-Litovsk. Returning from Wales on 1 January, Tom Jones, a member of the War Cabinet Secretariat, 'found the War Cabinet atmosphere completely changed. Everybody talking of peace.'[14] The speech was drafted by Lloyd George, Robert Cecil, and Jan Smuts, who had just returned from secret discussions with the former Austro-Hungarian ambassador to London, Albert von Mensdorff.

Since the November revolution in Russia the mood in London had been gloomy, but defiant. 'Balfour's favourite reading seemed to be novels with a happy ending of which he finds the supply far too short,' recorded Jones, a comment on the atmosphere as much as on Balfour's temperament.[15] More seriously, Andrew Bonar Law, Chancellor of the Exchequer, denounced Lord Lansdowne's peace letter in November 1917 as a 'national misfortune'. Lansdowne had proposed a negotiated settlement of the war that allowed Germany to retain Alsace and Lorraine, conceded the freedom of the seas, and established an arbitration treaty. Although Lansdowne hoped that the Hohenzollern dynasty would abdicate, 'this matter must be for the decision of the German people'.[16] Lloyd George had also criticized Lansdowne's letter as much for its timing and its assumptions as for its specific proposals. 'Lord Lansdowne,' the prime minister said, 'advocates making a treaty with a nation whom we are fighting because they have broken a treaty. He advocates that the treaty should be enforced by a League of Nations consisting of the nations who are now engaged in attempting to enforce the treaty already in existence'.[17] Nonetheless the collapse of Russian power had undermined Lloyd George's confidence in victory against the Central Powers.

The War Cabinet on 31 December discussed their statement of war aims as a reply to Czernin's statement.[18] The statement had to serve both international and domestic political purposes. As ever language and policy had to be reconciled. The members – Lloyd George, Cecil, Smuts, Edward Carson, leader of the Ulster Unionists, and George Barnes – agreed that the statement had to be couched in 'moderate and reasonable terms in order to show to the democracies, not only in allied, but also in enemy countries that we were not continuing the war for imperialistic or unreasonable aims'. Cecil pointed out that Trotsky's recent statements had denounced British imperial rule, so that a statement would require a defence of 'British methods of rule, including a reference to Ireland, India, and Egypt, which were governed for the benefit of the governed'. Barnes, the Labour Party minister, argued in favour of a precise statement of British war aims, which went beyond the articulation of principles to their application. Lloyd George, Smuts, and Cecil drafted statements, which became the basis of the prime minister's speech on 5 January. Hankey got Cecil to remove a general commitment to self-determination on the grounds that Germany – not the Bolsheviks – could exploit the commitment to undermine the British empire.[19]

Barnes had raised the issue of a socialist international conference at the War Cabinet. The legacy of the failed Stockholm Conference, the Labour Party statement on war aims, and the persistent importance of liberal internationalists in British politics also necessitated a statement of war aims. At the weekly meeting on 3 January of the Garton Foundation, founded in 1912 by the philanthropist, brewer, and chemist Richard Garton, liberal internationalists discussed the prospective statement. 'All agreed,' Jones recorded, 'that it was essential in order to keep our own people right to make some definite declaration of our minimum peace terms.' Moreover, they saw peace-making in terms of the balance of domestic politics in Germany. Alfred Zimmern, the historian and liberal internationalist, feared that Ludendorff had become the dominant figure, whereas others believed that the SPD was becoming a more powerful factor.[20]

Speaking to the assembled trade unionists at Caxton Hall on 5 January, Lloyd George set out his statement of British war aims. Unlike Wilson he did not number them, but his aims may be grouped into five sections. First, he insisted that the Central Powers withdraw from the occupied territories in Belgium, France, Italy, Romania, and Serbia, and make reparation for the damage inflicted. He defined reparations as a legal and moral problem, a righting of a wrong, rather than an economic imposition. It was also signifi-cant that the prime minister justified the return of Alsace and Lorraine to France on the grounds of undoing the 'great wrong of 1871' rather than on the basis of self-determination. Second, the consent of the governed was the basis for other alterations to the map of Europe. Lloyd George demanded the estab-lishment of an independent Polish state, 'an urgent necessity for the stability of western Europe', as well as meeting the claims of Italy and Romania 'for union with those of their own race and tongue'. While he warned that the German government was exploiting the principle of self-determination in the former Russian empire, he had no specific proposals for this vast region. Indeed, in early December he had imagined a compromise peace, in which Britain would take German colonies and a sphere of influence in Palestine and Mesopotamia, France would regain Alsace and Lorraine, and Germany would be compensated with a 'large slice of Russia'.[21] Lloyd George also applied the principle of the 'consent of the governed' to the Ottoman empire. While the Allies had no designs on Anatolia, the heartland of the Turkish nation, nor any longer on Constantinople now that imperial Russian war aims could be disregarded, the Ottoman territories of Armenia, Arabia, Mesopotamia, Syria, and Palestine were 'entitled to a recognition of their separate national conditions'. Given that Britain (and France and Italy) had extensive aims in these regions, Lloyd George's invocation of the consent of the governed demonstrated a similar marriage of principle and interest to that shown by the Central Powers at Brest-Litovsk. Moreover, while he was willing to consider some form of consultation with the inhabitants of former German colonies, the prime minister made no mention of British policy towards India and Egypt.

The other three issues had no parallel in Czernin's Christmas Day declaration, which had ignored international organization and law and economic terms, as well as denying that constitutional reform within the Central Powers was an issue of international relations. The third general issue of Lloyd George's speech concerned the constitutional structures of Germany and Austria-Hungary. This was a delicate matter. The speech was designed to appeal to liberals, socialists, and national minorities in the Central Powers. Though carefully phrased, his comments underlined the notion that peace required representative governments. The prime minister denied that the Allies aimed to destroy the 'imperial constitution of Germany', but he added that a 'military, autocratic constitution' was 'a dangerous anachronism in the twentieth century'. The 'adoption of a really democratic constitution' was the best means for Germans to signal the demise of the 'old military spirit' and secure a 'broad democratic peace'. If he was ambivalent about the German constitution, Lloyd George argued that 'unless genuine democratic government is granted to those Austro-Hungarian nationalities who have long desired it', politics in that part of Europe would continue to threaten the general peace. Fourth, he made clear that the Allies, who controlled the bulk of the world's raw materials, planned to 'help themselves and their friends first'. As German economic liberals read it, the economic war would continue after the end of the conflict. Finally, he called for the establishment of an international organization, the use of international law to regulate relations between states, and disarmament. War, he concluded, 'is a relic of barbarism' and law 'is destined ultimately to take the place of war in the settlement of controversies between nations'.[22]

'Epoch-making' was how Riddell described the speech, and it was precisely this prospect that unnerved Woodrow Wilson when he read the text. 'I also insisted that after the President had made his address,' noted Edward House, Wilson's confidant, on 6 January, 'it would so smother the Lloyd George speech, that it would be forgotten and that he, the President, would once more become the spokesman for the Entente, and indeed, the spokesman for the liberals of the world. The President was greatly heartened by this opinion, and set to work again with renewed zest.'[23] In addition to his enormous self-esteem, Wilson was suspicious of Allied war aims. The failure to agree on a joint statement of Allied and American war aims at a conference in late November had troubled Wilson, especially in the context of Lenin's peace decree and the imminent negotiations at Brest-Litovsk. He decided to set out his own aims. On 4 December 1917, in his Fifth Annual Message, the president addressed the 'crude formula' of peace without annexations and indemnities, which he asserted the Central Powers were exploiting to advance their power and claims to leadership in the world. 'But the fact that a wrong use has been made of a just idea,' Wilson said, 'is no reason why a right use should not be made of it.' Only a representative government could make the 'right use' of the principle. While he claimed that he did not seek to intervene in German internal affairs, the president made clear that peace between Germany and the United States and Allies could only be constructed if the 'present masters' of Germany were replaced by a government of the German people.[24]

Two weeks after this speech Wilson decided to make another public address in what would become his fourteen-point speech. He had multiple audiences in mind. Within the United States, he needed to affirm the progressive character of the war, tarnished by the suppression of dissent and the suspicion that interest groups, especially large corporations, were benefiting from government contracts. As in previous speeches, his intended international audience extended beyond the belligerent govern-ments to civilians and soldiers. In particular Wilson presented himself as the international leader of progressive interests that appealed to liberals and socialists alike. He also directed his speech towards war-weary popula-tions in the Allied states.

Much of the detailed work on territorial questions, at the core of his speech, was undertaken by the Inquiry. The Inquiry originated in August 1917 as the importance of planning for peace became increasingly evident. Supposedly a team of experts, many members had little specific training in the areas they wrote about. House had set up the Inquiry through a network of personal and academic contacts. Its existence was separate from the State Department and members were initially housed in the New York Public Library before moving to the American Geographical Society's home on the Upper West Side of New York. This was not too far from Columbia University, the academic home of prominent liberal internationalists such as James Shotwell and Nicholas Murray Butler, and across Central Park from House's New York residence.[25] By 2 January 1918 the Inquiry had completed a statement of peace terms, which House delivered to Wilson two days later, when the two men began to draft the seminal speech. The following day they spent fourteen hours working on the text.[26]

Wilson's speech to Congress on 8 January was more restrained and clearer than Lloyd George's.[27] The simplicity of breaking his speech down into fourteen points echoed the style of an official dispatch – it rendered in public the style of private statements of war aims, such as Bethmann Hollweg's six points in the September programme. Points six to thirteen dealt with specific territorial claims. Wilson never used the term 'self-determination' in the speech, despite his historic association with this term in the popular imagination. He demanded the evacuation of Russia, so that Russians were free to choose their own institutions, though he made no reference to the interests of nations within the borders of the former Russian empire. The restoration of and payment of reparation to Belgium, the president argued, was a moral as well as a territorial imperative. The Inquiry, in similar fashion to Lloyd George's speech, argued that the 'financial amounts involved are less important than the acknowledgment of wrong involved in Germany's consent to rehabilitate the country'.[28] Reparations were defined as part of an international moral reckoning rather than a purely financial concern. Wilson called for the return of Alsace and Lorraine to France. He and the Inquiry recognized that the application of the principle of nationality in this instance might have led to a plebiscite that recognized German sovereignty, owing to the immigration of Germans to the provinces. Such a plebiscite, however, would ratify the violent annexation of 1871. This was similar to French arguments about the two provinces. Italian borders were to be adjusted 'along clearly recognizable lines of nationality'. In the Balkans Romania, Serbia, and Montenegro were to be restored, Serbia given access to the sea, and the territorial integrity of the states guaranteed by international agreements. Wilson now demanded an independent Polish state, enjoying access to the sea and an international territorial guarantee. The president assured Austria-Hungary that he wished to see its place among nations 'safeguarded', but he also called for the nationalities to enjoy 'the freest opportunity to autonomous development'. Wilson used the same term – 'autonomous development' – in relation to the Ottoman empire, but he hinted at some form of international control or independence for subject nationalities, while guaranteeing the 'Turkish portion' its sovereignty.

The fifth point called for the settlement of 'all colonial claims' based on the principle that the interests – not the wishes – of the population had equal weight with the claims of the imperial government. In effect only German colonies were the subject of such claims, but the principle was framed in a loose way that gave it a much wider purchase.

The remaining first four points and the final point were statements about international institutions and principles necessary, in Wilson's view, to sustain peace. Open diplomacy, the freedom of the seas, the 'equality of trade conditions' and removal of barriers to international commerce, and the reduction of armaments were principles that liberal internationalists and many socialists had long espoused. His final point called for the 'association of nations' that would provide mutual guarantees of political independence and territorial integrity under 'specific covenants'. The word 'covenant', as we have seen, had a specific meaning for Wilson that distinguished it from the legal internationalist conception of an association, in which states were legally bound to support guarantees through the use of economic and military sanctions.

Wilson framed these points firstly as a response to the declaration of the Central Powers and the Bolsheviks. Whereas Lloyd George had been dismissive of Russia, Wilson extended the hand of friendship, in part to disrupt negotiations at Brest-Litovsk and in part to follow his idea that revolutionary nations should be encouraged to build their own institutions, free from external intervention. The president moved rapidly from the specific to the universal. The United States was fighting a war to change the world. 'The day of conquest and aggrandizement', he told Congress, 'is gone by'. Morality and political behaviour had to be aligned to provide a 'just and stable peace'. Because the war was a conflict of principles, Wilson returned to the argument that he had made on 4 December, namely that the United States needed to know with whom it was negotiating – 'the Reichstag majority' or the 'military party and men whose creed is imperial domination'. And because this was a war of principles, Wilson's concluding sentence fused war and peace in a millenarian vision of sacrifice and redemption: 'The moral climax of this the culminating and final war for human liberty has come and [the American people] are ready to put their own strength, their own highest purpose, their own integrity and devotion to the test.'

* * *

On 9 January 1918 the Bolshevik delegation, now headed by Trotsky, returned to Brest-Litovsk. Lloyd George's and Wilson's interventions made little difference to the negotiations. Neither the Allied nor American governments succeeded in projecting their power into eastern Europe following the Russian revolution. Issues such as the League of Nations did not intrude upon the negotiations, which were now taking place in secret.

In the days following the resumption of negotiations Trotsky and Kühlmann ranged far and wide in their debates about self-determination, but even that flexible principle was soon warped and broken. By 18 January, frustrated by Trotsky's delaying tactics, Hoffmann denounced Bolshevik claims to represent the ideals of self-determination. The suppression of dissent, the dissolution of representative assemblies, and the attack on the Ukrainian Rada contradicted the fine words and decrees.[29] Presented with an ultimatum, Trotsky sought to evade a treaty by adopting the strategy of 'no war, no peace'. Lenin favoured a separate and immediate peace to consolidate the revolution, but Trotsky's strategy was accepted by the Central Committee on 22 January. Trotsky calculated that the Central Powers would either have to tone down their demands or impose peace by the use of military force, but in doing so undermine their legitimacy and their representational strategy. In the 'No war! No peace!' decree issued on 10 February, Trotsky declared that Germany and Austria-Hungary were champions of the 'right of armed conquest'. It paid homage to the persistent scenario of a revolution in western Europe, though Lenin was rightly sceptical that German workers, despite a wave of strikes in January, were in a position to overthrow the Kaiser's regime.[30]

The decree placed German leaders in a quandary. Kühlmann warned against falling into Trotsky's trap and advised against resuming military operations. He wanted to accept the 'no war, no peace' formula. After all, German troops occupied the territory they wanted, the Bolsheviks did not pose a military threat, and troops could be transferred from the Eastern to the Western Front. German policy should develop relations with nationalist movements in the Ukraine and Finland. Czernin had threatened that Austria-Hungary would conclude a separate peace if Germany embarked on military operations. Whereas Kühlmann sought to exploit the ambiguity of Trotsky's formula, Ludendorff demanded clarity. In advance of a meeting of civilian and military leaders at Bad Homburg on 13 February, he argued that military action would achieve decisive outcomes, including security on the Eastern Front, the release of troops for the Western Front, and the possible overthrow of the Bolshevik regime and its replacement by a conservative regime. Nor were the German military concerned about Czernin's threat. Hindenburg even told Kühlmann that 'the next war will be between us and Austria'. Ludendorff and Hindenburg prevailed on this occasion. On 18 February military operations resumed. In operational terms the offensive was successful, conquering large swathes of Russian territory. Yet as Czernin stated on 19 February, the 'restless hunger for annexations of Germany have permanently ruined peace in the west'.[31]

The German government, which now occupied the Baltic provinces, Belarus, and the Ukraine, presented more exacting terms, including the Russian renunciation of any territorial claims to these territories. What seemed to be the definitive loss of the Ukraine was the most significant blow to the Bolsheviks, given the reliance of major cities on crops produced in this region. The German demands brought to a head the debate within the Central Committee about revolutionary Russia's place in the world. Nikolai Bukharin, Joffe, and others on the left wing of the party favoured the option of revolutionary war. Based on the heroic myth of revolutionary war they called for the total mobilization of revolutionary enthusiasm within Russia, the execution of domestic enemies (broadly defined), and the instigation of working-class revolution in Germany and Austria-Hungary. They envisioned a new international order constructed on the basis of revolutionary war.

Lenin had dropped the option of revolutionary war since late 1917. It was a hollow myth, he had written in January, 'that might perhaps answer the human yearning for the beautiful, dramatic, and striking, but that would totally disregard the objective balance of class forces and material factors at the present stage of the socialist revolution'.[32] The military collapse since the resumption of hostilities confirmed Lenin's determination to conclude peace. With the revolution already beset by food shortages, popular resistance, and fragmentation along ethnic and national lines, external peace was essential to defend the revolution at home. The crucial shift in thinking was to identify the primary threat to the revolution as a domestic, rather than a foreign, one. Yet the vision of revolutionary war remained so appealing that Lenin had to threaten to resign before the Central Committee agreed to accept the German terms. In this contest Lenin had strengthened his own authority within the party. By rejecting revolutionary war, he also began a process of socializing Soviet Russia into the international system. Although Lenin has earned the label 'realist' for his judgement of the balance of forces in the European war between January and March 1918, he still anticipated a world revolution. His decision in March was contingent on the 'balance of class forces and material factors', as he put it. The accommodation of Soviet Russia into the international order was jagged – and it also required the other powers to accept its membership.

Under the terms of the Treaty of Brest-Litovsk, Soviet Russia renounced all claims to Finland, the Baltic provinces, Belarus, and Ukraine. Article 3 stated that Germany and Austria-Hungary would 'determine the fate of the said territories with the consent of their inhabitants'. The Ottoman empire also secured Ardahan, Kars, and Batum, annexed by Tsarist Russia after the Ottoman–Russian War in 1877–8. The Central Powers did not impose an indemnity on Russia. From the perspective of the Russian empire in 1914 these terms constituted catastrophic demographic, economic, and strategic losses. Yet the territories shorn from the Russian empire reflected the dictates of nationality politics, as well as the balance of military power.

Assessing the Treaty of Brest-Litovsk requires taking into account how German and Austro-Hungarian policy shaped the future of these territories in the short term. The ambiguous character of the treaty was evident in Reichstag debates. The SPD abstained from voting on it. Scheidemann argued that the Central Powers perverted the notion of self-determination by demanding Russia renounce its claims to Poland, Lithuania, and Courland. By pursuing 'power politics' (*Machtpolitik*) Germany had undermined the possibility of a reconciliation and lasting peace with Russia. On the other hand the SPD demanded that 'the genuine right of self-determination of Poland, Lithuania, and Courland must be secured' in the coming months. SPD member Eduard David made a similar point during his speech, suggesting that the terms could be redeemed through granting the occupied territories self-determination, free from manipulation. The SPD distrusted the authors of the terms, rather than the terms themselves.[33] Matthias Erzberger insisted that the treaty reflected the previous year's peace resolutions. He argued that it met the criteria of self-determination, which promoted the 'general contentment' of Russia's western border, provided for a lasting peace, and secured Germany's own right to self-determination. Erzberger had developed close connections with Lithuanian elites and considered them instinctively favourable to close relations with Germany.[34] The newly formed Fatherland Party read the terms in a different way. It countered the principle of self-determination with the claim that the spoils go to the victor. In March the party approved the treaty, but it also pressed for greater expansion in the Baltics and a proto-colonial scheme, which would provide land for soldier-settlers.[35]

The policy of the German government in the Baltics edged towards incorporating the new states into the Reich. In Lithuania the Council (*Taryba*), established in September 1917, declared independence in February 1918. The members were not simply lackeys of the German occupying forces. Indeed, they resented the severe restrictions on their political remit. Where German officials viewed the Council as a conduit to the Lithuanian population, the members tried to preserve the faintest semblance of an autonomous political community. The Council sometimes proved a source of embarrassment to German occupation authorities. When the German government proposed a personal union between Lithuania and Germany under the Kaiser, the Council invited Duke Wilhelm of Urach, from Württemberg, to become king. Within Germany the SPD and Erzberger (later in 1918) criticized policy in Lithuania as a violation of self-determination and a sign of the military's influence on the settlement in eastern Europe.[36] Even in the context of a decisive military victory on the Eastern Front, German forces could not simply impose the political settlement.

The principle of self-determination quickly collapsed due to the dominance of Ludendorff within the German leadership, the weakness of Austria-Hungary, and the absence of stability in the region. These processes can be seen in the case of the Ukraine. Since the Rada's declaration of independence Ukrainian nationalists had become increasingly reliant on German support to fend off the threat from the Bolshevik offensive. 'From now on,' wrote the founder of the League for the Liberation of Ukraine, Andrij Žuk, on 16 February, 'the fate of our people is tightly linked to the fate of the German nation.'[37] Parallel to the growing dependency on Germany, the Ukrainian delegation at Brest-Litovsk confronted Czernin on 13 January with certain demands, rooted in the principle of self-determination and supported by food diplomacy. The first related to the province of Cholm, formerly part of the Russian empire, occupied by Austro-Hungarian troops, and claimed by Polish nationalists since 1916. Polish nationalists justified their claim on historic grounds, but they were not present at Brest-Litovsk. The Ukrainian delegate, Mykola Ljubynski, called for a plebiscite, aware that approximately 60 per cent of the province's population were Ukrainian and only 20 per cent Polish. 'In this room we can barely hear the voices of the people,' responded Czernin acidly.

The second Ukrainian demand was arguably even more far-reaching, particularly in light of Czernin's definition of self-determination as a domestic Austro-Hungarian issue. The Ukrainian delegation demanded that the Habsburg province of Galicia be divided into two separate provinces, with separate Ruthenian Crown Lands in eastern Galicia. Although Poles constituted a majority – 60 per cent – in the whole province, in eastern Galicia Ukrainians accounted for 70 per cent of the population.

On 8 February Czernin agreed to include a secret protocol for the establishment of the Ruthenian Crown Lands in the treaty between the Central Powers and the Ukraine, having already agreed to hand over Cholm to the newly independent state. These constituted two remarkable concessions. When Czernin met the Polish Club, an important constituency of his domestic political support, on 19 January, he could not bring himself to mention Cholm. When the news emerged, this concession destroyed Austro-Hungarian influence in Poland. It also created a new source of nationalist tensions in 1918 between the Ukraine and Poland, two emerging but very fragile states. The agreement on the Ruthenian Crown Lands was even more humiliating for Czernin, conceding to the Ukraine what he had refused to concede to Lloyd George and Woodrow Wilson. The reason for these concessions lay in the appalling shortages of food in the Habsburg monarchy and its dependence on Germany. Czernin had even briefly explored a separate peace with the United States, but he concluded that the fate of the monarchy was bound up with Germany. The promise of food deliveries from the Ukraine's bread basket was at the heart of Czernin's reasoning. 'The East Galician question,' he said on 19 January, 'I will leave to the Austrian Ministry; that must be decided in Vienna. The Cholm question I will decide on my own. I can and will not look on as hundreds of thousands starve, in order to preserve Polish sympathies.'[38] On 22 January the Ministerial Council met in Vienna. Czernin compared the monarchy's position to a man on the third floor of a burning house, deciding whether to jump. The proposed Ruthenian Crown Lands was a 'kowtow to Ukraine', while the Hungarian Minister President, Sándor Wekerle, appointed in 1917 to succeed István Tisza, warned that a concession to the Ukraine had unforeseen repercussions. 'The ethnographic structure of the monarchy,' he argued, 'forbids any foreign intervention, which, if it is accepted in one case, must create a dangerous precedent for other states.'[39] Yet the food issue trumped other considerations. The army had already diverted 40,000 well-trained troops to suppress internal unrest in January 1918.[40] The ministers decided to jump and accept the Ukrainian demands.

While the Ukrainian delegation asserted their national claims against Austria-Hungary, the state's dependency on Germany made a mockery of self-determination. German diplomats and politicians, including SPD member Eduard David, saw the Ukraine as a source of agricultural imports rather than as an equal state, while the Pan-German writer Paul Rohrbach evoked the imperial language of the civilizing mission to describe the relationship.[41] During the spring of 1918 the last vestiges of a German policy in eastern Europe based on any form of self-determination collapsed, as Ludendorff triumphed over Kühlmann. The latter's argument that German influence and power could best be achieved through the manipulation of newly independent nations had little purchase on the Supreme Command. Moreover, Wilhelm II had moved firmly into the annexationist camp following the conclusion of the Treaty of Brest-Litovsk. Referring to the Baltics, he wrote, with a touch of megalomania: 'I conquered it and no jurist can take it from me.'[42] Ludendorff failed to grasp the limits of German power. The search for total control weakened Germany – as Lenin had predicted it would – because it required the diversion of resources to the Eastern Front at a time when the German Army was preparing for an offensive in the west. In addition, revolution and occupation had destroyed state structures in the region, making it more difficult to extract food that Germany and Austria-Hungary needed for their war-weary populations.

Throughout March and April the German Supreme Command watched the development of Ukrainian politics with growing dismay. The Rada certainly made errors. The abolition of the private ownership of land in February undermined the social basis of the new nation, while violence and crime demoralized the urban population. 'The bourgeoisie,' noted Vladimir Vernadskii, a Russian academic living in the Ukraine, on 19 March, 'is beginning to think about the Germans. They will guarantee them protection against murder, violence, and plunder – but what about afterwards?'[43] German troops had already entered the Ukraine by the time Wilhelm Groener, one of the rising officers in the Supreme Command, met the conservative Ukrainian politician Pavlo Skoropadsky, a former Tsarist general and opponent of the Bolshevik revolution. On 29 April the Ukrainian Union of Landowners proclaimed Pavlo Skoropadsky *hetman* (chief) of the Ukraine. His new government had a narrow and elite social basis, it repealed the Rada's legislation, and allowed German forces to requisition grain from peasants.[44] Within months German occupation had thoroughly alienated the Ukrainian population. 'The Germans behave correctly,' noted Vernadskii on 31 March, 'but like masters.'[45] By June Ukrainian peasants had revolted unsuccessfully against the German requisitions.

By late June 1918, Ludendorff was thinking in terms of the creation of a German-dominated European-Asian bloc, in which Russia was dependent on the Reich. The rationale behind his vision was a world divided into three blocs, including a Pan-American one in the western hemisphere and one based on the British empire. To secure its future, Ludendorff believed, Germany had to build an empire in eastern Europe.

The evolution from proposals for self-determination to Ludendorff's plans for a German empire in eastern Europe was not simply the unveiling of long-standing plans. The idea of colonizing territory in eastern Europe and the Baltics had long been discussed within German foreign policy debates, but it was only one strand. The Foreign Ministry represented an alternative vision of the international order, in which German dominance was secured by adapting the emerging political norms of self-determination. This was undoubtedly cynical, but it was no more cynical than similar plans by Allied, American, and Russian politicians to exploit principles to further their states' security and power. Moreover, the existence of principles provided a yardstick against which policies and decisions could be measured. They often fell short – far short – of the lofty ideals, but they constituted a framework in which power was exercised.

The collapse of Russian power on the Eastern Front created a paradox. Germany's military predominance was now overwhelming, but it had become much more difficult to exercise power because the political institutions that replaced those of the Russian empire were weak and fragile. The proposed annexation of the Baltic states and military occupation in the Ukraine had the seductive appeal of political clarity. Wilhelm II's hubris also benefited Ludendorff, while Kühlmann's comparative restraint led to his dismissal in July 1918. The ideas, though not the practice, of self-determination and international revolution survived beneath the dominant German imperial position.

* * *

Beyond the German sphere of influence Wilson's fourteen-point speech resonated, sometimes in unpredictable ways. Two days after the speech, Secretary of State Robert Lansing set out some dilemmas in the interpretation of the points. When he considered the 'long-standing and complex situation in the Balkans', he doubted whether it could be resolved on the 'principle of self-determination'.[46] Wilson had never uttered the phrase 'self-determination', nor did he use it in a further elaboration of his ideas in a speech on 11 February. Nonetheless the concept became inextricably associated with the fourteen points. What had been a specific statement of aims was transformed into slogans and ideas that had an enormous purchase on international politics. In December 1918 Lansing, increasingly hostile towards Wilson, called him the 'phrase-maker par excellence. The gift of clever phrasing may be a curse unless the phrases are put to the test of sound, practical application before being uttered.'[47] This criticism was unfair, but Wilson's speech had widened the intellectual space in which a vast variety of groups – governments, national minorities, socialists, and colonial leaders – could assert their interests.

European socialists rallied to Wilson's programme, partly out of conviction and partly to manage increasing dissent amongst workers. In January 1918 strikes broke out in major armament production centres in France, while working-class discontent in Italy was contained by the threat of conscription for strikers. In the United States workers had become increasingly suspicious of the progressive claims that Wilson and Samuel Gompers, the leader of the American Federation of Labor (AFL), were making for the war. The lack of reform and the imprisonment of opponents compounded the privations of the war, such as the shortage of coal and deteriorating working conditions. 'The question of wages is nothing,' noted a French police report of the strikers' sentiments in February, 'that of Peace is every-thing; the working class must therefore organise itself in anticipation of a revolutionary movement which will break out simultaneously in all coun-tries to impose Peace.'[48] The French trade union leader Léon Jouhaux, who had called for a statement of war aims at a conference of the Confédération Générale du Travail (CGT) in late December, recalled how Wilson's fourteen-point speech had calmed 'the timid' and thrilled 'the humble, the innumerable, who did not despair of the war, but who feared being led off the path by evil shepherds.'[49]

Between 20 and 24 February an Inter-Allied Labour and Socialist Conference took place at Central Hall in Westminster. Thomas, Jouhaux, Vandervelde, and the Italian socialist Giuseppe Modigliani, the brother of the famous painter, travelled to London as did representatives of Czech and Polish trade union associations from the United States. The AFL turned down the invitation. Wilson's name was only mentioned once in the final memorandum, while the discussions concentrated on the statement of war aims drawn up by Webb, Henderson, and MacDonald for the Labour Party. The statement about colonial claims and the proposal for an association of nations chimed closely with Wilson's fourteen points. The conference did assert the 'right of all peoples to self-determination' in a general injunction. Its call for 'the complete democratisation of all countries' as a precondition for entry into the League of Nations articulated a long-standing theme of Allied and American thinking about the future international order, one that Wilson and Lloyd George had expressed tentatively in their war aims speeches. Finally, the conference reiterated that peace required the social and economic reconstruction of the world and restated demands for the international regulation of labour, the improvement of health and safety conditions, and the prohibition of cartels and protective tariffs. Further, the delegates emphasized the role of the state in managing the economy: 'It is now known that in this way it is quite possible for any government to prevent, if it chooses, the occurrence of any widespread or prolonged invol-untary unemployment; which if it is now allowed to occur in any country, is as much the result of Government neglect as any epidemic disease.'[50]

Trade union leaders struggled to contain the frustrations and weariness of the working classes. Britain was an exception in this respect – in spring 1918 the number of days lost to strikes was at its lowest point during the war. In Glasgow workers reportedly chipped in an extra day's work to show solidarity with the men in the trenches. In France 200,000 metalworkers went on strike between 13 and 18 May, which ended with the imprisonment of the strike leaders. The Italian Federation of Metalworkers (FIOM) had led 144 strikes in 1917, but 226 by September 1918. The response of the state propaganda office was revealing. In August 1918 it declared: 'The war is being fought for all those who suffer and live in poverty, in the countryside and in the towns. . . . The war is being fought for the proletariat. . . . But people will get all this only through the state.'[51] While socialist and trade union leaders were committed to a settlement based on national self-determination, a League of Nations, and democracy, they also recognized that binding the working classes to the peace settlement would require specific measures that would improve their daily lives. Promises of reform – as well as the gains made during the war – had become part of the expectation and meaning of peace. These ideas went beyond the Wilsonian prescription.

Ideas about the future peace spread in multiple trajectories. In Italy the Committee on Public Information, the American Red Cross, and other organizations had transformed Wilson into a 'great saint', who according to one elderly woman, 'was making peace for us. "Che bell santo quel grande Sante Americano".'[52] The insertion of America into everyday life in Italy had a profound effect. One million Italian soldiers ate in American canteens every month, while in April 1918, to mark the first anniversary of American entry into the war, the United States gave 6.4 million lire in financial aid to 290,000 Italian families. The scale and quality of the American presence in Italy reinforced the image of the United States, which had been transmitted by millions of migrants. Fiorella La Guardia, the first Italian American elected to Congress and later the mayor of New York, served with the American Army in Italy and went on a speaking tour after the Italian defeat at Caporetto in November 1917. 'America stands not only for democracy,' wrote Charles Merriam, the head of the Italian section of the Committee on Public Information, in June 1918, 'but for all the unrealized ideals of many of the European peoples; and they must not be disillusioned.'[53]

Woodrow Wilson appealed to people as well as governments. The sceptical response of the Italian government to Wilson's fourteen-point speech and his policies in general derived from their distaste for his conduct of international politics. Foreign Minister Sidney Sonnino preferred the conventional channels of diplomacy. He was perturbed by Lloyd George's and Wilson's speeches, which emphasized nationality as the guiding principle of the territorial settlement. This threatened the basis of the 1915 Treaty of London (which Sonnino had signed), driven by the logic of military security. In addition, Sonnino was depressed by his sense of guilt about the defeat at Caporetto. In an outburst at an Inter-Allied Conference in February 1918, he revealed his sense of helplessness, partly due to personal circumstances, and partly due to the rapidly shifting sands of international politics: 'I have read that this world war is due to the passage of the latest comet near the earth. The comet poisoned the earth. Sometimes I have thought about this explanation. Things that overwhelm our will must be in the world in these years. We have all become crazy. Boundless folly alone is the master of man. How then can we pretend to control destiny?'[54]

Sonnino feared that the principle of self-determination would favour Yugoslav claims in the Adriatic. The previous July the Serbian government and the Yugoslav Committee had issued the Corfu Declaration. Essentially, the declaration was a political compromise between the Serbian government, weakened by its exile to Corfu, and the Yugoslav Committee, which wanted a federal Yugoslav state. While each of the 'national denominations' – Serbs, Croats, and Slovenes – had equal cultural and linguistic rights, the balance between centralization and federalism was studiously ignored. In defining its geopolitical rationale, the declaration emphasized the Yugoslav state's role as a rampart 'against the pressure of the Germans'. The declaration demanded the cession of South Slav regions in the Habsburg empire. Defining the borders of the new state as the territory 'where our nation lives in compact masses and without discontinuity' was directed against Italian claims as well as Austro-Hungarian territory. At a lunch hosted by the Serbian Society of Great Britain on 8 August 1917, Cecil pretended not to discern any division between Serbian or Yugoslav and Italian ambitions. The Serbian prime minister Nikola Pašić, who responded, invoked self-determination to disguise the conflict politely, saying that he supported the unification of ethnic Italian regions with Italy as well as the unification of South Slavs.[55] Hence Sonnino's exasperation when he heard Lloyd George and Wilson justify Italian claims on the grounds of nationality – they had adopted the same logic as Pašić.

The Congress of Oppressed Nationalities in Rome in April 1918 was one Italian response to Wilson's fourteen-point speech and the growing importance of self-determination. While Sonnino was committed to the Treaty of London, democratic interventionists, such as Gaetano Salvemini, favoured a deal with the putative Yugoslav state based on self-determination. Wilson's speech gave a new fillip to the Italian debate. Salvemini, who had taken part in the 4th Isonzo Offensive in late 1915 before being taken ill, returned to Italian domestic political debate in 1916. He helped to convert Luigi Albertini, the influential editor of the *Corriere della Sera*, to a position of national self-determination. Albertini led the public campaign in early 1918 to hold a Congress of Oppressed Nationalities in Rome, while within the cabinet Leonida Bissolati championed the principle of self-determination. The prime minister, Vittorio Orlando, supported the proposal with a view to undermining Austria-Hungary.[56] The proposal drew support from outside Italy. The New Europe group in Britain, founded in October 1916 by Robert Seton-Watson, Alfred Zimmern, Henry Wickham Steed, and others, championed the formation of nation states in the Austro-Hungarian empire as a means of containing German power in Europe as well as securing the basis for a lasting peace. In addition, the French government supported the Congress in the hope that the resolution of differences between Italy and the South Slavs would strengthen Italy and a future Yugoslavia as barriers to German expansionism.[57]

The Congress of Oppressed Nationalities took place in Rome in April 1918. Orlando, underlining the tactical dimension of the Congress, stressed Italian sympathy for the nationalities oppressed by Austria-Hungary.[58] The resolutions of the Congress, attended by Czech, Slovak, and Romanian representatives as well as Italian and Yugoslav delegates, were directed against Austria-Hungary. They affirmed the right of these nationalities to their own states and the imperative of their common struggle against Austria-Hungary. Additional resolutions agreed by Ante Trumbic, the Yugoslav Committee's representative, and Andrea Torre, the Italian representative, reflected the democratic interventionist conception of the settlement in the Adriatic. Territorial disputes were to be settled on the 'principle of nationality', they would cooperate in the Adriatic Sea, and their goals were the 'completion of Italian national unity' and Yugoslav unity and independence.[59] Though Torre had no official status as a representative of the Italian government, he was in close contact with Orlando. The Congress also anticipated a split between democratic interventionists in Italy and their allies in Britain and the United States. During the Congress Salvemini had proposed to Steed – who had acted as go-between in negotiations between Trumbic and Torre – that Italy could forego its claims to Dalmatia in return for gaining Istria, including Fiume. This solution was more easily reconcilable with the principle of nationality, but Steed ignored it and had little sympathy for the political problems faced by democratic interventionists in Italy.

The resolutions of the Congress of Oppressed Nationalities fitted with changes in the Allied governments' policy towards Austria-Hungary and the future geopolitical settlement in Europe. In January 1918 both Wilson and Lloyd George had held open the prospect of a reformed Austria-Hungary retaining its place on the map of Europe. By April the political constellation had changed following the failure of a brief exchange between Czernin and Wilson on the possibility of a separate peace and the conclusion of the Treaty of Brest-Litovsk. On 6 April, speaking in Baltimore as part of the Third Liberty Loan campaign, Wilson condemned the German government for its imperial plans that violated 'the principle of free self-determination of nations'. This was the first occasion on which he used the term 'self-determination'. Although he rowed back from it a few days later and claimed that the Allies did not want to impose constitutions on other states, Wilson had finally said what people had imagined he had said three months previously. Moreover, the brief exchange between Wilson and Czernin in February and March had shown that their conceptions of self-determination were irreconcilable, precisely because Wilson did expect internal constitutional change in Austria-Hungary as part of a peace settlement.

The Allies had begun to adjust their nationality policy in 1917 as a reaction to the Russian revolution and the policy of the Central Powers towards Poland. Earlier in the war the Allies had regularly claimed that they were fighting in defence of nations, but this generally referred to existing states, such as Belgium, Serbia, and later Romania. The principle of nationality also justified certain territorial claims. From late 1917 this principle expanded to include the establishment of new nation states, accommodating security and principle in the emerging European order. Joseph Noulens, the French ambassador to Petrograd and opponent of the Bolsheviks, reported on 29 November that 'in the general shattering of ideas in Russia, the sentiment of nationalities seems like the only one capable of offering our policy a solid basis'. He and Jean Pélissier, who had worked with exiled nationalist leaders in Switzerland, called for immediate French support for the nascent Ukrainian state. However, the French government was slow to act and powerless in the region. Nor did the suggestion of the senior French military figure in the Ukraine, General Tabouis, help, namely that the Ukraine form a federation with Poland. 'They treat us like Zulus', was the revealing comment of one Ukrainian nationalist.[60] When the Rada declared independence, the French government did not recognize its existence. Ukrainian independence, with its evident dependence on Germany, held little attraction for French planners. In the longer term, however, Pierre de Margerie, a leading official in the French Foreign Ministry, saw Poland as a rampart – a voguish phrase – against German power. In a memorandum on 26 November de Margerie combined geopolitical interest and cultural bonds. As a 'centre of western culture', trapped between Germanic and Slavic nations, Poland would need to develop rapidly. Here de Margerie was adopting the cultural geopolitical arguments that Polish exiles had used in previous years.[61]

In the spring of 1918 Allied decisions underlined their shift towards a policy of independent nation states. The day after the Treaty of Brest-Litovsk was signed, the memorandum for Stephen Pichon, the French Foreign Minister who favoured national self-determination, called for the establishment of Polish, Czechoslovak, and Romanian states, which would form the 'indispensable barrier between Germanism and the Balkan states on one hand and the countries of the east on the other hand'.[62] In April and May Georges Clemenceau, the French prime minister, assured the exiled Czech nationalist leader Edvard Beneš of French support for Czechoslovak independence. Lloyd George was cautious about making promises that the Allies could not keep, fearing that any subsequent disappointment would alienate the nationalities from Britain. Although more cautious than their French counterparts, the Foreign Office promised support to the Czech National Council in April. On 9 August the Foreign Office recognized the Council as the provisional Czech government.[63] In a joint declaration on 3 June, Britain and France expressed their support for the establishment of an independent Poland with access to the sea.

Framed in the language of nationality the interests of the Allies were clear. Their first specific guarantee for the 'restoration of Poland in its histor-ical and geographic limits' was made on 2 March in an attempt to spur Poles in the rapidly dissolving Russian Army to desert and join forces with units from General Joseph Haller's nascent Polish Army.[64] The confluence of Allied strategy with the ambitions of separatist nationalists in central and eastern Europe created a new framework for the assertion of claims to national self-determination following the Treaty of Brest-Litovsk.

Words, however, could not be caged. Notions of self-determination were generally framed to coincide with Allied and American interests. Nationalist leaders articulated their demands in ways that appealed to their likely bene-factors amongst the great powers. Hence the Ukrainian self-presentation as a land of agricultural bounty or the Corfu Declaration's robust reference to the future Yugoslavia as a rampart against German expansionism. Thomas

Masaryk, in *The New Europe* published in 1918, provided a particularly fine example of the fusion of nationalist demands and Allied interests. He identified the 'moral significance' of the war in the conflict between two political conceptions – monarchical theocracies and modern nationalism. The war was ushering in a new historical epoch, defined by 'the New Man, homo Europeus', who was constructed by national democracy and 'growing interstatism and internationalism'. In less abstract terms Masaryk called for the break-up of Austria-Hungary and the establishment of independent Czechoslovak, Yugoslav, and Polish nation states. As he surveyed Europe, Masaryk argued that the only acute national issues in western Europe centred on the Danish population in Schleswig and the French population in Alsace and Lorraine. 'The Irish question,' he claimed without offering any explanation, 'is not a national question (not in the sense in which, for instance, the Polish or Czechoslovak questions are national).'[65]

Masaryk's claim would have surprised Irish nationalists, whether Home Rulers or separatist nationalists in Sinn Fein, and probably politicians of all hues in the United Kingdom. Irish nationalists regularly invoked the concept of self-determination. Writing to the *Irish Independent* on 16 January 1918, Eoin MacNeill, a Sinn Fein member and professor of early Irish history at University College Dublin, argued that Lloyd George's speech of 5 January constituted a 'solemn pledge' that 'self-determination would apply to Ireland no less than any other country. . . . In fact the pledge in the eyes of the world is necessarily more binding on the British government in the case of Ireland than in the case of Belgium, Servia[sic], etc, for the British government is absolutely free to bind this principle. . . in the settlement of the Irish difficulty, and is very far from being free in its application to those other countries.'[66] There was a certain degree of playfulness in MacNeill's interpretation of Lloyd George's speech, but it showed how Irish nationalists sought to use the language and emerging norms of the international system to further their own domestic political agenda. Since the 1916 Easter Rising, British and Irish politicians had tried on several occasions to bring about a resolution of the Irish question. Prospective solutions often linked constitutional change in Ireland to a wider reform of the British empire, reconstituted as a federation. These attempts foundered on coalition politics and Unionist opposition. Moreover, the basis for a solution that retained Ireland within the United Kingdom was rapidly eroding as Sinn Fein, the separatist party, won a string of by-elections in 1917. As its fortunes threatened to go into reverse in 1918, the conscription crisis – the application of conscription to Ireland, excluded from the 1916

Act – revived the party. Having failed to prevent the application of conscription to Ireland, the Irish Parliamentary Party withdrew from Westminster, a signal that Irish nationalists had lost faith in British constitutional politics.[67] During the debate in Ireland about conscription, nationalists claimed that its introduction represented a violation of Wilson's declaration of self-determination and the Allied claims that they were fighting a war for small nations.[68]

Nationalists in Egypt and India added Wilsonian ideas into their brew of justifications for self-government. His ideas were spread in the Arabic language press and they prompted debate over whether self-determination could be applied to Egypt. Figures such as Sa'd Zaghlul, the vice-president of the Legislative Assembly, couched their claims for self-government in the language of national self-determination rather than on religious or historical grounds.[69] Indian students and workers in the United States, largely in California, created networks that helped the transmission of Wilsonian ideals. San Francisco was the American base of the Ghadar movement, which wanted complete separation from Britain. After entering the war, American authorities had suppressed the Ghadar movement, notably during the Hindu-German conspiracy trial between November 1917 and April 1918.[70] Yet it was American words as much as practices that attracted Indian nationalists. 'Ideas, universal ideas,' wrote Lajpat Rai, a future president of the Indian Congress Party, in February 1918, 'have a knack of rubbing off all geographical limitations. It is impossible that the noble truths uttered by President Wilson in his War Message could be limited in their application. Henceforth his words are going to be the war cry of all small and subject and oppressed nationalities in the world. He has conferred a new character of democracy and liberty on the latter and the people of Asia are going to make as much use of this charter, if not even more, as are those of America and Europe.'[71]

There was a wide gap between intention and consequence in Wilson's policy. He could not control how his words ricocheted around the world, being reworked in local contexts that he had never even imagined. His intention had been to revive flagging spirits, to provide coherence to Allied and American aims, with a distinctive American twist, and to make clear his own aims for the peace settlement. Yet his words provided the ballast for the aims of others.

Meanwhile Allied unity in western Europe held in the face of the Russian revolution, the Italian defeat at Caporetto, and the massive gains of the Central Powers at Russia's expense at Brest-Litovsk. The United States was sending troops to Europe, over a quarter of a million between January and

April 1918, and another 244,000 in May alone. German troops were turning west, with the number of divisions on the Eastern Front falling from 85 to 47 and the number in the west rising from 147 to 191 between November 1917 and March 1918.[72] The final battles of the First World War were about to be joined. Their outcome would shape, as Masaryk put it, 'the question of organizing the Old and the New World, all mankind.'[73]

* * *

The decision to launch the Michael Offensive and the planning behind it remain some of the most controversial issues in the military history of the First World War.[74] By taking the initiative on the Western Front, Germany's military leaders staked the outcome of the war on this offensive. When Prince Max von Baden, the future Chancellor, asked Ludendorff what would happen if the offensive failed, the general replied that 'Germany must perish'. The Prince was as impressed with Ludendorff's boldness and air of authority as he was alarmed by the gamble.[75] This extreme either/or scenario, purposefully planned and casually articulated, was of a piece with other military decisions by the German leadership. It was the third attempt to win the war solely by military means, following the initial offensive in 1914 and the submarine campaign in 1917. The logic of the decision-making bore similarities to these previous attempts, especially the launching of the submarine campaign. First, the authors of the decision, Ludendorff, Hindenburg, and their advisers in the Supreme Command, opposed a compromise peace in the west. They were committed to retaining control of Belgium, which ruled out any deal with the Allies. Second, they recognized the superior resources of the Allied and American forces. They assumed that in a war of attrition these resources would determine victory. Third, they feared revolution within Germany owing to food shortages, political divisions, and general war-weariness. At the least these last two assumptions were open to question, given the enormous difficulty the Allies had in breaking through strong defensive positions and the absence of revolution to date. Nonetheless these assumptions formed an essential part of Ludendorff's reasoning. And this led to the final piece in the jigsaw – time. On 23 October 1917, before the Bolshevik revolution, Major Georg Wetzell, a close adviser to Ludendorff, argued that Germany needed to defeat Britain and France before the bulk of the American troops reached Europe in the second half of 1918.[76]

Detailed planning for the offensive in the west began on 11 November 1917. In discussions from this point up to January 1918, the original conception of a single offensive evolved into a plan for a series of offensives. Ludendorff devoted considerable attention to the tactical arrangements for the offensives. Troops were pulled out and retrained in storm-troop tactics. These emphasized small, mobile units with a wide scope for taking the initiative in engagements on the battlefield. In some respects these units represented the culmination of a change within European armies towards a more professional conception of the soldier. Armies were increasingly made up of specialists in particular skills rather than the massed ranks of infantrymen. However, the artillery remained the dominant arm on the battlefields of 1918. Colonel Georg Brüchmüller, who had risen from comparative obscurity to plan the artillery barrage to dramatic effect in the battle of Riga in August 1917, took charge of the artillery doctrine on the Western Front in 1918. His major insight was to use artillery to suppress the enemy, rather than destroy their positions. This required close coordination with storm troops and the centralized command of artillery. Due to the centralization of artillery command and the precise schedule of artillery barrages, the German offensives in 1918 were shaped by detailed bureaucratic systems rather than the power of initiative stressed in the storm-troop tactics.[77]

The German armies – 17th, 2nd, and 18th from north to south – that massed in readiness for the offensive were superior in numbers of troops, guns (a ratio of 5:2), and training to their British opponents. The Allies had already decided to stand on the defensive in early 1918, they were recovering from the losses in ill-conceived offensives in 1917, and they were awaiting the arrival of American troops. The British Army compounded its weaknesses with poor defensive preparations. The 3rd and 5th Armies, commanded by Generals Julian Byng and Hubert Gough respectively, had not completed work on their defensive positions and had stationed too many troops close to the front line in vulnerable positions.[78] 'I felt,' wrote Lieutenant Sergeant Ledger on 13 March, as he surveyed the defensive positions of the 5th Army, 'that I could understand the feeling of prisoners of the 16th century who had been sentenced to have their heads chopped off at dawn.'[79]

When the German armies attacked on 21 March, they captured over 21,000 British prisoners on the first day. Gough's 5th Army was wilting under the assault and the commander's nerves were fraying badly. When Louis Loucheur, Minister for Armaments, met Foch and Gough on the evening of 27 March, he found Foch in good form, but Gough had 'the air of a drunk'.[80] An Allied and American conference at Beauvais on 3 April effectively made Foch the commander-in-chief over Haig, Pétain, and Pershing. Foch's confidence and personal authority enabled him to direct the defensive operations. His most significant contribution was to insist on the defence of Amiens, the railway hub at the heart of Allied logistics.[81] On 5 April Ludendorff brought the Michael Offensive to an end, but his direction of the battle has been criticized for its concentration on tactical success and the failure to focus German fighting efforts on the capture of Amiens.[82]

The German offensive resumed on 9 April, in Operation Georgette, a smaller operation than originally planned, as the diminutive suggests. Nonetheless the German 4th and 6th Armies had superior numbers. They broke through a combination of British and Portuguese forces. By 11 April, as thirty-one German divisions faced thirteen British divisions, Haig implored Foch to send reinforcements. He also issued his famous order, an emotional appeal rather than an operational plan: 'Every position must be held to the last man: there must be no retirement. With our backs to the wall and believing in the justice of our cause, each one of us must fight on to the end. . . . Many amongst us are now tired. To those I would say that Victory will belong to the side that holds out longest. The French Army is moving rapidly and in great force to our support.'[83] Although the French army was doing nothing of the sort, the German offensive began to peter out the following day. In part this was due to dogged defence by British, Australian, and Canadian forces; but it also reflected the inherent problems in the German offensive – the loss of highly trained units and officers in the Michael Offensive took its toll, the logistical support was weak, and the troops, hopeful of victory in March, were now exhausted and dubious about the prospects for success. The Blücher–Yorck Offensive between 27 May and 4 June and the Gneisenau Offensive between 9 and 14 June – both named after heroes of the German Wars of Liberation against Napoleon – repeated the pattern of the frustrating failure to exploit rapid initial gains.

That said, the German spring offensive was a close-run thing. It created a sense of crisis amongst the Allied leaders. German guns were within range of Paris once again. Blanche Duhamel decided to leave the capital on 23 March, having heard the German artillery assault earlier that morning. Some 200,000 Parisians left the city between 18 March and 6 April. The trench journal, Sans tabac, mocked the civilian flight: 'The battle continued fierce at the Gare de Lyon and the Quai d'Orsay. After a violent struggle . . . a detachment of quitters managed to take the train. The civilians pursued their strategic retreat. . . . They withdrew to positions prepared in advance further to the south, at Biarritz, Nice, and Monte Carlo. Their morale is excellent.'[84] Civilians had withstood air raids since the beginning of the year, so arguably it was fear of a German invasion of Paris rather than the bombardments that led to flight. In any case the majority followed President Poincaré's example. During the crisis in March, Clemenceau, Loucheur, Pétain, and Poincaré had met at the Elysée Palace to discuss the question of unified command. When Pétain warned that it was going to be difficult to defend Paris – the sort of pessimistic attitude that enabled Foch to pip him to Supreme Command – Clemenceau urged Poincaré to leave the city. 'The moment when the Boche enters by one door,' the president replied, 'I will leave by the other. Me, I will not leave Paris again; Bordeaux [to where the French government fled in 1914] was enough for me.'[85]

Soldiers' morale also held up; indeed, in the British army the postal censor reported that the grumbling stopped when the German guns started. The high rate of surrender was caused by mobile warfare and rear echelon troops caught by surprise as well as by war-weariness. American troops also fought on a large scale for the first time in these battles. 'To see blood and carnage everywhere,' wrote Clarence Mahon, a twenty-three-year-old mechanic from Indiana, 'as men, horses, and mules are blown to bits developed in us a certain savagry [sic] and hate that pushed us on toward a terrible enemy with a willingness to see him destroyed.' As one officer noted, nine out of ten of his men 'do not know what they are fighting for, the idea is simply to kill the Boche'. When the American Expeditionary Force set up its Morale Division in May 1918, this was designed to promote a progressive view of the war's purpose, not a response to demoralization.[86]

On 15 July Aristide Briand was staying in Cocherel, in the department of the Seine-et-Marne, where he had bought two houses the previous year. 'At midnight,' he recorded in his diary, 'woken by a continuous rolling barrage in the distance. The windows tremble. It is the artillery at the front. The German offensive is beginning again. We have waited for it with our arms crossed. She responds to this passive attitude. I hope that this time we will not be surprised.'[87] After a month's break, German forces had resumed the offensive, but Ludendorff's strategy had lost any remnant of coherence by this point. By June he knew that the offensives would not win the war, but he ignored the exhaustion of the troops and refused to consider any political initiative for a negotiated settlement. The 7th Army was instructed to launch the offensive on 15 July, despite warnings that its troops needed rest and its artillery arm required further training.[88] As German confidence waned and the offensive lost its strategic purpose, Foch was planning an Allied offensive that, he believed, would deliver victory in 1919. The Allies were well prepared for the 7th Army's offensive on 15 July and organized a counter-attack. After halting German forces, General Charles Mangin's 10th Army attacked on 18 July with tanks and a rolling barrage. French forces captured 12,000 German soldiers, while the American 2nd Division made the largest gains of the day. 'This is the greatest day since the Marne,' one French officer said. For Foch it marked a return to the offensive. He sought to keep the German forces off balance by directing a series of offensives over a broad front in August and early September. On 8 August General Sir Henry Rawlinson's 4th Army began the battle of Amiens, during which, over a three-day period, Allied forces captured 30,000 German prisoners. The Allies had cast off the passivity of the spring and seized the initiative. They would not relinquish it before the ceasefire in November.[89]

Did the Allies and the United States win the war or did Germany lose it? The most recent study by David Stevenson argues that Ludendorff's strategy in the spring of 1918 had catastrophic results. Between 1915 and 1917 German defensive battles, with the exception of Verdun, had fought the Allies to a standstill. The offensive in 1918 wasted the best-trained soldiers, extended the German lines at a time of dwindling numbers, and demoralized troops, who now realized that the chance of victory had evaporated. By July 1918 the German Army had suffered 1 million casualties. The Spanish flu epidemic accounted for 520,000 ill soldiers during July 1918 alone. The thinning of German reserves made it easier for the Allies to attack. Moreover, Ludendorff had lost the sense of calm authority he had displayed earlier in the year. Colonel Fritz von Loßberg, the leading defensive expert in the German Supreme Command, recalled how he had travelled to the headquarters of the 7th Army as it was falling back before the Allied counter-offensive. His visit confirmed what the Chief of Staff, Walther Reinhardt, had said before the final German offensive, namely that the troops were exhausted. Loßberg also supported Reinhardt's proposal to withdraw to defensive positions on the River Aisne, but Ludendorff refused to make the final decision for several days. The centralization of the German army and the consequent loss of initiative, even amongst senior commanders, exacerbated an already precarious position.[90]

Deteriorating morale made operations more difficult. Desertions increased, including mass desertions. Some Alsaciens and Poles, who now regarded the German war effort as none of their business, organized some of these desertions. The majority remained, but their morale was poor. 'Now after four years of fighting,' wrote K. Reiter, in mid-August, 'a certain depression is taking hold of the soldiers; they know that they must die for a hopeless cause. To them better peace today at any respectable price rather than tomorrow.'[91] Discipline had already broken down during the offensive as German troops stopped off to plunder Allied trenches, while one study estimates that between 10 and 20 per cent of troops sent on trains from east to west 'disappeared'. A large proportion of those who could, therefore, were ending their own participation in the war. Although the thesis that the German Army engaged in a 'military strike' in the summer of 1918 has been disputed recently, it is clear that soldiers, once they decided that the war could not be won, wanted peace.[92]

Private Dominik Richert, never an enthusiastic soldier, embodied some of these features of demoralization. As an Alsacien he felt treated as a second-class citizen. He had served on the Eastern Front in 1917 and took an interest in the Russian revolutions. In July 1918, back on the Western Front, he claimed that he caught Spanish flu. By the end of the month he had decided to desert with his NCO and a fellow Alsacien soldier. These circumstances were important – desertion required opportunity as well as motive and it was highly risky. As they passed over no-man's-land on the night of 23 July, they cried out 'Vive la France' to unseen soldiers in the French trenches. His two fellow deserters were shot and injured. Afterwards Richert heard that they had been sentenced to death in absentia. 'Truly,' he wrote, 'in war everything is turned upside down. Therefore, because we did not want to kill and be killed, we were condemned to death.' For Richert the war had robbed him and others of dignity. Just before the story of his desertion in his memoirs, he wrote of how he saw an Italian prisoner of war, working in the rear echelon, stooping into a urinal to pick up a half-smoked cigarette.[93]

The Allied and American forces still had to take the initiative and exploit the German Army's weaknesses. While their task was made easier by the quality of their foe, they had also improved their operational capacity. They exploited their technological and industrial advantage. The offensives in the late summer of 1918 featured combined arms operations with tanks and aeroplanes. Innovation in operational doctrine in 1918 was not just the result of a 'learning curve' that had begun in 1914. The British and French high commands had learned more slowly than their German counterparts and had often neglected good advice. However, in 1918 they demonstrated energy and decisiveness after recovering from the shock of the Michael Offensive. The quality of Foch's decision-making contrasted with Ludendorff's ponderous and nervous reaction to setbacks. Haig's commitment to the offensive, for once, was suited to the military conditions.

The first moment of defeat is a moment of perception. Ludendorff was not far behind his soldiers in realizing that Germany had lost the First World War. On 26 September he told the civilian leadership and the Kaiser that the war was lost. Three days later he demanded that the government seek an immediate armistice. This coincided with news of the Bulgarian ceasefire. While Ludendorff's demand for an immediate armistice was a shock, Germany's defeat was not. On 22 July Hindenburg had 'admitted total failure' to the Kaiser. That evening Wilhelm II had spoken of himself as a 'defeated War Lord', while the following day he told Admiral von Müller that 'he had not closed an eye all night. He had seen visions of all the English and Russian relatives and all the ministers and generals of his own reign marching past and mocking him. Only the little Queen of Norway had been friendly to him.'[94] The self-pity was unappealing but it demonstrated that the German military and political leaders – at least those 'in the loop' – considered themselves defeated by the Allied counter-offensives in the summer of 1918. Granted the Kaiser's mood had been as defeatist when Romania entered the war in August 1916, but then others had redressed his bleak pessimism. Although Ludendorff's demand for an immediate ceasefire followed quickly upon the Bulgarian government's request for a ceasefire on 25 September (it was concluded on 30 September), the battles on the Western Front had determined the German decision and therefore the politics of defeat and victory in the war. Moreover, the recognition of the military defeat in mid-July was a response to events on the battlefield. Only later did Ludendorff, Hindenburg, and others incorporate the collapse of the home front into their explanation for defeat, an explanation that framed the poisonous stab-in-the-back legend. Indeed, the first portraits in this rogues' gallery were not of socialists, pacifists, or Jews, but of members of Berlin court circles, allegedly guilty of 'indiscretions' about German war plans.[95]

* * *

'There has been some excitement in England,' wrote Mary Wilson on 3 October to her husband serving in Palestine, 'about Bulgaria. . . . We all think it won't be long now. Wouldn't it be nice if we had peace by Christmas?'[96] The Bulgarian request for the ceasefire on 25 September marked the beginning of forty-seven days that culminated in the armistice on 11 November. Ending hostilities was also the occasion for stamping meaning on the war. This process occurred on three separate but related axes. First, the exchange of notes between Woodrow Wilson and the

German government framed the war in terms of a constitutional struggle between democracy and autocracy and the future international order. Second, the armistice agreements, largely drafted by the Allied governments and especially their military leaders, focused on military and territorial terms. These agreements were imposed on the defeated powers, Germany, Austria-Hungary, the Ottoman empire, and Bulgaria. They framed the war in the language of military security. Finally, individual soldiers and civilians wondered what war and peace meant as they anticipated the armistice. Their expectations were extremely diverse, but they tended to focus on the personal, most obviously survival, but also family and job prospects.

German military and political leaders carefully choreographed their request for a ceasefire. The first task was the reconstruction of the government on a broad national basis. On 1 October Prince Max von Baden was appointed Chancellor and his cabinet included two socialists, Philip Scheidemann and Gustav Bauer, a leading trade unionist. Scheidemann had opposed participating in government or, as he put it, a 'bankrupt operation'. At a meeting of the SPD on 3 October the argument of its chairman Friedrich Ebert prevailed, namely that participation in government was the national duty of the party. In political terms he saw a broadly based national government as the only means of preserving order and avoiding the radicalization and civil war that had occurred in the Russian revolution. He also had a strong personal patriotic conviction, rendered more poignant by the death of two of his sons during the war. In placing the government on this more representative basis, German leaders entertained a number of scenarios. First, it strengthened the planned appeal to Wilson to negotiate an armistice: German leaders bought into Wilson's argument that peace required a settlement between the Allies and United States and a government representing the German people. Second, a broadly based government held open the prospect of rallying the population to the defence of the Fatherland if ceasefire negotiations failed. Finally, as Scheidemann feared, it enabled the military and political elite to share that most unwanted commodity, responsibility for Germany's defeat in the war.[97]

On 3 October Max von Baden sent the German offer to Wilson. This began a month-long exchange of notes that transformed German politics and sought to establish Wilson's ideas as the basis of the international order. The German note was both a request for an immediate armistice and a peace proposal. It proposed peace negotiations on the basis of Wilson's fourteen-point speech of 8 January and referred to later elaborations by the president, most recently a speech he had given in New York on 27 September, opening the campaign for the Fourth Liberty Loan.[98] The president's speech in New York was wider-ranging than his proposals to Congress had been in January. Peace was a matter for peoples, not just governments. He pointed to the demands of labour for a peace that went beyond statesmen's terms of 'territorial arrangements and the division of power' towards a 'broad-visioned justice and mercy and peace and the satisfaction of those deep-seated longings of oppressed and distracted men and women and enslaved peoples that seem to them the only things worth fighting a war for'. Much of the speech concentrated on the rights of people and nations to freedom in their domestic and international affairs. Most importantly, from the perspective of the negotiations with Berlin, there was no ambiguity in Wilson's call for a change of government in Germany. He made clear that peace could not be negotiated with the German government that had concluded the treaties of Brest-Litovsk and Bucharest. That this did not mean a simple change in the cabinet, but a wider constitutional reform, was also clear. 'Shall people,' the president asked, 'be ruled and dominated, even in their own internal affairs, by arbitrary and irresponsible force or by their own will and choice?'[99]

The American response on 8 October pressed home this point, asking whether 'the Imperial Chancellor is speaking merely for the constituted authorities of the Empire that have so far conducted the war'.[100] Over the next month American diplomacy repeatedly pressed this issue of the constitutional basis of the German government. The change of government in early October had not been sufficient and it was clear to German leaders that they faced massive American intervention in their constitutional arrangements. This was the culmination of a war defined by the conflict between political principles. On 7 October before the transmission of the first American note, Robert Lansing had argued that the negotiations should be used to undermine the German military authorities, so that 'democracy becomes dominant in Germany'. Wilson and Lansing believed they had a lever in German popular opinion, which was so desirous of peace that it would provide the basis for constitutional change.[101]

Lansing recognized that many Germans remained fearful of Allied intentions. In an alternative scenario, the popular impetus behind political reform provided the basis for an uprising en masse. Paul von Hintze, the German Foreign Secretary, suggested this as an option on 29 September. As the Hohenzollern dynasty would hardly survive defeat, it could mobilize

popular enthusiasm for a *Volkskrieg* (people's war) by broadening the basis
of government.[102] This option offered a final, alternative roll of the dice, in
which a people's war would stave off defeat. Yet it was an inherently revolutionary proposal. A people's war was the antithesis of the self-conception of
the German military, a form of unrestrained warfare that contrasted with
their self-proclaimed expert management of violence. Walther Rathenau
saw the implications more clearly than Hintze did, or wanted to. Devastated
by the prospect of defeat and what he regarded as the obsequious acceptance of Wilson's fourteen points, he had broken down on 2 October. Five
days later, in the liberal *Vossische Zeitung*, he called for a popular war 'of
self-assertion and self-determination'. He decoupled this vision of war from
'militarism and feudalism', as a defence of German territory and economic
interest. The rising of the people was to be organized by an Office of
Defence, staffed by citizens and soldiers and enjoying dictatorial powers. In
the style of other national revolutionary wars, France in 1793 and Prussia
in 1813, the office would issue an appeal to the people, the starting point for
popular mobilization.[103] Rathenau's appeal was the most radical vision of a
war of national defence. The Inter-Party Committee, dominated by the
parties that had voted for the Reichstag resolution, also spoke of popular
resistance, while Scheidemann considered the possibility of a war in defence
of the nation. Yet his conception of the nation excluded the Kaiser and
required constitutional change. This debate had some similarities with
those that had taken place in other belligerents facing defeat, notably Serbia
in 1915 and Russia in 1917 and 1918. As in those cases German leaders did
not pursue a revolutionary people's war. Ludendorff warned that an uprising
en masse was bound to lead to catastrophe. Moreover, there was neither an
agreed political basis nor were there institutions on which this war could
take place, nor was there much popular enthusiasm.[104]

Once the option of *Volkskrieg* had been discounted, the pressures for
further constitutional reform became inescapable. The choice came down to
the Kaiser or peace, and both the nation and the army chose peace through
revolution rather than war and the Kaiser. In early November a series of
constitutional reforms were enacted in response to American diplomatic
pressure. Wilhelm II gradually handed over his powers and made ministers
responsible to the Reichstag, which also won the power over foreign policy
and military affairs. Anticipating an unstable new world, Carl Legien, on
behalf of the ADGB (General Commission of German Trade Unions), and
Hugo Stinnes, on behalf of industrialists, negotiated an agreement on labour
regulations, including the recognition of socialist trade unions in wage

bargaining and the introduction of the prized eight-hour day – as long as it was introduced in other industrialized states.

These amounted to radical political and social reforms, which satisfied Wilson's criteria of representative government. Yet by this stage, within Germany, the Kaiser was seen as an obstacle to peace. In Kiel the fantasies of catastrophic nationalism fired the dreams of naval officers, who proposed one final sortie into the North Sea to engage in a battle that would surely end in defeat, but rescue the honour of the individual officers, the navy, and the Fatherland – at least in their imagination. The sailors mutinied at the prospect of futile and deadly battle. In doing so they triggered a revolution against monarchical and military authority across Germany. The first dynasty to fall was that of the Wittelsbachs in Bavaria on 7 November. The army now faced the choice of marching back into Germany to suppress the incipient revolution and preserve the Hohenzollern dynasty or to forsake its oath to the Kaiser. After four years of national mobilization the army was a national, rather than a monarchical, institution. Early on 9 November thirty-eight commanders from ten different armies gathered at Spa, where they had been invited by the Supreme Command. Hindenburg told them that Wilhelm II wanted to lead them back to Germany to defeat the revolution. Twenty-three commanders said their men would not carry out these orders and the other fifteen doubted whether they would. When the army could no longer reconcile its oath to the Kaiser with its identity as a national army, its leaders chose the nation. Hindenburg evaded his responsibility to inform the Kaiser and the duty fell instead to Wilhelm Groener, whose awkward words to Wilhelm II stressed the primacy of peace and nation over loyalty to the Crown. Later that day the Kaiser abdicated and went into exile in the Netherlands, while Philipp Scheidemann appeared on the balcony of the Reichstag to declare the German Republic.

The following evening Reinhardt, who had left his post as Chief of Staff of the 7th Army just days earlier to organize the demobilization of the German Army, took down the ceasefire conditions over a phone in the Prussian Ministry of War. He likened the experience to the feeling 'a medieval delinquent must have had, as his body was broken bone by bone'.[105] On 5 November Lansing informed the German government that the Allies had accepted the fourteen points as the basis for negotiations with the exception of British reservations about the freedom of the seas and Allied demands for full compensation for the loss of civilian life and property on land, at sea, and from the air. The armistice terms amounted to more than a guarantee that Germany would not resume military operations after a respite, hence Reinhardt's shock. Allied governments, annoyed by Wilson's direct negotiations with Germany, saw in the armistice terms an opportunity to assert their interests in the peace settlement. They also represented a different conception of the international order and diplomatic style to Wilson's fourteen points. When Lloyd George and Balfour criticized what they regarded as the imprecision of the first American note to Germany, Lord Reading, the ambassador to Washington, asked 'What do you expect from a man who typewrites his message in his little room without consulting anyone?'[106] As Wilson duelled with the German Foreign Office over the meaning of representative government, the Allies scrambled to make their territorial claims. 'The only definitive territorial sacrifices,' Foch noted, 'will be those conceded by the enemy when the Armistice is signed.'[107] Foch played the leading role in shaping the terms of the armistice and other military leaders, Haig, Pétain, and Pershing, also had a large say in the discussions. The armistice agreement stipulated that the Allies and Americans occupy the left bank of the Rhine including the vital transport route of Mainz, Cologne, and Coblenz; that German troops evacuate the right bank of the Rhine; that Germany deliver locomotives and other economic goods to the Allies; and that the German Army surrender its planes, artillery, and machine guns. These clauses anticipated some of the territorial, military, and commercial aspects of the Treaty of Versailles.

The armistices between the Allies and the Ottoman empire and Austria-Hungary ensured territorial gains. On 1 October the CUP leader Talaat Pasha resigned, marking the end of CUP rule in the Ottoman empire. In any case the empire was fragmenting, following British occupation of Mesopotamia, Syria, and Palestine. In addition, the empire faced territorial claims from Greece and Armenia. Nonetheless Ottoman leaders invoked Wilson's fourteen points and a Wilson's Principles Society was formed. Wilson's principles, however, offered some value to an emerging Turkish state, rather than the Ottoman empire. As the empire collapsed, local councils were established by the Society for the Defence of National Rights, which rejected the dismemberment of Anatolia and asserted Turkish claims to Constantinople. While Enver Pasha fled, other CUP officials, including Mustafa Kemal, made the transition to this new Society, which emerged in ethnically contested regions, such as Izmir and Thrace.[108] On 22 October the British War Cabinet decided to exclude France from the armistice negotiations with the Ottoman empire. Lloyd George now regarded the Sykes-Picot agreement of 1916 as an unfortunate constraint and assuaged his conscience by claiming that British forces had done the fighting in the

Middle East. This was true, though, as Balfour noted, the Allies had originally agreed to 'pool' territory acquired during the war on the grounds that
fighting in one theatre might yield less in territorial terms, but represent an
equally important contribution to the war effort. These qualms were
ignored and the armistice of Mudros was concluded on 30 October between
British and Ottoman officials, permitting the Allies to occupy the Arabian
peninsula, Mesopotamia, Syria, and Palestine.[109]

A similar blend of Wilsonian aspiration and land-grabbing characterized the last days of Austria-Hungary and the foundational moments of the
emerging states in central Europe and the Balkans. Masaryk, who was in
the United States in October, was invited to Philadelphia by the city's mayor.
Here the newly minted Mid-European Union, representing Czechs,
Slovakians, Slovenes, Lithuanians, Poles, Ukrainians, Jews, and Romanians
issued a new declaration of independence. The iconography was irresist-
ible. The declaration was read out in Independence Hall and *The New York
Times* headline read 'New Liberty Bell Rung'. Having (figuratively) peeled
out freedom in 1915 at the San Francisco Exposition for the western hemisphere, the bell now rang in the birth of new nations in Europe, linking
them to the tradition of 1776.[110] On the ground in Europe, nationalist
groups proclaimed independence, bit by scrabbled bit. On 7 October the
Regent in Warzaw, the core of the future Poland, declared independence.
Polish representatives met in Lublin on 7 November to form a provisional
government, which announced elections to the Sjem (parliament) and
decreed the eight-hour day, now a customary badge of a 'civilized' community. On 10 November Josef Pilsudski arrived in Warzaw to take control of
the provisional government.[111]

A fragmentary process took place in the nascent Yugoslavia. As Serbian
soldiers fought their way towards Belgrade, the *komitadji*, the guerrilla resistance to the Habsburg and Bulgarian occupation, were renewing their fight,
causing Nikolai Pašić to fear that they might lay claim to an important place
in the new state. Other groups were also shaping the new Yugoslavia – on 1
November the Croatian National Council in Zagreb announced its readiness
to join a Yugoslav state, while in Geneva between 6 and 9 November Pašić
and representatives of the Croatian National Council and the Yugoslav
Committee discussed the structures of the new state.[112] The Czechoslovak
declaration of independence, published in Paris on 18 October and written
by Masaryk, Beneš, and Milan Stefanik, justified its claims with references to
the American constitutional tradition as well as a history of resistance to
Habsburg, German, and Magyar suppression of Czech rights.

Military success remained an important justification for territorial claims. Having remained on the defensive following Caporetto, the Italian Army needed some sort of victory to bolster Italian demands. Vittorio Orlando and Sidney Sonnino urged on the reluctant commander, General Diaz. Meanwhile in the Trentino, Alcide De Gasperi argued that as Austria-Hungary had accepted the principle of self-determination, it should apply to the Trentino. On 15 October an Italian deputation presented its demand for union with Italy.[113] Then on 24 October Italian forces launched their attack and could claim victory after entering the town of Vittorio Veneto on 30 October. In the armistice concluded three days later, Sonnino achieved his goal of Italian occupation of the territories assigned in the Treaty of London.[114] The combination of military action, self-determination, and anti-Bolshevism was evident in the nimble footwork of the Romanian government, which declared war against the Central Powers on 10 November, the same day as the Central Romanian Council in Transylvania, in the Hungarian half of the Habsburg empire, asked for aid against the threat of a 'Bolshevik' revolution.[115]

The Bulgarian armistice, concluded on 29 September, was perhaps the mildest. Although Italian, French, and British troops occupied Bulgaria, Greek and Serbian forces were restricted to areas that they had lost to Bulgaria since 1915. Moreover, the monarchy survived in Bulgaria. King Ferdinand abdicated on 4 October, but his son, Boris III, ascended to the throne. This limited the degree of political and constitutional change in Bulgaria, especially when compared to the revolution in Germany, let alone to the collapse of the House of Habsburg or the dissolution of the Ottoman empire.

The final dimension of the ending of the war was the popular response. As the armistice approached, the instinct of soldiers to survive heightened. The last few days of the war were particularly tense. 'Everyone knew,' wrote Private Robinson Shepherd, an American soldier, 'if he made it to eleven a.m. he would be o.k. and I never saw a more scared bunch of soldiers. Somehow we had not paid much attention before, but now we were most anxious to live until eleven o'clock.'[116] The war diary of a battalion in 33rd Landwehr Regiment noted that 'Soldiers were heard to say that they had no desire to be shot now just before the peace.'[117] Erich Maria Remarque described how the soldier's sense of time changed as the prospect of an armistice grew closer. 'Now that it has become known that peace may come any day, every hour has gained in weight a thousandfold, every minute under fire seems harder and longer than the whole time before.'[118] There is some evidence that the 'live and let live system', in which opposing soldiers agreed to minimize casualties, became more prevalent in the last weeks of the war. The reciprocal interest in survival even led to fraternization. American officers encouraged their soldiers to use these encounters to spread propaganda, just as German officers had on the Eastern Front in late 1917. French propaganda advised German troops not to die for an assortment of villains, including greedy businessmen and Ludendorff, as the war was on the verge of ending.[119]

Just as the shattering of family ties defined the war experience at the moment of mobilization, the prospect of families reunited had a powerful hold on the expectations of soldiers and civilians at the end of the war. In some instances fears about families hastened a crisis of morale. The Bulgarian Army did not mutiny, but it was unable to offer significant resistance to the Allied advance in mid-September. The crisis of morale amongst peasant soldiers owed much to concerns about their families and livelihoods.[120] In the German Army soldiers began to make the individual choice to return home, though the discipline of the front-line troops was maintained even during the first weeks of demobilization. Others looked forward with more optimism to renewing family life. Mary Wilson wondered whether she and her husband could take a holiday to Palestine, where he was serving: 'We could just eat some grapes & figs.'

The emotional register at the end of the war defies categorization and herein lies its significance. The personal response to the end of the conflict could not be accommodated within the political categories of victory and defeat. Yet this emotional register was an important element in international politics. Joy, grief, relief, fear, hatred, and empathy all seeped into the popular politics of making peace and ending the war. Indeed, it is worth bearing in mind that political and military leaders also shared an emotional response to the war. They were not simply desiccated theorists wallowing in their abstractions or hard-headed military men directing units to seize territory. Maxime Weygand, the commander of the French Army in 1940, recalled Foch's sentimental midnight visit to Metz two weeks after the armistice. The generalissimo had studied there in 1870–1, witnessing defeat and occupation.[121] For some, like Ludwig Beck, later a leading Wehrmacht general, opponent of the invasion of France in 1940, and a member of the military resistance to Adolf Hitler, personal and national crisis merged into one. The experience of the defeat and revolution was 'dreadful'. The destruction of a 500-year-old dynasty in what he considered a cowardly revolution that left Germany open to French depredations shattered him. Yet Beck concluded by urging his sister-in-law (and himself) not to give up hope.[122]

People were uncertain about the appropriate response to the end of the war. In New York, Sergey Prokofiev received a phone call 'with two pieces of news: first that peace has been declared, this time unambiguously and therefore there will be more public rejoicing, and second, that quite unexpectedly and unheralded Rachmaninoff [a fellow Russian composer] has arrived. This is a truly remarkable turn of events. Before I left Japan I heard that he did have plans to come here, and was receiving all kinds of glittering proposals, but he had turned them all down. Huge crowds on the streets, girls kissing sailors, with deep and voluptuous abandon.'[123] Georges Duhamel celebrated the first day of peace amidst peeling bells, singing, and champagne. To the side he saw German prisoners singing and laughing as they read the official notice of the armistice. 'Is it true,' he asked, 'that, in its distress, their country can also know an unforeseen joy, that of regeneration, of revolution?' His letter crossed with his wife's on the same day. She hoped Germans would be 'sad'.[124] Stanley Baldwin, a Conservative minister, whose son was serving in the Irish Guards, could hear Big Ben across the river as he made his way to a church service in Southwark. He met a Labour MP, with whom he was friendly, 'Old Bill Crooks'. '[T]aking both of my hands in his big paws [he] said tremulously: "This is a great day". To which I replied, "Yes, but I feel very much like crying myself", to which he replied "I've 'ad my cry this morning.' " 'My brain,' Baldwin concluded, 'is reeling at it all. I find three impressions strongest: thankfulness that the slaughter is stopped, the thought of the millions of dead, and the vision of Europe in ruins. And now to work! Pick up the bits.'[125] On 10 November Richard Wilson died in Egypt. For his wife Mary, as for others, victory and defeat, war and peace had little inherent meaning.

CHAPTER 8

DRAFTING PEACE, 1919

IN PARIS, ROBERT Lansing had little to do. Distrusted by Wilson, partly due to contrasting temperaments, partly due to political differences, the American Secretary of State was excluded from key policy debates. He turned his hand to writing fables, criticizing the slow pace of peace negotiations and raising the spectre of Bolshevik revolution throughout Europe. In one he ridiculed 'some greedy men squabbling over gold and title deeds', while the house they were in was on fire. The people of the world, who had looked forward with hope to the peace settlements in Paris, had now turned in their despair to the 'Red Demon'. For Lansing the problems the world faced in 1919 were more profound than the territorial and economic issues of peacemaking. The world was 'going mad', while 'crime and lust swagger through the streets at noonday'. 'Civilization,' he concluded, 'will crumble to barbarism. Let it crumble.'[1] Lansing's depiction of political and social chaos hinted at the scale of peacemaking after the First World War, which involved fashioning anew political communities and social relationships, as well as distributing territory, determining reparations, and ensuring military security. Making peace had been rendered more complex by the character of the war. Lansing also expressed frustration and disappointment with peacemakers in Paris in 1919, and other criticisms have echoed down the years. More recently, historians have placed the difficulties the peacemakers faced into context, leading to a more balanced assessment.[2] In 1919 peace was drafted, rather than made, in Paris. The negotiations and debates created new states, new institutions, and new norms that constituted the basis of the international order, but it would take several years for these institutions to stabilize.

* * *

Claims had been staked out during the interval between the armistice and the arrival of delegations in Paris. Domestic political concerns shaped many of these pronouncements. In December 1918 voters in the United Kingdom went to the polls for the first time since the closely fought elections of 1910. Then Lloyd George had been the scourge of the Conservative Party; now he was the Liberal prime minister of a Conservative-dominated coalition. To secure the prime ministership, he had made a pact with the Conservatives. The election resulted in a victory for the Conservatives and elevated Labour to the principal party of opposition. The patriotic temper of the electorate suited the Conservative platform of military security, empire, and national cohesion. Although Lloyd George has been criticized for pandering to the vindictive impulses of parts of the electorate, his campaign speeches struck a balanced tone. Eric Geddes had promised his constituents in Cambridge on 10 December that the government would squeeze Germany 'until the pips squeak'. The following day at Colston Hall in Bristol, Lloyd George told the audience that Germany should pay the costs of the war as the country was 'guilty of wrong'. Yet he also made clear that the financial settlement would take into account Germany's capacity to pay. In principle Germany was liable for the total costs of the war, but as that would overwhelm its capacity to pay, the final sum would be much less than the total costs.[3] Nonetheless the tenor of the campaign and the balance of the Conservative-dominated coalition informed British diplomacy at the Paris Peace Conference culminating in the Versailles Treaty.

In the United States Wilson ensured that party concerns shaped the American politics of peacemaking. Mid-term elections were scheduled for November 1918. On 25 October the president issued an appeal to voters to support Democratic candidates. Victory at the polls, he claimed, was necessary to bolster his negotiating position in the forthcoming peace talks. Quite apart from questions about the balance of the American constitution, Wilson had misjudged the political moment. The Republicans defeated the Democrats at the mid-term polls. Foreign policy issues were only one amongst many in the election, but the Republican brand of patriotism and concern at open-ended commitments to defend the peace settlement in distant parts of the world gained more prominence in American debates. 'Don't waste time arguing with an escaped lunatic, a mad bull, or Teddy Roosevelt,' quipped Lansing about one of the Republican Party's most effective campaigners in 1918.[4] As it turned out, Roosevelt died on 6 January 1919, but Wilson faced an equally obdurate opponent in Henry Cabot Lodge, the Republican senator from Massachusetts. He had long despised

Wilson and, elected chair of the Senate Foreign Relations Committee after the elections, he had a pulpit from which to speak. Wilson then compounded his error of judgement by failing to nominate a senior Republican figure to the American delegation.[5]

Italy did not hold elections until late 1919, but its negotiating positions at the Paris Peace Conference in January were shaped by popular pressure. Leonida Bissolati, the Socialist Minister, proposed giving up Italian claims to the Tyrol, Dalmatia, and Dodecanese islands, and instead seeking the city of Fiume and the peninsula of Istria at the head of the Adriatic, on the principle of nationality. This had been a recurrent theme in the war aims of democratic interventionists and nationalists. On 30 October the Italian commune in the city had declared union with Italy, whereas the previous day the Croat National Council had declared Fiume part of Croatia. When Sidney Sonnino, the Foreign Minister, rejected Bissolati's proposal, the latter resigned from the cabinet. Yet in response to nationalist pressure the Italian delegation simply added Fiume to the list of their demands.[6] In France it is difficult to identify popular pressure on the government. George Clemenceau's government censured the press, with *Le Temps* censured on twenty-two occasions and *Le Journal de Débats* on twenty-five occasions in the first six months of 1919.[7] More importantly, the French delegation shared the popular sentiment that Germany, even in its republican guise, remained a threat to French security. The delegation was divided, however, on how to contain the German threat.

The Paris Peace Conference opened on 18 January. Negotiations were unwieldy. There were fifty-two separate committees and commissions drafting various clauses. The Council of Ten was supplanted by the Council of Four. Clemenceau, Lloyd George, the Italian premier Vittorio Orlando, and Wilson were supposed to assert executive control over the negotiations, but their personal relationships were poor – at one point Lloyd George physically attacked Clemenceau – and their political interests so diverse that they failed to provide overall coherence to the treaty. The slow pace of proceedings worried those who feared that Europe was slipping into irreversible revolutionary chaos. 'Once upon a time,' wrote Lansing in his fable entitled 'The Men who Sat too Long',

> there were ten men, who sat in judgment on a wicked man, who had committed most terrible crimes. When the ten men after a long time could not agree what to do with the wicked man, the case was referred to Four Great Men. The Four sat and sat and talked for many

days about a fit Punishment. Finally when they were near to an Agreement, a rude man opened the Door of the Council Chamber and cried out: 'Never mind, Gentlemen, the wicked man has committed suicide. He got so nervous waiting that he could wait no longer for your decision.' So the Four Great Men lost their Job as Judges and could do nothing but go home.[8]

The German question was the major preoccupation in the negotiations, while the threat of a Bolshevik revolution lurked in the background. In approaching these issues, politicians thought in terms of establishing an international order that could withstand the revival of German power and the temptations of revolution, while also leaving open the possibility of accommodating a democratic Germany and a stable Russian state in the future. There was no single architect or purpose of design amongst the peacemakers at Paris, but the creation of the League of Nations, the territorial dispensation, the reparations settlement, the mandate system, and the establishment of the International Labour Organization heralded the emergence of a new international order. The order was not complete in 1919, but the architecture was sketched out.

The League of Nations was at the centre of Wilson's vision of international politics. Wilson had refused to discuss his plans for the League in any detailed way during the war. He kept Taft's League to Enforce Peace at arm's length, while he dismissed British wartime pressure, especially from Robert Cecil, the British delegation's adviser, to adopt a common Anglo-American stance on the League of Nations. In August 1918 Cecil had sent the Phillimore report, a British proposal for the League, to Colonel House, who passed it on to the League to Enforce Peace. Wilson prevented publication of the report. Instead he began work on his own draft, on the basis of a report by Colonel House and David Miller of the Inquiry. Wilson's draft had certain peculiarities that marked his ideas out from those of other supporters of the idea of the League in the United States, Britain, and France. He criticized the Phillimore report on the grounds that 'it has not teeth', but his own draft did not provide for effective sanctions against states which violated the covenant. His draft guaranteed equal representation for all states, great and small, in the League. While Wilson proposed the guarantee of each state's territorial sovereignty, he also proposed in what became known as the Magnolia Draft that borders would change in response to social and demographic change. These changes would be managed by the League on the basis of 'self-determination'. Wilson's vision of the guarantee was a political one, founded upon public opinion, rather than a legal one guaranteed by automatic military sanctions.[9]

Where Wilson departed most from supporters of the League of Nations in Britain and especially in France was in his conceptions of its political underpinnings. One of his reasons for not discussing the League with the Allies during the war was that he wished to avoid the new institution becoming too closely associated with wartime alliances. British and French advocates of the League saw it as an institution that could manage power politics, rather than repudiate it. Cecil viewed the League as a means to consolidate Anglo-American relations. Both states shared similar 'ideas of right and justice', whereas Britain and continental European states, he thought, had a different view of international politics. 'We are right,' he said, 'and the Continental nations are, speaking generally, wrong. If America accepts our point of view in these matters, it will mean the dominance of that point of view in all international affairs.'[10] Although Clemenceau paid little attention to the League, he was committed to perpetuating the wartime alliance into peacetime. The French premier was willing to make significant concessions to British and American interests because he viewed the alliance as the best means of achieving French security against a future German threat. Within this context Clemenceau initially supported the League as a means of reinforcing wartime relations. French supporters of the League were on the margins of French policymaking in 1919. Their ambitions for the League went far beyond what Wilson or even the League to Enforce Peace countenanced, including the establishment of a world court of justice, whose decisions would be implemented by military force. Law, rather than public opinion, formed the framework for security and international order.[11]

On 14 February Wilson presented the Covenant to the third plenary session. 'He stood there,' wrote his wife Ethel, who had sneaked into the room to listen, 'slender, calm, and powerful in his argument – I seemed to see the people of all depressed countries – men, women, and little children – crowding round and waiting on his words.'[12] Cecil, who by now entertained a strong dislike of Wilson, was much less generous: 'The Conference was indescribably hot and stuffy and the President, though he probably did well to read the Covenant right through, made his speech rather dull in consequence.' Léon Bourgeois, the French delegation's adviser on the League of Nations, chipped in with a 'dismal oration', while Cecil could not rise beyond stereotype in describing how Orlando spoke 'with an Italian excess of gesture, which was almost comic.'[13] Article 10, which featured at the heart of the American debate on the Versailles Treaty in the summer of 1919, stated that the members of the League would respect and defend the integrity and independence of its members against external aggression. The Executive Council would 'advise' members on how to fulfil 'this obligation'. This caused immense confusion in debates at the time and in diplomatic practice in the interwar period. How could a state be 'advised' on its 'obligation'? If it had an obligation, surely it did not need 'advice'. In his presentation, however, Wilson stressed that military sanctions were very much a last resort, only to be used if 'moral force' failed. The Covenant also set out the institutions of the League, including the Assembly and the Council. Britain, France, Italy, Japan, and the United States (provided the Senate ratified the treaty) were permanent members, while four members in the Assembly would also have temporary seats in the Council. These included Belgium and Greece as two small but significant allies, Spain as the leading neutral, and Brazil as a nod to regional balance. A permanent secretariat was established in Geneva. While most interest attached to the League's role in resolving international disputes and managing disarmament, its purview spread far beyond that. The Covenant specifically mentioned the League's role in international labour regulation and in supervising colonial mandates.[14] It was hardly a day for heated debate, but Bourgeois made clear French unease with the League when he pointed to the absence of any organized military force to sustain the Covenant. While the principles contained in the Covenant marked 'the Prevalence of Right over violence and barbarity', it remained 'the foundation on which we shall have to work'.[15]

The Covenant disappointed French internationalists and supporters of the wartime alliance. After listening to the presentation of the Covenant, Clemenceau concluded that the League of Nations lacked teeth to enforce its decisions and secure its members' safety, especially France from Germany. From mid-February he began to press for more extensive territorial guarantees. On 16 February he presented the Senate's Commission for Foreign Affairs with a plan to create an autonomous state in the Rhineland, which would be joined to France by a customs union and the annexation of the Saar.[16] Herein lay the grit in the construction of the new international order. Wilson conceived of the League as a means of transforming the norms of international politics through the practice of cooperation, sustained by public opinion. The League was the international order; in Wilson's view it offered a means of replacing military competition with international cooperation, which had the added benefit of easing the pressure on the United States to compete in an arms race and militarize its own society and political institutions. During his speaking tour in September he called the League an 'absolute revolution' in international affairs.[17] In Clemenceau's view the League did not provide the basis for a new international order because it had no mechanism to enforce international treaties and law. French diplomacy now pushed for territorial changes that tested the boundaries of self-determination and its application in the international system. This was a vision of an international system based on territorial buffer zones and military power, with no significant role for international institutions and arbitration.

The debate over the territorial dispensation, therefore, went beyond cutting here and stitching there on the map of Europe. It had its own logic and its own defenders. Often dismissed, especially by frustrated American diplomats, as 'old diplomacy', its defenders argued that prioritizing continental and regional balances over the wishes of the inhabitants remained the most effective way of constructing peace. In a debate on 11 February about the relative weight attached to ethnic, economic, and strategic concerns in setting Romania's borders, the Italian diplomat Giacomo De Martino intervened: 'It is necessary to recognise the significance of strategic and economic considerations and take them sufficiently into account; in particular, the strategic element is indispensable if one wishes to secure a lasting peace and the tranquillity of nations.' When the American delegate, Charles Seymour, accused him of returning to the diplomatic norms of the seventeenth century, Di Martino replied that the self-determination of tens of thousands of inhabitants was subordinate to providing secure communications and borders for a state. The security of the state trumped self-determination because the former provided the basis for peace.[18]

That said, principles created frameworks, within which political interest worked itself out. Self-determination was generally the starting point for discussions. There was no doubt concerning the return of Alsace and Lorraine to France, an act considered as righting an historic wrong. Wilson and Lloyd George opposed Clemenceau's demands for an autonomous Rhineland and annexation of the Saarland. Lloyd George recognized the French security dilemma and offered a guarantee of immediate military support against German aggression. He also persuaded Wilson to make a similar offer. Clemenceau took the offer, despite the vehement opposition of Marshal Foch. The final settlement allowed for occupation of the left bank of the Rhine for fifteen years, the demilitarization of the right bank of the Rhine, and the right of Allied troops to expand their zone of occupation if Germany failed to meet its reparations payments. The terms also enabled the French state to administer the Saarland, control the coalfields, and hold a plebiscite at the end of fifteen years to decide on sovereignty over the region. These terms provided ample scope for French policy to undermine German sovereignty, win over local support, and dismember the Reich in the west. Nonetheless Germany retained the title deeds to its core industrial regions in the west. It did lose a small region of Eupen-Malmédy to Belgium, and France was able to exploit its occupation of Luxembourg to engineer a customs union, which the local inhabitants voted for in a plebiscite on 28 September.[19]

Germany's borders in eastern Europe were also settled at Versailles. The application of self-determination posed great difficulties in eastern Europe, though this had been anticipated in advance of the peace conference. During the war the notion of self-determination had been expanded to include access to the sea and other criteria, considered essential to viable independence. The detailed application required innovative solutions. Since late 1916 the formation of a Polish state in eastern Europe was widely accepted, but its borders were heavily contested. The new Polish state incorporated Poznan, much of West Prussia, and a corridor to the Baltic Sea. These were predominantly Polish territories. The port of Danzig, Poland's point of access to the sea, was made a free city administered by the League of Nations. The future of Upper Silesia, initially granted *in toto* to Poland, was to be decided by plebiscites. Czechoslovakia's border with Austria and Germany also challenged the norms of self-determination, most notably with the inclusion of 3 million Germans in the Sudetenland, formerly part of the Habsburg monarchy, into the new central European state. French diplomats, supported by their Italian counterparts, argued that Czechoslovakia's viability required the inclusion of the economic resources and the more easily defended frontier in the Sudetenland. French and Italian politicians considered the strengthening of these states essential in their plans to contain German power.[20]

For the same reason they succeeded in preventing the Anschluss between Austria and Germany. In early 1919 socialists and Catholics in both Austria and Germany supported unification on the grounds of national self-determination. They depicted the union as a culmination of the national traditions of 1848, republican and democratic, rather than autocratic and militaristic. The Foreign Ministry and German military supported the union for different reasons, as a means of strengthening German security. That said, neither state undertook serious negotiations about union, beset as they were by a host of more pressing problems. During the war, Allied planning had entertained two alternative scenarios about Austria. If Austria united with Germany, it could balance Prussian militarist values with a powerful southern Catholic bloc; or, alternatively, Austria would remain independent to contain German power. French policy assumed that German political values remained wedded to militarism and authoritarianism despite the overthrow of the Kaiser and the establishment of a republic. This denied the logic of democratizing Germany by means of a union with Austria. As Lloyd George paid little attention to this part of the Versailles Treaty, Clemenceau, with the support of Orlando, was able to make union between the two German states conditional on the League of Nations' approval, over which French governments wielded a veto. In the light of this ban on a German-Austrian union, the incorporation of the Sudetenland into Czechoslovakia, and the favouring of Polish over German claims in disputed regions, the extent of self-determination in the treaty appears meagre.

However, an assessment of the significance of self-determination in the treaty needs to take into account three issues. First, the application of self-determination was always bound to lead to anomalies. Second, that those anomalies were always resolved against Germany was the result of its defeat in the war and its status as a pariah in international politics. Finally, the alternative to self-determination was the dismemberment of the Reich. Proposals had been aired during the war, in Paris and Petrograd, that went as far as breaking the Germany united in 1871 into its constituent states, such as Prussia, Bavaria, and Hanover. Indeed, proposals to detach the Rhineland from Prussia found their historical justification in the Rheinbund created by Napoleon in 1806. In 1919 plans to separate the Rhineland and even Bavaria from the Reich resurfaced. While these remained options in French policy, they were contained in 1919 – and many French policymakers doubted their feasibility because the proposals could not accommodate local German national sentiment in these regions. On the other (eastern) side of Germany the settlement in Upper Silesia was revised to enable a plebiscite, which limited initial Polish gains. In other words without the principle of self-determination the territorial settlement could have been much more severe, while, in geographical terms, it could hardly have been more generous to Germany following its defeat in a bitter war.

The tensions between the principle of self-determination and the logic of cabinet diplomacy were epitomized by Italian claims. As noted, their demands at the Paris Peace Conference combined the provisions of the

Treaty of London (1915) with new claims to Fiume, based on the dominant position of ethnic Italians in the city. Italian claims encroached on the new Yugoslavia, Woodrow Wilson's sensibilities, and French views of Yugoslavia as a rampart against German expansion. Each side adapted existing war cultures to the new conflict. The Yugoslav Committee quickly issued declarations, comparing Italian political values to 'German Kultur' and condemning the 'extermination of an innocent people'. Both Italian and Yugoslav publicists framed their claims in the language of self-determination. Italians privileged the ethnic composition in the cities, as they were centres of 'civilization', whereas the Yugoslav Committee held that the Italians in Rijeka (in Fiume) were a 'colony of immigrants', who were disqualified from self-determination.[21]

In the Adriatic, Italian policy had the advantages of overwhelming military power, but in Paris, Sonnino and Orlando had little political leverage. The United States had never approved the Treaty of London. Wilson restricted his support for Italian demands to clear instances of self-determination, such as the Trentino and Trieste, and Pula in Istria. The conflict between Wilson and Sonnino resulted from their very different styles of politics and their assumptions about the international order. Wilson had travelled around Italy between 2 and 6 January, where his enthusiastic reception led him to believe that he could appeal to the Italian people over the heads of the delegation in Paris. Sonnino cultivated relations with House, who was more favourable to Italian concerns. Whereas Wilson instinctively looked to the 'people' to legitimize his position, Sonnino remained faithful to the practice of cabinet diplomacy as a means to resolve conflicting claims. However, Sonnino's abrasive character hardly helped. Even his colleagues despaired of him. 'I was tempted to throw the inkwell at him,' wrote Salvatore Barzilai, a member of the Italian delegation, after one meeting, 'and thus create a pretext to escape that inferno.'[22] More fundamentally, Wilson believed in self-determination as a founding principle of the new international order, something Sonnino had never accepted. The American delegation itself was split on the issue of Italian demands. Thomas Page, the ambassador, warned that it was necessary to take into account 'the passions of the [Italian] people', whereas Seymour appealed to Wilson's 'inspiring moral direction'. On 23 April Wilson issued his appeal, denying Italian claims to Fiume on the basis that the port provided access to the Adriatic for the new Yugoslav state, and via rail, for Hungary and Romania – and also rejecting Italian claims to Dalmatia on the basis that the majority of the inhabitants were Croats, not Italians. At a broader level he argued that the principles of self-determination must be applied across Europe. Orlando and Sonnino promptly left Paris and received an enthusiastic reception on their return to Rome.[23]

The crisis had three outcomes. First, in leaving Paris, Orlando and Sonnino lost the ability to shape the treaty. Yugoslavia received the northern Dalmatian coast, while Fiume became a free state. Wilson had succeeded in inserting his view into the treaty. Second, Italian nationalists, led by Gabriele D'Annunzio, occupied Fiume in September 1919, beginning a five-year struggle between Italy and Yugoslavia for control of the city. This struggle illustrated the limits of the negotiations in Paris in determining borders in Europe after 1918. Military force on the ground – whether an army or a paramilitary formation – remained an important factor, even after the armistice, in shaping the post-war map of Europe, particularly in eastern Europe, the Balkans, and the former Ottoman empire. Finally, Wilson's appeal undermined his natural supporters within Italy, such as Bissolati, the Italian socialist now resigned from the cabinet, and Gaetano Salvemini, also a socialist. The editor of *Corriere della Sera*, Luigi Albertini, who had promoted the Congress of Oppressed Peoples, had as early as 14 November 1918 condemned the ingratitude of the Triple Entente for Italian sacrifices during the war. Italy actually gained much from the treaty. It added territory in the Trentino and Istria; its main threat, Austria-Hungary, was destroyed; and it blocked German expansion southwards. Yet the myth of a mutilated victory came to dominate interpretations of the peace. The sacrifice of war had not been fully redeemed. For Liberal Italy, which set so much store by its identity as a great power, the Versailles Treaty was a defeat. Orlando and Sonnino resigned on 19 June. In applying one set of principles – self-determination – Wilson had unwittingly undermined another basis of the peace settlement, namely fragile constitutional democracy in Italy.[24]

In one of the denunciations of the Treaty of London, Stojan Protić, prime minister of the nascent Yugoslav state, pointed out that whatever borders were drawn in Istria and Dalmatia, there would still be a national minority living there. Of course this was not a reason to deny Yugoslavia its territorial claims. Moreover, the Corfu Declaration had promised that all citizens would be equal under the law and all religions treated equally. In 1917 it would have been impolitic to identify the ethnic Italians in Dalmatia as the beneficiaries of Yugoslav tolerance, but once the conflict became public the Yugoslav state burnished its record of respect of different nationalities.[25] Other emerging states made similar claims about the new minorities within their borders. Good treatment of minorities – their right to education in their own language, cultural freedoms, and so on – was a badge of civilization. Before 1914, states that committed atrocities against their own subjects and citizens had been condemned for their uncivilized behaviour.

The great powers, however, had little faith in the capacity of the new states in eastern Europe to protect minorities. The first minority treaty was concluded with Poland on 28 June 1919. The principle of minority protection was not new, but its application and conceptual underpinnings had changed by this time. Minority protection had been written into treaties before 1914, though it generally applied to religious minorities rather than national minorities and terms were enforced (or often ignored) by the great powers. The minority treaties were a response to the emergence of national self-determination as the basis of states, the presence of large minorities in these states, and the catastrophes inflicted upon various national and religious minorities since the First Balkan War in 1912. Moreover, in early 1919 harrowing stories of the pogroms against Jews in Poland reached the delegations in Paris. In the city of Lvov, in the contested borderlands between Poland and the Ukraine, 150 Jews were killed and 500 shops destroyed in November 1918. 'Let all the burghers, the merchants, lawyers, and doctors, go buy land in Palestine', declared one threat against the Jewish community in the city.[26] These reports, however, confirmed the suspicions in Britain, France, and the United States that international treaties were necessary to secure the protection of minorities in central and eastern Europe.

The new states, particularly Poland, resented the intrusion upon their sovereignty and the implication that they were not as civilized as the Allies. Britain and France had their own minorities, not to mention colonial subjects, but they were not bound by these treaties. The new states were also concerned that the internationalization of minority protection could be used to undermine domestic stability. Under the treaties, minorities were able to petition the Council of the League of Nations. In the case of a dispute between the Council and the state in which the minority lived, the issue was referred to the Permanent Court of International Justice at The Hague. By vesting the supervision of these treaties in the League, it was hoped to avoid a situation where great power politics determined the reaction to any persecution of minorities.[27]

The third major pillar of the Versailles Treaty, after the League of Nations and self-determination, centred on reparations, an issue with moral and economic dimensions. During the war the Allies asserted that Germany was to pay reparations because it had destroyed Allied property as a result of its violations of international law. In economic terms the complexity of the reparations settlement was connected to the post-war international economic order. The Allies knew that payment of reparations depended on a German economic recovery, but French planners, notably Etienne Clémentel and Louis Loucheur, feared that Germany would come to dominate the European economy. The challenge, therefore, was to construct an international economic system that contained German economic power. Clémentel looked forward to the continued cooperation between the Allies and the United States, which had been tightened in 1917 and 1918 by a series of agreements on shipping, coal, and food supplies. 'It would negate all the effort of the war and the idealistic character of the struggle, in which nations have fought side by side,' Jean Monnet wrote to his boss, Clémentel, on 2 November 1918, 'not to prolong, during this necessary period of reconstruction, the application of the principles of mutual aid and the distribution of materials according to the most urgent needs, which permitted the Allies to conduct this struggle against the enemy to a successful end.'[28] French economic policy followed a similar pattern to its security policy. It sought to promote continued Allied cooperation, but if the wartime structures broke down, the alternative was a 'peace of reprisals and punishments', as a Ministry of Commerce memorandum put it.[29]

Granted French visions of the post-war economic order aimed to deny German manufacturers raw materials and markets, but this was considered just compensation for the illegal destruction of French and Belgian industrial resources. Woodrow Wilson was not particularly interested in the economic aspects of the peace settlement, though he adhered to the general idea that commercial barriers between states should be minimized. The American vision favoured a general restoration of trade and credit throughout Europe, including Germany. The revival of economic activity would boost employment, stave off revolution, and provide better trading opportunities for the United States. Trade acquired a moral value, as an agent of civilization and a means of sustaining peace. Herbert Hoover, Head of the American Relief Administration, pressed for the lifting of the blockade on Germany in order to deliver food supplies to hungry people. This served the immediate interests of American farmers, but Hoover saw a happy coincidence in American interests and the international economic order. 'There are seventy millions of people,' he wrote in 'Why we are Feeding Germany' in March 1919, 'who must either produce or die. ... their production is essential to the world's future and they cannot produce unless they are fed.'[30] By December 1918 the United States had already begun dismantling the institutions of Allied wartime cooperation, much to the dismay of Monnet and others.

Resolving reparations was the first step in constructing the post-war international economic system. 'We are most impressed by the urgency of settling the indemnity question,' John Foster Dulles, on the American delegation, wrote to Edwin Gay, his former boss in Washington, 'which is operating in considerable measure to arrest the renewal of trade and industry.'[31] As Dulles noted, the uncertainty over the extent of reparations payments hampered lending and the restoration of credit. He played a central role in the reparations commission, where French, British, and American diplomats haggled over the amount of reparations, their relative share, and the relationship between war debts and reparations. This proved a toxic combination. France was prepared to accept a lower amount if it received a higher proportion, Britain wanted a higher amount, and the United States rejected any linkages between war debts and reparations. In the end no sum was established in the Versailles Treaty, but instead a reparations commission was set up with British, French, American, and Belgian representatives to establish the amount and assess Germany's ability to pay.

One significant clause did emerge from the commission, drafted by Dulles. This was the so-called war guilt clause, Article 231 of the treaty, which attributed to Germany sole responsibility for the outbreak of the war. The article inscribed into the treaty the moral chasm that had separated the belligerents during the war. Moreover, because the reparations settlement was linked to the occupation regime, Article 231 became the moral core of the treaty, one rooted in a debate about the outbreak of the war. Reparations became the hinge on which the treaty turned in western Europe.

Germany's ability to pay the reparations was hampered by a separate section of the treaty, Part X, which dealt with commercial relations between the former enemies. The proposals aimed at limiting German trade drafted during the Paris economic conference in June 1916 shaped these clauses. The treaty prohibited Germany from raising its tariffs against Allied imports for a period of five years, during which Allied states would enjoy the benefits of most favoured nation status. Goods from Polish and French territories, formerly part of Germany, were exempt from tariffs for between three and five years. German goods, however, did not enjoy reciprocal treatment. These terms, supported by the American delegate, Bernard Baruch, repudiated the commercial freedoms promised in Wilson's fourteen points. German exports were also limited by the loss of 90 per cent of its merchant marine.[32] These terms exacerbated the dilemmas confronted in the reparations debate. The international economic order required the revival of German commerce, yet that revival also threatened the Allies, particularly France and, to a lesser extent, Britain. The commercial clauses most closely reflected British policy at the Paris Peace Conference, which aimed to limit German commerce, but did not want to tie the British economy into a putative Allied economic order. The idea that German business had cheated its way to prosperity before the war and must therefore be punished and contained trumped the liberal ideal that commerce had a civilizing quality, vital for the restoration of friendly relations between societies. Yet although failing to construct the basis for an international economic order, the treaty left open the space for the businessman and the politician (sometimes one and the same person) to create new commercial agreements between the erstwhile enemies.

The geographical remit of the Versailles Treaty stretched beyond Europe. The disposition of German colonies in Africa and Asia provided the occasion for reworking the imperial order. The first innovation was the mandate system, which assigned former German colonies (and later Mesopotamia, Syria, Palestine, and Arabia from the former Ottoman empire) to the control of one of the Allied powers. The Allied powers were supposed to administer the territory under the supervision of the League of Nations, in the interests of the inhabitants, and with a view to preparing those inhabitants for self-government. The mandate system served various purposes, not the least of which was to legitimize the expansion of the British, French, and Japanese empires. Italian claims to Ottoman territory were ignored in the absence of Orlando in Paris during late April and May.[33] As British policymakers surveyed their colonial agreements and imperial ambitions in late 1918, they used the mandates system to undo the Sykes-Picot agreement. The Foreign Secretary, Arthur Balfour, claimed not to understand the agreement, while Lord Curzon denounced it as 'wretched'. Nor did the Sykes-Picot agreement chime with the principle of self-determination. The mandates system offered a solution, in which British policymakers could wriggle out of awkward wartime agreements with their European allies, secure their territorial and economic interests in the region, and gesture towards the temper of the times.[34]

Nationalists in the Arab territories of the former Ottoman empire asserted their own claims to independence, invoking wartime agreements with the Allies, their participation in the war against the empire, and a dash of Wilsonian idealism. Amir Faysal, who had set up an Arab government in

Damascus in 1918, presented his case in Paris for an independent Greater Syrian state, including Syria, Transjordan, and Lebanon, that would serve as the core of a future independent Arab state. The Syrian Congress presented the King-Crane Commission, an American initiative to assess the popular mood amongst the Arab population, with a resolution on 2 July, demanding independence. Arabs were just as effective at the business of government, they claimed, as the emerging nation states in Europe.[35] However, the prevailing assumption was that the Arab population was not fit for self-government and British forces were on the ground throughout the Middle East to secure their war aims. The formal transfer of former Ottoman territory to the mandated great powers, Britain and France, rather than to the nationalist claimants, took place after the Treaty of Sèvres between the Allies and the Ottoman empire in August 1920.

The mandate system adopted the essential elements of the civilizing mission, the pre-war justification for European imperial expansion. The imperial administration had a duty to develop the colony and 'civilize' its subjects. Yet the mandate system had three important implications for the international order. First, the goal of self-government was explicitly stated as the purpose of the system, even as the mandates blocked the claims of Arab nationalists and others for immediate self-government or independence. In that sense the mandates system had been anticipated in wartime policy statements about the future of empire, such as the Montagu Declaration on Britain's India policy in 1917. Second, the League of Nations supervised the administration of the mandate, collected data, and heard petitions. While neither the Permanent Mandates Commission nor the League's secretariat could impose sanctions on states that fell short in their duties – as they regularly did – the practice of collecting and publicizing information created a new normative environment for imperial practice. This supervision did not extend to colonies already in the British and French empires. Finally, Australia, New Zealand, and South Africa used their position on the Mandates Commission to chart their own interests within the empire, while Japan valued its position on the Commission as a signal of its status in the civilized order of nations.[36]

In preparing for the Paris Peace Conference the Japanese government had concentrated on three issues – the confirmation of its wartime agreements concerning Shantung province, the possession of German islands in the Pacific, north of the equator, and securing the recognition of racial equality. The last issue reflected concerns in Tokyo that the League of Nations would become an instrument for the leading European states and the United States to control global politics and block Japanese interests due to racial prejudice. The proposal for a racial equality clause, put by Barons Makino and Chinda, aimed to secure Japan's place in the 'civilized' community, while it did away with racial hierarchies, at least in a formal sense, in the international order.[37] The presentation of the proposal challenged the European powers and the United States to articulate the racial limits of the international order. Makino presented the proposal as part of a revolution in the international order: 'It is not necessary to dwell on the fact that racial and religious animosities have constituted a fruitful source of warfare among different peoples throughout history often leading to deplorable excesses. ... What was deemed impossible before is about to be accomplished. The creation of this League is a notable example. If this organization can open a way to the solution of the question, the scope of the work will become wider and enlist the interest of a still greater part of humanity.'[38]

Some European states, notably France and Italy, accepted the proposal. However, the British empire and the United States successfully opposed it. The most forthright opponent was William Hughes, the Australian prime minister, who saw the proposal as a threat to the white Australia policy and a prelude to immigration from Asia to Australia. It also played on his fears of Japanese expansion into the South Pacific. Hughes, 'the smallest but most outspoken of all the delegates' in the words of the British journalist Vernon Bartlett, gave cover to other Dominion leaders as well as British and American politicians, who feared the implications of the racial equality clause. It is unlikely that the Australian prime minister could have successfully opposed the clause had the American and British governments added their weight in support of the Japanese proposal. By failing to act, both these governments ensured the clause would fail. The prospect of large numbers of immigrants from Asia and their claims to equal rights alarmed Dominion and American politicians. House thought the racial equality clause would stoke up racial tensions, not ease them, though he did not elaborate on his reasoning. The failure to support the proposal undermined the universal claims of European and American politicians. From the Japanese perspective the racial hierarchies of the pre-war era persisted. The conference had failed to deal with the racial fault lines in international politics.[39]

Nor was the rejection of the proposal without immediate costs. While Makino was drafting his proposal in Paris, the Hara government in Tokyo was committed to inheriting directly German concessions in Shantung. During the war Japanese diplomats had concluded agreements with the

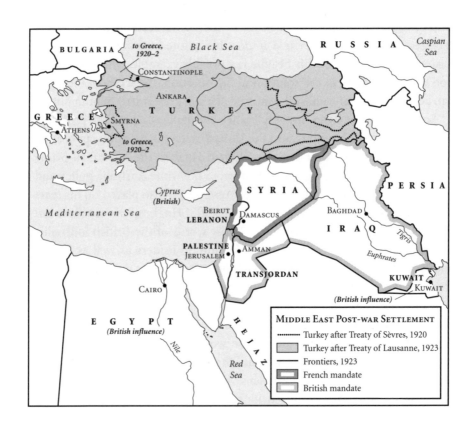

BULGARIA   to Greece,   *Black Sea*   R U S S I A   *Caspian*
                1920–2   *Sea*
            CONSTANTINOPLE

                    ANKARA
            T U R K E Y
G R E E C E   SMYRNA
    ATHENS
            to Greece,
            1920–2

    Cyprus   P E R S I A
    (British)   S Y R I A
Mediterranean Sea   BEIRUT DAMASCUS   BAGHDAD
            LEBANON   I R A Q   *Tigris*
            PALESTINE AMMAN   *Euphrates*
            JERUSALEM
                    TRANSJORDAN   KUWAIT
    CAIRO   KUWAIT
                            (British influence)
E G Y P T   *H E J A Z*
(British influence)   MIDDLE EAST POST-WAR SETTLEMENT
                                Turkey after Treaty of Sèvres, 1920
            Red   Turkey after Treaty of Lausanne, 1923
    Nile   *Sea*   Frontiers, 1923
                                French mandate
                                British mandate

Allies, the United States, and the Chinese government confirming its position. However, the Japanese position came under sustained pressure from the Chinese delegation at Versailles. Wellington Koo presented the Chinese case to the delegates on 28 January. He argued that the German concessions should be handed back directly to China. Japan's claims, he said, were undermined by its use of military threats to extract Chinese agreements in 1915 and 1917 and by atrocities it had committed against Chinese civilians. Koo had supported Makino's racial equality proposal, but he considered it, with some justification, as a guise for Japanese expansion in Asia. In the face of these charges by Koo, Japanese officials complained that their national prestige had been challenged and threatened the use of military force. At this stage, before the introduction of the racial equality clause, Wilson told the American minister in Beijing, Paul Reinsch, that the Chinese government should not cave in to Japanese threats.[40] By 22 April Wilson's position had changed. At the same time as he told Orlando and Sonnino that the Treaty of London could not be honoured, he told Koo that the war had been fought to show that treaties were inviolable. Better to fulfil the terms of a bad treaty than abandon this principle. Lloyd George and Clemenceau, principled to a fault in this case, also defended their countries' treaties with Japan.

On 21 April in Tokyo, Ito Miyoji, an influential conservative politician, concluded that Japan should withdraw from the League of Nations if its claims to Shantung were rejected. The Hara cabinet agreed and issued instructions to the delegation in Paris. In the face of this threat to withdraw, Wilson had decided to support the Japanese claims. Ironically, the American failure to support Chinese claims in Shantung was one of the most prominent arguments of Wilson's opponents in the Senate. The American president did a deal with Makino in which Japan would take possession of Shantung and then return it to Chinese sovereignty while retaining economic concessions. This process, he hoped, would be supervised by the League. At the Council of Four meeting on 22 April he claimed that 'I am above all concerned not to create a deep chasm between the East and the West'.[41] Wilson saw the League as a process as well as an institution, through which the unresolved and apparently intractable problems of the peace conference could be settled.

In his presentation of the Covenant, Wilson also made much of the inclusion of provisions for the international regulation of labour and work conditions. These provisions demonstrated that the scope of the League of Nations extended beyond conventional diplomacy to encompass social issues of international importance. Some delegates saw the labour provisions as a fundamental dimension of making peace. 'The mass remain a misfit in their present conditions,' said the British delegate George Barnes, in his presentation of the report of the Commission on Labour Regulation on 11 April, 'a source of concern to all lovers of their kind and a menace to the peace of the world. It is that latter aspect of it that makes labor regulation, and I should say labor improvement, an integral and urgent part of the work of the Peace Conference.' Emile Vandervelde, who had flown from Brussels to Paris especially to attend this plenary session, argued that the provisions were a means of compensating the working classes for their sacrifices during the war and thereby tying their substantial support into the peace settlement.[42] Socialists and trade unionists had long argued that incorporating labour provisions into the peace settlement would bolster its legitimacy.

Cecil gave a different twist to this argument when he claimed, in a meeting of the British Empire Delegation, that the League of Nations would bolster its authority as 'an instrument of international progress' by managing the labour regulations. It would provide the League with 'continuing activity' when international crises were not disturbing the repose of diplomats. The habit of international cooperation developed in regulating labour conditions would benefit the League's ability to manage international political crises. Arthur Fontaine, the French member who worked on the Commission of International Labour Regulation, understood 'peace as a continual creation, which in order to be maintained, demands vigilant attention all the time, a patient and sustained effort in education to restrain the bellicose instincts engendered by a history of rivalries and national struggles.'[43]

Allied and American trade unionists and socialists had considerable influence on the labour provisions in the Versailles Treaty. The Commission on International Labour Regulation was established on 25 January and its members included Barnes, Samuel Gompers, Vandervelde, and Léon Jouhaux, as well as representatives from Japan, Italy, Poland, Czechoslovakia, and Cuba. These members often wore two hats. They were officially representing their governments, but they also had met each other in previous years at international meetings of socialists and trade unionists. Between 5 and 9 February in Berne the first post-war meeting of the International Federation of Trade Unions took place, attended by German as well as Allied trade unionists (with the notable exception of Belgian and American representatives). The conference developed the resolutions passed at Leeds in 1916 and Berne in 1917 as the basis for future international labour regu-lation.[44] Others on the Commission, such as Arthur Fontaine, one of the founders of the International Association for the Legal Protection of Workers, had been active as 'professional social experts' before the war.[45] The Commission marked the incorporation of the professional expert into conventional diplomacy. Before the war international gatherings of experts (and enthusiasts) had provided a platform from which to press govern-ments to undertake reforms. The rise of the expert in international rela-tions during and after the First World War reflected the increasing awareness of the complexities of international politics and the interconnec-tions between the different facets – political, economic, and cultural – of relations between states.

Part 13 of the Versailles Treaty was devoted to the provisions for the international regulation of labour. The preamble stated that 'universal peace . . . can be established only if it is established upon social justice'. The terms provided for the establishment of a general conference and an International Labour Office. The conference would vote on regulations, which it would then propose to governments for adoption into their national legislation, while the International Labour Office was to review the implementation of international regulations, gather data, and provide expert advice. All members of the League of Nations were members of the International Labour Organization, as it became known. Membership was also quickly expanded to include former enemies, notably Germany, so that German industry could not evade international scrutiny of its work practices. Each state had four representatives, one each for workers and employers and two government appointees. The first head of the International Labour Organization was Albert Thomas, who could draw on his experience in managing labour relations in France during the war. Part 13 also sketched out some preliminary principles, including the right of association into trade unions, the adoption of the eight-hour day and forty-eight-hour week, the abolition of child labour, and equal pay for work of 'equal value' for men and women. Article 427 noted that strict uniformity of practice was impossible owing to different economic conditions, histor-ical legacies, and climatic environments.

Hughes had objected to the qualification enshrined in Article 427, fearing that it would benefit low-wage economies in Asia, particularly Japan, and undermine the 'white man's wage' in Australia. Balfour and Cecil argued that it was better to insert this qualification, so that Japan would have to 'defend her position in the face of international and internal public opinion'.[46] While trade unionists wanted to raise their workers' living standards, they also saw the International Labour Organization as a means of protecting their members' working conditions against competition, whether it be from women or from lower-wage economies. The greatest possible degree of harmonization of work conditions was the only means of preventing employers from exploiting 'the unfair competition of backward countries', as a Labour Party pamphlet put it. In May 1926 James Shotwell, professor of history at Columbia University and a progressive internationalist, revealed the double-edged thinking behind the International Labour Organization, when he praised 'this notable extension of the idea of human rights', which expanded 'the ideals of justice prevalent in countries of higher civilization within lands of lower culture'.[47] As with other parts of the Versailles Treaty, implementation of the terms of labour provisions remained the test of its significance. Yet the inclusion of this section in the treaty marked a victory for trade unions, including those in the Central Powers, that had campaigned for this since 1916. More traditional notions of peace had been expanded to include concepts of social justice, while the institutions and the regulations, even if they lacked teeth, had the power to establish international norms concerning working conditions.

* * *

On 4 May, 3,000 students gathered in Tiananmen Square in Beijing. One of them, Luo Jialun, recalled how the protesters surged forward. The Minister of Communication, Cao Rulin, was chased from his house, demonstrating a 'rare agility' as he leapt over walls to escape the angry protesters. When he returned home he found his family's belongings smashed. Cao was associated with the pro-Japanese faction in Chinese politics; news of the deal over Shantung had just arrived. Other protesters carried placards, some in English, condemning the deal. From Brisbane to San Francisco, Chinese migrant workers and students gathered in a worldwide protest.[48] This was the first protest against the specific terms of the Versailles Treaty. Around the world it was condemned for failing to fulfil the far-reaching aspirations that had arisen during the war. The meaning of peace was measured against promises made during the war, be they for national self-determination or international cooperation. In addition, the treaty challenged the domestic legitimacy of political regimes, which had staked their authority on delivering peace.

The Chinese delegation did not attend the ceremony in the Hall of Mirrors at Versailles, where Johannes Bell and Hermann Müller signed the treaty on 28 June 1919 on behalf of Germany. The West, Japan, and the Chinese political institutions and traditional social mores were all held responsible for the failure to achieve a just peace settlement. The treaty exacerbated fault lines in Chinese politics, between Asia and the West, within Asia between Japan and China, and within China. 'China is now at the parting of the ways,' noted Koo. 'She has come to the West for justice. If she should fail to get it, the people may perhaps attribute its failure not so much to Japan's insistence on her own claims as to the attitude of the West, merely because some of its leading Powers had privately pledged to support Japan.'[49] The West was as much a construct as the East. Koo had cast Chinese demands – territorial integrity, sovereignty, economic and fiscal independence – as an affirmation of the spirit of Wilson's fourteen points, which would unite East and West.[50] In Paris, however, the West's traditions of secret diplomacy had cut the ground from underneath a Wilsonian settlement in the Far East, deepening the cultural chasm between Asia and the West. The Chinese reaction to the treaty cast it as a betrayal of the principles for which the war was fought, not just by China, but by the Allies and the United States in particular.

In denouncing the treaty, however, Chinese publicists and diplomats used the language of Allied and American peace politics. In the United States, Chinese groups lodged protests and published pamphlets. The Chinese Patriotic Committee, established on New York's Upper West Side, explained in *Why China Refused to Sign the Peace Treaty* that Japan's claim to Shantung continued the original violation of international rights committed by Germany's seizure of the region in 1897. Japanese diplomacy, backed by military threats, had bullied the Chinese government into making concessions during the war. Japanese militarism represented a continuation of German methods, while China was cast as the 'weaker nation', compelled by might to surrender what was its territory by right. The China Society in America declared that the 'principles enunciated' at Paris were 'admittedly sound', but they had not been applied: 'The New Order does not come to China.'[51] Despite the sense of betrayal, Chinese writers and societies continued to appeal to Western opinion to protect China from Japanese ambitions. If the war was about the triumph of right over might, then the successful Japanese claims to Shantung, based as they were on force, rendered the war meaningless. One appeal, issued by a broad range of Chinese civil society, warned that in failing to secure a durable peace in East Asia, the powers risked a 'world conflagration'. It ended with a somewhat plaintive plea that China be allowed to become part of the 'whole human family'. The treaty terms, it was implied, confirmed the persistent hierarchies within the international order, which denied equal rights to all states. By consolidating these divisions, based on power, culture, and race, the leaders at Versailles were storing up tensions for the future.[52]

The memorandum also identified Chinese politicians, such as Cao Rulin, who were condemned for their 'treachery'. Since 1911 popular protests in China, particularly in urban areas, had been stimulated by international challenges. In turn the challenges of international politics required domestic political and cultural change. After a brief efflorescence in 1912 and 1915, this form of popular politics had waned. Consistent failures in foreign policy had undermined the credibility of the Republic. The protests on 4 May became the starting point of what became known as the Fourth of May Movement, which both fed into the channels of the Chinese revolution and diverted it. Although not a coherent movement with a set of political objectives, its cultural and intellectual output challenged Confucian ideals, which stressed stability and carefully constructed social relationships. Writers and activists in the Fourth of May Movement regarded Confucianism as too restrictive for the modern world. The two major parties, the Nationalists and the Communist Party, that emerged to dominate Chinese politics from the mid-1920s until the end of the Second World War, shared this rejection of Confucianism and looked to modernize China.[53]

While the Chinese protests focused on the terms of the Versailles Treaty, other nationalist groups, whose hopes for independence and autonomy had been stoked by wartime rhetoric, were simply excluded from the Paris Peace Conference. Nationalists from Korea, which had been subsumed within the Japanese empire between 1895 and 1910, called for independence. The Japanese government complained that Wilsonian ideals had triggered Korean nationalist protests. Only one Korean representative arrived in Paris, but he had no formal status. In the United States and China, Korean émigrés organized protests and petitions at their exclusion from the peace conference. Reprising the Middle-European Union declaration of independence in October 1918, Syngman Rhee, later president of South Korea after the Second World War, organized the First Korean Congress, in Philadelphia in April. Here he burnished Korea's credentials to independence as a democratic and Christian society in the Far East. He defended the dignity and capacity for self-government of the individual Korean and he denounced Japanese atrocities, comparing incidents in Korea to those in

Belgium. The Congress ended in a carefully staged parade that concluded with Rhee reading the declaration of Korean independence at Independence Hall, before delegates passed by the Liberty Bell.[54] The only concession granted by Japan was a minimal amount of cultural autonomy.

When Robert Lansing criticized the concept of self-determination, he was primarily concerned about its application in the British empire, from Ireland to India, from Egypt to South Africa. 'The phrase is simply loaded with dynamite,' he noted. 'It will raise hopes which can never be realized. It will, I fear, cost thousands of lives.'[55] While the Dominion politicians, particularly Jan Smuts and Hughes, played a central role in the Paris Peace Conference negotiations, nationalist politicians from India, Egypt, and Ireland were excluded, not to mention the absence of any international interest in the future of black South Africans. The 1918 election in the United Kingdom had destroyed the Irish Parliamentary Party and the Home Rule solution to the Irish question. Sinn Fein had returned seventy-five MPs, who set up a parliament, or Dail, in Dublin rather than go to Westminster. Arthur Griffith, the Sinn Fein leader, realized that Irish nationalists would not get a seat at the conference table, but Sinn Fein leaders saw some value, as Griffith put it, in 'stand[ing] on the stairs and harangu[ing] the world outside'. The Dail's Message to the Free Nations of the World made unflattering comparisons between Britain and Austria-Hungary and compared Irish claims to those of Polish and Czechoslovak nationalists. England took the place of Germany as the offender against the values of the 'civilized world'. Eamon de Valera, the leading survivor of the 1916 Easter Rising, brought Sinn Fein's campaign to the United States. Other leaders, notably Michael Collins, remained sceptical about 'eyes turning to Paris or to New York'. Although Sinn Fein got no succour from American or European leaders in 1919, the changing normative environment in the international order was of critical importance to its later successes.[56]

In Egypt the British administration arrested and deported nationalist leaders, including Sa'd Zaghlul, to Malta, when they attempted to travel to Paris. This sparked a revolt in Egypt on 9 March, fuelled by disappointed expectations of reform, urban unrest, and the frustration of the peasants (*fellahin*), wearied by the strictures of the Egyptian war economy. Egyptian nationalists' dismay at the absence of constitutional reform was compounded by American silence at the British crackdown. There was an Indian delegation at Paris, but not a delegation that was representative of the Indian National Congress. The Congress sent its own representatives, including

B. G. Tilak. Tilak had been sceptical of British intentions towards India before the war – he had been exiled to Burma for his troubles – but in Paris he was momentarily hopeful that the spirit of the times would lead to self-government for India, which went beyond what he viewed as the limited scope of the Montagu–Chelmsford proposals. However, by April, Tilak had made no progress at Paris. Meanwhile in India economic privation and the death toll from the Spanish influenza – estimated between 6 and 18 million – fuelled anger. Political unrest and a repressive response by British authorities undermined the hopes generated by wartime promises of reform. The arrest of Mohandas Gandhi in March sparked riots throughout northern India. On 13 April, following the deaths of three Europeans in the city of Amritsar, imperial troops opened fire on demonstrators, killing 379 people and wounding over 1,000.[57] Whereas in Egypt the revolt had been triggered by the Paris Peace Conference, in India and in Ireland the radicalization of opposition to imperial rule was already under way and new political movements subsumed the global politics of remaking the world into their own local agendas. Nationalist leaders in all three countries were disappointed to different degrees by Wilson's support for the British empire. Nonetheless they did not abandon their reading of Wilsonian principles or their campaigns to win public support in the United States. Wilsonianism without Wilson – in all its local iterations – still had a powerful purchase on people's imagination.

Ho Chi Minh, either alone or as part of a Vietnamese group in Paris, issued 'The Demands of the Annamite People' on 18 June 1919. The demands were moderate, including the abolition of forced labour (*corvée*), equal rights for Vietnamese and French citizens, and freedoms of association and speech. There was no direct reference to Wilsonian ideals in the document; rather it framed its demands within the Allied themes of a war between civilization and barbarism, the principle of nationalities, and universal fraternity.[58] It demanded autonomy, rather than independence. Wilson was not the only inspiration for anti-colonial nationalists, who could use the language of the Allied war for civilization and justice to undermine the claims of Allied empires.

When Bell and Müller walked through the Hall of Mirrors to sign the Versailles Treaty on 28 June 1919, they passed by a number of *gueules cassées*, French soldiers whose faces had been disfigured by war injuries. Clemenceau had invited these men, blinded and unable to speak, to be present at the signing of the treaty. It was a vivid demonstration of the suffering of war, which Clemenceau and the other Allied leaders had charged Germany with starting.[59] Seven weeks earlier, the draft treaty had been presented to the German Foreign Minister, Ulrich von Brockdorff-Rantzau, who responded with a speech. He rejected Article 231, which assigned sole responsibility to Germany for the outbreak of the war, and against allegations of German war crimes he set the deaths of 'hundreds of thousands of [German] non-combatants' as a result of the continued blockade since the armistice. 'Remember that,' he told the delegates, 'when you speak of guilt and atone-ment.' His speech expressed the genuine convictions of millions of Germans that they were being unjustly treated and blamed. Brockdorff-Rantzau framed the clauses of the treaty – the reparations, territorial losses, disarma-ment – within an international moral economy. Germany, he claimed, was willing to recognize its wrongs and make reparations, but the accounts of guilt and innocence had to be balanced. He appealed to Wilson's principles, which Germany, the United States, and Allies had agreed upon as the foun-dation for peace in November 1918. Only on the basis of economic coopera-tion could Germany afford to pay reparations, but international solidarity was undermined by Germany's exclusion from the League of Nations and the moral judgement of the Versailles Treaty.[60] The speech was heartfelt, but highly impolitic. Nor did it help that Brockdorff-Rantzau was, as one contemporary described him, every inch the aristocrat. The Allies simply refused to entertain any notion of moral equivalence. By failing to repent, Brockdorff-Rantzau merely reinforced the sense that the German revolution of November 1918 had been superficial.

The Foreign Minister's view resonated across Germany. At a meeting of the National Assembly on 12 May, Philipp Scheidemann, now Chancellor of the Weimar Republic, condemned the treaty. 'The hand that places us in such fetters,' he said, 'must wither.' The moral chasm between Germany and its erstwhile enemies created by the experiences of the war was widened by the debate over Versailles. The SPD could unite briefly with the parties on the right, the German National People's Party (DNVP) and the German People's Party (DVP), to defend Germany against the calumnies of the 'shame' paragraphs, which attributed to Germany responsibility for the outbreak of war. Gustav Stresemann, the DVP leader, claimed that the treaty amounted to 'a moral, political, and economic death sentence'.[61]

The German government was given five weeks to draft a response to the Versailles Treaty. It was able to secure minor revisions, notably in the plebi-scites in Upper Silesia, but in essence it faced a clear choice – accept or reject the terms. It was a similar choice to the one in November 1918. If Germany rejected the terms, its political and military leaders expected an

Allied invasion. There was less agreement on the implications of accepting the terms, whether it was truly a 'death sentence' or whether it represented the unpalatable, but only viable, option. General Walther Reinhardt, the Prussian Minister of War, was amongst a small group who called for a resumption of war. In this scenario western Germany would be occupied by the Allies and separated from the Reich. Civilians would wage resistance against the occupation, while the core of the German state would defend itself behind the River Elbe. This rump state, in the historical heart of the German Reich in East Prussia, would preserve national honour and prepare for territorial reunification in the future. The plan for an eastern German state was predicated on the idea that saving national honour was more important than retaining territory. This was the logic of a moral reading of the war without moorings in the material realities of geography and economic resources. Only by rejecting the treaty could Germans redeem the sacrifice of the war.[62]

Ultimately there was little appetite to pile more sacrifice upon sacrifice. Reports from western Germany, which would bear the brunt of an Allied invasion, made clear the lack of popular support for rejection and further military conflict. 'National viewpoints,' reported one officer on 3 June, 'have retreated to the background. Many people are indifferent whether they are under German or French rule, as long as they get along well.'[63] The government barely cobbled together enough votes to pass the treaty through the National Assembly. Scheidemann resigned as Chancellor, while the members of the German Democratic Party (DDP) resigned from the cabinet, only to return in October. Friedrich Ebert, now the president, Matthias Erzberger, and others recognized the futility of rejection. Accepting the treaty provided a platform from which to revise its terms. On 23 July Hermann Müller, now the Foreign Minister, set out an agenda for the Republic's foreign policy that stressed international cooperation and the rejection of militarism. He spoke of a 'true League of Nations'. He also outlined possibilities for integrating Germany into the international order on the basis of its economic power, through trade with the United States and Britain and cooperation with France on the reconstruction of its devastated territory. The Republic never accepted the moral underpinnings of the treaty, but politicians from the Weimar coalition – the SPD, the Centre Party, the DDP – pursued a foreign policy that sought international cooperation and the revival of trade. Having placed its faith in Wilson's fourteen points and been disappointed, the Weimar government realized it had little option but to stake its foreign policy on revising the treaty in accordance with German notions of self-determination, reparations, and the international order.[64]

The Versailles Treaty, however, did considerable damage to the Weimar Republic. In January 1919 the SPD, the Centre Party, and the DDP won 75 per cent of the popular vote, an overwhelming confirmation of popular German support for the new regime. In the next national elections in June 1920 these three parties, the backbone of the Republic, won less than 50 per cent and they would never again win a majority of the popular vote before 1933. There were many reasons for the collapse in popular support, not least economic and social problems and a succession of domestic political crises. Nonetheless the credibility of the German revolution had been closely linked to the coming of peace. Many Germans associated the social and economic difficulties, such as unemployment and inflation, with the treaty. The revolution had been both a means of ending the war and of securing a more favourable peace. As a constitutional democracy, Germany might have expected to accelerate its return to the civilized international order, but the 'shame paragraphs' in the treaty excluded Germany from this community. Moreover, many Germans across the political spectrum suspected that the international order was based on power politics, conducted primarily by the French government. Defeated and disarmed, Germans felt vulnerable to French military aggression. If the international system operated on the logic of military power, then the SPD's vision of international cooperation was woefully naive.

There is a strong case that Germany emerged more secure from the war. The largest economy in Europe, with small states on its eastern and southern flanks, and a weakened France to its west, Germany had the potential to re-emerge as the dominant European power.[65] Yet this perception was not widely shared in 1919. The major preoccupations centred on foreign occu-pation, the scale of reparations, and Germany's exclusion from the League of Nations. The Versailles Treaty undermined German democracy, but not fatally by any means. The survival of the Republic depended on interna-tional politics as well as domestic conditions.

Marshal Foch was another prominent figure who decided not to attend the signing ceremony in the Hall of Mirrors. He was convinced that France had failed to achieve the necessary guarantees for its future security. 'Shall we make of France an accursed country,' he wrote on 18 April, 'which after losing 1,500,000 men in 1914 will be obliged soon to begin again, so that the women who gave their husbands in 1914 will have to give their sons in the next war?'[66] On 31 July the Deuxième Bureau of the French General

Staff produced a report that claimed that the German military were
following the historical example of the Prussian Reform period, when
Gerhard von Scharnhorst had established militia forces. German military
policy, on this reading, sought to evade the restrictions of the 100,000-man
army prescribed by the Versailles Treaty and build a large trained reserve in
readiness for another shot across the Rhine. French officers needed no
reminding that just nine years after Napoleon's crushing victory over
Prussia at the battle of Jena in 1806, Prussian troops were strolling around
Paris. 'The example of 1806,' the report concluded, 'is there to warn us,
history is in perpetual renewal.'[67] While the Army and those on the right
were dissatisfied with the security guarantees, liberal internationalists in
the French Association for the League of Nations (AFSDN) and the League
of the Rights of Man criticized the shortcomings of the League of Nations,
which did not have the military power to enforce the Covenant.[68] The
contest between these two different strands in French thinking on international affairs and their impact on German policy would do much to shape
the European settlement over the coming years. In the meantime,
Clemenceau was able to shepherd the treaty through the Chamber, though
deputies accepted it in the spirit of being the least bad option.

In Britain there was widespread dissatisfaction with the Versailles Treaty.
Between the presentation of the draft in May and the signing in June,
Winston Churchill and Henry Wilson urged Lloyd George to make concessions to ensure Germany signed and accepted the peace. Even Lloyd George
considered revisions, as British delegates suddenly appeared to realize the
overall impact of the treaty. Even members of the delegation professed to be
shocked at the cumulative severity of the terms. Opposition to the treaty
was founded on diverse assumptions. Philip Snowden, a Labour Party
member, dismissed the League of Nations as the mere instrument of the
victorious Allies, while Ramsay MacDonald condemned the terms as 'an
act of madness unparalleled in history'. Edmund Hammond, a British
liberal journalist already fulminating about the contrasts between extreme
poverty and wealth on display in Paris, argued that the treaty was infected
with the spirit of jingoism. Within the Labour Party there was a growing
sense that Germany had been harshly treated, a distrust of French military
power, and a strong belief in arbitration, disarmament, and international
trade as panaceas for the general crisis.[69]

Italian criticism of the peace settlements concentrated on the Adriatic,
while highlighting the hypocrisy of their Allies' decisions. Orlando told
Clemenceau that 'For the Italians, the Yugoslavs are what the boches are for

you. To accept Wilson's proposal would be the equivalent to Clemenceau's accepting a solution of the war proposed by the boches.' Salvemini mocked Wilson's claims that all states enjoy 'equality of rights', while the United States adhered to the Monroe Doctrine.[70] Nationalists of all hues were outraged by the peace settlement. Some, led by D'Annunzio, seized Fiume in September 1919, an act of nationalist power politics by a band of adventurers. While the government struggled to assert control over Italy's foreign relations, the dilemma for adherents of power politics remained Italy's limited capability to assert its claims in the face of great power opposition.

Clemenceau's major coup in the negotiations had been the Anglo-American security guarantee against German aggression. Yet even before he secured the guarantee, it was clear that the ratification of the Versailles Treaty would face difficulties in the American Senate. On 3 March Henry Cabot Lodge put a tactical resolution to the outgoing Senate, stating that the Covenant of the League, which was part of the treaty, was unacceptable in its present terms. Wilson, the first serving president to leave American soil, had returned to the United States in late February, to make an initial attempt to win over sceptics. However, a meeting with senators on 26 February went badly. Frank Brandegee, the Republican senator from Connecticut, lamented that the lunch in the White House was a 'miserable affair' due to the absence of any alcohol. More seriously, Lodge complained of Wilson's vagueness about the proposed League of Nations.[71]

The opposition to the treaty centred on Article 10 of the Covenant. Opponents had other objections – the absence of any mention of the Monroe Doctrine, the concession of Shantung to Japan, the voting rights of British Dominions in the League's Assembly, British rule in Ireland, and a strong personal dislike of Wilson in some cases. It was, however, rival interpretations of Article 10 that dominated the debate over the treaty. Whereas French critics were disappointed with the lack of military sanctions in the Covenant, many American opponents feared that the United States would be compelled to send military forces abroad at the behest of the League's Council. The debate revolved around the tensions between American constitutional politics and its place in the new world order. The different positions were given an early public airing in a debate between Lodge and a fellow Boston Brahmin, the president of Harvard, A. Lawrence Lowell, on 19 March. Lodge argued that Article 10 undermined the Senate's right, and therefore the liberty of the American people, to decide on the most fundamental sovereign issue, the decision to go to war. Lodge was not an isolationist. He had supported American entry into the war. However, he wanted the United States to retain absolute control over its foreign policy, rather than sending 'the hope of their families, the hope of the nation, the best of our youth' into conflicts and wars where there was no direct American interest. Lowell, a leading member of the League to Enforce Peace, proffered a different conception of international politics. The United States faced the question 'whether our country shall take its place, like a true and generous nation, side by side with others as guardians of law and order, or whether it shall turn its face away from a world in agony'. The United States had gone to war to preserve international law; law without force to implement it was merely 'a scrap of paper'. Lowell, therefore, had a much more expansive interpretation of Article 10 than had Wilson. Like William Taft, Elihu Root, and others in the League to Enforce Peace, Lowell was much closer to French visions of the League of Nations. In his view the threat of automatic military action against a state that violated the Covenant offered the soundest way of securing peace because it would most likely deter aggression. The constraints on the American Senate were a small – and perhaps even theoretical – price to pay for securing peace.[72]

The legalist interpretation of Article 10 was marginalized once Wilson returned to the United States in July 1919. Already suffering from poor health, Wilson's political nous was absent in the treaty debate. His consistent failure to reach out to the League to Enforce Peace weakened the contribution of this powerful (and Republican-dominated) association to the public debate. His interpretation of Article 10 lacked clarity. In August he rejected a proposed reservation to the treaty in the Senate that interpreted League instructions on military and economic sanctions under Article 10 as advisory rather than obligatory. Yet at the same time Wilson claimed that Article 10 did not oblige American military action each time the Covenant was violated in distant parts of the globe. Instead he argued that the weight of public opinion and the practice of the League would socialize states into a peaceful international order.

Unwilling to compromise with his opponents in the Senate, Wilson decided to embark on a speaking tour. He saw himself as educating the American public about the League of Nations and international politics, while also building a political base to overwhelm Senate opposition. His train left Washington on 3 September, setting out for the Midwest and then the West Coast. He attracted large crowds and struck local notes. In St Louis he spoke of the treaty's importance in restoring world trade; in Omaha he compared the international system to a territory with no settled land laws, in which 'all the farmers would be sitting on fences with shotguns'. In Oakland in California he warned that the rejection of the treaty would mean that little children in the audience would fight 'another and final war' in years to come. These speeches were distributed to 1,400 local newspapers, while journalists from the major newspapers travelled on the presidential train. It was a remarkable political and physical performance, but the wheel of speeches around America finally broke Wilson. On 25 September, after speeches in Denver and Pueblo, he was taken ill. His doctor, who had advised against the trip, now got Joseph Tumulty, Wilson's secretary, to cancel the remaining stops. Wilson returned to Washington where on 2 October he suffered a stroke that paralyzed his left side.[73]

The fate of the Versailles Treaty was now determined in the Senate. Two thirds of the Senate had to ratify it, including any reservations. In March Lodge had already secured the backing of thirty-seven senators (out of ninety-six) to oppose the Covenant as it stood. By the autumn he had secured more support. Lodge submitted several reservations to the treaty, the two most important of which were that the United States accepted no obligation under Article 10 to undertake military or naval action at the behest of the Council and that Congress retained the authority to declare war and conclude peace.

Wilson had been unwilling to compromise in the spring and summer. Now incapacitated, he could not give any effective direction to his supporters in the Senate and other advocates of the League of Nations. Taft urged compromise as the only means of securing American participation in the League. His view that it was better to accept the League and work to improve it was similar to that of Bourgeois (and many other disappointed supporters of the League). Even had Wilson enjoyed full health it is unlikely that he would have compromised with Lodge. He thought the reservations would hollow out the American commitment to the League. The Covenant was supposed to consecrate the sacrifices of the war. Compromise would sully the legacy of the war. The League was the bridge, in Wilson's mind, between war and peace. 'Many terrible things have come out of this war,' he told the delegates on 14 February, 'but some very beautiful things have come out of it. Wrong has been defeated, but the rest of the world has been more conscious than it ever was before of the majesty of Right. People who were suspicious of one another can now live as friends and comrades in a single family, and desire to do so. The miasma of distrust, intrigue is cleared away. Men are looking eye to eye and saying "We are brothers and have a common purpose. We did not realize it before, but now we do realize it, and this is our Covenant of fraternity and friendship." '[74] Wilson took the notion of the

Covenant absolutely. Although the text was the work of a few men, and especially Wilson, the president viewed it as a Covenant with the people of the world. Within this conceptual framework, compromise made no sense.

Without Wilson directing his supporters to endorse Lodge's reservations, neither side could secure the two-thirds majority to ratify the Versailles Treaty with or without its amendments. Occasionally the debate turned nasty. Robert La Follette denounced Wilson for betraying the American heritage of foreign policy founded on George Washington's principle of non-entanglement. He dismissed Wilson as a 'gentleman who failed as a lawyer and had become a college professor'. Despite the likelihood of failure for both sides, senators spent two days, on 18 and 19 November, debating the treaty. Neither side mustered a majority and when they returned for another attempt in March 1920, they failed again. The United States was the only signatory that failed to ratify the treaty.

The absence of the United States from the League of Nations was a significant blow to that organization, one that made the task of constructing peace more difficult. Yet even had the United States joined, much of the task of enforcing peace in Europe would still have fallen to the British and French governments. They remained the dominant military and economic powers in Europe, indeed around much of the globe. It was not their capacity, but their willingness, to construct peace that was in question. The same questions would have applied to American foreign policy, even if Wilson had won a resounding victory in the Senate. In early 1919 the American government was already demobilizing. It was certainly not on the verge of setting up the kind of national security state which enabled it to project its power after the Second World War – and those institutions emerged only fitfully after 1945. Moreover, by the time the United States Senate had rejected the Versailles Treaty, much of the Wilsonian mystique had faded around the world. Socialists in Germany, nationalists in Egypt, liberals in Italy, and diplomats in China had their expectations of a Wilsonian peace dashed.

That, however, did not mean that the ideas he symbolized had been abandoned. Many of the critics and opponents of the treaty framed their condemnations in terms of self-determination, democracy, international cooperation, commercial freedom, arbitration, and disarmament. Others, particularly in the colonies, sought equality with European states and nations, to become equal members of the civilized community. Wilson had synthesized ideas that were already prominent in different war cultures, embodied those ideas, and associated them with American power.

'The real work of making peace,' Smuts declared the day after the signing ceremony in the Hall of Mirrors, 'will only begin after this treaty [of Versailles] has been signed and a definite halt has been called to the destructive passions that have been desolating Europe for nearly five years.' The signing ceremony, in Smuts's view, marked the end of the war and the armistice, but the work of peace had barely begun. In central and eastern Europe government structures, economic relations, and social bonds were rent asunder by the crisis at the end of the war. Yet while the conflict had undermined 'civilization', Smuts argued, it had also ended with the destruction of Prussian militarism. The 'pacific ideals born of the war' had produced the League of Nations. These two results of the war, he believed, provided the basis for a 'real peace of peoples', which 'ought to follow, complete, and amend the peace of statesmen in this treaty'. He imagined that this could be managed best by the cooperation of the peoples of the British empire and the United States.[75] The normative transformation of the international system had found expression, even if it was imperfect, in the Versailles Treaty. Self-determination, minority rights, a permanent international organization to manage international affairs, disarmament, and international labour regulation were inscribed in the treaty. Racial and cultural hierarchies continued to shape the international order, but the mandates system from the perspective of European imperialists represented a new form of international control over empire. The treaty provided a starting point for making peace.

CHAPTER 9

THE WARS THAT WOULD NOT END, 1919–1923

'So THE WAR is over,' Field Marshal Sir Henry Wilson wrote to General Pershing on 13 November 1918. 'It is difficult to believe that after these 4 ghastly years.'[1] On 22 June 1922 two Irish republicans, Joseph O'Sullivan and Reggie Dunne, shot and killed Wilson outside the front door of his home at Eaton Place in the Knightsbridge district of London. The assassins viewed Wilson as the embodiment of hardline Unionism, responsible for obstructing the goals of Irish nationalists and for atrocities against Catholics in the newly formed Northern Irish state. O'Sullivan had joined the Munster Fusiliers in January 1915, while Dunne had volunteered for the Irish Guards the following year. 'We both joined voluntarily for the purpose of taking human life,' Dunne declared, 'in order that the principle for which this country [Britain] stood should be upheld and preserved. These principles, we were told, were self-determination and freedom for small nations. We came back from France to find that Self-Determination had been given to some Nations we had never heard of, but that it had been denied for Ireland.'[2] When Pershing was asked for his reaction to Wilson's death, he said 'this is an outrage that must shock civilization'.[3] The First World War had ended on 11 November 1918, but the issues over which it had been fought, including what it meant to be civilized and the freedom of small nations, continued to shape violent conflict after 1918.

The international order had been drafted at the Paris Peace Conference, but it was made, in part, through the violence that dominated large parts of global politics between 1918 and 1923.[4] These conflicts centred on the formation of new states, regimes, and nations in the 'shatter zones'[5] of empire in eastern and central Europe, the Middle East, and Italy; the working out of imperial control, especially in the territories under the mandates system; and the financial, territorial, and moral conflicts in western Europe, particularly between France and Germany. Finally, the accommodation of revolutionary Russia within the international order had to be worked out. The different issues intersected with each other, in terms of geography and the different logics of political violence. People were fighting different wars – national, revolutionary, imperial – even as they fought on the same battlefield. Yet from these entangled strands a patch-work settlement was made between 1919 and 1923.

* * *

Arguably, revolutionary Russia posed the greatest challenge to the international order in the years after 1918 because Lenin and other Bolsheviks still adhered to fantasies of world revolution, even as they fought a civil war at home to consolidate Soviet power. A world order based on communist revolution could not be accommodated within the international order in the same way as an adjustment of borders or even ethnic violence was. Soviet Russia's place in the world was worked out in the Russian Civil War and its overlapping contexts of foreign intervention, state formation, and the export of revolution between 1918 and 1921.

From its very inception the Bolshevik revolution was a civil war. It involved a violent struggle to establish political authority in Russia, to secure borders, and to remake the social and economic basis of the country. The labels of Reds and Whites do not do justice to the complex conflicts that, in total, led to the death of between 7 and 10 million people, including around 5 million people from famine in 1921–2, a direct result of the upheavals of world and civil war.[6] Civil war became an all-encompassing term for conflicts that pitted revolutionary against conservative, Russian against Ukrainian, worker and peasant against party official.

One reason for the emergence of the Soviet dictatorship from the civil war was that it managed to accommodate the different strands of the revolution more successfully than any alternative. As one historian has argued, the Bolshevik programme was attractive not as a set of abstract ideas, but as a 'compelling interpretation' of people's 'lived experiences'. For officers who made the transition from the imperial to the revolutionary army the practice of violence was a bridge. The use of deportations, mass executions, and concentration camps against civilians in the civil war were devices with which officers had become familiar during service on Russia's imperial frontier and then in the First World War.[7] Land reform after 1918 left many peasants dissatisfied, but they turned to local soviets and courts to resolve their claims. Soldiers and their relatives invoked service in the imperial and later Red Army to support their claims for land. The act of petitioning and the practice of response created its own habit of authority for Bolshevik institutions. Enacting promises of social reform, which dated back to the early years of the war, was a means of building the Soviet state and creating constituencies of support.[8] The scarcity of food supplies exacerbated and overlaid the more ostensibly political conflicts of the civil war. In January 1918 only 7 per cent of the grain scheduled to arrive in Petrograd and Moscow reached its destination. Concerned by the prospect of losing authority in their urban centres of power, the Bolsheviks mobilized to requisition supplies.

In mobilizing to secure food and economic productivity, suppress internal opponents, and repel foreign invasion, the Bolshevik Party founded the Soviet state. In January 1918 Lenin wrote an essay, describing the proletarian dictatorship as a 'state of simmering war, a state of military measures against the enemies of the proletariat power'.[9] A massive apparatus of coercion was required to secure the Soviet state. Felix Dzerzhinsky, from a noble Polish family, set up the Cheka in December 1917, while the following summer the Central Committee resumed and expanded the Tsarist use of concentration camps. In February 1918 Trotsky set up the Red Army, rejecting the revolutionary model of the militia and soldiers' councils in favour of a centralized, conscript force.

The civil war escalated in May 1918.[10] More than 40,000 Czechoslovak men, who had been taken prisoner from the Austro-Hungarian Army and formed into a legion in prisoner-of-war camps, were making their way out of Russia to rejoin the world war and the struggle for Czechoslovak independence. As they crossed the Trans-Siberian Railway line, they clashed with Hungarian prisoners on 14 May, a Habsburg conflict thousands of miles from Prague and Budapest. Trotsky overreacted, ordering the immediate execution of any Czechoslovak soldiers. The Czech Legion now captured stations along the Trans-Siberian railway, cutting the eastern half of the Russian empire off from Petrograd. The Czech Legion created opportunities for counter-revolutionary White forces opposed to the revolution to emerge and consolidate their position. However, the Red Army was able to halt the advance of White forces and by March 1920, following victory over General Denikin's White forces, the Bolsheviks had established control over Russia.

They also warded off foreign meddling. The intervention by British, French, and American forces had been half-hearted, without clear aims and beset by limited resources. Initially these governments had sent troops to deny Germany access to Russian resources. Once the German menace disappeared some Allied military and political leaders such as Winston Churchill wanted to overthrow the Bolshevik regime. Japan's intervention in March 1918 aimed to carve out a sphere of influence for itself in Siberia and northern Manchuria. Woodrow Wilson considered armed intervention futile as well as unprincipled. 'You could not defeat ideas by armies,' he told C. P. Scott.[11] Gradually Allied forces were withdrawn from Russian territory.

Out of the confusion of Allied policies, the Bolshevik leaders, including Stalin, drew a single lesson – that the capitalist world was ready to prey on Soviet weakness. Foreign intervention and domestic opposition were welded into a grand narrative of counter-revolutionary ambition. This reinforced the revolutionary dimension of Soviet foreign policy. Lenin had accepted the Treaty of Brest-Litovsk in March 1918 in order to provide space for the consolidation of the revolution. He continued to look out for opportunities to pursue world revolution. In March 1919, as a response to the meeting of the Social Democratic Conference at Berne the previous month and to the revolutionary potential across central Europe following the collapse of the Central Powers, Lenin set up the Comintern (the Third International). The Comintern sought to bring European communist parties under Russian control, while also channelling funds for propaganda.[12]

By 1920 the Red Army had become the most likely institution to export revolution to central Europe. Trotsky, its founder, was a leading exponent of world revolution. When the Red Army was established, the decree referred to its role as a 'support for the coming socialist revolution in Europe'. More realistically the Red Army supported revolutionary movements in the Baltics in 1919 and was only driven back by German paramilitary forces, which had remained in the region at the request of the Allies.[13] Amidst an ongoing theoretical debate over whether the proletarian revolution could be given a helping hand by the Red Army or emerge from popular communist revolution, the conflict between Poland and the Ukraine and the territorial ambitions of the Polish state provided an opportunity to hasten the revolution in central Europe.

In the borderlands of the Russian empire, revolutionary and national wars intersected.[14] The fragile Ukrainian state, without German support since November 1918, was caught in the middle of the Russian Civil War and Polish and Russian territorial ambitions. Simon Petlura, the head of the Ukrainian government, recognized the need for external support. Yet in turning first to the White Russian forces and then to General Josef Pilsudski in Poland, he allied the Ukrainian state to forces that had no place for an independent Ukraine. The White Russians would have incorporated the Ukraine back into the Russian empire, while Pilsudski pursued the Jagiellonian ideal, the dream of restoring the old Polish Commonwealth that incorporated Lithuania and the western Ukraine. Exponents of this vision, such as the conservative journalist Stanislav 'Cat' Mackiewiecz, viewed Poland's security as dependent on carving out the dominant position in eastern Europe, whereas Roman Dmowski, head of the Polish National Committee during the war, favoured limiting Poland's territorial expansion and avoiding the incorporation of further national minorities.[15] Pilsudski adopted the more expansive view of Polish territorial ambitions. Following a typhus epidemic that killed 70 per cent of Ukrainian troops, and the Red Army's capture of Kiev, Petlura signed a military convention with Poland that gave up eastern Galicia – one of the Ukraine's gains under the Treaty of Brest-Litovsk. The Polish offensive reached Kiev by 7 May 1920. Pilsudski returned to Warzaw and a hero's welcome. However, in advancing so rapidly Polish forces had overstretched themselves. The Red Army's counter-offensive broke through Polish lines on 5 June and advanced towards Warzaw.

A national war had been transformed into a potential revolutionary war by the Red Army's success. Lenin saw opportunities to move directly from a victorious revolutionary war in Russia to aiding revolutions in Europe. In March 1920, on the occasion of the general strike against the right-wing Kapp Putsch in Berlin, he had urged Stalin to accelerate the 'capture of the Crimea in order to have entirely free hands, as a civil war in Germany may force us to move west to aid the Communists'.[16] The specific plan remained inchoate, but the scenario of using the Red Army to bolster revolution in central Europe was an important preoccupation of Lenin's thinking about international politics. In July he spoke of the knock-on effect of revolution in Poland, Hungary, Czechoslovakia, and Romania. The Comintern met in Moscow between 7 July and 8 August, adding to the febrile expectations of international revolution. With the prospect of revolution throughout central Europe, Lenin turned down the mediation attempt of George Curzon, the British Foreign Secretary. The offer of a border between Bialystok and Brest-Litovsk would have enabled Soviet Russia to incorporate within its borders eastern Galicia, a territory that had been successively occupied by Tsarist Russia, the Habsburgs, the Ukraine, and Poland since 1915. This refusal of mediation amounted to more than a rejection of a territorial compromise; it was a rejection of the international order in favour of revolutionary war.[17]

At a closed meeting of the 9th Conference of the Communist Party on 20 September, Lenin cast the Soviet-Polish War as the central event in the contest between international imperialism and international revolution. Having defeated the White armies, which Britain and France had supported, in the Civil War, Lenin told the delegates that 'the defensive period of the war with world-wide imperialism was over, and we could, and had the obligation to launch an offensive war'. Poland, he argued, was at the heart of the imperialist system, a buffer zone between western Europe and revolutionary Russia. If Poland fell to Soviet Russia, then a bridge between the two powers opposed to the Versailles Treaty – Germany and Russia – would be complete. Conservatives in Germany, Lenin believed, would swallow their ideological scruples to ally with Soviet Russia in overthrowing the Versailles order, reprising the historic 1813 alliance against Napoleon. By bringing the Red Army's offensive to the gates of Warzaw, Soviet Russia was 'making politics not in Poland, but in Germany and England'. The refusal of British (and Belgian and German) workers to transport weapons to Poland, Lenin argued, was another sign that the 'English proletariat has raised itself to an entirely new revolutionary level'.[18]

The battle of Warzaw, therefore, had become a 'turning point for the world', in Lenin's view. On 16 August Pilsudski launched a counter-attack, cutting off three Red Army divisions. Within three days Pilsudski had reached Brest-Litovsk. Military operational factors were the main reasons for the failure of the Red Army, whose forces were overstretched and exhausted. The Polish government also took decisive political measures. It formed a Council for State Defence, mobilized 100,000 volunteers, and issued a decree on land reform within the first two weeks in July. National cohesion held under the duress of crisis in July and August 1920. Karl Radek, an Austrian-born Bolshevik, condemned the Polish working classes and farmers for acting 'nationally and imperialistically', rather than 'socially and revolutionarily'. Lenin's revolutionary strategy lacked a popular basis. The flipside of rallying the nation through reforms was a sharpening of anti-Semitic attitudes and policy as Jews were persecuted on the basis that they were agents of the Bolshevik revolution (as happened elsewhere in Europe and North America). Some 17,000 Jewish men were interned in a camp near Warzaw until September.[19]

By October 1920 the two sides had agreed a ceasefire and the following March, Poland and Soviet Russia had concluded the Treaty of Riga.[20]

Poland's eastern border incorporated western Volhynia and eastern Galicia, though under Article 2 Poland and Soviet Russia agreed to recognize the independence of the Ukraine and White Ruthenia (Belarus) 'in accordance with the principle of national self-determination'. What was left of the Ukraine became a federal state in the Russian Socialist Federated Soviet Republic, to give it its full title, under the terms of a treaty in December 1920 between the Soviet Ukrainian government and Soviet Russia. The following year the official death toll in the Ukrainian famine, a result of the wars, was 235,000, though historians estimate the real figure to be closer to 1 million. The settlement of the Polish–Soviet war marked a further step in the socialization of Soviet Russia into the international order. 'Given the international situation,' Lenin concluded after the defeat of the Red Army outside Warzaw, 'we must limit ourselves to a defensive posture with regard to the Entente, but despite the complete failure in the first instance, our first defeat, we will keep shifting from a defensive to an offensive policy over and over again until we finish them off for good.'[21] The last phrase was partly brave talk, but it also reflected the faith, derived from knowing the laws of history, in world revolution. Yet two more failed attempts to foment revolution in Germany, in 1921 and 1923, gradually transformed socialism in one country from a conditional tactic into the basis of Soviet foreign policy.

* * *

In December 1923 the Hungarian intellectual Oskar Jászi assessed the dismal prospects for peace in central Europe. Taking Thomas Masaryk's book *The New Europe*, published in 1918, as his foil, he argued that the Paris peace settlement had created economic barriers and 'national and race hatred' in central Europe. Democracy had failed to take root in many of the successor states, national self-determination had created territorial rivalries, and minorities had been ill-treated. Masaryk's vision of a new Europe, based on democratic nation states with safeguards for minorities, and limited sovereignty, had failed on every count. Although the old multi-national empires, especially Austria-Hungary, had been destroyed, their values – in Jászi's mind – persisted. 'The Old Europe,' he wrote in *Foreign Affairs*, 'is corroded by imperialism, by foreign war and civil war. The vicious feudal dogma of an absolute national sovereignty makes almost impossible all social life worthy of the name. Nations have no consideration for each other in economics and politics. This system destroys all moral unity in Europe. European distress, misery, anarchy, and civil war are, in their deepest roots, a moral problem.' Moral transformation, however, could only come through political institutions. Jászi proposed a European confederation, like the United States, based on democratic states, free trade, and cultural autonomy for minorities.[22]

There was potential in the region to develop democracy and international cooperation. Peasant parties in largely agrarian societies were inclined towards domestic reform rather than foreign adventure, following years of war. Figures like Jászi and Masaryk articulated coherent plans for political liberties and regional cooperation. By the mid-1920s, however, the basis for a peace founded on democratic states, regional cooperation, and the revival of trade had been destroyed in a geographical strip running from Finland to Turkey, through the lands of the former German, Russian, Austro-Hungarian, and Ottoman empires. Competing claims to national self-determination in the region shaped border wars, violence against minorities, and the collapse of democratic regimes. Whereas British intellectuals in the New Europe group during the war had argued that democracy would temper the aggression of nationalist ambitions in central and eastern Europe, the perceived demands of the international environment – national cohesion and a strong military – undermined the potential for constitutional democracy. The peace settlement in this region was worked out between 1918 and 1923 in wars between Romania and Hungary and also Greece and Turkey, in Poland's border conflicts in the Baltics and Upper Silesia, in the often violent process of state formation in Yugoslavia, and in the vengeful politics of Bulgaria. Moreover, the radicalization of Italian politics, culminating in Mussolini's coming to power in 1922, both contributed to and was shaped by instability in the Balkans and eastern Mediterranean.

Jászi's brief political career had ended due to the demands of the Romanian National Council in Transylvania, the first post-armistice demonstration of how competing foreign policy concerns shaped domestic politics in Hungary and Romania. At a meeting in Arad on 14 November 1918 Jászi proclaimed his devotion to Woodrow Wilson's fourteen points. Noting that 3 million of the 7 million inhabitants of Transylvania were not Romanian, but Hungarian, Serbian, and Saxon, he proposed working towards a Danubian confederation, as a means of reconciling national demands within a stable regional framework. It was a way of escaping the primacy of foreign policy. The Romanian National Council had no interest in this solution and declared the union of Transylvania with Romania on 1 December. Romanian troops secured the union by occupying Transylvania.

Serb, Croat, and Czechoslovak forces and nationalist groups acted in similar ways so that by Christmas 1918 Hungary had been dismembered. The reformist government under Count Karolyi collapsed. Karolyi handed power to a coalition of Social Democrats and Communists, which was effectively led by Bela Kun, who had been a prisoner of war in Russia and then fought for the Bolsheviks in the Russian Civil War. Kun's conversion to Bolshevism seems to have been due as much to circumstances as conviction, but by the time he returned to Hungary his commitment to revolution was clear. On 22 March 1919 the new government declared Hungary a Soviet Republic. Kun implemented radical policies, including the expropriation of large landed estates and the holding of elections to Soviets between 7 and 10 April.[23]

The Romanian prime minister, Ion Bratianu, decided to continue the offensive in an effort to create facts on the ground that could be transformed into territorial gains in the peace settlement. Kun responded by instituting a Red Terror against suspected opponents. Relations with the peasants deteriorated amidst food shortages and requisitioning. In turn this radicalization of Hungarian politics prompted the establishment of an anti-Bolshevik Committee, in which the dominant figure was Rear Admiral Miklós Horthy. The polarization within Hungarian politics eased the advance of the Romanian forces, which occupied Budapest on 3 August. Kun went into exile, first to Vienna and then to Moscow. In 1937 he was executed in one of Stalin's purges.

From Bratianu's perspective the invasion of Hungary in the spring of 1919 made good the wartime promises. As far as he was concerned the British and French governments were reneging on the 1916 treaty that had ushered Romania into the war. Romania 'was treated like a wretch which merited pity,' Bratianu noted bitterly, 'and not as an ally who has a right to justice.'[24] The only means of ensuring justice, therefore, was the use of military force, which both achieved and was legitimized by the principles of self-determination. The population of the newly expanded Romanian state had increased from 7 million to 17 million between 1914 and June 1920, when the Treaty of Trianon between Hungary and its former enemies was signed. Around 9 per cent of the population were Hungarian, 5 per cent Jewish, and 4 per cent German. While the latter groups adapted to the new state, the Hungarian minority looked towards Budapest.

It is impossible to speculate how defeat would have shaped Romanian domestic politics in the 1920s, but it is instructive to compare the relative quiescence of Romanian affairs of state with the violence in Hungarian politics. For most of the 1920s, Romanian politics was dominated by the Liberal Party, which had close links with banking and industrial interests. While the Liberals favoured a strong centralized state, a Peasant Party emerged as a powerful voice in opposition and won 70 per cent of the vote in the 1928 election, after which it formed a government. The 1923 constitution granted the king important powers over ministers and parliament, storing up problems for the future.[25]

In Hungary, by contrast, the collapse of Bela Kun's Soviet regime, brutal as it was, was followed by a much more severe repression, the White Terror. Resentment at defeat and the humiliation of the peace settlement fuelled right-wing violence. Former officers and Hungarian nationalists identified socialists, trade unionists, and Jews as enemies of the social order and national prestige. 'We shall see to it,' wrote Miklós Kozma, a former officer, 'that the flame of nationalism leaps high. . . . We shall also punish. Those who for months have committed heinous crimes must receive their punishment. It is predictable . . . that the compromisers and those with weak stomachs will moan and groan when we line up a few red rogues and terrorists against the wall. The false slogans of humanism and other "isms" have helped to drive the country into ruin before. This second time they will wail in vain.'[26] Between August 1919 and the end of 1921 an estimated 3,000 people were murdered in Hungary, including between 1,000 and 1,300 Jews in sixty pogroms. In addition, approximately 75,000 people were thrown into jail, while 100,000 went into exile, including Jászi. The constitution of 1920 allowed for elections, though on a restricted franchise and with an open ballot.[27]

As in Hungary, defeat and territorial loss radicalized politics in Bulgaria. The terms of the Treaty of Neuilly between Bulgaria and the Allies returned the country to its borders at the end of the Second Balkan War, restricted its army to 20,000 men, and imposed a reparations payment of 2.5 billion francs. Alexander Stamboliski, now the Bulgarian prime minister, signed the treaty in November 1919. His party, the BANU, had emerged as the largest party in Bulgaria in the elections of August 1919, winning 28 per cent of the vote. Primarily representing peasants, BANU offered a programme of land reform at home and peace abroad. Stamboliski had been a vocal critic of Bulgaria's wars since 1912, spending time in jail due to his protests. Once in power, he did not shy away from using violence, setting up paramilitary forces to suppress workers' strikes and tampering with election results. Peace abroad was a precondition of social and economic reform. His policies favoured disarmament and the diversion of resources to social reform, while they also reflected BANU voters' disenchantment with war. To this end Stamboliski envisioned a coalition of states in eastern Europe, held together by common agrarian interests. He achieved some notable foreign policy successes. In 1921 Bulgaria became the first defeated state to enter the League of Nations. In the same year the International Agrarian Bureau, sometimes known as the Green International, was founded, including BANU and peasant parties from Czechoslovakia and Poland.

Stamboliski's government, however, could not escape the pressures of foreign affairs, which derailed domestic reform. First, the reparations bill and occupation expenses amounted to 213 per cent of Bulgarian GNP. The reparations commission, dominated by its French representative, prioritized reparations payments over social and economic reforms. This slowed down land reform, particularly pressing owing to the influx of 450,000 refugees into Bulgaria after the war. Second, the presence of defeated White Russian army officers destabilized Bulgarian politics. About 15,000 soldiers from White Russian forces came to Bulgaria following Allied pressure on Stamboliski to accept them. These Whites regarded Stamboliski's reforming government as little more than a Bulgarian version of Bolshevism and they developed close links with militant nationalists, who felt humiliated by the Treaty of Neuilly and rejected Stamboliski's peace policy. These groups, particularly in the army and the IMRO (Internal Macedonian Revolutionary Organization), were most dangerous to the BANU government. Since 1920 IMRO had carried out raids into Macedonia across the Bulgarian–Yugoslav border, partly in response to the suppression of Bulgarian cultural and religious institutions in the region, often undertaken by Serbian paramilitaries. IMRO claimed Macedonia on the grounds of self-determination. In February 1923 Stamboliski signed the Yugoslav–Bulgarian treaty at Nis, which permitted Yugoslav forces to pursue IMRO groups over the border.

The Bulgarian Army had never been brought under parliamentary control after 1918. Senior officers joined with IMRO to launch a coup in the summer of 1923. On 9 June a group of officers surrounded the villa where Stamboliski was staying, protected by his party's paramilitary organization, the Orange Guard. In the subsequent fight Stamboliski managed to escape, taking refuge in the mountains. On 14 June he was found, then tortured and stabbed sixty times. His brother, Vasilii, was also murdered. Twenty BANU deputies were arrested and shot in the days after the coup. The Communists, on instructions from Moscow, launched their own meagre rising in September. In the subsequent repression an estimated 16,000 BANU and Communist Party members were killed between 1923 and 1925. Britain and France quickly recognized the new Bulgarian government, as did Nikola Pašić, the Yugoslav prime minister.[28]

In Pašić's Yugoslavia the task of integrating nationalities with different historical experiences into a single state tested political stability. The Corfu Declaration had left open the balance between centralization and federalism in the Yugoslav state. This had been negotiated between Croats on the Yugoslav Committee and Pašić. Stjepan Radić, the leader of the Croatian Peasants Party, the largest party in Croatia, instinctively opposed the Yugoslav project and suspected Pašić wanted a highly centralized Serbian-dominated state. Tensions between Serbian institutions and Croatian peasants were heightened by the ending of the war. In 1918 Croatian prisoners of war returning from Russia brought home stories of land reform and an end to war. Soldiers and peasants formed Green Cadres, roving paramilitary units, which, at the end of the war, began to seize land. The National Council in Zagreb, with little appreciation of the Green Cadres movement, invited Serbian troops to occupy Croatia.[29] However, Radić viewed the Serbian army as an occupation force. When he refused to recognize the Yugoslav state, Radić was thrown into jail for eleven months until his release in February 1920. He was imprisoned again in August and ordered to fast on 1 December, the day of Yugoslav unification.

Released two days before the appointed fast, Radić participated in the Yugoslav elections to the Constituent Assembly. While the Croatian Peasant Party emerged as the largest in Croatia, Radić's decision to abstain from the Assembly made it easy for Pašić to push through a centralizing constitution. The Karageorgovich dynasty was confirmed as the ruling house of Yugoslavia, while there was a single-chamber parliament. By centralizing the state, Pašić had institutionalized historical tensions between Serbs and Croatians. Serbian claims to privilege in the state and its institutions were based on their blood sacrifice during the war. Serbs saw the new state as their creation, which restricted the space for the other nationalities. Radić's opposition to the state gradually ebbed, a result of his campaign's futility. By 1925 he had accepted the state and entered parliament. In August of that year King Alexander paid his first visit to Zagreb. As the key figures in Yugoslav politics moved away from their wartime stances, the institutions of the state began to function more effectively, though the assassination of Radić in parliament in 1928 underlined the persistent threat of political violence.

Even the paragon of interwar European democracy, Czechoslovakia, was founded on exclusions and violence as well as votes and debate. Masaryk and Foreign Minister Edvard Beneš consistently highlighted the state's democratic credentials, as a means of binding Czechoslovak identity into a putative western European community of democracies, while also placing a claim for support on Britain and France. Democratic values, therefore, seemed to be an integral part of foreign policy. However, Beneš also warned that internal national struggles created divisions, which the surrounding states could exploit. 'We must at all times,' he told the National Assembly in September 1919, 'bear in mind our difficult international position ... enemies surround us on all sides ... and that the only strength which can for ever save us is inner discipline, consolidation and high moral level of all our national endeavour.'[30] This created a tension between the normative demands of democracy and the security requirements of national cohesion. From the outset there were significant limitations on representative politics in Czechoslovakia. The provisional assembly provided only 40 out of 256 seats to Slovaks, while there were no representatives from the German, Hungarian, or Polish minorities. State institutions, especially the army, were dominated by Czechs. The Slovak population resented their exclusion from state jobs. Owing to the electoral system, party bureaucracies accumulated considerable power, which limited the significance of elections.[31] Despite these problems Czechoslovakia managed to achieve political stability. Critically, Beneš avoided entanglements with neighbouring states, which could have unpicked the domestic political settlement.

In the early 1920s Polish claims on Teschen in Czechoslovakia were more concerning for the government in Prague than threats from the Sudeten Germans who pined for the Reich. In October and November 1921 Beneš negotiated a pact with the Polish Foreign Minister, Konstantin Skirmunt, but the Polish parliament never ratified the deal owing to the failure to resolve claims to Teschen. However, the attention of Polish governments was directed north. In repelling the Red Army from Warzaw in the autumn of 1920 Polish forces also helped themselves to Vilna in Lithuania. Polish claims were based on the Jagiellonian vision of historic right and, eventually, a vote by the Central Lithuanian Sejm in January 1922, which declared for union with Poland. Although the vote had taken place under Polish military occupation, the Council of the League of Nations confirmed Vilna as Polish territory in 1923. The Lithuanian government did not accept this decision and remained in a state of (unwaged) war with Poland until 1927.[32]

A vote was also supposed to settle the future of Upper Silesia. The plebiscite took place in March 1921 with 60 per cent of the population voting for union with Germany. The Polish government backed a rising in Upper Silesia, which was suppressed by German Freikorps troops. In October, however, the League of Nations, which had the right to 'interpret' the plebiscite's results, decided largely in favour of Poland, granting it 30 per cent of the territory, 46 per cent of the population, and most of the significant industrial resources. Despite these border conflicts and the war against Soviet Russia, democratic constitutional structures survived in Poland in the early 1920s. On the other hand the drive for national loyalty alienated minorities, while successive governments – like others in Europe – failed to bring inflation under control before it caused an economic and political crisis in 1923. It was only in 1926 that executive powers were strengthened in Poland, paving the way for Josef Pilsudski's dictatorship.

Meanwhile unrequited territorial claims had led to the Greco-Turkish War. The ambitions of Eleftherios Venizelos to expand territory in Anatolia were encouraged at the Paris Peace Conference. British and French officials admired the Greek prime minister and saw in his ambitions a means of thwarting Italian claims in Anatolia. With Sidney Sonnino and Vittorio Orlando brooding in Rome, the Greek forces landed in Smyrna (Izmir) on the Aegean coast of Anatolia on 15 May 1919. Venizelos variously argued that the predominantly local Muslim population would accept Greek rule and fiddled the numbers of ethnic Greeks living in the region. Given the atrocities of the Balkan Wars the Allied support of Greek ambitions was particularly reckless, both from a political and a humanitarian point of view. The Greek forces and ethnic Greeks resident in the city committed atrocities against the Muslim population, including murder, rape, and the destruction of homes; ethnic Greeks had been subjected to atrocities by Turkish paramilitaries before the invasion.[33]

The Greek occupation began a process that transformed Turkish as well as Greek politics and the demography of the region as well as the final territorial settlement. 'The barbarous Greek attacks and crimes perpetrated upon our Anatolia,' declared Hacim Muhittin at the National Congress in Balikesir in June, 'have brought to pass a true and firm national movement among the Muslim and Turk in this realm.'[34] In fact, it took some time for a cohesive Turkish resistance to emerge. General war-weariness, persistent divisions within Ottoman politics, and ambiguity about who and what even constituted Turkey made it difficult to organize resistance.

The central figure was Mustafa Kemal, who benefited from his burgeoning reputation as an effective military commander and his comparative distance from the CUP leadership during the First World War. On 19 May 1919 he landed at the Black Sea port of Samsun to resist Armenian claims to provinces in eastern Anatolia. Eastern Anatolia provided a secure base from which to organize resistance. Moreover, the defence of Anatolia was both a geopolitical project and a statement of identity. Unionist groups, including paramilitary organizations, party officials, and bureaucrats who had kept a low profile since November 1918, began to organize. Congresses met at Erzerum and Sivas in July and September 1919, the latter presenting itself as the Society for the Defence of National Rights of Anatolia and Thrace. It issued the National Pact in January 1920. The text was a fusion of long-time CUP demands, notions of self-determination, and geopolitical interests. It asserted the indivisibility of Ottoman Muslim territories, but it proposed plebiscites in regions with an Arab majority, in Batum, Kars, and Ardahan, and western Thrace; it accepted the application of minority rights treaties concluded in Paris; and it called for full economic sovereignty (meaning the end to capitulations).[35]

The war between Greece and Turkey culminated in September 1922, in which the intersecting dynamics of imperial, nationalist, and domestic politics shaped the crisis. As Turkish forces advanced towards Thrace, both these and the retreating Greek units committed atrocities against enemies defined by their ethnicity. Changing the demographic composition of the region had become a means of securing territory. Turkish troops expelled ethnic Greeks from Smyrna and burned down the Armenian quarter of the city. The Greek government appealed to the British government for support, but only the most limited assistance was available. On 1 October Kemal agreed to open ceasefire negotiations, which paved the way for the Treaty of Lausanne concluded in July 1923.

Under the terms of the treaty, Turkey secured Anatolia, Constantinople, and eastern Thrace. It also involved the transfer of ethnic Greeks from Turkey to Greece and Muslims from Greece to Turkey. Fridtjof Nansen, the Norwegian Arctic explorer and humanitarian activist, suggested the idea of a population exchange in December 1922 as a way to end the cycle of ethnic violence in the region. Both governments saw advantages in the exchange. The system of minority protection treaties that covered eastern and central Europe was not applied to the region where ethnic violence had been most destructive since 1912. 'The frontiers will never be secure,' Venizelos had argued, 'if western Thrace and Macedonia are ethnologically as well as politically Greek territories.'[36] From the point of view of regional stability the population exchange was a striking success. There were no irredentist claims or national minorities to cause tensions in the relations between the two states until the Cyprus crisis arose in the 1950s. From the point of view of the people forced to leave their homes it was a time of immense suffering. Many wished to remain in their communities, oblivious to the tug of a nationalist identity they did not recognize. The scale of the operation meant departure points were overcrowded. Thousands of Greek Orthodox Christians died while waiting to leave Constantinople, and thousands more died of starvation on arriving in Greece. The American Red Cross, the Red Crescent, and the League of Nations set up relief operations for the forced migrants.[37]

The population exchange coincided with the formation of the emerging Turkish state, based on the notion of a homogeneous national population. Nation was to replace religion as the touchstone of identity and loyalty in the new Turkey. Kemal viewed French republicanism, with its anti-clericalism and national claims on citizens' loyalty, as the model of a strong state. He abolished the Sultanate on 1 November 1922 and the Caliphate the following year. In April 1923 Kemal's People's Party won 60 per cent of the vote and in October he proclaimed Turkey a republic. However, his rule was authoritarian, involving the imprisonment and execution of political opponents and murderous campaigns against ethnic minorities. Following a rising of Kurds in February 1925, the Turkish government responded with aerial bombardment and a scorched-earth campaign.[38]

While Kemal brought authoritarian stability to the new Turkish state, the First World War had further destabilized politics in Greece. The defeat in Asia Minor prompted a coup in Greece as divisions dating back to 1915 came to the fore once again. Over the following five years abdication, referendum, coup, and counter-coup shaped Greek politics. The monarchy was abolished in 1924, but the bitter legacies of the schism between Venizelos and King Constantine persisted into the 1930s. This offered the Greek officer corps considerable scope to intervene in domestic politics.[39]

Meanwhile in Italy between 1919 and 1922 disappointed foreign policy expectations, fear of revolution, and paramilitary violence exacerbated a chronic crisis of authority. Mussolini's Fascist movement would eventually take advantage of this instability, but in the aftermath of the war Italian Fascism was weak. In the November 1919 elections, in Mussolini's Milan stronghold, the party won just 5,000 votes compared to 70,000 for the Popular Party and 168,000 for the Italian Socialist Party. Most veterans voted for these parties.[40] However, the dominant parties failed to form a stable government, discrediting parliamentary politics. Relations between workers and employers deteriorated through the *bienno rosso* in 1919 and 1920, while Gabriele D'Annunzio's presence in Fiume underlined the foreign policy weaknesses of Italian governments. During these crises Mussolini was able to build alliances with employers, nationalists, students, and others. Giovanni Giolitti, who had returned as prime minister in June 1920, called an election in May 1921, which enabled the Fascists to make their electoral breakthrough. In tandem with the ballot box, they also intimidated political opponents. Many of the leading figures in the *squadristi*, such as Italo Balbo and Roberto Farinacci, having served in the war, considered violence against 'internal enemies', notably socialists, entirely justified. However, it was the absence of political authority, rather than the war, that was the most important factor in shaping violent disorder in Italy between 1919 and 1922.[41] In October 1922 Mussolini was appointed prime minister by the king, Victor Emmanuel III. Conservatives hoped that Mussolini would establish public order and political authority. Yet even then Mussolini's grip on power was not secure. Gaetano Salvemini, now in exile in Britain, expected that Fascist rule would collapse owing to budgetary and foreign policy problems.[42] Only after the conclusion of the Matteotti crisis in 1924 – the brutal murder of the Socialist Giacomo Matteotti by Fascist *squadristi* and the subsequent scandal – did Mussolini consolidate the Fascist regime.

By 1923 politics in eastern and southern Europe appeared to represent a travesty of the wartime visions of Jászi, Masaryk, Salvemini, Stamboliski, Radic, and others. The promise of a region of nation states, tolerating minorities, practising democracy, and forging peaceful bonds through commerce and intellectual exchange, had evaporated in war, ethnic cleansing, assassinations, and the vicious repression of political opponents. States had claims on each other's territory, variously justified by nationality, historical rights, and irredentism. International tensions encouraged authoritarian domestic politics, the exclusion of minorities, and the intrusion of the military into politics. Out of the fragments of four empires, an international system had emerged characterized by a wary balance of power. Turkey's identity had been so radically altered by territorial and demographic change that Kemal in his 1927 Great Speech could convincingly portray the Republic as the victor power by opening his historical account in May 1919 with the Greek invasion of Anatolia.

Kemal's historical starting point demonstrates the importance of perspective in judging any peace settlement, including the patchwork peace that existed in eastern Europe and the Balkans by the mid-1920s. Given the circumstances of eastern European states between the end of the war and the mid-1920s, the stabilization of regional inter-state politics was a notable achievement, though it came at an appalling cost. Some states had emerged from the ruins of empire, with uncertain institutional and territorial bases. Other states, notably Romania and Serbia, had been all but destroyed during the war. The scale of social and economic dislocation was generally greater in eastern Europe than in western Europe due to occupation and refugee crises. Not only had several of the states fought against each other, but they also existed in the shadow of Soviet Russia, which viewed eastern Europe as a bridge to a European-wide revolution. Nationalist politicians and army officers in the Weimar Republic resented Poland's existence, while Italian governments, particularly the Fascist regime after 1922, had designs to expand their influence in the eastern Mediterranean and the Balkans.

To escape this anarchical system, in which the existence of states, social classes, and ethnic groups seemed to be at stake, required guarantees of security. The League of Nations made some stuttering progress in this unstable region. The resolution of the Åland Islands dispute between Finland and Sweden represented an early success for the League. The islanders, subject to Finnish sovereignty, appealed on the grounds of self-determination for union with Sweden. In the summer of 1921, following a commission of inquiry, the League confirmed Finnish sovereignty over the islands as a means of bolstering the government in Helsinki against Soviet Russia, but it also ensured that the islanders enjoyed a high degree of autonomy, a solution that has persisted to the present day. In the case of the dispute over Vilna between Poland and Lithuania the League largely ratified a decision achieved by force of Polish arms.

The first major test of the League of Nations in the region had highly ambiguous results. In 1923, following the murder of General Tellini, an Italian member of the commission demarcating the Greek–Albanian border, Mussolini decided to occupy Corfu. British diplomats immediately saw this as whether 'we shall or shall not be forced to retreat from the position of upholding the Covenant and the public law of Europe'. William Tyrrell, the deputy undersecretary at the Foreign Office, favoured submitting the dispute to the League, a proposal supported by the Foreign Secretary, George Curzon. Mussolini affected outrage that the dispute would be resolved by the League, which placed states like 'Haiti and Ireland on equality with great powers'. Ultimately, Mussolini withdrew from Corfu

in return for compensation of £500,000. His final decision to withdraw from the island owed much to the Italian navy's warning against risking war with Britain.[43] It was a grubby deal – 'To such a state of immorality have we sunk,' Curzon commented. Moreover, as Mussolini refused to accept the League's jurisdiction in the Corfu crisis, its recommendations had to be communicated to Italy through the Conference of Ambassadors, the Allied organization based in Paris that oversaw the implementation of the Versailles Treaty. Yet the Corfu incident did not represent a singular defeat for the League. It had created a negotiating process to resolve the dispute, Mussolini paid some heed to international public opinion as represented in the League, and the Italian and Yugoslav governments registered treaties on the status of Fiume with the League in 1924.[44]

The following year the League of Nations resolved a border dispute in the Balkans, following an incursion by Greek forces into Bulgarian territory. The Bulgarian government appealed to the League, and the Council acted quickly, threatening sanctions, which forced Greece to back down. Between 1924 and 1926 the League facilitated the resolution of a dispute between Turkey and Britain over Mosul, confirming the city's place in the British mandate of Iraq. Compared to the major crises between France and Germany in the early 1920s, these incidents were less significant. Nonetheless they demonstrated that the League, if used by the great powers, principally Britain and France, provided a flexible and new means of maintaining international peace.[45]

By the mid-1920s there was regional stability of sorts in eastern and southern Europe. Domestic politics had stabilized on the basis of the formation of authoritarian regimes, rather than the pluralist democracies anticipated during the war. These regimes neither threatened a regional war nor undermined the broader construction of the international order. They were socialized into the international order through the League of Nations, the admittedly patchy application of minority treaties, and their role in a wider European balance of power. The last was achieved through French agreements with Poland and Czechoslovakia in 1921, aimed at containing the latent power of Germany.[46]

* * *

The competing claims of empire and nation were at the core of imperial politics after 1918, a legacy of the promises made, treaties signed, and aspirations proclaimed during the war years. The promise of reform had to be redeemed, but the politics of redemption had changed during the course of the war. Nationalists of a more radical hue had come to the fore in Ireland, Egypt, and India, while in the mandates, especially in Syria and Iraq, nationalist expectations cut across wartime deals that Britain had concluded with Husayn ibn Ali, sharif of Mecca. Moreover, the experience of war had undermined European claims to moral and political superiority in Africa and Asia.[47]

Ireland lay at the intersection between the European and imperial order. On 21 January 1919 a group of nationalist Volunteers ambushed a Royal Irish Constabulary unit in Tipperary, killing two policemen. The same day the Dail – the parliament established in the Mansion House in Dublin by Sinn Fein MPs abstaining from the Westminster parliament – issued its Declaration of Independence. This document emphasized the continuity of the Irish people's resistance to 'foreign usurpation'. Although the ambush was not approved by the self-proclaimed provisional government established in the Dail, violence and democracy were intertwined in the constitution of Irish self-determination. Sinn Fein hollowed out the United Kingdom in southern Ireland by constructing its own parastate with a parliament, courts, the launch of a national loan, and local government reforms. Alongside the practice of government, the Irish Republican Army, a paramilitary force that included men who had served in the British Army during the war, undertook a campaign of ambushes and assassinations against the British forces and the Royal Irish Constabulary. The IRA also killed individuals deemed enemies of the nation, often socially marginal figures, including some Protestants, women, and ex-servicemen.[48] In Ulster, Unionists were also busy making their own nation, expelling Catholics from workplaces and homes. The Home Rule government established in Ulster in 1920 was explicit about the privileges of the Protestant majority

By late 1919 British authority had collapsed throughout much of southern Ireland. One response was the employment of paramilitary forces, the Black and Tans, who were variously supposed to terrorize the population and defeat the IRA. The military response was organized by Sir Nevil Macready, a man who loathed Ireland 'with a depth greater than the sea and more violent than that which I feel against the Boche'.[49] The cycle of violence reached its height in 1920 and 1921. Sinn Fein and particularly Michael Collins had begun to consider a negotiated settlement by late 1920.[50] Sir Henry Wilson believed that he could destroy Sinn Fein within six months, if given a free hand under martial law – but, significantly, Lloyd George's government recoiled from ratcheting up violent repression. The political restraints on British military power reflected changing international norms. British politicians across the spectrum recognized the legitimacy of some form of autonomy for southern Ireland. Liberals had supported Home Rule since 1886 and during the war Conservatives had entertained proposals for Irish autonomy within the empire. Moreover, the military option of crushing Sinn Fein would have required a heavy and severe military occupation of southern Ireland with all the likely consequences of violence against the civilian population. Events such as the burning of Cork City in December 1920 and other atrocities committed by the Black and Tans were the subject of intense and widespread criticism in Britain. There were condemnations of the transplantation of 'German' methods of barbarism to the United Kingdom, while Labour politicians feared that paramilitaries could be transported across the Irish Sea to suppress strikes. The brutalization of British politics was not a price worth paying for the suppression of self-determination.[51] The Anglo-Irish Treaty, concluded in December 1921, did not bring immediate peace to Ireland. In the Free State there was a brief Civil War, during which there were some further atrocities against the Protestant minority. However, by 1924, following the quashing of the Army mutiny, the Irish Free State had become a functioning democracy. In Northern Ireland the Catholic minority faced systematic discrimination in what James Craig, its first prime minister, described in 1934 as a 'Protestant parliament and a Protestant state'.

While Irish nationalists' claims to self-determination could be accommodated within a framework of British imperial interests, the competing conceptions of nation and empire were less easily resolved in the Middle East. In Egypt the arrest in March 1919 of Sa'd Zaghlul, the vice-president of the Legislative Assembly, triggered the Egyptian uprising. The revolt derived its popularity from the combination of thwarted nationalist political goals and social discontent. Grievances ranged from the resentment of educated Egyptians, whose opportunities for promotion were curtailed by the preference for Europeans in the upper echelons of the civil administration, to the refusal of Brigadier Macauley of Egyptian State Railways to give employees time off for prayers on Friday, to families living in overcrowded housing.[52] The aspirations of everyday life intersected with the geopolitics of empire. British policymakers came to see Egypt as the fulcrum of empire. After suppressing the revolt the British government negotiated with the Wafd, Zaghlul's nationalist party. In February 1922 Britain granted Egypt independence, but it was hedged with significant constraints, including the retention of imperial communications, control of the Suez Canal, and the

stationing of troops in Egypt. While the settlement of 1922 did not reconcile British conceptions of a protectorate with Egyptian understandings of
independence, Egypt entered the League of Nations in the 1930s, its status
and relationship with Britain radically altered since the 1882 occupation.[53]

In the mandates in the former Ottoman territories French and British
imperial policymakers confronted their own wartime promises to regional
potentates, political and religious divisions, and organized nationalist
groups. In addition, British and French officials were divided on how to
manage their inheritance from the Ottoman empire. Working out the
legacy of the First World War among these conflicting interests led to a
series of colonial wars. In Mesopotamia the initial belief in Allied promises
of self-determination gave way to protests and violent revolt by mid-1920.
In what was to become Iraq, members of the Sunni and Shiite communities
supported the nationalist organization, the Guardians of Iraqi Independence
founded in 1919. In 1920 Iraqi nationalists launched their uprising for an
independent state. The British Army there was increased from 60,000 to
100,000, including a large contingent from India. In the subsequent
campaign, which ended in October, an estimated 8,450 Iraqis and 2,200
British and Indian soldiers died. An Iraqi journalist, Muhammad Abd
al-Husayn, described how the British army 'had no other interest than our
extermination. . . . there has been bloodshed and the destruction of populous towns and the violation of the sanctity of places of worship to make
humanity weep'.[54] The Anglo-Iraqi Treaty of 1922, concluded with King
Faysal, gave Britain effective control of Iraq. British forces suppressed the
popular uprising against the treaty, before a Constituent Assembly ratified
it and established a new constitution in 1924. Like Egypt, Iraq entered the
League of Nations in the 1930s.

Faysal's biography between 1919 and 1922 reflected the patchwork settlement in the Middle East. As the ambitions of his father, Sharif Husayn of
Mecca, to establish an Arab kingdom in the Middle East withered, Faysal set
up a government in Damascus in October 1918 with the support of Arab
nationalists, with whom he had fought during the Arab revolt against the
Ottomans. Hopes for independence receded rapidly after the First World
War. Following Britain's transfer of control of Syria to French forces in late
1919, the Syrian National Congress made its move and declared independence in March 1920. Faysal was declared king of Syria, including Lebanon
and Palestine. However, French colonial forces easily crushed the incipient
revolt in Syria. Faysal now made his way to Iraq, where British officials
supported his successful bid to become king. His brother, Abdullah, became

the first king of Transjordan, another mandate controlled by Britain. Both brothers had gained their crowns as consolation prizes, granted by Britain, and their subjects were well aware of this. Meanwhile in Syria, French forces faced uprisings in 1922 and, most notably in 1925, as nationalists continued to seek independence.[55] In France's other mandate, Lebanon, there was less violence, but bitter resentment at broken promises of independence prevailed amongst Lebanese nationalists. In the British mandate of Palestine, there was periodic violence. The first eruption of inter-communal violence between Muslims, Christians, and Jews took place during the Muslim pilgrim festival of Nebi Musa in April 1920, resulting in the deaths of nine people, including five Jews. However, it was not until the 1930s that violence intensified in Palestine, notably in the Arab rebellion of 1936.[56]

In Britain's most important colony, the Government of India Act of 1919 embodied the principles of constitutional reform set out by Edwin Montagu in 1917. This created a dual system of government in which ministers were responsible to provincial councils for areas of local government, such as health and education. The Imperial Legislative Council became a bicameral legislature in which the majority of members were elected but a substantial proportion were imperial nominees. While the Indian National Congress had accepted the constitutional reforms at a conference in December 1919, Gandhi mobilized Hindu and Muslim opinion and managed to reverse that decision in September 1920. Congress's campaign of non-cooperation tested the political reforms and it might have undone them, had the non-cooperation held together. Yet it splintered into its constituent groups of Muslims and Hindus, peasants and landlords, and the Indian middle classes in late 1921 and early 1922. These groups remained dissatisfied with the constitutional reforms after 1917, but in the absence of an alternative and with the support of local notables, civil servants, and other beneficiaries, the British empire held its position in India.[57]

By the mid-1920s the British imperial settlements had established a framework within which further reform and change could take place. Indian and Egyptian nationalists had not given up their hope of independence, but events such as the entry of Iraq and Egypt into the League of Nations in the 1930s showed the scope for significant change within the frameworks established in the early 1920s. The French colonial settlement was more unstable, however, and offered less flexibility in adapting to the changing environment of the interwar era.

* * *

The fulcrum of the emerging post-war order was Germany. Here the different strands of international and domestic politics were interwoven. Domestic politics had to engage with paramilitary violence, ethnic conflict, polarization between right and left, the struggle to preserve democracy and public order, and economic dislocation. In addition, Germany's neighbours sought to weaken the potential aggressor further, fearing its future revival, while many Germans entertained fantasies of revanche and revisionist war. A stable international order required German domestic political stability, but this also required resolving Germany's place in Europe. The interaction between domestic and foreign politics reached its zenith in the Weimar Republic's crisis of 1923.

The French government's decision to occupy the Ruhr in January 1923, on the basis of German violations of the reparations agreements, was the culmination of four years of frustration, missed opportunities, and sporadic violence. In some ways it was the final act in a war that neither side believed had ended in November 1918. Although reparations were at the centre of Franco-German relations and therefore the working out of the peace settlement in western Europe, they amounted to much more than a financial transaction. Reparations represented a moral reckoning of the war, they served as a proxy for territorial disputes, and they framed and ultimately derailed the reconstruction of the post-war economic order between 1919 and 1923. The absence of 'moral disarmament' ensured that the moral chasm between French and German war cultures tended to dominate relations after 1918. 'The situation of France in the world,' wrote Abbé Pradel of the French Institute in Cologne to Philippe Berthelot, the secretary of the Ministry of Foreign Affairs, in December 1920, 'will always be precarious as long as its neighbour to the east, still strong and populous, nourishes hostile sentiments towards it. Physical disarmament will only result in incessant mutual coldness. Above all moral disarmament is important. Everything that one can do to enlighten and bring the two nations closer will serve this aim.'[58] Key figures on both sides of the Rhine considered enmity between France and Germany as the natural historical relationship between the two nations.[59] The fears generated by this reading of history reflected, especially in France, the absence of any sense of security, particularly following rejection of the Versailles Treaty by the American Senate.

The French search for security, however, was destabilizing and often violent. The same considerations about national homogeneity were evident in French policy towards the provinces of Alsace and Lorraine as they were in the new states of eastern Europe. During the war French justifications for the return of the two provinces had purposefully ignored self-determination as policymakers recognized the demographic transformation that had taken place over four decades. In 1910, 87.2 per cent of the Alsatian population spoke a German dialect as their first language. That amounted to 1.5 million people, equivalent to 4 per cent of France's population. There was no minority protection treaty to defend these people after 1918. The French government regarded them with suspicion and imposed restrictions on their civil liberties. The inhabitants were divided into three categories (or four if one includes the small number of Allied citizens) and assigned 'cartes'. A minority was given a clean bill of national health, as long they had been born before 1870 or their parents had been French citizens. Two other groups included people with one French and one German parent or those who had moved to Alsace and Lorraine since 1870, over half a million people. Their freedom of movement was limited as were their employment opportunities. They also faced economic restrictions, the purpose of which was to make life sufficiently uncomfortable that they would move to Germany. Over 200,000 people left Alsace after the war. These included French-speaking women married to German men. One of these, Hélène Herr, protested that she was 'forced to leave my birthplace with my four children, to finish my life in exile'. Others were expelled because they were unemployed and/or impoverished. In these cases the nationalizing project became a means of getting rid of a social nuisance.[60]

However, identity politics could be flexible, as some strands of French policy demonstrated during the occupation of the Rhineland. The occupation served various purposes – as a means to secure reparation payments and the fulfilment of other treaty terms including disarmament, as an opportunity to increase French political and cultural influence in the region, and as a way to detach the Rhineland from Germany. These projects jostled for priority amongst the various agencies of French and Allied policy, including the Ministry of Foreign Affairs, the army, and the Rhineland Commission, headed by Paul Tirard. The idea of separating off the Rhineland drew on notions of cultural affinities between that region and French civilization. In this case inherent and essential differences were ignored that proved difficult to accommodate within the borders of the French Republic. Encouraging separatism in the Rhineland meant at a minimum detaching the region from the Prussian state as a means of decentralizing power in Germany. This scenario assumed that there was a fundamental economic, political, and cultural conflict between the historic heart of the Prussian state and its westerly provinces. 'It is necessary to let the population understand that their particular interests have in us a defender against the Prussian intrusion', advised a note from the Direction des Affaires Politiques et Commerciales in January 1920, 'as much on the economic as on the political terrain and that we will look with sympathy on the development of any emancipatory movement.'[61]

There were a number of separatist coups in the Rhineland after the war, though they had extremely limited popular support. To the extent that there was backing for a Rhineland state in Germany, it was considered a means to prevent French annexation of the region and to maintain the Rhineland within the Reich. In 1919 and 1923 the mayor of Cologne, Konrad Adenauer, contemplated a Rhenish state within the Reich as a means of preserving German unity, while assuaging French security concerns by decentralizing the Reich.[62]

Other French initiatives in the occupied region varied widely. Most were in the realm of cultural politics, such as the establishment of French language courses in universities. Certain moments exposed the tin ear of the French occupation, such as the parade organized by Tirard to commemorate Napoleon's contribution to civilizing the Rhineland.[63] The encounter between Allied occupying troops and German civilians ran the spectrum between friendly and hostile. 'Shortly after they reach a town,' one American officer wrote, 'it is common enough to find that some old woman is baking cakes for them and giving them rooms in her house instead of the stable in which they are billeted. This is a form of propaganda which it is practically impossible to combat.'[64] The French military authorities frowned on these good relations. Whereas American troops considered the German election results of January 1919 as proof of the triumph of democracy, French authorities fretted about the persistence of militarism in German politics.[65] One of the most contentious aspects of the French occupation of the Rhineland was the presence of 25,000 colonial troops from Senegal and north Africa as part of the occupying force. German publicists considered this a violation of shared European values, a further means of punishing the German nation for a crime it had not committed. The post-war denunciations of 'barbarous African troops' drew on images established during the war.

From the French perspective the occupation was justified by German atrocities during the war as well as security considerations. The moral perspectives of the different parties exacerbated the difficulties of resolving the reparations payments and war debts question. The Versailles Treaty had established a reparations commission, but it had not set an amount or a schedule. When the United States rejected the treaty, John Foster Dulles warned that it had lost its seat on the 'committee on the reorganization of Allied Europe'. From his perspective and that of other American policy-makers the chief goal of international politics was to restore economic growth. 'Allied Europe is financially indebted to the United States in a sum approximating thirteen billion dollars,' he wrote on 8 August 1919. 'It should be our customer annually for several billion dollars worth of our products. Upon the successful financial and economic rehabilitation of Europe depends Europe's ability to repay what she owes and her ability to buy from us what we wish to sell.'[66] This was a dollar and cents approach to the legacy of the war, but Dulles considered the revival of trade and economic activity to have civilizing consequences by creating employment and economic bonds between former enemies. British policymakers like-wise stressed the restoration of international commerce. It was a means of bringing about peace as well as an economic benefit. Reparations payments had to be subordinated to the priority of the economic restoration of Europe.

French politicians, on the other hand, reminded their former allies of the devastated regions in the north-east of the country and the blood sacri-fice paid over four years of war. French casualties, as a proportion of the population, were almost double the level of British casualties. German reparations were a means of levelling the economic playing field. Moreover, French leaders linked reparations to war debts, a relationship which the United States absolutely rejected. From the French perspective its devas-tated regions and dead sons had been sacrificed to defend civilization and justice for the benefit of other nations as well as its own security. André Tardieu, Minister for the Liberated Regions in Clemenceau's cabinet, played with these notions when in October 1920 he asked the American Committee for Devastated France to continue its philanthropic work, including recon-structing homes and improving children's healthcare. To withdraw the aid would be a blow to France, which had 'legitimately counted' on British and American support for its demands against Germany. The divisions between the Allies meant that Germany had evaded reparations payments. 'France merits more than ever the sympathy,' he wrote to Myron Herrick, later ambassador to France between 1921 and 1929, 'which until now has faith-fully supported her.'[67] The fusion of economic need, anxiety about national security, and a sense of frustrated justice shaped French reactions to German reparations policy.

German governments simply rejected the war guilt clause as the flawed moral basis for reparations payments. Successive foreign ministers claimed that Germany could not pay reparations on the scale demanded. Whether Germany could not pay or would not pay continues to attract scholarly attention. The London Schedule of Payments in April 1921 fixed the reparations total at 132 billion marks. The structures of the payments meant that Germany would pay 50 billion marks. In theory this sum was within Germany's ability to pay. Annual payments worked out at over 5 per cent of national income. Extracting this sum required a strong state and the Weimar Republic did not belong in this category, particularly in the wake of the Versailles Treaty. The reparations issue was a political, rather than an economic, problem. As J. P. Morgan put it in June 1922, 'the Allies must make up their minds as to whether they wanted a weak Germany who could not pay or a strong Germany who could pay. If they wanted a weak Germany, they must keep her economically weak; but if they wanted her to be able to pay they must allow Germany to exist in a condition of cheerfulness. This meant, however, that you would get a strong Germany, and a Germany that was strong economically would, in a sense, be strong from a military point of view also.'[68]

In this nexus of the weak German state, beset by foreign policy setbacks and challenges to its legitimacy at home, lies the relationship between inflation and reparations. French governments dismissed (rightly) German claims that reparations caused inflation. The inflationary pressures dated to the mismanagement of the war economy, including the inflationary price and wage settlements in the Hindenburg programme of December 1916. Nor, as French governments claimed, was inflation a device to evade reparations payments through a self-induced economic catastrophe. Rather the Weimar Republic could not pay the demanded reparations for the same reason that it could not rein in inflation. It lacked the authority to impose the kind of economic settlement that could have generated reparations and brought inflation under control – the reduction of imports, the increase in exports, longer working hours, higher taxes, and less domestic consumption. Such an economic settlement was rejected as politically explosive. Moreover, given that the German population, almost to a person, repudiated the moral underpinnings of reparation, the war guilt clause, it was impossible to extract that percentage of national income to pay the bills to her erstwhile enemies. If the Allies wanted democracy to survive in Germany, they needed to accommodate the widely held German understanding of the war within the international settlement.

Instead French governments responded to German failure to pay its reparations bill and other violations of the Versailles terms by extending their zone of occupation. Aggressive vigilance appeared to be the most reliable option to secure France's future and redeem the sacrifices of the war.

The events of the Kapp Putsch in March 1920 show the vortex in which the German Republic found itself, as it was confronted with Allied, and particularly French, demands. The Putsch was undoubtedly the result of domestic right-wing opposition to the Republic, but foreign policy issues contributed to the coup, led by Wolfgang Kapp, a leading figure in the Fatherland Party, and Walther von Lüttwitz, a senior officer. In July 1919, following German acceptance of the Versailles Treaty, they began to plan the overthrow of the republican government. Their plans depended on the Ehrhardt brigade, a Freikorps unit that had fought in the Baltics in 1919. The Allies had supported the German Freikorps as a means of checking the advances of the Red Army into the newly independent Baltic states. However, when the success of the Freikorps threatened to establish a German sphere of influence in the region, the Allies demanded their withdrawal. The individual soldiers, having been promised land as a reward for fighting in the Baltics, now threatened to mutiny. Only with the greatest difficulty did the Weimar government persuade them to return to Germany. In late 1919 the Allies demanded that the German Army demobilize in accordance with the agreed schedule, despite warnings that this would precipitate a mutiny. Faced with Allied sanctions, however, the Republic decided to comply with the demobilization schedule. The Ehrhardt brigade was identified for demobilization in March 1920. The soldiers, already resentful at their treatment in the Baltics, were now prepared to march on Berlin, while Kapp and Lüttwitz accelerated their plot before the brigade was dissolved. On 13 March the brigade marched into Berlin, the republican government fled, and Kapp proclaimed his government. At this point the socialist trade unions declared a general strike and the vast majority of bureaucrats decided not to cooperate with the Kapp government. Within days Kapp had fled and the republican government returned to Berlin. However, the general strike had escalated into a left-wing rising in the Ruhr. When the Weimar government asked for permission to send troops into the demilitarized zone to suppress the uprising, the Allies refused. After the Reichswehr and Freikorps entered the region, the French government responded to this violation of the Versailles Treaty by occupying Frankfurt and five other cities. From the Baltics to the Rhineland the cumulative effect of the working out of policy decisions was the weakening of the Republic and the chances for stability in post-war Europe. Allied policy was short-sighted, undermining the Republic that represented the best chance of peaceful stability in central Europe. Or as Lloyd George put it, following the French occupation of these cities: 'In a couple of years the Germans will have fed themselves up with sausages and be as virile as ever.'[69]

This pattern of Allied demand, German failure to comply, Allied punishment, and setback for the Weimar Republic was repeated on several occasions between 1919 and 1923.

There were attempts to break out of this cycle, notably the Wiesbaden Agreement of October 1921 and the Genoa Conference in April 1922, proposed by Lloyd George to revive Europe's economy. On both sides of the Rhine there were parties who favoured conciliation and cooperation. As Jacques Seydoux, who had established the commercial section of the Quai d'Orsay in 1919, told an American diplomat, France and Germany had to 'live in the same house'. In his view the 'violent solution' might leave France 'master of Germany', but the German state and economy would be destroyed and therefore become a burden on France. Better then, he argued, to 'exhaust all formulas of conciliation and understanding that we can accept'. Aristide Briand, who had become premier and Foreign Minister yet again in January 1921, was more open to Seydoux's reasoning than the other men who passed through the revolving door of the Third Republic's cabinet in the early 1920s, notably Alexandre Millerand and Raymond Poincaré. Briand appointed Louis Loucheur as the Minister for Liberated Regions. His technocratic temperament led him to consider alternative ways of extracting reparations and rebuilding the devastated regions of northern France.[70] In Germany, Joseph Wirth, the Centre Party Chancellor, appointed Walther Rathenau as the Minister of Reconstruction in May 1921. While Rathenau considered the London schedule of payments unworkable, he looked for alternative solutions. Finally, he picked up the threads of his pre-war ideas for economic cooperation between France and Germany, now recast as a means of integrating Germany into the international order.[71] In three meetings in Wiesbaden between June and October 1921, Loucheur and Rathenau worked out an agreement under which Germany would pay reparations in kind rather than in cash. The agreement, however, rapidly came unstuck due to the opposition of French industrialists, who feared German products would displace their own, German industrialists, such as Hugo Stinnes, who opposed any form of reparation settlement, and the British government, which feared it would lose its share of the reparations as a result of Franco-German cooperation.

Lloyd George countered with a grand plan for a summit on European reconstruction to be held in Genoa in April 1922. Taking place outside the

League of Nations, the conference was supposed to reintegrate Germany and Soviet Russia into the international order through the economic reconstruction of the continent. It represented an imaginative proposal, but the conference foundered on the persistent conflicts between the great powers, victors and defeated alike. Even before the conference had taken place the political basis for a deal was cut away. Briand resigned as premier in January 1922, following parliamentary criticism of his conciliatory policy. Poincaré, the new premier, favoured strict implementation of the Versailles Treaty. Lenin sought to exploit the conference to prevent reconciliation between the Allies and Germany as part of the Soviet strategy to divide the capitalist world. 'It suits us that Genoa be wrecked,' he wrote to Georgi Chicherin, 'but not by us of course.'[72] In this Chicherin succeeded brilliantly. At the conference in April, playing on German fears of a deal between the Allies and Soviet Russia that would further isolate the Weimar Republic, Chicherin negotiated a treaty with Rathenau at Rapallo, a seaside resort outside Genoa. The Treaty of Rapallo provided for full diplomatic relations and the renunciation of reparations claims by both states. The treaty, a conventional stroke of great power cabinet politics, destroyed the multilateral conference and with it the hope for cooperation between the great powers in restoring the economic order. The American judgement that the basis for international cooperation was still absent in Europe was sound. Herbert Hoover, now Secretary of Commerce, and Charles Hughes, now Secretary of State, would have welcomed a cooperative solution at Genoa, but considered that things would need to get worse before opinion in Europe would coalesce around cooperation.[73]

The ideas to restore the international order were present, but the political constellations were not yet in place. In Germany prominent supporters of the Republic and advocates of reconciliation with the Allies were intimidated and even assassinated by right-wing terrorists. On 26 August 1921 two members of the Organisation Consul, a right-wing terrorist group in Weimar Germany, Heinrich Tillessen and Heinrich Schulz, shot Matthias Erzberger as he was out walking in Griesbach in the Black Forest. Erzberger's crime, in the view of his killers, was his signature of the armistice in 1918 and his role in the Reichstag peace resolutions in 1917. The conservative *Kreuzzeitung* compared his killers to Charlotte Corday who had stabbed Jean-Paul Marat, the radical Jacobin, in his bath in July 1793. Other right-wing papers claimed that Erzberger's assassination was necessary in order to save the Fatherland from further catastrophe. His assassins escaped to Hungary with the help of the Bavarian authorities and were only imprisoned following trials after 1945.

On 24 June 1922 Walther Rathenau was driving from his villa in the Grünewald district of Berlin to the Foreign Office when two gunmen pulled up beside his car and shot him. Erwin Kern and Hermann Fischer were also members of the Organisation Consul; surrounded by police three weeks later, Kern was shot, while Fischer committed suicide. The murder of Rathenau was a protest against the policy of fulfilment, liberalism, and Jews in German public life.[74] Three months after his murder, Karin Glaser, a friend of Max Lotz, whom Rathenau had helped find a job in June 1914, wrote to Paul Kahn: 'In October 1915 Max Lotz died an agonising death as the dreadful consequence of being buried alive. He and his family were only permitted one month to enjoy the happy change that their lives had taken. And now he is also resting forever, he who, for thousands, was a help, a comfort, a source of fortune, and who might have saved the German people. I did not have the fortune to know Dr Rathenau, but I suffer the loss of this incomparably great man, as the most difficult and bitter that this terrible war has brought.'[75]

On 27 November 1922, following continued failures by Germany to deliver reparation payments, the French cabinet decided on the strict enforcement of the terms of the Versailles Treaty. On 9 January 1923 the Reparations Commission concluded that Germany had defaulted on its payments and this provided the justification for French and Belgian troops to occupy the Ruhr. The German government responded by declaring a campaign of passive resistance to French occupation.[76] On both sides the occupation was cast as a continuation of the First World War. The French memorandum on 2 January, calling for sanctions against Germany, referred to the destruction of mines in Nord-Pas de Calais between 1914 and 1918. The Weimar government issued an 'Appeal to the German People', evoking the memories of August 1914. This time the German government high-lighted the 'breach of peace and law'. Some German publicists, such as the historian Hermann Oncken, framed it as part of a longer historical enmity, claiming Poincaré's policy represented the continuity of French aggression towards Germany since the reign of Louis XIV.[77]

Friedrich Ebert of the SPD spoke of a 'true people's war', based on popular passive resistance. The French occupation, however, entailed considerable violence against civilians in the Ruhr. By October 1923, 130,000 Germans, mainly civil servants, had been expelled from the region. The health of the civilian population deteriorated due to inflation and food shortages. The cost of a pound of potatoes increased from 3,000 marks on 20 July to 6,800 marks on 23 July, and 10,000 marks the following day. Some 10 per cent of children in Dortmund between the ages of two and ten suffered from rickets, while 75 per cent of children in Hamborn were malnourished, compared to the still high figure of 50 per cent before the occupation. By October, 214,097 children had been evacuated from the province of Westphalia.[78] On 31 March French soldiers had shot workers demonstrating at the Krupp plant in Essen, killing thirteen of them. While the German government blamed the French Army for shooting without cause, the French authorities blamed the directors of Krupp for inciting trouble. There is some disagreement on the number of civilian deaths during the Ruhr occupation – German sources put the figure at 154 and French sources at 118. German sources claim that 87 rapes took place, French sources 59.[79]

There was violent German resistance to the occupation, primarily by members of Freikorps units, who travelled to the Ruhr to engage in sabotage and kill Allied troops. On 30 June 1923 eight Belgians were killed. On 10 March two French soldiers were killed in Buer, a suburb of Gelsenkirchen. The funeral of twenty-two-year-old Lieutenant Colpin was choreographed as an act in a war that had begun in 1914. *La Croix du Nord* claimed that Colpin had been killed by the same hands which had devastated his home-town of Lille. Colpin's biography fitted the narrative of the war, based on the myth of the Union Sacrée. Born into a Catholic family in Lille in 1900, he had been deported to Germany in 1916. Now he had died in Germany, defending the victory of 1918 against a nation that had not admitted its responsibility for the war.[80]

The occupation was not responsible for the hyper-inflationary spiral in the German economy. However, the costs of occupation, the political weakness of the government, and the throttling of industrial activity in the Ruhr meant that inflation accelerated. Hyper-inflation not only distorted economic value, it is also undermined established social status and cultural values.[81] The terms of everyday life were transformed by hyper-inflation, as prices and wages changed on a daily basis. People were desperate to spend their paper money as soon as they received it, as its value depreciated rapidly. On 15 October one dollar was worth 3,760,000,000 paper marks; a week later it was worth more than ten times that, 40,000,000,000 paper marks. By 1 November the mark had depreciated a further 400 per cent, while on 20 November one dollar was worth 4,200,000,000,000 paper marks, more than one hundred times its value just four weeks previously. Waiting in a queue risked a minor financial calamity.[82]

The crisis of the Weimar Republic reached its height between August and November 1923, as hyper-inflation and occupation combined to expose the deep clefts in German politics. Society, the state, and the

European system were on the verge of disintegration. Observers compared the popular mood to the autumn of 1918. 'The mass of the population is in a similar mood with respect to the decisive battle on the Rhine and Ruhr,' reported officials from Würzburg in northern Bavaria in July, 'as it was regarding the war in the fall months of 1918. . . . They often no longer believe in success. The word "swindle", which played such a fateful role at the end of the war, is frequently heard again.' Others condemned any sign of weakening on the part of the government, as amounting to a second stab in the back, this time of civilians waging passive resistance in the Ruhr. Rumours circulated that 'Stresemann will have to follow Rathenau and Erzberger as soon as possible.'[83] Gustav Stresemann had been appointed Chancellor in August 1923, completing the journey from wartime annexationist to *Vernunftrepublikaner*, a republican due to circumstances rather than conviction. Even compared to 1918 Germany's possibilities seemed to have shrivelled. Stresemann's decision in September 1923 to call off the campaign of passive resistance was a second German defeat at the hands of France, one he compared to signing the Treaty of Versailles.[84]

Yet he had little option but to accept defeat. The extremes on the right and left had been strengthened by economic collapse and foreign occupation. As the authority of the republic ebbed, Nazi and Communist Party leaders were plotting their coups and revolutions. The Republic seemed to have few resources of support. The possibility of a military dictatorship under the head of the Army command, Hans von Seeckt, was touted. Stresemann's government was also without friends in the wider world. Once Poincaré had rejected British offers to mediate, Stresemann knew that he had no alternative but to accept France's continued occupation of the Ruhr, call off passive resistance, and place his faith in future negotiations.

The dissolution of Germany continued apace. In Saxony and Thuringia the Communist Party had organized paramilitary groups, known as 'hundreds', in preparation for revolution. Moscow was supporting plans for the German 'October'. The German Army acted with alacrity to dissolve the communist 'hundreds'. The Reich government also dissolved regional Socialist governments in Saxony and Thuringia for failing to maintain public authority, a sign of the republic's increasingly authoritarian approach. This snuffed out the threat of a revolution from the radical left.

When it came to dealing with the radical right, the Reich was hampered by the protection offered by the Bavarian government to figures such as Hitler and by the army's ambivalent attitude. In late October the army commander in Bavaria, Otto von Lossow, spoke of a march on Berlin to establish a dictatorship. The example of Mussolini's march on Rome echoed around Bavarian politics in 1923. The Bavarian government refused to countenance any intervention from Berlin in its internal affairs. Without a reliable military force to carry out its order, the government in Berlin could only watch nervously. The divisions within the radical right in Bavaria saved the Republic. Hitler, fearing that rivals would steal a march on him, had launched his Putsch on the evening of 8 November. The following day, five years after the German revolution, Hitler and his supporters marched through Munich. As they reached the Odeonsplatz, where Hitler had celebrated the outbreak of war in 1914, a brief firefight broke out between police and Putschists. Hitler survived narrowly, but fourteen Putschists and four policemen lay dead. The Putsch had fizzled out.[85]

Six days later, on 15 November, a new currency, the Rentenmark, was issued. The decision had been taken a month earlier. By November 1923 there was no functioning German currency. The proliferation of local currencies was arguably a greater risk to unity than the threats from the radical right and left. The Mayor of Bochum told Stresemann of 'hordes of people starving and wandering about'. Food riots and looting were regular occurrences, while rioters attacked Jewish districts in cities.[86] The introduction of the new currency marked a moment of stabilization. A week later, Stresemann explained in the Reichstag his conception of the relationship between currency stabilization in Germany and the construction of the international order: 'The increase of the purchasing power of the German population is not just a German concern. It is an issue of the maintenance of normal relations in the world economy.' Stresemann's vision of the world economy underpinned the political reconstruction of the European order. Europe, he argued, was 'not a creation that could live by itself. Europe is only possible within the world and within the world economy. If, in this Europe between the Rhine and the Urals, only "louse-poor" people live, that will have consequences for the world economy, which embraces all peoples.'[87] The following day the Reichstag passed a motion of no confidence in Stresemann's cabinet. Even within his hundred days as Chancellor he had accomplished a considerable amount, often through necessity, but underpinned by clear judgement and an occasional grain of good fortune. The threats from the radical left and right had fizzled out, as neither provided an alternative political system. The process of bringing inflation and the economy under control had begun. And German unity and democracy held.

* * *

Between 1918 and 1923 post-war stabilization had taken different forms, many of them anathema to the liberal vision of peace based on democracy, commercial exchange, and international law. The consolidation of the Soviet dictatorship in Russia and the Fascist coming to power in Italy were notable setbacks for democracy. Authoritarian regimes had come to power in eastern and central Europe. Crucially, however, democracy survived in the fulcrum of the post-war order, Germany, though republicans had received little support from the great powers. The relationship between domestic and international politics was complex. It is striking that authoritarian regimes, including Fascist Italy and Soviet Russia, were being socialized into the international order, rather than overturning it. This acceptance of the emerging international order derived from the recognition that individual states were not sufficiently powerful to achieve their expansionist aims. International revolution had proved a chimera for Soviet Russia, Fascist Italy did not have sufficient power to defy Britain in the Mediterranean, and France could not convince Rhinelanders to break away from Prussia. The same logic applied to states from the Baltics to Turkey, as revisionist and expansionist projects no longer shaped the immediate foreign policy agenda, instead being postponed to a distant future. Yet the significance of this postponement is that it provided an opportunity to construct other paths to peace. On the basis of this patchwork stabilization statesmen and others tried to fashion a more durable order.

CHAPTER 10

MAKING REAL PEACE, 1922–1925

'PEACE AT LAST' declared *The Times* on 17 October 1925. The town of Locarno on the shores of Lake Maggiore had staged the 'first real Peace Congress of Europe' in the words of Austen Chamberlain, the Conservative British Foreign Secretary. The editorial noted the scaled-down aspirations in the Treaty of Locarno, which guaranteed the existing borders in western Europe and affirmed that Germany's borders in eastern Europe could only be changed by arbitration and the consent of the individual state. 'How many people in Europe eleven years ago,' asked the editorial, 'were cherishing generous dreams of the liberation and expansion of human enterprise? How few they are now! Humbled and chastened by an unimaginable calamity, the peoples of Europe, struggling with a thousand fantastic problems in a changing world, have learned to limit their hopes and purposes. Safety for a time that may be foreseen, some real confidence that the work done today will not be undone tomorrow, even that would mean a marvellous release of energy in the present state of Europe.'[1] The details of the treaty seemed mundane, but the text stood for more than a guarantee of borders. It embodied what became known as the 'spirit of Locarno', an ethos of international reconciliation and cooperation. 'Locarno may be interpreted,' said Gustav Stresemann, now the German Foreign Minister, in a radio broadcast on 3 November, 'as signifying that the states of Europe at last realize that they cannot go on making war upon each other without being involved in common ruin.'[2] On the same day Paul Painlevé, the French premier, told the Chamber of Deputies that Europe was 'condemned to perish' if it persisted in 'its hatreds and divisions'. Locarno had not ended the 'era of difficulties', but it had 'purified the atmosphere'. This opened the 'paths to peace'.[3]

Between 1922 and 1925 states and societies constructed a peaceful international order. This process was framed by two conferences and regional treaties, one in Washington that concentrated on East Asian and Pacific politics, and one in Locarno that dealt with Europe. While diplomats and foreign ministers did the detailed work, the construction of peace rested upon the demobilization of the mind.[4] This took place in a myriad of ways, from the return of soldiers to civilian life to the restoration of transnational cultural and commercial networks. Groups mobilized in support of what can be termed a 'peace culture'. This privileged cooperation over confrontation, mutual respect over hatred, and welfare over armaments. It adapted wartime language about justice, welfare, and humanity to the detailed work of constructing peace. The practice of peace spanned the daily act of work as well as the daily act of wading through Foreign Office correspondence. This process of cultural demobilization and the construction of a culture of peace remained incomplete. Nor were the diplomatic and high political processes without their flaws. Negotiations and bargains established hierarchies within the international order, excluded important states and questions, and left fundamental problems unresolved. Nonetheless by the mid–1920s people were more optimistic about their futures and about peace. The expectations that had greeted Woodrow Wilson in 1918 and 1919 as he arrived in Europe had faded. The new optimism derived from the processes of negotiation rather the prospect of an absolute and immediate solution.

* * *

In the Far East and Pacific international tensions rose steadily following the First World War. Many American observers regarded Japan as an expansionist militarist power, while Japanese politicians feared their dwindling chances to secure economic resources in a world dominated by the United States and the British empire. Prince Konoe Fumimaro, one of the delegates at Paris, denounced the Versailles Treaty as an Anglo-American peace. British and American politicians were concerned that the Japanese government was exploiting instability in China with a view to expanding its imperial possessions on the Asian mainland. One of the many reasons the United States refused to grant independence to the Philippines was the fear of Japanese expansion in the Pacific. Nor were Anglo-American relations entirely without their difficulties. All three states were engaged in major naval armaments programmes, the seeds of an arms race. 'This meant that the Pacific,' said George Curzon, the Foreign Secretary, to Auckland Geddes, the ambassador in Washington, on 29 June 1921, 'would speedily become the centre and pivot of world politics, and that it would play an enormous part in the determination of the destinies of the future.'[5] The Washington Conference, attended by representatives from nine states between November 1921 and February 1922, provided a framework to manage international relations in this 'pivot of world politics'.

The decision to hold a conference arose from discussions about the renewal of the Anglo-Japanese alliance. Concluded in 1902, this alliance had been part of the geopolitical landscape in East Asian politics for two decades. Its original purpose – to contain Russia in the Far East – had long dissipated, and its more recent use against German possessions and threats in East Asia was also redundant. In the summer of 1921 delegates from the Dominions gathered in London to discuss imperial relations and they expressed their concern about the renewal of the alliance. Australian politicians saw Japan as a potential threat while Arthur Meighen, the Canadian prime minister, passed on American concerns about the continuation of the Anglo-Japanese alliance. Charles Hughes, the American Secretary of State, had made clear that he considered a renewal of the alliance as directed against the United States, now that the Russian and German threats in the region no longer existed. His principal concern was that the alliance would encourage Japanese policy to adopt a more aggressive stance in the Far East. The prospect of having to support Japan in a war against the United States, due to the terms of the alliance, alarmed officials in the Foreign Office.[6] Underlying these geopolitical calculations were conceptions of the racial order in world politics, of a global community of white Anglo-Saxon nations, and distinctive Western and 'Oriental' diplomatic cultures.[7] Nonetheless Japanese officials had good reasons to support the conference. Admiral Katō Tomosaburō argued that Japan could not win a naval race against the United States, but was well placed to expand its interests in China through trade. Japan's trade and investments in China had transformed its source of influence on the Asian mainland. Dampening down an arms race could work in Japan's favour.[8]

While Curzon and Hughes shared similar goals of easing tensions in East Asia, protecting British and American commercial interests, and creating international conditions for stability in Chinese politics, they approached the problem in distinctive ways. One solution was for the United States to conclude an alliance with Japan, setting a framework for their relations in East Asia. However, Hughes favoured calling a major conference in Washington to resolve naval competition and China's relations with the powers in the region. While Hughes acknowledged the primacy of the United States, Japan, and Britain in the Pacific region, he embedded the great power relationships into a multilateral framework that accommodated other powers, notably China and France.

The day before the conference opened, Warren Harding, the American president, led the ceremony in dedicating the grave of the unknown soldier at Arlington National Cemetery. This ceremony endowed the Washington Conference with wider meanings – as the conclusion of the war and the harbinger of a more peaceful international order. The conference, while restricted to East Asian affairs, was purposefully staged as an event with global implications. The remains of the American soldier had been taken from the village of Châlons sur Marne and lay in state in the Capitol, from whence they were taken via the White House to the cemetery at Arlington. The former president Wilson was only able to accompany the procession to the White House, as he remained too frail to walk the rest of the way to Arlington – and the War Department did not permit him to make the journey in a horse-drawn carriage, as he requested. It fell, in any case, to Harding to fuse American and universal values in the dedication. Having run on a platform of 'America first', Harding did not try to replicate Wilson's idiom. Yet his message was no less effective for that. In a speech witnessed by Americans and foreign delegates and diplomats gathered for the Washington Conference, he paid tribute to the American soldier. 'It is fitting to say that his sacrifice', Harding told the crowds, 'and that of the millions of dead, shall not be in vain. There must, there shall be, the commanding voice of a conscious civilization against armed warfare.' This Armistice Day marked the 'beginning of a new and lasting era of peace on earth, good will among men'.[9] American, Christian, and universal, the rhetoric framed the meaning of the Washington Conference.

The following day Harding opened the conference, attended by representatives from Britain, Japan, France, China, Italy, the Netherlands, Portugal, and Belgium. Acknowledging that he only spoke for the United States, the American president emphasized that the shocking destructiveness of the war and the burdens of debt made international peace imperative. He then handed over to Hughes, who chaired the conference. 'The world looks to the conference', Hughes told the delegates, 'to relieve humanity of the crushing burden created by competition in armament, and it is the view of the American government that we should meet that expectation without any unnecessary delay.' Hughes framed the conference within the matrix of the liberal peace, between democracies, and enabling economic growth through the reduction of wasteful military expenditure. He went beyond these principles to reveal his proposal for a naval armaments agreement. He had refused to divulge the contents of his speech to the other delegations. By setting out the proposals in this public forum, Hughes intended to bolster their force with the support of public opinion. It was a form of open diplomacy, used to striking effect. Paradoxically, Hughes was able to put forward his proposals because American intelligence had broken the Japanese code, which enabled them to have a good idea of what kind of deal would be acceptable to the Japanese government. Hughes proposed an immediate naval holiday ending current plans for ship construction, the scrapping of older ships, and fixing ratios between the signatories. Under these terms the ratio between the size of the American, British, Japanese, French, and Italian navies would be: 5:5:3:1.75:1.75.[10] Hughes introduced the concept of 'relative naval security' to the negotiations. He did not propose disarmament, but rather an arms limitations agreement. Moreover, he understood that absolute security was a mirage, and a costly one that fuelled arms races. Balancing each state's naval requirements within a binding agreement was a more effective means to reconcile the requirements of national security and stability in the international order. Indeed, order was created by the rules and balances within the proposal.

Over the subsequent three months the conference negotiated three pacts, which became the basis for the Washington system. The first pact was the Five Power Treaty on naval armaments, which reflected Hughes's proposals. It also included detailed agreements prohibiting the construction of naval fortifications across large swathes of the Pacific, though Japan, Singapore, and Hawaii were exempt from this prohibition.

Rivalries in the Pacific owed much to the mutual suspicion of the great powers in China. The Nine Power Pact, concluded on 6 February 1922, was designed to regulate relations between foreign states, principally Japan, the United States, and Britain, and China. It has often been seen as a victory for American diplomacy as it enshrined the concept of the Open Door in an international agreement. The Open Door, first advocated by John Hay, American Secretary of State at the turn of the century, sought to eliminate special privileges for individual states within China. By ending spheres of influence, the United States expected that its commercial strengths would triumph in competition with other nations. The signatories in 1922 agreed to respect Chinese sovereignty, allow China to develop its own political institutions, and uphold equal rights for all states within the country. In return China, represented by Wellington Koo, agreed not to grant special privileges to any state and to observe the obligations of neutrality in times of war.

In addition, Japan returned Shantung to Chinese sovereignty in 1922. This deal was negotiated on the sidelines of the conference, with British and American mediation. For Hughes the return of Shantung was important to the politics of getting any treaty through the Senate. For Japan it marked a considerable concession, even though the government had already promised at Paris in 1919 that it would return Shantung to China. The Chinese government, which had never recognized the Shantung clauses in the Versailles Treaty, almost missed the opportunity by overstating their demands. Hughes had to warn Koo that if he did not accept the deal in Washington, the United States would not support Chinese claims in the future. Koo and his fellow delegates, however, faced considerable resistance from sections of Chinese public opinion. On 1 December 1921 the Chinese delegation had to take refuge in the bathroom of their legation on Massachusetts Avenue, as they were besieged by Chinese students protesting against negotiations with Japan. Hughes had to send a military escort to bring the Chinese delegates to the conference at the Pan-American Building. The return of Shantung vindicated the decision of Koo not to sign the Versailles Treaty two and a half years earlier, but Chinese domestic politics remained unstable, in large part the result of China's efforts to find its place in the international order.

The Washington treaties represented a set of ideas and assumptions about the international order that went beyond specific clauses. The ideal of Washington gained currency in discussions about international politics as people invested the treaty with wider meanings. Arthur Lee, the First Lord of the Admiralty, who bemoaned the 'unwillingly dry hospitality' he had received in Prohibition America, told the Royal Colonial Institute on 9 May 1922 that the 'conference produced a complete change in the attitude of mind of the nations there assembled, and if I may so describe it, made them think in terms of peace rather than in terms of war'. In the United States the treaty easily made its way through the Senate, though Frank Brandegee, the Republican senator from Connecticut, appended a reservation to the treaty which made it clear that the United States stood under no military obligation according to its terms. Hughes and Harding had selected Henry Cabot Lodge, Elihu Root, and Oscar Underwood, the Democrat Senate Minority Leader for the American delegation, which meant that the treaty already had strong backing in the Senate. While the terms of the treaty were far less controversial than Article 10 of the Covenant, the Secretary of State and president had clearly learnt from Wilson's mismanagement of the Versailles delegation. The treaty, from the American perspective, had reconciled the divergent claims of national security, fiscal restraint, and commercial opportunity.[11]

On 4 November 1921, between the calling of the conference and its beginning, the Japanese prime minister, Hara Kei, was stabbed to death by a radical nationalist. He was the first of three premiers assassinated between 1918 and 1931 (there were fourteen prime ministers in Japan during this period). In all three cases their assassins were motivated by a rejection of the prime ministers' conciliatory foreign policy.[12] Appointed prime minister a week after Kei's assassination, Takahashi Korekiyo, who had called the agreement a 'blessing for mankind', fell from power in the summer of 1922 over foreign policy issues. However, his replacement, Admiral Kato, had been one of the delegates at Washington. Many within Japan regarded the Washington treaty as an Anglo-American barrier to legitimate Japanese expansionism in China, but opponents of the treaty could not yet offer a practical alternative. The Washington system was supposed to buy time for China to stabilize its domestic politics. However, instability persisted, leading to increasingly destructive conflicts between the central government and warlords in 1924 and 1925 and the militarization of politics. Once the fragile balance of China's domestic political system collapsed, the temptations (or perceived necessity) of intervention became too great for the powers, notably Japan, that stood to lose most.[13]

Constructing peace in the Far East and Pacific also required the careful negotiation of racial issues. From this perspective the United States took a disastrous step in passing an immigration act in 1924, the Johnson Act, that specifically prohibited the immigration of Asians on racial grounds. Immigration politics had become increasingly restrictive after the First World War, as broad swathes of American opinion, from labour to business, from Protestant churches to the nativist movements, feared that immigration from anywhere save northern Europe threatened the American stock with degeneracy. Since the early twentieth century the Japanese government had been sensitive to American immigration restrictions based on racial grounds. Disputes over immigration and the treatment of Japanese immigrants in the United States had been a source of tension between the two states, a racial mark of the barriers to cooperation. When Congress debated further immigration restrictions in 1923 and 1924, Hughes kept a close eye on proceedings, appreciating its links with wider American interests in the Far East. 'It is useless to argue,' he wrote to Albert Johnson, the chair of the House Committee on Immigration and Naturalization, 'whether or not such a feeling would be justified; it is quite sufficient to say that it would exist. It has certainly been manifested in the discussions in Japan with respect to the tendency of this measure and no amount of argument can avail to remove it.'[14] The Japanese ambassador, Masanao Hanihara, stressed that the prohibition of immigration would undercut those in Japan who promoted cooperation with the United States.

The Johnson Act cut the annual number of Japanese immigrants from 246 to zero. It also caused immense damage to relations between the United States and Japan. Hanihara resigned as ambassador, after he warned of 'grave consequences' from the Act, a phrase seized upon by Lodge and other senators. The Act, according to Hughes, 'implanted the seeds of antagonism, which are sure to bear fruit in the future.'[15] He was not thinking of war between the United States and Japan, but rather the collapse of the spirit of Washington. Antagonism and suspicion replaced cooperation and trust in relations. Nitobe Inazo, a Quaker convert who had studied in the United States, vowed never to set foot in the United States again as long as the Act was in force. Nitobe was one of Japan's leading internationalists, the first Japanese undersecretary general of the League of Nations.[16]

By mid-1924 the spirit of the Washington Conference had dissipated. The racial hierarchies in the international order remained, undermining the legitimacy of the settlement in the Far East. In China the failure of the Peking Tariff Conference in 1925 illustrated the tensions between the great powers and the persistent weaknesses of central authority in China. The great powers failed to agree on fundamental issues, while they continued to develop relations with local warlords in order to promote their own interests. A great power war in the Far East and Pacific remained unlikely in the mid-1920s, but peace was undercut by domestic political interests, ingrained prejudices, and frustrated ambitions.

* * *

In the Far East the Washington Conference had stimulated, briefly, a mood of peace. In western Europe the Treaty of Locarno was possible because of changing popular attitudes to the war, especially in France, Germany, and Britain. In turn the agreements at Locarno embodied and kindled the 'spirit of Locarno', which eased further diplomatic negotiations. The 'spirit of Locarno' was itself a product of a long process of demobilization that had started during the First World War, from the construction of transnational anti-war networks, to the desertion of soldiers, to the preparations of states for a post-war era. Demobilization was a pivot between war and peace. It involved leaving the war behind in a material and a cultural sense. However, demobilization also channelled the war experience into new directions, as former soldiers and civilians asserted their claims in the reconstruction of post-war societies and the international order. Many of these claims were embedded in broadly conceived notions of peace, embracing social reform and transnational cooperation.

The myriad pathways to demobilization are evident in an intersection between Norbert Elias and Erich Maria Remarque. Elias, following his injury at the battle of the Somme in 1916, had served in the infirmary at Breslau. At the end of the war he joined his unit's soldiers' council and was demobilized in February 1919. He had enrolled at university in 1918, which marked the beginning of his academic career. This successful demobilization may have accounted for his argument that the First World War did not fundamentally upset social etiquette. 'Strong regressive moments,' he argued in his discussion of table manners, 'are certainly not inconceivable either. It is well-known that, for example, the conditions of life in World War I automatically enforced a breakdown of some of the taboos of peacetime civilization. In the trenches officers and soldiers again ate when necessary with knives and hands. The threshold of repugnance shrank rather rapidly under the pressure of the inescapable situation.'[17] As Elias could observe all around him following demobilization, young German men did not eat with their hands and a knife. This was part of a wider argument that stressed the 'civilizing process' within modern European history.

However, the transition from trench habits to domestic habits, even in the realm of table manners, was uneven. Ernst, the returning veteran in Remarque's novel *The Road Back*, was invited to his wealthy uncle's house for a dinner party. After the food was served he ate it with his hands, without speaking. He was embarrassed that the guests saw him eat in this way, but he was also angry at the manner in which they gaped at him. In his view they were the ones who had benefited from the war, while he had run the risks. In this story manners reveal the gap in the moral economy of demobilization and the lack of empathy between civilians and soldiers. Ernst drifts for some time after the war, alienated within his own community, before finding a job as a teacher.[18] Accommodating the radically different experiences and expectations of war was at the core of the challenge of demobilization.

Demobilization, therefore, was a complex process. For the individual soldier the arrival home marked an important stage in the process. Soldiers compared the war to a task or piece of work that had been completed and now they could return home. In the case of the Allied armies, having saved their country, they now returned to the basis of the nation, their families.[19] 'Home via Victoria and then a taxi. Clean up and then to Brixton where I met Louie and the rest of the story doesn't concern anybody but our two sweet selves and does not require the aid of a diary. Therefore THE END!!!', so concluded George Riches' wartime diary on 12 November 1919.[20] On 13 March 1919 Blanche Duhamel received a telegram informing her that her husband Georges was due back on Sunday, three days later. 'I was expecting this departure,' she wrote, 'but now that I know you will be home, the hours seem very long to me. Ah! But how happy I am with the idea that on Sunday all three of us will eat lunch at ours, my dear love. Until Sunday, my love. I love you, I love you.'[21] Other soldiers were less fortunate. Family structures had come under great strain during the war and there was a surge of divorces, for example, in Germany after the war. In Saxony between 1920 and 1924 the percentage of divorces following less than five years of marriage rose from 27 per cent to 37 per cent, suggesting that a proportion of the rise was due to hasty marriages concluded during the conflict.[22] One survey of British files concluded that 16 per cent of marriages in which the man suffered from neurasthenia as a result of the war broke down due to the strains of living with and caring for a shell-shocked man.[23]

Men were also anxious to return to their jobs. Troops feared that late demobilization would mean they would lose out on employment opportunities. Governments sought to manage this in various ways, generally releasing older men and workers with key skills for the post-war economy. What seemed efficient from the point of view of government planners did not necessarily meet the criteria of fairness set by the soldiers. American soldiers petitioned congressmen and senators to accelerate demobilization. Riots at Folkestone in January 1919 amongst British troops being returned to France owed much to the sense of frustration at the slow pace of demobilization. In late 1920s Britain, 80 per cent of unemployed men between the ages of thirty and thirty-four were veterans.[24]

Work was interwoven with a broad concept of peace based on reconstructing communities and strengthening the nation. Putting veterans to work was partly a means of recivilizing them after years of war as well as doing the necessary work of rebuilding the economy. This emphasis on work had important consequences for the labour market, as women were fired from jobs reserved for returning soldiers. The restoration of gender relations had been a central aim of trade unions during the war. Unemployed soldiers were a threat to the social (and international) order, so one of the costs of restoring peace at the end of the war was the often unceremonious dismissal of women war workers. Even then there was a serious unemployment crisis across the belligerent countries. In part this was due to the end of military production. At the National Filling Factory in Manchester, 27 per cent of 22,701 men and 71 per cent of 17,721 women lost their jobs. In Munich, 52,000 people were unemployed in January 1919. In Germany, employment rates were nevertheless maintained by an inflationary boom that temporarily helped to stabilize the new Republic.[25]

The disappointments of demobilization gave rise to strikes and protests. Much of the discontent was directed inwards, towards domestic political opponents and social groups, including women, Jews, capitalists, and trade unionists. In the case of paramilitary groups, such as the Freikorps, the IRA, the Black and Tans, and others, the frustrations of demobilization led back to violent conflict. However, the vast majority of soldiers did not channel their frustrated expectations and military experiences back into violent conflict. Crucially, the vast majority of veterans looked forward to peace. They were not necessarily brutalized or traumatized by the war, nor did they always see the war as a futile waste. Their experiences of war were rechannelled into mobilization for peace.

Veterans' organizations represented a distinctive peace culture shaped by soldiers' experiences of the war, the rights of disabled veterans to welfare provisions, and the claims to political participation, based on military service, in post-war society. In many cases a number of interlocking claims were made. The grim experience of war, the suffering, and the grief for lost comrades created a public political space in which veterans campaigned against militarist values. Veterans were not pacifists, but they opposed the heroization of war and the elevation of martial values into an exemplary code for civil society. By challenging those values at home, they sought to prevent the easy resort to war. On the eve of Bastille Day in 1919 the *Journal des Mutilés* declared: 'The Feast of 14 July 1919 consecrates [France's] triumph. Let it be majestic, let it be dazzling, but let it at the same time sound the passing bell of military pomp and all its works.'[26] The German Franz Osterroth was born in 1900 and was called up in 1918. After the war he joined the SPD and became a member of the Reichsbanner, the centre-left veterans association founded in 1924. In his brief essay, 'Schreie eines Aufgewachten', penned in late 1918, he described the destruction of intimacy and human relationships wrought by the war. 'Entangled in the violence of animal-like anger,' he declared, 'man has murdered his brother, has destroyed his young body with grenades, has bored through him with life-eating bullets, and has suffocated his youthful hope in poisonous clouds.' He called on his fellow soldiers to fight a 'war of extermination' against weapons, so that war would never be repeated.[27]

Prisoners of war experienced demobilization in different ways to their uncaptured comrades. There were an estimated 8 million prisoners in Europe during the war and each one had a story to tell. In some ways they (and civilian internees) encountered enemy societies more directly than any other social group during the war. Their stories, however, reflected political and social pressures as well as personal experiences. When soldiers' and workers' councils in Germany issued pamphlets to returning Allied prisoners lamenting that they had not seen 'our arts, our sciences, our model cities, our theatres, our schools, our industries, our social institutions', they faced a hostile audience.[28] As death rates spiked amongst returning prisoners due to the influenza pandemic, scientists in France blamed the German authorities for deliberate neglect.[29] Some 300,000 Russian prisoners were detained in Germany, as the Weimar Republic used them to make good labour shortages, especially in the agricultural sector. The exploitation of Russian prisoners, according to the Soviet government, showed that the Weimar Republic represented the same aggressive capitalist elites that had dominated Wilhelmine Germany.[30]

Beneath the politics of prisoner return emotional ties shaped the response. Families in Germany considered the delay in returning prisoners as yet another Allied punishment. A small proportion of prisoners managed to transform their captivity into domesticity, setting up families or establishing themselves in local communities through work. About 20,000 Russians remained in Germany in this way – the German Nationalist People's Party, representing agrarian interests, was an active supporter of their right to stay. Most prisoners, however, just wanted to get home. 'Ahead of me I saw my home village,' recalled Dominik Richert of his return home in January 1919, 'which I had left in October 1913, so almost 5½ years ago. Suddenly tears came to my eyes. Now I was finally home. The one wish, which I had during the war and of whose fulfillment I had so often doubted, was now realised.'[31] Richert was one of those soldiers whose home was now in a new country, Alsace having been returned to France. Unlike thousands of other German speakers in the region he stayed, began farming, and got married in 1922.

Disabled veterans had rights to pensions, depending on the scale of their injuries. These pensions amounted to a significant proportion of governments' post-war budgets – about 7 per cent in the British case and 20 per cent in the German case. Welfare became a path to peace, as well as a matter of social justice. The Reichsbanner, according to its guidelines, 'will work for the economic and social reconstruction of Germany and will stand up vigorously for the interests of participants in the war and especially the war wounded and those left behind'.[32] The less money that was spent on armaments, the more could be devoted to helping those left injured or widowed by the war. The legacy of the moral economy of the war in peacetime militated against military spending. Veterans' associations were a visible presence in public spaces in Germany, France, Britain, and the United States after the war. They held frequent demonstrations and rallies to promote their interests and their wider political agenda. The Reichsbanner was founded by Otto Hörsing and other veterans who were members of the SPD, with the avowed purpose of defending the Weimar Republic. It was the largest veterans' association in the Republic.[33] From their perspective the Republic, by pursuing a foreign policy of reconciliation and cooperation, was the very institutionalization of a war fought for peace.

The Reichsbanner leaders also viewed their public presence as an act of foreign policy. It represented a different version of Germany that defended 'republican values, democratic institutions, and international cooperation'.[34] However, French veterans' associations found it difficult to distinguish between the different political persuasions amongst German veterans' associations. The problem lay in the presentation. 'Patriotic festivals,' noted one French account in October 1924, 'organised on the other side of the Rhine look remarkably like a return to arms. Nothing is missing except weapons. In uniform once again Fritz and Dudule, today as yesterday and despite their civilian status, goose-step past in front of the same generals and under the command of the same officers. Yes, truly these men are different from us.'[35] There were two international veterans' associations set up after the war, FIDAC and CIAMAC. Both were based on veterans' networks in Allied states. CIAMAC was more willing to allow German veterans' associations to join the network. By the mid-1920s some tentative steps had been taken to promote international cooperation between the veterans' associations in the Allied states and Germany. They found common ground in their wartime suffering and their rejection of militarism.

These groups sought to mobilize the sacrifice of their fallen comrades in the service of international cooperation, whereas radical nationalist groups claimed that the defence of victory (in the Allied states) or revenge (in

Germany) was the only suitable redemption of the war dead. During the war the sculptor Wilhelm Lehmbrück had refused to make an 'heroic figure' for the Kaiserberg Cemetery of Honour in his hometown of Duisburg. In 1922, three years after Lehmbrück had committed suicide, his sculpture, *Sitting Youth*, a study in human despair and loneliness, was placed in the cemetery. During the Third Reich there were plans to get rid of the sculpture, as it was considered to represent a degenerate view of war, but the work was destroyed in an air raid.[36] In August 1919 Alcide de Gasperi, on a visit to a mountain battlefield in the Alps, came across a mass of bones. He suggested that the bones should be gathered in a single ossuary, dedicated to fraternity and liberty. As a leading figure in Trentino politics he had an interest in promoting good relations with Austria. De Gasperi also used Catholic networks to establish bonds with politicians in former enemy states, such as Konrad Adenauer, whom he met in 1921 on a visit to Germany.[37] However, once Mussolini came to power public architecture in the Trentino celebrated Italy's victor. In Bolzano in 1928 the Fascist government constructed the Victory Gate, dedicated to the Italian dead of the war and bearing an inscription drawn from one of the more aggressive pages of Roman imperial history. Each state confronted the ambiguities of victory and defeat in its efforts to commemorate the war. On Armistice Day in Britain surviving soldiers often celebrated their own fortune and victory, the relatives of the fallen mourned, and disabled veterans protested at the state's neglect. Accommodating the different emotional and material legacies of the war in a single national narrative was a challenge that defied resolution.[38]

The international women's movement stressed the grief of mothers, wives, and children who had lost sons, husbands, and fathers during the war. Grief was not bound by borders. Ruptured family bonds provided a means of creating empathy between erstwhile enemies and mobilizing for international peace and reconciliation. The Women's International League for Peace and Freedom (WILPF) staged ceremonies that symbolized the restoration of empathetic bonds between nations. They organized summer schools, petitions, and demonstrations. Founded in 1915 following the Hague Conference, their first major post-war conference took place in Zurich in 1919, where the delegates denounced the Versailles Treaty. On the platform Lida Gustava Heymann, the German suffragette, presented the French representative, Jeanne Mélin, with roses and a stylized but resonant greeting: 'A German woman holds out a hand to a French woman, and says in the name of the German delegation: We hope that we women will throw a bridge from France to Germany and from Germany to France.' Mélin replied: 'I take the hand of my German sisters; with them we will work from now on, not against man, but for him.' In 1926 the WILPF staged a tree-planting ceremony in north-eastern France, where a French widow, Camille Prevet, and a German woman who had lost her son, Frida Perlen, jointly planted a tree.[39] These women represented a small, middle-class, internationalist elite, but their emphasis on the shared human experience of family resonated widely. At a conference in July 1922, Jane Addams, one of the founding members of the WILPF, argued that the grief of mothers, widows, and orphans was to be directed towards ensuring an end to war, rather than revenge. She recognized that the 'intense and sacred feeling' of the bereaved could be mobilized in either direction. Addams played an important role in the campaign that resulted in the League of Nations adopting the Declaration of Children's Rights in 1924. This campaign was led by the International Association for the Promotion of Child Welfare, based in Brussels, and supported by Save the Children, which had been established in 1919 in Britain to provide humanitarian relief in Europe.[40] Family relationships became a site on which peace could be built, both as the fundamental unit in a stable society and as a source for generating empathy across national borders.

Despite their long traditions of international cooperation and their common devotion to international labour regulation, the re-establishment of links between Allied and German socialists and trade unions proved challenging. Emile Vandervelde believed that post-war socialists never recaptured the commitment to internationalism or even the sensibilities for it that had characterized pre-war European socialism. The persistent differences between German and Allied socialists over the meaning of the war and the post-war crises over the Versailles Treaty, reparations, and the occupation of the Ruhr undermined rapprochement. It also reflected the increased presence of socialists in national government. 'Never has Socialism been stronger within each individual country,' Vandervelde commented to Ramsay MacDonald on 31 January 1920, 'but never has the International been so weak.'[41] MacDonald was to become Britain's first Labour prime minister in 1924.

The immediate difficulty in 1919 was the refusal of German trade unionists and socialists to confess to their sin of supporting the government for over four years of war and failing to condemn atrocities. Belgian socialists refused to attend the Berne Conference owing to the presence of their German counterparts. Léon Jouhaux countered German complaints about the detention of prisoners of war in France by pointing to the deportation of Belgian workers and the mistreatment of Russian civilians in Germany during the war. Between 28 July and 2 August 1919 trade unionists met in Amsterdam to re-establish the International Federation of Trade Unions. The Belgian representative, Martens, denounced German trade unions for failing in their international duty to Belgian workers and for tolerating atrocities and deportations. Before opening talks on institutional and labour matters he demanded a declaration of regret from the German delegation for these 'misdeeds'. The German delegation offered a staunch defence of its conduct and that of the German government. After arguing that war guilt could only be established following the opening of all states' archives, they denounced Allied atrocities, including the blockade and alleged Belgian civilian atrocities against German soldiers. Finally, they sought to dissociate themselves from Wilhelm II's regime by citing the revolutionary transformation in German politics: 'One commits an injustice, if one lays the deeds of our government upon us. We cannot accept responsibility for these deeds, we who have brought down this government.'[42] When Johannes Sassenbach, who had been active in international trade union circles before the war, admitted that the Belgian people had been mistreated, his own delegation disowned him and there was widespread anger in Germany. One of the outcomes of the Amsterdam meeting was the dominance of the Allied trade unions in the International Federation of Trade Unions, as William Appleton became the president and Jouhaux the vice-president.[43]

Between 1919 and 1924 European socialists and trade unions engaged in two parallel relationships. First, they cooperated on labour policy, particularly through conferences of the International Labour Organization and the work of the International Labour Office, headed by Albert Thomas. The International Federation of Trade Unions ensured that its affiliates nominated each state's 'worker representative' in the International Labour Organization. By 1924 there had been 142 ratifications of measures recommended by the International Labour Organization. However, key demands, such as the eight-hour day ratified by seven states, fared less well than measures on unemployment insurance (seventeen ratifications), limits to nightime work (thirteen ratifications), and the right of agricultural labourers to form associations (eleven ratifications). The Dutch trade unionist Edo Fimmen concluded in 1925 that the International Labour Organization was 'absolutely no use to the workers'. That said, its supporters saw a value in establishing the principle of international regulations and the practice of working together. For example, in March 1922 the International Labour Organization hosted a meeting, together with the International Red Cross and Health Section of the League of Nations, of disabled veterans from Europe and North America. Participants discussed medical practices and pension rights. This meeting was representative of 'a new spirit which cannot fail to give courage to those who believe in the permanence of the ideas upon which the League is founded', according to the publicity produced by the League of Nations Union.[44]

Second, trade unionists began to cooperate on international political issues. In 1920 the International Federation of Trade Unions organized a short boycott of Miklós Horthy's regime in Hungary and its members refused to send weapons to Poland. At the conference in London in November 1920 Carl Legien, just a month before his death, denounced reparations for destroying the health and welfare of the German working class. He distinguished between French socialists and the French government, whose brand of militarism 'is going further than the Prussian'.[45] This comparison only served to alienate their French counterparts, but Jouhaux and others were critics of French foreign policy. Before the occupation of the Ruhr, international socialists had inched away from their national war cultures and towards a practice and an ethos of international cooperation.

While socialists and trade unionists tried to pick up the threads of pre-war cooperation, the League of Nations inspired its own international movement. Before the end of the war the League of Nations Union in Britain, the League to Enforce Peace in the United States, and the French Association for the League of Nations had established personal networks. In some cases these built on pre-war networks of liberal internationalists, but they also recruited a new generations of activists. These included soldiers who had served in the war. For example, René Cassin, severely wounded during the war, became influential in League of Nations circles and the international veterans' movement. Others had been too young to serve in the war, but old enough, as Bertrand de Jouvenel, born in 1903, put it, 'to understand the horrors, to suffer losses in their families'. Robert Lange, whose brother Henry's death in 1918 inspired his internationalist sensibilities, became an influential figure in the French League of Nations movement.[46] In Britain the League of Nations Union had 60,000 members by the end of 1920, with important bastions of support amongst Liberals, churches, and the left. Robert Cecil, the leading League of Nations advocate in Britain, was a Conservative. Following the rejection of the Versailles Treaty, American internationalists pursued a lower-key campaign that sought to emphasize the effectiveness of the League rather than push for American entry.[47] In Germany the association of the League of Nations with the Versailles Treaty was so close that public support was extremely restricted. Matthias Erzberger, who had written in support of the idea of a League in 1918, had been assassinated in 1921. Erzberger was one of the founding members of the German League for the League of Nations (Liga für das Völkerbund), which included prominent socialists, liberals, and businessmen.

The post-war period witnessed an almost immediate revival of cultural and academic internationalism. Romain Rolland, who had spent the war in Switzerland trying to hold together what remained of the pre-war spirit of international intellectual exchange, issued the Declaration of the Independence of the Spirit on 16 March 1919. Signed by 145 intellectuals when it was published in *Humanité* on 26 June, and a further 900 from Spain, Italy, and Germany by August, the declaration called on the 'workers of the spirit' to deepen fraternal union. Rolland restated his case that intellectuals had contributed to the hatred that fuelled the war, which betrayed their duty to 'thought'. By prostituting their creativity for national, rather than universal, ends, they had corrupted the value of thought. In the act of demobilizing the mind, Rolland proposed the remobilization of intellectuals in the service of humanity, unconstrained by borders and the imaginary barriers of race and caste. The supporting cast of signatories included Georges Duhamel, Stefan Zweig, Benedetto Croce, Albert Einstein, Maxim Gorky, Bertrand Russell, and Rabindranath Tagore.[48] It was impossible to measure their impact on attitudes to international politics after 1918, but they contributed to widening the space for cultural reconciliation. The intellectual became a site for forming international bonds. This soon seeped into the ambit of the League of Nations. Leading pre-war internationalists, such as Paul Otlet and Henri La Fontaine, who had founded the International Institute of Bibliography and the Union of International Associations before the war, urged the League to promote international intellectual cooperation. The League established an International Committee on Intellectual Cooperation in 1922. Chaired by Henri Bergson, it included other luminaries such as Einstein, Marie Curie, and Hendrik Lorentz, a Dutch physicist and winner of the Nobel Prize. Einstein's inclusion, however, disguised the difficulties of reintegrating the German academic community into the international order. In 1924, for example, German universities were left out of an appeal to raise funding for universities in need, following objections from Bergson and the Polish historian Oscar Halecki. Of course, international academic and intellectual politics was not simply a matter of inclusion and exclusion by committees in the League of Nations. In 1924, for example, representatives from universities throughout Europe, North America, and Japan gathered at Königsberg for the bicentenary of Kant's birth. Speakers celebrated Kant as the educator of Prussia and mankind.[49]

There were also specific networks of cooperation between French and German intellectuals. Paul Desjardins used the surroundings of the Cistercian abbey in Pontigny, which he had purchased before the war, to host annual meetings between writers, artists, and academics from France and Germany. Ernst Robert Curtius, Heinrich Mann, and Edmond Vermeil were amongst the participants at the 'Décades de Pontigny' in the early 1920s. Vermeil, an increasingly influential French academic specialist on Germany, had been called up in 1914, been awarded the Croix de Guerre the following year, and worked in war propaganda in 1917 and 1918. After the war Vermeil worked in the French occupation zones in western Germany. By 1923 he argued that it was in France's interest to support democracy in the Weimar Republic rather than dismember it. On the occasion of Walther Rathenau's assassination he reflected on the division between 'the German organisational dream' and 'western individualism'. Neither was adequate in coping with the problems left by the war. The national formula had been exhausted, according to Vermeil, and in its place was required a 'European synthesis' integrating individualism and organization.[50]

Pierre Viénot, who had become addicted to cocaine after suffering severe injuries in July 1918, also attended meetings at Pontigny in 1922 and 1923. He had supported the Bloc National in the 1919 elections, but after spending some time in Germany on the staff of Paul Tirard (Chair of the Inter-Allied Rhineland Commission), Viénot considered that Raymond Poincaré's policies were stimulating German demagogic nationalism. He told Hubert Lyautey, his former commander in Morocco in the early 1920s, that the rise of Hitler in Bavaria or Léon Daudet, the French right-wing activist and journalist, in France, were symptoms of 'prolongation of the state of war after the material peace'.[51] Viénot established a connection with the Luxembourg steel magnate Émile Mayrisch, who supported the young Frenchman's proposal to set up a Franco-German Student Committee. Viénot's brand of internationalism favoured elites, whom he believed had the educational background to detach themselves from the passions of nationalism and to understand other cultures. Viénot was part of a broader discussion in France and Germany after 1923 that redefined security. A purely military conception of security missed the underlying politics of national identity. The practice of tolerance, rather than the elimination of national difference, was Viénot's solution to the European security dilemma.[52]

Viénot's project intersected with the interests of businessmen on both sides of the Rhine to cooperate in the restoration of western Europe's economy. Before the Ruhr occupation there had been several attempts to bridge the Franco-German political divide through economic deals, notably by Rathenau and Louis Loucheur in 1921. Even Hugo Stinnes, often marked out as the embodiment of the German commercial revanchism by French politicians, tried to broker deals with French partners that would have resolved the reparations question. Evidently there was a large dose of self-interest amongst businesses, which sought profits – though the same could be said of other groups from trade unionist to elite intellectual cooperation. Reconceiving self-interest – and the national interest – in terms of international cooperation offered the best opportunity to ensure that the practice of cooperation stuck. By the end of 1923 German industrialists in the Ruhr were prepared to cooperate with French heavy industry as a means of saving what they could from the economic distress caused by the occupation of the Ruhr. 'Peace could be achieved in Europe,' claimed the Mining Association in November 1923, 'only by linking together the respective major economic interests of France and Germany.'[53] By October 1926 industrialists from Germany, France, Belgium, and Luxembourg (including Émile Mayrisch) had founded the International Steel Cartel to fix rates of production in each country. Although the Cartel meetings were the occasion of fraught negotiations, these powerful figures had an interest in political stability and cooperation.[54]

The experience of the post-war years was essential in breaking down the war cultures that had existed in western Europe. The futility of Franco-German relations had become increasingly apparent after 1919. Important social groups in both countries supported international cooperation. They often arrived at the idea of international cooperation not through thinking about the specific problems of war and peace, but by thinking about their own interests. The process of cultural demobilization was not complete by the mid–1920s, but the balance had shifted sufficiently to provide a political basis for rapprochement.

The political basis for the Treaty of Locarno resulted from the rapid changes in electoral politics in France, Germany, and Britain between 1923 and 1926. Voters had many preoccupations, including inflation, the costs of stabilization, and unemployment, but improved international relations came to be seen as a condition of general economic revival. The centre-left bloc in France, the Cartel des Gauches, formed the government after the May 1924 elections, in which they had attacked Poincaré's foreign, financial, and religious policies. Governments remained unstable but the three premiers and foreign ministers between May 1924 and March 1926, Edouard Herriot, the long-time mayor of Lyons and admirer of German social reforms, Paul Painlevé, and Aristide Briand, favoured cooperation with Germany. French supporters of the League of Nations viewed the 1924 elections as a choice on foreign policy, 'war or peace', as Émile Borel put it. The umbrella group, the French Federation of Associations of the League of Nations, saw the ascent of Labour in Britain as evidence of a wider change in western European political attitudes.[55] In Britain there was a rapid turnover of governments between 1922 and 1924, which included the first Labour government, headed by Ramsay MacDonald, between January and November 1924. George V complained about the singing of the Marseillaise and the Red Flag at a Labour rally, but MacDonald's performance as prime minister and Foreign Secretary demonstrated that Labour would transform the political and social system rather than tear it down by revolution. Finally, in Germany, the SPD was out of government for four years between 1924 and 1928, but the right-wing DVP and DNVP came into government and provided the Republic with an expanded base in German politics, while the SPD could be relied upon to support Stresemann's foreign policy.

* * *

Locarno was not only a result of electoral coincidence in the three major western European powers. The shift in the positions of politicians, such as Stresemann, Briand, and Austen Chamberlain, all three of whom would win the Nobel Peace Prize over the coming years, showed how experience could change perception in international politics. Stresemann's wartime support for annexations and generally belligerent tone had long been abandoned, while Briand had begun to rethink the trajectory of French foreign policy in the early 1920s. The settlement in western Europe, reached in the Dawes Plan in 1924 and the Treaty of Locarno in 1925, sought to depoliticize reparations, stabilize borders, and integrate Germany into the international order.

An essential element of the new settlement was the participation of the United States. Woodrow Wilson's successors, Warren Harding (1921–3) and Calvin Coolidge (1923–9), concentrated on domestic politics. However, the United States had not withdrawn from world affairs. The immediate

post-war prescription of Herbert Hoover, John Foster Dulles, and others of
stimulating economic recovery as a means of securing political stability
remained an important strand in American thinking on foreign policy.
Charles Hughes was reluctant to waste American political capital on intervening in western Europe when there was little prospect of success. In
December 1922 at the meeting of the American Historical Association in
New Haven, Connecticut, Hughes condemned the prospective French
occupation of the Ruhr. He proposed a depoliticized reparations regime, in
which the payments were regulated by financial experts. In fact, instituting
such a regime was an inherently political act, as it would involve American
financial and technical participation and it would put an end to any possibility that French policy could use reparations to dismember Germany.[56] A
reconstruction of the international order based on economic and financial
power was bound to benefit the United States and Germany. This option
remained on the agenda throughout 1923, but as Hoover, the Commerce
Secretary and supporter of Hughes's proposal, noted in January 1923, 'this
experience [of occupation] will be disastrous to both Germany and France,
but it will at some stage offer an opportunity when the rule of reason can be
brought into play'.[57] By late 1923 Hughes was playing a more active role in
advocating a settlement of the Franco-German dispute. The conclusion of
a trade agreement between Germany and the United States in December
1923 signalled American sympathies in European politics.

Stresemann favoured American participation in any general settlement.
This distinguished his policy from that of Rathenau, who sought a direct
deal with the French government and businesses. Stresemann saw the
incorporation of the United States into the settlement as a means of
balancing French power while also magnifying German economic power.
American trade with and investment in Germany, Stresemann believed,
meant that the interests of these states were closely aligned. In addition, he
recognized the importance of German access to world markets and feared
that French policy tended towards a more closed European bloc.[58] Economic
interdependence was central to Stresemann's strategy in 1924 and 1925 as
he stressed the mutual benefits of political stability and economic recovery.
On Christmas Day 1923 he made the case to German voters in an article
entitled 'Is this Peace?' Germany's geopolitical position had made it over
the centuries the 'battleground of Europe'. The occupation of the Ruhr –
'the continuation of a war in time of peace against a defenceless and
disarmed people' – resulted from the anarchical international system.
Transforming the system to reflect economic interdependence was the only

means of achieving peace. 'The statesmen of many States,' he claimed with justification, 'are troubled by the economic problems that have resulted from the Versailles Treaty. Unemployment and financial stress are not a phenomenon confined to the economic life of Germany. The effort to find a solution leads from one international conference to another.'[59] Stresemann's last sentence struck a weary tone, but he was increasingly preaching to the converted, abroad even more so than at home

Even before MacDonald's appointment as prime minister in 1924, British leaders had become exasperated with Poincaré. Stanley Baldwin, who had become prime minister in May 1923 following Andrew Bonar Law's brief tenure, claimed he was going to 'try to settle Europe, though he failed and failed again'. By the time of the Conservative Party Conference in October, Baldwin, now frustrated, was turning away from Europe, towards imperial reform and tariff protection. Fighting a general election on tariff reform proved a disastrous political choice in 1923 for the Conservatives. Had Baldwin won the election it would likely have strengthened figures like Leo Amery, the heir to Joseph Chamberlain, who saw Britain's security and economic future in the empire rather than Europe. Defeat in 1923 also had consequences for the balance of the Conservative government elected in late 1924. Austen Chamberlain, an ardent Francophile and fluent in French, became Foreign Secretary. Unlike his father he appreciated the importance of stability in Europe for British security, arguing that Britain needed both to 'allay French fears' and to 'bring Germany back into the concert of Europe.'[60] Occasionally he threatened to resign over foreign policy, or as he put it in a letter to his sister in March 1925: 'If the servants get out of hand, it is Mrs Watson's business (I do not mean in her capacity as a plain cook where she is admirable, but as head of the household) to keep them in order. And yesterday I sent her a wire to say that either my apartment must be run as I wished and the meals served as I ordered them or I should leave her lodgings . . . I can't do my work if the other tenants are always making a racket and sticking their brooms and buckets just where I am bound to fall over them.'[61]

In between the two Conservative governments, MacDonald took charge of foreign policy. Since 1919 he had been a critic of the Versailles Treaty. He and his fellow Labour ministers considered Britain's economic problems to be the result of international upheaval. Moreover, they saw foreign policy as a field in which Labour had to prove their governing credentials. MacDonald also brought his distinctive view of international affairs, developed since 1914, to the negotiations. He was instinctively suspicious of great power politics, alliances, and military commitments. He feared that the continued exclusion of Germany from a settlement in western Europe would inevitably lead to a revival of that staple option in international politics, an alliance between Germany and Russia. This combination would overwhelm France and the remnants of the Versailles Treaty. His suspicions of great power politics led MacDonald to underplay French security concerns, in a way that Chamberlain did not. MacDonald sought a normative transformation as a path to safeguarding the security of European states. 'The one thing that matters,' he argued, 'is psychology.... Unless we change the qualities of our minds we had better arm to the teeth.'[62]

Across the Channel, by October 1923 Poincaré was coming to favour a collective agreement between the Allies and Germany to settle reparations. His change of mind owed more to routine political calculation than to a conversion to new thinking on international politics. He had confronted the limits of French military power in the Ruhr and his policy risked financial catastrophe at home, the irrevocable alienation of Britain, and isolation in the future against Germany.[63] Briand, who had been out of office for over three years, had also begun to reconsider the European constellation. According to one source, as early as 1922 he had mentioned the idea of a United States of Europe – but as a means for Europe to compete with the United States and Soviet Russia.[64] As Jules Laroche, a senior figure in the French Foreign Ministry, argued, the preponderance of French military power on the continent had ended up undermining French security. The presence of MacDonald in 10 Downing Street required French policy to adapt to the newly emerging international order, in which multilateral negotiations, economic integration, and treaty law shaped relations between the great powers.[65] This complex of ideas had remained an important strand of French foreign policy thinking since the war, but the failure of the Ruhr occupation, the collapsing value of the franc, and the victory of the Cartel des Gauches in May 1924 provided the political space for its exponents in government and the Ministry of Foreign Affairs to come to the fore. Herriot was more instinctively favourable to conciliation with Germany. Moreover, as he pointed out in his speech on becoming premier, the problems facing France would be easier to resolve if 'everywhere in the world one was finally able to breathe the pure atmosphere of peace'.[66] Having been a reforming mayor in Lyons, Herriot wanted a stable international order so that his government could devote more attention and resources to domestic affairs. The new government planned reductions in the size of the French Army and a reduction in the duration of conscription from eighteen months to one year.

Important differences between and within the four powers – the United States, Germany, Britain, and France – remained. There were different geopolitical scenarios, ranging from an Atlantic community to a European bloc to the integration of empire. There were different priorities concerning the reparations payments, war debts, the process of disarmament, the League of Nations, and the establishment of arbitration mechanisms. These issues provided the substance of international debate in the late 1920s, but governments discussed them in multilateral summits and the League of Nations. The settlement in 1924 and 1925 did not attempt to resolve all problems; rather it provided the mechanisms that could be adapted to different disputes.

This was also the age of the expert. The banking expert, supposed to be an impartial arbiter of international disputes, became a central figure in the financial settlement. The expert figure had already emerged in the new arenas of international politics, such as labour regulation and intellectual cooperation. Now the expert made the leap into the realm of conventional security issues in the reparations question and, later, disarmament.[67] The authority of the expert derived from their professional training and ethos, though their elevation was in itself a political move, designed to shield the negotiating process from the pressures of popular opinion. It also reflected the technical complexity of international relations, as the minutiae of issues such as bond schedules and comparative tax rates assumed fundamental importance. That said, the results of the negotiations in 1924 and 1925 were still subject to parliamentary approval.

The Dawes Plan on reparations resulted from the work of an expert committee, chaired by a banker from Chicago, Charles Dawes. The plan, completed on 9 April 1924, set out a new reparations system. Germany would pay a small amount of reparations in 1924 and 1925, before annual payments increased to 2.5 billion marks in 1929. The administration of payments was removed from the Reparations Commission, dominated by France, to a reparations agent. There was also international supervision of the German budget, an international loan to Germany, and the issue of bonds backed by the German railway system. The French government lost its capability to impose sanctions on Germany in the case of default, effectively ratifying the outcome of the occupation of the Ruhr, which had demonstrated the limited utility of these sanctions. By removing the threats and calibrating reparations payments against the recovery of the German economy, the Dawes Plan was part of a wider international economic settlement. Money flowed east from the United States to Europe, especially

Germany, which was supposed to stimulate economic recovery and enable European states to pay reparations and war debts. Although the United States government had no formal role in the Dawes Plan, the visit of Hughes to Germany in the summer of 1924 signalled the American support for the settlement. American money was also essential in underwriting the financial basis of the settlement.

The second feature of the settlements was the practice of multilateral diplomacy. The integration of Germany into the international order depended on the process as well as the outcome of negotiations. The Versailles Treaty had been denounced as a diktat owing to the absence of German participation. In the summer of 1924 Stresemann underlined the importance of German representation at the conference of London, which convened to discuss the amendments necessary to the Versailles Treaty due to the Dawes Plan. Stresemann warned the British and French governments that he would be unable to steer the Dawes Plan through the Reichstag unless the German government could send delegates to London. In particular the DNVP, whose members were reluctant to pay even the comparatively small amounts of reparations due under the Dawes Plan, criticized Stresemann's policy of cooperation on the grounds that Germany remained an outsider. The United States, which had an informal presence at the conference, insisted that a German delegation be invited. The legitimacy of the settlement required inclusive talks. American bankers used their financial leverage to ensure German participation. On 1 August, Ramsay MacDonald issued the requisite invitation.

The London Conference has often been portrayed as a victory for German over French foreign policy.[68] Isolated and financially weakened by the devaluation of the franc, Herriot made significant concessions in return for vague promises. The French government gave up its right to impose sanctions and agreed to withdraw its forces from the Ruhr within twelve months and to accelerate the evacuation of Allied forces from the Rhineland. The occupation of the Rhineland had been designed, at a minimum, to ensure German compliance with the treaty, but it now constituted a sign of lingering distrust between Germany and its former enemies. At the final session of the London Conference, MacDonald claimed: 'We are now offering the first really negotiated settlement since the war. This agreement may be regarded as the first peace treaty, because we sign it with a feeling that we have turned our backs on the terrible years of war and war mentality.'[69]

To chivvy Herriot along and provide cover in French domestic politics, MacDonald hinted at an agreement that would alleviate French security concerns. Establishing a multilateral security system was an important prize for French foreign policy, one that had remained an option since 1919. In the light of the failure of the Ruhr occupation, the policy of achieving security through unilateral military measures had already come to a dead end before the London Conference. From this perspective Herriot had given up little at London, although the hue and cry in Paris suggested otherwise. Equally, while the London Conference marked a gain for Stresemann's foreign policy, he also conceived of gains and losses in multi-lateral terms. While he valued American and British participation in the settlement as a means of countering French military power, Stresemann did not seek to divide France from Britain. That would simply recreate or even worsen the security dilemma in Europe. He redefined realpolitik as the achievement of security through European consensus rather than a zero-sum duel between the great powers. His success was in demonstrating the common interests of western Europe in German economic recovery. 'I am too much of a Realpolitiker,' he told the Reichstag on 6 March 1924, 'to expect that somebody would do something out of love for us or sympathy for Germany. No, this appeal by the experts [Dawes committee] is some-thing else, it is an appeal to the genuine reason of the businessmen of the world not to allow themselves to collapse by allowing Germany to collapse.'[70]

One of the outcomes of the London Conference was the Geneva Protocol. In June MacDonald had promised Herriot a deal on security issues. In September, following speeches from Herriot and MacDonald to the Assembly at Geneva, two committees, one chaired by Edvard Beneš, the other by Nicolas Politis, the Greek delegate, worked out a system of arbitra-tion and security. The protocol proposed a test of aggression. Any states in dispute would resort to arbitration. A state that launched war in contraven-tion of the arbitration process would be considered the aggressor, and would be subject to sanctions. While some French diplomats and soldiers had reservations about the value of the sanctions, Herriot and Briand saw the protocol as the basis for achieving a system of collective security, based on a clear legal test of aggression. The Geneva Protocol would also bind Britain into the system of collective security. At a meeting of military and civilian leaders in Paris in November 1924, Briand argued, in the face of objections from Foch and Pétain, that French security depended on the conclusion of a mutual security pact that included Germany. As German membership of the League of Nations was on the agenda, the Geneva Protocol represented a solution to the security dilemma, not just in western Europe but also in eastern Europe, where states would also be covered by the protocol.

However, the extensive commitments of the Geneva Protocol rendered it unacceptable to Britain. The security guarantee was so broad that it was difficult to see how it could be applied – the source of the scepticism of French generals towards the protocol. By November 1924 the Conservatives were back in power and even Chamberlain, the most Eurocentric-minded Conservative Foreign Secretary, baulked at the prospect of having to fight in defence of the Polish corridor. Yet while turning away from the Geneva Protocol Chamberlain worked towards a narrower British commitment to the continent concentrated on the territorial integrity of France, Germany, and Belgium.[71] At the same time Stresemann, with some encouragement from the British ambassador in Berlin, Lord D'Abernon, drafted a memorandum on a security pact that proposed the guarantee of the post-war territorial settlement in western Europe (including the demilitarization of the Rhineland), the use of arbitration to settle disputes in western and eastern Europe, and the renunciation of war as an instrument of policy. It was designed to appease French security fears, which Stresemann had identified as the most significant obstacle to a general settlement.

Moreover, Stresemann believed that by easing French security concerns, Germany's integration into the international order would be facilitated. Stresemann's memorandum presented the Republic as a force for peace in European politics. From the German perspective the proposal was linked to the evacuation of the Rhineland. In January French forces had not evacuated certain zones in the Rhineland as scheduled owing to the failure of Germany to comply with disarmament terms in the Versailles Treaty. The guarantee would secure Germany's borders as much as it would secure French borders – after all, as Stresemann pointed out in late 1925, it was Germany's territorial integrity that had been under threat most recently.[72] French policy continued to work towards a system of guarantees, despite the disappointment at Britain's rejection of the Geneva Protocol. 'We do not have an option,' Herriot told the Chamber of Deputies on 11 March 1925, 'we must engage with Britain and Germany in a durable system of security and such a regime can only be achieved under the juridical system of the League of Nations.'[73] Although Britain, France, and Germany, as ever, had different priorities, they agreed that a multilateral security treaty was required to complement the reparations settlement and stabilize western European politics.

Yet in making the proposal Stresemann also divided European peace and security into two spheres, in the east and west. While Stresemann was willing to accept as permanent the territorial settlement in the west, including the integration of Alsace into France, German leaders did not countenance a similar deal with Poland. Ulrich Rauscher, the German envoy in Poland since 1922, suggested concluding a treaty with Poland guaranteeing territorial integrity and then repudiating it in the future if the military balance changed and Germany could successfully fight a war against Poland. Stresemann rejected this option. In any case he considered war a catastrophe and only countenanced military action in defence of German territory. Instead his policy sought to keep the status of the borders in eastern Europe open so that they could be revised at a later date – one scenario contemplated border revision at a peace conference in the wake of a war between Poland and Soviet Russia.[74] This created difficulties for French security policy, which had developed its network of alliances in central Europe. However, German interests coincided with British reluctance to make extensive commitments. Faced with the choice between losing Britain's guarantee of the treaty and downgrading their relationship with Poland, Czechoslovakia, and Yugoslavia, French ministers chose the British option.[75] Stresemann, however, was also making a choice, privileging cooperation with Britain and France in western Europe over the option of developing a more overtly revisionist alliance with Soviet Russia, as favoured by Hans von Seeckt, the head of the Reichswehr, who had developed links with the Red Army since 1920.

Between Stresemann's initial proposal in February 1925 and the meeting of foreign ministers at Locarno in October 1925, the principal protagonists faced considerable pressures that might have derailed the negotiations. The election of Paul von Hindenburg as president of the Weimar Republic in April 1925 alarmed Stresemann, who feared that it represented the persistent strength of militarism in Germany to the wider world. French politicians were concerned, but financial problems were more pressing. Herriot had failed to bring the budget under control and his government fell in April, to be replaced by Painlevé, who appointed Briand as Foreign Minister. In Britain Chamberlain had to negotiate the challenges of those in the cabinet who repudiated any British commitment to European security. 'All our greatest wars have been fought,' he reminded the House of Commons on 24 March 1925, 'to prevent one great military power dominating Europe, and at the same time dominating the coasts of the Channel, and the ports of the Low Countries.' In addition to this geopolitical destiny Britain had obligations under the Versailles Treaty to prevent the remilitarization of the Rhineland.[76]

Stresemann arrived in Locarno on 2 October. The gathering of foreign ministers from seven different states – Germany, France, Britain, Belgium,

Italy, Poland, and Czechoslovakia – was important in itself. 'I hate having to go away again,' Chamberlain told his sister, 'but at any rate it marks progress that the time for a personal meeting has come.'[77] Especially in the age of mass politics, personal connections between political leaders constituted an important element of diplomatic practice. Meetings had not always been happy occasions – Lloyd George's assault on Clemenceau comes to mind – but at Locarno the foreign ministers formed good relations. 'Atmosphere of the negotiations: courteous, with noticeable and increasing cordiality,' noted Stresemann.[78] He formed a close bond with Briand, which endured until the German Foreign Minister's death in October 1929.

The major points of the Treaty of Locarno had been anticipated in negotiations since February. The preamble noted the 'desire for security and protection which animates the peoples upon whom fell the scourge of the war of 1914–1918' and ensuring peace 'in the area which has so frequently been the scene of European conflicts'. Germany, France, and Belgium renounced aggressive war against each other, set out to identify aggression, and benefited from the guarantee of Britain and Italy to uphold the treaty. In eastern Europe, Germany signed arbitration agreements with Poland and Czechoslovakia, though in a clear demonstration of the emerging hierarchies in the European order both foreign ministers from these countries were forced, as Stresemann put it, 'to sit in a side room, until we allowed them in'. Germany also agreed to enter the League of Nations, though Stresemann secured an interpretation of Article 16 which ensured that Germany would not have to participate in any military action against a state that violated the Covenant. This eased Soviet fears that Germany's entry into the League was the prelude to a capitalist war of aggression against Russia – and it also preserved the option of squeezing Poland between Germany and Russia. On the other hand Germany's entry into the League of Nations, Briand hoped, would secure its adherence to the peaceful conduct of international relations.[79]

The Treaty of Locarno and Germany's subsequent entry into the League of Nations the following year marked the reintegration of Germany into the European order. It came at a substantial price. In geopolitical terms Europe was divided between west and east. In the west the use of force had been renounced and guaranteed by the major powers. In eastern Europe the use of force remained an option in international politics. That said, the Weimar Republic was in no position to use military force to secure border changes in eastern Europe. Stresemann did not contemplate using military force in the foreseeable future. Even in the 1930s after large-scale German rearmament had begun, conservative military leaders and diplomats were sceptical about using military force to achieve foreign policy goals, fearing the preponderance of French military power. If the option of going to war was off the table, then the Treaty of Locarno was an opportunity to bind Germany into an international order based on arbitration. The treaty held out several advantages for Germany. In practical terms, now that their security concerns had been alleviated, French forces accelerated their withdrawal from the Rhineland. Germany also benefited from its participation as an equal member of the European order. While German nationalists' demands for a repudiation of the war guilt clause were rejected by Chamberlain and Briand, the text of the Locarno treaty ignored notions of guilt for the war and emphasized common suffering. This was part of a wider process of revision, which depicted the war as tragedy rather than crime. 'We have undertaken,' Stresemann declared in his final speech at the conference, 'the responsibility of initialling the treaties because we live in the faith that only by peaceful cooperation of States and peoples can that development be secured, which is nowhere more important than for that great civilized land of Europe, whose peoples have suffered so bitterly in the years that lie behind.' A European order was being remade at Locarno, both as a concept and as a geopolitical reality, with new hierarchies, divisions, rules, norms, and practices.

CONCLUSION

IN 1928 KONRAD ADENAUER welcomed Edouard Herriot, who had made his political career as mayor of Lyon, to Cologne. The meeting of the two mayors represented the spirit of Locarno. Adenauer's address placed the First World War and its lessons in this Locarno context:

> I am not a diplomat nor a government representative. I am a free man and a citizen and therefore I can speak openly. . . . We have experienced something terrible, we have seen what fate threatens humanity, if the means of advanced technology, if the masses of people of this time, if the capability for organization of this era is used for the purpose of destruction. The old Europe lies in ruins, we stand on the eve of a new era, a new epoch for humanity. This new era must be a better one, if the well-meaning people in all countries want it and work for it. Want it and work for it seriously, with perseverance, with devotion, not discouraged by ridicule and failure, in the certain conviction that the idea of peace and understanding must triumph, if Europe is not to come to an end. The ideas of the condemning of war, of disarmament, of reconciliation, of the peaceful resolution of conflicts, of gathering all peoples in a society of equal members are marching forwards, even if slowly. Many in Germany – and I belonged to them – had at first regarded these ideas full of doubt and scepticism, but we have let ourselves be convinced. The path is long and the destination is high. It will progress in stages, and setbacks will not fail to materialize. There will be heights and troughs to be overcome. But the destination, the understanding between peoples, the equality of all peoples, the welfare of all peoples can only be reached by this path.[1]

Twenty years later Adenauer spoke to the CDU conference at Recklinghausen in the British occupied zone in western Germany:

> If you think back to the time 45 years ago, and see clearly what Europe then was, when Germany was the most powerful land power in Europe, when France and Italy were great powers, when England was the greatest sea power, whose fleet was bigger than the next two largest navies taken together, when the United States was still a debtor country, when Austria-Hungary connected the whole Balkans, the Balkan states to western Europe, when in Russia the Asiatic side did not rule exclusively, but the west Russian part had influence – and if you then look at today's Europe, then you can recognise the shattering decline.[2]

Two decades earlier Adenauer could hardly have imagined the depth of the setbacks that the spirit of Locarno had suffered. He himself had been dismissed as mayor of Cologne after the Nazi seizure of power, had been arrested twice, including once following the failed July 1944 assassination attempt on Hitler, and witnessed the defeat of Germany and the destruction of Cologne.

Adenauer was hardly politically naive. In the late 1920s he and millions of others had good reasons for their confidence in the future peace and stability of the international order. Power politics had been tamed. In addition to the international treaties, the League of Nations was functioning, promoting international cooperation in a wide range of fields, such as health and social reform. Internationalist ideals flourished with the expansion of transnational civil society, from veterans' associations to humanitarian organizations. Trade and finance bound the major economies of the world more closely together. Perhaps most important of all, attitudes towards war had changed. In 1928 the Kellogg–Briand pact, signed by forty-seven countries, renounced war as an instrument of national policy. Between the grand declarations of principle and the daily work of international cooperation, peace seemed assured for the future.

Yet despite these achievements, the international orders negotiated at Locarno and Washington certainly proved fleeting, even by the standards of rapidly changing international politics. Comparisons with other peace settlements may offer some cautious instruction. The Vienna order, established in 1815, lasted for over thirty years until collapsing under the weight of revolution and great power war between 1848 and 1854. The post-Second World War settlement lasted for over four decades until the collapse of the

Soviet Union and the revolutionary process of decolonization took place without triggering a great power war. By contrast, within four years of the Treaty of Locarno the Great Depression undermined the fragile economic and financial basis of peace. Two years later, in 1931, Japanese forces seized northern Manchuria from China and established a puppet state, Manchukuo. The militarization of politics in East Asia coincided with the frustration of disarmament negotiations at Geneva. Even before Hitler came to power in Germany in 1933, the bonds of peace had frayed during the Great Depression that had taken hold of Europe and North America. Committed to waging war in Europe, Hitler's aggressive revisionism sundered what remained of peace throughout the 1930s. In August 1936 De Gasperi, now in internal exile in Italy and writing for the Vatican press, dismissed the League of Nations, which spawned 'an endless flow of formulae to save the world that tomorrow will vanish like soap bubbles'.[3] Fourteen years after the conclusion of the Treaty of Locarno, Hitler initiated a general European war.

The transient period of stability in international politics suggests bad peace settlements and enduring bitter legacies that connect the two world wars. The narrative of a second Thirty Years War, as destructive of life and social fabric as the conflict between 1618 and 1648, has a powerful attraction. Significant issues at stake – the question of German power, the emergence of nation states in place of empires, making race the basis of political communities – remained important in both wars.[4] The modes of violence in the Second World War had their roots in the First World War – racist imperialism, genocide, violence against civilians, the militarization of civilian life, atrocities against prisoners of war, the murderous culling of the weak, sick, and marginal in the name of strengthening the nation and the race. Framing the First World War as part of a broader epoch of violence, the first act in a Thirty Years' War underlines the violent legacies and the unresolved conflicts of this period. The legacies of the First World War had been contained in the 1920s, before emerging in radicalized forms in the 1930s as the Great Depression, the militarization of international affairs, and the rise of Nazism in Germany destroyed the Locarno and Washington treaties.

Yet Adenauer was neither politically naive in 1928 nor in 1948. His address greeting Herriot represented the common sense of the day. It was possible to halt the dynamics of violence.[5] The narrative of a second Thirty Years' War is useful as a means of identifying the connections between the two conflicts, but it also marginalizes other legacies, more peaceful legacies, of the First World War. These endured beyond 1945 into the international order dominated by the Cold War and decolonization. The Cold War undoubtedly changed the dynamics of making peace in Europe after 1945. Soviet military power now extended as far as Berlin, rather than stalling outside Warzaw, while the American commitment to security was military and political, as well as financial and economic. Yet in other respects peacemaking after 1945 drew on ideas, institutions, and personnel shaped by the First World War and its aftermath. The reconstruction of the European economy with American aid, the integration of national economies in Europe, the promotion of transnational civil society, tying the Federal Republic of Germany into the Atlantic world, and the support for democracy in western Europe echoed the ambitions of a previous generation of politicians. The founders of the United Nations learned from the flaws of the League of Nations and drew on the expertise of League officials.[6]

After the Second World War, Jean Monnet contemptuously referred to the League of Nations as a 'telephone exchange', but his experiences of inter-Allied cooperation and the League's secretariat shaped his approach to remaking the international order after 1945. It was not so much that people could reach into their desks and draw out ready-made plans, but rather that their experiences and ideas had been shaped by two global conflicts and the peacemaking attempts of the 1920s.[7] These personal continuities were important in shaping peace. Many of the leaders associated with remaking western Europe after 1945, such as Adenauer, De Gasperi, and Monnet, had been politically active during the First World War. Their ideas and assumptions about the international order had been formed during that conflict, though refined through later experiences and worked out in different conditions. Others like Harold Macmillan had actually fought in the First World War, an experience that led them to view international politics as the primary preoccupation of statesmen.[8] After 1945 old ideas were adapted to new circumstances, and projects conceived in the 1920s were pushed towards more radical solutions. Just as the violent inheritance from the First World War was inscribed in the biographies of men like Hitler, Mussolini, and Horthy, the more peaceful legacies were evident in the careers of Adenauer, De Gasperi, and Monnet. None of these three men had fought, but veterans of the First World War also played a role in rebuilding Europe and the international order after 1945. From René Cassin, who was influential in framing the Universal Declaration of Human Rights, to Macmillan, who became British prime minister in 1957 and managed withdrawal from empire as well as Britain's first application to join the Common Market, veterans of the First World War continued to explore different ways of creating and sustaining peace.[9]

The collapse of Europe as the arbiter of world politics, which had begun during the long First World War, was completed after the Second World War. The two global conflicts shaped the process of decolonization, arguably the most significant transformation in global politics in the twentieth century. The 'winds of change', to use Macmillan's catchy phrase, had been gathering force for some time. 'In the twentieth century, and especially since the ending of the war,' Macmillan told his white (and indifferent) audience at Cape Town in 1960, 'the processes which gave birth to the nation states of Europe have been repeated all over the world.'[10] Granted, as Macmillan made clear, the process intensified dramatically after 1945, while the expectations of anti-colonial nationalists were much greater. The declaration of independence issued by Ho Chi Minh in 1945 was a much more radical document than the call for autonomy he had presented in Paris in June 1919. He also made the declaration of independence in Ba Dinh Square in Hanoi, whereas in 1919 he had been a supplicant in Paris.[11] Anti-colonial leaders after 1945 were less willing to compromise, to accept lengthy and uncertain pathways to independence. That said, figures like Ho Chi Minh and Syngman Rhee, the president of South Korea, had started their political careers before and during the First World War, deployed Wilsonian rhetoric, and learned from the bitter disappointments of Paris in 1919.

The First World War was the crucible of twentieth-century visions of peace. Ideas formulated in the war and then experimented with in the 1920s were bequeathed to a later post–1945 generation of peacemakers. If politics as diverse as Nazi racism, European integration, and decolonization have their roots in the First World War, then the legacy of the war was open-ended and contingent on future developments. Judgements on the legacies of the war have inevitably varied with chronological and geographical perspectives. Indeed, in 1925 European integration and decolonization were more likely future developments than genocidal war. Judgements about the war owe much to the author's own historical perspective. Speaking in Oxford in 1929 the French historian Élie Halévy concluded that 'happy as may have been, happy as I think have been on the whole, the European results of the war', further challenges and difficulties remained. He did not mean that the war had been a positive experience, rather that its legacies tended towards the benign and peaceful. Yet when the lecture was published in *The Era of Tyrannies* in 1938, the year after Halévy's death, the introductory preface by his friend and pacifist, Celestin Bouglé, was markedly more pessimistic.[12] The First World War was the seminal event of the twentieth century, but concentrating on its evidently catastrophic consequences neglects the ways in which the experience of the war redefined what peace meant and how it might be forged.

Peace as a political process rather than simply ending a state of war was not, of course, an invention of the First World War. At Vienna, and arguably before that in Münster and Osnabrück in 1648 and Utrecht in 1713, European states established institutions, conventions, and norms that provided a process for the maintenance of peace and the adjustment of future conflicts of interest. What had changed was the increasingly expansive conception of peace, the prescriptions in the treaties, the unspoken diplomatic assumptions, and the dense network of international and domestic institutions designed to sustain peace. It now embraced a wider set of claims, from welfare to constitutional reform, from minority rights to national self-determination, from internationalist associations to diplomatic institutions, such as summits and the League of Nations. These ideas were neither the product of a Wilsonian moment nor of the Bolshevik revolution. Wilson and Lenin promoted certain ideas about making peace, which resonated because they adopted ideas already widely discussed and responded to the experience of the war. Granted ideas and proposals for these forms of international cooperation had proliferated in the nineteenth century, but they had often been marginal to the practice of peace, which remained embedded in elite cabinet politics. Offering a defence of Realpolitik in the mid–1920s, the German historian Friedrich Meinicke argued that 'war ... became more intensive than earlier, but peace also became more intensive and complete'. He was referring to Bismarck's wars and peace, but his judgement reflected more recent experiences.[13] The experiences of the First World War, the mobilization of societies, and the moral issues proclaimed to be at stake in that conflict changed what peace meant. The totalizing logic of the war, according to which each side ratcheted up its efforts and aims in response to their opponents' mobilization, expanded expectations of peace.

As peace was interwoven with war, from the moment war was declared it became increasingly difficult to make peace. Governments eschewed a compromise settlement in favour of their vision of peace. The traditional distinctions between war and peace were blurred. War became an instrument to achieve peace, peace a future condition that justified the war. This relationship between violence and peace continued after the formal end to the major conflicts at Brest-Litovsk, in the armistices, and at Paris in 1918 and 1919. Ending this violence led to a patchwork of settlements in international, imperial, and domestic politics. From welfare regimes to international borders the compromises involved in these settlements disappointed individual expectations of peace. These compromises marked a return to less exalted visions of peace, cast in prose, rather than declaimed in poetry. Peace required daily affirmation and this thicker understanding of peace was reflected in the revival of older internationalist groups, such as the labour movement, and the establishment of new ones, such as the international veterans' associations. These varieties of internationalism presented themselves as part of the peacemaking process. At the diplomatic level the treaties of Washington and Locarno represented the culmination of peacemaking after 1918. These treaties were important not only for their resolution of conflicts, but in creating diplomatic institutions and practices that enabled further negotiation. Because the great powers had bought into these treaties, they created confidence that peace would continue.

Working in Berlin as a journalist in the early 1920s, Joseph Roth described a shelter for the homeless on Fröbelsstrasse in Berlin. Here he met a former Russian army officer, Bersin, who knew nothing of the fate of his family, lost in the tumult of war and revolution. 'History has performed a somersault,' Roth concluded, 'and a lieutenant colonel winds up in the shelter for homeless people.'[14] Finding an equilibrium after this historical somersault was a significant, and often painful, achievement. The settlements in the mid–1920s did not mark an end to history, but they pointed towards the peaceful evolution of international politics. Revision and change could be accommodated within the flexible international orders worked out at Washington and Locarno. The League of Nations was functioning and broadening its membership, Soviet Russia was gradually brought into the European order, and the United States was playing a central role in the key pivotal areas of world politics, East Asia and western Europe. With the enormously important exception of the Chinese revolution, the two other great national revolutions of this period, in Mexico and Russia, had been settled, and no longer provided an occasion for foreign intervention. Reforms in the British empire channelled the post-war imperial crisis and created scope for further constitutional change.

In the 1930s as another general war became increasingly likely, peace remained a powerful dream. Even Hitler, determined on war, resorted to the essential vocabulary of peace in his speeches and presentation to the German and international public, twisting the conventional meaning of words. By late 1938 Hitler concluded, in angry reaction to crowds cheering him as the Peace Chancellor, that he had spoken too much of peace since becoming Chancellor and needed now to 'make it clear [to the German people] that there are things which must be achieved by force if peaceful means fail'.[15] Hitler's deceptive peace talk was itself a legacy of the war to end all wars. Visions of peace provided powerful sources to legitimize political action in twentieth-century history. These visions shaped the political context, in which international, imperial, and domestic politics were conducted. Since the First World War, with its catastrophic experience of violence, peace had become a repository of demands and expectations for a better future. War and peace, as experience and expectation, condition and aim, dystopia and utopia, were interwoven over the course of the twentieth century – but gradually, despite the brutal legacies of violence bequeathed by the First World War and replenished in other conflicts over the course of the past one hundred years, peace has survived, even flourished.

NOTES

Chapter 1 Introduction

1. Elihu Root, 'The Outlook for International Law', *Proceedings of the American Society of International Law at its Annual Meeting (1907–1917)*, vol. 9 (28–30 December 1915), p. 10; see also Stephen Wertheim, 'The League that Wasn't: American Designs for a Legalist-Sanctionist League of Nations and the Intellectual Origins of International Organization, 1914–1920', *Diplomatic History*, 35, 5 (2011), p. 818.
2. Root, 'Outlook', p. 10.
3. Norman Naimark, *Fires of Hatred: Ethnic Cleansing in Twentieth-Century Europe* (Cambridge, MA, 2001).
4. George Kennan, *The Decline of Bismarck's European Order: Franco-Russian Relations, 1875–1890* (Princeton, NJ, 1981); John Lewis Gaddis, *George F. Kennan: An American Life* (London, 2011), pp. 618–21.
5. Fritz Fischer, *Germany's Aims in the First World War* (London, 1967).
6. David Blackbourn and Geoff Eley, *The Peculiarities of German History: Bourgeois Society and Politics in Nineteenth-Century Germany* (Oxford, 1984).
7. Mark Mazower, *Dark Continent: Europe's Twentieth Century* (London, 1998); Tony Judt, *Post-War: A History of Europe since 1945* (London, 2006); Niall Ferguson, *The War of the World: History's Age of Hatred* (London, 2006); see also the conclusion, Niall Ferguson, *The Pity of War* (London, 1998), pp. 460–2.
8. Ian Kershaw, 'War and Political Violence in Twentieth-Century Europe', *Contemporary European History*, 14, 1 (2005), p. 112; Mark Mazower, 'Violence and the State in the Twentieth Century', *American Historical Review*, 107, 4 (2002), p. 1,175.
9. Alan Kramer, *The Dynamics of Destruction: Culture and Mass Killing in the First World War* (Oxford, 2007).
10. Uğur Ümit Üngör, *The Making of Modern Turkey: Nation and State in Eastern Anatolia, 1913–1950* (Oxford, 2011); Naimark, *Fires of Hatred*; John Horne and Alan Kramer, *German Atrocities, 1914: A History of Denial* (New Haven, CT, 2001); Peter Holquist, *Making War, Forging Revolution: Russia's Continuum of Crisis, 1914–1921* (Cambridge, MA, 2002); David Stevenson, *1914–1918: The History of the First World War* (London, 2005); Roger Chickering and Stig Förster, *Great War, Total War: Combat and Mobilization on the Western Front* (Cambridge, 2000).
11. Georges Duhamel, *Civilization, 1914–1917* (New York, 1919), pp. 86–7.
12. John Horne, *Labour at War: France and Britain, 1914–1918* (Oxford, 1991); Annie Kriegel, *Histoire du mouvement ouvrier français, 1914–1920* (Paris, 1964); Peter Jackson, 'French Security and a British "Continental Commitment" after the First World War: A Reassessment', *English Historical Review*, 126, 519 (2011), pp. 345–85; Adrian Gregory, *The Last Great War: British Society and the First World War* (Cambridge, 2008); Annette Becker, *Oubliés de la grande guerre. Humanitaires et cultures de guerre 1914–1918. Populations occupées, déportés civils, prisonniers de guerre* (Paris, 1998); Frank Ninkovich, *The Wilsonian Century: US Foreign Policy since 1900* (Chicago, IL, 2001); Alan Dawley, *Changing the World: American Progressives in War and Revolution* (Princeton, NJ,

2003); Erez Manela, *The Wilsonian Moment: Self-Determination and the International Origins of Anti-Colonial Nationalism* (Oxford, 2007); Peter Yearwood, *Guarantee of Peace: The League of Nations in British Policy, 1914–1925* (Oxford, 2009); Patrick Cohrs, *The Unfinished Peace after World War I: America, Britain, and the Stabilization of Europe, 1919–1932* (Cambridge, 2006); Zara Steiner, *The Lights that Failed: European International History, 1919–1933* (Oxford, 2005).

13. Pierre Allan and Alexis Keller, eds, *What Is a Just Peace?* (Oxford, 2006); Michael Howard, *The Invention of Peace: Reflections on War and International Order* (London, 2001); see the special issue of *Contemporary European History*, 17, 3 (2008), edited by Holger Nehring and Helge Pharo, *A Peaceful Europe? Negotiating Peace in the Twentieth Century*.

14. 'A Million Homes after the War', report by the Parliamentary Committee of the Trade Union Congress (London, 1917).

15. 'Le basi morali della democrazia', speech, Brussels, 20 November 1948: http://www.degasperi.net/ scheda_fonti.php?id_obj=5921&obj_type=f2&parent_cat=

16. Cited in Ute Daniel, *The War from Within: German Working-Class Women in the First World War* (Oxford, 1997), p. 152.

17. Hew Strachan, *The First World War: To Arms* (Oxford, 2001), pp. 1,114–39.

18. 'Are We Pro-German?', 18 December 1915, in Arthur Schlesinger, ed., *Walter Lippmann: Early Writings* (New York, 1970), pp. 23–5.

19. 'Deutschland unter der europäischen Weltmächten', in Wolfgang Mommsen and Gangolf Hübinger, eds, *Max Weber. Zur Politik im Weltkrieg. Schriften und Reden 1914–1918*, series 1, vol. 15 (Tübingen, 1984), p. 180.

20. 'Perpetual Peace' (1795), in Immanuel Kant, *Perpetual Peace*, in Mary J. Gregor, ed., *Political Philosophy* (Cambridge, 1996), p. 327; David Bell, *The First Total War: Napoleon's Europe and the Birth of Warfare As We Know It* (Boston, MA, 2007).

21. 'International Government', 1916, in Don H. Lawrence and Daniel J. Levy, eds, *Bernard Shaw: The Complete Prefaces* (London, 1995), vol. 2, pp. 265–6.

22. H. G. Wells, *The War that Will End War* (New York, 1914), pp. 14, 97–100.

23. Robert Gerwarth and John Horne, eds, *War in Peace: Paramilitary Violence after the Great War* (Oxford, 2012).

24. 'The World in Revolution', 5 May 1917, in Schlesinger, ed., *Lippmann*, p. 77.

Chapter 2 The Failure of Great Power Peace, 1911–1914

1. 'Mr Lloyd George on British Prestige', *The Times*, 22 July 1911, p. 7.

2. Cited in Marilyn Lake and Henry Reynolds, *Drawing the Global Colour Line: White Men's Countries and the International Challenge of Racial Equality* (Cambridge, 2008), p. 258; also see Mansour Bonakdarian, 'Negotiating Universal Values and Cultural and National Parameters at the First Universal Races Congress', *Radical History Review*, 92 (spring 2005), pp. 118–32.

3. John P. Campbell, 'Taft, Roosevelt, and the Arbitration Treaties of 1911', *Journal of American History*, 53, 2 (1966), pp. 279–98.

4. Diary entry for 11 June 1913, in Anthony Philips, ed., *Sergey Prokofiev: Diaries, 1907–1914, Prodigious Youth* (Ithaca, NY, 2006), pp. 436–7.

5. Alan Knight, *The Mexican Revolution*, 2 vols (London, 1986); Paolo Riguzzi, 'From Globalisation to Revolution? The Porfirian Political Economy: An Essay on Issues and Interpretations', *Journal of Latin American Studies*, 41 (2009), pp. 347–68; Myrna Santiago, 'Culture Clash: Foreign Oil and Indigenous People in Northern Veracruz, Mexico, 1900–1921', *Journal of American History* (June 2012), pp. 62–73.

6. Xu Guoqi, *China and the Great War* (Cambridge, 2005), pp. 24–48; Richard Phillips, *China since 1911* (Basingstoke, 1996), pp. 8–13.

7. Hintze to Bethmann Hollweg, 7 November 1911, 3 January 1913, in Johannes Hürter, ed., *Paul von Hintze, Marineoffizier, Diplomat, Staatssekretär. Dokumente einer Karriere zwischen Militär und Politik, 1903–1918* (Munich, 1998), pp. 303–5, 311–12.

8. John Milton Cooper, 'Making a Case for Wilson', in John Milton Cooper, ed., *Reconsidering Woodrow Wilson: Progressivism, Internationalism, War, and Peace* (Baltimore, MD, 2008), p. 13.

9. 'An Address in New York to the National League of Commission Merchants', 11 January 1912, *Papers of Woodrow Wilson* (hereafter *PWW*), vol. 24 (Princeton, NJ, 1977), p. 40.

10. 'A Statement on the Pending Chinese Loan', 18 March 1913, *PWW*, vol. 27, p. 193.

11. Diary entry by Josephus Daniels, 18 April 1913, *PWW*, vol. 27, pp. 328–30.

12. Diary entry by Josephus Daniels, 4 April 1913, *PWW*, vol. 27, pp. 261–2.

13. Peter Calvert, *The Mexican Revolution, 1910–1914: The Diplomacy of Anglo-American Conflict* (Cambridge, 1968), p. 119.

14. Thomas J. Knock, *To End all Wars: Woodrow Wilson and the Quest for a New World Order* (New York, 1992), pp. 25-8.
15. 'The Causes Behind the Mexican Revolution', *The New York Times*, 27 April 1914, in John Newsinger, ed., *John Reed: Shaking the World: Revolutionary Journalism* (London, 1998), p. 55.
16. Bernhard Rosenberger, *Zeitungen als Kriegstreiber? Die Rolle der Presse im Vorfeld des Ersten Weltkrieges* (Cologne, 1998), pp. 188-201.
17. Friedrich Kiessling, *Gegen den 'großen Krieg'. Entspannung in den internationalen Beziehungen 1911-1914* (Munich, 2002), p. 38.
18. Pichon in Turin, 19 May 1916, in Maurice Barrès, *Mes cahiers 1896-1923* (Paris, 1963), p. 761.
19. 'Erlaß nach Konstantinopel, Rom', 31 July 1911, in L. Bittner and H. Uebersberger, *Österreich Ungarns Aussenpolitik von der bosnischen Krise 1908 bis zum Kriegsausbruch 1914* (hereafter *ÖUA*), 9 vols (Vienna, 1930), vol. 3, pp. 289-90.
20. Jules Cambon to Selvès, 24 September 1911, *Documents diplomatiques français* (hereafter *DDF*), 14 vols (Paris, 1930-55), 2nd series, vol. 14, pp. 503-4.
21. 'Beginn des Kampfs um Tripolis', *Neue Freie Presse*, 25 September 1911, p. 1.
22. Aldo Mola, *Giolitti. Lo statisto della nuova Italia* (Milan, 2003), pp. 327-30.
23. Cited in Timothy Childs, *Italo-Turkish Diplomacy and the War over Libya, 1911-1912* (Leiden, 1990), p. 39.
24. Avarna to San Giuliano, 28 July 1911, and Promemoria di San Giuliano, 28 July 1911, in Aldo Mola and Aldo Ricci, eds, *Giovanni Giolitti. Al Governo, in Parlamento, nel Carteggio*, 3 vols (Foggia, 2007), vol. 3, pp. 201-7.
25. Avarna to San Giuliano, 28 July 1911, in ibid., p. 201.
26. C. J. Lowe and F. Marzari, *Italian Foreign Policy, 1870-1940* (London, 1978), pp. 82-90, 96-110; Childs, *Italo-Turkish Diplomacy*, p. 7.
27. Ibid., pp. 37-8.
28. 'Grave situazione a Tripoli', *La Stampa*, 23 September 1911, p. 1; 'La volontà d'agire', *La Stampa*, 28 September 1911, p. 1.
29. Telegram from Pallavicini, Constantinople, 10 August 1911, *ÖUA*, vol. 3, p. 304; Childs, *Italo-Turkish Diplomacy*, p. 44.
30. Hasan Kayali, *Arabs and Young Turks: Ottomanism, Arabism, and Islamism in the Ottoman Empire, 1908-1918* (Berkeley, CA, 1997); Feroz Ahmad, *The Young Turks: The Committee of Union and Progress in Turkish Politics, 1908-1914* (Oxford, 1969).
31. E. Grant Duff to Grey, 24 June 1911, TNA FO 421/273, p. 8.
32. Churchill to Nicolson, 26 September 1911, *British Documents on the Origins of the War* (hereafter *BD*), 11 vols (London, 1926-38), vol. 9, p. 278.
33. Rodd to Drummond, 14 September 1911, Grey Papers, TNA FO 800/64, fo. 169.
34. Childs, *Italo-Turkish Diplomacy*, pp. 60-70.
35. Freiherr von Jenisch to Kiderlen, 28 September 1911, in Johannes Lepsius, Albrecht Mendelsohn Bartholdy, and Friedrich Thimme, eds, *Die Grosse Politik der europäischen Kabinette 1871-1914*, 40 vols (Berlin, 1922-27), vol. 30, part I, pp. 65-7.
36. 'Bericht aus London', 29 September 1911, *ÖUA*, vol. 3, p. 366.
37. 'The Attack on Turkey', *Manchester Guardian*, 29 September 1911, p. 8.
38. Diary entry for 29 September 1911 in Fritz Fellner, ed., *Schicksalsjahre Österreichs 1908-1918. Das politische Tagebuch Josef Redlichs*, 2 vols (Graz, 1953), vol. 1, p. 100.
39. 'The War', *The Times*, 5 October 1911, p. 7.
40. Klaus Wilsberg, *'Terrible ami - ennemi aimable'. Kooperation und Konflikt in den deutsch-französischen Beziehungen 1911-1914* (Bonn, 1998), pp. 32-3.
41. John Gooch, ' "The Moment to Act has Arrived": Italy's Libyan War, 1911-1912', in Peter Dennis and Jeffrey Grey, eds, *1911: Preliminary Moves* (Canberra, 2012), pp. 184-209.
42. Ibid., pp. 195-7.
43. Andrew Mango, *Atatürk* (London, 1999), pp. 101-8.
44. David Herrmann, 'The Paralysis of Italian Strategy in the Italian-Turkish War, 1911-1912', *English Historical Review*, 104, 411 (1989), pp. 332-56.
45. 'Il conflitto entra nella nuova fase. La pace e la guerra a fondo', *La Stampa*, 6 November 1911, p. 2.
46. Andrea Ungari, 'The Italian Airforce from the Eve of the Libyan Conflict to the First World War', *War in History*, 17, 4 (2010), p. 404.
47. Erik Jan Zürcher, *Turkey: A Modern History* (London, 1997), pp. 107-8.
48. Charles Killinger, *Gaetano Salvemini: A Biography* (Westport, CT, 2002).
49. Douglas Forsyth, *The Crisis of Liberal Italy: Monetary and Financial Policy, 1914-1922* (Cambridge, 1993), pp. 3-6.

50. Christopher Clark, *The Sleepwalkers: How Europe Went to War in 1914* (London, 2012), pp. 251–7.
51. Mark Biondich, *The Balkans: Revolution, War, and Political Violence since 1878* (Oxford, 2011), pp. 31, 67–70.
52. Cited in R. J. Crampton, *Bulgaria* (Oxford, 2007), p. 192.
53. Cited in Uğur Ümit Üngör, *The Making of Modern Turkey: Nation and State in Eastern Anatolia, 1913–1950* (Oxford, 2011), p. 44.
54. Cited in Syed Tanvir Wasti, 'The 1912–13 Balkan Wars and the Siege of Edirne', *Middle Eastern Studies*, 40, 4 (2004), pp. 62, 68.
55. Justin McCarthy, *Death and Exile: The Ethnic Cleansing of Ottoman Muslims, 1821–1922* (Princeton, NJ, 1995), pp. 135–64.
56. Üngör, *Making of Modern Turkey*, p. 45; Eyal Ginio, 'Mobilizing the Ottoman Nation during the Balkan Wars (1912–1913): Awakening from Ottoman Dreams', *War in History*, 12, 2 (2005), pp. 156–77.
57. Cited in Mustafa Aksakal, *The Ottoman Road to War in 1914: The Ottoman Empire and the First World War* (Cambridge, 2008), p. 21.
58. M. Sukru Honioglu, *Ataturk: An Intellectual Biography* (Princeton, NJ, 2011), pp. 49–53.
59. Crampton, *Bulgaria*, pp. 200–5; David Mackenzie, *Serbs and Russians* (New York, 1996), pp. 43, 181–3.
60. Norbert Elias, *The Civilizing Process*, trans. and ed. Eric Dunning, Johan Goudsblom and Stephen Mennell (London, 2000), p. 161.
61. 'Montenegrin Warriors', *Penny Illustrated Press*, October 1912.
62. Cited in Florian Keisinger, *Unzivilisierte Krieg im zivilisierten Europa? Die Balkankriege und die öffentliche Meinung in Deutschland, England und Irland 1876–1913* (Paderborn, 2008), p. 124.
63. Ibid., p. 103.
64. Cited in Joshua Rubenstein, *Leon Trotsky: A Revolutionary's Life* (New Haven, CT, 2011), p. 61.
65. 'L'ordre sanglant', *L'Humanité*, 22 April 1912, p. 1; also reprinted in Jean-Pierre Rioux, ed., *Jean Jaurès. Rallumer tous les soleils* (Paris, 2006), pp. 845–7.
66. 'L'odeur de ce charnier', *La Dépêche de Toulouse*, 25 November 1912, in Rioux, ed., *Jaurès*, pp. 877–80.
67. Dzovinar Kévonian, 'L'enquête, le délit, la preuve: les "atrocités" balkaniques de 1912–1913 à l'épreuve du dossier de la guerre', *Le mouvement social*, 222 (2008), pp. 13–40.
68. Paul Miliukov, *Political Memoirs, 1905–1917* (Ann Arbor, MI, 1967), p. 203.
69. Ibid., p. 201.
70. Nicholas Murray Butler, 'Preface', *Report of the International Commission to Report into the Causes and Conduct of the Balkan Wars* (Washington, DC, 1914).
71. Miliukov, *Memoirs*, pp. 203–4.
72. Keisinger, *Unzivilisierte Kriege*, pp. 153–70.
73. Cited in Mark Biondich, *Stjepan Radic, the Croat Peasant Party, and the Politics of Mass Mobilization, 1904–1928* (Toronto, 2000), p. 117; Elena Tonezzer, 'Alcide De Gasperi and Trentino', *Modern Italy*, 14, 4 (2009), p. 404.
74. Robert Musil, *The Man without Qualities*, trans. Sophie Wilkins and Burton Pike (London, 1997), p. 215.
75. Cited in Hugo Hantsch, *Leopold Graf Berchtold*, 2 vols (Graz, 1963), vol. 2, p. 518.
76. Keisinger, *Unzivilisierte Kriege*, p. 154.
77. Jagow to Kiderlen, 12 December 1911, in Ernst Jäckh, *Kiderlen-Wächter der Staatsmann und Mensch. Briefwechsel und Nachlass*, 2 vols (Stuttgart, 1924), vol. 2, p. 167.
78. 'Notes on Letters Contained in My Boxes', Haldane Papers, NLS, MS 5923, fo. 5.
79. Rodd to Grey, 4 September 1911, Grey Papers, TNA FO 800/64, fo. 168.
80. Laroche to Selves, 20 September 1911; J. Cambon to Caillaux, 24 September 1911; Boppe to Selves, 26 September 1911, *DDF*, 2nd series, vol. 14, pp. 90–2, 503–5, 519–22.
81. Abraham Ascher, *P. A. Stolypin: The Search for Stability in Late Imperial Russia* (Stanford, CA, 2001).
82. Childs, *Italo-Turkish Diplomacy*, pp. 108–12.
83. Cited in Ralf Forsbach, *Alfred von Kiderlen-Wächter (1852–1912)*, 2 vols (Göttingen, 1997), vol. 2, p. 683.
84. A. Nekludoff, *Diplomatic Reminiscences before and during the World War, 1911–1917* (London, 1920), p. 45; Clark, *Sleepwalkers*, pp. 259–62.
85. 'Bericht aus St Petersburg', 4 November 1912; telegram aus St Petersburg, 5 November 1912, *ÖUA*, vol. 4, pp. 771, 779.
86. 'Konzept', 30 October 1912, in *ÖUA*, vol. 4, pp. 727–9.
87. Kiessling, *Gegen den 'Großen Krieg'*, pp. 42–50.
88. Jäckh, *Kiderlen-Wächter*, pp. 191–2.

89. Cited in Jost Dülffer, Martin Kröger, and Rolf-Harald Wippich, *Vermiedene Kriege. Deeskalation von Konflikten der Grossmächte zwischen Krimkrieg und Erstem Weltkrieg (1865–1914)* (Munich, 1997), p. 654.
90. Cited in Kiessling, *Gegen den 'Großen Krieg'*, p. 153.
91. 'Konzept, Egon Freiherr von Berger von Waldenegg', 11 November 1912, *ÖUA*, vol. 4, pp. 841–2.
92. Günther Kronenbitter, *'Krieg im Frieden'. Die Führung der k.u.k. Armee und die Grossmachtpolitik Österreich-Ungarns 1906–1914* (Munich, 2003), pp. 414–24; David Stevenson, *Armaments and the Coming of War: Europe, 1904–1914* (Oxford, 2000), pp. 266–71; MacDonald, *United Government*, pp. 188–90; R. J. Crampton, *Hollow Détente: Anglo-German Relations in the Balkans, 1911–1914* (London, 1980), pp. 83–96.
93. Hantsch, *Berchtold*, pp. 499–503.
94. Richard S. Wortman, *Scenarios of Power: Myth and Ceremony in the Russian Monarchy*, 2 vols (Princeton, NJ, 2000), vol. 2, pp. 464–78.
95. MacDonald, *United Government*; Roderic Dawson, 'The Armenian Crisis, 1912–1914', *American Historical Review*, 53, 3 (1948), pp. 481–505; William Mulligan, ' "We Can't Be more Russian than the Russians": British Policy in the Liman von Sanders Crisis, 1913–1914', *Diplomacy & Statecraft*, 17, 2 (2006), pp. 261–82.
96. 'Journal einer Sonderkonferenz', 21 February 1914, in Otto Hoetzsch, ed., *Die internationalen Beziehungen im Zeitalter des Imperialismus*, 1st series, 5 vols (Berlin, 1931), vol. 1, pp. 283–96; Sean McMeekin, *The Russian Origins of the First World War* (Cambridge, MA, 2011), pp. 31–40.

Chapter 3 The End of Civilization, 1914

1. Hugo Hantsch, *Leopold Graf Berchtold* (Graz, 1963), p. 521.
2. Nicolson to Bunsen, 19 January 1914, Nicolson Papers, TNA FO 800/372, fos 81–3.
3. Stephen Schröder, *Die englisch-russische Marinekonvention. Das deutsche Reich und die Flottenverhandlungen der Tripelentente am Vorabend des Ersten Weltkrieges* (Göttingen, 2006); Stefan Schmidt, *Frankreichs Außenpolitik in der Julikrise. Ein Beitrag zur Geschichte des Ausbruches des Ersten Weltkrieges* (Munich, 2009).
4. Grey to Goschen, 24 June 1914, TNA FO 425/380, fos 119–20.
5. Stephen Schröder, ' "Ausgedehnte Spionage": Benno von Sieberts geheime Zusammenarbeit mit dem Auswärtigen Amt (1909–1926)', *Militärgeschichtliche Zeitschrift*, 64 (2005), pp. 425–63.
6. Schröder, *Marinekonvention*, p. 674.
7. Diary entry for 28 June 1914, in Michael Epkenhans, ed., *Albert Hopman. Das ereignisreiche Leben eines "Wilhelminers". Tagebücher, Briefe, Aufzeichnungen 1901–1920* (Munich, 2004), p. 380.
8. Diary entry for 28 June 1914, in Fritz Fellner, ed., *Schicksalsjahre Österreichs 1908–1918. Das politische Tagebuch Josef Redlichs* (Graz, 1953), vol. 1, p. 235.
9. Christopher Clark, *The Sleepwalkers: How Europe Went to War in 1914* (London, 2012), pp. 367–553.
10. Hantsch, *Berchtold*, p. 558; G. Kronenbitter, *'Krieg im Frieden', Die Führung der k.u.k. Armee und die Grossmachtpolitik Österreich-Ungarns 1906–1914* (Munich, 2003), p. 462; Bernd Wegner, 'Hitler, der zweite Weltkrieg, und die Choreographie des Untergangs', *Geschichte und Gesellschaft*, 26 (2000), pp. 493–518.
11. Hantsch, *Berchtold*, pp. 560–4.
12. Clark, *Sleepwalkers*, pp. 379–87.
13. Hantsch, *Berchtold*, pp. 562–9.
14. Cited in Fritz Fellner, 'Die Mission Hoyos', in Wilhelm Alff, ed., *Deutschlands Sonderung von Europa 1862–1945* (Frankfurt, 1984), pp. 312–13.
15. William Mulligan, *The Origins of the First World War* (Cambridge, 2010), p. 212.
16. Falkenhayn to Moltke, 5 July 1914, in Imanuel Geiss, ed., *July 1914: The Outbreak of the First World War: Selected Documents* (London, 1967), pp. 76–7.
17. The minutes are reprinted in Miklós Komjáthy, ed., *Protokolle des Gemeinsamen Ministerrates der Österreichisch-Ungarischen Monarchie (1914–1918)* (Budapest, 1966), pp. 141–8.
18. Hantsch, *Berchtold*, pp. 588–9.
19. Berchtold to Giesl, 20 July 1914, in Geiss, ed., *July*, pp. 142–6.
20. Andrej Mitrovic, *Serbia's Great War, 1914–1918* (London, 2007), p. 42.
21. Hantsch, *Berchtold*, p. 605.
22. Ibid., pp. 590–7.
23. Serbian government to Giesl, Belgrade, 25 July 1914, in Geiss, ed., *July 1914*, pp. 201–4; Mitrovic, *Serbia's Great War*, pp. 41–51; Richard Hall, 'Serbia', in Holger Herwig and Richard F. Hamilton, eds, *The Origins of the First World War* (Cambridge, 2003), pp. 105–11.

24. Cited in Dominic Lieven, *Russia and the Origins of the First World War* (London, 1983), pp. 141–4.

25. Cited in Schmidt, *Frankreichs Außenpolitik*, p. 103.

26. Ibid., p. 87.

27. Günther Kronenbitter, 'Austria-Hungary', in Richard Hamilton and Holger Herwig, eds, *War Planning 1914* (Cambridge, 2010), pp. 45–7.

28. Bruce Menning, 'War Planning and Initial Operations in the Russian Context', in Hamilton and Herwig, eds, *War Planning*, pp. 115–26; David Alan Rich, 'Russia', in Herwig and Hamilton, eds, *Origins*, pp. 221–5.

29. Ulrich Trumpener, 'War Premeditated? German Intelligence Operations in July 1914', *Central European History*, 9, 1 (1976), pp. 58–85.

30. Egmont Zechlin, *Krieg und Kriegsrisiko. Zur deutschen Politik im Ersten Weltkrieg* (Düsseldorf, 1979), pp. 64–89; Annika Mombauer, *Helmuth von Moltke and the Origins of the First World War* (Cambridge, 2001).

31. Diary entry, 19 November 1916, in J. M. McEwen, ed., *The Riddell Diaries 1908–1923* (London, 1986), p. 173.

32. 'Conversation échangée à la fin de juillet et le 1er août 1914 entre l'Ambassadeur de l'Allemagne et le docteur Hugenschmidt et communiquée à M de Berckheim par ce dernier', Jules Cambon Papers, MAE PA-AP 43/62, fo. 3.

33. Rathenau to Emil Rathenau, 4 August 1914, in Alexander Jager, Clemens Picht, and Ernst Schulin, eds, *Walther Rathenau. Briefe*, 2 vols (Düsseldorf, 2006), vol. 2, p. 1,349.

34. Thomas Weber, *Hitler's First War* (Oxford, 2010), pp. 11–17.

35. Jeffrey Verhey, *The Spirit of 1914: Militarism, Myth and Mobilization in Germany* (Cambridge, 2000), p. 39.

36. Cited in Guido Müller, *Europäische Gesellschaftsbeziehungen nach dem Erstem Weltkrieg. Das Deutsch-Französische Studienkomitee und der Europäische Kulturbund* (Munich, 2005), p. 94.

37. Cited in Adrian Gregory, *The Last Great War: British Society and the First World War* (Cambridge, 2008), pp. 33–4.

38. Simon Ball, *The Guardsmen: Harold Macmillan, Three Friends, and the World they Made* (London, 2004), p. 30.

39. Max Lotz to Rathenau, 24 August 1914, in *Rathenau. Briefe*, vol. 2, p. 1,319.

40. Colleen M. Moore, 'Demonstrations and Lamentations: Urban and Rural Responses to War in Russia in 1914', *Historian* (2009), pp. 565–8.

41. Sven Oliver Müller, *Die Nation als Waffe und Vorstellung. Nationalismus in Deutschland und Großbritannien im Ersten Weltkrieg* (Göttingen, 2002), p. 65.

42. Dominik Richert, *Beste Gelegenheit zum Sterben. Meine Erlebnisse im Kriege 1914–1918*, ed. Angelika Tramitz and Bernd Ulrich (Munich, 1989), pp. 15–16.

43. Cited in Geoffrey Hodges, 'Military Labour in East Africa and its Impact on Kenya', in Melvin Page, ed., *Africa and the First World War* (Basingstoke, 1987), pp. 141–2.

44. Maurice Barrès, *Mes cahiers, 1896–1923* (Paris, 1963), p. 739.

45. Jean-Jacques Becker, *The Great War and the French People* (Leamington Spa, 1985), pp. 16–21.

46. Georges Duhamel, *Civilization, 1914–1917* (New York, 1919), p. 106.

47. Müller, *Nation*, pp. 62–3, 74.

48. Diary entry for 18 July 1914 (OS), in Anthony Philips, ed., *Sergey Prokofiev: Diaries, 1907–1914, Prodigious Youth* (Ithaca, NY, 2006), p. 717.

49. Joshua Sanborn, *Drafting the Russian Nation: Military Conscription, Total War, and Mass Politics, 1905–1925* (DeKalb, IL, 2003), pp. 23–31.

50. Aaron Retish, *Russia's Peasants in Revolution and Civil War: Citizenship, Identity, and the Creation of the Soviet State, 1914–1922* (Cambridge, 2008), pp. 23–7.

51. Diary entry, 4 August 1914, in Georges Dethan, ed., *Gabriel Hanotaux. Carnets (1907–1925)* (Paris, 1982), p. 111.

52. Retish, *Russia's Peasants*, p. 27.

53. Alex Watson, *Enduring the Great War: Combat, Morale and Collapse in the German and British Armies, 1914–1918* (Cambridge, 2008), pp. 45–54; Bart Ziino, 'Enlistment and Non-Enlistment in Wartime Australia: Responses to the 1916 Call to Arms Appeal', *Australian Historical Studies* 41, 2 (2010), pp. 217–32.

54. Emily Pyle, 'Peasant Strategies for Obtaining State Aid: A Study of Petitions during World War I', *Russian History/Histoire russe*, 24, 1–2 (1997), pp. 41–64.

55. Maureen Healy, *Vienna and the Fall of the Habsburg Empire: Total War and Everyday Life in World War I* (Cambridge, 2004), p. 194.

56. Ute Daniel, *The War from Within: German Working-Class Women in the First World War* (Oxford, 1997), pp. 24–31, 176–81.

57. Susan Pedersen, *Family Dependence and the Origins of the Welfare State: Britain and France, 1914–1945* (Cambridge, 1993), pp. 107–19.

58. Mitrovic, *Serbia*, p. 70.

59. Janet Polasky, *The Democratic Socialism of Emile Vandervelde: Between Reform and Revolution* (Oxford, 1995), p. 113; Sophie de Schaepdrjiver, *La Belgique et la Première Guerre Mondiale* (Frankfurt, 2004), pp. 60–6.

60. Keith Jeffery, *Ireland and the Great War* (Cambridge, 2000), pp. 10–16; Senia Pašeta, 'Thomas Kettle: An Irish Soldier in the Army of Europe?', in Adrian Gregory and Senia Pašeta, eds, *Ireland and the Great War: A War to Unite Us All?* (Manchester, 2002), p. 10; Joseph Finnan, *John Redmond and Irish Unity, 1912–1918* (Syracuse, NY, 2004), pp. 78–84.

61. Nigel Keohane, *The Party of Patriotism: The Conservative Party and the First World War* (Farnham, 2010), pp. 71–2; Finnan, *Redmond*, pp. 81–7; Cecil to Grey, 11 September 1914, Cecil Papers, British Library, Add MS 51073, fos 69–73.

62. Cited in Sanborn, *Drafting*, p. 75.

63. Wladzimierz Borodziej, *Geschichte Polens im 20. Jahrhundert* (Munich, 2010), p. 76.

64. Cited in Zbynek Zeman, *The Break-Up of the Habsburg Empire* (London, 1964), p. 44.

65. Andrea Orzoff, *Battle for the Castle: The Myth of Czechoslovakia in Europe, 1914–1948* (Oxford, 2009), pp. 37–9.

66. Rathenau to Bethmann Hollweg, 6 August 1914, *Rathenau. Briefe*, vol. 2, p. 1,354.

67. Wolfgang Kruse, *Krieg und nationale Integration. Eine Neuinterpretation des sozialdemokratischen Burgfriedensschlusses 1914/15* (Essen, 1993), pp. 76–89; Müller, *Nation*, pp. 292–4.

68. Bernard Georges and Denise Tintant, *Léon Jouhaux. Cinquante ans de syndicalisme*, 2 vols (Paris, 1962), vol. 1, pp. 144–58; John Horne, *Labour at War: France and Britain, 1914–1918* (Oxford, 1991), pp. 43–7, 60–1; Annie Kriegel, *Histoire du mouvement ouvrier français, 1914–1920*, 2 vols (Paris, 1964), vol. 1, pp. 60–74.

69. David Marquand, *Ramsay MacDonald* (London, 1977).

70. Paul Bridgen, *The Labour Party and the Politics of War and Peace, 1900–1924* (Woodbridge, 2009), pp. 46–60; Royden Harrison, 'The War Emergency Workers' National Committee 1914–1920', in Asa Briggs, ed., *Essays in Labour History, 1886–1923* (London, 1971), pp. 211–15.

71. Cited in Melissa Stockdale, *Paul Miliukov and the Quest for a Liberal Russia, 1880–1918* (Ithaca, NY, 1996), p. 218.

72. Cited in Heinz Hagenlücke, *Deutsche Vaterlandspartei. Die nationale Rechte am Ende des Kaiserreichs* (Düsseldorf, 1997), p. 50.

73. Orzoff, *Castle*, p. 37.

74. Cited in Michael Laffan, *The Resurrection of Ireland: The Sinn Fein Party, 1916–1923* (Cambridge, 1999), p. 35.

75. 'The Tasks of Revolutionary Social Democracy in the European War', 6 September 1914, in V. I. Lenin, *Collected Works*, 45 vols (London, 1964), vol. 21, pp. 15–19.

76. Karl Christian Führer, *Carl Legien 1861–1920. Ein Gewerkschafter im Kampf um 'möglichst gutes Leben' für alle Arbeiter* (Essen, 2009), pp. 307–9.

77. Stefan Zweig, *Journey into the Past*, translated by Anthea Bell (London, 2009), pp. 66–8.

78. Bill Albert, *South America and the First World War: The Impact of the War on Brazil, Argentina, Peru, and Chile* (Cambridge, 1988), pp. 1–4, 41–53.

79. Cited in David Patterson, *The Search for Negotiated Peace: Women's Activism and Citizen Diplomacy in World War I* (London, 2008), p. 21.

80. Phillips Payson O'Brien, 'The American Press, Public, and the Reaction to the Outbreak of the First World War', *Diplomatic History*, 378, 3 (2013), pp. 446–75.

81. John A. Moses, 'An Australian Empire Patriot and the Great War: Professor Sir Archibald T. Strong (1876–1930)', *Australian Journal of Politics and History*, 53, 3 (2007), pp. 411–16.

82. Bill Nasson, 'War Opinion in South Africa, 1914', *Journal of Imperial and Commonwealth History*, 23, 2 (1995), pp. 248–76.

83. 'Indian Conferences: Ideals of the Congress, 29 December 1914', *Times of India*, 29 December 1914, p. 9.

84. 'The Loyalty of the Madras', *Times of India*, 23 November 1914, p. 9.

85. Albert E. Altman and Harold Z. Schiffrin, 'Sun Yat-Sen and the Japanese, 1914–16', *Modern Asian Studies*, 6, 4 (1972), p. 389.

86. Frederick Dickinson, *War and National Reinvention: Japan in the Great War, 1914–1919* (Cambridge, MA, 1999), p. 56.

87. Robert Dubarle to Charlotte, 9 November 1914, in Jacques Benoist-Méchin, ed., *Ce qui demeure. Lettres de soldats tombés au champ d'honneur 1914–1918* (Paris, 2000), p. 137.

88. Barrès, *Cahiers*, p. 741.

89. Cited in Annika Mombauer, 'The Battle of the Marne: Myths and Reality of Germany's "Fateful Battle"', *Historian*, 68, 4 (200) p. 758.

90. Alexander Solzhenitsyn, *August 1914*, trans. Misha Glenny (London, 1972), p. 300.

91. William Fuller, 'The Eastern Front', in Jay Winter, Geoffrey Parker, and Mary Habeck, eds, *The Great War and the Twentieth Century* (New Haven, CT, 2000), p. 40; Dennis Showalter, *Tannenberg: Clash of Empires* (Hamden, CT, 1991).

92. John R. Schindler, 'Disaster on the Drina: The Austro-Hungarian Army in Serbia, 1914', *War in History*, 9, 2 (2002), pp. 159–95.

93. Xu Guoqi, *China and the Great War* (Cambridge, 2005), p. 90.

94. Duhamel, *Civilization*, pp. 18–19.

95. Cited in Bernd Ulrich, *Die Augenzeugen. Deutsche Feldpostbriefe in Kriegs- und Nachkriegszeit 1914–1933* (Essen, 1997), p. 60.

96. Cited in Michael Finn, ' "Local Heroes": War News and the Construction of "Community" in Britain, 1914–1918', *Historical Research*, 83, 221 (2010), p. 527.

97. Heather Jones, *Violence against Prisoners of War in the First World War: Britain, France, and Germany, 1914–1918* (Cambridge, 2010), pp. 45–57; Annette Becker, *Oubliés de la grande guerre. Humanitaires et cultures de guerre 1914–1918. Populations occupées, déportés civils, prisonniers de guerre* (Paris, 1998), p. 99.

98. Joseph Roth, *The Radetzky March*, trans. Michael Hofmann (London, 2002), pp. 348–9.

99. John Horne and Alan Kramer, *German Atrocities 1914: A History of Denial* (New Haven, CT, 2001), pp. 1–78.

100. Laura Engelstein, ' "Belgium of Our Own": The Sack of Russian Kalisz, August 1914', *Kritika*, 10, 3 (2009), pp. 441–73.

101. Horne and Kramer, *Atrocities*, pp. 78–82.

102. Jonathan Gumz, *The Resurrection and Collapse of Empire in Habsburg Serbia, 1914–1918* (Cambridge, 2009), pp. 52–7.

103. Peter Gattrell, *A Whole Empire Walking: Refugees in Russia during World War I* (Bloomington, IN, 1999), p. 17.

104. Annette Becker, *Les cicatrices rouges 14–18. France et Belgique occupées* (Paris, 2010), p. 56.

105. H. G. Wells, *The War that Will End War* (New York, 1914), pp. 12–14, 97–100.

106. Georges-Henri Soutou, *L'or et le sang. Les buts de guerre économiques de la Première Guerre Mondiale* (Paris, 1989), p. 114.

107. Paléologue to Delcassé, 22 November 1914, documents 561 and 563, in Jean Claude Montant, ed., *Documents diplomatiques français 1914, 3 août–31 décembre* (Paris, 1999), pp. 550–3.

108. Wells, *War*, pp. 52–9.

109. 'The Lord Mayor's Banquet', *The Scotsman*, 10 November 1914, p. 7.

110. Hubertus Jahn, *Patriotic Culture in Russia during World War I* (Ithaca, NY, 1995), pp. 36–8.

111. Nicoletta Gullace, 'Sexual Violence and Family Honor: British Propaganda and International Law during the First World War', *American Historical Review*, 102, 3 (1997), pp. 714–47.

112. 'La force qui s'use et celle qui ne s'use pas', 4 November 1914; 'Discours en séance publique de l'Académie des sciences morales et publiques', 12 December 1914, in Henri Bergson, *Mélanges* (Paris, 1977), pp. 1,107–14.

113. Gumz, *Resurrection*, pp. 45–7.

114. Horne and Kramer, *Atrocities*, pp. 238–47.

115. Jürgen von Ungern-Sternberg and Wolfgang von Ungern-Sternburg, *Der Aufruf 'An die Kulturwelt'. Das Manifest der 93 und die Anfänge der Kriegspropaganda im Ersten Weltkrieg* (Stuttgart, 1996), pp. 144–5.

116. Christian Koller, *'Von wilden aller Rassen niedergemetzelt'. Die Diskussion um die Verwendung von Kolonialtruppen in Europa zwischen Rassismus, Kolonial- und Militärpolitik (1914–1930)* (Stuttgart, 2001), pp. 85–95, 103–19; Daniel Steinbach, 'Challenging European Colonial Supremacy: The Internment of "Enemy Aliens" in British and German East Africa during the First World War', in James Kitchen, Alisa Miller and Laura Rowe, eds, *Other Combatants, Other Fronts: Competing Histories of the First World War* (Newcastle, 2011), pp. 153–72.

117. Karl Lamprecht, *Zur neuen Lage* (Leipzig, 1914).

118. Diary entry, 4 September 1914, in Kurt Riezler, *Tagebücher, Aufsätze, Dokumente*, ed. Karl Dietrich Erdmann, intro. Holger Afflerbach (Göttingen, 2008), p. 205.

119. http://germanhistorydocs.ghi-dc.org/docpage.cfm?docpage_id=1811 is a translation of this key document; Soutou, *L'or*, pp. 24–31; Fritz Fischer, *Germany's Aims in the First World War* (London, 1967), pp. 100–11; Niall Ferguson, *The Pity of War* (London, 1998), pp. 168–73.

120. Hantsch, *Berchtold*, pp. 699–701.

121. 'Au dessus de la melée', in Jean Albertini, ed., *Roman Rolland. Textes politiques, sociaux et philosophiques choisis* (Paris, 1970), pp. 135–42.

122. Rathenau to Hermann Stehr, 14 August 1914, in *Rathenau. Briefe*, vol. 2, p. 1,357.

Chapter 4 Empires and Nations, 1915

1. Thomas Masaryk, *The Problem of Small Nations in the European Crisis* (London, 1916), pp. 11, 16, 23.

2. I have benefited from discussions with Stuart Ward and Mark McKenna about the significance of the battle of Gallipoli.

3. Cited in Wolfdieter Bihl and Erwin A. Schmidt, 'Österreich-Ungarns Präsenz und Ambitionen im Nahen Osten', in Jürgen Angelow, ed., *Der Erste Weltkrieg auf dem Balkan* (Berlin, 2011), p. 81.

4. Mustafa Aksakal, *The Ottoman Road to War in 1914: The Ottoman Empire and the First World War* (Cambridge, 2008), pp. 42–7; Ryan Gingeras, *Sorrowful Shore: Violence, Ethnicity, and the End of the Ottoman Empire, 1912–1923* (Oxford, 2009), pp. 38–41.

5. Uğur Ümit Üngör, *The Making of Modern Turkey: Nation and State in Eastern Anatolia, 1913–1950* (Oxford, 2011), pp. 56–60.

6. Cited in Aksakal, *Ottoman Road*, p. 163.

7. Ibid., p. 19.

8. Ronald Park Bobroff, *Roads to Glory: Late Imperial Russia and the Turkish Straits* (London, 2006), pp. 109–15.

9. Diary entry, 27 November 1914, in Trevor Wilson, ed., *C. P. Scott, 1911–1928* (London, 1970), p. 112.

10. 'Editorial', *The Scotsman*, 10 November 1914.

11. Hardinge to Nicolson, 6 January 1915, Nicolson Papers TNA FO 800/377, fos 112–13.

12. Sean McMeekin, *The Berlin–Baghdad Express: The Ottoman Empire and Germany's Bid for World Power, 1898–1918* (London, 2010).

13. Mustafa Aksakal, '"Holy War Made in Germany?" Ottoman Origins of the 1914 Jihad', *War in History*, 18, 2 (2011), pp. 184–99.

14. Robin Prior, *Gallipoli: The End of the Myth* (London and New Haven, CT, 2009), pp. 7–11.

15. Georges Suarez, *Briand, 1914–1916*, 6 vols (Paris, 1938), vol. 3, pp. 85–98.

16. Thanos Veremis and Helen Gardikas-Kotsiadakis, 'Protagonist in Politics, 1912–20', in Paschalis Kitromilides, ed., *Eleftherios Venizelos: The Trials of Statesmanship* (Edinburgh, 2006), pp. 118–21.

17. Prior, *Gallipoli*, pp. 57, 102.

18. Jeffrey Grey, *A Military History of Australia* (Cambridge, 1999), pp. 89–94.

19. Edward Erickson, 'Strength against Weakness: Ottoman Military Effectiveness at Gallipoli, 1915', *Journal of Military History*, 65, 4 (2001), pp. 981–1,001; M. Şükrü Hanioğlu, *Ataturk: An Intellectual Biography* (Princeton, NJ, 2011), pp. 73–9.

20. Nicolson to Hardinge, 11 March 1915, Nicolson Papers, TNA FO 800/377, fos 137.

21. Bobroff, *Straits*, pp. 128–31; William C. Fuller, *The Foe Within: Fantasies of Treason and the End of Imperial Russia* (Ithaca, NY, 2006), pp. 130–2.

22. Buchanan to Nicolson, 24 February 1915, Nicolson Papers, TNA FO 800/377, fos 49–52.

23. Grey to Buchanan, 10 March 1915, TNA FO 371/2481, fo. 141; see also the minute 'Russia and the Eventual Settlement', 8 March 1915, in ibid., fo. 148.

24. Delcassé to Paléologue, 6 March 1915, *Documents diplomatiques français*, 1915, vol. 1, pp. 260–1.

25. C. M. Andrew and A. S. Kanya-Forstner, 'The French Colonial Party and French Colonial War Aims, 1914–1918', *Historical Journal*, 17, 1 (1974), pp. 83–6.

26. Mark Levene, 'The Balfour Declaration: A Case of Mistaken Identity', *English Historical Review*, 107, 422 (1992), pp. 59–77.

27. Gingeras, *Sorrowful Shore*, pp. 43–5.

28. Donald Bloxham, 'The Armenian Genocide of 1915–1916: Cumulative Radicalization and the Development of a Destruction Policy', *Past & Present*, 181 (November 2003), pp. 141–91.

29. Ibid., pp. 162–4; Edward Erickson, 'The Armenians and Ottoman Military Policy, 1915', *War in History*, 15, 2 (2008), pp. 141–67.

30. Donald Bloxham, 'Terrorism and Imperial Decline: The Ottoman-Armenian Case', *European Review of History*, 14, 3 (2007), pp. 316–17.

31. Cited in Hans-Lukas Kieser, 'From Patriotism to Mass-Murder: Dr Mehmed Resid (1873–1919)', in Ronald Grigor Suny, Fatma Müge Göçek, and Norman Naimark, eds, *A Question of Genocide: Armenians and Turks at the End of the Ottoman Empire* (Oxford, 2011), p. 137.

32. Üngör, *Making of Modern Turkey*, pp. 71–7.

33. Ibid., pp. 39–42.

34. 'Bulletin du jour', *Le Temps*, 29 July 1916, p. 1; 'Les intérêts de la Russie et la conquête de l'Asie-Mineure', *Le Temps*, 29 March 1916, p. 3.

35. Department of State to the American embassy, Constantinople, 29 May 1915, www.armeniangenocide.org; Daniel Marc Segesser, 'Dissolve or Punish? The International Debate amongst Jurists and Publicists on the Consequences of the Armenian Genocide for the Ottoman Empire, 1915–1923', *Journal of Genocide Research*, 10, 1 (2008), pp. 99–100.

36. Ibid., p. 107.

37. Barrère to Delcassé, 6 March 1915, *DDF*, vol. 1, pp. 395–6.

38. Meeting of 8 March 1915, in Miklós Komjáthy, ed., *Protokolle des Gemeinsamen Ministerrates der Österreichisch-Ungarischen Monarchie (1914–1918)* (Budapest, 1966), p. 221.

39. C. J. Lowe and F. Marzari, *Italian Foreign Policy, 1870–1940* (London, 1978), p. 389.

40. 'Il sacro egoismo per l'Italia', 18 October 1914, in Antonio Salandra, *I discorsi della guerra con alcune note* (Milan, 1922), pp. 1–8.

41. Lyncker to his wife, 9 January 1915, in Holger Afflerbach, ed., *Kaiser Wilhelm II als oberster Kriegsherr im Ersten Weltkrieg: Quellen aus der militärischen Umgebung des Kaisers 1914–1918* (Munich, 2005), p. 213.

42. Cited in Alberto Monticone, *Deutschland und die Neutralität Italiens 1914–1915* (Wiesbaden, 1982), p. 116.

43. Geoffrey Heywood, *Failure of a Dream: Sidney Sonnino and the Rise and Fall of Liberal Italy, 1847–1922* (Florence, 1999), pp. 407–11.

44. Frédéric Le Moal, *La France et l'Italie dans les Balkans 1914–1919. Le contentieux adriatique* (Paris, 2006), p. 37; Glenn Torrey, *Romania and World War I: A Collection of Studies* (Portland, OR, 1998), p. 15.

45. Monticone, *Deutschland*, p. 14.

46. Monts to Redlich, 26 August 1914, 12 September 1914, in Fritz Fellner, 'Aus der Denkwelt eines kaiserlichen Botschafters a. D. Die Briefe des Grafen Monts an Josef Redlich aus den Jahren 1914/15', *Mitteilungen des Österreichischen Staatsarchiv*, 31 (1978), pp. 394–5.

47. Lyncker to his wife, 6 March 1915, in Afflerbach, ed., *Kaiser Wilhelm II*, p. 220.

48. Diary entries, 6 and 7 March 1915, in Walter Görlitz, ed., *The Kaiser and his Court: The Diaries, Notebooks and Letters of Admiral Georg Alexander von Müller, Chief of the Naval Cabinet, 1914–1918* (London, 1961), p. 69.

49. Cited in Hugo Hantsch, *Leopold Graf Berchtold* (Graz, 1963), p. 700.

50. Cited in Monticone, *Deutschland*, p. 97.

51. Meeting, 8 August 1914, in Komjáthy, ed., *Protokolle*, p. 162.

52. Meeting, 3 February 1915, in ibid., p. 195.

53. Hantsch, *Berchtold*, pp. 720–4; Monticone, *Deutschland*, pp. 77–82.

54. Meeting, 8 March 1915, in Komjáthy, ed., *Protokolle*, pp. 215–32.

55. Heywood, *Sonnino*, pp. 415–18; William A. Renzi, 'Italy's Neutrality and Entrance into the Great War: A Re-Examination', *American Historical Review*, 73, 5 (1968), pp. 1,430–1; Delcassé to Barrère, 16 October 1914, *DDF*, 1914, pp. 401–2.

56. Andrej Mitrovic, *Serbia's Great War, 1914–1918* (London, 2007), pp. 95–9.

57. British embassy, Petrograd, to the Foreign Office, 31 March 1915, TNA FO 371/2508, fos 4–10.

58. Le Moal, *France*, pp. 46–51, 100–1.

59. Delcassé to Paléologue, Cambon, Barrère, 8 March 1915; Barrère to Delcassé, 11 March 1915, *DDF*, 1915, vol. 1, pp. 410–11, 441–2.

60. Grey to Foreign Office, 31 March 1915, Grey Papers, TNA FO 800/75, fo. 105.

61. Grey to Buchanan, 19 April 1915, TNA FO 371/2508, fo. 161.

62. Lowe and Marzari, *Italian Foreign Policy*, pp. 148–50.

63. Lord Eustace Percy, 'Memorandum', 2 May 1915, Grey Papers, TNA FO 800/95, fos 41–3.

64. Antonio Gibelli, *La grande guerra degli italiani 1915–1918* (Milan, 1998), p. 30; Paul Corner, *Fascism in Ferrara, 1915–1925* (Oxford, 1975), p. 21.

65. Cited in Walter Adamson, *Avant-Garde Florence: From Modernism to Fascism* (Cambridge, MA, 1993), p. 197.

66. Gibelli, *Grande guerra*, pp. 74–80.

67. 'Manifesto della direzione socialista per la neutralità assoluta', 20 October 1914, in Renzo De Felice, *Mussolini, il rivoluzionaria 1883–1920* (Turin, 1965), p. 682.

68. 'Primo manifesto-appello del Fascio rivoluzionario d'azione internazionalista', 5 October 1914, in ibid., pp. 679–80.

69. Charles Killinger, *Gaetano Salvemini: A Biography* (Westport, CT, 2002), pp. 87–92.

70. Massimo Bucarelli, 'Mussolini, la questione adriatica e il fallimento dell'interventismo democratica', *Nuova Rivista Storica*, 95, 1 (2011), pp. 137–40.

71. Klaus Epstein, *Matthias Erzberger and the Dilemma of German Democracy* (New York, 1971), pp. 133–5.
72. Heywood, *Sonnino*, p. 433.
73. Elena Tonezzer, 'Alcide De Gasperi and Trentino', *Modern Italy*, 14, 4 (2009), pp. 404–5.
74. Rathenau to Georg von Diezelsky, 3 May 1915, in Alexander Jager, Clemens Picht, and Ernst Schulin, eds, *Walther Rathenau. Briefe*, 2 vols (Düsseldorf, 2006), vol. 2, p. 1,430.
75. Cited in Timothy C. Dowling, *The Brusilov Offensive* (Bloomington, IN, 2008), p. 23.
76. Robert Foley, *German Strategy and the Path to Verdun: Erich von Falkenhayn and the Development of Attrition, 1871–1916* (Cambridge, 2005), pp. 126–50.
77. Alexander Morrison, *Russian Rule in Samarkand: A Comparison with British India* (Oxford, 2008); Richard Wortman, *Scenarios of Power: Myth and Ceremony in the Russian Monarchy: From Alexander II to the Abdication of Nicholas II* (Princeton, NJ, 2000).
78. Cited in Corinne Gaudin, 'Rural Echoes of World War I: War Talk in the Russian Village', *Jahrbücher für Geschichte Osteuropas*, 56, 3 (2008), pp. 401–2.
79. Sergei Kudryashev, 'The Revolts of 1916 in Russian Central Asia', in Jan Erik Zürcher, ed., *Arming the State: Military Conscription in the Middle East and Central Asia, 1775–1925* (London, 1999), pp. 139–44; Alexander Morrison, 'Metropole, Colony, and Imperial Citizenship in the Russian Empire', *Kritika*, 13, 2 (2012), pp. 354–8.
80. Cited in Aaron Retish, *Russia's Peasants in Revolution and Civil War: Citizenship, Identity, and the Creation of the Soviet State, 1914–1922* (Cambridge, 2008), pp. 52–3; Joshua Sanborn, *Drafting the Russian Nation: Military Conscription, Total War, and Mass Politics, 1905–1925* (DeKalb, IL, 2003), p. 105.
81. Hubertus Jahn, *Patriotic Culture in Russia during World War I* (Ithaca, NY, 1995), pp. 1–8.
82. Peter Gattrell, *A Whole Empire Walking: Refugees in Russia during World War I* (Bloomington, IN, 1999), pp. 37–58
83. See Fuller, *The Foe Within*.
84. Eric Lohr, *Nationalizing the Russian Empire: The Campaign against Enemy Aliens during World War I* (Cambridge, MA, 2003), pp. 31–45.
85. Ibid., pp. 129–35.
86. Ibid., pp. 137–50; Gattrell, *A Whole Empire Walking*, pp. 143–8.
87. Levene, 'The Balfour Declaration', pp. 55–63.
88. Paul Miliukov, *Political Memoirs, 1905–1917* (Ann Arbor, MI, 1967), pp. 310–11.
89. Melissa Stockdale, *Paul Miliukov and the Quest for a Liberal Russia, 1880–1918* (Ithaca, NY, 1996), pp. 224–30; Joshua Sanborn, 'Liberals and Bureaucrats at War', *Kritika*, 8, 1 (2007), pp. 143–7.
90. Scott Seregny, 'Zemtsvos, Peasants, and Citizenship: The Russian Adult Education Movement and World War I', *Slavic Review*, 59, 2 (2000), pp. 290–315.
91. Cited in Miliukov, *Memoirs*, p. 322.
92. Cited in Stockdale, *Miliukov*, p. 228.
93. Wortman, *Scenarios of Power*, pp. 512–21.
94. Wladzimierz Borodziej, *Geschichte Polens im 20. Jahrhundert* (Munich, 2010), pp. 80–83.
95. Jan Styka, 'Appeal to the French People', 28 May 1915; and Joseph de Lipkowski, 'Memorandum', July 1915, both in BDIC 4 delta 280, dossier France, question polonaise 1914–1919, fo. 2.
96. 'Discours de M. A. Briand', *Journal des débats politiques et littéraires*, 5 November 1915, p. 3; Eric Drummond, 'Poles in America', 12 March 1915, TNA FO 371/2450, fos 27–9; Ghislain de Castelbajac, 'La France et la question polonaise (1914–1918)', in Georges-Henri Soutou, ed., *Recherches sur la France et le problème des nationalités pendant la Première Guerre Mondiale* (Paris, 1995), p. 54.
97. Ronald Bobroff, 'Revolution in Wartime: Sergei D. Sazonov and the Future of Poland, 1910–1916', *International History Review*, 22, 3 (2000), pp. 512–18.
98. Theobald von Bethmann Hollweg, *Sechs Kriegsreden des Reichskanzlers* (Berlin, 1916), pp. 39–40, 58–61.
99. Diary entry, 16 July 1915, in Kurt Riezler, *Tagebücher, Aufsätze, Dokumente*, ed. Karl Dietrich Erdmann, intro. Holger Afflerbach (Göttingen, 2008), p. 285.
100. Nicolson to Hardinge, 27 May 1915, Nicolson Papers, TNA FO 800/378, fo. 91.
101. Wolfgang-Uwe Friedrich, *Bulgarien und die Mächte 1913–1915. Ein Beitrag zur Weltkriegs- und Imperialismusgeschichte* (Stuttgart, 1985), pp. 237–64.
102. Paléologue to Delcassé, 23 November 1914, *DDF*, 1914, p. 557.
103. Diary entry, 7 February 1915, in Anthony Philips, ed., *Sergey Prokofiev: Diaries 1915–1923, Behind the Mask* (Ithaca, NY, 2008), p. 13; Bax-Ironside to Nicolson, 8 March 1915, Nicolson Papers, TNA FO 800/377, fos 22–3; Friedrich, *Bulgarien*, pp. 157–62.

104. John D. Bell, *Peasants in Power: Alexander Stamboliski and the Bulgarian Agrarian National Union, 1899–1923* (Princeton, NJ, 1977), pp. 113–21; Snezhona Dimitrova, ' "Taming the Death": The Culture of Death (1915–18) and its Meaning and Commemorating through First World War Soldier Monuments in Bulgaria (1917–44)', *Social History*, 30, 2 (2005), pp. 175–94; Evelina Kelbetcheva, 'Between Apology and Denial: Bulgarian Culture during World War I', in Aviel Roshwald and Richard Stites, eds, *European Culture in the Great War: The Arts, Entertainment, and Propaganda, 1914–1918* (Cambridge, 1999), p. 236.

105. Mitrovic, *Serbia's Great War*, pp. 145–60.

106. Ibid., p. 154.

107. Jonathan Gumz, *The Resurrection and Collapse of Empire in Habsburg Serbia, 1914–1918* (Cambridge, 2009), p. 74.

108. Mitrovic, *Serbia's Great War*, pp. 200–24.

109. David Stevenson, *1914–1918: The History of the First World War* (London, 2005), pp. 99–105.

110. Cited in J. P. Harris, *Douglas Haig and the First World War* (Cambridge, 2008), pp. 108–10.

111. Ibid., p. 112.

112. Ibid., pp. 127–9; Robert Doughty, *Pyrrhic Victory: French Strategy and Operations in the Great War* (Cambridge, MA, 2005), pp. 253–6; Elizabeth Greenhalgh, *Foch in Command: The Forging of a First World War General* (Cambridge, 2011), pp. 133–9.

113. Gerd Hardach, 'Industrial Mobilization in 1914–1918: Production, Planning, and Ideology', in Patrick Fridenson, ed., *The French Home Front, 1914–1918* (Providence, RI, 1992), pp. 64–5; John Keiger, *Raymond Poincaré* (Cambridge, 1997), pp. 221–4.

114. Trevor Wilson, *The Downfall of the Liberal Party, 1914–1935* (London, 1966), pp. 51–68; Stephen E. Koss, 'The Destruction of Britain's Last Liberal Government', *Journal of Modern History*, 40, 2 (1968), pp. 257–77.

115. Nicholas Lambert, *Planning Armageddon: British Economic Warfare and the First World War* (Cambridge, MA, 2012), pp. 185–322.

116. Cited in Epstein, *Erzberger*, pp. 410–12.

117. Janes Addams, Emily Balch, and Alice Hamilton, *Women of The Hague* (New York, 1915), p. 80; David Patterson, *The Search for Negotiated Peace: Women's Activism and Citizen Diplomacy in World War I* (London and New York, 2008), pp. 51–81; Leila J. Rupp, *Worlds of Women: The Making of an International Women's Movement* (Princeton, NJ, 1997), p. 115.

118. Stephen Wertheim, 'The League that Wasn't: American Designs for a Legalist-Sanctionist League of Nations and the Intellectual Origins of International Organization, 1914–1920', *Diplomatic History*, 35, 5 (2011), p. 808.

119. 'Liberty Bell', *Indianapolis Star*, 22 November 1915, p. 1; 'Thousands View the Liberty Bell at the Exposition', *San Francisco Chronicle*, p. 7; 'Bell Gives New Message of Freedom', *San Francisco Chronicle*, 18 July 1915, p. 29.

120. Alan Dawley, *Changing the World: American Progressives in War and Revolution* (Princeton, NJ, 2003), pp. 83–93.

121. Cited in Thomas J. Knock, *To End all Wars: Woodrow Wilson and the Quest for a New World Order* (New York, 1992), pp. 43–4.

122. 'Pan-Americanism, an Address by Robert Lansing', 27 December 1915, Pan-American Scientific Congress, Washington, Lansing Papers, Seeley G. Mudd Library, Princeton, MC 083, Box 10, folder 3, p. 8.

123. 'Are There Specific American Problems of International Law?', Pan-American Scientific Congress, Washington, 27 December 1915–8 January 1916, Dulles Papers, Seeley G. Mudd Library, Princeton, MC 016, Box 1.

124. Mark T. Gilderhus, 'Revolution, War, and Expansion: Woodrow Wilson in Latin America', in John Milton Cooper, ed., *Reconsidering Woodrow Wilson: Progressivism, Internationalism, War, and Peace* (Baltimore, MD, 2008), p. 177.

125. Cited in John Milton Cooper, *Woodrow Wilson* (New York, 2011), p. 285.

126. Department of State to Ambassador Gerard, 13 May 1915, in *Foreign Relations of the United States* (Washington DC, 1915), supplement, p. 393.

127. 'Cruel and Inhuman Acts of War', 25 May 1915, Lansing Papers, Seeley G. Mudd Library MC083, Box 7, folder 2, fo. 20.

128. Diary entry, 20 March 1915, in Riezler, *Tagebücher*, p. 261.

129. Roger Chickering, *Imperial Germany and the Great War, 1914–1918* (Cambridge, 1998), pp. 89–90.

130. Cooper, *Wilson*, p. 290.

131. Lambert, *Armageddon*, pp. 424–31.

132. Drummond, telegram, 7 June 1915, Grey Papers, TNA FO 800/95, fos 73–4.

133. 'Freedom of the Seas', 11 June 1915, Grey Papers, TNA FO 800/95, fos 86–90.

134. Ibid., fos 79–85.
135. Grey to Crewe, 14 June 1915, Grey Papers, TNA FO 800/95, fos 107–9.
136. Lambert, *Armageddon*, pp. 431–50; Stephen Roskill, *Hankey: Man of Secrets, 1877–1918*, 3 vols (London, 1970), vol. 1, p. 158.
137. Diary entry, 26 August 1915, Görlitz, ed., *The Kaiser and his Court*, p. 102.
138. Graham Cross, *The Diplomatic Education of Franklin D. Roosevelt, 1882–1933* (Basingstoke, 2012), p. 35.
139. 'Exposition Crowds Hail Liberty Bell', *The New York Times*, p. 10.
140. 'Timid Neutrality', 21 November 1914, in *Walter Lippmann: Early Writings*, ed. Arthur Schlesinger (New York, 1970), p. 13.
141. Knock, *To End All Wars*, pp. 59–63; Cooper, *Wilson*, pp. 296–8.
142. Nicolson to Hardinge, 6 February 1915, Nicolson Papers, TNA FO 800/377, fos 116–17; Delcassé to Cambon, Paléologue, 25 January 1915, *DDF*, vol. 1, p. 146.
143. Frederick Dickinson, *War and National Reinvention: Japan in the Great War, 1914–1919* (Cambridge, MA, 1999), pp. 93–113, 123–5.
144. Cited in Xu Guoqi, *China and the Great War* (Cambridge, 2005), p. 317.
145. Wai-Hung Ho, 'Social Change and Nationalism in China's Popular Songs', *Social History*, 31, 4 (2006), pp. 437–8.
146. Zhitian Luo, 'National Humiliation and National Assertions: The Chinese Response to the Twenty-One Demands', *Modern Asian Studies*, 27, 2 (1993), pp. 298–309.
147. Xu Guoqi, *China*, pp. 93–8.
148. Ibid., pp. 99–113.
149. Richard Phillips, *China since 1911* (Basingstoke, 1996), pp. 24–8; Albert E. Altman and Harold Z. Schiffrin, 'Sun Yat-sen and the Japanese, 1914–16', *Modern Asian Studies*, 6, 4 (1972), pp. 385–400.

Chapter 5 Making War and Offering Peace, 1916

1. Robert Doughty, *Pyrrhic Victory: French Strategy and Operations in the Great War* (Cambridge, MA, 2005), pp. 250–2.
2. Diary entry by Hans Georg von Plessen, 3 December 1915, in Holger Afflerbach, ed., *Kaiser Wilhelm II als oberster Kriegsherr im Ersten Weltkrieg: Quellen aus der militärischen Umgebung des Kaisers 1914–1918* (Munich, 2005), pp. 844–5; Holger Afflerbach, *Falkenhayn. Politisches Denken und Handeln im Kaiserreich* (Munich, 1994), pp. 360–70; Robert Foley, *German Strategy and the Path to Verdun: Erich von Falkenhayn and the Development of Attrition, 1871–1916* (Cambridge, 2005), pp. 187–90.
3. Doughty, *Pyrrhic Victory*, p. 260; Foley, *Path to Verdun*, pp. 204–17.
4. Georges Dethan, ed., *Gabriel Hanotaux. Carnets (1907–1925)* (Paris, 1982), p. 170.
5. Doughty, *Pyrrhic Victory*, pp. 271–87; Afflerbach, *Falkenhayn*, pp. 404–9; Foley, *Path to Verdun*, pp. 259–61.
6. Maurice Paléologue, *An Ambassador's Memoirs*, 3 vols (London, 1924), vol. 2, p. 221.
7. J. P. Harris, *Douglas Haig and the First World War* (Cambridge, 2008), pp. 208–10.
8. Timothy C. Dowling, *The Brusilov Offensive* (Bloomington, IN, 2008), pp. 62–84.
9. Graydon A. Tunstall, 'Austria-Hungary and the Brusilov Offensive of 1916', *Historian*, 70, 1 (2008), pp. 40–3.
10. Dowling, *Brusilov*, pp. 99–106.
11. Ibid., p. 130.
12. Lyncker to his wife, 26 July 1916, in Afflerbach, ed., *Wilhelm II*, p. 403.
13. Afflerbach, *Falkenhayn*, pp. 442–8; Glenn Torrey, *Romania and World War I: A Collection of Studies* (Portland, OR, 1998), pp. 102–16; Wolfram Pyta, *Hindenburg. Herrschaft zwischen Hohenzollern und Hitler* (Munich, 2009), pp. 215–17.
14. Robin Prior and Trevor Wilson, *The Somme* (New Haven, CT, and London, 2005), p. 51; Harris, *Haig*, pp. 216–28.
15. Cited in Doughty, *Pyrrhic Victory*, p. 291.
16. Ibid., p. 304.
17. Prior and Wilson, *Somme*, pp. 112–18; Harris, *Haig*, p. 232.
18. Diary entry, 26 November 1916, in J. M. McEwen, ed., *The Riddell Diaries 1908–1923* (London, 1986), p. 174; Stephen Roskill, *Hankey: Man of Secrets, 1877*, 3 vols (London, 1970), vol. 2, p. 308.
19. Prior and Wilson, *Somme*, pp. 186–96.
20. Cited in Alexander Watson, *Enduring the Great War: Combat, Morale and Collapse in the German and British Armies, 1914–1918* (Cambridge, 2008), p. 150.

21. Bernd Hüppauf, 'Langemarck, Verdun, and the Myth of a "New Man" in Germany after the First World War', *War & Society*, 6, 2 (1988), pp. 70–103.
22. Jay M. Winter, *Socialism and the Challenge of War: Ideas and Politics in Britain, 1912–1918* (London, 1974), pp. 158–62.
23. Brian K. Feltman, 'Tolerance as a Crime? The British Treatment of German Prisoners of War on the Western Front, 1914–1918', *War in History*, 17, 4 (2010), pp. 443, 449–50.
24. Simon Ball, *The Guardsmen: Harold Macmillan, Three Friends, and the World they Made* (London, 2004), p. 42.
25. Stéphane Audoin-Rouzeau, 'Norbert Elias et l'expérience oubliée de la Première Guerre mondiale', *Vingtième Siècle*, 2 (2010), p. 107.
26. Norbert Elias, *The Civilizing Process*, trans. and ed. Eric Dunning, Johan Goudsblom, and Stephen Mennell (London, 2000), pp. 106–7.
27. Sigmund Freud, 'The Disillusionment of War' and 'Our Attitude to Death', in *Civilization, Society, and Religion: The Penguin Freud Library*, 15 vols (London, 1985), vol. 12, pp. 61–88.
28. Bernhard Dernburg, 'Neujahrsgedanken', 1 January 1916, in *Von beiden Ufern. Flugschriften des Berliner Tagesblatt* (Berlin, 1917), pp. 7–16.
29. Annette Becker, *Oubliés de la grande guerre. Humanitaires et cultures de guerre 1914–1918. Populations occupées, déportés civils, prisonniers de guerre* (Paris, 1998), p. 203.
30. Ibid., p. 282; Jeanne Halbwachs, 'Guerre de religion', Articles de Jeanne Halbwachs-Alexandre parus dans Populaire du Centre (1914–1918), BDIC, GF delta res 99.
31. Gabriele Paolini, *Offensive di pace. La Santa Sede e la prima guerra mondiale* (Florence, 2008), p. 154.
32. For a different view, see Joanna Bourke, *An Intimate History of Killing: Face-to-Face Killings in Twentieth-Century Warfare* (London, 1999).
33. Elias, *Civilizing Process*, p. 270.
34. Oxana Nagornaja, 'United by Barbed Wire: Russian PoWs in Germany, National Stereotypes, and International Relations, 1914–1922', *Kritika*, 10, 3 (2009), p. 481.
35. Jonathan Gumz, *The Resurrection and Collapse of Empire in Habsburg Serbia, 1914–1918* (Cambridge, 2009), pp. 109–25.
36. Gabriel Vejas Liulevicius, *War Land on the Eastern Front: Culture, National Identity, and German Occupation in World War I* (Cambridge, 2000), pp. 176–92; Christian Westerhoff, *Zwangsarbeit im Ersten Weltkrieg. Deutsche Arbeitskräftepolitik im besetzten Polen und Litauen 1914–1918* (Paderborn, 2008).
37. Becker, *Oubliés*, p. 61; Annette Becker, *Les cicatrices rouges 14–18. France et Belgique occupées* (Paris, 2010), p. 126; Jochen Oltmer, 'Einführung. Funktionen und Erfahrungen von Kriegsgefangenschaft im Europa des Ersten Weltkrieges', in Jochen Oltmer, ed., *Kriegsgefangene in Europa des Ersten Weltkrieges* (Paderborn, 2006), pp. 11–22; Jens Thiel, *Menschenbassin Belgien. Anwerbung, Deportation und Zwangsarbeit im Ersten Weltkrieg* (Essen, 2004), pp. 141–7.
38. Becker, *Cicatrices rouges*, p. 106.
39. Cited in Giovanna Procacci, *Soldati e prigionieri italiani nella Grande Guerra* (Turin, 2000), p. 451; Vanda Wilcox, ' "Weeping Tears of Blood": Exploring Italian Soldiers' Emotions in the First World War', *Modern Italy*, 17, 2 (2012), pp. 175–82; Stéphane Audoin-Rouzeau, *Men at War 1914–1918: National Sentiment and Trench Journalism in France during the First World War* (Oxford, 1992), pp. 93–101; Watson, *Enduring the Great War*, pp. 76–7.
40. Bernard Georges and Denise Tintant, *Léon Jouhaux. Cinquante ans de syndicalisme*, 2 vols (Paris, 1962), vol. 1, p. 158.
41. Karl Christian Führer, *Carl Legien 1861–1920. Ein Gewerkschafter im Kampf um 'möglichst gutes Leben' für alle Arbeiter* (Essen, 2009), p. 308.
42. Giovanna Procacci, 'Popular Protest and Labour Conflict in Italy, 1914–1918', *Social History*, 14, 1 (1989), pp. 31–58; Peter Gattrell, *Russia's First World War: A Social and Economic History* (Harlow, 2005), pp. 67–72.
43. Jean-Jacques Becker, *The Great War and the French People* (Leamington Spa, 1985), pp. 25–8.
44. Adrian Gregory, *The Last Great War: British Society and the First World War* (Cambridge, 2008), p. 189.
45. Gerd Hardach, 'Industrial Mobilization', in Patrick Fridenson, ed., *The French Home Front, 1914–1918* (Providence, RI, 1992), pp. 74–80.
46. Gerald Feldman, *Army, Industry and Labor in Germany, 1914–1918* (Princeton, NJ, 1966), pp. 222–49.
47. Luigi Tomassini, 'Industrial Mobilization and the Labour Market in Italy during the First World War', *Social History*, 16, 1 (1991), pp. 77–83.
48. Gattrell, *Russia's First World War*, pp. 113–17.

49. Gerry D. Rubin, *War, Law, and Labour: The Munitions Act, State Regulation, and the Unions, 1915–1921* (Oxford, 1987), pp. 1–14, 47.
50. Cited in ibid., p. 24.
51. Hardach, 'Industrial Mobilization', pp. 67–72; Douglas Forsyth, *The Crisis of Liberal Italy: Monetary and Financial Policy, 1914–1922* (Cambridge, 1993), pp. 84–5.
52. Jasmien van Daele, 'Engineering Social Peace: Networks, Ideas, and the Founding of the International Labor Organization', *International Review of Social History*, 50 (2005), pp. 435–66.
53. Copy of Appleton's letter to Asquith, 30 August 1916, in Shotwell Papers, Columbia University Archives, Shotwell Box 109.
54. Georges and Tintant, *Jouhaux*, p. 234.
55. 'Generalkommission der Gewerkschaften Deutschlands, 25 November 1917', BArch R 703/47, fos 3–7.
56. 'Report of the Proceedings of the International Conference of Trade Unions, Held in Bern, Maison du Peuple, 1–4 October 1917', Shotwell Papers, Columbia University Archives, Shotwell Box 103a.
57. David Stevenson, 'The First World War and European Integration', *International History Review*, 34, 4 (2012), pp. 841–63.
58. Bund deutscher Landwirte, Deutsche Bauernbund, Westfälischer Bauernverein, Centralverband deutscher Industrie, Bund deutscher Industrie, Reichsdeutscher Mittelstandsverband to Bethmann Hollweg, 20 May 1915, reprinted in 'Auskunftsstelle Vereinigter Verbände', *Gedanken und Wünschen zur Gestaltung des Friedens* (1916), pp. 12–19.
59. Rathenau to Admiral von Capelle, 31 December 1914, Rathenau to Oscar Caro, 15 February 1915, in Alexander Jager, Clemens Picht, and Ernst Schulin, eds, *Walther Rathenau. Briefe*, 2 vols (Düsseldorf, 2006), vol. 2, pp. 1,409–10, 1,420.
60. Georges-Henri Soutou, *L'or et le sang. Les buts de guerre économiques de la Première Guerre Mondiale* (Paris, 1989), pp. 76–85; Hans Peter Schwarz, *Adenauer. Der Aufstieg, 1876–1952* (Stuttgart, 1986), pp. 173, 186.
61. Ministerial Council meeting, 18 June 1915, in Miklós Komjáthy, ed., *Protokolle des Gemeinsamen Ministerrates der Österreichisch-Ungarischen Monarchie (1914–1918)* (Budapest, 1966), p. 259.
62. Memorandum du Gouvernement allemand, 13 November 1915, in André Scherer and Jacques Grunewald, eds, *L'Allemagne et les problèmes de la paix pendant la Première Guerre Mondiale* (Paris, 1962–78), pp. 211–15.
63. Cited in Éric Roussel, *Jean Monnet* (Paris, 1996), p. 50.
64. Marc Trachtenberg, *Reparations in World Politics: France and European Economic Diplomacy, 1916–1923* (New York, 1980), pp. 1–4.
65. Soutou, *L'or et le sang*, pp. 145–53.
66. Deuxième séance, 27 March 1916, Conférence des Alliées, Jules Cambon Papers, MAE PA-AP 43, Cambon 84, fos 61–84.
67. Cited in Soutou, *L'or et le sang*, p. 263.
68. Ibid., pp. 261–7; Conférence Economique des Gouvernements Alliées, 14–17 June 1916, Jules Cambon Papers, MAE PA-AP 43, Cambon 84, fos 101–3.
69. Soutou, *L'or et le sang*, pp. 185–7.
70. David M. Kennedy, *Over Here: The First World War and American Society* (New York, 1980), p. 95.
71. Cited in Priscilla Roberts, 'Willard D. Straight and the Diplomacy of International Finance during the First World War', *Business History*, 40, 3 (1998), p. 33.
72. Frederick Dickinson, *War and National Reinvention: Japan in the Great War, 1914–1919* (Cambridge, MA, 1999), pp. 160–4.
73. Erik van Ree, 'Lenin's Conception of Socialism in One Country, 1915–1917', *Revolutionary Russia*, 23, 2 (2010), pp. 159–81; 'On the Slogan for a United States of Europe', *Sotsial-Demokrat*, 23 August 1915, in V. I. Lenin, *Collected Works*, 45 vols (London, 1964), vol. 21, pp. 339–42.
74. Diary entry, 14 June 1916, in Kurt Riezler, *Tagebücher, Aufsätze, Dokumente*, ed. Karl Dietrich Erdmann, intro. Holger Afflerbach (Göttingen, 2008), p. 359.
75. John Milton Cooper, *Woodrow Wilson* (New York, 2011), p. 348.
76. Cited in Keith Neilson, *Strategy and Supply: The Anglo-Russian Alliance, 1914–1917* (London, 1984), p. 155.
77. Diary entries, 24 and 25 August 1916, in Walter Görlitz, ed., *The Kaiser and his Court: The Diaries, Notebooks and Letters of Admiral Georg Alexander von Müller, Chief of the Naval Cabinet, 1914–1918* (London, 1961), pp. 196–7.
78. Diary entry, 1 August 1916, in Riezler, *Tagebücher*, pp. 366–8.
79. Diary entry, 6 July 1916, in ibid., p. 365.
80. Anna von der Goltz, *Hindenburg: Power, Myth, and the Rise of the Nazis* (Oxford, 2011), pp. 35–6.
81. Pyta, *Hindenburg*, pp. 205–22.

82. Diary entry, 27 August 1916, in Görlitz, ed., *The Kaiser and his Court*, p. 198.

83. Plessen to Gräfin Brockdorff, 29 August 1916, in Afflerbach, ed., *Kaiser Wilhelm II*, pp. 873–5.

84. David French, *British Strategy and War Aims, 1914–1916* (London, 1986), pp. 210–13; Victor Rothwell, *British War Aims and Peace Diplomacy, 1914–1918* (Oxford, 1971), pp. 42–8; Erik Goldstein, *Winning the Peace: British Diplomatic Strategy, Planning, and the Paris Peace Conference, 1916–1920* (Oxford, 1991), pp. 9–13; Čedomir Antić, *Ralph Paget: A Diplomat in Serbia* (Belgrade, 2006), pp. 95–107.

85. Sir R. Paget and W. Tyrrell, 'Peace Terms', TNA FO 371/2804, fos 405–14.

86. Diary entry, 7 October 1916, McEwen, ed., *Riddell Diaries*, p. 170.

87. Michael Fry, *Lloyd George and Foreign Policy: The Education of a Statesman, 1890–1916* (Montreal, 1977), pp. 243–8.

88. David Lloyd George, *War Memoirs* (London, 1938), pp. 504–12.

89. Lord Newton (Thomas Legh), *Lord Lansdowne: A Biography* (London, 1929), pp. 449–52; Frank Winters, 'Exaggerating the Efficacy of Diplomacy: The Marquis of Lansdowne's "Peace Letter" of November 1917', *International History Review*, 32, 1 (2010), pp. 28–33.

90. 'Proposals for Diminishing the Occasion of Future Wars', October 1916, in Cecil Papers, British Library, MS Add. 51102, fos 1–5.

91. Notes by Sir E. Crowe on Lord R. Cecil's proposals for the maintenance of future peace, TNA FO 371/3082, fo. 9.

92. Soutou, *L'or et le sang*, pp. 279–82; David Stevenson, *French War Aims against Germany, 1914–1919* (Oxford, 1982), pp. 41–5; see also Peter Jackson's forthcoming book on French security policy, *Beyond the Balance of Power: France and the Politics of National Security in the Era of the First World War* (Cambridge University Press) – my reading of the normative changes in international politics owes much to discussions with him.

93. Comité National d'Etudes Politiques et Sociales, séance du lundi 20 novembre 1916, MAE PA-AP 10, Bourgeois 16, fos 2–13.

94. Note, 'Provinces Rhénanes', October 1916, MAE Serie A–Paix, vol. 223, fos 35–47.

95. Keith Hitchins, *Rumania, 1866–1947* (Oxford, 1994), pp. 262–5.

96. Scott to Hobhouse, 25 November 1916, in Trevor Wilson, ed., *The Political Diaries of C. P. Scott, 1911–1928* (London, 1970), p. 233.

97. Ronald Bobroff, 'Revolution in Wartime: Sergei D. Sazonov and the Future of Poland, 1910–1916', *International History Review*, 22, 3 (2000), pp. 522–5.

98. Diary entry, 3 November 1916, in Görlitz, ed., *The Kaiser and his Court*, p. 215; Wolfgang Steglich and Wilhelm E. Winterhagen, 'Die Polenproklamation vom 5. November 1916', *Militärgeschichtliche Mitteilungen*, 78, 1 (1978), pp. 114–15.

99. Diary entry, 9 November 1916, in Riezler, *Tagebücher*, pp. 379–80.

100. 'Deutschland und der europäischen Weltmächten', in Wolfgang Mommsen and Gangolf Hübinger, eds, *Max Weber. Zur Politik im Weltkrieg. Schriften und Reden 1914–1918*, series 1, vol. 15 (Tübingen, 1984), pp. 180–2, 188.

101. Bethmann Hollweg to Ferdinand I of Bulgaria, 23 October 1916, Bethmann Hollweg to embassy in Vienna, 28 October 1916, in Scherer and Grunewald, eds, *L'Allemagne*, pp. 522, 534–5.

102. Note de Bethmann Hollweg, Berlin, 18 October 1916; Note de Jagow, Pless, 18 October 1916, in ibid., pp. 515–20.

103. 'Manifest des deutschen Generalgouverneurs', 5 November 1916, *Ursachen und Folgen*, vol. 1, p. 39.

104. Ingeborg Meckling, *Die Aussenpolitik des Grafen Czernin* (Munich, 1969), p. 170.

105. Birgitt Morgenbrod, *Wiener Großbürgertum im Ersten Weltkrieg. Die Geschichte der Österreichischen Politischen Gesellschaft 1916–1918* (Vienna, 1998), pp. 86–90; Petronilla Ehrenpreis, *Kriegs- und Friedensziele im Diskurs. Regierung und deutschsprachige Öffentlichkeit während des Ersten Weltkrieges* (Innsbruck, 2005), pp. 119–29.

106. Wladzimierz Borodziej, *Geschichte Polens im 20. Jahrhundert* (Munich, 2010), pp. 83–6; Alexander Watson, 'Fighting for Another Fatherland: The Polish Minority in the German Army, 1914–1918', *English Historical Review*, 126, 522 (2011), pp. 1,152–4.

107. Cooper, *Wilson*, p. 347.

108. For example, Hughes's speech, Star Casino, New York, 24 October 1916, Hughes Papers, Library of Congress, Container 178, reel 137, fo. 2.

109. Bullard to House, Mandeville, Jamaica, 8 November 1916, in Bullard Papers, Seeley G. Mudd Library, Princeton, MC008, box 9.

110. Cooper, *Wilson*, pp. 326–7.

111. Diary entry, 2 December 1916, in Riezler, *Tagebücher*, pp. 384–6.

112. Diary entry, 9 December 1916, in ibid., p. 387.

113. 'Friedensangebot der Mittelmächte', 12 December 1916, Reichstag speech, 12 December 1916, *Ursachen und Folgen*, pp. 68–71.
114. Cooper, *Wilson*, p. 365; Arthur S. Link, *Wilson: Campaigns for Progressivism and Peace, 1916–1917* (Princeton, NJ, 1965), pp. 214–19.
115. Blanche Duhamel to Georges Duhamel, 23 December 1916, in Georges Duhamel and Blanche Duhamel, *Correspondance de guerre, 1914–1919*, ed. Arlette Lafay, intro. Jean-Jacques Becker (Paris, 2007–8), vol. 1, p. 1,383.
116. 'Cri de détresse', *Le Figaro*, 1 October 1916; Manon Pignot, *La guerre des crayons. Quand les petits Parisiens dessinaient la Grande Guerre* (Paris, 2004), pp. 48–51.
117. James Bone to C. P. Scott, 21 December 1916, in Wilson, ed., *Political Diaries*, p. 253; Paul Cambon to his son, 15 December 1916, in Henri Cambon, ed., *Paul Cambon. Correspondance 1870–1924*, 3 vols (Paris, 1946), vol. 3, p. 134.
118. Minute, 14 December 1916, TNA FO 371/2805, fo. 283.
119. Balfour to Bertie, 15 December, TNA FO 371/2805, fo. 312.
120. Draft reply by Briand, 22 December 1916, TNA FO 371/2805, fos 469–72.
121. Draft reply by Briand, 23 December 1916, TNA FO 371/2805, fos 517–19.
122. Bertie to Foreign Office, 22 December 1916, TNA FO 371/2805, fo. 501; Rodd, telegram to the Foreign Office, 24 December 1916, TNA FO 371/2806, fos 13–14.
123. Conférence du 26 décembre 1916, Mantoux Papers, BDIC, F delta res 0858/01/04.
124. Blanche Duhamel to Georges Duhamel, 28 December 1916, in *Correspondance de guerre*, vol. 1, pp. 1,396–7.
125. Entente reply to the peace note of Germany and her Allies, 30 December 1916, in Carnegie Endowment for International Peace, *Official Communications and Speeches Relating to Proposals, 1916–1917* (Washington DC, 1917), pp. 38–41.
126. Entente reply to President Wilson's Peace Note, 10 January 1917, in ibid., pp. 47–50.
127. Diary entries, 31 December 1916, 2 January 1917, in Görlitz, *The Kaiser and his Court*, p. 227; diary entry, 6 January 1917, in Riezler, *Tagebücher*, p. 391.

Chapter 6 Great Movements for Peace, 1917

1. Cited in Bernd Ulrich, *Die Augenzeugen. Deutsche Feldpostbriefe in Kriegs- und Nachkriegzeit 1914–1933* (Essen, 1997), p. 70.
2. Aufruf Wilhelm II, 5 January 1917, in Herbert Michaelis and Ernst Schraepeler, eds, *Ursachen und Folgen. Vom deutschen Zusammenbruch 1918 und 1945 bis zur staatlichen Neuordnung Deutschlands in der Gegenwart*, 26 vols (Berlin, 1958–), p. 85.
3. 'Ce que la vie m'a enseigné', manuscript written in 1949 by Count Emmanuel de Benningsen, Bakhmeteff Archive, Columbia University, BAR-Benningsen, Box 1, fo. 12.
4. William Fuller, *The Foe Within: Fantasies of Treason and the End of Imperial Russia* (Ithaca, NY, 2006), pp. 203–13.
5. Rex Wade, *The Russian Revolution, 1917* (Cambridge, 2000), pp. 22–3; Joshua Sanborn, 'Liberals and Bureaucrats at War', *Kritika*, 8, 1 (2007), pp. 151–8; Paul Miliukov, *Political Memoirs, 1905–1917* (Ann Arbor, MI, 1967), pp. 376–8; Melissa Stockdale, *Paul Miliukov and the Quest for a Liberal Russia, 1880–1918* (Ithaca, NY, 1996), pp. 231–7; Paul Miliukov, *The Russian Revolution*, 3 vols (Gulf Breeze, FL, 1978), vol. 1, pp. 17–18.
6. Cited in Corinne Gaudin, 'Rural Echoes of World War I: War Talk in the Russian Village', *Jahrbücher für Geschichte Osteuropas*, 56, 3 (2008), p. 400.
7. Ibid., p. 399; Joshua Sanborn, *Drafting the Russian Nation: Military Conscription, Total War, and Mass Politics, 1905–1925* (DeKalb, IL 2003), pp. 35–8.
8. Peter Holquist, *Making War, Forging Revolution: Russia's Continuum of Crisis, 1914–1921* (Cambridge, MA, 2002), pp. 26–46.
9. Cited in Barbara Alpern Engel, 'Not by Bread Alone: Subsistence Riots in Russia during World War I', *Journal of Modern History*, 69, 4 (1997), p. 717.
10. Diary entry, 24 February 1917, in Anthony Philips, ed., *Sergey Prokofiev: Diaries 1915–1923, Behind the Mask* (Ithaca, NY, 2008), pp. 175–6.
11. Diary entry, 28 February 1917, in ibid., p. 182; Wade, *Revolution*, pp. 32–42.
12. Wade, *Revolution*, pp. 45–50; Fuller, *Fantasy*, p. 232; Miliukov, *Memoirs*, p. 396; Stockdale, *Miliukov*, pp. 242–9.
13. Cited in Miliukov, *Revolution*, p. 64; Wade, *Revolution*, pp. 60–1.
14. 'Russia Leads the Way', *The Tribunal*, 22 March 1917, in Richard A. Reppel, Louis Greenspan, Beryl Haslam, Albert Lewis, and Mark Lippincourt, eds, *The Collected Papers of Bertrand Russell: Pacifism and Revolution, 1916–1918*, 29 vols (London, 1995), vol. 14, pp. 118–19.

15. Jean-Jacques Becker, *The Great War and the French People* (Leamington Spa, 1985), p. 241.
16. Miliukov, *Revolution*, pp. 43–6.
17. Wade, *Revolution*, p. 151.
18. Ibid., pp. 66–71.
19. Ibid., pp. 82–3.
20. Letter to the Chair of Soviet Workers' and Soldiers' Deputies, from Yegorov in the 753rd Reserve Regiment, late April 1917, in Mark D. Steinberg, ed., *Voices of Revolution, 1917* (New Haven, CT, 2001), p. 119.
21. Ibid., p. 98.
22. David Stevenson, *French War Aims against Germany, 1914–1919* (Oxford, 1982), pp. 65–8; Keith Neilson, *Strategy and Supply: The Anglo-Russian Alliance, 1914–1917* (London, 1984), pp. 262–3.
23. Diary entry, 16 March 1917, in Trevor Wilson, ed., *The Political Diaries of C. P. Scott, 1911–1928* (London, 1970), pp. 267–8.
24. Ingeborg Meckling, *Die Aussenpolitik des Grafen Czernin* (Munich, 1969), pp. 221–5; Konrad Jarausch, *The Enigmatic Chancellor: Bethmann Hollweg and the Hubris of Imperial Germany* (New Haven, CT, 1973), pp. 222–8.
25. House to Wilson, 17 March 1917; Lansing to Wilson, 19 March 1917; Diary of Josephus Daniels, 20 March 1917, in Arthur Link, *Papers of Woodrow Wilson*, 69 vols (Princeton, NJ, 1966–94), vol. 41, pp. 422–3, 425–7, 444–5.
26. Heinz Hagenlücke, *Deutsche Vaterlandspartei. Die nationale Rechte am Ende des Kaiserreichs* (Düsseldorf, 1997), pp. 75–81.
27. *Durch Deutschen Sieg zum Deutschen Frieden. Mahnruf ans deutsche Volk* (Berlin, 1917), p. 42.
28. Diary entry, 8 January 1917, Walter Görlitz, ed., *The Kaiser and his Court: The Diaries, Notebooks and Letters of Admiral Georg Alexander von Müller, Chief of the Naval Cabinet, 1914–1918* (London, 1961), p. 229.
29. Dirk Steffen, 'The Holtzendorff Memorandum of 22 December 1916 and Germany's Declaration of Unrestricted U-Boat Warfare', *Journal of Military History*, 68, 1 (2004), pp. 215–24.
30. Klaus Epstein, *Matthias Erzberger and the Dilemma of German Democracy* (New York, 1971), pp. 158–62; John G. Williamson, *Karl Helfferich, 1872–1924: Economist, Financier, Politician* (Princeton, NJ, 1971), pp. 163–8; Holger Herwig, 'Total Rhetoric, Limited War: Germany's U-Boat Campaign, 1917–1918', in Roger Chickering and Stig Förster, eds, *Great War, Total War: Combat and Mobilization on the Western Front* (Cambridge, 2000), pp. 189–206.
31. Diary entry, 9 January 1917, in Görlitz, *The Kaiser and his Court*, pp. 229–31; Diary entry, 25 January 1917, in Kurt Riezler, *Tagebücher, Aufsätze, Dokumente*, ed. Karl Dietrich Erdmann, intro. Holger Afflerbach (Göttingen, 2008), p. 401.
32. Arthur Link, *Wilson: Campaigns for Progressivism and Peace, 1916–1917* (Princeton, NJ, 1965), p. 290.
33. 'Notes on the Probable Resumption of Submarine Warfare', 24 January 1917, Lansing Papers, Seeley G. Mudd Library, MC083, Box 7, Folder 2, fos 53–4.
34. Cited in John Milton Cooper, *Woodrow Wilson* (New York, 2011), p. 369.
35. Ibid., pp. 369–70; Thomas J. Knock, *To End All Wars: Woodrow Wilson and the Quest for a New World Order* (New York, 1992), pp. 111–15.
36. Cooper, *Wilson*, p. 370; Knock, *To End All Wars*, pp. 114–15.
37. Diary entry by House, 1 February 1917; memorandum by Louis Paul Lochner, 1 February 1917, in Link, *Papers of Woodrow Wilson*, vol. 41, pp. 86–91.
38. Cooper, *Wilson*, pp. 374–5.
39. Address to Joint Session of Congress, 3 February 1917, in Link, *Papers of Woodrow Wilson*, vol. 41, pp. 109–12.
40. Link, *Campaigns*, pp. 334–8; Alan Knight, *The Mexican Revolution: Counter-Reconstruction*, 2 vols (Cambridge, 1986), vol. 2, pp. 470–1.
41. Link, *Campaigns*, pp. 423–7; Cooper, *Wilson*, pp. 384–6.
42. 'The Defence of the Atlantic World', 17 February 1917, in Arthur Schlesinger, ed., *Walter Lippmann: Early Writings* (New York, 1970), pp. 69–75.
43. Jennifer D. Keene, 'W. E. B. DuBois and the Wounded World: Seeking Meaning in the First World War for African-Americans', *Peace & Change*, 26, 2 (2001), pp. 140–1.
44. Anthony Goughan, 'Woodrow Wilson and the Rise of Militant Interventionism in the South', *Journal of Southern History*, 65, 4 (1999), pp. 789–94.
45. American Federation of Labor, *American Labor's Position in Peace or in War* (Washington DC, 1917) .
46. Alan Dawley, *Changing the World: American Progressives in War and Revolution* (Princeton, NJ, 2003), pp. 210–15.

47. 'Hughes Enlists All for Service', *The New York Times*, 13 April 1917.
48. Taft Address on Behalf of the Red Cross Fund at the Boston Opera House, 19 June 1917, Taft Papers, Library of Congress, Series 9A, vol. 39, reel 574, fo. 96.
49. Erez Manela, *The Wilsonian Moment: Self-Determination and the International Origins of Anti-Colonial Nationalism* (Oxford, 2007), pp. 20–2.
50. 'Germany, 1917', Dulles Papers, Seeley G. Mudd Library, Princeton, MC016, Box 1; Ronald Pruessen, *John Foster Dulles: The Road to Power* (New York, 1982), pp. 24–5.
51. 'Discours au banquet de la Société France-Amérique à New York', 12 March 1917, in Henri Bergson, *Mélanges* (Paris, 1977), pp. 1,243–8.
52. 'Fighting France', Hoover Institution Archives, Lauzanne Papers, Box 2.
53. Cited in Xu Guoqi, *China and the Great War* (Cambridge, 2005), p. 159.
54. Ibid., pp. 164–7.
55. Ibid., p. 178.
56. Ibid., pp. 203–31; Richard Phillips, *China since 1911* (Basingstoke, 1996), pp. 28–32; Edward A. McCord, 'Warlords against Warlordism: The Politics of Anti-Militarism in Early Twentieth-Century China', *Modern Asian Studies*, 30, 4 (1996), pp. 795–827.
57. Frederick Dickinson, *War and National Reinvention: Japan in the Great War, 1914–1919* (Cambridge, MA, 1999), pp. 176–9.
58. 'British Policy in India', *The Times*, 21 August 1917, p. 8.
59. Robin Moore, 'Curzon and Indian Reform', *Modern Asian Studies*, 27, 4 (1993), pp. 729–32.
60. Ronan Fanning, *Fatal Path: British Government and Irish Revolution, 1910–1922* (London, 2013), pp. 155–9.
61. Richard Fogarty, *Race and War in France: Colonial Subjects in the French Army, 1914–1918* (Baltimore, MD, 2008), pp. 233–41.
62. Joe Lunn, 'Kamara Speaks', in Melvyn Page, ed., *Africa and the First World War* (Basingstoke, 1987), p. 45.
63. Cited in Radikha Singha, 'The Recruiter's Eye on "the Primitive": To France – and Back – in the Indian Labour Corps, 1917–1918', in James Kitchen, Alisa Miller, and Laura Rowe, eds, *Other Combatants, Other Fronts: Competing Histories of the First World War* (Newcastle, 2011), p. 216; Radikha Singha, 'Front Lines and Status Lines: Sepoy and Menial in the Great War, 1916–1920', in Heike Liebau, Katrin Bromber, Katharina Lange, Dyala Hamzah, and Ravi Ahuja, eds, *The World in World Wars: Experiences, Perceptions and Perspectives from Africa and Asia* (Leiden, 2010), pp. 56–106.
64. William Duiker, *Ho Chi Minh: A Life* (New York, 2000), pp. 54–8.
65. Jennifer D. Keene, *Doughboys, the Great War, and the Remaking of America* (Baltimore, MD, 2001), p. 108.
66. Cited in Robert Doughty, *Pyrrhic Victory: French Strategy and Operations in the Great War* (Cambridge, MA, 2005), p. 339.
67. Ibid., pp. 349–59; Leonard Smith, Stéphane Audoin-Rouzeau, and Annette Becker, *France and the Great War, 1914–1918* (Cambridge, 2003), pp. 120–31.
68. Cited in Antonio Gibelli, *La grande guerra degli italiani 1915–1918* (Milan, 1998), pp. 89–92.
69. Alexander Watson, *Enduring the Great War: Combat, Morale and Collapse in the German and British Armies, 1914–1918* (Cambridge, 2008), pp. 153, 168.
70. Ulrich, *Augenzeugen*, p. 138.
71. Maureen Healy, *Vienna and the Fall of the Habsburg Empire: Total War and Everyday Life in World War I* (Cambridge, 2004), p. 42; Richard Wall and Jay Winter, 'Introduction' in idem, eds, *The Upheaval of War: Family, Work, and Welfare in Europe, 1914–1918* (Cambridge, 1988), pp. 2–39.
72. John D. Bell, *Peasants in Power: Alexander Stamboliski and the Bulgarian Agrarian National Union, 1899–1923* (Princeton, NJ, 1977), pp. 123–6.
73. Healy, *Vienna*, pp. 83–4.
74. Ute Daniel, *The War from Within: German Working-Class Women in the First World War* (Oxford, 1997), p. 233.
75. John Horne, 'The Comité d'Action (CGT-Parti Socialiste) and the Origins of Wartime Labor Reformism (1914–1916)', in Patrick Fridenson, ed., *The French Home Front, 1914–1918* (Providence, RI, 1992), pp. 246–8; Becker, *The Great War*, p. 231.
76. Adrian Gregory, *The Last Great War: British Society and the First World War* (Cambridge, 2008), p. 215.
77. Becker, *The Great War*, pp. 209–10.
78. Cited in Karl Christian Führer, *Carl Legien 1861–1920. Ein Gewerkschafter im Kampf um 'möglichst gutes Leben' für alle Arbeiter* (Essen, 2009), p. 205.
79. Cited in Gibelli, *Grande guerra*, p. 218.

80. Cited in Stéphane Audoin-Rouzeau, *Men at War 1914–1918: National Sentiment and Trench Journalism in France during the First World War* (Oxford, 1992), p. 139.

81. Healy, *Vienna*, pp. 249–55.

82. Daniel, *War from Within*, p. 155.

83. Paul Corner, *Fascism in Ferrara, 1915–1925* (Oxford, 1975), p. 34.

84. Gregory, *Last Great War*, pp. 208–12.

85. Maurice Barrès, *Mes cahiers, 1896–1923* (Paris, 1963), p. 773.

86. Corner, *Fascism in Ferrara*, p. 39.

87. Rathenau to Mathilde von Leixner, 28 December 1916, in Alexander Jager, Clemens Picht, and Ernst Schulin, eds, *Walther Rathenau. Briefe*, 2 vols (Düsseldorf, 2006), vol. 2, p. 1,594.

88. Cited in Janet Polasky, *The Democratic Socialism of Emile Vandervelde: Between Reform and Revolution* (Oxford, 1995), p. 125.

89. Sitzung der holländischen ISB-Delegation in Laren, 15 April 1917, http://labourhistory.net/stockholm1917/documents/p1a.php.

90. David Kirby, 'International Socialism and the Question of Peace: The Stockholm Conference of 1917', *Historical Journal*, 25, 3 (1982), p. 710.

91. Jay M. Winter, *Socialism and the Challenge of War: Ideas and Politics in Britain, 1912–1918* (London, 1974), pp. 245–56.

92. 'L'attitude de la Russie dans les questions des buts de guerre', 22 July 1917, MAE, Série A, *Paix*, vol. 55, fos 91–4.

93. 'Internationale de Guerre au Internationale de Paix', Parti Socialiste, Fédération de la Haute-Loire, BDIC, GF delta res 95, Dossier: France SFIO: Fédération de la Marne.

94. See the text of the Commission's report in *Le Parti Socialiste, la guerre et la paix* (Paris, 1918), pp. 4–65.

95. Emile Vandervelde, *Three Aspects of the Russian Revolution* (London, 1918), pp. 243–67.

96. Meckling, *Czernin*, pp. 74–6; Francesco Marin, 'Die deutsch-österreichische Sozialdemokratie und die Friedensbestrebungen 1917', in Andreas Gottmann, ed., *Karl I. (IV.), der Erste Weltkrieg und das Ende der Donaumonarchie* (Vienna, 2007), pp. 33–46.

97. Sitzung der Holländisch-skandinavischen Komitees mit der Delegation der MSPD am 13. Juni 1917, http://labourhistory.net/stockholm1917/documents/p34b.php

98. Marin, 'Die deutsch-österreichische Sozialdemokratie', pp. 38–42.

99. Cited in Führer, *Legien*, p. 204.

100. Sven Oliver Müller, *Die Nation als Waffe und Vorstellung. Nationalismus in Deutschland und Großbritannien im Ersten Weltkrieg* (Göttingen, 2002), pp. 86–8.

101. 'Parlament und Regierung im neugeordneten Deutschland. Zur politischen Kritik des Beamtentums und Parteiwesens' in Wolfgang Mommsen and Gangolf Hübinger, eds, Max Weber. Zur Politik im Weltkrieg. Schriften und Reden 1914–1918, series 1, vol. 15 (Tübingen, 1984), pp. 421–521; this was published in March 1918, but it was based on six articles published in the *Frankfurter Zeitung* between April and June 1917.

102. Epstein, *Erzberger*, pp. 189–90.

103. Müller, *Nation als Waffe*, p. 295.

104. Ibid., pp. 302–10.

105. Erzberger speech, 6 July 1917, and Scheidemann speech, 7 July 1917, in Herbert Michaelis and Ernst Schraepeler, eds, *Ursachen und Folgen. Vom deutschen Zusammenbruch 1918 und 1945 bis zur staatlichen Neuordnung Deutschlands in der Gegenwart*, 26 vols (Berlin, 1958–), vol. 2, pp. 3–12.

106. http://germanhistorydocs.ghi-dc.org/sub_document.cfm?document_id=987 – the text of 'Reichstag's Peace Resolution' (19 July 1917).

107. Gabriele Paolini, *Offensive di pace. La Santa Sede e la prima guerra mondiale* (Florence, 2008), pp. 152–7; Hans-Georg Aschoff, 'Benedict XV (1914–1922), Profil eines Pontifikats', *Historisches Jahrbuch*, 127 (2007), pp. 307–10.

108. Cited in Cooper, *Wilson*, p. 417.

109. 'Defining the Issue', *The Times*, 27 July 1917, p. 7.

110. Ibid.; Pierre Renaudel, 'Obscurité', *L'Humanité*, 21 July 1917, p. 1.

111. Hagenlücke, *Vaterlandspartei*, pp. 87–9, 248–60; Wolfram Pyta, *Hindenburg. Herrschaft zwischen Hohenzollern und Hitler* (Munich, 2009), pp. 271–82; Anna von der Goltz, *Hindenburg: Power, Myth, and the Rise of the Nazis* (Oxford, 2009).

112. Paolini, *Offensive di pace*, pp. 166–75; Aschoff, 'Benedict XV', pp. 312–13.

113. John Horne, *Labour at War: France and Britain, 1914–1918* (Oxford, 1991), pp. 311–14; Smith, Becker, and Audoin-Rouzeau, *France*, pp. 138–41; Winter, *Socialism*, pp. 259–62; Paul Bridgen, *The Labour Party and the Politics of War and Peace, 1900–1924* (Woodbridge, 2009), pp. 100–6.

114. Neilson, *Strategy and Supply*, pp. 273–81; Stevenson, *French War Aims*, pp. 86–7; Ghislain de Castelbajac, 'La France et la question polonaise', in Georges-Henri Soutou, ed., *Recherches sur la France et le problème des nationalités pendant la Première Guerre mondiale* (Paris, 1995), p. 71.

115. Wade, *Russian Revolution*, pp. 175–81.

116. Beryl Williams, *Lenin: Profiles in Power* (Harlow, 2000), p. 66.

117. Resolution of workers of twenty-seven small enterprises, Peterhof district, 27 July 1917, pp. 189–90; Letter to the Soviet from the soldier Yurchenko at the front, 8 July 1917, p. 199; Letter to the Central Executive Committee of Soviets from soldiers at the front, 9 August 1917, pp. 214–15, all in Steinberg, ed., *Voices of Revolution*.

118. Wade, *Russian Revolution*, pp. 194–5; Serhy Yekelchyk, *Ukraine: Birth of a Modern Nation* (Oxford, 2007), pp. 68–70.

119. Stockdale, *Miliukov*, pp. 257–60; William Gleason, 'Alexander Guchkov and the End of the Russian Empire', *Transactions of the American Philosophical Society*, New Series, 73, 3 (1983), pp. 76–7.

120. 'The Tasks of the Revolution', 9–10 October 1917, in V. I. Lenin, *Collected Works*, 45 vols (London, 1964), vol. 26, pp. 62–4.

Chapter 7 Victory and Defeat, 1918

1. Richard Georg Plaschka, Horst Haselsteiner, and Arnold Suppon, *Innere Front. Militärassistenz, Widerstand und Umsturz in der Donaumonarchie 1918*, 2 vols (Munich, 1974), vol. 1, pp. 107–40.

2. 'Proclamation of the Assumption of Power by Congress of Soviets', 7–8 November 1917, in Rex Wade, ed., *Documents of Soviet History*, vol. 1, *The Triumph of Bolshevism, 1917–1919*, 6 vols (Gulf Breeze, FL, 1991), pp. 5–6.

3. 'Decree on Peace', 8 November 1917', in ibid., pp. 6–8.

4. Trotsky's Report on Soviet Foreign Policy, 21 November 1917; 'Appeal to the Belligerents on Peace', 27 November 1917, in Wade, ed., *Documents*, pp. 44–6, 49–50.

5. Mark Cornwall, *The Undermining of Austria-Hungary: The Battle for Hearts and Minds* (Basingstoke, 2000), pp. 54–62.

6. Speech by Georg von Hertling, 29 November 1917, http://www.reichstagsprotokolle.de/Blatt_k13_bsb00003407_00085.html.

7. 'Declaration of the Rights of the Peoples of Russia', 15 November 1917, in Wade, ed., *Documents*, pp. 24–5.

8. 'Report on the National Question', 28 January 1918, in Wade, ed., *Documents*, pp. 93–4.

9. 'Ukrainian Declaration of Independence', 22 January 1918, in ibid., pp. 87–8; Serhy Yekelchyk, *Ukraine: Birth of a Modern Nation* (Oxford, 2007), pp. 67–73; Frank Golczewski, *Deutsche und Ukrainer 1914–1939* (Paderborn, 2010), pp. 181–6.

10. Wolfdieter Bihl, *Österreich-Ungarn und die Friedensschlüsse von Brest-Litovsk* (Vienna, 1970), pp. 43–6; Andrea Orzoff, *Battle for the Castle: The Myth of Czechoslovakia in Europe, 1914–1948* (Oxford, 2009), p. 46.

11. Birgitt Morgenbrod, *Wiener Großbürgertum im Ersten Weltkrieg. Die Geschichte der Österreichischen Politischen Gesellschaft 1916–1918* (Vienna, 1998), pp. 112–23.

12. Cited in Bihl, *Brest-Litovsk*, p. 51.

13. Diary entry, 5 January 1918, in J. M. McEwen, ed., *The Riddell Diaries 1908–1923* (London, 1986), p. 212.

14. Stephen Roskill, *Hankey: Man of Secrets, 1877–1918*, 3 vols (London, 1970), vol. 1, p. 474; Diary entry, 1 January 1918, in Thomas Jones, *Whitehall Diary*, ed. Keith Middlemass, 3 vols (Oxford, 1969), vol. 1, p. 42.

15. Diary entry, 16 November 1917, in Jones, *Whitehall Diary*, vol. 1, p. 39.

16. Frank Winters, 'Exaggerating the Efficacy of Diplomacy: The Marquis of Lansdowne's "Peace Letter" of November 1917', *International History Review*, 32, 1 (2010), pp. 34–41.

17. Diary entry, 3 December 1917, in Riddell, *Diaries*, p. 208.

18. Draft minutes of a meeting held at 10 Downing Street, 31 December 1917, TNA CAB 23/13/33, fos 2–3.

19. Roskill, *Hankey*, p. 479.

20. Diary entry, 3 January 1918, in Jones, *Diary*, p. 43.

21. Diary entry, 9 December 1917, in Riddell, *Diary*, p. 210.

22. 'Mr Lloyd George's Statement', *The Times*, 7 January 1918, pp. 7–8.

23. Cited in Lawrence Gelfand, *The Inquiry: American Preparations for Peace, 1917–1919* (New Haven, CT, 1963), p. 151.

24. Fifth annual address, 4 December 1917, http://www.presidency.ucsb.edu/ws/index.php?pid=29558.

25. Gelfand, *Inquiry*, pp. 25–102.
26. John Milton Cooper, *Woodrow Wilson* (New York, 2011), p. 421.
27. Address at the joint session of Congress, 8 January 1918, in Ray Stannard Baker and William E. Dodd, eds, *War and Peace: Presidential Messages, Addresses, and Public Papers (1917–1924) by Woodrow Wilson*, 2 vols (New York, 1927), vol. 1, pp. 155–62.
28. Gelfand, *Inquiry*, p. 138.
29. Winfried Baumgart, *Deutsche Ostpolitik 1918. Von Brest-Litovsk bis zum Ende des Weltkrieges* (Vienna, 1966), pp. 20–2.
30. 'No war! No peace!', in Wade, ed., *Triumph of Bolshevism*, pp. 100–1.
31. Baumgart, *Ostpolitik*, pp. 23–6; Ingeborg Meckling, *Die Aussenpolitik des Grafen Czernin* (Munich, 1969), p. 297.
32. 'On the History of the Question of the Unfortunate Peace', 7 January 1918, in V. I. Lenin, *Collected Works* (London, 1964), p. 447.
33. Reichstag debate, 22 March 1918, http://www.reichstagsprotokolle.de/Blatt_k13_bsb00003407_00674.html
34. Klaus Epstein, *Matthias Erzberger and the Dilemma of German Democracy* (New York, 1971), pp. 234–9.
35. Heinz Hagenlücke, *Deutsche Vaterlandspartei. Die nationale Rechte am Ende des Kaiserreichs* (Düsseldorf, 1997), pp. 206–11.
36. Joachim Tauber, 'Stubborn Collaborators: The Politics of the Lithuanian Taryba, 1917–1918', *Journal of Baltic Studies*, 37, 2 (2006), pp. 194–209.
37. Cited in Golczewski, *Deutsche und Ukrainer*, p. 195.
38. Bihl, *Brest-Litovsk*, p. 85.
39. Miklós Komjáthy, ed., *Protokolle des Gemeinsamen Ministerrates der Österreichisch-Ungarischen Monarchie (1914–1918)* (Budapest, 1966), pp. 627–33.
40. Plaschka et al., *Innere Front*, p. 84.
41. Golczewski, *Deutsche und Ukrainer*, pp. 241–3.
42. Cited in Baumgart, *Ostpolitik*, p. 68.
43. Oleksandr I. Syč, 'Die Tagebücher von Vladimir I. Vernaskij als Quelle für die Erforschung der deutsch-österreichisch-ungarischen Okkupation der Ukraine 1918', in Wolfram Dornik and Stefan Korner, eds, *Die Besatzung der Ukraine 1918. Historischer Kontext – Forschungsstand – wirtschaftliche und soziale Folgen* (Graz, 2008), p. 192.
44. Yekelchyk, *Ukraine*, pp. 73–6.
45. Syč, 'Tagebücher', p. 194.
46. 'Subjects in the President's Statement of War Aims, on January 8, 1918, which are Open to Debate', 10 January 1918, in Lansing Papers, Seeley G. Mudd Library, Princeton, MC083, Box 7, folder 2, fo. 125.
47. 'Certain phrases of the president contain the seeds of trouble', 20 December 1918, in Lansing Papers, Seeley G. Mudd Library, Princeton, MC 083, Box 7, folder 2, fo. 208.
48. John Horne, *Labour at War: France and Britain, 1914–1918* (Oxford, 1991), pp. 181–4; Giovanna Procacci, 'Popular Protest and Labour Conflict in Italy, 1914–1918', *Social History*, 14, 1 (1989), pp. 50–2; Elizabeth McKillen, 'Integrating Labor into the Narrative of Wilsonian Internationalism', *Diplomatic History*, 34, 4 (2010), pp. 656–9.
49. Cited in Bernard Georges and Denise Tintant, *Léon Jouhaux. Cinquante ans de syndicalisme*, 2 vols (Paris, 1962), vol. 1, p. 256.
50. 'Memorandum on War Aims Agreed at Central Hall, Westminster', 20–24 February 1918, Inter-Allied Labour and Socialist Conference, Shotwell Papers, Columbia University Archives, Box 103.
51. Cited in Procacci, 'Popular Protest', p. 54; Adrian Gregory, *The Last Great War: British Society and the First World War* (Cambridge, 2008), pp. 203–6; Gilbert Hatry, 'Shop Stewards at Renault', in Patrick Fridenson, ed., *The French Home Front, 1914–1918* (Providence, RI, 1992), pp. 229–34.
52. Daniela Rossini, *Woodrow Wilson and the American Myth in Italy: Culture, Diplomacy, and War Propaganda* (Cambridge, MA, 2008), p. 135.
53. Ibid., p. 128.
54. Geoffrey Heywood, *Failure of a Dream: Sidney Sonnino and the Rise and Fall of Liberal Italy, 1847–1922* (Florence, 1999), p. 461.
55. Andrej Mitrovic, *Serbia's Great War, 1914–1918* (London, 2007), pp. 291–4; 'The Freeing of Serbia', *The Times*, 8 August 1917.
56. Heywood, *Sonnino*, pp. 466–9; Charles Killinger, *Gaetano Salvemini: A Biography* (Westport, CT, 2002), pp. 123–7.
57. Elizabeth Fordham, 'Le combat pour le New Europe. Les radicaux britanniques et la Première Guerre mondiale', *Mil neuf cent. Revue d'histoire intellectuelle*, 23, 1 (2005), pp. 111–18; Frédéric

Le Moal, *La France et l'Italie dans les Balkans 1914–1919. Le contentieux adriatique* (Paris, 2006), pp. 238–9.

58. 'Le dichiarazioni di Orlando ai rappresentanti del Congresso della nazionalità', *La Stampa*, 12 April 1918, p. 4.

59. 'I postulati del Congresso delle nazionalità oppresso dall'Austria', *La Stampa*, 11 April 1918, p. 2.

60. Georges Henri Soutou, 'Jean Pélissier et l'Office central des nationalités, 1911–1918: un agent du gouvernement français auprès des nationalités', p. 31; Sébastian de Gasquet, 'La France et les mouvements nationaux ukrainiens (1917–1919)', p. 125, both in Georges-Henri Soutou, ed., *Recherches sur la France et le problème des nationalités pendant la Première Guerre Mondiale* (Paris, 1995).

61. Ghislain de Castelbajac, 'La France et la question polonaise', in Georges-Henri Soutou, ed., *Recherches sur la France et le problème des nationalités pendant la Première Guerre Mondiale* (Paris, 1995), p. 87.

62. Ibid., p. 93.

63. David Stevenson, *French War Aims against Germany, 1914–1919* (Oxford, 1982), pp. 103–7; Victor Rothwell, *British War Aims and Peace Diplomacy, 1914–1918* (Oxford, 1971), pp. 222–6.

64. Norman Davies, *God's Playground: A History of Poland*, 2 vols (Oxford, 1981), vol. 2, pp. 186–7.

65. Thomas G. Masaryk, *The New Europe* (Lewisburg, PA, 1972), pp. 63, 93, 189.

66. 'Self-Determination Principle. Mr J. MacNeill and the Premier's Pledge', *Irish Independent*, 16 January 1918.

67. Michael Laffan, *The Resurrection of Ireland: The Sinn Fein Party, 1916–1923* (Cambridge, 1999), pp. 56–70, 128–39.

68. 'Bishops' Addresses', *Irish Independent*, 18 April 1918; 'Mr Devlin, MP at Toome', *Irish Independent*, 24 April 1918; P. O'Loughlin to the editor, 'The Position of Ireland', *Irish Independent*, 17 April 1918.

69. Erez Manela, *The Wilsonian Moment: Self-Determination and the International Origins of Anti-Colonial Nationalism* (Oxford, 2007), pp. 63–7.

70. Maia Ramnath, 'Two Revolutions: The Ghadar Movement and India's Radical Diaspora, 1913–1918', *Radical History Review*, 92 (Spring 2005), pp. 15–17.

71. Cited in Manela, *Wilsonian Moment*, p. 90.

72. David Stevenson, *1914–1918: The History of the First World War* (London, 2004), pp. 398–9; David Stevenson, *With our Backs to the Wall: Victory and Defeat in 1918* (London, 2011), p. 345.

73. Masaryk, *New Europe*, p. 52.

74. Stevenson, *Backs to the Wall*, is the most recent, comprehensive, and best analysis of the military conflict in 1918.

75. Prinz Max von Baden, *Erinnerungen und Dokumente* (Stuttgart, 1968), p. 242; Rüdiger Schütz, 'Einführende Bemerkungen. Die militärischen Operationen der Mittelmächte an der Westfront 1918', in Jorg Düppler and Gerhard P. Groß, eds, *Kriegsende 1918. Ereignis, Wirkung, Nachwirkung* (Oldenbourg, 1999), pp. 46–8.

76. Schütz, 'Einführende Bemerkungen', p. 47.

77. Dabid Zabecki, *Steel Wind: Colonel Georg Brüchmüller and the Birth of Modern Artillery* (Westport, CT, 1994), pp. 21–38; Dieter Storz, ' "Aber was hätte anders geschehen sollen?" Die deutschen Offensive an der Westfront 1918', in Düppler and Groß, eds, *Kriegsende*, pp. 63–6.

78. Stevenson, *Backs to the Wall*, pp. 43–52.

79. Cited in Alexander Watson, *Enduring the Great War: Combat, Morale and Collapse in the German and British Armies, 1914–1918* (Cambridge, 2008), p. 179.

80. 'Mars 1918', Loucheur Papers, Hoover Institution Archives, Box 12, folder 10.

81. Elizabeth Greenhalgh, *Foch in Command: The Forging of a First World War General* (Cambridge, 2011), pp. 300–11.

82. Stevenson, *Backs to the Wall*, pp. 67–8.

83. Cited in J. P. Harris, *Douglas Haig and the First World War* (Cambridge, 2008), p. 469.

84. Cited in Stéphane Audoin-Rouzeau, *Men at War 1914–1918: National Sentiment and Trench Journalism in France during the First World War* (Oxford, 1992), p. 111; Jean-Jacques Becker, *The Great War and the French People* (Leamington Spa, 1985), p. 311; Blanche Duhamel to Georges Duhamel, in Georges and Blanche Duhamel, *Correspondance de guerre, 1914–1919*, ed. Arlette Lafay, intro. Jean-Jacques Becker, 2 vols (Paris, 2007–8), vol. 2, pp. 994–5.

85. Loucheur, note, 9 October 1918, Loucheur Papers, Hoover Institution Archives, Box 2, folder 1.

86. Jennifer D. Keene, *Doughboys, the Great War, and the Remaking of America* (Baltimore, MD, 2001), pp. 75–8; Alan Dawley, *Changing the World: American Progressives in War and Revolution* (Princeton, NJ, 2003), pp. 193–4.

87. Georges Suarez, *Briand: Sa vie, son oeuvre*, 6 vols (Paris, 1938), vol. 3, p. 371.

88. Report, 241 Inf-D, No. 871/I geh., Artl-Kder, 24 June 1918, BA-MA, PH 5 II/482, fo. 152.

89. Robert Doughty, *Pyrrhic Victory: French Strategy and Operations in the Great War* (Cambridge, MA, 2005), pp. 461–74.
90. Fritz von Loßberg, *Meine Tätigkeit im Weltkriege 1914–1918* (Berlin, 1939), pp. 348–51.
91. Watson, *Enduring the Great War*, pp. 185–95.
92. Wilhelm Deist, 'Verdeckter Militärstreik im Kriegsjahr 1918?', in Wolfram Wette, ed., *Der Krieg des kleinen Mannes. Eine Militärgeschichte von unten* (Munich, 1992), pp. 146–67.
93. Dominik Richert, *Beste Gelegenheit zum Sterben. Meine Erlebnisse im Kriege 1914–1918*, ed. Angelika Tramitz and Bernd Ulrich (Munich, 1989), p. 386.
94. Diary entries, 22 and 23 July 1918, in Walter Görlitz, ed., *The Kaiser and his Court: The Diaries, Notebooks and Letters of Admiral Georg Alexander von Müller, Chief of the Naval Cabinet, 1914–1918* (London, 1961), pp. 373–4.
95. Ibid., p. 373; Boris Barth, *Dolchstosslegenden und politische Desintegration. Das Trauma der deutschen Niederlage im Ersten Weltkrieg 1914–1933* (Düsseldorf, 2003), pp. 173–9.
96. Mary Wilson to Richard Wilson, 3 October 1918, R. H. Wilson Papers, Imperial War Museum, London, 05/53/1.
97. 'Aufzeichnung, Auswärtiges Amt', by Fréderic Hans von Rosenberg, Diego von Bergen and Wilhelm von Stumm, 28 September 1918; 'Aufzeichnung, Paul von Hintze', 29 September 1918, both in Klaus Schwabe, ed., *Quellen zum Friedensschluss von Versailles* (Darmstadt, 1997), pp. 50–3; von Baden, *Erinnerungen*, pp. 323–37; Philipp Scheidemann, *Memoirs of a Social Democrat* (London, 1929), pp. 482–90.
98. Von Baden, *Erinnerungen*, p. 337.
99. Address opening the campaign for the Fourth Liberty Loan, New York City, 27 September 1918, in Ray Stannard Baker and William E. Dodd, eds, *War & Peace: Presidential Messages, Addresses, and Public Papers (1917–1924)*, 2 vols (New York, 1970), vol. 1, pp. 253–60.
100. 'Secretary of State to the Swiss Chargé d'Affaires', 8 October 1918, in *Foreign Relations of the United States (FRUS)*, Supplement 1, 'The World War', 2 vols (Washington DC, 1933), vol. 1, p. 343; see also Brian Kampmark, ' "No Peace with the Hohenzollerns": American Attitudes on Political Legitimacy towards Hohenzollern Germany, 1917–1918', *Diplomatic History*, 34, 5 (2010), pp. 784–7.
101. 'Policy as to Overtures of Peace by Germany and Austria', 7 October 1918, in Lansing Papers, Seeley G. Mudd Library, MC083, Box 7, folder 2, fos 179–80.
102. Paul von Hintze, 'Aufzeichnung', in Schwabe, ed., *Quellen*, p. 53.
103. Text of article in von Baden, *Erinnerungen*, pp. 362–3.
104. Michael Geyer, 'Insurrectionary Warfare: The German Debate about a Levée en Masse in October 1918', *Journal of Modern History*, 73, 4 (2001), pp. 475–90.
105. Cited in William Mulligan, *The Creation of the Modern German Army: General Walther Reinhardt and the Weimar Republic, 1914–1930* (Oxford, 2005), p. 35.
106. Diary entry, 15 October 1918, in T. Jones, *Whitehall Diary*, ed. Keith Middlemass, 3 vols (Oxford, 1969), vol. 1, p. 70.
107. Cited in Stevenson, *French War Aims*, p. 122.
108. M. Şükrü Hanioğlu, *Ataturk: An Intellectual Biography* (Princeton, NJ, 2011), pp. 89–96.
109. Rothwell, *War Aims*, pp. 241–8; David Fromkin, *A Peace to End all Peace: Creating the Modern Middle East, 1914–1922* (London, 1989), p. 365.
110. 'Independence Hall Sees Nations Born. New Liberty Bell Rung', *The New York Times*, 27 October 1918, p. 6.
111. Wladzimierz Borodziej, *Geschichte Polens im 20. Jahrhundert* (Munich, 2010), pp. 89–93.
112. Mark Biondich, *Stjepan Radic, the Croat Peasant Party, and the Politics of Mass Mobilization, 1904–1928* (Toronto, 2000), pp. 135–9; Mitrovic, *Serbia*, pp. 313–23.
113. Elisa Carrillo, *Alcide De Gasperi: The Long Apprenticeship* (Notre Dame, IL, 1965), p. 42.
114. Heywood, *Sonnino*, pp. 471–3.
115. Glenn Torrey, *Romania and World War I: A Collection of Studies* (Portland, OR, 1998), pp. 274–5, 366–7.
116. Cited in Keene, *Doughboys*, p. 117.
117. Cited in Scott Stephenson, *The Final Battle: Soldiers of the Western Front and the German Revolution of 1918* (Cambridge, 2009), p. 63.
118. Erich Maria Remarque, *The Road Back* (London, 1979), p. 11.
119. 'Service Spécial Propagande aux armées', 3 November 1918; 'Services renseignements aux armées à Lt Col de Cointet', October 1918, in Bibliothèque de Documentation Internationale Contemporaine, F delta res 926, 'Échanges entre soldats français et allemands', folder 2; Keene, *Doughboys*, pp. 111–16.
120. Richard Hall, ' "The Enemy is behind Us": The Morale Crisis in the Bulgarian Army during the Summer of 1918', *War in History*, 21, 2 (2004), p. 219.

121. Maxime Weygand, *Mémoires. Mirages et réalité*, 3 vols (Paris, 1957), vol. 2, p. 17.
122. Beck to Gertrud Beck (sister-in-law), 28 November 1918, in Klaus-Jürgen Müller, *General Ludwig Beck. Studien und Dokumente zur politisch-militärischen Vorstellungswelt und Tätigkeit des Generalstabschefs des deutschen Heeres 1933–1938* (Boppard am Rhein, 1980), pp. 323–8.
123. Diary entry, 11 November 1918, in Anthony Philips, ed., *Sergey Prokofiev: Diaries 1915–1923, Behind the Mask* (Ithaca, NY, 2008), pp. 351–2.
124. Georges Duhamel to Blanche Duhamel, 11 November 1918, in *Correspondance*, pp. 1,366–7.
125. Baldwin to his mother, Louise, 11 November 1918, in Philip Williamson and Philip Baldwin, eds, *Baldwin Papers: A Conservative Statesman, 1908–1947* (Cambridge, 2004), pp. 39–40.

Chapter 8 Drafting Peace, 1919

1. 'Some greedy men squabbling over gold and title deeds', Lansing Papers, Seeley G. Mudd Library, MC083, Scraps, 1918–1920, Box 10, Folder 29, fos 5–8.
2. Manfred F. Boemeke, Gerald D. Feldman, and Elisabeth Glaser, eds, *The Treaty of Versailles: A Reassessment after 75 Years* (Cambridge, 1998); Margaret Macmillan, *Paris 1919: Six Months that Changed the World* (New York, 2002).
3. 'Prime Minister on Conscription. The Limits of Capacity Explained', *The Times*, 12 December 1918, p. 6; Neville Meaney, *Australia and the World Crisis, 1914–1923* (Sydney, 2009), p. 332.
4. Untitled, Lansing Papers, Seeley G. Mudd Library, MC083, Scraps, 1918–1920, Box 10, Folder 29, fos 1–2.
5. John Milton Cooper, *Breaking the Heart of the World: Woodrow Wilson and the Fight for the League of Nations* (Cambridge, 2001), pp. 39–42; John Milton Cooper, *Woodrow Wilson* (New York, 2011), pp. 445–7.
6. Geoffrey Heywood, *Failure of a Dream: Sidney Sonnino and the Rise and Fall of Liberal Italy, 1847–1922* (Florence, 1999), pp. 475–83; Massimo Bucarelli, 'Mussolini, la questione adriatica e il fallimento dell'interventismo democratica', *Nuova Rivista Storica*, 95, 1 (2011), pp. 178–82.
7. Pierre Miquel, 'Le Journal de Débats et la paix de Versailles', *Revue Historique*, 232 (1964), pp. 380–1.
8. 'The Men who Sat too Long', Lansing Papers, Seeley G. Mudd Library, MC083, Scraps, 1918–1920, Box 10, Folder 29, fos 9–10.
9. Cooper, *Breaking the Heart*, pp. 28–30; Lloyd Ambrosius, *Woodrow Wilson and the American Diplomatic Tradition: The Treaty Fight in Perspective* (Cambridge, 1987), pp. 44–5.
10. Cited in Peter Yearwood, *Guarantee of Peace: The League of Nations in British Policy, 1914–1925* (Oxford, 2009), p. 75.
11. Jean-Michel Guieu, *Le rameau et le glaive. Les militants français pour la Société des Nations* (Paris, 2008), pp. 54–61.
12. Cooper, *Breaking the Heart*, p. 10.
13. Diary entry, 14 February 1919, Cecil Papers, British Library, MS Add 51131, fo. 38.
14. Plenary Session, 14 February 1919, in *Foreign Relations of the United States*, 1919, supplement Paris, vol. 3, pp. 212–13.
15. Ibid., p. 228.
16. David Stevenson, *French War Aims against Germany, 1914–1919* (Oxford, 1982), pp. 165–6; Georges-Henri Soutou, 'La France et les Marches de l'Est', *Revue Historique*, 260 (1978), p. 384.
17. Ross A. Kennedy, 'Woodrow Wilson, World War I, and an American Conception of National Security', *Diplomatic History*, 25, 1 (2001), p. 27.
18. Cited in Francesco Caccomo, *L'Italia e la 'Nuova' Europa. Il confronto sull' Europa orientale alla conferenza di pace di Parigi (1919–1920)* (2000), p. 63.
19. Zara Steiner, *The Lights that Failed: European International History, 1919–1933* (Oxford, 2005), pp. 48–50.
20. Ibid., pp. 50–5.
21. 'A tous les peuples amis', 16 June 1919, 'Comment les Italiens répandent la Civilisation en Istrie', 'Les italiens de Rijeka (Fiume) constituent une colonie d'immigrés', BDIC, 4 delta 1589, Yougoslavie.
22. Cited in Heywood, *Sonnino*, p. 491.
23. Daniela Rossini, *Woodrow Wilson and the American Myth in Italy: Culture, Diplomacy, and War Propaganda* (Cambridge, MA, 2008), pp. 177–88.
24. Bucarelli, 'Mussolini', pp. 191–202.
25. 'Exposé du président du Conseil, M. Protič, fait à Belgrade devant la Représentation nationale', 22 March 1919, BDIC, 4 delta 1589, Yougoslavie.

26. William W. Hagen, 'The Moral Economy of Ethnic Cleansing: The Pogrom in Lwów, November 1918', *Geschichte und Gesellschaft*, 31 (2005), pp. 207-9, 225.

27. Carole Fink, *Defending the Rights of Others: The Great Powers, the Jews, and the International Minority, 1878-1938* (Cambridge, 2004); Mark Mazower, 'Minorities and the League of Nations in Interwar Europe', *Daedalus*, 126, 2 (1997), pp. 47-54.

28. Cited in Éric Roussel, *Jean Monnet* (Paris, 1996), p. 73.

29. Marc Trachtenberg, *Reparations in World Politics: France and European Economic Diplomacy, 1916-1923* (New York, 1980), p. 34.

30. Cited in Robert H. van Meter, 'Herbert Hoover and the Economic Reconstruction of Europe, 1918-1921', in Lawrence Gelfand, ed., *Herbert Hoover: The Great War and its Aftermath, 1914-1923* (Iowa City, IA, 1979), p. 154.

31. Cited in Ronald W. Pruessen, *John Foster Dulles: The Road to Power* (New York, 1982), p. 52.

32. Georges-Henri Soutou, *L'or et le sang. Les buts de guerre économiques de la Première Guerre Mondiale* (Paris, 1989), pp. 840-3.

33. Luciano Monzali, 'Il "Partito Coloniale" e la politica estera italiana', *Clio*, 44, 3 (2008), pp. 401-10.

34. Erik Goldstein, *Winning the Peace: British Diplomatic Strategy, Peace Planning, and the Paris Peace Conference, 1916-1920* (Oxford, 1991), pp. 151-64.

35. Eugene Rogan, *The Arabs: A History* (London, 2009), pp. 193-200.

36. Susan Pedersen, 'The Meaning of the Mandates System: An Argument', *Geschichte und Gesellschaft*, 32, 4 (2006), pp. 560-82.

37. Naoko Shimazu, *Japan, Race, and Equality: The Racial Equality Proposal of 1919* (London, 1998).

38. Cited in Kristoffer Allerfeldt, 'Wilsonian Pragmatism? Woodrow Wilson, Japanese Immigration, and the Paris Peace Conference', *Diplomacy & Statecraft*, 15, 3 (2004), p. 547.

39. Ibid., pp. 545-72; Marilyn Lake and Henry Reynolds, *Drawing the Global Colour Line: White Men's Countries and the International Challenge of Racial Equality* (Cambridge, 2008), pp. 285-92.

40. Noriko Kawamura, 'Wilsonian Idealism and Japanese Claims at the Paris Peace Conference', *Pacific Historical Review*, 66, 4 (1997), pp. 521-3; Xu Guoqi, *China and the Great War* (Cambridge, 2005), pp. 245-61.

41. Kawamura, 'Wilsonian Idealism', p. 525.

42. Plenary Session, 11 April 1919, in *FRUS*, 1919, supplement Paris, vol. 3, p. 242.

43. British Empire Delegation, meeting 8 April 1919, Shotwell Papers, Columbia Archives, Box 106; 'Arthur Fontaine, l'homme et son oeuvre', in *L'Europe Nouvelle* in Shotwell Papers, Columbia Archives, Box 104.

44. Geert van Goethem, *The Amsterdam International: The World of the International Federation of Trade Unions, 1913-1945* (Aldershot, 2006), pp. 21-2.

45. Jasmien van Daele, 'Engineering Social Peace: Networks, Ideas, and the Founding of the International Labour Organization', *International Review of Social History*, 50 (2005), pp. 435-66.

46. British Empire Delegation, meeting 8 April 1919, Shotwell Papers, Columbia Archives, Box 106.

47. Labour Party, 'International Labour and Peace' (1919); James Shotwell, 'International Labor Organization', May 1926, Shotwell Papers, Columbia Archives, Box 103a.

48. Rana Mitter, *A Bitter Revolution: China's Struggle with the Modern World* (Oxford, 2004), pp. 3-9; Xu, *China*, pp. 266-70.

49. Cited in Xu, *China*, p. 266.

50. Memorandum of Chinese delegation in Washington, 25 November 1918, Lansing Papers, Seeley G. Mudd Library, MC083, Box 3, folder 2.

51. Chinese Patriotic Committee, *Why China Refused to Sign the Peace Treaty* (New York, 1919); Erez Manela, *The Wilsonian Moment: Self-Determination and the International Origins of Anti-Colonial Nationalism* (Oxford, 2007), pp. 190-6.

52. 'Memorandum, being an Appeal for the Moral Support of Friendly Powers Made by the People of China concerning Japan's Aggressive Policy in China', Kiangsu Educational Association, World's Chinese Students Federation, Shanghai City Chamber of Commerce, Shanghai Educational Association, National Vocational Education Association, Shanghai YMCA, Western Returned Students Union, China Overseas Federation, Shanghai Fire Brigade Association, Shanghai Chinese Christian Union, Cotton Mill Owners' Association, Cotton Guild of Shanghai, Cotton Merchants' Association, 24 July 1919, Shotwell Papers, Columbia Archive, Box 41.

53. Mitter, *Bitter Revolution*, pp. 41-51, 105-21.

54. Manela, *Wilsonian Moment*, pp. 198-211.

55. 'Self-Determination and the Dangers', 30 December 1918, Lansing Papers, Seeley G. Mudd Library, MC083, Box 7, folder 2, fo. 210.

56. Michael Laffan, *The Resurrection of Ireland: The Sinn Fein Party, 1916–1923* (Cambridge, 1999), pp. 243–51; 'Message to the Free Nations of the World', 21 January 1919, in Ronan Fanning, Michael Kennedy, Dermot Keogh, and Eunan O'Halpin, eds, *Documents on Irish Foreign Policy, 1919–1922* (Dublin, 1998), p. 2; Ronan Fanning, *Fatal Path: British Government and Irish Revolution, 1910–1922* (London, 2013), pp. 206–7.

57. Manela, *Wilsonian Moment*, pp. 141–75; John Darwin, *The Empire Project: The Rise and Fall of the British World System, 1830–1970* (Cambridge, 2009), pp. 346–53, 380–2.

58. William Duiker, *Ho Chi Minh: A Life* (New York, 2000), pp. 58–61.

59. Gerd Krumeich, 'Der Krieg in den Köpfen', in Gerd Krumeich, ed., *Versailles. Ziele – Wirkung – Wahrnehmung* (Essen, 2001), p. 64.

60. Speech of the German delegation, Versailles, 7 May 1919, in Anton Kaes, Martin Jay, and Edward Dimendberg, eds, *The Weimar Republic Sourcebook* (Berkeley, CA, 1995), pp. 9–12; Christiane Scheidemann, *Ulrich Graf Brockdorff-Rantzau (1869–1928). Eine politische Biographie* (Frankfurt, 1998), pp. 369–72.

61. Fritz Klein, 'Versailles und der deutsche Linke', in Krumeich, ed., *Versailles*, pp. 314–16; Jonathan Wright, *Gustav Stresemann: Weimar's Greatest Statesman* (Oxford, 2002), p. 131.

62. William Mulligan, *The Creation of the Modern German Army: General Walther Reinhardt and the Weimar Republic, 1914–1930* (Oxford, 2005), pp. 97–104.

63. Ibid., p. 100.

64. Peter Krüger, *Die Aussenpolitik der Republik von Weimar* (Darmstadt, 1985), pp. 89–99.

65. Gerhard L. Weinberg, 'The Defeat of Germany in 1918 and the European Balance of Power', *Central European History*, 2, 3 (1969), pp. 248–60.

66. Cited in Elizabeth Greenhalgh, *Foch in Command: The Forging of a First World War General* (Cambridge, 2011), p. 505.

67. EMA, 2e Bureau, 'Note sur l'armée allemande', 31 July 1919, MAE, Série Z, Allemagne, 56, fo. 246.

68. Guieu, *Le rameau*, pp. 58–62.

69. Antony Lentin, *Guilt at Versailles: Lloyd George and the Pre-History of Appeasement* (Leicester, 1984), pp. 132–54; Michael Graham Fry, 'British Revisionism', in Boemeke et al., eds, *Versailles*, pp. 565–80; Paul Bridgen, *The Labour Party and the Politics of War and Peace, 1900–1924* (Woodbridge, 2009), pp. 111–19; Peter Clarke, *Liberals and Social Democrats* (Cambridge, 1978), pp. 202–4.

70. H. James Burgwyn, *The Legend of the Mutilated Victory: Italy, the Great War, and the Paris Peace Conference, 1915–1919* (Westport, CT, 1993), pp. 276–81.

71. Cooper, *Breaking the Heart*, pp. 55, 62–6.

72. 'Lodge v Lowell: A Joint Debate on the Covenant of the League of Nations', Symphony Hall, 19 March 1919, reprinted from the *Boston Evening Transcript*; Cooper, *Breaking the Heart*, pp. 74–7; Stephen Wertheim, 'The League that Wasn't: American Designs for a Legalist-Sanctionist League of Nations and the Intellectual Origins of International Organization, 1914–1920', *Diplomatic History*, 35, 5 (2011), pp. 821–7.

73. Cooper, *Breaking the Heart*, pp. 158–98.

74. Plenary Session, 14 February 1919, in *FRUS*, 1919, supplement Paris, vol. 3, p. 215.

75. 'Smuts Calls Peace Terms too Harsh', *The New York Times*, 30 June 1919.

Chapter 9 The Wars that Would Not End, 1919–1923

1. Wilson to Pershing, 13 November 1918, Pershing Papers, Library of Congress, Container 213.

2. Cited in Keith Jeffery, *Ireland and the Great War* (Cambridge, 2000), p. 65.

3. Pershing statement on H. Wilson's assassination, 22 June 1922, Pershing Papers, Library of Congress, Container 213.

4. Robert Gerwarth and John Horne, eds, *War in Peace: Paramilitary Violence in Europe after the Great War* (Oxford, 2012).

5. Robert Gerwarth, 'The Central European Counter-Revolution: Paramilitary Violence in Germany, Austria, and Hungary after the Great War', *Past & Present*, (2008), pp. 175–209.

6. Evan Mawdsley, *The Russian Civil War* (Boston, MA, 1987), pp. 285–8.

7. Peter Holquist, 'Violent Russia, Deadly Marxism? Russia in the Epoch of Violence, 1905–1921', *Kritika*, 4, 3 (2003), p. 645.

8. David L. Hoffmann, *Cultivating the Masses: Modern State Practices and Soviet Socialism, 1914–1939* (Ithaca, NY, 2011), pp. 48–54; Aaron Retish, *Russia's Peasants in Revolution and Civil War: Citizenship, Identity, and the Creation of the Soviet State, 1914–1922* (Cambridge, 2008), pp. 145–56.

9. Beryl Williams, *Lenin: Profiles in Power* (Harlow, 2000), p. 107.

10. See Mawdsley, *Russian Civil War*, for the history of the conflict.

11. Betty Miller Unterberger, 'Woodrow Wilson and the Bolsheviks: The Acid Test of Soviet-American Relations', *Diplomatic History*, 11, 1 (1987), p. 89; Frederick Dickinson, *War and National Reinvention: Japan in the Great War, 1914–1919* (Cambridge, MA, 1999), pp. 184–96.

12. Williams, *Lenin*, pp. 171–3.

13. Dmitri Volkogonov, *Trotsky: The Eternal Revolutionary* (London, 1996), pp. 204–5; R. Craig Nation, *Black Earth, Red Star: A History of Soviet Security Policy, 1917–1991* (Ithaca, NY, 1992), p. 29.

14. Norman Davies, *White Eagle, Red Star: The Polish–Soviet War, 1919–1920* (London, 1972).

15. Serhy Yekelchyk, *Ukraine: Birth of a Modern Nation* (Oxford, 2007), pp. 79–84; Wladzimierz Borodziej, *Geschichte Polens im 20. Jahrhundert* (Munich, 2010), pp. 111–15; Stefanie Zloch, *Polnischer Nationalismus. Politik und Gesellschaft zwischen den beiden Weltkriegen* (Cologne, 2010), pp. 111–27.

16. Lenin to Stalin, 17 March 1920, in Richard Pipes, ed., *The Unknown Lenin: From the Secret Archives* (New Haven, CT, 1996), p. 79.

17. Cited in Craig Nation, *Black Earth*, p. 29.

18. 'Lenin's Speech to a Closed Meeting of the 9th Party Conference of the Communist Party', 20 September 1920, in Pipes, ed., *Unknown Lenin*, pp. 95–114.

19. Zloch, *Polnischer Nationalismus*, pp. 143–7.

20. Jerzy Borzecki, *The Soviet–Polish Peace of 1921 and the Creation of Interwar Europe* (New Haven, CT, 2008).

21. Pipes, ed., *Unknown Lenin*, p. 114.

22. Oskar Jászi, 'Dismembered Hungary and Peace in Central Europe', *Foreign Affairs*, December 1923, pp. 270–82.

23. Jörg Hoensch, *A History of Modern Hungary, 1867–1994* (London, 1996), pp. 85–98; Keith Hitchins, *Rumania, 1866–1947* (Oxford, 1994), pp. 284–6.

24. Glenn Torrey, *Romania and World War I: A Collection of Studies* (Portland, OR, 1998), p. 229.

25. Hitchins, *Rumania*, pp. 377–87, 406–15.

26. Cited in Robert Gerwarth, 'Fighting the Red Beast: Counter-Revolutionary Violence in the Defeated States of Central Europe', in Gerwarth and Horne, eds, *War in Peace*, p. 62.

27. Ibid., pp. 61–3; Bela Bodo, 'Hungarian Aristocracy and the White Terror', *Journal of Contemporary History*, 45, 4 (2010), pp. 703–6; Hoensch, *Hungary*, pp. 98–106, 115.

28. John D. Bell, *Peasants in Power: Alexander Stamboliski and the Bulgarian Agrarian National Union, 1899–1923* (Princeton, NJ, 1977), pp. 140–245; Adam Tooze and Martin Ivanov, 'Disciplining the "Black Sheep of the Balkans": Financial Supervision and Sovereignty in Bulgaria, 1902–1938', *Economic History Review*, 64, 1 (2011), pp. 37–9; John Paul Newman, 'The Origins, Attributes, and Legacies of Paramilitary Violence in the Balkans', in Gerwarth and Horne, eds, *War in Peace*, pp. 152–3.

29. Cited in Mark Biondich, *Stjepan Radic, the Croat Peasant Party, and the Politics of Mass Mobilization, 1904–1928* (Toronto, 2000), p. 144; John Paul Newman, 'Post-Imperial and Post-War Violence in the South Slav Lands, 1917–1923', *Contemporary European History*, 19, 3 (2010), pp. 253–8.

30. Cited in Zbyněk Zeman, with Antonín Klimek, *The Life of Edvard Beneš, 1884–1948: Czechoslovakia in Peace and War* (Oxford, 1997), p. 51; Andrea Orzoff, *Battle for the Castle: The Myth of Czechoslovakia in Europe, 1914–1948* (Oxford, 2009).

31. Michael Walsh Campbell, 'The Making of "March Fallen": March 4, 1919 and the Subversive Potential of Occupation', *Central European History*, 39, 1 (2006), pp. 1–20.

32. Zara Steiner, *The Lights that Failed: European International History, 1919–1933* (Oxford, 2005), pp. 258, 297–303.

33. Cited in Ryan Gingeras, *Sorrowful Shore: Violence, Ethnicity, and the End of the Ottoman Empire, 1912–1923* (Oxford, 2009), pp. 70–1.

34. Ibid., pp. 73–4.

35. Erik Jan Zürcher, *Turkey: A Modern History* (London, 1997), p. 144.

36. Cited in Michael Llewellyn-Smith, 'Venizelos' Diplomacy, 1910–1923', in Paschalis Kitromilides, ed., *Eleftherios Venizelos: The Trials of Statesmanship* (Edinburgh, 2006), p. 172.

37. Bruce Clark, *Twice a Stranger: How Mass Expulsions Shaped Modern Greece and Turkey* (London, 2006), pp. 131–8.

38. M. Şükrü Hanioğlu, *Ataturk: An Intellectual Biography* (Princeton, NJ, 2011), pp. 135–57; Uğur Ümit Üngör, 'Seeing like a Nation-State: Young Turk Social Engineering in Eastern Turkey, 1913–1950', *Journal of Genocide Research*, 10, 1 (2008), pp. 28–32.

39. Ioannis Tossopoulos, 'The Experiment of Inclusive Constitutionalism, 1909–1932', in Kitromilides, ed., *Venizelos*, pp. 260–3.

40. John Whittam, *Fascist Italy* (Manchester, 1995), pp. 19–20.

41. R. J. B. Bosworth, *Mussolini's Italy: Life under the Dictatorship, 1915–1945* (London, 2007), pp. 121–49.

42. Charles Killinger, *Gaetano Salvemini: A Biography* (Westport, CT, 2002), p. 165.

43. John Gooch, *Mussolini and his Generals: The Armed Forces and Fascist Foreign Policy, 1922–1940* (Cambridge, 2007), pp. 44–7; C. J. Lowe and F. Marzari, *Italian Foreign Policy, 1870–1940* (London, 1978), pp. 194–9.

44. Peter Yearwood, *Guarantee of Peace: The League of Nations in British Policy, 1914–1925* (Oxford, 2009), pp. 252–73.

45. Steiner, *The Lights that Failed*, pp. 357–9.

46. Piotr S. Wandycz, *France and her Eastern Allies, 1919–1925: French–Czechoslovak–Polish Relations from the Paris Peace Conference to Locarno* (Westport, CT, 1962).

47. Michael Adas, 'Contested Hegemony: The Great War and the Afro-Asian Assault on the Civilizing Mission Ideology', *Journal of World History*, 15, 1 (2004), pp. 31–63.

48. Julia Eichenberg, 'The Dark Side of Independence: Paramilitary Violence in Ireland and Poland after the First World War', *Contemporary European History*, 19, 3 (2010), pp. 238–41.

49. Cited in Keith Jeffery, *The British Army and the Crisis of Empire, 1918–1922* (Manchester, 1984), p. 80.

50. Cited in Michael Hopkinson, 'Negotiation: The Anglo-Irish War and Revolution', in Joost Augusteijn, ed., *The Irish Revolution, 1913–1923* (Basingstoke, 2010), p. 125.

51. Jon Lawrence, 'Forging a Peaceable Kingdom: War, Violence, and Fear of Brutalization in Post-First World War Britain', *Journal of Modern History*, 75, 3 (2003), pp. 572–87.

52. W. J. Berridge, 'Object Lessons in Violence: The Rationalities and Irrationalities of Urban Struggle during the Egyptian Revolution of 1919', *Journal of Colonialism and Colonial History*, 12, 3 (2011); http://muse.jhu.edu/journals/journal_of_colonialism_and_colonial_history/v012/12.3.berridge.html

53. Eugene Rogan, *The Arabs: A History* (London, 2009), pp. 209–10, 238–40; John Darwin, *The Empire Project: The Rise and Fall of the British World System, 1830–1970* (Cambridge, 2009), p. 384.

54. Cited in Rogan, *Arabs*, pp. 214–15; Priya Satia, 'The Defense of Inhumanity: Air Control in Iraq and the British Idea of Arabia', *American Historical Review*, 111 (2006), pp. 16–51.

55. Rogan, *Arabs*, pp. 285–92.

56. Bernard Wasserstein, *Divided Jerusalem: The Struggle for the Holy City* (London, 2001), p. 204.

57. Darwin, *Empire Project*, pp. 385–93.

58. Abbé Pradel to Berthelot, 27 December 1920, MAE, Série Z, Allemagne, 401, fos 101–5.

59. William Mulligan, 'Weimar and the Wars of Liberation: German and French Officers and the Politics of History', *European History Quarterly*, 38, 2 (2008), pp. 266–93.

60. Tara Zahra, 'The Minority Problem and National Classification in the French and Czech Borderlands', *Contemporary European History*, 17, 2 (2008), pp. 138–58; Carolyn Grohmann, 'From Lothringen to Lorraine: Expulsion and Voluntary Repatriation', *Diplomacy and Statecraft*, 16, 3 (2005), pp. 571–87.

61. 'Note de la direction des affaires politiques et commerciales', Paris, 27 January 1920, in Stefan Martens, ed., *Documents diplomatiques français sur l'Allemagne – Französische Diplomatenberichte aus Deutschland. 9. Januar–31. Dezember 1920*, 2 vols (Bonn, 1992–3), vol. 1, pp. 83–5; Walter McDougall, *France's Rhineland Diplomacy, 1914–1924: The Last Bid for a Balance of Power in Europe* (Princeton, NJ, 1978), pp. 97–206.

62. Hans Peter Schwarz, *Adenauer. Der Aufstieg, 1876–1952* (Stuttgart, 1986), pp. 218–27.

63. Peter Schöttler, 'The Rhine as an Object of Historical Controversy in the Interwar Years: Towards a History of Frontier Mentalities', *History Workshop Journal*, 39 (1995), pp. 1–17.

64. Cited in Jennifer D. Keene, *Doughboys, the Great War, and the Remaking of America* (Baltimore, MD, 2001), p. 121.

65. Cited in Gerd Krumeich, ' "Der Ruhrkampf" als Krieg: Überlegungen zu einem verdrängten deutsch-französischen Konflikt', in Gerd Krumeich and Joachim Schröder, eds, *Der Schatten des Weltkrieges. Die Ruhrbesetzung 1923* (Essen, 2004), p. 15.

66. Cited in Ronald Pruessen, *John Foster Dulles: The Road to Power* (New York, 1982), p. 143.

67. Tardieu to Herrick, 22 October 1920, Papers of the American Committee for Devastated France, Seeley G. Mudd Library, MC026, Box 1, Folder 2.

68. Gerald D. Feldman, *The Great Disorder: Politics, Economics, and Society in the German Inflation, 1914–1924* (Oxford, 1993), p. 446.

69. Cited in Marc Trachtenberg, *Reparations in World Politics: France and European Economic Diplomacy, 1916–1923* (New York, 1980), p. 127.

70. Ibid., pp. 163–71; Peter Jackson, 'French Security and a British "Continental Commitment" after the First World War: A Reassessment', *English Historical Review*, 126, 519 (2011), pp. 352–7; Stanislas Jeannesson, 'Jacques Seydoux et la diplomatie économique de la France dans l'après-guerre', *Relations internationales*, 121, 1 (2005), pp. 9–27.

71. Hartmut Pogge von Strandmann, ed., *Walther Rathenau: Industrialist, Banker, Intellectual, and Politician: Notes and Diaries, 1907–1922* (Oxford, 1985), pp. 250–2; Manfred Berg, 'Germany and the United States: The Concept of World Economic Interdependence', in Carole Fink, Axel Fröhn and Jürgen Heideking, eds, *Genoa, Rapallo and European Reconstruction in 1922* (Cambridge, 2002), pp. 80–4.

72. Cited in Pipes, ed., *Unknown Lenin*, p. 145.

73. Manfred Berg, 'Germany and the United States: The Concept of World Economic Interdependence', in Fink, Fröhn, and Heideking, eds, *Genoa, Rapallo and European Reconstruction*, pp. 82–7.

74. Martin Sabrow, *Der Rathenaumord. Rekonstruktion einer Verschwörung gegen die Republik von Weimar* (Munich, 1994); Heinrich August Winkler, *Weimar, 1918–1933. Die Geschichte der ersten deutschen Demokratie* (Munich, 1993), pp. 164–75.

75. Glaser to Kahn, 25 September 1922, in Alexander Jager, Clemens Picht, and Ernst Schulin, eds, *Walther Rathenau. Briefe*, 2 vols (Düsseldorf, 2006), vol. 2, p. 1,319.

76. On the Ruhr crisis see Conan Fischer, *The Ruhr Crisis, 1923–1924* (Oxford, 2003); Stanislas Jeannesson, *Poincaré, la France et la Ruhr (1922–1924)* (Strasbourg, 1998); Krumeich and Schröder, eds, *Der Schatten*.

77. Gerd Krumeich, 'Der Ruhrkampf', in Gerd Krumeich and Joachim Schröder, eds, *Der Schatten*, pp. 16–18; Christoph Cornelißen, 'Vom "Ruhrkampf" zur Ruhrkrise: die Historiographie der Ruhrbesetzung', in Krumeich and Schröder, eds, *Der Schatten*, pp. 25–45.

78. Fischer, *Ruhr Crisis*, pp. 110–32.

79. Jeannesson, 'Übergriffe der französischen Besatzungsmacht und deutsche Beschwerden', in Krumeich and Schröder, eds, *Der Schatten*, pp. 207–31.

80. Annette Becker-Doureux, 'Das Begräbnis des Leutnants Colpin in Lille am 21. März 1923', in Krumeich and Schröder, eds, *Der Schatten*, pp. 257–63.

81. Martin Geyer, *Verkehrte Welt. Revolution, Inflation und Moderne* (Göttingen, 1998); for a specific example, see Gideon Reuveni, 'The "Crisis of the Book" and German Society after the First World War', *German History*, 20, 4 (2002), pp. 446–55.

82. Feldman, *The Great Disorder*, pp. 782–4.

83. Cited in ibid., pp. 704–6.

84. Jonathan Wright, *Gustav Stresemann: Weimar's Greatest Statesman* (Oxford, 2002), p. 219.

85. Ian Kershaw, *Hitler, 1889–1936: Hubris* (London, 1998), pp. 200–12.

86. Feldman, *The Great Disorder*, pp. 768–80; Winkler, *Weimar*, p. 237.

87. Speech, 22 November 1923, http://www.reichstagsprotokolle.de/Blatt2_w1_bsb00000045_00446.html

Chapter 10 Making Real Peace, 1922–1925

1. 'Peace at Last', *The Times*, 13 October 1925, p. 13.

2. Cited in William Mulligan, 'Weimar and the Wars of Liberation: German and French Officers and the Politics of History', *European History Quarterly*, 38, 2 (2008), p. 286.

3. 'La déclaration ministerielle', *Le Temps*, 4 November 1925, p. 6.

4. John Horne, 'Guerres et reconciliations européenes au 20e siècle', *Vingtième Siècle*, 104 (October–December 2009), pp. 3–16; John Horne, 'Kulturelle Demobilmachung 1919–1939. Ein sinnvoller historischer Begriff?', in Wolfgang Hardtwig, ed., *Politische Kulturgeschichte der Zwischenkriegszeit 1918–1939* (Göttingen, 2005), pp. 129–50.

5. Curzon to Geddes, 29 June 1921, in *Documents on British Foreign Policy, 1919–1939* (*DBFP*), 22 vols, 1st series, vol. 14, p. 318.

6. Geddes to Curzon, 24 June 1921, *DBFP*, 1st series, vol. 14, pp. 311–12; Merlo J. Pusey, *Charles Evans Hughes*, 2 vols (New York, 1963), vol. 2, pp. 454–63.

7. See for example 'Memorandum by Sir J. Jordan, Respecting American Suggestions for Agenda for the Conference', 17 October 1921, and 'General Survey of Political Situation in Pacific and the Far East with Reference to the Forthcoming Washington Conference, 20 October 1921', in *DBFP*, 1st series, vol. 14, pp. 426–8, 434–8.

8. Walter LaFeber, *The Clash: A History of U.S.–Japan Relations* (New York, 1997), pp. 138–48.

9. Cited in Robert K. Murray, *The Harding Years: Warren G. Harding and his Administration* (Minneapolis, MN, 1969), p. 149.

10. Cited in Pusey, *Hughes*, pp. 468–9.

11. 'The Washington Ideal', *The Times*, 8 March 1922, p. 6; Akira Iriye, *The Origins of the Second World War in the Pacific* (London, 1987), pp. 1–21.

12. Marius B. Jensen, *The Making of Modern Japan* (Cambridge, MA, 2000), p. 504.

13. Arthur Waldron, *From War to Nationalism: China's Turning Point, 1924–1925* (Cambridge, 1995), pp. 161–77; Edward A. McCord, 'Warlords against Warlordism: The Politics of Anti-Militarism in Early Twentieth-Century China', *Modern Asian Studies*, 30, 4 (1996), pp. 795–827.
14. Pusey, *Hughes*, p. 513.
15. Ibid., p. 516.
16. Jensen, *Modern Japan*, p. 522.
17. Norbert Elias, *The Civilizing Process*, trans. and ed. Eric Dunning, Johan Goudsblom, and Stephen Mennell (London, 2000), p. 106.
18. Erich Maria Remarque, *The Road Back* (London, 1979), pp. 72–4.
19. Bruno Cabanes, *La victoire endeuillée. La sortie de guerre des soldats français, 1918–1920* (Paris, 2004), pp. 72–6.
20. Diary entry, 12 November 1919, in George John Riches, *War Diaries, 1914–1919* (quoted by kind permission of Ann Hirst).
21. Blanche to Georges Duhamel, 13 March 1919, in Georges and Blanche Duhamel, *Correspondance de guerre, 1914–1919*, ed. Arlette Lafay, intro. Jean-Jacques Becker (Paris, 2007–8), p. 1,589.
22. Richard Bessel, *Germany after the First World War* (Oxford, 1993), pp. 231–2.
23. Jessica Meyer, ' "Not Septimus now": Wives of Disabled Veterans and Cultural Memory of the First World War in Britain', *Women's History Review*, 13, 1 (2004), p. 128.
24. Jennifer D. Keene, *Doughboys, the Great War, and the Remaking of America* (Baltimore, MD, 2001), pp. 133–8; Stephen Ward, 'Great Britain: Land Fit for Heroes Lost', in Stephen Ward, ed., *The War Generation: Veterans of the First World War* (New York, 1975), p. 30; Andrew Rothstein, *The Soldiers' Strike of 1919* (London, 1980).
25. Adam Seipp, *The Ordeal of Peace: Demobilization and the Urban Experience in Britain and Germany, 1917–1921* (Farnham, 2009), pp. 147–50, 188–90.
26. Cited in Antoine Prost, *In the Wake of War: 'Les anciens combattants' and French Society, 1914–1939* (Oxford, 1992), p. 59.
27. 'Schreie eines Aufgewachten', probably late 1918, NL Franz Osterroth, Mappe 13, Friedrich Ebert Stiftung, Bonn.
28. Heather Jones, *Violence against Prisoners of War in the First World War: Britain, France, and Germany, 1914–1918* (Cambridge, 2010), p. 283.
29. Cabanes, *Victoire endeuillée*, p. 372.
30. Oxana Nagornaja, 'United by Barbed Wire: Russian PoWs in Germany, National Stereotypes, and International Relations, 1914–1922', *Kritika*, 10, 3 (2009), pp. 490–2.
31. Dominik Richert, *Beste Gelegenheit zum Sterben. Meine Erlebnisse im Kriege 1914–1918*, ed. Angelika Tramitz and Bernd Ulrich (Munich, 1989), p. 390; Jones, *Violence against Prisoners of War*, pp. 291–305; Reinhard Nachtigal, 'Die Repatrierung der Mittelmächte – Kriegsgefangene aus dem revolutionären Rußland', and Jochen Oltmer, 'Repatrierungspolitik im Spannungsfeld von Antibolschewismus, Asylgewährung und Arbeitsmarktentwicklung', in Jochen Oltmer, ed., *Kriegsgefangene im Europa des Ersten Weltkrieges* (Paderborn, 2006), pp. 239–90.
32. [*Reichsbanner*], *Wegweiser für Funktionäre, Führer und alle Bundeskameraden* (1926), p. 8.
33. Benjamin Ziemann, 'Republikanische Kriegserinnerung in einer polarisierten Öffentlichkeit. Das Reichsbanner Schwarz-Rot-Gold als Veteranenverband der sozialistischen Arbeiterschaft', *Historische Zeitschrift*, 267, 2 (1998), pp. 357–98.
34. 'Der republikanische Tag von Bielefeld', *1. Beilage der Volkswacht*, 23 Mar. 1925, NL Carl Severing, Mappe 8, Friedrich Ebert Stiftung.
35. Cited in Prost, *Wake of War*, pp. 51–4.
36. http://www.volksbund.de/kriegsgraeberstaette/duisburg-kaiserberg-kriegsgraeberstaette-erster-welt.html; August Hoff, *Das Werk Wilhelm Lehmbrücks* (Duisburg, 1932); Jay Winter, *Sites of Memory, Sites of Mourning: The Great War in European Cultural History* (Cambridge, 1998), pp. 78–116.
37. Elisa Carrillo, *Alcide De Gasperi: The Long Apprenticeship* (Notre Dame, IL, 1965), pp. 58–65; I would like to thank Georg Grote and Lindsey Earner-Byrne for the information concerning Bolzano.
38. Sean A. Forner, 'War Commemoration and the Republic in Crisis: Weimar Germany and the Neue Wache', *Central European History*, 35, 4 (2002), pp. 513–49.
39. Cited in Leila J. Rupp, *Worlds of Women: The Making of an International Women's Movement* (Princeton, NJ, 1997), p. 118.
40. *Bulletin of the Women's International League for Peace and Freedom*, June/August 1922, p. 7, Hoover Institute Archives, Peace Subject Collection, Box 3; Dominique Marshall, 'The Construction of Children as an Object of International Relations: The Declaration of Children's Rights and the Child Welfare Committee of the League of Nations, 1900–1929', *International Journal of Children's Rights*, 7 (1999), pp. 108–38; Emily Baughan, ' "Every Citizen of Empire Implored to Save the

Children!" Empire, Internationalism, and the Save the Children Fund in Inter-War Britain', *Historical Research*, 86, 231 (2013), pp. 116–37.

41. Cited in Janet Polasky, *The Democratic Socialism of Emile Vandervelde: Between Reform and Revolution* (Oxford, 1995), p. 192.
42. Cited in Karl Christian Führer, *Carl Legien 1861–1920. Ein Gewerkschafter im Kampf um 'möglichst gutes Leben' für alle Arbeiter* (Essen, 2009), p. 340.
43. Bernard Georges and Denise Tintant, *Léon Jouhaux. Cinquante ans de syndicalisme*, 2 vols (Paris, 1962), vol. 1, pp. 344–7; Geert van Goethem, *The Amsterdam International: The World of the International Federation of Trade Unions, 1913–1945* (Aldershot, 2006), pp. 23–31.
44. Goethem, *Amsterdam International*, p. 142; League of Nations Union, *The International Labour Organisation of the League of Nations* (London, 1922), p. 16; Hans Fehlinger, *Erfolge der internationalen Arbeitsorganisation* (Lepizig, 1925).
45. Führer, *Legien*, pp. 347–8; Goethem, *Amsterdam International*, pp. 32–6.
46. Jean-Michel Guieu, *Le rameau et le glaive. Les militants français pour la Société des Nations* (Paris, 2008), pp. 107–15.
47. Arthur Bullard, 'Memel: A European Aspect of the League', *Annals of the American Academy of Political and Social Science*, July 1924, pp. 102–4, in Bullard Papers, Seeley G. Mudd Library, MC008, Box 4; Page W. Bobson, 'The League and Foreign Securities', 18 November 1924, in William Hard Papers, Seeley G. Mudd Library, Box 2, Folder 12.
48. 'Déclaration d'Indépendance de l'Esprit', in Jean Albertini, ed., *Roman Rolland. Textes politiques, sociaux et philosophiques choisis* (Paris, 1970), pp. 179–80.
49. 'Kant's Bicentenary', *The Times*, 23 April 1924, p. 17; Daniel Laqua, 'Transnational Intellectual Cooperation: The League of Nations and the Problem of Order', *Journal of Global History*, 6, 2 (2011), pp. 223–6, 234–7.
50. Katja Marmetschke, *Feindbeobachtung und Verständigung. Der Germanist Edmond Vermeil (1878–1964) in den deutsch-französischen Beziehungen* (Cologne, 2008), pp. 188–97, 201–12, 266–84, 306–8.
51. Guido Müller, *Europäische Gesellschaftsbeziehungen nach dem Erstem Weltkrieg. Das Deutsch-Französische Studienkomite und der Europäische Kulturbund* (Munich, 2005), pp. 96–8.
52. Ibid., pp. 102–15.
53. Cited in Conan Fischer, 'Scoundrels without a Fatherland? Heavy Industry and Transnationalism in Post-First World War Germany', *Contemporary European History*, 14, 4 (2005), p. 461.
54. Daniel Barbezat, 'Cooperation and Rivalry in the International Steel Cartel, 1926–1933', *Journal of Economic History*, 49, 2 (1989), pp. 435–7.
55. Jean-Marie Mayeur, *La vie politique sous la Troisième République 1870–1940* (Paris, 1984), pp. 271–7; Guieu, *Le rameau et le glaive*, pp. 135–8.
56. Patrick Cohrs, *The Unfinished Peace after World War I. America, Britain and the Stabilization of Europe, 1919–1932* (Cambridge, 2006), pp. 85–8.
57. Cited in Royal J. Schmidt, 'Hoover's Reflections on the Versailles Treaty', in Lawrence Gelfand, ed., *Herbert Hoover: The Great War and its Aftermath, 1914–1923* (Iowa City, IA, 1979), p. 78.
58. Manfred Berg, 'Germany and the United States: The Concept of World Economic Interdependence', in Carole Fink, Axel Fröhn, and Jürgen Heideking, eds, *Genoa, Rapallo and European Reconstruction in 1922* (Cambridge, 2002), pp. 80–2.
59. Gustav Stresemann, *His Diaries, Letters, and Papers*, ed. Eric Sutton, 3 vols (London, 1935), vol. 1, pp. 262–5.
60. Philip Williamson, *Stanley Baldwin: Conservative Leadership and National Values* (Cambridge, 1999), pp. 28–31; Richard Grayson, 'The Historiography of Inter-War Politics: Competing Conservative World Views in High Politics, 1924–1929', in William Mulligan and Brendan Simms, eds, *The Primacy of Foreign Policy in British History, 1660–2000* (Basingstoke, 2010), pp. 284–5.
61. Cited in Robert C. Self, ed., *The Austen Chamberlain Diary Letters: The Correspondence of Sir Austen Chamberlain with his Sisters, Hilda and Ida, 1916–1937* (Cambridge, 1995), p. 268.
62. Cited in Cohrs, *Unfinished Peace*, p. 94; David Marquand, *Ramsay MacDonald* (London, 1977), pp. 329–37.
63. John Keiger, *Raymond Poincaré* (Cambridge, 1997), pp. 304–5.
64. Bernard Oudin, *Aristide Briand. La Paix, une idée neuve en Europe* (Paris, 1987), p. 445.
65. Peter Jackson, 'French Security and a British "Continental Commitment" after the First World War: A Reassessment', *English Historical Review*, 126, 519 (2011), pp. 365–8.
66. 'Le message du président de la République', *Le Temps*, 18 June 1924, p. 6.
67. Andrew Webster, 'The Transnational Dream: Politicians, Diplomats, and Soldiers in the League of Nations' Pursuit of International Disarmament, 1920–1938', *Contemporary European History*, 14, 4 (2005), pp. 493–518.

68. Zara Steiner, *The Lights that Failed: European International History, 1919–1933* (Oxford, 2005), pp. 244–5.
69. Cited in ibid., p. 248.
70. Cited in Klaus Hildebrand, *Das vergangene Reich. Deutsche Aussenpolitik von Bismarck bis Hitler, 1871–1945* (Stuttgart, 1995), p. 446; see also Peter Krüger, *Die Aussenpolitik der Republik von Weimar* (Darmstadt, 1985), pp. 239–42.
71. Steiner, *The Lights that Failed*, p. 381.
72. Krüger, *Aussenpolitik*, pp. 269–76; Jonathan Wright, *Gustav Stresemann: Weimar's Greatest Statesman* (Oxford, 2002), pp. 301–3.
73. Cited in Jackson, 'French Security', p. 377.
74. Wright, *Stresemann*, p. 313.
75. Jackson, 'French Security', pp. 381–3.
76. Speech to the House of Commons, 24 March 1925, *Hansard*, vol. 182, p. 316.
77. Chamberlain to Ida, 2 October 1925, in Self, ed., *Chamberlain Letters*, pp. 280–1.
78. Diary entry, 5 October 1925, in Stresemann, *Diaries*, p. 173.
79. Wright, *Stresemann*, pp. 331–9.

Conclusion

1. Hans Peter Schwarz, *Adenauer. Der Aufstieg, 1876–1952* (Stuttgart, 1986), pp. 297–8.
2. Ibid., pp. 148–9.
3. Sara Lorenzini, 'The Roots of a Statesman: De Gasperi's Foreign Policy', *Modern Italy*, 14, 4 (2009), p. 475.
4. Michael Howard, 'A Thirty Years' War: The Two World Wars in Historical Perspective', *Transactions of the Royal Historical Society*, 6th Series, 3 (1993), pp. 171–84; Niall Ferguson, *The War of the World: History's Age of Hatred* (London, 2006); Bruno Thoß and Hans-Erich Volkmann, eds, *Erster Weltkrieg – Zweiter Weltkrieg. Ein Vergleich. Krieg, Kriegserlebnis, Kriegserfahrung in Deutschland* (Paderborn, 2002).
5. Alan Kramer, *The Dynamics of Destruction: Culture and Mass Killing in the First World War* (Oxford, 2007), pp. 328–38.
6. Mark Mazower, *Governing the World: The History of an Idea* (London, 2012), pp. 205–13; Patricia Clavin, *Securing the World Economy: Reinventing the League of Nations, 1920–1946* (Oxford, 2013), pp. 4–6.
7. François Duchêne, *Jean Monnet: The First Statesman of Interdependence* (New York, 1994), pp. 42–3; Gérard Bossuat and Andreas Wilkens, eds, *Jean Monnet. L'Europe et les chemins de la paix* (Paris, 1999).
8. Simon Ball, *The Guardsmen: Harold Macmillan, Three Friends, and the World they Made* (London, 2004), p. 401.
9. Jay Winter and Antoine Prost, *René Cassin and Human Rights: From the Great War to the Universal Declaration* (Cambridge, 2013), pp. 215, 348.
10. For the text of the speech, see http://www.isn.ethz.ch/Digital-Library/Publications/Detail/?ots591=0c54e3b3-1e9c-be1e-2c24-a6a8c7060233&lng=en&id=125398; see also Ronald Hyam, *Britain's Declining Empire: The Road to Decolonisation, 1918–1968* (Cambridge, 2006), pp. 30–7, 258–61.
11. William Duiker, *Ho Chi Minh: A Life* (New York, 2000), pp. 58, 323.
12. Élie Halévy, *The Era of Tyrannies: Essays on Socialism and War* (London, 1967), pp. xxii, 189–90.
13. Friedrich Meinicke, *Machiavellism: The Doctrine of Raison d'État and its Place in Modern History* (London, 1957), p. 416.
14. 'With the Homeless', published in *Neue Berliner Zeitung*, 23 September 1920, in Joseph Roth, *What I Saw: Reports from Berlin, 1920–33*, introduced by Michael Hoffmann (London, 2003), pp. 63–7.
15. J. Noakes and G. Pridham, eds, *Nazism, 1919–1945: Foreign Policy, War, and Racial Extermination* (Exeter, 1997), pp. 723–4; Ian Kershaw, *The Hitler Myth: Image and Reality in the Third Reich* (Oxford, 1987), pp. 121–39.

BIBLIOGRAPHY

Primary Sources

Archives

Archives de Ministère des Affaires Étrangères, Paris
MAE PA-AP: Jules Cambon Papers, Léon Bourgeois Papers
MAE Série A – Paix
MAE, Série Z – Allemagne

Bibliothèque de Documentation Internationale et Contemporaine, Paris
4 delta 280, dossier France, question polonaise 1914–1919
4 delta 1589, Yougoslavie
GF delta res 99, Halbwachs dossier
GF delta res 95, Dossier: France SFIO: Fédération de la Marne
F delta res 0858/01/04, Mantoux Papers
F delta res 926, Échanges entre soldats français et allemands, folder 2

British Library, London
Cecil Papers

Bundesarchiv, Lichterfelde-Berlin
R 703: Stellvertreter des Reichskanzlers
R 43: Cabinet Papers

Bundesarchiv-Militärarchiv, Freiburg
BA-MA, PH 5 II: Armeeoberkommandos

Columbia University Archives
Bakhmeteff Archive: Benningsen Papers
Shotwell Papers

Friedrich Ebert Stiftung, Bonn
NL Carl Severing
NL Franz Osterroth

Hoover Institute, Stanford University, CA
Lauzanne Papers
Loucheur Papers
Peace Subject Collection

Imperial War Museum, London
R. H. Wilson Papers

Library of Congress, Washington DC
Hughes Papers
Pershing Papers
Taft Papers

Seeley G. Mudd Library, Princeton, NJ
Bullard Papers, MC008
Dulles Papers, MC016
Lansing Papers, MC083
William Hard Papers, MC145
Papers of American Committee for Devastated France, MC026

The National Archive, Kew, London
CAB 23: Cabinet Papers
FO 800: Grey Papers, Nicolson Papers
FO 425: Confidential Print
FO 371: Foreign Office files

The National Library of Scotland, Edinburgh
Haldane Papers

George John Riches, 'War Diaries, 1914–1919', by kind permission of Ann Hirst

Printed Primary Sources

Addams, Jane, Balch, Emily, and Hamilton, Alice, *Women of The Hague* (New York, 1915)
Afflerbach, Holger, ed., *Kaiser Wilhelm II als oberster Kriegsherr im Ersten Weltkrieg: Quellen aus der militärischen Umgebung des Kaisers 1914–1918* (Munich, 2005)
Albertini, Jean, ed., *Roman Rolland. Textes politiques, sociaux et philosophiques choisis* (Paris, 1970)
American Federation of Labor, *American Labor's Position in Peace or in War* (Washington DC, 1917)
Auskunftsstelle Vereinigter Verbände, *Gedanken und Wünschen zur Gestaltung des Friedens* (1916)
Baden, Prinz Max von, *Erinnerungen und Dokumente* (Stuttgart, 1968)
Barrès, Maurice, *Mes cahiers, 1896–1923* (Paris, 1963)
Benoist-Méchin, Jacques, ed., *Ce qui demeure. Lettres de soldats tombés au champ d'honneur 1914–1918* (Paris, 2000)
Bergson, Henri, *Mélanges* (Paris, 1977)
Bethmann Hollweg, Theobald von, *Sechs Kriegsreden des Reichskanzlers* (Berlin, 1916)
Bittner, L. and Uebersberger, H., *Österreich-Ungarns Aussenpolitik von der bosnischen Krise 1908 bis zum Kriegsausbruch 1914* (Vienna, 1930)
Bulletin of the Women's International League for Peace and Freedom (June/August 1922)
Cambon, Henri, ed., *Paul Cambon. Correspondance 1870–1924* (Paris, 1946)
Carnegie Endowment for International Peace, *Official Communications and Speeches Relating to Peace Proposals, 1916–1917* (Washington DC, 1917)
Chinese Patriotic Committee, *Why China Refused to Sign the Peace Treaty* (New York, 1919)
Clemenceau, Georges, *France Facing Germany: Speeches and Articles* (New York, 1919)
Dernburg, Bernhard, *Von beiden Ufern. Flugschriften des Berliner Tageblatt* (Berlin, 1917)
Dethan, Georges, ed., *Gabriel Hanotaux. Carnets (1907–1925)* (Paris, 1982)
Documents diplomatiques français, 1871–1914, 2nd Series (Paris, 1930–55)
Duhamel, Georges, *Civilization, 1914–1917* (New York, 1919)
Duhamel, Georges and Blanche, *Correspondance de guerre, 1914–1919*, ed. Arlette Lafay, intro. Jean-Jacques Becker (Paris, 2007–8)
Durch Deutschen Sieg zum Deutschen Frieden. Mahnruf ans deutsche Volk (Berlin, 1917)
Elias, Norbert, *The Civilizing Process*, trans. and ed. Eric Dunning, Johan Goudsblom, and Stephen Mennell (London, 2000)
Epkenhans, Michael, ed., *Albert Hopman. Das ereignisreiche Leben eines 'Wilhelminers'. Tagebücher, Briefe, Aufzeichnungen 1901–1920* (Munich, 2004)
Fanning, Ronan, Kennedy, Michael, Keogh, Dermot, and O'Halpin, Eunan, eds, *Documents on Irish Foreign Policy, 1919–1922* (Dublin, 1998)
Fehlinger, Hans, *Erfolge der internationalen Arbeitsorganisation* (Lepizig, 1925)
Fellner, Fritz, 'Aus der Denkwelt eines kaiserlichen Botschafters a. D. Die Briefe des Grafen Monts an Josef Redlich aus den Jahren 1914/15', *Mitteilungen des Österreichischen Staatsarchiv*, 31 (1978)

Fellner, Fritz, ed., *Schicksalsjahre Österreichs 1908-1918. Das politische Tagebuch Josef Redlichs* (Graz, 1953)

Freud, Sigmund, 'The Disillusionment of War' and 'Our Attitude to Death', in *Civilization, Society, and Religion: The Penguin Freud Library*, 15 vols (London, 1985), vol. 12

Geiss, Imanuel, ed., *July 1914: The Outbreak of the First World War: Selected Documents* (London, 1967)

Gooch, G. P. and Temperley, Harold, eds, *British Dcouments on the Origins of the War, 1898-1914* (London, 1926-38)

Görlitz, Walter, ed., *The Kaiser and his Court: The Diaries, Notebooks and Letters of Admiral Georg Alexander von Müller, Chief of the Naval Cabinet, 1914-1918* (London, 1961)

Halévy, Élie, *The Era of Tyrannies: Essays on Socialism and War* (London, 1967)

Hoetzsch, Otto, ed., *Die internationalen Beziehungen im Zeitalter des Imperialismus*, 1st Series, (Berlin, 1931)

Hürter, Johannes, ed., *Paul von Hintze, Marineoffizier, Diplomat, Staatssekretär. Dokumente einer Karriere zwischen Militär und Politik, 1903-1918* (Munich, 1998)

Jäckh, Ernst, *Kiderlen-Wächter der Staatsmann und Mensch. Briefwechsel und Nachlass* (Stuttgart, 1924)

Jager, Alexander, Picht, Clemens, and Schulin, Ernst, eds, *Walther Rathenau. Briefe*, 2 vols (Düsseldorf, 2006), vol. 2

Jászi, Oskar, 'Dismembered Hungary and Peace in Central Europe', *Foreign Affairs* (December 1923), pp. 270-82.

Jones, Thomas, *Whitehall Diary*, ed. Keith Middlemass, 3 vols (Oxford, 1969), vol. 1

Kaes, Anton, Jay, Martin, and Dimendberg, Edward, eds, *The Weimar Republic Sourcebook* (Berkeley, CA, 1995)

Kant, Immanuel, *Perpetual Peace*, in Mary J. Gregor, ed., *Political Philosophy* (Cambridge, 1996)

Komjáthy, Miklós, ed., *Protokolle des Gemeinsamen Ministerrates der Österreichisch-Ungarischen Monarchie (1914-1918)* (Budapest, 1966)

Lamprecht, Karl, *Zur neuen Lage* (Leipzig, 1914)

Lawrence, Don H. and Levy, Daniel J., eds, *Bernard Shaw: The Complete Prefaces*, 3 vols (London, 1995), vol. 2

Le Parti Socialiste, la guerre et la paix (Paris, 1918)

League of Nations Union, *The International Labour Organisation of the League of Nations* (London, 1922)

Lenin, V. I., *Collected Works* (London, 1964)

Link, Arthur, *Papers of Woodrow Wilson* (Princeton, NJ, 1966-94)

Lloyd George, David, *War Memoirs* (London, 1938)

Lodge v Lowell: A Joint Debate on the Covenant of the League of Nations, Symphony Hall, Boston, 19 March 1919

Loßberg, Fritz von, *Meine Tätigkeit im Weltkriege 1914-1918* (Berlin, 1939)

Martens, Stefan and Kessel, Martina, eds, *Documents diplomatiques français sur l'Allemagne 1920* (Bonn, 2002-3)

Masaryk, Thomas G., *The Problem of Small Nations in the European Crisis* (London, 1916)

Masaryk, Thomas G., *The New Europe* (Lewisburg, PA, 1972)

McEwen, J. M., ed., *The Riddell Diaries 1908-1923* (London, 1986)

Medlicott, W. N., Dakin, Douglas, and Lambert, M. E., *Documents on British Foreign Policy, 1919-1939*, 1st Series (London, 1966-)

Meinicke, Friedrich, *Machiavellism: The Doctrine of Raison d'État and its Place in Modern History* (London, 1957)

Michaelis, Herbert and Schraepeler, Ernst, eds, *Ursachen und Folgen. Vom deutschen Zusammenbruch 1918 und 1945 bis zur staatlichen Neuordnung Deutschlands in der Gegenwart* (Berlin, 1958-)

Miliukov, Paul, *Political Memoirs, 1905-1917* (Ann Arbor, MI, 1967)

Miliukov, Paul, *The Russian Revolution*, 3 vols (Gulf Breeze, FL, 1978), vol. 1

Mola, Aldo and Ricci, Aldo, eds, *Giovanni Giolitti. Al Governo, in Parlamento, nel Carteggio*, 3 vols (Foggia, 2007), vol. 3

Mommsen, Wolfgang and Hübinger, Gangolf, eds, *Max Weber. Zur Politik im Weltkrieg. Schriften und Reden 1914-1918*, 1st Series, vol. 15 (Tübingen, 1984)

Montant, Jean Claude, ed., *Documents diplomatiques français 1914-1915* (Brussels, 1999-2004)

Müller, Klaus-Jürgen, *General Ludwig Beck. Studien und Dokumente zur politisch-militärischen Vorstellungswelt und Tätigkeit des Generalstabschefs des deutschen Heeres 1933-1938* (Boppard am Rhein, 1980)

Musil, Robert, *The Man without Qualities*, trans. Sophie Wilkins and Burton Pike (London, 1997)

Nekludoff, A., *Diplomatic Reminiscences before and during the World War, 1911-1917* (London, 1920)

Newsinger, John, ed., *John Reed: Shaking the World: Revolutionary Journalism* (London, 1998)

Noakes, J. and Pridham, G., eds, *Nazism, 1919–1945: Foreign Policy, War, and Racial Extermination* (Exeter, 1997)

Paléologue, Maurice, *An Ambassador's Memoirs*, 3 vols (London, 1924), vol. 2

Philips, Anthony, ed., *Sergey Prokofiev: Diaries, 1907–1914, Prodigious Youth* (Ithaca, NY, 2006)

Philips, Anthony, ed., *Sergey Prokofiev: Diaries 1915–1923, Behind the Mask* (Ithaca, NY, 2008)

Pogge von Strandmann, Hartmut, ed., *Walther Rathenau: Industrialist, Banker, Intellectual, and Politician: Notes and Diaries, 1907–1922* (Oxford, 1985)

Remarque, Erich Maria, *The Road Back* (London, 1979)

Report of the International Commission to Report into the Causes and Conduct of the Balkan Wars (Washington DC, 1914).

Reppel, Richard A., Greenspan, Louis, Haslam, Beryl, Lewis, Albert, and Lippincourt, Mark, eds, *The Collected Papers of Bertrand Russell: Pacifism and Revolution, 1916–1918*, 29 vols (London, 1995), vol. 14

Richert, Dominik, *Beste Gelegenheit zum Sterben. Meine Erlebnisse im Kriege 1914–1918*, ed. Angelika Tramitz and Bernd Ulrich (Munich, 1989)

Riezler, Kurt, *Tagebücher, Aufsätze, Dokumente*, ed. Karl Dietrich Erdmann, introduction by Holger Afflerbach (Göttingen, 2008)

Rioux, Jean Pierre, ed., *Jean Jaurès. Rallumer tous les soleils* (Paris, 2006)

Root, Elihu, 'The Outlook for International Law', *Proceedings of the American Society of International Law at its Annual Meeting (1907–1917)*, 9 (28–30 December 1915), pp. 2–11.

Roth, Joseph, *The Radetzky March*, trans. Michael Hofmann (London, 2002)

Roth, Joseph, *What I Saw: Reports from Berlin, 1920–33*, introduction by Michael Hoffmann (London, 2003)

Salandra, Antonio, *I discorsi della guerra con alcune note* (Milan, 1922)

Scheidemann, Philipp, *Memoirs of a Social Democrat* (London, 1929)

Scherer, André and Grunewald, Jacques, eds, *L'Allemagne et les problèmes de la paix pendant la Première Guerre Mondiale* (Paris, 1962–78)

Schlesinger, Arthur, ed., *Walter Lippmann: Early Writings* (New York, 1970)

Schwabe, Klaus, ed., *Quellen zum Friedensschluss von Versailles* (Darmstadt, 1997)

Self, Robert C., ed., *The Austen Chamberlain Diary Letters: The Correspondence of Sir Austen Chamberlain with his Sisters, Hilda and Ida, 1916–1937* (Cambridge, 1995)

Solzhenitsyn, Alexander, *August 1914*, trans. Michael Glenny (London, 1972)

Stannard Baker, Ray and Dodd, William E., eds, *War & Peace: Presidential Messages, Addresses, and Public Papers (1917–1924)* (New York, 1970)

Steinberg, Mark D., ed., *Voices of Revolution, 1917* (New Haven, CT, 2001)

Stresemann, Gustav, *His Diaries, Letters, and Papers*, ed. Eric Sutton (London, 1935)

Trade Union Congress, *A Million Homes after the War* (London, 1917)

United States Department of State, *Papers Relating to the Foreign Relations of the United States, 1919: The Paris Peace Conference* (Washington DC, 1942)

Vandervelde, Emile, *Three Aspects of the Russian Revolution* (London, 1918)

Wade, Rex, ed., *Documents of Soviet History*, 8 vols, vol. 1, *The Triumph of Bolshevism, 1917–1919* (Gulf Breeze, FL, 1991)

Wells, H. G., *The War that Will End War* (New York, 1914)

Weygand, Maxime, *Mémoires. Mirages et réalité* (Paris, 1957)

Williamson, Philip and Baldwin, Philip, eds, *Baldwin Papers: A Conservative Statesman, 1908–1947* (Cambridge, 2004)

Wilson, Trevor, ed., *The Political Diaries of C. P. Scott, 1911–1928* (London, 1970)

Zweig, Stefan, *Journey into the Past*, trans. Anthea Bell (London, 2009)

Newspapers

Indianapolis Star
Irish Independent
Journal des Débats politiques et littéraires
La Stampa
Le Figaro
Le Temps
L'Humanité
Manchester Guardian
Neue Freie Presse

Penny Illustrated Press
San Francisco Chronicle
The New York Times
The Scotsman
The Times
The Times of India

Websites

www.armeniangenocide.org – collection of documents on Armenian genocide
http://www.degasperi.net/ – collection of sources from the career of Alcide De Gasperi
http://germanhistorydocs.ghi-dc.org/ – German history documents
http://hansard.millbanksystems.com/
http://labourhistory.net/stockholm1917/ – documents concerning the Stockholm Peace Conference, 1917
http://www.presidency.ucsb.edu/ – Presidents' public papers and speeches
http://www.reichstagsprotokolle.de/ – Reichstag debates
http://www.volksbund.de/kriegsgraeberstaette/ – German war graves

Secondary Sources

Adamson, Walter, *Avant-Garde Florence: From Modernism to Fascism* (Cambridge, MA, 1993)
Adas, Michael, 'Contested Hegemony: The Great War and the Afro-Asian Assault on the Civilizing Mission Ideology', *Journal of World History*, 15, 1 (2004), pp. 31–63
Afflerbach, Holger, *Falkenhayn. Politisches Denken und Handeln im Kaiserreich* (Munich, 1994)
Ahmad, Feroz, *The Young Turks: The Committee of Union and Progress in Turkish Politics, 1908–1914* (Oxford, 1969)
Aksakal, Mustafa, *The Ottoman Road to War in 1914: The Ottoman Empire and the First World War* (Cambridge, 2008)
Aksakal, Mustafa, ' "Holy War Made in Germany?" Ottoman Origins of the 1914 Jihad', *War in History*, 18, 2 (2011), pp. 184–99
Albert, Bill, *South America and the First World War: The Impact of the War on Brazil, Argentina, Peru, and Chile* (Cambridge, 1988)
Alff, Wilhelm, ed., *Deutschlands Sonderung von Europa 1862–1945* (Frankfurt, 1984)
Allan, Pierre and Keller, Alexis, eds, *What Is a Just Peace?* (Oxford, 2006)
Allerfeldt, Kristoffer, 'Wilsonian Pragmatism? Woodrow Wilson, Japanese Immigration, and the Paris Peace Conference', *Diplomacy & Statecraft*, 15, 3 (2004), pp. 545–72
Alpern Engel, Barbara, 'Not by Bread Alone: Subsistence Riots in Russia during World War I', *Journal of Modern History*, 69, 4 (1997), pp. 696–721
Altman, Albert E. and Schiffrin, Harold Z., 'Sun Yat-sen and the Japanese, 1914–16', *Modern Asian Studies*, 6, 4 (1972), pp. 385–400
Ambrosius, Lloyd, *Woodrow Wilson and the American Diplomatic Tradition: The Treaty Fight in Perspective* (Cambridge, 1987)
Andrew, C. M. and Kanya-Forstner, A. S., 'The French Colonial Party and French Colonial War Aims, 1914–1918', *Historical Journal*, 17, 1 (1974), pp. 79–106
Angelow, Jürgen, ed., *Der Erste Weltkrieg auf dem Balkan* (Berlin, 2011)
Antić, Čedomir, *Ralph Paget: A Diplomat in Serbia* (Belgrade, 2006)
Ascher, Abraham, *P. A. Stolypin: The Search for Stability in Late Imperial Russia* (Stanford, CA, 2001)
Aschoff, Hans-Georg, 'Benedict XV (1914–1922), Profil enies Pontifikats', *Historisches Jahrbuch*, 127 (2007), pp. 295–329
Audoin-Rouzeau, Stéphane, *Men at War 1914–1918: National Sentiment and Trench Journalism in France during the First World War* (Oxford, 1992)
Audoin-Rouzeau, Stéphane, 'Norbert Elias et l'expérience oubliée de la Première Guerre mondiale', *Vingtième Siècle*, 2 (2010), pp. 104–14
Augusteijn, Joost, ed., *The Irish Revolution, 1913–1923* (Basingstoke, 2010)
Ball, Simon, *The Guardsmen: Harold Macmillan, Three Friends, and the World they Made* (London, 2004)
Barbezat, Daniel, 'Cooperation and Rivalry in the International Steel Cartel, 1926–1933', *Journal of Economic History*, 49, 2 (1989), pp. 435–47
Barth, Boris, *Dolchstosslegenden und politische Desintegration. Das Trauma der deutschen Niederlage im Ersten Weltkrieg 1914–1933* (Düsseldorf, 2003)

416   BIBLIOGRAPHY

Baughan, Emily, ' "Every Citizen of Empire Implored to Save the Children!" Empire, Internationalism, and the Save the Children Fund in Inter-War Britain', *Historical Research*, 86, 231 (2013), pp. 116–37

Baumgart, Winfried, *Deutsche Ostpolitik 1918. Von Brest-Litovsk bis zum Ende des Weltkrieges* (Vienna, 1966)

Becker, Annette, *Oubliés de la grande guerre. Humanitaires et cultures de guerre 1914–1918. Populations occupées, déportés civils, prisonniers de guerre* (Paris, 1998)

Becker, Annette, *Les cicatrices rouges 14–18. France et Belgique occupées* (Paris, 2010)

Becker, Jean-Jacques, *The Great War and the French People* (Leamington Spa, 1985)

Bell, Daniel, *The First Total War: Napoleon's Europe and the Birth of Warfare as We Know It* (Boston, MA, 2007)

Bell, John D., *Peasants in Power: Alexander Stamboliski and the Bulgarian Agrarian National Union, 1899–1923* (Princeton, NJ, 1977)

Berridge, M. J., 'Object Lessons in Violence: The Rationalities and Irrationalities of Urban Struggle during the Egyptian Revolution of 1919', *Journal of Colonialism and Colonial History*, 12, 3 (2011)

Bessel, Richard, *Germany after the First World War* (Oxford, 1993)

Bihl, Wolfdieter, *Österreich-Ungarn und die Friedensschlüsse von Brest-Litovsk* (Vienna, 1970)

Biondich, Mark, *Stjepan Radić, the Croat Peasant Party, and the Politics of Mass Mobilization, 1904–1928* (Toronto, 2000)

Biondich, Mark, *The Balkans: Revolution, War, and Political Violence since 1878* (Oxford, 2011)

Blackbourn, David and Eley, Geoff, *The Peculiarities of German History: Bourgeois Society and Politics in Nineteenth-Century Germany* (Oxford, 1984)

Bloxham, Donald, 'The Armenian Genocide of 1915–1916: Cumulative Radicalization and the Development of a Destruction Policy', *Past & Present*, 181 (November 2003), pp. 141–91

Bloxham, Donald, 'Terrorism and Imperial Decline: The Ottoman-Armenian Case', *European Review of History*, 14, 3 (2007), pp. 301–24

Bobroff, Ronald, 'Revolution in Wartime: Sergei D. Sazonov and the Future of Poland, 1910–1916', *International History Review*, 22, 3 (2000), pp. 505–28

Bobroff, Ronald, *Roads to Glory: Late Imperial Russia and the Turkish Straits* (London, 2006)

Bodo, Bela, 'Hungarian Aristocracy and the White Terror', *Journal of Contemporary History*, 45, 4 (2010), pp. 703–24

Boemeke, Manfred F., Feldman, Gerald D., and Glaser, Elisabeth, eds, *The Treaty of Versailles: A Reassessment after 75 Years* (Cambridge, 1998)

Bonakdarian, Mansour, 'Negotiating Universal Values and Cultural and National Parameters at the First Universal Races Congress', *Radical History Review*, 92 (Spring 2005), pp. 118–32

Borodziej, Wladzimierz, *Geschichte Polens im 20. Jahrhundert* (Munich, 2010)

Borzecki, Jerzy, *The Soviet–Polish Peace of 1921 and the Creation of Interwar Europe* (New Haven, CT, 2008)

Bossuat, Gérard and Wilkens, Andreas, eds, *Jean Monnet. L'Europe et les chemins de la paix* (Paris, 1999)

Bosworth, R. J. B., *Mussolini's Italy: Life under the Dictatorship, 1915–1945* (London, 2007)

Bourke, Joanna, *An Intimate History of Killing: Face-to-Face Killings in Twentieth-Century Warfare* (London, 1999)

Bridgen, Paul, *The Labour Party and the Politics of War and Peace, 1900–1924* (Woodbridge, 2009)

Briggs, Asa, ed., *Essays in Labour History, 1886–1923* (London, 1971)

Bucarelli, Massimo, 'Mussolini, la questione adriatica e il fallimento dell'interventismo democratica', *Nuova Rivista Storica*, 95, 1 (2011), pp. 137–205

Burgwyn, H. James, *The Legend of the Mutilated Victory: Italy, the Great War, and the Paris Peace Conference, 1915–1919* (Westport, CT, 1993)

Cabanes, Bruno, *La victoire endeuillée. La sortie de guerre des soldats français, 1918–1920* (Paris, 2004)

Caccomo, Francesco, *L'Italia e la 'Nuova' Europa. Il confronto sull' Europa orientale alla conferenza di pace di Parigi (1919–1920)* (2000)

Calvert, Peter, *The Mexican Revolution, 1910–1914: The Diplomacy of Anglo-American Conflict* (Cambridge, 1968)

Campbell, John P., 'Taft, Roosevelt, and the Arbitration Treaties of 1911', *Journal of American History*, 53, 2 (1966), pp. 279–98

Carrillo, Elisa, *Alcide De Gasperi: The Long Apprenticeship* (Notre Dame, IL, 1965)

Chickering, Roger, *Imperial Germany and the Great War, 1914–1918* (Cambridge, 1998)

Chickering, Roger and Förster, Stig, eds, *Great War, Total War: Combat and Mobilization on the Western Front* (Cambridge, 2000)

Childs, Thomas, *Italo-Turkish Diplomacy and the War over Libya, 1911–1912* (Leiden, 1990)

Clark, Bruce, *Twice a Stranger: How Mass Expulsions Shaped Modern Greece and Turkey* (London, 2006)

Clark, Christopher, *The Sleepwalkers: How Europe Went to War in 1914* (London, 2012)

Clarke, Peter, *Liberals and Social Democrats* (Cambridge, 1978)

Clavin, Patricia, *Securing the World Economy: Reinventing the League of Nations, 1920–1946* (Oxford, 2013)

Cohrs, Patrick, *The Unfinished Peace after World War I: America, Britain, and the Stabilization of Europe, 1919–1932* (Cambridge, 2006)

Cooper, John Milton, *Breaking the Heart of the World: Woodrow Wilson and the Fight for the League of Nations* (Cambridge, 2001)

Cooper, John Milton, *Woodrow Wilson* (New York, 2011)

Cooper, John Milton, ed., *Reconsidering Woodrow Wilson: Progressivism, Internationalism, War, and Peace* (Baltimore, MD, 2008)

Corner, Paul, *Fascism in Ferrara, 1915–1925* (Oxford, 1975)

Cornwall, Mark, *The Undermining of Austria-Hungary: The Battle for Hearts and Minds* (Basingstoke, 2000)

Craig Nation, R., *Black Earth, Red Star: A History of Soviet Security Policy, 1917–1991* (Ithaca, NY, 1992)

Crampton, R. J., *Bulgaria* (Oxford, 2007)

Crampton, R. J., *Hollow Détente: Anglo-German Relations in the Balkans, 1911–1914* (London, 1980)

Cross, Graham, *The Diplomatic Education of Franklin D. Roosevelt, 1882–1933* (Basingstoke, 2012)

Daele, Jasmien van, 'Engineering Social Peace: Networks, Ideas, and the Founding of the International Labor Organization', *International Review of Social History*, 50 (2005), pp. 435–66

Daniel, Ute, *The War from Within: German Working-Class Women in the First World War* (Oxford, 1997)

Darwin, John, *The Empire Project: The Rise and Fall of the British World System, 1830–1970* (Cambridge, 2009)

Davies, Norman, *White Eagle, Red Star: The Polish-Soviet War, 1919–1920* (London, 1972)

Davies, Norman, *God's Playground: A History of Poland*, 2 vols (Oxford, 1981)

Dawley, Alan, *Changing the World: American Progressives in War and Revolution* (Princeton, NJ, 2003)

Dawson, Roderic, 'The Armenian Crisis, 1912–1914', *American Historical Review*, 53, 3 (1948), pp. 481–505

De Felice, Renzo, *Mussolini, il rivoluzionaria 1883–1920* (Turin, 1965)

De Schaepdrjiver, Sophie, *La Belgique et la Première Guerre Mondiale* (Frankfurt, 2004)

Dennis, Peter and Grey, Jeffrey, eds, *1911: Preliminary Moves* (Canberra, 2012)

Dickinson, Frederick, *War and National Reinvention: Japan in the Great War, 1914–1919* (Cambridge, MA, 1999)

Dimitrova, Snezhona, ' "Taming the Death": The Culture of death (1915–18) and its Meaning and Commemorating through First World War Soldier Monuments in Bulgaria (1917–44)', *Social History*, 30, 2 (2005), pp. 175–94

Dornik, Wolfram and Korner, Stefan, eds, *Die Besatzung der Ukraine 1918. Historischer Kontext – Forschungsstand – wirtschaftliche und soziale Folgen* (Graz, 2008)

Doughty, Robert, *Pyrrhic Victory: French Strategy and Operations in the Great War* (Cambridge, MA, 2005)

Dowling, Timothy C., *The Brusilov Offensive* (Bloomington, IN, 2008)

Duchêne, François, *Jean Monnet: The First Statesman of Interdependence* (New York, 1994)

Duiker, William, *Ho Chi Minh: A Life* (New York, 2000)

Dülffer, Jost, Kröger, Martin, and Wippich, Rolf-Harald, *Vermiedene Kriege. Deeskalation von Konflikten der Grossmächte zwischen Krimkrieg und Erstem Weltkrieg (1865–1914)* (Munich, 1997)

Düppler, Jorg and Groß, Gerhard P., eds, *Kriegsende 1918. Ereignis, Wirkung, Nachwirkung* (Oldenbourg, 1999)

Ehrenpreis, Petronilla, *Kriegs- und Friedensziele im Diskurs. Regierung und deutschsprachige Öffentlichkeit während des Ersten Weltkrieges* (Innsbruck, 2005)

Eichenberg, Julia, 'The Dark Side of Independence: Paramilitary Violence in Ireland and Poland after the First World War', *Contemporary European History*, 19, 3 (2010), pp. 231–48

Engelstein, Laura, ' "Belgium of Our Own": The Sack of Russian Kalisz, August 1914', *Kritika*, 10, 3 (2009), pp. 441–73

Epstein, Klaus, *Matthias Erzberger and the Dilemma of German Democracy* (New York, 1971)

Erickson, Edward, 'Strength against Weakness: Ottoman Military Effectiveness at Gallipoli, 1915', *Journal of Military History*, 65, 4 (2001), pp. 981–1,001

Erickson, Edward, 'The Armenians and Ottoman Military Policy, 1915', *War in History*, 15, 2 (2008), pp. 141–67

Fanning, Ronan, *Fatal Path: British Government and Irish Revolution, 1910–1922* (London, 2013)

Feldman, Gerald, *Army, Industry and Labor in Germany, 1914–1918* (Princeton, NJ, 1966)

Feldman, Gerald, *The Great Disorder: Politics, Economics, and Society in the German Inflation, 1914–1924* (Oxford, 1993)

Feltman, Brian K., 'Tolerance as a Crime? The British Treatment of German Prisoners of War on the Western Front, 1914–1918', *War in History*, 17, 4 (2010), pp. 435–58

Ferguson, Niall, *The Pity of War* (London, 1998)

Ferguson, Niall, *The War of the World: History's Age of Hatred* (London, 2006)

Fink, Carole, *Defending the Rights of Others: The Great Powers, the Jews, and the International Minority, 1878–1938* (Cambridge, 2004)

Fink, Carole, Fröhn, Axel, and Heideking, Jürgen, eds, *Genoa, Rapallo and European Reconstruction in 1922* (Cambridge, 2002)

Finn, Michael, ' "Local Heroes": War News and the Construction of "Community" in Britain, 1914–1918', *Historical Research*, 83, 221 (2010), pp. 520–38

Finnan, Joseph, *John Redmond and Irish Unity, 1912–1918* (Syracuse, NY, 2004)

Fischer, Conan, *The Ruhr Crisis, 1923–1924* (Oxford, 2003)

Fischer, Conan, 'Scoundrels without a Fatherland? Heavy Industry and Transnationalism in Post-First World War Germany', *Contemporary European History*, 14, 4 (2005), pp. 441–64

Fischer, Fritz, *Germany's Aims in the First World War* (London, 1967)

Fogarty, Richard, *Race and War in France: Colonial Subjects in the French Army, 1914–1918* (Baltimore, MD, 2008)

Foley, Robert, *German Strategy and the Path to Verdun: Erich von Falkenhayn and the Development of Attrition, 1871–1916* (Cambridge, 2005)

Fordham, Elizabeth, 'Le combat pour le New Europe. Les radicaux britanniques et la Première Guerre mondiale', *Mil neuf cent. Revue d'histoire intellectuelle*, 23, 1 (2005), pp. 111–41

Forner, Sean A., 'War Commemoration and the Republic in Crisis: Weimar Germany and the Neue Wache', *Central European History*, 35, 4 (2002), pp. 513–49

Forsbach, Ralf, *Alfred von Kiderlen-Wächter (1852–1912)*, 2 vols (Göttingen, 1997), vol. 2

Forsyth, Douglas, *The Crisis of Liberal Italy: Monetary and Financial Policy, 1914–1922* (Cambridge, 1993)

French, David, *British Strategy and War Aims, 1914–1916* (London, 1986)

Fridenson, Patrick, ed., *The French Home Front, 1914–1918* (Providence, RI, 1992)

Friedrich, Wolfgang-Uwe, *Bulgarien und die Mächte 1913–1915. Ein Beitrag zur Weltkriegs- und Imperialismusgeschichte* (Stuttgart, 1985)

Fromkin, David, *A Peace to End all Peace: Creating the Modern Middle East, 1914–1922* (London, 1989)

Fry, Michael, *Lloyd George and Foreign Policy: The Education of a Statesman, 1890–1916* (Montreal, 1977)

Führer, Karl Christian, *Carl Legien 1861–1920. Ein Gewerkschafter im Kampf um 'möglichst gutes Leben' für alle Arbeiter* (Essen, 2009)

Fuller, William, *The Foe Within: Fantasies of Treason and the End of Imperial Russia* (Ithaca, NY, 2006)

Gaddis, John Lewis, *George F. Kennan: An American Life* (London, 2011)

Gattrell, Peter, *A Whole Empire Walking: Refugees in Russia during World War I* (Bloomington, IN, 1999)

Gattrell, Peter, *Russia's First World War: A Social and Economic History* (Harlow, 2005)

Gaudin, Corinne, 'Rural Echoes of World War I: War Talk in the Russian Village', *Jahrbücher für Geschichte Osteuropas*, 56, 3 (2008), pp. 391–414

Gelfand, Lawrence, *The Inquiry: American Preparations for Peace, 1917–1919* (New Haven, CT, 1963)

Gelfand, Lawrence, ed., *Herbert Hoover: The Great War and its Aftermath, 1914–1923* (Iowa City, IA, 1979)

Georges, Bernard and Tintant, Denise, *Léon Jouhaux. Cinquante ans de syndicalisme*, 2 vols (Paris, 1962), vol. 1

Gerwarth, Robert, 'The Central European Counter-Revolution: Paramilitary Violence in Germany, Austria, and Hungary after the Great War', *Past & Present*, (2008), pp. 175–209

Gerwarth, Robert and Horne, John, eds, *War in Peace: Paramilitary Violence in Europe after the Great War* (Oxford, 2012)

Geyer, Martin, *Verkehrte Welt. Revolution, Inflation und Moderne* (Göttingen, 1998)

Geyer, Michael, 'Insurrectionary Warfare: The German Debate about a Levée en Masse in October 1918', *Journal of Modern History*, 73, 4 (2001), pp. 459–527

Gibelli, Antonio, *La grande guerra degli italiani 1915–1918* (Milan, 1998)

Gingeras, Ryan, *Sorrowful Shore: Violence, Ethnicity, and the End of the Ottoman Empire, 1912–1923* (Oxford, 2009)

Ginio, Eyal, 'Mobilizing the Ottoman Nation during the Balkan Wars (1912–1913): Awakening from Ottoman Dreams', *War in History*, 12, 2 (2005), pp. 156–77

Gleason, William, 'Alexander Guchkov and the End of the Russian Empire', *Transactions of the American Philosophical Society*, New Series, 73, 3 (1983), pp. 1–90

Goethem, Geert van, *The Amsterdam International: The World of the International Federation of Trade Unions, 1913–1945* (Aldershot, 2006)

Golczewski, Frank, *Deutsche und Ukrainer 1914–1939* (Paderborn, 2010)

Goldstein, Erik, *Winning the Peace: British Diplomatic Strategy, Peace Planning, and the Paris Peace Conference, 1916–1920* (Oxford, 1991)

Goltz, Anna von der, *Hindenburg: Power, Myth, and the Rise of the Nazis* (Oxford, 2009)

Gooch, John, *Mussolini and his Generals: The Armed Forces and Fascist Foreign Policy, 1922–1940* (Cambridge, 2007)

Gottmann, Andreas, ed., *Karl I. (IV.), der Erste Weltkrieg und das Ende der Donaumonarchie* (Vienna, 2007)

Goughan, Anthony, 'Woodrow Wilson and the Rise of Militant Interventionism in the South', *Journal of Southern History*, 65, 4 (1999), pp. 771–808

Greenhalgh, Elizabeth, *Foch in Command: The Forging of a First World War General* (Cambridge, 2011)

Gregory, Adrian, *The Last Great War: British Society and the First World War* (Cambridge, 2008)

Gregory, Adrian and Pašeta, Senia, eds, *Ireland and the Great War: A War to Unite Us All?* (Manchester, 2002)

Grey, Jeffrey, *A Military History of Australia* (Cambridge, 1999)

Grohmann, Carolyn, 'From Lothringen to Lorraine: Expulsion and Voluntary Repatriation', *Diplomacy and Statecraft*, 16, 3 (2005), pp. 571–87

Guieu, Jean-Michel, *Le rameau et le glaive. Les militants français pour la Société des Nations* (Paris, 2008)

Gullace, Nicoletta, 'Sexual Violence and Family Honor: British Propaganda and International Law during the First World War', *American Historical Review*, 102, 3 (1997), pp. 714–47

Gumz, Jonathan, *The Resurrection and Collapse of Empire in Habsburg Serbia, 1914–1918* (Cambridge, 2009)

Hagen, William H., 'The Moral Economy of Ethnic Cleansing: The Pogrom in Lwów, November 1918', *Geschichte und Gesellschaft*, 31 (2005), pp. 203–26

Hagenlücke, Heinz, *Deutsche Vaterlandspartei. Die nationale Rechte am Ende des Kaiserreichs* (Düsseldorf, 1997)

Hall, Richard, ' "The Enemy is behind Us": The Morale Crisis in the Bulgarian Army during the Summer of 1918', *War in History*, 21, 2 (2004), pp. 209–19

Hamilton, Richard and Herwig, Holger, eds, *War Planning 1914* (Cambridge, 2010)

Hanioğlu, M. Şükrü, *Ataturk: An Intellectual Biography* (Princeton, NJ, 2011)

Hanks, Robert K., ' "Generalissimo" or "Skunk"? The Impact of Georges Clemenceau's Leadership on the Western Alliance in 1918', *French History*, 24, 2 (2010), pp. 197–217

Hantsch, Hugo, *Leopold Graf Berchtold* (Graz, 1963)

Hardtwig, Wolfgang, ed., *Politische Kulturgeschichte der Zwischenkriegszeit 1918–1939* (Göttingen, 2005)

Harris, J. P., *Douglas Haig and the First World War* (Cambridge, 2008)

Healy, Maureen, *Vienna and the Fall of the Habsburg Empire: Total War and Everyday Life in World War I* (Cambridge, 2004)

Herrmann, David, 'The Paralysis of Italian Strategy in the Italian-Turkish War, 1911–1912', *English Historical Review*, 104, 411 (1989), pp. 332–56

Herwig, Holger and Hamilton, Richard F., eds, *The Origins of the First World War* (Cambridge, 2003)

Heywood, Geoffrey, *Failure of a Dream: Sidney Sonnino and the Rise and Fall of Liberal Italy, 1847–1922* (Florence, 1999)

Hildebrand, Klaus, *Das vergangene Reich. Deutsche Aussenpolitik von Bismarck bis Hitler, 1871–1945* (Stuttgart, 1995)

Hitchins, Keith, *Rumania, 1866–1947* (Oxford, 1994)

Ho, Wai-Chung, 'Social Change and Nationalism in China's Popular Songs', *Social History*, 31, 4 (2006), pp. 435–53

Hoensch, Jörg, *A History of Modern Hungary, 1867–1994* (London, 1996)

Hoff, August, *Das Werk Wilhelm Lehmbrücks* (Duisburg, 1932)

Hoffmann, David L., *Cultivating the Masses: Modern State Practices and Soviet Socialism, 1914–1939* (Ithaca, NY, 2011)

Holquist, Peter, *Making War, Forging Revolution: Russia's Continuum of Crisis, 1914–1921* (Cambridge, MA, 2002)

Holquist, Peter, 'Violent Russia, Deadly Marxism? Russia in the Epoch of Violence, 1905–1921', *Kritika*, 4, 3 (2003), pp. 627–52

Horne, John, *Labour at War: France and Britain, 1914–1918* (Oxford, 1991)

Horne, John, 'Guerres et reconciliations européenes au 20e siècle', *Vingtiéme Siècle*, 104 (October–December 2009), pp. 3–16

Horne, John and Kramer, Alan, *German Atrocities, 1914: A History of Denial* (New Haven, CT, 2001)

Howard, Michael, 'A Thirty Years' War: The Two World Wars in Historical Perspective', *Transactions of the Royal Historical Society*, 6th Series, 3 (1993), pp. 171–84

Howard, Michael, *The Invention of Peace: Reflections on War and International Order* (London, 2001)

Hüppauf, Bernd, 'Langemarck, Verdun, and the Myth of a "New Man" in Germany after the First World War', *War & Society*, 6, 2 (1988), pp. 70–103

Hyam, Ronald, *Britain's Declining Empire: The Road to Decolonisation, 1918–1968* (Cambridge, 2006)

Iriye, Akira, *The Origins of the Second World War in the Pacific* (London, 1987)

Jackson, Peter, 'French Security and a British "Continental Commitment" after the First World War: A Reassessment', *English Historical Review*, 126, 519 (2011), pp. 345–85

Jahn, Hubertus, *Patriotic Culture in Russia during World War I* (Ithaca, NY, 1995)

Jarausch, Konrad, *The Enigmatic Chancellor: Bethmann Hollweg and the Hubris of Imperial Germany* (New Haven, CT, 1973)

Jeannesson, Stanislas, *Poincaré, la France et la Ruhr (1922–1924)* (Strasbourg, 1998)

Jeannesson, Stanislas, 'Jacques Seydoux et la diplomatie économique de la France dans l'après-guerre', *Relations internationales*, 121, 1 (2005), pp. 9–27

Jeffery, Keith, *The British Army and the Crisis of Empire, 1918–1922* (Manchester, 1984)

Jeffery, Keith, *Ireland and the Great War* (Cambridge, 2000)

Jensen, Marius B., *The Making of Modern Japan* (Cambridge, MA, 2000)

Jones, Heather, *Violence against Prisoners of War in the First World War: Britain, France, and Germany, 1914–1918* (Cambridge, 2010)

Judt, Tony, *Post-War: A History of Europe since 1945* (London, 2006)

Kampmark, Brian, ' "No Peace with the Hohenzollerns": American Attitudes on Political Legitimacy towards Hohenzollern Germany, 1917–1918', *Diplomatic History*, 34, 5 (2010), pp. 769–91

Kawamura, Noriko, 'Wilsonian Idealism and Japanese Claims at the Paris Peace Conference', *Pacific Historical Review*, 66, 4 (1997), pp. 503–26

Kayali, Hasan, *Arabs and Young Turks: Ottomanism, Arabism, and Islamism in the Ottoman Empire, 1908–1918* (Berkeley, CA, 1997)

Keene, Jennifer D., *Doughboys, the Great War, and the Remaking of America* (Baltimore, MD, 2001)

Keene, Jennifer D., 'W. E. B. DuBois and the Wounded World: Seeking Meaning in the First World War for African-Americans', *Peace & Change*, 26, 2 (2001), pp. 135–52

Keiger, John, *Raymond Poincaré* (Cambridge, 1997)

Keisinger, Florian, *Unzivilisierte Krieg im zivilisierten Europa? Die Balkankriege und die öffentliche Meinung in Deutschland, England und Irland 1876–1913* (Paderborn, 2008)

Kennan, George, *The Decline of Bismarck's European Order: Franco-Russian Relations, 1875–1890* (Princeton, NJ, 1981)

Kennedy, David M., *Over Here: The First World War and American Society* (New York, 1980)

Kennedy, Ross A., 'Woodrow Wilson, World War I, and an American Conception of National Security', *Diplomatic History*, 25, 1 (2001), pp. 1–32.

Keohane, Nigel, *The Party of Patriotism: The Conservative Party and the First World War* (Farnham, 2010)

Kershaw, Ian, *The Hitler Myth: Image and Reality in the Third Reich* (Oxford, 1987)

Kershaw, Ian, *Hitler, 1889–1936: Hubris* (London, 1998)

Kershaw, Ian, 'War and Political Violence in Twentieth-Century Europe', *Contemporary European History*, 14, 1 (2005), pp. 107–23

Kévonian, Dzovinar, 'L'enquête, le délit, la preuve: les "atrocités" balkaniques de 1912–1913 à l'épreuve du dossier de la guerre', *Le mouvement social*, 222 (2008), pp. 13–40

Kiessling, Friedrich, *Gegen den 'großen Krieg'. Entspannung in den internationalen Beziehungen 1911–1914* (Munich, 2002)

Killinger, Charles, *Gaetano Salvemini: A Biography* (Westport, CT, 2002)

Kirby, David, 'International Socialism and the Question of Peace: The Stockholm Conference of 1917', *Historical Journal*, 25, 3 (1982), pp. 709–16

Kitchen, James, Miller, Alisa, and Rowe, Laura, eds, *Other Combatants, Other Fronts: Competing Histories of the First World War* (Newcastle, 2011)

Kitromilides, Paschalis, ed., *Eleftherios Venizelos: The Trials of Statesmanship* (Edinburgh, 2006)

Knight, Alan, *The Mexican Revolution*, 2 vols (London, 1986)

Knock, Thomas J., *To End All Wars: Woodrow Wilson and the Quest for a New World Order* (New York, 1992)

Koller, Christian, *'Von wilden aller Rassen niedergemetzelt'. Die Diskussion um die Verwendung von Kolonialtruppen in Europa zwischen Rassismus, Kolonial- und Militärpolitik (1914–1930)* (Stuttgart, 2001)

Koss, Stephen E., 'The Destruction of Britain's Last Liberal Government', *Journal of Modern History*, 40, 2 (1968), pp. 257–77

Kramer, Alan, *The Dynamics of Destruction: Culture and Mass Killing in the First World War* (Oxford, 2007)

Kriegel, Annie, *Histoire du mouvement ouvrier français, 1914–1920*, 2 vols (Paris, 1964), vol. 1

Kronenbitter, Günther, *'Krieg im Frieden'. Die Führung der k.u.k. Armee und die Grossmachtpolitik Österreich-Ungarns 1906–1914* (Munich, 2003)

Krüger, Peter, *Die Aussenpolitik der Republik von Weimar* (Darmstadt, 1985)

Krumeich, Gerd, ed., *Versailles. Ziele – Wirkung – Wahrnehmung* (Essen, 2001)

Krumeich, Gerd and Schröder, Joachim, eds, *Der Schatten des Weltkrieges. Die Ruhrbesetzung 1923* (Essen, 2004)

Kruse, Wolfgang, *Krieg und nationale Integration. Eine Neuinterpretation des sozialdemokratischen Burgfriedensschlusses 1914/15* (Essen, 1993)

LaFeber, Walter, *The Clash: A History of U.S.–Japan Relations* (New York, 1997)

Laffan, Michael, *The Resurrection of Ireland: The Sinn Fein Party, 1916–1923* (Cambridge, 1999)

Lake, Marilyn and Reynolds, Henry, *Drawing the Global Colour Line: White Men's Countries and the International Challenge of Racial Equality* (Cambridge, 2008)

Lambert, Nicholas, *Planning Armageddon: British Economic Warfare and the First World War* (Cambridge, MA, 2012)

Laqua, Daniel, 'Transnational Intellectual Cooperation: The League of Nations and the Problem of Order', *Journal of Global History*, 6, 2 (2011), pp. 223–47

Lawrence, Jon, 'Forging a Peaceable Kingdom: War, Violence, and Fear of Brutalization in Post-First World War Britain', *Journal of Modern History*, 75, 3 (2003), pp. 557–89

Le Moal, Frédéric, *La France et l'Italie dans les Balkans 1914–1919. Le contentieux adriatique* (Paris, 2006)

Lentin, Antony, *Guilt at Versailles: Lloyd George and the Pre-History of Appeasement* (Leicester, 1984)

Levene, Mark, 'The Balfour Declaration: A Case of Mistaken Identity', *English Historical Review*, 107, 422 (1992), pp. 59–77

Liebau, Heike, Bromber, Katrin, Lange, Katharina, Hamzah, Dyala, and Ahuja, Ravi, eds, *The World in World Wars: Experiences, Perceptions and Perspectives from Africa and Asia* (Leiden, 2010)

Lieven, Dominic, *Russia and the Origins of the First World War* (London, 1983)

Link, Arthur, *Wilson: Campaigns for Progressivism and Peace, 1916–1917* (Princeton, NJ, 1965)

Liulevicius, Gabriel Vejas, *War Land on the Eastern Front: Culture, National Identity, and German Occupation in World War I* (Cambridge, 2000)

Lohr, Eric, *Nationalizing the Russian Empire: The Campaign against Enemy Aliens during World War I* (Cambridge, MA, 2003)

Lorenzini, Sara, 'The Roots of a Statesman: De Gasperi's Foreign Policy', *Modern Italy*, 14, 4 (2009), pp. 473–84

Lowe, C. J. and Marzari, F., *Italian Foreign Policy, 1870–1940* (London, 1978)

Luo, Zhitian, 'National Humiliation and National Assertions: The Chinese Response to the Twenty-One Demands', *Modern Asian Studies*, 27, 2 (1993), pp. 298–309

McCarthy, Justin, *Death and Exile: The Ethnic Cleansing of Ottoman Muslims, 1821–1922* (Princeton, NJ, 1995)

McCord, Edward A., 'Warlords against Warlordism: The Politics of Anti-Militarism in Early Twentieth-Century China', *Modern Asian Studies*, 30, 4 (1996), pp. 795–827

McDougall, Walter, *France's Rhineland Diplomacy, 1914–1924: The Last Bid for a Balance of Power in Europe* (Princeton, NJ, 1978)

Mackenzie, David, *Serbs and Russians* (New York, 1996)

McKillen, Elizabeth, 'Integrating Labor into the Narrative of Wilsonian Internationalism', *Diplomatic History*, 34, 4 (2010), pp. 643–62

Maclaren McDonald, David, *United Government and Foreign Policy in Russia, 1900–1914* (Cambridge, MA, 1992)

McMeekin, Sean, *The Russian Origins of the First World War* (Cambridge, MA, 2011)

McMeekin, Sean, *The Berlin–Baghdad Express: The Ottoman Empire and Germany's Bid for World Power, 1898–1918* (London, 2010)

Macmillan, Margaret, *Paris 1919: Six Months that Changed the World* (New York, 2002)

Manela, Erez, *The Wilsonian Moment: Self-Determination and the International Origins of Anti-Colonial Nationalism* (Oxford, 2007)

Mango, Andrew, *Atatürk* (London, 1999)

Marmetschke, Katja, *Feindbeobachtung und Verständigung. Der Germanist Edmond Vermeil (1878-1964) in den deutsch-französischen Beziehungen* (Cologne, 2008)

Marquand, David, *Ramsay MacDonald* (London, 1977)

Marshall, Dominique, 'The Construction of Children as an Object of International Relations: The Declaration of Children's Rights and the Child Welfare Committee of the League of Nations, 1900-1929', *International Journal of Children's Rights*, 7 (1999), pp. 108-38

Mawdsley, Evan, *The Russian Civil War* (Boston, MA, 1987)

Mayeur, Jean-Marie, *La vie politique sous la Troisième République 1870-1940* (Paris, 1984)

Mazower, Mark, 'Minorities and the League of Nations in Interwar Europe', *Daedalus*, 126, 2 (1997), pp. 47-54

Mazower, Mark, *Dark Continent: Europe's Twentieth Century* (London, 1998)

Mazower, Mark, 'Violence and the State in the Twentieth Century', *American Historical Review*, 107, 4 (2002), pp. 1,158-78

Mazower, Mark, *Governing the World: The History of an Idea* (London, 2012)

Meaney, Neville, *Australia and the World Crisis, 1914-1923* (Sydney, 2009)

Meckling, Ingeborg, *Die Aussenpolitik des Grafen Czernin* (Munich, 1969)

Meyer, Jessica, ' "Not Septimus now": Wives of Disabled Veterans and Cultural Memory of the First World War in Britain', *Women's History Review*, 13, 1 (2004), pp. 117-38

Miller Unterberger, Betty, 'Woodrow Wilson and the Bolsheviks: The Acid Test of Soviet-American Relations', *Diplomatic History*, 11, 1 (1987), pp. 71-90

Miquel, Pierre, 'Le Journal de Débats et la paix de Versailles', *Revue Historique*, 232 (1964), pp. 379-414

Mitrovic, Andrej, *Serbia's Great War, 1914-1918* (London, 2007)

Mitter, Rana, *A Bitter Revolution: China's Struggle with the Modern World* (Oxford, 2004)

Mola, Aldo, *Giolitti. Lo statisto della nuova Italia* (Milan, 2003)

Mombauer, Annika, *Helmuth von Moltke and the Origins of the First World War* (Cambridge, 2001)

Mombauer, Annika, 'The Battle of the Marne: Myths and Reality of Germany's "Fateful Battle" ', *Historian*, 68, 4 (2006), pp. 747-69

Monticone, Alberto, *Deutschland und die Neutralität Italiens 1914-1915* (Wiesbaden, 1982)

Monzali, Luciano, 'Il "Partito Coloniale" e la politica estera italiana', *Clio*, 44, 3 (2008), pp. 401-10

Moore, Colleen H., 'Demonstrations and Lamentations: Urban and Rural Responses to War in Russia in 1914', *Historian* (2009), pp. 555-75

Moore, Robin, 'Curzon and Indian Reform', *Modern Asian Studies*, 27, 4 (1993), pp. 719-40

Morgenbrod, Birgitt, *Wiener Großbürgertum im Ersten Weltkrieg. Die Geschichte der Österreichischen Politischen Gesellschaft 1916-1918* (Vienna, 1998)

Morrison, Alexander, *Russian Rule in Samarkand: A Comparison with British India* (Oxford, 2008)

Morrison, Alexander, 'Metropole, Colony, and Imperial Citizenship in the Russian Empire', *Kritika*, 13, 2 (2012), pp. 327-64

Moses, John A., 'An Australian Empire Patriot and the Great War: Professor Sir Archibald T. Strong (1876-1930)', *Australian Journal of Politics and History*, 53, 3 (2007), pp. 407-19

Müller, Guido, *Europäische Gesellschaftsbeziehungen nach dem Erstem Weltkrieg. Das Deutsch-Französische Studienkomitee und der Europäische Kulturbund* (Munich, 2005)

Müller, Sven Oliver, *Die Nation als Waffe und Vorstellung. Nationalismus in Deutschland und Großbritannien im Ersten Weltkrieg* (Göttingen, 2002)

Mulligan, William, *The Creation of the Modern German Army: General Walther Reinhardt and the Weimar Republic, 1914-1930* (Oxford, 2005)

Mulligan, William, ' "We Can't Be more Russian than the Russians": British Policy in the Liman von Sanders Crisis, 1913-1914', *Diplomacy & Statecraft*, 17, 2 (2006), pp. 261-82

Mulligan, William, 'Weimar and the Wars of Liberation: German and French Officers and the Politics of History', *European History Quarterly*, 38, 2 (2008), pp. 266-93

Mulligan, William, *The Origins of the First World War* (Cambridge, 2010)

Mulligan, William and Simms, Brendan, eds, *The Primacy of Foreign Policy in British History, 1660-2000* (Basingstoke, 2010)

Murray, Robert, *The Harding Years: Warren G. Harding and his Administration* (Minneapolis, MN, 1969)

Nagornaja, Oxana, 'United by Barbed Wire: Russian PoWs in Germany, National Stereotypes, and International Relations, 1914-1922', *Kritika*, 10, 3 (2009), pp. 475-98

Naimark, Norman, *Fires of Hatred: Ethnic Cleansing in Twentieth-Century Europe* (Cambridge, MA, 2001)

Nasson, Bill, 'War Opinion in South Africa, 1914', *Journal of Imperial and Commonwealth History*, 23, 2 (1995), pp. 248–76

Nehring, Holger and Pharo, Helge, eds, *A Peaceful Europe? Negotiating Peace in the Twentieth Century*, special issue of *Contemporary European History*, 17, 3 (2008)

Neilson, Keith, *Strategy and Supply: The Anglo-Russian Alliance, 1914–1917* (London, 1984)

Newman, John Paul, 'Post-Imperial and Post-War Violence in the South Slav Lands, 1917–1923', *Contemporary European History*, 19, 3 (2010), pp. 249–65

Newton, Lord (Thomas Legh), *Lord Lansdowne: A Biography* (London, 1929)

Ninkovich, Frank, *The Wilsonian Century: US Foreign Policy since 1900* (Chicago, IL, 2001)

O'Brien, Phillips Payson, 'The American Press, Public, and the Reaction to the Outbreak of the First World War', *Diplomatic History*, 378, 3 (2013), pp. 446–75

Oltmer, Jochen, ed., *Kriegsgefangene im Europa des Ersten Weltkriegs* (Paderborn, 2006)

Orzoff, Andrea, *Battle for the Castle: The Myth of Czechoslovakia in Europe, 1914–1948* (Oxford, 2009)

Oudin, Bernard, *Aristide Briand. La Paix, une idée neuve en Europe* (Paris, 1987)

Page, Melvyn, ed., *Africa and the First World War* (Basingstoke, 1987)

Paolini, Gabriele, *Offensive di pace. La Santa Sede e la prima guerra mondiale* (Florence, 2008)

Patterson, David, *The Search for Negotiated Peace: Women's Activism and Citizen Diplomacy in World War I* (London and New York, 2008)

Pedersen, Susan, *Family Dependence and the Origins of the Welfare State: Britain and France, 1914–1945* (Cambridge, 1993)

Pedersen, Susan, 'The Meaning of the Mandates System: An Argument', *Geschichte und Gesellschaft*, 32, 4 (2006), pp. 560–82

Phillips, Richard, *China since 1911* (Basingstoke, 1996)

Pignot, Manon, *La guerre des crayons. Quand les petits Parisiens dessinaient la Grande Guerre* (Paris, 2004)

Pipes, Richard, ed., *The Unknown Lenin: From the Secret Archives* (New Haven, CT, 1996)

Plaschka, Richard Georg, Haselsteiner, Horst, and Suppon, Arnold, *Innere Front. Militärassistenz, Widerstand und Umsturz in der Donaumonarchie 1918* (Munich, 1974)

Polasky, Janet, *The Democratic Socialism of Emile Vandervelde: Between Reform and Revolution* (Oxford, 1995)

Prior, Robin, *Gallipoli: The End of the Myth* (New Haven, CT, 2009)

Prior, Robin and Wilson, Trevor, *The Somme* (New Haven, CT, 2005)

Procacci, Giovanna, 'Popular Protest and Labour Conflict in Italy, 1914–1918', *Social History*, 14, 1 (1989), pp. 31–58

Procacci, Giovanna, *Soldati e prigionieri italiani nella Grande Guerra* (Turin, 2000)

Prost, Antoine, *In the Wake of War: 'Les anciens combattants' and French Society, 1914–1939* (Oxford, 1992)

Pruessen, Ronald, *John Foster Dulles: The Road to Power* (New York, 1982)

Pusey, Merlo J., *Charles Evans Hughes* (New York, 1963)

Pyle, Emily, 'Peasant Strategies for Obtaining State Aid: A Study of Petitions during World War I', *Russian History/Histoire russe*, 24, 1–2 (1997), pp. 41–64

Pyta, Wolfram, *Hindenburg. Herrschaft zwischen Hohenzollern und Hitler* (Munich, 2009)

Ramnath, Maia, 'Two Revolutions: The Ghadar Movement and India's Radical Diaspora, 1913–1918', *Radical History Review*, 92 (Spring 2005), pp. 7–30

Ree, Erik van, 'Lenin's Conception of Socialism in One Country, 1915–1917', *Revolutionary Russia*, 23, 2 (2010), pp. 159–81

Renzi, William A., 'Italy's Neutrality and Entrance into the Great War: A Re-Examination', *American Historical Review*, 73, 5 (1968), pp. 1,414–32

Retish, Aaron, *Russia's Peasants in Revolution and Civil War: Citizenship, Identity, and the Creation of the Soviet State, 1914–1922* (Cambridge, 2008)

Reuveni, Gideon, 'The "Crisis of the Book" and German Society after the First World War', *German History*, 20, 4 (2002), pp. 438–61

Riguzzi, Paolo, 'From Globalisation to Revolution? The Porfirian Political Economy: An Essay on Issues and Interpretations', *Journal of Latin American Studies*, 41 (2009), pp. 347–68

Roberts, Priscilla, 'Willard D. Straight and the Diplomacy of International Finance during the First World War', *Business History*, 40, 3 (1998)

Rogan, Eugene, *The Arabs: A History* (London, 2009)

Rosenberger, Bernhard, *Zeitungen als Kriegstreiber? Die Rolle der Presse im Vorfeld des Ersten Weltkriegs* (Cologne, 1998)

Roshwald, Aviel and Stites, Richard, eds, *European Culture in the Great War: The Arts, Entertainment, and Propaganda, 1914-1918* (Cambridge, 1999)

Roskill, Stephen, *Hankey: Man of Secrets, 1877-1918*, 3 vols (London, 1970), vol. 1

Rossini, Daniela, *Woodrow Wilson and the American Myth in Italy: Culture, Diplomacy, and War Propaganda* (Cambridge, MA, 2008)

Rothstein, Andrew, *The Soldiers' Strike of 1919* (London, 1980)

Rothwell, Victor, *British War Aims and Peace Diplomacy, 1914-1918* (Oxford, 1971)

Roussel, Éric, *Jean Monnet* (Paris, 1996)

Rubenstein, Joshua, *Leon Trotsky: A Revolutionary's Life* (New Haven, CT, 2011)

Rubin, Gerry D., *War, Law, and Labour: The Munitions Act, State Regulation, and the Unions, 1915-1921* (Oxford, 1987)

Rupp, Leila J., *Worlds of Women: The Making of an International Women's Movement* (Princeton, NJ, 1997)

Sabrow, Martin, *Der Rathenaumord. Rekonstruktion einer Verschwörung gegen die Republik von Weimar* (Munich, 1994)

Sanborn, Joshua, *Drafting the Russian Nation: Military Conscription, Total War, and Mass Politics, 1905-1925* (DeKalb, IL, 2003)

Sanborn, Joshua, 'Liberals and Bureaucrats at War', *Kritika*, 8, 1 (2007), pp. 143-7

Santiago, Myrna, 'Culture Clash: Foreign Oil and Indigenous People in Northern Veracruz, Mexico, 1900-1921', *Journal of American History* (June 2012), pp. 62-73

Satia, Priya, 'The Defense of Inhumanity: Air Control in Iraq and the British Idea of Arabia', *American Historical Review*, 111 (2006), pp. 16-51

Scheidemann, Christiane, *Ulrich Graf Brockdorff-Rantzau (1869-1928). Eine politische Biographie* (Frankfurt, 1998)

Schindler, John R., 'Disaster on the Drina: The Austro-Hungarian Army in Serbia, 1914', *War in History*, 9, 2 (2002), pp. 159-95

Schmidt, Stefan, *Frankreichs Außenpolitik in der Julikrise. Ein Beitrag zur Geschichte des Ausbruches des Ersten Weltkrieges* (Munich, 2009)

Schöttler, Peter, 'The Rhine as an Object of Historical Controversy in the Interwar Years: Towards a History of Frontier Mentalities', *History Workshop Journal*, 39 (1995), pp. 1-17

Schröder, Stephen, ' "Ausgedehnte Spionage": Benno von Sieberts geheime Zusammenarbeit mit dem Auswärtigen Amt (1909-1926)', *Militärgeschichtliche Zeitschrift*, 64 (2005), pp. 425-63

Schröder, Stephen, *Die englisch-russische Marinekonvention. Das deutsche Reich und die Flottenverhandlungen der Tripelentente am Vorabend des Ersten Weltkriegs* (Göttingen, 2006)

Schwarz, Hans Peter, *Adenauer. Der Aufstieg, 1876-1952* (Stuttgart, 1986)

Segesser, Daniel Marc, 'Dissolve or Punish? The International Debate amongst Jurists and Publicists on the Consequences of the Armenian Genocide for the Ottoman Empire, 1915-1923', *Journal of Genocide Research*, 10, 1 (2008), pp. 95-110

Seipp, Adam, *The Ordeal of Peace: Demobilization and the Urban Experience in Britain and Germany, 1917-1921* (Farnham, 2009)

Seregny, Scott, 'Zemstvos, Peasants, and Citizenship: The Russian Adult Education Movement and World War I', *Slavic Review*, 59, 2 (2000), pp. 290-315

Shimazu, Naoko, *Japan, Race, and Equality: The Racial Equality Proposal of 1919* (London, 1998)

Showalter, Dennis, *Tannenberg: Clash of Empires* (Hamden, CT, 1991)

Smith, Leonard, Audoin-Rouzeau, Stéphane, and Becker, Annette, *France and the Great War, 1914-1918* (Cambridge, 2003)

Soutou, Georges-Henri, 'La France et les Marches de l'Est', *Revue Historique*, 260 (1978)

Soutou, Georges-Henri, *L'or et le sang. Les buts de guerre économiques de la Première Guerre Mondiale* (Paris, 1989)

Soutou, Georges-Henri, ed., *Recherches sur la France et le problème des nationalités pendant la Première Guerre Mondiale* (Paris, 1995)

Steffen, Dirk, 'The Holtzendorff Memorandum of 22 December 1916 and Germany's Declaration of Unrestricted U-Boat Warfare', *Journal of Military History*, 68, 1 (2004), pp. 215-24

Steglich, Wolfgang and Winterhagen, Wilhelm E., 'Die Polenproklamation vom 5. November 1916', *Militärgeschichtliche Mitteilungen*, 78, 1 (1978), pp. 105-46

Steiner, Zara, *The Lights that Failed: European International History, 1919-1933* (Oxford, 2005)

Stevenson, David, *French War Aims against Germany, 1914-1919* (Oxford, 1982)

Stevenson, David, *Armaments and the Coming of War: Europe, 1904-1914* (Oxford, 2000)

Stevenson, David, *1914-1918: The History of the First World War* (London, 2005)

Stevenson, David, *With our Backs to the Wall: Victory and Defeat in 1918* (London, 2011)

Stevenson, David, 'The First World War and European Integration', *International History Review*, 34, 4 (2012), pp. 841–63

Stockdale, Melissa, *Paul Miliukov and the Quest for a Liberal Russia, 1880–1918* (Ithaca, NY, 1996)

Strachan, Hew, *The First World War: To Arms* (Oxford, 2001)

Suarez, Georges, *Briand: Sa vie, son oeuvre*, 3 vols (Paris, 1938)

Suny, Ronald Grigor, Göçek, Fatma Müge, and Naimark, Norman, eds, *A Question of Genocide: Armenians and Turks at the End of the Ottoman Empire* (Oxford, 2011)

Tauber, Joachim, 'Stubborn Collaborators: The Politics of the Lithuanian Taryba, 1917–1918', *Journal of Baltic Studies*, 37, 2 (2006), pp. 194–209

Thiel, Jens, *Menschenbassin Belgien. Anwerbung, Deportation und Zwangsarbeit im Ersten Weltkrieg* (Essen, 2004)

Thoß, Bruno and Volkmann, Hans-Erich, eds, *Erster Weltkrieg – Zweiter Weltkrieg. Ein Vergleich. Krieg, Kriegserlebnis, Kriegserfahrung in Deutschland* (Paderborn, 2002)

Tomassini, Luigi, 'Industrial Mobilization and the Labour Market in Italy during the First World War', *Social History*, 16, 1 (1991), pp. 59–87

Tonezzer, Elena, 'Alcide De Gasperi and Trentino', *Modern Italy*, 14, 4 (2009), pp. 399–413

Tooze, Adam and Ivanov, Martin, 'Disciplining the "Black Sheep of the Balkans": Financial Supervision and Sovereignty in Bulgaria, 1902–1938', *Economic History Review*, 64, 1 (2011), pp. 30–51

Torrey, Glenn, *Romania and World War I: A Collection of Studies* (Portland, OR, 1998)

Trachtenberg, Marc, *Reparations in World Politics: France and European Economic Diplomacy, 1916–1923* (New York, 1980)

Trumpener, Ulrich, 'War Premeditated? German Intelligence Operations in July 1914', *Central European History*, 9, 1 (1976), pp. 58–85

Tunstall, Graydon A., 'Austria-Hungary and the Brusilov Offensive of 1916', *Historian*, 70, 1 (2008), pp. 30–53

Ulrich, Bernd, *Die Augenzeugen. Deutsche Feldpostbriefe in Kriegs- und Nachkriegszeit 1914–1933* (Essen, 1997)

Ungari, Andrea, 'The Italian Airforce from the Eve of the Libyan Conflict to the First World War', *War in History*, 17, 4 (2010), pp. 403–34

Ungern-Sternberg, Jürgen von and Ungern-Sternburg, Wolfgang von, *Der Aufruf 'An die Kulturwelt'. Das Manifest der 93 und die Anfänge der Kriegspropaganda im Ersten Weltkrieg* (Stuttgart, 1996)

Üngör, Uğur Ümit, 'Seeing like a Nation-State: Young Turk Social Engineering in Eastern Turkey, 1913–1950', *Journal of Genocide Research*, 10, 1 (2008), pp. 15–39

Üngör, Uğur Ümit, *The Making of Modern Turkey: Nation and State in Eastern Anatolia, 1913–1950* (Oxford, 2011)

Verhey, Jeffrey, *The Spirit of 1914: Militarism, Myth and Mobilization in Germany* (Cambridge, 2000)

Volkogonov, Dmitri, *Trotsky: The Eternal Revolutionary* (London, 1996)

Wade, Rex, *The Russian Revolution, 1917* (Cambridge, 2000)

Waldron, Arthur, *From War to Nationalism: China's Turning Point, 1924–1925* (Cambridge, 1995)

Wall, Richard and Winter, Jay, eds, *The Upheaval of War: Family, Work, and Welfare in Europe, 1914–1918* (Cambridge, 1988)

Walsh Campbell, Michael, 'The Making of "March Fallen": March 4, 1919 and the Subversive Potential of Occupation', *Central European History*, 39, 1 (2006), pp. 1–20

Wandycz, Piotr S., *France and her Eastern Allies, 1919–1925: French-Czechoslovak-Polish Relations from the Paris Peace Conference to Locarno* (Westport, CT, 1962)

Ward, Stephen, ed., *The War Generation: Veterans of the First World War* (New York, 1975)

Wasserstein, Bernard, *Divided Jerusalem: The Struggle for the Holy City* (London, 2001)

Wasti, Syed Tanvir, 'The 1912–13 Balkan Wars and the Siege of Edirne', *Middle Eastern Studies*, 40, 4 (2004), pp. 59–78

Watson, Alexander, *Enduring the Great War: Combat, Morale and Collapse in the German and British Armies, 1914–1918* (Cambridge, 2008)

Watson, Alexander, 'Fighting for Another Fatherland: The Polish Minority in the German Army, 1914–1918', *English Historical Review*, 126, 522 (2011), pp. 1,137–66

Weber, Thomas, *Hitler's First War* (Oxford, 2010)

Webster, Andrew, 'The Transnational Dream: Politicians, Diplomats, and Soldiers in the League of Nations' Pursuit of International Disarmament, 1920–1938', *Contemporary European History*, 14, 4 (2005), pp. 493–518

Wegner, Bernd, 'Hitler, der Zweite Weltkrieg, und die Choreographie des Untergangs', *Geschichte und Gesellschaft*, 26 (2000), pp. 493–518

Weinberg, Gerhard L., 'The Defeat of Germany in 1918 and the European Balance of Power', *Central European History*, 2, 3 (1969), pp. 248–60

Wertheim, Stephen, 'The League that Wasn't: American Designs for a Legalist-Sanctionist League of Nations and the Intellectual Origins of International Organization, 1914–1920', *Diplomatic History*, 35, 5 (2011), pp. 797–836

Westerhoff, Christian, *Zwangsarbeit im Ersten Weltkrieg. Deutsche Arbeitskräftepolitik im besetzten Polen und Litauen 1914–1918* (Paderborn, 2008)

Wette, Wolfram, ed., *Der Krieg des kleinen Mannes. Eine Militärgeschichte von unten* (Munich, 1992)

Whittam, John, *Fascist Italy* (Manchester, 1995)

Wilcox, Vanda, ' "Weeping Tears of Blood": Exploring Italian Soldiers' Emotions in the First World War', *Modern Italy*, 17, 2 (2012), pp. 175–82

Williams, Beryl, *Lenin: Profiles in Power* (Harlow, 2000)

Williamson, John, *Karl Helfferich, 1872–1924: Economist, Financier, Politician* (Princeton, NJ, 1971)

Williamson, Philip, *Stanley Baldwin: Conservative Leadership and National Values* (Cambridge, 1999)

Wilsberg, Klaus, *'Terrible ami–ennemi aimable'. Kooperation und Konflikt in den deutsch-französischen Beziehungen 1911–1914* (Bonn, 1998)

Wilson, Trevor, *The Downfall of the Liberal Party, 1914–1935* (London, 1966)

Winkler, Heinrich August, *Weimar, 1918–1933. Die Geschichte der ersten deutschen Demokratie* (Munich, 1993)

Winter, Jay, *Socialism and the Challenge of War: Ideas and Politics in Britain, 1912–1918* (London, 1974)

Winter, Jay, *Sites of Memory, Sites of Mourning: The Great War in European Cultural History* (Cambridge, 1998)

Winter, Jay, Parker, Geoffrey, and Habeck, Mary, eds, *The Great War and the Twentieth Century* (New Haven, CT, 2000)

Winters, Frank, 'Exaggerating the Efficacy of Diplomacy: The Marquis of Lansdowne's "Peace Letter" of November 1917', *International History Review*, 32, 1 (2010), pp. 25–46

Wortman, Richard S., *Scenarios of Power: Myth and Ceremony in the Russian Monarchy: From Alexander II to the Abdication of Nicholas II* (Princeton, NJ, 2000), pp. 464–78

Wright, Jonathan, *Gustav Stresemann: Weimar's Greatest Statesman* (Oxford, 2002)

Xu Guoqi, *China and the Great War* (Cambridge, 2005)

Yearwood, Peter, *Guarantee of Peace: The League of Nations in British Policy, 1914–1925* (Oxford, 2009)

Yekelchyk, Serhy, *Ukraine: Birth of a Modern Nation* (Oxford, 2007)

Zabecki, David, *Steel Wind: Colonel Georg Brüchmüller and the Birth of Modern Artillery* (Westport, CT, 1994)

Zahra, Tara, 'The Minority Problem and National Classification in the French and Czech Borderlands', *Contemporary European History*, 17, 2 (2008), pp. 138–58

Zechlin, Egmont, *Krieg und Kriegsrisiko. Zur deutschen Politik im Ersten Weltkrieg* (Düsseldorf, 1979)

Zeman, Zbynek, *The Break-Up of the Habsburg Empire* (London, 1964)

Zeman, Zbyněk, with Antonín Klimek, *The Life of Edvard Beneš, 1884–1948: Czechoslovakia in Peace and War* (Oxford, 1997)

Ziemann, Benjamin, 'Republikanische Kriegserinnerung in einer polarisierten Öffentlichkeit. Das Reichsbanner Schwarz-Rot-Gold als Veteranenverband der sozialistischen Arbeiterschaft', *Historische Zeitschrift*, 267, 2 (1998), pp. 357–98

Ziino, Bart, 'Enlistment and Non-Enlistment in Wartime Australia: Responses to the 1916 Call to Arms Appeal', *Australian Historical Studies*, 41, 2 (2010), pp. 217–32

Zloch, Stefanie, *Polnischer Nationalismus. Politik und Gesellschaft zwischen den beiden Weltkriegen* (Cologne, 2010)

Zürcher, Erik Jan, *Turkey: A Modern History* (London, 1997)

Zürcher, Erik Jan, ed., *Arming the State: Military Conscription in the Middle East and Central Asia, 1775–1925* (London, 1999)

INDEX

ACKNOWLEDGEMENTS

THERE IS NO shortage of scholars working on the First World War – as the increasing number of publications testifies. I am fortunate that these scholars have been generous in their advice and convivial in their company. In the endnotes and bibliography the reader can see how much I have relied on the work of others. Over the past decade I have been privileged to work at the University of Glasgow and University College Dublin, where I have benefited from discussions with colleagues and the seminars run by the Scottish Centre for War Studies and the Centre for War Studies at UCD. In particular I am grateful for the advice and support of Phil O'Brien, Simon Ball, Evan Mawdsley, Robert Gerwarth, Stephan Malinowski, Stuart Ward, Mark McKenna, Suzanne d'Arcy, John Paul Newman, Uğur Ümit Üngor, Julia Eichenberg, Thomas Balkelis, James Kitchen, Gajendra Signh, Matthew Lewis, Mark Jones, and Jamie Matthews. Long before the idea of a 'research corridor' between UCD and Trinity College Dublin entered the lexicon of Irish research policy, I benefited from participating in seminars at Trinity on the history of the First World War, organized by John Horne and Alan Kramer, and more recently by Edward Madigan.

I have had numerous opportunities at conferences and seminars to discuss international politics in the first quarter of the twentieth century and I would like especially to thank Mustafa Aksakal, Altay Cengizer, Chris Clark, Peter Dennis, Dominik Geppert, Eckart Goebel, Jeffrey Grey, Jean-Michel Guieu, Peter Jackson, Oliver Janz, Jack Levy, Annika Mombauer, Thomas Otte, Jan Rüger, Andreas Rose, Josh Sanborn, Brendan Simms, Gul Tokay, and John Vasquez.

Yale University Press has provided outstanding support for this project. In particular Heather McCallum has been a constant source of encouragement and well-directed advice. Richard Mason, through rigorous copy-editing, has greatly improved the text and saved me from several howlers.

In spring 2012 I had the great fortune to be a member of the Institute for Advanced Study at Princeton. It was a wonderful personal and intellectually enriching experience, during which much of the research and many of the ideas in this book matured. I would like to thank the benefactors of the Herodotus Fund for making my stay at the Institute possible and Michael van Walt van Praag and Jonathan Israel for their interest in my project. As I complete the book, I am in Berlin, at the Wissenschaftskolleg, which is home like Princeton to an outstanding Institute for Advanced Study. I am grateful to the Rector, Luca Giuliani, and staff for creating an atmosphere so conducive to thinking. In view of this bounty of support and advice, I can only say that any errors in the book are mine, and mine alone.

Researching and writing this book have also depended on the generosity of family and friends. I am extremely grateful to Ann Hirst, who gave me a copy of the diary of her grand-father, George Riches, and who generously granted me permission to quote from it. For their company in New York I would like to thank Glenn Carroll, Joe Dargan, Hugh Eakin, Niall McMahon, Ranu Nandy, and most especially Gerry Frewen, who generously put me up and travelled down to Washington DC with me, where we visited Woodrow Wilson's final home – amongst other sights. In London I would like to thank my sisters, Helen and Kate, and my brother-in-law, Rich Sinclair, for putting me up and taking me out. In Dublin my parents, Deirdre and Herbert, have been untiring in their support of my interest in history.

Most of all I am grateful to my wife, Kate. She has supported me day in, day out, despite my lengthy absences and erratic working and living habits as I researched and wrote the book. She also took the author's picture on the cover jacket, which demanded considerable skill and tact as she dealt with an awkward subject. Without her patience, support, and love I could not have written it. So I dedicate this book to her.